CW00676628

TITO

By the same author

NICHOLAS RIDLEY
THOMAS CRANMER
JOHN KNOX
LORD PALMERSTON
MARY TUDOR
GARIBALDI
THE ROUNDHEADS
NAPOLEON III AND EUGÉNIE
HISTORY OF ENGLAND
THE STATESMAN AND THE FANATIC
HENRY VIII
ELIZABETH I
THE TUDOR AGE
MAXIMILIAN AND JUÁREZ

TITO

———— ❖ ————

JASPER RIDLEY

CONSTABLE · LONDON

First published in Great Britain 1994
by Constable and Company Limited
3 The Lanchesters
162 Fulham Palace Road
London W6 9ER
Copyright © Jasper Ridley 1994
The right of Jasper Ridley to be identified as the author
of this work has been asserted by him in accordance
with the Copyright, Designs and Patents Act 1988
ISBN 0 09 471260 3
Set in Linotron Sabon 11pt by
Rowland Phototypesetting Limited
Bury St Edmunds, Suffolk
Printed in Great Britain by
St Edmundsbury Press Limited
Bury St Edmunds, Suffolk

A CIP catalogue record for this book
is available from the British Library

To Duška, Emina, Jasna and Ljerka

Contents

	Illustrations	9
	Acknowledgements	11
	A Note on Spelling and Pronunciation	15
	Maps	16
1	Funeral of a Communist	19
2	The Yugoslavs	26
3	The Marxists	35
4	Young Josip Broz	42
5	The Metalworker	51
6	Sergeant-Major Broz	62
7	The Russian Civil War	69
8	Return to Yugoslavia	77
9	The Professional Revolutionary	86
10	In King Alexander's Prisons	102
11	From Kumrovec to Moscow	109
12	The Hotel Lux	119
13	The Hitler–Stalin Pact	144
14	The German Invasion	157
15	From Užice to Bihać	175
16	The March Negotiations and the Sutjeska	196
17	Fitzroy Maclean	214
18	From Drvar to Belgrade	233
19	Victory and Revenge	253
20	The Cold War	264

21 The Break with Stalin   280
22 Defying the Lightning   290
23 The Triumphant Tito   316
24 Khrushchev: The Crisis of 1956   331
25 Non-Alignment   345
26 Liberals and Hardliners   364
27 The Prague Spring and the Crisis of 1968   381
28 Curbing the Croats   391
29 The Last Days   410
30 Yugoslavia after Tito   416
    Sources and References   421
    Bibliography   455
    Interviews   464
    Index   467

Illustrations

between pages 96 and 97

1. The house in Kumrovec where Tito was born. The statue of Tito is by Antun Augustinčić
2. Tito's school in Kumrovec, *c.* 1900. The picture on the wall is of the Emperor Franz Joseph
3. Tito's house in Veliko Trojstvo where he lived from 1922–5
4. Tito with his first wife Pelagea Belousova (Polka) and their zon Žarko in 1927
5. Tito's file in the records at the Zagreb police, 4 May 1928
6. Tito at the time of his trial in Zagreb in November 1928
7. Tito at the Seventh Congress of the Cominterm in Moscow in August 1935
8. One of the false passports used by Tito in 1937–9

between pages 192 and 193

9. The house in Zagreb, where the illegal conference of the Communist Party was held in October 1940
10. Ribnikar's villa in Belgrade, where the decision to launch the insurrection was taken on 4 July 1941
11. The German proclamation of July 1943 offering a reward of 100,000 Reichsmarks for the capture of Tito
12. Milka Kufrin during her Partisan years, 1941–5
13. Tito with Davorjanka Paunović (Zdenka) in 1942
14. Tito and his comrades at Jajce in 1943
15. A meeting of the Politburo of the CPY in the cave on Vis in June 1944
16. Tito and Churchill in Naples, August 1944

between pages 320 and 321

17. Tito on Vis in 1944
18. Tito and Nazor in Zagreb in May 1945
19. Part of the letter to the Central Committee of the CPY of 27 March 1948 signed by Molotov and Stalin
20. The Fifth Congress of the CPY in Belgrade in July 1948
21. The Fifth Conference of the CPY in Zagreb in 1952
22. Tito with Queen Elizabeth II, Queen Elizabeth the Queen Mother, the Duke of Edinburgh and Princess Margaret in London in March 1953
23. Tito at a supper with the schoolteachers in his native village of Kumrovec in December 1953
24. Tito welcomes Khrushchev at Belgrade airport in May 1955
25. Tito at the Acropolis in Athens in June 1954
26. Tito on a hunting expedition
27. Tito and Churchill in Split in 1960
28. Tito and his wife Jovanka Budisavljević at the home of his cousin Martin Broz in Kumrovec in 1962
29. Left to right: Kardelj, Tito, Ranković
30. Tito (dressed in native Serb costume) with his wife Jovanka at a New Year's Eve party
31. Statue of Tito by Antun Augustinčić

Acknowledgements

I wish to thank His Excellency Franjo Tudjman, the President of Croatia, for receiving me and giving me information about Tito;

Tito's sons, Žarko Broz and Miša Broz; his second wife, Herta Haas; and his cousins Josip Broz of Kumrovec and Martin Broz of Zagreb;

His former colleague on the Politburo of the Communist party of Yugoslavia and later opponent, Milovan Djilas;

The members of his government: Miloš Minić (foreign minister), Josip Vrhovec (foreign minister), Vladimir Velebit (minister of foreign trade and ambassador to Great Britain) and Milka Kufrin (minister of tourism);

Živadin Simić (his ambassador to the Sudan and to Canada) and Colonel-General Miloš Šumanja (his ambassador to the Netherlands);

Colonel-General Petar Babić (the chief of his military Cabinet), Lieutenant-Colonel-General Milan Basta and Colonel-General Djoko Jovanič;

The leader of the Croatian movement of 1971, Mika Tripalo;

Tito's private secretaries Ranko Bugarčić and Olga Humo (who was also his interpreter);

Dr Pero Damjanović, the distinguished Belgrade historian, who was Tito's colleague and biographer;

The director of the Yugoslav National Archives, Dr Miodrag Zečević, who was formerly on the committee drafting the Yugoslav constitution of 1974 and was Tito's master of the hunt;

Dr Branko Pavićević, the former chairman of the Academy of Arts and Sciences of Montenegro, who was often in attendance on Tito and travelled with him to the United States in 1978;

Slavenka Oughtred (formerly Petnički), of the Yugoslav embassy in

Addis Ababa and New Delhi (who also taught Tito's grandchildren English) and Milena Glušac of the Yugoslav consulate in New York;

Sir Fitzroy Maclean of Dunconnell; Sir William Deakin; Rear-Admiral Sir Morgan Morgan-Giles; Geoffrey Harris; Hilary King; George Mason; and E. D. Roberts, all of whom served in Yugoslavia on missions to Tito's Partisans in the Second World War;

Sir Anthony Nutting (formerly British minister of state for foreign affairs) and Dr Gert Feine (of the German embassy in Belgrade in 1939–41);

Dušanka Barović (who served at Tito's headquarters during the Second World War) and Niko Barović, the wife and son of the defence lawyer Jovan Barović; Marijo and Marina Bauer of Zagreb; Dr Ralph Bennett of the 'Ultra' team at Bletchley in the Second World War; Mrs Vasja Brown (Slavenka Oughtred's sister) for her information about the murder of her father and brother in Split in 1943; Margarete Buber-Neumann, for her information about life in the Hotel Lux in Moscow in 1937; Mladen Čaldarović for his information about the fate of dissidents expelled from the Communist party of Yugoslavia before and during the Second World War; Vladislav Celik; Peter Elstob, the former international secretary of PEN; Giovanni and Marion Greco; Profesor Dr Milan Jovanović; Milan Jovanović the painter; Dušan Makavejev, the film director; John Platts-Mills, QC, for his information about his encounters with Tito and with Churchill; Ivor Porter, who served in the British embassy in Bucharest after the Second World War; Dr Lav Znidarčić for his information on the capture of Zagreb by the Partisans in 1945; Odvjetnica Zvjezdana Znidarčić-Begović for her information about her experiences in the demonstrations in Zagreb after the suppression of the Croatian movement in November 1971; and a prisoner in Jasenovac and Goli Otok who does not wish to be identified 'because you never know what may happen in the Balkans';

All of whom gave me information about their encounters with Tito and other personal experiences.

This book could not have been written without the help of my assistants Duška Jovanović, Emina Kurtagić, Ljerka Radović and Jasna Srdar, and I wish to express my gratitude to them. They are not, of course, in any way responsible for the opinions expressed in my book, about which they were not consulted. This also applies to Živadin Simić and to Branka Magaš, both of whom read my type-script, and to Sir William Deakin, Hilary King and Dr Velebit, who most kindly agreed to read some sections of it which referred to their experiences.

I am most grateful to Dr Pero Damjanović and Živadin Simić for their help and encouragement.

I wish to thank all those who have helped me by undertaking occasional research, by offering me hospitality, and in other ways: Betty Armstrong, Roy and Lyn Armstrong, Nana Baranac, Ada Beck, the staff of the Worshipful Company of Carpenters, David Cheeseman, Stuart Collins, Libuše Edererová, Slavica Esnault-Pelterie (née Barović), Antonia Fraser, Theo Fründt, Victoria Glendinning, Ronald Harewood, Jean Howard, Christine Howe, Rosemary Hull, Judith Ann Kerr, Dr Margaret King, Marianne Lowe, Beba Marković, Miloš Nekvasil, Michael O'Hagan, Elfreda Powell, Ingrid Price-Gschlössl, Isabel Quigly, John Radon, my daughter Barbara Ridley, my stepmother Jane Ridley, Klaus and Lile Schulyok, Professor Stoyan Sedmak, Dr Maria D. Simon, Christopher and Margaret Small, Dr Michael Smith, Boszi Tomalin, and Mrs Vera Velebit;

The staff of the Arkiv Jugoslavije in Belgrade; the British Library in London; English PEN in London; the Hrvatska Povijesni Muzej in Zagreb (and Rhea Ivanuš); the Imperial War Museum in London; the Josip Broz Tito Memorial Centre in Belgrade; the Kent County Library in Tunbridge Wells; the London Library in London; the Public Record Office in Kew; the Royal Institute of International Affairs (Chatham House) in London; the Spomen Park in Kumrovec; the United Nations Information Centre in London; and the United States National Archives in Washington, DC.

I wish to thank my wife Vera for reading and advising on the typesecript, and my son John for reading the proofs.

JASPER RIDLEY
Tunbridge Wells
29 March 1994

A Note on Spelling and Pronunciation

In referring to the names and places and people in the former Yugoslavia, I have adopted the spelling which is used there when these names are written in the Latin alphabet, except in a few cases where the spelling has been anglicized, as in 'Belgrade', 'Chetnik' and 'Ustasha'. Serbian names written in the Cyrillic alphabet have been changed into the Latin alphabet as used in Yugoslavia. In the case of Russian (as opposed to Serbian) names, the Cyrillic spelling has been changed into the accepted English spelling.

In the language which was once called 'Serbo-Croat' (a name which is highly objectionable today to both Serbs and Croats) the letters of the Latin alphabet are pronounced in the following way:

a *a* as in *far*.
c *ts*, as in *gets*.
č *ch*, as in check.
ć a slightly softer *ch*, as in church.
dj *j* as in *judge*, or *dy*.
e *e* as in *fetch*.
g *g* as in *get*.
i *ee* as in *been*.
j *y* as in *yes* (except where following a *d*; see *dj*).
o a short *o*, as in *hot*.
s *s* as in *soft* (not as in *was*).
š *sh*, as in *shoot*.
u *oo*, as in *pool*.
z *z*, as in *zone*.
ž *zh*, as the French *j* in the French word *je*.

b, d, f, h, k, l, m, n, p, r, t and *v* are pronounced as in English. There is no *q, w, x* or *y* in Serbo-Croat.

Frontiers 1940–90

VOJVODINA

ROMANIA

Novi Sad
(Peterwardein)

rnji Zabar

Sava

Zemun

BELGRADE

Danube

• Požarevac

• Smederevska Palanka

Cralova •

• Krupanj

Veliko Plana •

Ravna Gora

• Veliko Popov

• Gornji Milanovac

• Čačak

Užice •

Pozega

SERBIA

RAJEVO

oča •

MONTENEGRO

KOSOVO

BULGARIA

• Cetinje

■ SKOPJE

ALBANIA

MACEDONIA

GREECE

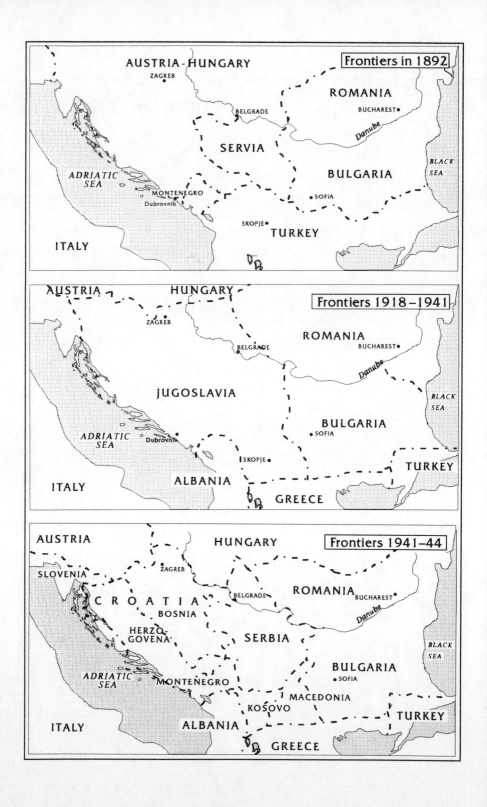

CHAPTER 1

❖

Funeral of a Communist

P LANE after plane carrying Very Important Persons flew into
Surčin Airport near Belgrade on 7 May 1980. They had come
to attend the funeral of the president of Yugoslavia, Josip Broz
Tito. Three days before, at 15.05 hours, the code message 'The match
is postponed' had been sent out to the leaders of the state, the army
and the Communist party; and soon afterwards the nation was
solemnly informed on television that Tito had died, after a long
illness, in Ljubljana in Slovenia.[1] He would have been eighty-eight
on 7 May. His official birthday had been celebrated for many years
in Yugoslavia on 25 May, but he was born on 7 May 1892.

Never before had so many world leaders attended a state funeral.
There were many more than at Queen Victoria's funeral in London
in 1901, and even more than at President Kennedy's and Winston
Churchill's. They included four kings, thirty-one presidents, six
princes, twenty-two prime ministers and forty-seven ministers for
foreign affairs. They came from 128 nations in every part of the
world, from both sides in the Cold War between the superpowers,
and from the neutral Non-Aligned states.

Tito was the last survivor of the great Allied leaders of the
Second World War. He had outlived Roosevelt, Stalin, MacArthur,
Churchill, Eisenhower, de Gaulle, Truman, Zhukov, Haile Selassie,
Chiang Kai-shek, Mao Tse-tung and Montgomery. But there was a
more important reason why the VIPs came to his funeral. They came
because he had been the leader of the Non-Aligned states. The statesmen of the American and the Russian blocs came to impress the
Non-Aligned states, and the Non-Aligned states came to honour their
foremost champion.

The Cold War had lasted for more than thirty years. From time to time it had seemed as if the United States and the Soviet Union were on the point of making peace, but every improvement in their relations was always followed by new and increased tensions.

In 1980 relations between East and West were at their worst. At Christmas 1979 the Soviet army invaded Afghanistan to help one faction in the Communist government of Afghanistan against another. The United States and its allies were not interested in these feuds between Afghan Communists, but were alarmed to see the Soviet army approaching the Red Sea and the oilfields of the Middle East. So they sent arms to the Muslim nationalists in Afghanistan who were waging guerrilla warfare against the Russians. Many of these guerrillas were ardent supporters of the Ayatollah Khomeini in Iran, who was outraging public opinion in the United States by imprisoning American citizens; but sentiment and ideology have little influence when a Great Power decides to help guerrillas who are killing the soldiers of its enemy. The United States and Britain were also trying to organize a boycott of the Olympic Games in Moscow, in which the Soviet government had invested a great deal of money. But these bitter enemies of East and West came together in Belgrade for Tito's funeral; and so did other equally bitter enemies from weaker states who had been engaged in their own localized wars.

From Britain came the Queen's husband, Prince Philip, Duke of Edinburgh, with the prime minister Margaret Thatcher; the leaders of both the Opposition parties, James Callaghan and David Steel; two British officers who had served with Tito during the Second World War, Sir Fitzroy Maclean and Sir William Deakin; and in a humbler position, with the representatives of the political parties, Gordon McLennan, the general secretary of the British Communist party, which had joined in the attack on Tito in 1948. From the Soviet Union came the prime minister, Leonid Brezhnev, and his foreign minister, Andrei Gromyko; from France the foreign minister, Raymond Barre; from Italy President Cosiga, though Italian relations with Yugoslavia had been very strained over Trieste; from Belgium King Baudouin, from Sweden King Carl Gustaf, and from Norway King Olaf; from West Germany Chancellor Helmut Schmidt and foreign minister Hans Dietrich Genscher; from Communist East Germany President Erich Honecker.

All the other Communist countries of Eastern Europe, Russia's satellites in the Warsaw Pact, who had once denounced Tito in the most violent language, sent their leaders to his funeral. The foreign minister of Communist Cuba attended. President Ceauşescu's Communist government in Romania was pursuing an anti-Russian foreign policy; but he too came to the funeral. Four leaders came from Communist China, which had continued to denounce Tito when the other Communist states had stopped doing so. Kim il Sung, the Communist dictator of North Korea, was there, though he rarely travelled abroad; so were the leaders of Communist Vietnam; Mrs Indira Gandhi from India and her great enemy, General Zia from Pakistan; President Kaunda of Zambia; President Sadat of Egypt, who had proclaimed a seven-day fast in his country when he heard of Tito's death; King Hussein of Jordan; President Assad of Syria; President Saddam Hussein of Iraq; the Sultan of Soviet-controlled Afghanistan; and the secretary-general of the United Nations, Kurt Waldheim (a former foreign minister and a future president of Austria). Waldheim has been accused of having committed war crimes while serving in the German army in Yugoslavia during the Second World War; but he had always been on friendly terms with Tito.

There was one notable absentee. The President of the United States, Jimmy Carter, did not come, though he sent his mother, his vice-president Walter Mondale, and his secretary of state. This caused very little adverse comment in Yugoslavia; but *The Times* of London linked his absence from the funeral with his other recent failures in foreign policy. In a leading article, headed 'He ought to have gone',[2] it castigated Carter for allowing Brezhnev to gain a march on him by attending the funeral; but a spokesman at the White House declared that the American people would greatly resent this criticism of the president, who could not go to Belgrade because of ill-health. The spokesman added that 'the President refuses to get involved in diplomatic one-up-manship with the Kremlin in a matter like this.'

Carter made it clear that the United States would continue to support the independence of Yugoslavia, and said that Tito was 'a towering figure on the world stage'. Mrs Thatcher said that she 'was deeply saddened to hear of the death of President Tito', who 'was a staunch ally of the United Kingdom in time of war'.[3] The leaders of both the countries that had once tried to crush him, Germany and the Soviet Union, paid their tributes. Helmut Schmidt said that he was a great fighter for his country's independence. The Russian press praised him as an 'outstanding leader'.

His body was brought by special train from Ljubljana to Belgrade. All Yugoslavia stopped work while the train was on its eight-hour journey through the Slovenian, Croatian and Serbian countryside and through the little railway stations where people stood bare-headed in silence. In Belgrade, great crowds stood in the streets in the late afternoon of a warm day in early summer to watch the hearse drive from the Central Station to the Federal Assembly building where the coffin lay in state for forty-eight hours. Thousands of people came to see him for the last time, though there was nothing to see except the simple wooden coffin. Many came during the day, and even more during the night. They stood in line for three hours to reach and pass the dead president, in silence, or speaking softly in awe-struck voices to their neighbours in the queue.

To some extent the mourners were organized. The factories, offices, trade unions and other organizations fixed a time when their employees and members were to assemble so that they could go together to the Federal Assembly building; but no one was obliged to go, and some critics and cynics made a point of staying away. If the attendance times of some of the mourners was organized, the grief of all of them was spontaneous, sincere and profound. Even those Yugoslavs who today vilify Tito will usually have the honesty to admit that in May 1980 they were stricken with grief by his death. Nearly the whole nation mourned, as a nation mourns only when a wartime leader dies; as the people of London mourned at Churchill's funeral in 1965, and the people of Moscow at Stalin's; and as the people of Berlin would perhaps have mourned at Hitler's, had he won the war and died in his bed.

Important people who did not have to queue also came to see the coffin. Margaret Thatcher was photographed looking sadly down upon it.[4] Tito's widow made her first public appearance for many months. She had been living apart from Tito for the last three years, and there had been many rumours as to why the marriage had broken down; but Jovanka took her rightful place, standing beside the coffin at the lying-in-state.

Next day thousands of people again lined the streets for the funeral, which was seen by millions more on television in Yugoslavia and in fifty-eight foreign countries. After Stevan Doronjski had made a speech at the Federal Assembly building, the procession set off. The car carrying Tito's body drove slowly along the two-mile route, down Prince Miloš Street and up to Tito's private residence at 15 Užička Street where he was to be buried. The marching soldiers, the officials, the sports organizations and Communist party groups walked slowly all the way, as did all the kings, presidents and prime ministers. Only the aged Mrs Lillian Carter was driven in a car.

During the closing months of his life, Tito had discussed with his intimate advisers where he was to be buried. Should it be at his birthplace in Kumrovec in Croatia? Or on the River Sutjeska, the site of the bloodiest battle in Yugoslavia of the Second World War, with 35,000 of his soldiers and comrades? He himself had at first favoured the Sutjeska, but then decided on Belgrade, the capital of Yugoslavia, where he had taken the most important decisions about the government of the country during his thirty-five years of power.[5]

The grave had been prepared in the Hall of Flowers, one of the eight buildings in the grounds of his residence; he used to sit there sometimes in the afternoons to rest in a chair on the marble terrace between the flower beds. He was to be buried beneath that marble terrace. A stage had been erected for the distinguished guests in the garden, facing the entrance to the Hall of Flowers. There they listened to the funeral oration by Lazar Koliševski. This was an atheist's funeral, and there was no religious ceremony. It was also a Communist's funeral. Koliševski, in his speech, praised 'dear Comrade Tito' not primarily for his thirty-five years as president of Yugoslavia but for his devotion to duty and his great leadership since 'you assumed the leadership of our glorious party forty-three years ago'.[6] The crowds in the streets mourned the president and wartime leader of Yugoslavia. But the organizers of the funeral, the men who governed Yugoslavia, mourned Tito the Communist, the general secretary and leader for forty-three years of the organization to which he and they had rendered total allegiance – the Communist party.

The mourners in the procession had marched to the music of the famous funeral marches, to the more doleful of Yugoslav traditional songs, and to the anthems of the Pan-Slav movement. But when, after all the marching and speeches, the coffin was lowered into the grave, it was to the accompaniment of music composed by a Belgian Socialist, Pierre Degeyter in honour of the International Working Men's Association which Karl Marx had founded in 1864. The words of 'L' Internationale' which the French Socialist Eugène Pottier wrote to Degeyter's music had been translated into many languages and had replaced 'La Marseillaise' as the song of the international revolution. It was adopted by the Third (Communist) International in 1919 and was the national anthem of the Soviet Union until Stalin replaced it with a patriotic song in 1943.

It was the most appropriate end for the Communist funeral of Josip Broz Tito, who had been a devoted Communist ever since he joined the party at the age of twenty-eight; first as an agitator and shop steward in Croatia, then as a full-time party organizer in the illegal underground movement in Yugoslavia, in King Alexander's prisons, and in Moscow at the height of Stalin's purges, then as leader of the Yugoslav national resistance against the German invader during the Second World War, then as dictator of a repressive police state, as the rebel who defied Stalin and freed Yugoslavia from Russian domination, and finally as the elder statesman of the Non-Aligned world, preaching the benefits of peaceful co-existence between capitalism and Communism to the two sides in the Cold War. Tito had always been, first and last, a Communist, working for the triumph of Communism in his own country and throughout the world. If he had sometimes denied it, this was only a trick to deceive the enemy and to further the victory of his cause. During these years his lifestyle and his strategy had changed; but his devotion to Communism had not changed.

At his wish, his grave was marked with a simple inscription: 'Josip Broz Tito 1892–1980'. There was no other decoration on his tombstone – not even the red star of the Communist Partisans. Many people believed that this proved that Tito was a Freemason. Tito had never been a Freemason, but on his last visit to America in 1978 he had been impressed by Franklin D. Roosevelt's grave, with only Roosevelt's name and the dates of his birth and death on the tombstone; and he wished to have nothing more on his own grave.[7]

For twelve years four sentries stood permanently on guard over the tomb; but in 1992 the guard was withdrawn after Yugoslavia had ceased to exist as a state. The Germans, whom Tito had fought successfully in the Second World War, had helped to bring this about by encouraging Tito's Croat fellow-countrymen to declare their independence, with the active support of Margaret Thatcher. In 1980 she had stood respectfully beside Tito's grave while they played the 'International'; but in 1991–2 she called on the nations of Europe and the United States to aid the struggle of the Croats and the Bosnian Muslims against the 'Communist acts of aggression' committed by the Serbs.[8]

Tito, like Alexander the Great twenty-three centuries earlier, the Great Mogul Aurangzeb in India in 1707, and Tsar Dušan of Serbia in the fourteenth century, had died triumphant at the height of his power, unaware that within a few years his empire would collapse and disappear in the chaos of anarchy and civil war.

CHAPTER 2

❖

The Yugoslavs

IN the second century BC the Roman legions invaded the land of the Illyrians, a territory which is today Slovenia, Croatia, Serbia, Bosnia-Herzegovina and Montenegro. They also invaded Dalmatia, a region along the Adriatic coast, which had recently revolted against the King of the Illyrians and won its independence. The Romans easily subdued the Dalmatians, but it took them 150 years before they had finally conquered the Illyrians. The Romans made Illiricum a new province of the Roman Empire. Many of the Illyrians were assimilated with the Latin immigrants in Illiricum, but some of them fled into the mountains of the south-west, where they were left undisturbed by the Romans in the country that is now called Albania.

The Romans built towns along the Adriatic coast of Illiricum which became centres of urban civilization, like the other towns in the Roman Empire from Constantinople to York. At the end of the third century AD, the Emperor Diocletian established his principal place of residence in Illiricum, where he had several palaces, including a magnificent one at Spalato.

Six hundred miles to the north-east of the frontier of Illiricum some tribes known as the Southern Slavs (in their own language 'Yugoslavs') lived in what is today western Ukraine, between the upper reaches of the rivers Dniester and Bug. The Yugoslavs cultivated the soil as well as hunting animals for food, but they did not remain for very long in one area, and after a few years moved on to new pastures. When they fought other tribes they showed exceptional courage and ferocity. They frequented the river banks, exploring the length of the rivers in their territory, and from childhood the boys were strong swimmers. They worshipped their tribal gods – the Father of the Gods, Perun the Thunderer (Suarog), the three sons of

Suarog – Dazbog the God of the Sun, Ċors, and Veles the God of
Cattle – and the lesser gods. They feared the evil gods Stribog, the
God of Storms, and Črt the God of Hate, who would cause great
harm and spread much evil unless they were bridled by Perun and
his sons.

When the Roman Empire in the West was overrun by barbarian
tribes, the Eastern Empire continued in Constantinople. After the
death of the Eastern Emperor Justinian in 565 he was succeeded by
a series of weak emperors who lost control of Illiricum. In the seventh
century the Yugoslavs in their wanderings moved further than usual
to the south-west and began to enter Illiricum. They did not move
as an organized invading army but as a straggling horde of immigrants. By about 635 several Yugoslav tribes had settled in Illiricum:
the Serbs in the eastern and central parts, the Bosnians further
west, the Montenegrins on the Adriatic coast in the south, the Croats
on the coast in Dalmatia and further north, and the Slovenes still
further north. Most of the Yugoslavs continued to live in the countryside of Illiricum as they had lived along the banks of the Dniester
and the Bug; but in the west the Croats could not resist the lure of
urban civilization. They intermarried with the Romans and settled
down to share their lifestyle in Spalato and Ragusa, which they
called, in their language, Split and Dubrovnik.[1]

Christianity had been the state religion of the Roman Empire since
the fourth century; but the Christian Church in the West and East
became involved in organizational and theological controversies. The
Eastern Orthodox Church separated from the Roman Catholic
Church under the Pope in Rome and became the state religion of
the Eastern Roman Empire. Missionaries from Constantinople went
to the territory of the Serbs, the Montenegrins and some of the
Bosnians and to the Bulgarian tribes who had settled in the eastern
part of the Balkans. They persuaded the inhabitants to join the
Orthodox Church; but the people in the towns of Dalmatia remained
Roman Catholics. Missionaries went from Italy and Dalmatia to
Croatia and parts of Bosnia and converted the Croats and some
Bosnians to Roman Catholicism.

A few people, most of them priests, learned to read and write. In
Dalmatia, Croatia and parts of Bosnia they learned the Latin alphabet from Rome. The missionaries from Constantinople taught the
Serbs, Montenegrins, Bulgarians and some of the Bosnians to use
the Greek alphabet which had been adopted in Constantinople. This

alphabet was afterwards inappropriately called 'the Cyrillic alphabet' after a missionary named Constantine, who in the ninth century had unsuccessfully tried to convert the Croats to the Orthodox faith, and who then went to Rome and became a monk, changing his name to Cyril;[2] but Cyril played only a very minor part in the development of the alphabet.

The emperors in Constantinople tried from time to time to reconquer Illiricum, and sometimes succeeded; but the Yugoslavs, particularly the Serbs, were fierce fighters, and they always rebelled and broke away again from the Eastern Empire. When the Serbs were not fighting the emperor they were often waging war against the Bulgarians and the Croats, who also went to war with their northern neighbours, the Hungarians.

In all these wars great cruelties were committed, which shocked even the hardened warriors of Western Europe. In earlier times the Romans had punished rebels by crucifying them; in the Eastern Empire, rebels had their hands amputated. When the Bulgarian ruler Krum succeeded in capturing Constantinople in 811, he killed the Emperor Nicephorus, cut off his head, gouged out the eyes, skinned it, and used the skull as a drinking goblet. Balkan wars were just as fierce two hundred years later, when the Emperor Basil II, after defeating the Bulgarians, put out the eyes of 15,000 prisoners.

At the end of the eighth century the King of the Franks, Charlemagne, established himself as the strongest ruler in Western Europe. His armies invaded Hungary and Slovenia, and they also crossed the Adriatic and penetrated Dalmatia and Croatia. On Christmas Day 800, Charlemagne was crowned by the Pope in Rome as Holy Roman Emperor. Charlemagne was a devout Christian, and saw to it that his subjects became Christians by ordering that any heathen who refused to convert to Christianity should be put to death. He ensured that Dalmatia, Croatia and Slovenia remained Roman Catholic and did not convert to Orthodox Christianity. But his armies never reached Serbia or Bosnia.

In 1102 the Hungarians conquered Croatia, which for more than eight hundred years remained part of the kingdom of Hungary. They also conquered the northern parts of Dalmatia; but the southern Dalmatian cities of Split and Dubrovnik and the surrounding country were annexed by the thriving commercial republic of Venice, whose ships regularly crossed the Adriatic to Dalmatia and went as far as Greece and Smyrna. Slovenia was conquered and governed by a series of German dukes, and in the fourteenth century the Habsburg family acquired it and held it as their personal possession for six hundred years. When the Habsburgs became Archdukes of Austria, Slovenia became part of Austria.

Charlemagne's Holy Roman Empire was the centre of the civilization of Western and Central Europe during the Middle Ages. Its economic and social system was feudalism; the great nobles held their lands from the king as his tenants-in-chief in return for serving him in wartime with their men; the peasants were serfs of the lords, holding their lands from the lords by labour service and working for the lords on a specified number of days in the year. The feudal system was more oppressive in the east than in the west. In eastern France the serf's lot was worse than in western France and in England; it was worse in Germany and Austria than in eastern France; it was worse in Poland, Hungary and Croatia than in Germany and Austria.

Sometimes the serfs rebelled. Peasant revolts occurred all over feudal Europe, but they were always ultimately suppressed by the lords. The atrocities committed by both sides were far more savage in the East than in the West. In 1573 it was the turn of Croatia. The immediate cause of the revolt was the serfs' resentment against a local lord who, after his wife died, consoled himself by raping many of the peasant girls. One of the centres of the uprising was the district north of Zagreb where Josip Broz Tito was born three centuries later. After the revolt was suppressed many serfs were hanged, and their leader, Matija Gubec, suffered the usual punishment in Hungary for rebellious peasant leaders. The Bishop of Zagreb wrote to the Emperor Maximilian II: 'We shall crown him as an example, with Your Sacred Majesty's permission, with an iron crown, and a red-hot one too'.[3] The emperor granted his permission; lumps of Gubec's flesh were torn out by red-hot pincers, and he died after several hours of torture.

Feudalism was never established in Serbia or in the Balkans beyond Croatia. The economic and social system there resembled the pre-feudal system of Anglo-Saxon England before 1066. The people were organized in large families or groups of families, and elected their chief. The chiefs of all the families attended the National Council where they elected the Prince of Serbia. This system was not as democratic as it was supposed to be, because in practice the chiefs and the prince were chosen by the most powerful lords. There were a few serfs in Serbia, but the great majority of the people were free tenants. Their lords lived on the product of their labour, as they did under the feudal system of Croatia and Western Europe; but only a few of the most influential lords had the judicial powers of life and death over their tenants held by the feudal lords. The codes of law drawn up by the princes of Serbia were administered by the local communities with a jury system. The prince could not declare war without the consent of the National Council, but under a strong prince this was something of a formality. In wartime, every Serb had a duty to serve in the army – a duty which they all performed with great willingness.

The culture of Western Europe, like its feudalism, did not extend to Serbia. The legends of chivalry, of valiant knights tilting with villains and wooing beautiful ladies with submissive courtly love, are very similar in the stories of Sir Launcelot and Sir Gareth in England, Roland and Ogier the Dane in France, the Cid in Spain, and Dietrich von Berne in Central Europe. The Serbian legends are of fairies, witches and vampires, and of the heroes who encounter them in the mountains and the forests. The Serbian national hero, Prince Marko Kraljević (a historical character who in fact betrayed his King and fought for the Turkish invaders against Serbia) is as wily as Odysseus in ancient Greek legend. His greatest achievement was his victory over the bandit Musa in single combat. Musa had got Marko on the ground and was about to strangle him when a beautiful fairy, who was on Marko's side, distracted Musa's attention; and while Musa was looking at the fairy, Marko stabbed him with a knife and killed him.

Marko's most valuable asset was his horse Šarac, who could out-distance any other horse and could leap from one mountain crag to another and over the widest rivers. Thanks to Šarac, Marko always escaped from his enemies. This is a different hero from King Arthur's Knights of the Round Table and Charlemagne's paladins who never fled from the foe; but throughout most of their history the Serbs were a small tribe, surrounded by powerful enemies from whom they could escape only by guile or flight. They knew that if they were taken prisoner they would not be honourably entertained by their captor and his beautiful sister until the ransom money was paid, but would have their eyes put out or their hands cut off, if they were not immediately put to death.

It was different in the middle of the fourteenth century, when Tsar Dušan of Serbia dominated the Balkans, defeating the Hungarians, conquering Bulgaria, Albania and Macedonia, and advancing to within forty miles of Constantinople where he died in mysterious circumstances. After his death his empire collapsed, and soon the Muslim Turks were advancing from the east. Bypassing Constantinople, they invaded Serbia, and on the most famous and tragic day in Serbian history, 15 June* 1389, they annihilated the Serbian army on the battlefield of Kosovo, killing the Serbian prince, 'Tsar' Lazar, and most of his nobles. The Eastern Empire was saved for a generation by the Mongol hordes of Tamburlane, who defeated and temporarily conquered the Turks; but the Mongols disappeared after Tamburlane's death. In 1453, to the dismay of all Europe, the Turks captured Constantinople, and in 1455 they completed the conquest of Serbia which was incorporated into the Ottoman Empire. Even Albania, which had held out against the Romans, had been annexed by the Turks before the end of the fifteenth century; but the Turks never conquered Montenegro.

In parts of the conquered territories, particularly in Albania and Bosnia, many of the inhabitants converted to Islam. The Turks did not persecute the Orthodox Christian religion, but oppressed the conquered Slavs in every other way. The Serbian democratic institutions were abolished, and the country was governed by Turkish officials who were sometimes understanding, but more often brutal. Heavy taxes were imposed on the people. Their sons were often taken from them when they were boys and trained for the Turkish army; unlike most of the population, these boys were forced to become Muslims. The people felt they were an oppressed nation ruled by the foreign conqueror.

In 1526 the Turks invaded Hungary and destroyed the Hungarian army at Mohacs; the young King Ladislaus II (who was also King of Bohemia) was drowned escaping from the battlefield. His Habsburg brother-in-law, Ferdinand, assumed the title of King of Hungary and Bohemia; but the Hungarian nobleman, Jan Zapolya, persuaded the Turks to appoint him as King of Hungary in opposition to Ferdinand. After fighting each other for some years, Zapolya and Ferdinand made peace and agreed that Ferdinand should have Croatia and Zapolya the rest of Hungary. When Zapolya died, the Turks annexed his part of Hungary, which they held for 150 years; but

* By the twentieth century this date had become 28 June by the modern Gregorian calendar.

Ferdinand retained Croatia, which was never under the Turks. The frontier between Croatia and Serbia was still the frontier between Western Europe and the East, as it had been for nearly a thousand years. Slovenia remained under the Habsburgs as part of Austria.

In 1582 Pope Gregory XIII reformed the calendar. This introduced another difference between the Yugoslavs. All Roman Catholic countries, including Slovenia, Croatia and Dalmatia, adopted the Gregorian calendar. The Orthodox Christians of Serbia, Bosnia-Herzegovina, Montenegro and Bulgaria, like Russia and Greece, retained the Julian calendar, which was ten days behind the Gregorian calendar in the sixteenth century. By the beginning of the twentieth century it was thirteen days behind.

In 1683 the Turks marched on Vienna, but were defeated by the King of Poland, Jan Sobieski, who arrived in time to save Christendom from the infidel. In the long war with Austria which followed, they were driven out of Hungary. The Austrian armies were commanded by Prince Eugène of Savoy; when he was not engaged in fighting the French in Bavaria, in alliance with the British and his comrade-in-arms, John Churchill, Duke of Marlborough, he was winning a series of victories over the Turks in the Balkans. The Croats were good fighters, and Eugène's Croatian soldiers were among the best units in his army.

Eugène's last battle was the capture of Belgrade in 1717. By the peace treaty next year, the Turks ceded all Hungary, and Belgrade, to Austria; but they retained most of Serbia, and recaptured Belgrade in 1739. The little town of Zemun across the Danube, which is now a suburb of Belgrade, remained in Croatia and the Austrian empire. Today the people of Zemun still say: 'The West begins in Zemun.'

The Serbs were not sure where their sympathies lay in the wars between the Turks and Austria. They hated the Turks; but the Austrians, unlike the Turks, persecuted the Orthodox Church. A story, which was certainly apocryphal, was told in Serbia about the Serb who had gone to the sultan in Constantinople and asked him what he would do if he conquered Serbia. 'I will build a mosque in every town and village where the faithful can worship,' replied the sultan. 'You may then, if you wish, build a Christian church beside the mosque, and I do not care in the least what you do in that church as long as you pay your taxes to me and obey my laws.' The Serb then went to Vienna, and asked the Emperor of Austria what he would do if he liberated Serbia. 'I will see to it that you go to a Roman

Catholic church and worship according to the only true faith,' said the emperor. 'I will not tolerate heresy anywhere in my empire.'[4] The Serb decided to let the Turks and the Austrians fight it out, and to help neither one side nor the other.

In Croatia and Slovenia the people had no doubt where they stood. They were loyal subjects of the Habsburg emperor of Austria and king of Hungary who defended their Roman Catholic faith; and the great majority of them did not object when the handful of Protestants were persecuted and burned.

When the French Revolution broke out in 1789, and the sovereigns of Europe united to crush the French republic, the Croats served in the Austrian army and fought against Napoleon in Italy. After Napoleon's armies had overrun the Venetian republic, they crossed the Adriatic and occupied the Venetian territories in Dalmatia. Napoleon set up a Dalmatian republic, and forced Austria to cede Croatia and Slovenia to Dalmatia; but when he was at last overthrown, the Great Powers at the Congress of Vienna returned Slovenia and Croatia to Austria, and also gave Austria all the territories of the former Venetian republic in Italy and Dalmatia.

So Slovenia, Croatia and Dalmatia felt the full impact of the French Revolution and Napoleon; but Serbia, Bosnia and Montenegro were unaffected. The Turks encountered Napoleon not in the Balkans but at the other end of their empire, when he invaded Egypt and Syria. The revolution against the Turks which broke out in Serbia in 1804 was not inspired by the French Revolution, but was the third revolt in Serbia in forty years. The Serbian rebels did not look to revolutionary France for help, but to the Tsar of Russia, the most autocratic of the European royal despots.

The Serbs were led by Karadjordj (Black George), who was so called because of his swarthy complexion and also his violent temper. He is said to have killed 125 men with his own hand in outbursts of anger, apart from those whom he slew in war. One of the 125 was his own father; Karadjordj killed him because his father refused to leave his holding and enlist with Karadjordj in the anti-Turkish forces. Some historians doubt the truth of this story; but it was firmly believed by Karadjordj's Serbian followers, who thought the better of him because of it.

The Russians, who were at war with Napoleon, did not give the Serbs the help that they expected, and the revolt was crushed. When another rising broke out in 1815 it was led by the Serbian peasant,

[33]

Miloš Obrenović, who took the precaution of eliminating Karadjordj, his rival for the leadership of the revolution. He sent agents to murder Karadjordj while he slept.

—————— ❖ ——————

CHAPTER 3

The Marxists

T HE French revolutionaries of 1792 proclaimed Liberty, Equality and Fraternity. There were a few individuals who believed that this should be extended to economic affairs, that society should not be divided into rich and poor, and that goods should be held in common. During the next fifty years, Socialist ideas were formulated in England, France and Germany by various visionaries. In January 1848 two young middle-class Germans living in Brussels wrote a short pamphlet which they called *The Manifesto of the Communist Party*. Karl Marx, aged twenty-nine, was a journalist who had written articles for a Radical newspaper in the Rhineland; Friedrich Engels, aged twenty-seven, was the son of a German who owned a factory in Manchester.

In *The Communist Manifesto*[1] Marx and Engels claimed to put forward a new kind of Socialism. It was not the Utopian Socialism of earlier writers, but 'scientific Socialism', which showed that Socialism would be achieved not because well-meaning visionaries thought that it was desirable, but because it would inevitably be the next phase in historical development. Mankind had originally been organized in a primitive communist society, with all goods held in common; but this had come to an end when the division of labour was introduced, and a society was established in which a minority were the masters and the majority were their slaves. Slavery had been replaced by feudalism, which in due course was followed by capitalism. Marx and Engels followed the current French political jargon in calling the capitalist class the 'bourgeoisie', because in the Middle Ages the merchants, the predecessors of the later capitalists, lived in towns. It is one of many examples of how a word can completely change its meaning after it has been used in controversy.

In *The Communist Manifesto* Marx and Engels paid a glowing tribute to the achievements of the bourgeoisie in replacing feudalism and developing industry throughout the world; but the time had now come for them to give way to the proletariat – the industrial workers in their factories. This would require a violent political revolution, for no ruling class had ever peacefully surrendered its power. The bourgeoisie had been obliged to resort to violence (the English Civil War in the seventeenth century and the French Revolution of 1789) in order to seize power from the feudal kings and lords, and the proletariat would have to use violence to capture power from the bourgeoisie. When the proletarian revolution had been accomplished, and the proletariat had become the ruling class, there would be no other class for the proletariat to exploit and oppress. They would establish Socialism, which would in due course develop peacefully into a classless society and Communism, and everyone would live happily ever after.

Communists would put an end to feelings of hatred between the working class of different nations. 'The workers have no Fatherland,' proclaimed *The Communist Manifesto*.[2] In later years, when Marx was considering the oppression of Ireland by the British, he wrote: 'A nation that oppresses another nation forges its own chains.'[3]

Marx claimed that he had given his followers scientific Socialism. He had in fact given them something much more valuable – a religion. Marxism was a religion, and not merely a cause. Marx and the Marxists loudly proclaimed that they did not believe in God, but this was not really true. They did not believe in the Christian, Jewish, Muslim, Hindu or Buddhist God, but they believed in their own God of Historical Development. 'Men make their own history, but not just as they please,' wrote Marx;[4] they had to make history in obedience to the ordinances of the God of Historical Development, in whose hands all men, both His servants the Communists and His enemies the bourgeoisie, were mere clay to be moulded according to His will. Like all other gods, the God of Historical Development was not only all-powerful but also all-good; He would allow the forces of evil to reign for a time, but would ensure that they would ultimately be overthrown, that good would triumph, and that a perfect paradise, in which everyone would be happy, would reign throughout all the earth. So the ultimate victory of Communism was inevitable.

This was the religion that millions of Communists throughout the world were to adopt in the twentieth century, and none of them more devotedly than Josip Broz Tito. Academic theorists, whose logic is stronger than their knowledge of human nature, have argued that it is illogical of the Marxists, if they believe that the victory of Communism is inevitable in any case, to make such efforts to achieve it; but belief that ultimate victory is inevitable has never lulled the supporters of a religion into inactivity; it has always spurred them on to greater efforts, to greater sacrifices, to greater ruthlessness.

Marx and Engels had just finished writing *The Communist Manifesto* when the revolution of 1848 broke out in Palermo, and rapidly spread to Paris and throughout central Europe; but nowhere did these revolutions against the old monarchies develop into Marx's proletarian revolution. The Communists were a threat only in Paris, where they were suppressed after four days' street fighting by the Republican Liberal, General Cavaignac. After his victory, Cavaignac ordered the summary execution of several thousand Communists.

When the revolution reached Germany, Marx and Engels went to join the Radicals in the Rhineland. Less than six months earlier they had written in *The Communist Manifesto* that the workers had no fatherland, and had ended their pamphlet with the stirring appeal: 'Proletarians of all countries, unite!'[5] But in Germany and in the Austrian Empire the revolution, far from uniting the proletarians of the various nations, aroused the most bitter hatreds between them. Marx and Engels themselves were completely carried away by the nationalist passions. The Germans, Hungarians and Poles supported the revolution, but the Czechs and the Croats opposed it; while Radical revolutionaries seized power in Vienna and Budapest, Prague and Zagreb remained quiet.

As the revolutionary government of Hungary refused to grant the demand of the Croats for autonomy, the Croats decided to save the Austrian monarchy. Count Jelačić, a Croatian landowner who was a general in the Austrian army, led 40,000 ardent Croatian volunteers to suppress the revolution in Vienna and Budapest, though the Hungarians were not defeated until the Tsar of Russia had sent an army to help the forces of the young Emperor of Austria, Franz Joseph.

In Prague a Czech historian, Palacký, initiated a Pan-Slav movement, calling for a union of all the Slav nations to restore the liberties of the Slav race. Marx and Engels vigorously denounced Pan-Slavism. Whatever Pan-Slavism claimed to be, wrote Engels, it was in practice an instrument of the autocratic Tsar of Russia, 'the Russian knout'. The Southern Slavs 'rose up in 1848 to establish their national independence only in order to suppress at the same time the German-Magyar revolution. They represent the counter-revolution.' Engels foretold that the Germans and Magyars 'will become free and will take bloody revenge on the Slav barbarians'.[6] It is going too far to claim, as some recent writers have done, that Engels seriously advocated a policy of genocide, of the extermination of all Slavs; but if he had been told in 1849 that Hungarian revolutionaries had slaughtered a Croatian peasant, Martin Broz (thereby preventing the procreation of Josip Broz Tito), he would certainly have cheered, and Marx would have joined in the applause.[7]

Serbia, Bosnia and Montenegro were as untouched in 1848 as they had been in 1789 by the revolutions of Western Europe. As usual they were busy with their own quarrels; but the Great Powers did not allow them to solve their problems by themselves, and the fights between the factions and the regions were used by Turkey, Russia and Austria, and to a lesser extent by Britain and France, for their own ends. A revolt led by Miloš Obrenović was sufficiently successful for the Turks to grant home rule to Serbia in 1830, with Miloš as their viceroy and the local dictator; but as Miloš became pro-Turk, Russia turned against him and supported his discontented nobles. The Russian Tsars were determined to use the revolts of the Orthodox Christians in the Balkans as an excuse to overthrow Turkish power in Europe; but British policy was expressed in the words of the famous music-hall song 'By Jingo' that Londoners sang with such enthusiasm during the war crisis of 1878: 'The Russians shall not have Constantinople.' The British therefore thwarted every attempt by the Christian peoples in the Balkans to win independence from Turkey, and insisted that they should rest content with home rule and that they should be divided into a number of small semi-independent states which were unlikely to unite against Turkey.

At the Congress of Berlin in 1878 the Great Powers attempted to settle the fate of the peoples of the Balkans by a compromise which was greatly resented, for different reasons, by everyone who lived there. Romania and Serbia were to be independent states. Bulgaria was to be divided into two provinces, Bulgaria and Roumelia; both were to have home rule under Turkish overlordship. Bosnia and Herzegovina were to remain part of the Turkish Empire, but were to be occupied by Austria until law and order were restored there. Albania was to continue under Turkey, and Montenegro was to stay independent as it had been for 522 years.

In London Dr Charles Marx, as his English acquaintances called him, was living in a small house in Dean Street, Soho, on money sent to him by Engels from the profits of Engels's capitalist factory in Manchester. In 1864 he began to write his great work, *Das Kapital*; when it was ultimately published in three volumes, it ran to 875,000 words, a little longer than the Bible. Engels called it 'the Bible of the working class',[8] and it did indeed serve as a bible, if not for the working class, at least for the Marxists. Like other bibles it was very long, difficult to understand, and capable of conflicting interpretations, and it was read by only a small proportion of the believers who venerated it; but they were impressed to hear that Marx had proved in its pages, by algebraical formulas, that the collapse of the capitalist system was inevitable.

In the same year, 1864, Marx founded the International Working Men's Association, with its headquarters in London. One of the first actions of the International was to send a message of congratulation to Abraham Lincoln on his re-election as president of the United States and his measures to win the American Civil War and abolish slavery.[9] But soon the French section was organizing strikes and street demonstrations against the government of Napoleon III which led to violent clashes with the police. After the defeat of Napoleon III in the Franco·German war and the establishment of the Third Republic in France, the Commune seized power in Paris. It was only coincidence that the word 'Commune' and the name of its supporters, the Communards, resembled the words 'Communism' and 'Communists', because the Commune took its name from the Paris Commune of 1792 which had played a leading part in the French Revolution; and the *commune* had for many centuries been the title of the local government bodies in France. But the link with Communism was appropriate, because Marx and the International supported the Commune, though its leaders were mostly old Jacobins and Red Republicans.

The French republican government sent General Galliffet to suppress the Commune. Galliffet gave orders to shoot the rebels who were captured. In reprisal, the Communards shot several hundred hostages, who were all members of the wealthier classes, and included the Archbishop of Paris. They demolished the Vendôme column and set fire to the Tuileries Palace, the Hôtel de Ville, and large parts of the city centre. When Paris fell after a week's street fighting, Galliffet's troops executed 30,000 of their Communard prisoners. The rest were tried for treason and sent to prison camps in New Caledonia, where they remained until they were freed by an amnesty nine years later.

A few days after the fall of the Commune, Marx addressed the General Council of the International in London. He denounced the atrocities of Galliffet's troops and praised the Communards' courage, but he criticized them for having remained on the defensive; if, at the start of the revolt, they had taken the offensive and marched on the government headquarters at Versailles, they would have won.[10] During the next fifty years, the Marxists never forgot the Paris Commune; they longed for revenge, and drew the lesson that the Communards had failed because they had not been sufficiently ruthless in dealing with their enemies. This is the usual reaction of the losing side in a cruel war.

Queen Victoria's daughter Victoria, the German crown princess (she was later to become the Empress Frederick) heard that there was a German living in London called Karl Marx who was instigating revolution throughout Europe. She wrote to her friend Mountstuart Elphinstone Grant Duff, MP, who had been a junior minister in Gladstone's Liberal government, and asked him if he could find out something about Marx and his doctrines. Grant Duff thought that the best way to find out would be to invite Marx to lunch. He wrote to the crown princess that Marx was not at all the fiery revolutionary type: 'Carl Marx spoke several times both of Your Imperial Highness and of the Crown Prince, and invariably with due respect and propriety.' Duff thought that Marx's opinions were 'interesting and often, as I thought, showing very correct ideas when he was conversing of the past and the present, but vague and unsatisfactory when he turned to the future.'[11]

The Paris Commune, the International and Marx's doctrines were one of the two factors which shaped Tito's life. The other was the violent history of the Balkans. After the Congress of Berlin, the killing continued in the Balkans; it sometimes stopped for a few years, but always began again.

Within seven years of the Treaty of Berlin, Bulgaria united with Roumelia, whereupon Serbia attacked Bulgaria. A short but very savage war took place which is remembered in Britain today only because it forms the background of George Bernard Shaw's play *Arms and the Man*. The Bulgarians were trouncing the Serbs when a threat of Austrian intervention forced them to halt and make peace.

In Bosnia there was spasmodic fighting between bands of Serb, Croat and Muslim irregulars which provided the excuse for the Austrian army to continue their occupation of the country. From time to time the Serbs and Albanians killed each other in the Turkish province of Kosovo.

There were violent political disagreements within each Balkan country which often led to political assassinations; some of the factions were supported by Russia and others by Austria. In 1903 King Alexander Obrenović of Serbia and his wife Queen Draga were murdered in their palace in Belgrade by the supporters of the Karadjordjević family, who threw their bodies out of the window into the great square below. Many people thought that the British government had instigated the assassination. The British government did not approve of murdering kings and queens and throwing their bodies out of a window, even if the queen was as scandalous a character as Draga. They withdrew the British diplomatic representatives from Belgrade and refused to attend the coronation of the new king, Petar Karadjordjević; but they resumed diplomatic relations after a year, and preferred the Karadjordjević to the Obrenović dynasty.

———— ❖ ————

CHAPTER 4

Young Josip Broz

T ITO was born Josip Broz, the son of Franjo and Marija Broz, in the village of Kumrovec in Croatia on 7 May 1892. There is not the slightest doubt about this, although many people in all parts of the former Yugoslavia still refuse to believe it. Throughout his life and after his death, rumours were always circulating that Tito was not really Josip Broz, but that when he became an agent of the Communist International (the Comintern) he was given forged papers in the name of Josip Broz, a Croat who had served in the Austrian army in the First World War and had died as a prisoner-of-war in Russia. It was said that the birth certificate of a Josip Broz, born in Vienna, is in the archives there. According to one story, the death certificate of Josip Broz, killed on the Carpathian front in 1915, was also in Vienna; but it was sent to Tito when he was President of Yugoslavia by the Austrian government as a return for some *quid pro quo*. After Tito died, Josip Broz's death certificate was found in his desk, but it was quickly removed and placed in the closed section of the secret archives in the War Office in Belgrade.

Many of these stories contradict each other, and none of them can be verified. They rest on two assumptions: the well-known practice of the Comintern to give their agents forged documents in the name of persons whom they knew were dead, and the fact that when Tito returned to Kumrovec in 1920, and again after 1945, no one in the village recognized him. But this last assertion is quite untrue; on both occasions Josip Broz was recognized by all his family and friends.

The mystery of Tito's true identity is a mystery only because people are determined that it should be a mystery. According to the various stories, Tito was really the son of a middle-class family in Slovenia; the illegitimate son of a Hungarian nobleman who held an important position under the Austro-Hungarian monarchy; a Russian; and a Jew. The latest story, which is taken very seriously in some quarters in Belgrade today, is that Tito was the illegitimate son of Winston Churchill, and this, they say, provides a complete explanation of British policy towards Yugoslavia during the Second World War.

The Roman Catholic clergy in Croatia were particularly inclined to believe that Tito was a Jew. Bishop Lach was firmly convinced of it until in 1946 he reluctantly accepted the fact that Tito was indeed Josip Broz after several members of the Broz family, some of whom were personal friends of the bishop, assured him that Tito was their cousin.[1]

The date of Tito's birth is recorded as 7 May 1892 in the church registers where the dates of birth of all children in Croatia had been recorded since the seventeenth century. When Tito was called up for military service in the Austrian army in 1913, his date of birth was given as 5 March 1892. Afterwards his dossier in the Yugoslav police files stated that he was born on 12 March 1892. In 1943 the German occupation authorities noted that he was born on 7 March 1892; and when he was president of Yugoslavia his birthday was celebrated every year on 25 May, apparently because his birthday was first celebrated on that day by the Partisans in error and it was never afterwards changed. When he himself wrote a short biographical *curriculum vitae* for the Comintern in Moscow in 1935, he stated that he was born in 1893. He may have had some reason for making out that he was a year younger than he really was, or it may have been an absentminded error; but it is unlikely to have the sinister implication which has been placed on it, or to provide any serious evidence that Tito was not really Josip Broz. There can be little doubt that 7 May 1892 is the true date of his birth.[2]

The Broz family had originally come from Bosnia, but they emigrated to Croatia in the fifteenth century to escape the Turkish occupation. They settled near Kumrovec, though they did not move into the village until about 1840.[3] Kumrovec is in a valley in the highlands of the Zagorje district of Croatia about twenty miles north of Zagreb and five miles east of the River Sutla, which was the border not only between Croatia and Slovenia but also between Hungary and Austria. Tito's grandfather, Martin Broz, like his ancestors for several generations, was born a serf of the Counts of Erdödy, one of the great Hungarian landowning families; but he had been emancipated when serfdom was hastily abolished by the Emperor Ferdinand during the revolution of 1848, and the serfs were allowed to buy their freedom by instalments. He became one of the more prosperous of the small peasant proprietors in Kumrovec, owning a hundred acres and adding to his income by setting up as a carrier, transporting produce on his cart between the neighbouring villages. He married the daughter of a local family who had been free peasants, not serfs, since the seventeenth century. They had one son, Franjo, and six daughters.

Franjo Broz was born eight years after the abolition of serfdom; but he was adversely affected by another piece of reforming legislation. A law of 1853 enacted that every son and daughter was entitled to share in their father's inheritance. When Martin Broz died after being crushed by his carrier's cart in 1878, Franjo had to share the farm with his six sisters, and inherited only fifteen acres. He tried to earn more money by buying and selling timber, for the law that abolished serfdom had ended the serfs' right to take timber from their lords' lands, and wood for fuel was in short supply in Kumrovec.

One of Franjo's journeys took him to the village of Posreda, eight miles from Kumrovec, just across the border in Slovenia. Here he met Marija Javeršek, the eldest of fourteen children of Martin Javeršek, who owned sixty-five acres of pasture and woodlands. Franjo married her in January 1881, when he was twenty-four and she was sixteen. It was quite common for Croats and Slovenes in the border areas to intermarry. Even among the Yugoslavs who hated each other far more than the Croats and the Slovenes, intermarriage was not unusual. Croats, Serbs, Bosnians and Montenegrins intermarried. This did not stop the husband from continuing to kill his wife's fellow-countrymen. The wife, after her marriage, was expected to join her husband's side and cheer him on when he slaughtered her kinsfolk.

After enjoying the traditional peasant wedding feast at Posreda, Franjo Broz returned home with his wife and her usual peasant dowry of beds, household furniture and linen. Marija then settled down to performing her principal duty of bearing children. During the first eleven years of the marriage she gave birth to seven children. Four of them died within a few months, but two sons and one daughter survived, and so did her eighth child, Josip, who lived to be eighty-eight and president of Yugoslavia. After his birth Marija produced seven more children, three of whom survived.[4] This was well above the usual survival rate, for, according to Tito, before the First

World War eighty per cent of Croatian peasant children died before they reached the age of fifteen.[5] The deaths of children in infancy was so common an occurrence that Tito was not even aware of how many of his brothers and sisters had died. He told his biographer and friend Vladimir Dedijer that his parents had had ten children. Dedijer discovered from the church registers that another five had died in early infancy, four of them before Tito was born.[6]

Tito, like all his father's and mother's family for centuries, was christened and brought up as a Roman Catholic. Crucifixes, pictures and images of the Virgin, and the stations of the cross were to be seen in the family home and all around him in the village. The parish priest was a significant figure in the villages of Croatia; he was one of the adults who played an important role in the lives of the children. Tito's statements to Dedijer about his encounters as a child with the clergy all describe unpleasant incidents. He told how he was chosen by the parish priest to be his acolyte, and how their relationship ended. 'Once after the service I could not remove the vestments from the big fat priest, who was in a hurry. He was irritated and slapped me. I never went to church again.'[7]

Did these painful experiences play their part in making Tito a Communist? It is more likely that the Communist beliefs he held in later life made him remember only the occasions when the priests behaved badly to him as a child.

He told Dedijer: 'My childhood was hard.'[8] But the lives of many children in Kumrovec were harder. Josip Broz grew up in one of the better houses of the village, a well-built brick structure, very different from the hovels of poor peasants in the Austrian Empire at the time. But it was certainly overcrowded, for Franjo Broz shared the five-room house with his cousin, and they all lived in their separate parts of the house with their wives and their many small children.[9]

The hardness of Tito's childhood was chiefly caused by his father's financial difficulties. Franjo Broz was determined to become rich enough to buy back from his sisters the land they had inherited from his father. He borrowed money from the banking firm of Deutsch & Grünwald who had bought the estates of Count Erdödy after the abolition of serfdom in 1848. But neither the sale of his farm produce nor the profits of his carrier's business brought in the necessary money. Franjo ran heavily into debt, and instead of buying the ninety acres from his sisters, he had to sell five of his fifteen acres to repay the bank with the eight per cent interest that they demanded.

It is significant that when Tito spoke to his biographer as president of Yugoslavia he pointed out that Deutsch and Grünwald, representatives of finance capital, had replaced the feudal aristocrats, the Erdödys, as exploiters of the people of Croatia; but he did not mention that Deutsch and Grünwald were Jews.[10] Many Croats were very conscious of this, and often mentioned it, for anti-Semitism had increased in Croatia, as it had in other parts of the Austrian Empire, in the last years of the nineteenth century.

Josip's happiest time as a child was when he was sent to live with his grandfather in Slovenia, at the age of five or six, in order to ease the financial burden on his father, until he was old enough to work on the farm. His grandfather lived in a house in a wood above the river. Josip played in the wood and cut twigs to make whips for the horses. It was here that he first came to love horses.[11] It was probably in his grandfather's house that he learned to play the piano, which he often did as a relaxation later in life. When Slavenka Petnički, who taught his grandchildren English, asked him when he had learned to play the piano, he told her that he had learned on a beautiful white piano when he was a small child.[12]

Old Martin Javeršek loved his grandson. People who knew the family said afterwards that Tito took after him, both in looks and build, and in his broad sense of humour.[13]

But in 1900, when Josip was eight, he had to return to his father's house to work in the fields. He enjoyed driving the cows and looking after the animals, but found work on the corn-mill tiring, and by the time he had finished his shirt was soaked with sweat. He disliked even more having to go round the village asking the neighbours to lend money to his father, who thought that they would be more likely to contribute if he sent the child.[14]

Franjo Broz could not keep Josip at work all the time, because he had to go to the village school in Kumrovec. Compulsory elementary education had been introduced throughout the Austrian Empire by the Empress Maria Theresia in the eighteenth century, more than a hundred years earlier than in England. On 7 July 1900 Josip attended the village school for the first time. He sat on a long narrow wooden bench at a narrow wooden desk, facing a crucifix and a photograph of the Emperor Franz Joseph which hung side by side on the wall above the schoolmaster's rostrum, with the crucifix marginally higher than the emperor's photograph.[15]

Franjo realized that education would enable his sons to obtain better jobs which would bring in more money to the family. He was pleased that the schoolmaster stressed the advantages of learning mathematics. During the five years that Josip attended school, he had reasonably satisfactory reports. He sometimes missed school, but this was more often because his father had told him to work on the farm than because he was playing truant on some prank of his own.[16]

When Tito was being interviewed for his biography by Dedijer, it suited him and the Communist party to emphasize the hardships and sufferings of the peasants in Croatia under the old regime; but his childhood was not entirely unhappy. If there were the cuffs from his father, his school teachers and the priest, and the tragedy of the deaths of his infant brothers and sisters from diphtheria (which he himself caught and survived), there were also the games with the other boys, the practical jokes on the school teachers, the security of a village community and of a large family, and the kindness to children which is usually found in those primitive communities in which the children play an essential part in the family economy. The family sometimes had to go hungry in periods of dearth; but there were also, at least in some years, the family and village feasts during the seasons of plenty.

One of the great pleasures of the peasants of the district was fully shared by Josip Broz from his childhood. They enjoyed dressing up in their best clothes on holidays and special occasions when they had finished their hard day's work. When urban influences spread to the villages, they fancied smart suits as much as they had loved their striking peasant garb. All his life Josip Broz enjoyed wearing smart clothes. Like the common people in other parts of the world, the peasants could not understand why aristocrats liked wearing shoddy old clothes. One day a baron drove into Kumrovec in his motor car at fifteen miles an hour, the maximum speed which cars in those days were capable of achieving. The villagers were most impressed, as they had never before seen a car. But their admiration turned to contempt when the baron got out of the car and they saw that he had a patch in his trousers. Tito told Dedijer: 'We said, "What kind of a baron is he supposed to be with trousers mended like ours?" '[17]

Josip Broz's greatest delight in his childhood was his sheepdog, Polak, the first of many dogs whom he was to love throughout his life. He and his brothers and sisters were heartbroken when their father decided to sell Polak to a gamekeeper in exchange for two cords of wood. But Polak ran home at once. Franjo Broz took him back to the gamekeeper, but he ran home again. This time the children decided to hide Polak in a cave in a wood. They kept him there for a fortnight, bringing him food and water every day. Franjo then relented and agreed not to sell the dog.[18]

At his trial in 1928, Tito said that he became a Communist because of the oppression that he had seen all around him as a child in his native village.[19] His chief reason for saying so was undoubtedly because this was the Communist party line; but it was at least half true. From his earliest childhood he was conscious of the wrongs that the peasants of Kumrovec had suffered in the past and present. When he cried in the night as a very small child he was told, like other children, that if he did not keep quiet and go to sleep at once, the Black Queen of Cesargrad would come and get him. This Black Queen was the Countess Barbara Erdödy of Cesargrad Castle, who had treated the defeated serfs with great cruelty after the suppression of the peasant revolt in 1573. The peasant followers of Gubec had stormed Cesargrad during that revolt, and after beheading the hated bailiff, had burned the castle. The ruin could be seen on the hill above the village from the window of the Broz house; and when Josip was a little older he and his schoolmates used to go to the castle and enact in the ruins the storming of the castle by the peasants. He was thoroughly familiar with the tragic end of the story, how Gubec had been tortured to death and how nearly 6,000 of his followers had been hanged along the roads in the neighbourhood of Kumrovec.[20]

There had been a more recent revolt in the district which was caused by the resentment of the Croats against the Hungarians who governed them from Budapest. The Croats had received no reward from the government in Vienna for having fought for the counter-revolution in 1848. On the contrary, the Emperor Franz Joseph and his ministers decided to win the goodwill of the Hungarians by granting them many privileges within the empire. The Hungarian control over Croatia was increased, for although the Ban (governor) of Croatia was still nominally appointed by the emperor, he was in practice chosen by the prime minister of Hungary. Slovenia, being part of Austria, was not affected by these conflicts.

The trouble came to a head in 1903. All the jobs on the railways in Croatia had been given to Hungarians; when Croats went to the station to buy a ticket for a train journey, they had to ask for it in

Hungarian. One day the Croats in the village next to Kumrovec burned the Hungarian flag that flew over the railway station, and rioting broke out all over northern Croatia. Hungarian troops were brought in; they fired on the people on several occasions, killing thirty-six demonstrators and wounding several hundreds. To the great resentment of the local inhabitants, the troops were billeted in their houses. Franjo Broz was forced to have four Hungarians in his house for a month and to feed them at his own expense when his family were already short of food.[21]

Josip Broz knew about the injustices that had been inflicted upon his family and their fellow-Croats; but this did not make him a political activist. There were many young Highlanders in Scotland in 1900 who felt strongly about the Massacre of Glencoe two hundred years before, the slaughter at Culloden in 1746 and the eviction of the tenants in the Highland Clearances at the beginning of the nineteenth century; but their immediate aim was not to avenge historic wrongs, but to find work, and perhaps to emigrate to America. Josip Broz was in the same situation.

When he left school at the age of thirteen, he worked for three years on his father's farm, and sometimes for other peasants. Once he took a job tending cattle for one of his mother's brothers. The arrangement was that he would receive no wages, but would be supplied with his food and that at the end of the year his uncle would give him a new pair of boots to replace his worn ones. His uncle took Josip's boots, repaired them, and gave them to his own son, giving Josip in exchange a pair of boots of much poorer quality.[22] Josip was beginning to learn that peasants can be mean, and that apparent benefactors may be fraudulent.

Franjo Broz, like his ancestors for many centuries and most of the other inhabitants of the district, had never in his life travelled more than fifty miles from his village. But he was reluctantly beginning to realize that in the modern world, with conditions so hard at home, it was better to send his sons to other parts of the world where they could earn good money and send it home to the family in Kumrovec. He agreed that his son Martin should go to work as a railwayman in Vienna. But many Croats were emigrating to the United States; according to Tito, a quarter of a million went there between 1899 and 1913.[23] It was still possible to enter the United States without a visa or even a passport; all that was needed was money for the fare.

Franjo decided to send Josip to the United States as soon as he could raise the money. But as usual he was too optimistic. After a few months he told Josip that he could not afford to buy his ticket to America. So Josip was sent to the town of Sisak, about sixty miles to the south, to try to find work there. His first idea was that he might become a tailor, and make smart clothes for the peasants to wear at their weddings and parties; but he could not find anyone who would train him in tailoring. He found work at Sisak in a restaurant, where he had to wash the dishes and put up the skittles in the skittle-alley for the soldiers of the local garrison who came to play there.[24] This did not satisfy him; but he soon found an old locksmith in Sisak who was prepared to take him as an apprentice. The locksmith was a Czech who had moved to Croatia and had built up a flourishing business in Sisak.

Broz worked as the locksmith's apprentice for three years until he was eighteen. The apprentices had to work twelve hours a day, from six in the morning to six in the evening, and were sometimes bullied and cuffed by the journeymen who worked in the locksmith's bicycle repair shop; but the food was reasonably good, and the locksmith himself was usually kind. Once he came into the workshop and found Josip reading aloud to the other apprentices a Serbo-Croat translation of Conan Doyle's *Adventures of Sherlock Holmes* when they should all have been working. The locksmith crept up behind Josip and slapped his face. Josip was so angry that he ran away and spent the night in a nearby brick factory. The police found him there and took him off to prison as a runaway apprentice; but the old locksmith did not prosecute him or terminate his apprenticeship.[25]

CHAPTER 5

The Metalworker

ANARCHISTS had made life dangerous for heads of state and their families. The assassination of rulers had been used as a political weapon for many centuries, but it became much more frequent at the end of the nineteenth century. The Russian revolutionary Mikhail Bakunin,* under the influence of his more extreme follower, Sergei Nechayev, advocated a policy of murdering heads of state, brutal police chiefs, and capitalists. Marx and Engels disagreed, and expelled Bakunin from the International; but his ideas were popular in countries with a terrorist tradition, like Italy and Spain; and they also spread to other countries. In the twenty-seven years between 1881 and 1908 Tsar Alexander II of Russia, President Carnot of France, the Empress Elizabeth of Austria, King Umberto of Italy, President McKinley of the United States, Alexander and Draga of Serbia, and King Carlos of Portugal and his son the crown prince, were assassinated; and unsuccessful assassination attempts were made on other princes and rulers, including Queen Victoria of England and her son the Prince of Wales.

The Social-Democratic parties rejected terrorism and revolution in favour of legal political activity through trade unions and the ballot box. Engels explained that the development of modern weapons, and the building of cities with wide boulevards to replace the narrow streets of 1848, had made it much more difficult to make a successful insurrection by the erection of barricades and by street fighting.[1]

---

* Bakunin, Mikhail (1814–76). Russian Anarchist leader; imprisoned in Saxony and later in Siberia after the defeat of the revolution in 1849, he escaped to England in 1861; a founder with Marx of the First International in 1864, his disagreements with Marx split the International after 1872.

In 1889 the Second International was formed to replace the First International which had been destroyed by the split between Marx and Bakunin. The International fixed May Day as a workers' holiday, and called for a general strike in all countries on 1 May every year. At first the movement was strongest in the Austrian empire; but after the fall of Bismarck and the repeal of his Anti-Socialist Law in 1890 it became very strong in Germany, and soon afterwards in France. A Social-Democratic party was formed in Croatia in 1894, in Slovenia in 1896, in Serbia in 1903, and in Bosnia in 1909. The Socialists agitated for universal suffrage. By 1907 this had been granted in Austria and Slovenia, but there was only a slight extension of the franchise in Hungary and Croatia. Less than two per cent of the population of Croatia had the right to vote; in Kumrovec only three of the two hundred families had it.[2]

Pan-Slavism was also developing among the Yugoslavs, though the Socialists still opposed it as Marx and Engels had done in 1848. Its adherents looked to the Tsar of Russia to support them against both Austria and Turkey. Pan-Slavism was strong in Bulgaria and Serbia, and it was beginning to gain supporters in Croatia. Socialism and Pan-Slavism were the first ideologies for 1,500 years to take root in both Croatia and Serbia. They were the first links between the two parts of Europe which since the sixth century had always followed different roads.

In 1908 a revolution took place in Turkey; the Young Turks overthrew the autocratic and antiquated rule of the sultan and installed a modern, liberal system of government. In October Bulgaria took advantage of the political confusion in Constantinople to proclaim her independence from Turkey, which in practice meant merely that the prince of Bulgaria took the title of king. Eight days later, Franz Joseph issued an imperial rescript annexing Bosnia and Herzegovina to the Austrian Empire.

These events did not immediately affect the life of the apprentice, Josip Broz; there was no Socialist or Pan-Slav activity in Sisak. In April 1909 one of the journeymen working at the locksmith's factory, who was kinder to the apprentices than were many of the others, told Broz that they ought to decorate the workshop on 1 May because the Socialists everywhere celebrated May Day as a holiday;[3] but no one in Sisak went on strike on May Day, as the Socialist workers did wherever they were strong enough to do so.

In the autumn of 1910 the eighteen-year-old Josip Broz finished his apprenticeship and qualified as a trained metalworker. He heard that there were jobs for metalworkers at an engineering works in Zagreb. He wanted to return home to Kumrovec, but first he must earn enough money to buy a smart new suit which would impress the villagers there. So for the first time in his life he went to the capital of Croatia. It was a thriving city. It had doubled its population in the last twenty years, and had 80,000 inhabitants in 1910. The city had suffered badly in an earthquake in 1901, but had been rebuilt in the massive classical style of the houses in the city centres of Prague and Munich, and had a Central European look very different from the oriental appearance of Sarajevo in Bosnia.

Josip Broz worked at the engineering factory for ten hours a day, and received two crowns thirty hellers for a day's work. The other workers in the factory told him that he ought to join the metalworkers' trade union, which was affiliated to the Social-Democratic party. He was soon drawn into political activity for the first time. The party and the union called on its members to take part in a march through the streets of Zagreb protesting against the low wages and the high cost of living; the party's posters in the city stated that in England and Belgium a worker ate five times as much meat as the Croatian worker could afford. The police charged the demonstrators, injuring several of them with their batons.[4]

After Broz had worked in the factory for two months he had saved enough money to buy a smart suit for twenty crowns. He took it back to his lodgings and then went to the factory to say goodbye to his friends. When he returned to his lodgings he found that his new suit had been stolen. He had enough money to go to a second-hand shop and buy another suit for four crowns. It was not new and smart like the stolen one, but at least it was better than if he had returned to Kumrovec in the same clothes in which he had left.

He arrived home in December 1910. On the first evening his mother cooked his favourite dish for dinner. Forty-two years later, he still remembered her chicken soup with noodles and her cheese pies called *štrukli*.[5] All his life he preferred the cheese dishes of the peasants of Kumrovec to the fare that was served at state banquets.[6]

Josip loved his native village and was tempted to stay there helping his brother at his job of making tiles and cement pipes; but he overheard his father and mother say that he was wasting his training as a metalworker, and in any case he would no doubt before long have gone off in search of adventure and better prospects. In January 1911 he left home again and went to Ljubljana in Slovenia, but was unable to find work there. He was told that casual employment could be found in the Austrian port of Trieste, and as he could not afford the fare he walked the sixty miles to Trieste through the snow, sleeping in barns along the road. On the last night of his journey he slept in a barn where a cow, mistaking him for a pile of salt, tore his suit as he slept. He told Dedijer: 'I was not lucky with suits.'[7]

In London, Lloyd George was piloting the National Insurance Bill through the House of Commons; it enacted that workers could draw unemployment benefit from the government. But no such system had been introduced in the Austrian Empire. Broz went to the Trieste branch of the Metalworkers Union and drew unemployment pay from the union. He spent ten days walking around Trieste, but failed to find work; so he went home to Kumrovec, hitching a lift for part of the way and walking the rest of the journey.

He had now learned another painful lesson: that a qualified workman cannot necessarily find work. But he found a job as a metalworker in Zagreb, where he was able to take part in the twenty-four-hour general strike that the Social-Democratic party and all the trade unions called on May Day. The local priests throughout Croatia preached sermons telling the workers in their congregations that they would be committing a mortal sin, and joining the ranks of Antichrist, if they joined in the strike on May Day. In Croatia, as in Italy, France, Spain and Mexico, the Catholic Church was at war with the Socialist movement. The sermons had some effect on the workers, and more on their wives; but the stoppage of work in Zagreb on May Day 1911 was almost complete.[8]

Broz soon left Zagreb and took another job in Ljubljana before settling down to work in an engineering works in the little Slovenian town of Kamnik. He stayed there for nearly a year. Then he and the other workmen in Kamnik were told that better-paid jobs were available at the Kolben-Daněk steel works at Jince-Čenkov near Klatovy in southern Bohemia.[9] When they arrived there, they found that the local Czech workers were on strike and that the men from Kamnik had been hired as strike-breakers. This was pointed out to them by the pickets, and they refused to scab. The management gave way within a week and accepted the strikers' demands. Broz and the Slovenes from Kamnik then agreed to work in Jince-Čenkov.

Broz enjoyed himself in Bohemia. He afterwards said that it was one of the happiest times of his life. He was young, healthy, and earning good money. He liked the evenings in the inns and dance-halls, and the picnics in the country at weekends. He said nothing to Dedijer about his friendships with young women, but in 1953 it was not considered essential, even in Western Europe and America, for someone to describe his sexual experiences in detail in his memoirs. It would have been undesirable for a Communist president of Yugoslavia to say anything about this side of his life in Jince-Čenkov; but since his death a great deal has been written about it by the more popular of his biographers. They have provided their readers with the names of various women who were his mistresses; he is said to have married one of them, who is still alive today, aged about a hundred. According to these stories, his first wife was a Czech whom he met in Bohemia in 1912, and she, like each of these women, had one son and no other children by Josip Broz.[10] It would be almost impossible to verify the truth of these stories and the identities of these wives, mistresses and bastards, though the names of some of them have been published; but in view of Tito's personality and the interest in women which he showed in later life, we can safely assume that the pretty Czech girls were noticed and pursued by the good-looking and daring young Croatian metalworker.

Like young men of his age two generations later, he wanted to see more of the world, and to travel within the limitations imposed by his lack of funds and by the transport available in 1912. If there were no aeroplanes and long-distance lorry drivers who would give him lifts, he had the advantage that he could travel throughout the Austrian Empire and across international frontiers without a pass-port and that he did not require a labour permit to work abroad. After passing through Pilsen, where he was not impressed by the Škoda works, he went to Munich. He worked there for a short time before going on to Mannheim. The first motor car had been built by the Daimler-Benz factory in Mannheim in 1885; now there were 40,000 cars in Germany. Broz worked at the Daimler-Benz factory. He then visited, and greatly admired, the modern factories in the Ruhr; but before the end of 1912 he had arrived at his brother's house in a village near Vienna.

He stayed for several months with his brother and sister-in-law.[11] His brother was still working on the railways, but Josip found employment as a metalworker in the Daimler-Benz factory in Wiener-Neustadt, forty miles south of Vienna. From his brother's house in the village he could travel by train every day to Wiener-Neustadt and to Vienna on Sundays and holidays.

He enjoyed his stay with his brother. He liked the work in the Daimler-Benz factory; apart from working there as a skilled metal-worker, he was often asked to drive and test the cars. They were large cars with heavy brasswork; the brakes were outside the door by the driver's seat. He had a nasty accident in the factory, when the tip of his left-hand index finger was badly mutilated in a machine. He did not lose the finger tip, but kept the scar all his life.[12]

On Sundays he went to Vienna. The city, with a population of nearly two million, was at the pinnacle of its glory in 1912. The Emperor Franz Joseph lived in the Hofburg in the city centre and in his other palace at Schönbrunn on the outskirts. He was aged eighty-two, and had reigned for sixty-four years, a little longer than Queen Victoria or than any European sovereign except Louis XIV of France in the seventeenth century. Commercially, the city was thriving. It was a brilliant intellectual centre, the birthplace of revolutionary ideas that shocked the more conservative inhabitants. In music there was Schönberg, Webern, Berg, Mahler and Richard Strauss; in paint-ing, Klimt, Schiele and Kokoschka; Loos, with his very controversial architectural buildings; and Freud, whose theories of psychoanalysis still outraged many people. In the cafés and theatres the music and operettas of Johann Strauss were as popular as the more recent successes of Franz Lehar, *The Merry Widow* and *The Count of Luxemburg*.

A young man from Braunau-am-Inn, Adolf Hitler, was living in Vienna at this time. He was aged twenty-three, three years older than Josip Broz. He was unemployed, frustrated and embittered, blaming his troubles on the many Jews who lived in Vienna. 'Wher-ever I went', he wrote in his book *Mein Kampf*, 'I began to see Jews, and the more I saw the more strongly they became distinguished in my eyes from the rest of humanity . . . Was there any form of filth or profligacy, particularly in cultural life, without at least one Jew involved in it? . . . Gradually I began to hate them.'[13]

Unlike Hitler, Broz was very happy in Vienna. All his life he was fond of music. He hated jazz, which was becoming popular in 1912, and in later life he said that he did not like modern music; but he loved the Viennese dance music and light operas. He could not afford to go to the expensive cafés, but he would lean against the railings outside, listening to the top orchestras playing the waltzes of Johann

Strauss and Lehar, till the head waiter chased him away. But there were plenty of cheaper cafés, and the Orpheum music hall where there were clowns, conjurors, and the music of the dances and operettas that he loved. He wished to become a good dancer, and attended dancing lessons; he had no difficulty in learning to waltz, but it took him much longer to master the quadrille and the polonaise. He also learned fencing at a gymnasium which he attended in Wiener-Neustadt.

During his year in Germany and Vienna, he learned to speak German fluently. Again he said nothing to Dedijer about girls, but we can be sure that he noticed the attractions of the sophisticated *Wienerin*, even if his popular biographers are wrong when they write that he married his second wife and had another son in Vienna.[14]

There was a shadow over life in Vienna and in other European cities in 1912. The fear of war was quite widespread among the more intelligent sections of the population, and many people realized that, if war came, it would be a far more terrible war than any that had been fought in the past. The large conscript armies that had come in with the French Revolution and Napoleon, and the development of modern weapons, caused a great increase in casualties in war during the course of the nineteenth century. In 1908 there had been a war-scare when Austria annexed Bosnia and Herzegovina, and another in 1911, after an incident between France and Germany at Agadir in Morocco. There was further international tension during the Balkan Wars of 1912–13, when Serbia, Bulgaria and Greece went to war with Turkey and won and then fought a second war between themselves to decide how they would divide the spoils.

The Socialist parties of the Second International were particularly alarmed at the danger of war. Marx and Engels had always supported every war against Russia, even when it was waged by the Sultan of Turkey or Napoleon III, because they hoped that if Russia were defeated in war, this would bring about the overthrow of Tsarism, the greatest enemy of the revolutionary movement in Europe. But after Engels's death, Socialism became associated with pacifism and opposition to war. The new policy, thanks largely to the influence of the French Socialist, Jean Jaurès, had been adopted at the congress of the Second International in Stuttgart in 1907.[15] Wars were caused by rivalries between the capitalists of different countries about their shares of international markets and colonial territories, and the capitalist government in every country used the workers as cannon-fodder in these wars. The international Socialist movement must therefore prevent war by threatening to call a general strike in every belligerent country if war broke out.

Lenin and Rosa Luxemburg,* who led the left-wing factions in the Russian and German Social-Democratic parties, went further: they believed that the workers in each country should welcome the defeat of their own country, because defeat in war might lead to revolution, as it had done in France in 1870 and in Russia in 1905.

The policy of preventing war by a general strike was loudly pro-claimed at the congress of the Second International in Basle during the war crisis of 1912, without reference to the more extreme course of action proposed by Lenin and Rosa Luxemburg. Next year Rosa Luxemburg declared, at a great Socialist rally near Frankfurt-am-Main: 'If they think we are going to lift the weapons of murder against our French and other brothers, then we shall shout: "We will not do it!" '[16] She was prosecuted for inciting the soldiers to mutiny, and sentenced to one year's imprisonment; but the fear of a general strike to prevent war worried the governments of the Great Powers. It was also a consolation to some members of the bour-geoisie. Ordinary middle-class ladies who hated Socialism reassured themselves that they need not worry about the possibility of war breaking out, because the Socialists would not permit it.[17]

In May 1913 Josip Broz reached the age of twenty-one, and became liable to do his two years' military service. His call-up papers were sent to his home in Kumrovec, and he was ordered to report to the barracks in Zagreb. On his first day in the army he encountered a bullying corporal who made life a hell for the recruits. The corporal thought that Broz's hair was too long and cut it with his clippers. At night, the corporal slept in the barrack room with thirty of the men. When he wanted to smoke he would put his cigarette in his mouth and make a hissing sound, at which all the men were required to jump out of bed and hurry to strike a match and light his cigarette. He also made them learn and recite the names and titles of all the archdukes in the Habsburg imperial family. One of the recruits, whom Josip Broz knew in Kumrovec, was slow-witted, and could

---

* Luxemburg, Rosa (1871–1919). Polish Socialist leader; joined the German Social-Democratic party; imprisoned for opposing the First World War; founder of the German Communist party; after leading the Spartakist revolt in January 1919 was assassinated by Right-wing irregulars.

not memorize the names of all Their Imperial Highnesses. The corporal made him sit on top of an unlit stove, tap himself on the forehead, and say over and over again: 'I am stupid!' When he was at last allowed to come down, Broz found him weeping in a corner of the barrack square.[18]

In the army Broz learned, by unpleasant personal experience, still more about the nasty side of human nature. He had already discovered that an uncle can cheat a nephew out of a pair of boots, and that a fellow-lodger can steal a new suit from a young man who has just bought it with his savings. Now he found out how an NCO can abuse his power when placed in a position of absolute authority over his soldier comrades. But Broz was tough enough to survive and clever enough to prosper in the conditions in which he unfortunately found himself, perhaps by keeping as far as possible out of the corporal's way, by obeying him, by doing his job efficiently, and by impressing the corporal with his personality. Did his experiences in the army barracks at Zagreb in 1913 prove useful to him when he was a Comintern *apparatchik* in Moscow during the Great Purge in 1937–39?

He did well in the army. Within less than six months, by Christmas Day 1913, he had been promoted to the rank of sergeant-major; at twenty-one, he was the youngest sergeant-major in the Austro-Hungarian army. He spent that winter learning to ski on the nursery slopes of the Sljeme mountains just outside Zagreb, and became a proficient skier.[19]

He entered for the army fencing championships, in which normally only officers took part, and came second in the finals in Budapest. In the deciding match he fenced against the other finalist, an Austrian count. The umpire repeatedly announced that the count had won a round when Broz thought that he himself had won, and Broz felt that the umpire was toadying to the count because of his rank. In the end Broz lost his temper and dealt the count a foul blow, slightly wounding him. Broz was disqualified and the count proclaimed the winner. When Tito told his son Miša many years later about this final of the fencing tournament, he said that he was now ashamed that he had dealt the count a foul blow, but that he had been sorely provoked and had lost control of himself.[20]

On 28 June 1914 Archduke Franz Ferdinand, who was Franz Joseph's nephew and the heir to the imperial throne, was assassinated in Sarajevo by a Bosnian nationalist while the archduke was paying the first official visit of an Austrian prince to the province Austria had annexed six years before. The Austrian government made it the excuse to declare war on Serbia, hoping to extend the empire still further by annexing Serbia. Russia threatened to declare war on Austria in support of Serbia; Germany supported Austria against Russia; France was bound by treaty to intervene in support of Russia; and Britain was prepared to go to war if the Germans invaded Belgium in their campaign against France.

This was the moment for the Socialist International to act in accordance with the resolution adopted at Basle in 1912, and on 29 July the Executive Committee of the International met in Brussels.[21] All the Social-Democratic parties declared that if war came they would call a general strike, except the Austrian Social-Democrats. Their leader, Viktor Adler, said that it would be impossible for the Social-Democrats to oppose the invasion of Serbia because of public opinion in Vienna; the people were enthusiastically clamouring for war. In 1914, as in 1848 and 1991, the masses showed that they were patriots and nationalists first and Socialists nowhere.

Within a few days the leaders of the other Socialist parties had followed Adler's example. Jaurès was assassinated in Paris by a young conservative who thought that he was a traitor to his country; but at his funeral the Socialist prime minister, Viviani, said that the best way of honouring Jaurès's memory was to support the war. The Belgian Socialist leader, Vandervelde, joined the Belgian government and appealed to the Russian Socialists to forget their opposition to the Tsar and to support the Russian war effort. The German Social-Democrats held out longer than the others; but they found that their party members and all the workers whom they encountered were insisting that they should support the defence of the Fatherland against the Russians and the French. They gave way, and declared their support for Germany in the war. A minority of the German Socialists, led by Karl Liebknecht* and Rosa Luxemburg, opposed the war and were imprisoned.

Only two of the Socialist parties adhered to their policy of opposing the imperialist war. The Serbian Socialists said that their Pan-Slav government should not use the Serbian workers to fight against Aus-

---

* Liebknecht, Karl (1871–1919). German left-wing Socialist leader; imprisoned for opposing the First World War; joined with Rosa Luxemburg in leading the Spartakist revolt and was assassinated with her in January 1919.

tria in the interests of Russian Tsarism. Several of their leaders were called up for the army; one of them was killed in action, and was posthumously awarded a high military decoration for valour.

The Russian Socialist MPs in the Duma in St Petersburg opposed the war. They were arrested and sent to Siberia. Lenin, in Zurich, called on the workers in every country to oppose the war and 'turn the imperialist war into civil war'.[22]

The decision of the Second International in 1912 to oppose imperialist war, and its failure to implement it in 1914, shaped the future of the Communist movement in which Josip Broz would play so important a part. The Socialist leaders in France, Germany and Austria supported the imperialist war because the pressure from their rank-and-file forced them to do so. They felt, as Viktor Adler said in July 1914, that 'it is better to be wrong with the working class than to be right against them'.[23] They were legal and democratic parties and hoped to come to power and introduce Socialism after winning a free election; and they knew that they would not win the next election if they outraged patriotic feeling by opposing the war and betraying the boys in the army. Lenin had never thought of winning power at a free election. He believed that it was necessary to create a party of dedicated Communists, of 'professional revolutionaries' who would be ready to make a revolution and seize power when the opportunity arose.[24] In the meantime the Communists must defy popular chauvinism, and oppose the war.

Lenin and his followers, convinced that the Social-Democratic leaders and the majority of the working class had betrayed the principles of international solidarity in 1914, saw themselves as a small body of saints in a world of sinners. In their variety of Marxism-Leninism, the God of Historical Development, who had decreed that the victory of Communism was inevitable, had also ordained that the majority of men were reprobates and that only a small minority of Communists were the Elect. No wonder that Lenin and Trotsky, who in this respect was a true Leninist, often compared the role of the Communists in the 'proletarian' revolution to that of the Calvinists in the bourgeois revolutions of the sixteenth and seventeenth centuries.

But in August 1914 Josip Broz was not yet a Marxist-Leninist, a member of the Communist Elect, a professional revolutionary. He was one of many millions of young men who found themselves in the army of one of the belligerent powers at the outbreak of the First World War.

CHAPTER 6

❖

Sergeant-Major Broz

S OON after Austria declared war on Serbia, Broz marched with his regiment towards the Serbian frontier; but before he reached it he was arrested and imprisoned in Peterwardein Castle in Novi Sad on the Danube, some twenty miles on the Hungarian side of the Serbian frontier. This historic fort, which had been Prince Eugène's headquarters during his Belgrade campaign in 1717, was now a military prison. This much is certain, but Tito gave three different versions as to why this occurred.

When Dedijer was writing his biography, Tito told him a Marxist-Leninist version, that 'we peasants and workers in the regiment' hoped that Austria would be defeated and that this would lead to the downfall of the Austrian Empire and the Habsburg monarchy. He was overheard saying this to his comrades in the regiment by an old sergeant-major who was loyal to Franz Joseph. The sergeant-major denounced him to the military authorities and he was imprisoned in Peterwardein. He was told by his cellmates that the prisoners had been incarcerated in the castle for many weeks without being brought to trial; but he repeatedly banged on the door of his cell and demanded a court-martial. At his trial he denied the old sergeant-major's story and persuaded a young soldier to give evidence on his behalf. The court believed him and his witness, and acquitted him.

According to Djilas,* Tito also told a Pan-Slav version of this story

* Djilas, Milovan (1911–   ). Yugoslav Communist leader; a close collaborator of Tito on the Politburo from 1937–54; expelled from the Communist party for wishing to introduce democracy in Yugoslavia; imprisoned several times between 1955 and 1966; lives today in Belgrade.

to Dedijer which is much the same as the Marxist-Leninist version except that he was overheard saying, not that he hoped that Austria would be defeated, but that he intended to desert to the Russians. But Djilas says that Tito once said that he had been arrested because of a clerical error, and that he was released after being imprisoned for a few hours in Peterwardein. This is the most likely explanation of why, after he had been arrested on such a charge, he was still trusted as a loyal and able sergeant-major. There may be a grain of truth in the Marxist-Leninist version, but the Pan-Slav version is certainly wrong.

There are contradictions in detail between these different versions; but there is no doubt that Broz was arrested on a charge of sedition and imprisoned in the first cell on the left when entering Peterwardein Castle, and held there either for a few days or for a few hours before being released, acquitted, vindicated and restored to his position as a sergeant-major without a stain on his character as a loyal soldier of Franz Joseph.[1]

At the outbreak of war the Russian army immediately took the offensive and invaded Germany and Austria. The Germans drove them out of East Prussia, but they advanced against the Austrians and penetrated deep into the Polish provinces of Austria, crossing the Carpathians and arriving within 125 miles of Budapest. Broz's regiment was quickly diverted from the campaign against Serbia and sent to stop the Russians.[2] On the Western front the armies were settling down to the slow horror of trench warfare; but in the Carpathians they fought an old-fashioned war in which the cavalry played a leading part. It was bitterly cold in the Carpathians in the winter of 1914–15. Some of the soldiers in Broz's unit froze to death.

Broz's company commander was a Croatian officer, Captain Tomašević, who was loyal to the Austrian Empire; but many of the Slavs in the Austrian army were affected by the secret propaganda of the Pan-Slavists who urged them to desert to the Russians and fight on the side of their Slav brothers against the Austrians. The Tsarist government encouraged the Pan-Slavists, and warned the Russian sentries in the army in the Carpathians to welcome any deserters who tried to come over to them. The Pan-Slavists had great success with the Czech soldiers, and many thousands of them crossed to the Russian lines at night. They were much less successful with the Croats. A few Croatian soldiers deserted to the Serbs and the

Russians, but not many. Broz had no intention of deserting to the Russians; he had never been a Pan-Slavist.

During that cold winter in the Carpathians, Broz continued to be a good and energetic NCO. He did not like his company commander. Captain Tomašević was a very severe disciplinarian, and meted out punishments for the slightest offence; but he had no reason to punish Sergeant-Major Broz, who had been falsely accused of subversion but had been acquitted and in every other way was a model NCO. Broz was acting in the way in which the Communist parties in future years would instruct their members to behave when they were serving in a bourgeois army during an imperialist war. By being a good soldier he would win the respect of the other men, who would then be more likely to listen favourably to his seditious propaganda.

Broz was chosen to lead small reconnaissance parties which raided the Russian outposts and captured prisoners. He enjoyed performing this duty, for it gave him scope to use his personal initiative. He often volunteered to lead these raids. On one of them he and his men captured eighty Russians who were sleeping in a house and had not posted sentries. 'Some of my men proposed killing them,' he told Dedijer, 'but I have never believed in useless bloodshed, so we brought them all back to our lines.'

On Easter Sunday, 4 April 1915 (22 March by the Russian calendar) the Russians launched an attack on the Austrian positions in the Carpathians. Broz's company was stationed near Okno, which today is in northern Romania near the Ukrainian frontier. They were successfully holding off an attack by the Russian infantry when a unit of Circassian cavalry broke through and attacked the Austrians in the rear. A Circassian stabbed Broz in the back below his left arm with a long two-pronged lance which just missed his heart but inflicted a very serious wound. He lost consciousness. He told Dedijer that he believed that the Circassians would have massacred all the wounded men if some Russian troops had not arrived and stopped the slaughter. Broz and the other survivors were taken prisoner.

Broz was sent to a Russian military hospital at Sviashsk near Kazan, about 1,500 miles behind the battlefront. He was well cared for, but his wound was serious, and complications set in. He developed pneumonia, and caught typhus. Once, when he had a high fever and was unconscious, a nurse tied a red ribbon to his bed, which was a sign that the patient was incurable and was to be left to die; but he was tough, and he recovered. During his convalescence he learned to speak Russian. He was able to use the hospital library and read Tolstoy, Turgenev, and Kuprin's brutally realistic novels and short stories about army life and brothels.

When he was cured he was sent 400 miles further east to Kungur, near Perm, where there was a big camp of German, Austrian and Hungarian prisoners-of-war. The prisoners were put to work repairing the railway line to Siberia. The Russians appointed Broz to be in command, under the Russian military authorities, of all the prisoners-of-war in the camp. As an NCO he was not obliged to work, under the provisions of the Hague Convention; but he volunteered for work, to avoid becoming bored. Many of the Czech and some of the Croatian prisoners-of-war in Russia volunteered to join the Russian army and fight against Austria for the Pan-Slav cause; but not Broz.

The war went on, with more and more casualties. The British lost 70,000 men in one day's fighting on the Somme; by 1917, they had suffered higher casualties than the total in all their wars in the previous thousand years. The French and German casualties had been equally heavy; but the Russian losses were much heavier. They lost five million men, more than all the other combatants combined.

The International Red Cross was organizing the supply of parcels to the prisoners-of-war, and parcels were duly sent, through the American and Swedish Red Cross, to the Austrian prisoners-of-war working on the railway at Kungur. They did not reach the prisoners. Broz discovered that they were being stolen by the Russian chief engineer on the railway. He complained to the representative of the Swedish Red Cross, who discovered the chief engineer's thefts. The old Russian countess who was in charge of the Red Cross in the district was indignant, and the chief engineer was severely reprimanded. He decided to be revenged on Broz. One day some prisoners-of-war were late for work. The chief engineer accused Broz, who was in charge of them, of being responsible, and sentenced him to be locked up in a cellar. There he was assaulted by three Cossacks, who beat him with their knouts – the whip with three thongs made of leather and wire with a metal spike at the end. Few victims survived more than a hundred blows with the knout. The three Cossacks gave Broz about thirty blows. He told Dedijer that he would remember these blows all his life.

He was kept in the cellar for some weeks, but after the three Cossacks had left he was guarded by other Russian soldiers, who treated him kindly. Then one day, in the spring of 1917, the news reached Kungur that there had been a revolution in the capital, Petrograd (as St Petersburg was now called) and that the Tsar had abdicated. Discipline in the army was breaking down all over Russia. Broz was released from the cellar and sent to work on repairing the railway at a small station near Perm. He became friendly at the station with some railway workers who supported Lenin's Bolshevik party. They showed him some pamphlets by Lenin, and talked to him about the revolution.

Lenin had returned from Switzerland to Petrograd in April; he had travelled through Germany with the assistance of the German government, who hoped that he would cause disaffection in Russia. He immediately launched a propaganda campaign against the war. But the Allied leaders insisted that Russia should continue the war. Russia was now led by the moderate Social-Democrat, Alexander Kerensky.* In response to the appeals of the Western Allies, he ordered the Russian army to launch a new offensive in the summer of 1917. Initially successful, it was then repulsed with heavy losses.

Lenin and the Bolsheviks offered the people 'bread, peace and land': bread for the workers in the capital suffering from food shortages, peace to the soldiers at the front, and land to the peasants who hoped to seize and divide the great estates of the nobility. The British diplomatic representative in Russia, Robert Bruce Lockhart, had no doubt which of these slogans was the most important. 'The revolution', he wrote, 'was a revolution for land, bread and peace – but, above all, for peace. There was only one way to save Russia from going Bolshevik. That was to allow her to make peace. It was because he would not make peace that Kerensky went under. It was solely because he promised to stop the war that Lenin came to the top.'[3]

One of the Bolshevik railwaymen told Broz that his son worked in the big Putilov engineering works in Petrograd and could probably find a job there for Broz; so Broz decided to go to Petrograd. He escaped from the prisoner-of-war camp without any difficulty, as the guards, like so many other Russian soldiers, had deserted and gone

---

* Kerensky, Alexander (1881–1970), Russian moderate Socialist leader; prime minister after the overthrow of the Tsarist regime in 1917; overthrown by the Bolshevik revolution of October 1917, escaped from Russia, and lived for the rest of his life in exile.

home. He climbed on to a goods train that was going to Petrograd, hiding between some sacks of wheat, and reached the capital after several days' travel. He stayed with his friend's son in Petrograd and worked in the Putilov factory.

The Bolsheviks had a good deal of support in the factory, and Broz soon found himself drawn into political activity. Less than a month after he arrived in Petrograd, the abortive insurrection took place which became known as 'the July Days'. It began with a spontaneous demonstration by factory workers and the discontented soldiers in the city, who brought their arms with them on the demonstration; it ended in a half-hearted attempt by the Bolsheviks to seize power. The demonstrations continued for three days, with desultory firing taking place between the armed demonstrators and the police and military units supporting Kerensky's government; then reinforcements arrived for the government troops, and the revolt was suppressed.

Kerensky now revealed that the German government had sent money to Lenin and the Bolsheviks. It was strongly denied by the Bolsheviks at the time, and later, but we now know that it was true.[4] The Bolshevik newspapers were suppressed, their party offices were raided and wrecked, and their supporters were beaten up by the soldiers and by anti-Bolshevik workers. Trotsky was arrested, but Lenin escaped from Petrograd disguised as a stoker on a train; after hiding for a month in a forest in the country, he reached Viborg in Finland, and stayed in the house of the chief of police, who was a secret Bolshevik sympathizer.

Broz took part in the demonstrations during the July Days, and came under fire from the government troops. After the suppression of the revolt he expected to be arrested, and decided to escape to Finland, for, though Finland was a province of the Russian empire, the police control had always been less rigid there. But he was stopped at the frontier of the province, and as he had no identity papers he was arrested, taken back to Petrograd, and imprisoned in the famous Peter and Paul Fortress. He was held here for three weeks in a cell that was cold and damp even in August, with the waters of the River Neva washing the outer wall of the cell.

He was then interrogated by a police official. Broz told him that he was an escaped Austrian prisoner-of-war. The interrogator was relieved to hear it, for he had thought that his prisoner might be an important Bolshevik agent. 'Fool,' he said to Broz. 'Why didn't you say so earlier? You have spent three weeks in here when you could already have been outside.'

The authorities decided to send him back to the prisoner-of-war camp in Kungur, and he was put on a train, under escort. When the train stopped at a station along the line, he asked the guard's permission to fetch some water so that they could make some tea, and took his opportunity to run out of the station and escape. He told Dedijer that the station where he escaped was Ekaterinburg (later called Sverdlovsk); but it is surprising, even allowing for the chaotic state of the railways in 1917, that a train from Petrograd to Kungur should have passed through Ekaterinburg. He jumped on another train travelling to Siberia, and a friendly conductor allowed him to travel without a ticket. The police searched the train for an escaped prisoner-of-war, but did not suspect that Broz was the man they were looking for, because he spoke such fluent Russian.

When the train reached Omsk in western Siberia, some 2,000 miles from Petrograd, it was stopped and searched by Bolshevik supporters who called themselves the Red Guard. They told the passengers that news had just arrived that the Bolsheviks had seized power in Petrograd by a revolution on 7 November (25 October by the Russian calendar) and that they were looking for escaping bourgeois and counter-revolutionaries. Broz explained that he was an Austrian prisoner-of-war, 'a worker like you are', and they accepted him as a friend. He left the train at Omsk, and enrolled in the Red Guard himself.

CHAPTER 7

❖

The Russian Civil War

B ROZ spent the next three years in Omsk and the surrounding countryside. They were momentous years in the history of Russia and Europe; but Broz, after all his travels and adventures since August 1914, lived quietly in Siberia from the day of the October Revolution to the final victory of the Bolsheviks in the civil war. Djilas has accused him of telling exaggerated tales about his exploits,[1] but he frankly admitted to Dedijer that he had done very little during the Russian Revolution. 'It has been written on many occasions that I took considerable part in the October Revolution and civil war in Russia. Unfortunately, that is not so.'[2]

When the Bolsheviks seized power in Petrograd, they formed a coalition government with the left Social Revolutionaries, who were the successors to the terrorists of the People's Will party and drew their support from the peasants. In November 1917 free elections were held throughout Russia to elect a Constituent Assembly. The voters elected 532 Social Revolutionaries and candidates of other parties and 175 Bolsheviks. When the Assembly met in January 1918 Lenin, imitating Cromwell and Napoleon, sent a handful of Bolshevik soldiers to drive the deputies from the parliament building at the point of the bayonet.

Lenin had no intention of establishing parliamentary democracy. 'History teaches us', he wrote, 'that an oppressed class has never and can never come to power without passing through a period of dictatorship, that is . . . the forcible suppression of the most desperate and frenzied resistance, that shrinks from no crime, which is always put up by the exploiters. . . . It would be monstrous to promise the exploiters freedom of association in times and situations in which they are resisting their overthrow and defending their privileges.

Neither in England in 1649 nor in France in 1793 did the revolutionary bourgeoisie guarantee freedom of association to the royalists and nobility when these summoned alien troops to the country and "assembled" to organize an attempt at restoration.'[3] When Lenin spoke of the dictatorship of the proletariat he meant the dictatorship of the Communist party, which was immediately imposed in those areas of Russia which were under Bolshevik control.

Lenin was convinced that the Bolsheviks could not resist the advance of the German army and would have to make peace and accept the German terms, however harsh. But the Social Revolutionaries wished to wage a revolutionary war against the Germans, and tried to provoke the war by assassinating the German ambassador who had just arrived in Moscow, the new Russian capital. The Bolsheviks then shot a number of Social Revolutionaries and suppressed the Social Revolutionary party. The Allies decided that the Japanese should seize Vladivostok, the French Odessa, and the British Archangel, and carry on the war against Germany on Russian soil; and British agents made secret contact with the illegal Social Revolutionaries in Bolshevik territory. A young Social Revolutionary woman tried to assassinate Lenin and wounded him severely; the Bolsheviks, as a reprisal, shot 500 'counter-revolutionaries' indiscriminately chosen from among all their opponents. They set up a secret police, the Cheka, under Felix Dzerzhinsky, a Polish aristocrat who had become a devoted Bolshevik. He said that the men who served in the Cheka would all have to be either saints or scoundrels. During the next three years the Cheka shot thousands of anti-Bolsheviks on the slightest excuse.

Trotsky wrote that the Bolsheviks, between the Germans and the Allies, 'were between hammer and anvil'.[4] But even in this uncomfortable position it is possible to gain a good deal by skilful manoeuvring. Trotsky's handling of the situation was not very skilful. Broz did much better twenty-five years later when he was between the hammer and the anvil of Hitler, Churchill and Stalin.

There were 70,000 Czechs in Russia who had deserted from the Austrian army and crossed to the Russian lines. They wished to continue fighting against the Germans. The Bolsheviks agreed with the Czech political leader, T. G. Masaryk* that they would be sent

* Masaryk, Tomaš Garrigue (1850–1937), Czechoslovak philosopher and Liberal politician; leader of the Czech movement in exile in the First World War; founder of the Czechoslovak Republic in 1918; president of Czechoslovakia 1918–35.

by train to Vladivostok and go from there in French ships to France where they could join the Allied troops on the Western Front. But on their way to Vladivostok they started fighting with some Hungarian prisoners-of-war who were sympathetic to the Bolsheviks, and a Czech and a Hungarian were killed. Trotsky then issued an order that any Czech found armed on the railway should be shot. The Czechs joined up with Tsarist White Guards in Siberia under the command of Admiral Kolchak and marched west against the Bolsheviks. They captured Ekaterinburg, where the Tsar and his family were imprisoned, but the Bolsheviks had murdered the whole family before the Czechs arrived.

Broz, at Omsk, was in the very middle of these events, and yet they touched him only marginally. When the Bolsheviks came to power they released all the prisoners-of-war in Russia and concentrated their propaganda on them, hoping that when they returned home they would spread Communism in their native countries. Broz was welcomed by the Bolsheviks at Omsk and joined the Red Guard which was being formed by Bolsheviks all over Russia. The Red Guards were ordered to fight against any Czechs and White Guards who arrived in their district. But when the Czechs and Admiral Kolchak's White forces captured Omsk in July 1918 they were in such strength that the Red Guards could not offer any effective resistance. Broz and his comrades went into hiding in the town.[5] This was wise of them, for Kolchak's troops shot many of the Red Guards whom they captured, or flogged them with the knout. When they took Ufa, they locked the Red Guards in a house and set it on fire, burning the prisoners alive.[6]

Broz hid in the house of a beautiful girl of fifteen, Pelagea Belousova (she was known as 'Polka'), until it was safe for him to leave Omsk and go into the country. There he became friendly with the chief of a Kirghiz tribe who had a small watermill in his territory. The chief, hearing that Broz was an engineer, engaged him to service and operate the mill.

Kolchak's White Guards often raided the Siberian villages, flogging any peasant whom they thought supported the Bolsheviks; but they did not come to the village where Broz was living, and Broz heard about what was happening in the civil war only by reading the newspapers. In 1952 he told his biographer Dedijer: 'Of all the leaders of the October Revolution, we heard most about Lenin. Trotsky was also mentioned. Less was known about the others. As to Stalin, during the time I stayed in Russia I never once heard his name.'[7] He would not have said this when he was in Moscow in 1938.

In November 1918 revolution broke out in Germany; the Kaiser abdicated, the new Social-Democratic German government accepted the Allies' terms, and the war ended. The German Communists tried to make a second revolution and seize power in Berlin, but the insurrection was suppressed, and the Communist leaders, Karl Liebknecht and Rosa Luxemburg, were murdered by the government forces who captured them. The Bolsheviks had more success in their propaganda with the Hungarians in Russia than with any of the other prisoners-of-war, and when the Hungarians returned home in the spring of 1919 they seized power in Budapest and proclaimed a Communist government. Lenin was delighted. He told the Hungarian Communists: 'You have given the world a still finer example than Soviet Russia.'[8] He had convened an international congress to form a Third, Communist, International, and those delegates who could reach Moscow through the Allied blockade passed a resolution founding the Comintern in March 1919.

They were very optimistic. On May Day they issued a message to the workers of the world: 'Before a year has passed the whole of Europe will be Soviet . . . Workers and soldiers of France, England, America, Italy, Serbia, Romania, Poland: turn your weapons against your own bourgeoisie. Your enemy is in your own country . . . In 1919 the great Communist International was born. In 1920 the great International Soviet Republic will come to birth.'[9]

The Allied leaders, meeting at Versailles to draft the peace treaty, had other plans for Europe. Germany was to cede territory to France and Poland, but it was the Austro-Hungarian Empire which was to be almost completely dismembered. Poland was to be restored by being given the lands that Russia, Prussia and Austria had annexed in the eighteenth century. The eastern part of Hungary (Transylvania) was ceded to Romania. Two new states, which had never existed, were created, chiefly out of former Austrian territory. Czechoslovakia was to have Austrian Bohemia and Moravia, and Hungarian Slovakia and Ruthenia. Yugoslavia was created by the union of Serbia and Montenegro, and the Austrian provinces of Croatia, Slovenia and Bosnia. Part of southern Hungary (the Vojvodina) was also granted to Yugoslavia. Austrian Trieste and Istria went to Italy.

King Peter Karadjordjević of Serbia, whose son Prince Alexander had led the Serbian army during the war, was chosen to be King of Yugoslavia, which was officially known as 'the kingdom of Serbs, Croats and Slovenes'. The new kingdom came into existence on 1 December 1918.

Czechoslovakia, Yugoslavia and Romania were closely linked to France. The three nations later signed a formal alliance which was known as 'the Little Entente'.

It was inevitable from the first that Serbia would dominate the new Yugoslavia, and this had been intended by the Allies. The people of Britain and France had admired the conduct of the Serbs during the war — their initial resistance to the Austrian invasion and their heroic retreat across the mountains in the snow to the French ships in the Adriatic when the Germans came to the help of the Austrians, and their steadfast endurance of very heavy casualties. Serbian children had been welcomed as refugees in Britain. The popular press praised 'gallant little Serbia'. Historians and other academics joined in, showing how, throughout the ages, the Serbs had always been braver, more faithful, and more successful than the other Yugoslavs, and how in 1914, when Austria, Hungary, Bulgaria and Turkey had all gone over to the German side, only Serbian resistance had stood in the way of the German advance to Constantinople.[10] The governments and public opinion in the West created a Serbian-dominated Yugoslavia in 1918 as surely as they destroyed it in 1991.

The Allied statesmen at Versailles expected the Yugoslavs, like the Czechs and Romanians, to play their part in destroying the Communist government of Hungary. While Yugoslav troops occupied the frontier region of the Vojvodina, which was granted to Yugoslavia under the peace treaty, the Czechs launched a full-scale invasion of Slovakia. They were repulsed by the Hungarian Red Army, but the Romanians were more successful and advanced on Budapest. In July 1919, the Comintern called for a general strike in all the Allied countries to save Communist Hungary. There was more support for the strike in Yugoslavia than in most other countries. In later years it was the proud boast of the Yugoslav Communist party that they had prevented the Yugoslav government from sending troops to crush the Hungarian revolution; but in fact it seems that the French commander in the Balkans, General Franchet d'Esperey, had already decided that the Yugoslavs should merely occupy the Vojvodina, leaving it to the Czechs and the Romanians to overthrow Communism in Hungary.[11] The general strike did not prevent Romanian troops from entering Budapest on 1 August. The Communist leaders escaped to Russia, but many other Communists were caught and shot.

But the Bolsheviks were still in power in Russia. The Red Army that Trotsky had hastily created fought against a variety of opponents, as first one side and then the other captured, lost and recaptured towns and advanced and retreated over vast distances. The enemies of the Bolsheviks consisted of Tsarist officers in the White Guards, the Czechs, the Social Revolutionaries, the Menshevik* faction of the Social-Democrats, Ukrainian nationalists, Anarchists, and people who hated Jews. There were many of these in Russia, particularly in the Ukraine; the anti-Jewish pogroms there in 1881, 1903 and 1905 had shocked public opinion in Western Europe. In 1919 thousands of Jews were massacred in the Ukraine by nationalists who were fighting against both the Bolsheviks and the Whites. The anti-Semitic propaganda made much of the fact that so many of the first-and second-rank leadership of the Bolsheviks were Jews.

By the spring of 1919 it was clear to the Allied leaders that the Bolsheviks in Russia would not be overthrown by half-hearted intervention; the blockade and the piecemeal aid to the Russian Whites was not enough. They would either have to accept the Bolshevik regime and reach some kind of *modus vivendi* with it, or intervene with Allied troops on a massive scale. The French prime minister, Georges Clemenceau, who had once been accused of being a Communard and had visited Marx in London, favoured large-scale intervention to destroy Bolshevism. President Wilson opposed this. The British prime minister, Lloyd George, also opposed it, but his secretary of state for war, Winston Churchill, was the strongest advocate of all in favour of intervention. In a series of speeches he whipped up hatred of the Bolsheviks. 'Of all the tyrannies in history, the Bolshevist tyranny is the worst, the most destructive, the most degrading.' He condemned the atrocities of Lenin and Trotsky, and accused the Bolsheviks of betraying their allies by making peace with Germany. 'Every British and French soldier lost last year was really done to death by Lenin and Trotsky.' He denounced 'the international Soviet of the Russian and Polish Jew'.[12]

* The Mensheviks (meaning 'Minority') were so called because the moderates were the minority at the congress of the Russian Social-Democratic Party in London in 1903, when the Bolsheviks (meaning 'Majority') followed Lenin.

Churchill used his influence in the government to authorize the publication of a government White Paper, *A Collection of Reports of Bolshevism in Russia*. It described the horrors of Bolshevik rule, how the Bolsheviks imported Chinese experts to inflict fiendish oriental tortures on their opponents, how churches were turned into brothels, and aristocratic and middle-class women were held there by force so that they could be raped by Bolsheviks.[13]

Churchill gave every encouragement to the Social Revolutionaries who were waging a terrorist campaign against Lenin's government, as they had done against the Tsar. They succeeded in assassinating several prominent Bolsheviks. The most prominent terrorist leader was Boris Savinkov, who had distinguished himself before the revolution by assassinating Tsarist officials. Most of the Allied leaders were nauseated by his past record and his personality, but Churchill was fascinated by his dark and gloomy character; he thought he looked exactly as a Russian terrorist ought to look. Churchill took Savinkov to see Lloyd George at Chequers; they travelled down from London in the same car, and got on very well. Churchill was sad a few years later when a Bolshevik *agent provocateur* lured Savinkov back to Russia on a terrorist mission, and betrayed him to the Cheka, who shot him.[14]

Churchill sent stocks of poison gas to the British forces at Archangel and in the spring of 1919 they were used against the Bolsheviks. When a Labour MP protested in the House of Commons against the use of poison gas, Churchill justified it on the grounds that the Bolsheviks had used gas first, though in fact the Bolsheviks had neither poison gas nor gas masks on the Archangel front. 'It is a very right and proper thing to employ poison gas against them,' said Churchill.[15]

But Churchill and Clemenceau failed to persuade Lloyd George and the Allied governments to intervene on a massive scale. The British soon evacuated Archangel, leaving their White Guard and Social-Democratic allies there to face the Bolsheviks alone. The Bolsheviks soon captured Archangel, and the Cheka shot thousands of prisoners. By the summer of 1919 Kolchak's forces were retreating from the Urals to the east. On 12 November they evacuated Omsk, and the Bolsheviks took control there.

Broz left the Kirghiz community and their watermill. The Kirghiz chief had hoped that he would remain with them permanently and marry the chief's daughter. But Broz did not enjoy Kirghiz food; he never liked foreign dishes. He declined the offer of the chief's daughter, and returned to Omsk. He found Polka, who had hidden him in her house when the Whites took Omsk, and soon afterwards he married her. They were married in an Orthodox church in Omsk, with all the ancient rites of the Orthodox marriage ceremony. Broz was twenty-seven and Polka not quite sixteen.[16]

The Bolsheviks continued their advance through Siberia. Most of the Czech soldiers, though anti-Bolshevik, held democratic or liberal opinions, and they became increasingly hostile to Kolchak's dictatorship. When they reached Irkutsk they arrested Kolchak and handed him over to the Mensheviks, who locked him in the local prison when they evacuated the town. The Bolsheviks shot him when they entered Irkutsk.

By the summer of 1920 the Bolsheviks had won the civil war and were in control of the whole of Russia. The Allied governments lifted the blockade and reluctantly accepted the fact that Russia had gone Bolshevik.

—— ❖ ——

CHAPTER 8

Return to Yugoslavia

B ROZ wanted to return home, to see Kumrovec and his family and friends again after his six-year absence. In later years it was often said that he joined the Communist party in Russia and was sent back to Yugoslavia by the Bolsheviks as an agent of the Comintern. He was certainly not an agent of the Comintern at this time; but there is some doubt as to whether or not he joined the Communist party in Omsk before he left Russia. Several people who knew him, including as close a collaborator as Djilas, have said that he did, but he himself stated that he first joined the Party in Zagreb after he arrived in Yugoslavia.[1]

Polka was pregnant, but she agreed to go with him to Croatia and in the spring of 1920 they left Omsk and travelled slowly via Petrograd and Estonia to Stettin, and through Germany and Austria to Yugoslavia. Broz was wearing the cap, with the red star at the front, which he had been given when he joined the Red Guard. On the advice of his travelling companions, he removed the star before he reached the Yugoslav frontier, in case it aroused the suspicion of the immigration officers. The other travellers were still worried that the officers would notice the mark on the cap where the star had been, and would guess what had made the mark; but no one asked Broz any questions at the frontier.

If he had been looking forward to his mother's *štrukli*, he was disappointed. Marija Broz had died in 1918, at the age of fifty-four. His father and brothers and sisters were still living, and Josip Broz and Polka were welcomed by his old friends in Kumrovec. But he was unable to find work as a skilled metalworker. He looked for it in Zagreb; but Yugoslavia, like the rest of Europe, was suffering from the postwar slump, and he was soon made redundant at the factory where he worked. For a time he worked as a waiter, as he had done when he took his first job at the age of fifteen. But after he had organized a strike among the waiters, he was sacked.[2]

He saw an advertisement in a newspaper for a job as manager of a flour mill in the village of Veliko Trojstvo (the Holy Trinity) about sixty miles east of Zagreb. The owner was an easy-going and friendly old Jew named Samuel Polak, who treated his employees well and never pursued his search for profits at the expense of their happiness. Polak and Broz liked each other at first sight, and Broz was offered and accepted the job. He moved to Veliko Trojstvo with Polka early in 1921, and stayed there for more than four years.[3]

When Broz returned to Yugoslavia in October 1920 local government elections had just been held. Many new political parties were quickly formed in time for the elections. One of them was the Social-Democratic party of Yugoslavia, which split into two factions. The moderate one affiliated to the Second International; the extremist group joined the Comintern, and adopted the name of the Communist party of Yugoslavia. Everyone was surprised by the Communists' success at the local elections. They won a majority on the city councils of Belgrade and Zagreb, and also did well in Macedonia and Montenegro, winning the support of the peasants in districts where there were no industrial proletarians.

The constitution required all elected MPs and local councillors to take an oath of allegiance to the king. The Communist councillors in Belgrade and Zagreb took the oath, but the Communist newspaper *Borba* published a statement that the Communists were taking it only as a necessary formality, and would not feel bound by the oath. The minister of the interior issued an order that in view of this statement the Communist councillors would not be allowed to take their seats. The Communist mayor of Zagreb protested, and was forcibly thrown out of the town hall by the police.

The Communist councillors appealed to the Constitutional Court, arguing that their ejection violated the constitution. The court agreed that it did, but refused to grant any relief to the councillors of Belgrade and Zagreb on the grounds that they had lodged their appeal out of time. Only in Montenegro, where the Communists applied in time, were they allowed to occupy the places to which they had been elected on the local parish councils.

The Communists stood for the elections to the Constituent Assembly in October 1920. Broz joined the party, and helped to distribute its election literature in Zagreb. Again the Communists did well in the elections. They obtained thirty-eight per cent of the votes in Montenegro and fifteen per cent in Serbia, but less than ten per cent in Slovenia, Croatia and Bosnia.

In December 1920 the Communists called a miners' strike in Slovenia. The government drafted the strikers into the army; the Communists replied by protest demonstrations and called for a general strike in support of the miners. On 29 December the government issued a decree suppressing the Communist party and all its affiliated organizations and trade unions. Anyone who called for a general strike was liable to one month's imprisonment; civil servants who sympathized with Bolshevism were to be dismissed; Communist students who had won scholarships to the universities were to be prohibited from studying there; and many street demonstrations were banned.

Liberals, as well as Communists, protested against the decree. The Liberals were genuinely shocked at the suppression of the Communists' democratic rights. The Communists protested because protest was a form of struggle and a way of winning the support of the people; but they expected nothing less than the suppression of their rights by the class enemy, the bourgeoisie, and had no intention of giving such rights to the bourgeoisie in Russia or in any other country where they came to power.

The Communist deputies withdrew from the Constituent Assembly in protest against the decree, and during their absence the constitution was adopted on 28 June 1921, by 223 votes to 35, with 165 abstentions, among them the absent Communists. Next day Prince Alexander, who was acting as regent for the king, took the oath of loyalty to the constitution. As the regent left the hall, a young Serbian Communist threw a bomb at his car. The regent escaped unhurt, but seven of the bystanders in the street were wounded. A month later, another young Communist from a Muslim family in Bosnia assassinated the minister of the interior who had promulgated the anti-Communist decree of 29 December. The Socialist movement in Serbia and Bosnia had always drawn its inspiration from Bakunin and the Anarchists, and the terrorist handbooks of the German Anarchist, Johann Most, had been more widely read than the works of Marx and Engels.

The Communist party denied any responsibility for these terrorist acts, and claimed that the two young men had acted on their own initiative without the knowledge of the party; but when the minister's assassin was sentenced to death, the Communists organized a campaign to obtain a reprieve. After they had failed and he had been executed, they staged a great demonstration of sympathy for him at his funeral.[4]

The Yugoslav government was determined to destroy Communism. The prince regent, in his youth, had been a page of the Tsar of Russia,[5] and his right-wing Conservative Pan-Slav prime minister, Nikola Pašić, was so old that very few people remembered that he had once been close to Bakunin and the Anarchists.[6] The Serbian ambassador in Russia was convinced that Lenin was a German spy and an enemy of the Pan-Slav cause. He had been involved in a plot to assassinate Lenin, and when the plot failed, he had consoled himself by spitting in Lenin's face and breaking off diplomatic relations.[7]

Yugoslavia had granted asylum to 80,000 anti-Bolshevik refugees from Russia,[8] including many prominent Tsarist White Guards. These refugees hated the Bolsheviks who had deprived them of their property and had murdered the Tsar and his children and many of their friends. They published newspapers and books in Belgrade inciting hatred of the Bolsheviks and their Yugoslav Communist agents.

Pašić summoned an emergency session of parliament which passed the Law for the Protection of the State. Communist propaganda was made punishable by death; no supporter of Communist doctrines was to be permitted to hold any government employment or study at a university; the Communist deputies and councillors were expelled from parliament and from local government bodies. In January 1922 the members of the Executive Committee of the Communist party were arrested and sentenced to two years' imprisonment for violating this law.

The government was very successful, as the Communists themselves admitted, in destroying the Communist movement in Yugoslavia. Many members left the party, including several of the former Communist deputies, and joined other left-wing parties that were permitted to function legally. But a man was sent from Moscow to reorganize the party, to look for new intakes to replace the members who had been arrested or who had fallen away. He was Stevo Sabić, a Croat who had served as an officer in the Austrian army and had joined the Bolsheviks as a prisoner-of-war in Russia. He had been a more active Bolshevik than Broz, for he had become an officer in the Red Army, and later a full-time agent of the Comintern.

Under Sabić's direction, the Communists concentrated on two forms of activity. One was to agitate through the legal liberal organizations for the repeal of the ban on the Communist party; the other was to work in the trade unions. It was now illegal for trade unions to engage in any political activity, but they were permitted to exist, to negotiate with the employers, and to call non-political strikes.

Some party members advised Sabić to contact Broz at the mill in Veliko Trojstvo. Broz agreed to work for the illegal Communist party. He distributed illegal party leaflets and contacted workers in factories, urging them to be active in their trade unions and to go on strike against the reductions in wages which the employers were imposing to reduce their production costs in a period of recession; they came at a time when the cost of living was high in comparison with wages.

Broz attended illegal party meetings and took part in the discussions, which were sometimes heated. Some comrades believed that the difficulties which the party now faced had been caused by the hot-blooded terrorists who had provided the government with the excuse to suppress the party; they thought that by repudiating violence and pursuing moderate policies they would be able to persuade the liberals to insist on the repeal of the Law for the Protection of the State and enable the Communists to function again as a legal and moderate Socialist party. But other party members took the view that the suppression of the party showed that they would never be granted democratic rights by a bourgeois government and that a violent revolution was the only way out. Broz agreed with them. He made a speech at one of these meetings at which he denounced the leader of the moderate faction. 'With such leadership', said Broz, 'the Communist party of Yugoslavia will never be able to come to power.' The leader told one of the comrades that he believed that Broz was a police *agent provocateur*.[9] It is typical of Tito's self-confidence and sense of humour that he mentioned this to his biographer Dedijer.

At the beginning of 1924 Broz was elected a member of the party district committee for the area; but he was not yet a full-time agent of the Comintern, one of Lenin's 'professional revolutionaries'. He engaged in his political activities in his spare time, and continued his work at the mill. The kindly old Jew took care not to know anything about Broz's work for the illegal Communist party. He told Broz that as long as he did his job well, he could do whatever he liked in his spare time.

Soon after Broz was elected to the district committee, another member of the committee died of consumption; he was a carpenter who had led a number of successful strikes. The Communists and the Social-Democrats united to give their departed comrade a socialist funeral. But the dead man's family were Roman Catholics who wanted him to have a Roman Catholic funeral, and the Catholic priest was determined to prevent a political demonstration at the funeral. As the coffin left the family home, a Social-Democrat began to make a speech, but he stopped when the priest and the family objected. The Communists marched to the cemetery in front of the coffin carrying a wreath in the form of their emblem, the hammer and sickle.

The Communists remained quiet during the religious ceremony, but afterwards Broz made a short speech at the graveside. He ended with the words: 'Comrade, we swear to fight to the end of our lives for the ideas to which you were so devoted.' The Communists then unfurled a red flag over the grave.

The priest and the dead man's family complained to the authorities, who discovered that Broz was the man who had made the speech at the funeral. When the police came to the mill at Veliko Trojstvo and questioned him, he admitted it. They arrested him and marched him to the nearby town, chained to another man who had attended the funeral. Broz's wrists were bleeding from the tightness of the chains as he and his colleague were paraded through the streets before being taken to the prison.

They were kept in prison for eight days and then charged in the local magistrate's court with creating a public disturbance at a funeral. But the government's prosecuting attorney was a member of the Orthodox Church, who hated Roman Catholics. He told the prisoners what he thought of the Catholic priest who had instigated the prosecution, and advised them on the best line of defence for them to adopt at the hearing. The magistrate found them not guilty.[10]

But one thing was leading to another, and events were shaping the destiny of Josip Broz. He had come home to Croatia after six years of travel, adventures and hardships, and might perhaps have settled down to a quiet life with a good job, a beautiful and loving wife, and a happy family. He had joined the Communist party out of sympathy for the oppressed workers and peasants, and would have continued for a time distributing Communist leaflets and organizing strikes; then he would gradually have become disillusioned by the apparent futility of the struggle and by the constant bickering among the party leadership. It would gradually have dawned on him that when he and his comrades went on strike and lost their jobs, were baton-charged on street demonstrations, and were beaten up in prison, they were being sacrificed in the interests of a small ruling clique in the Kremlin in Moscow who wished to further its doctrinaire theories and the national interests of the Soviet Union. He would then have left the party and devoted all his time to his job, his wife and family.

He had found a good job with his tolerant employer at Veliko Trojstvo. He never revealed whether his married life was happy at this time, but as the marriage broke up some years later, it may not have been going well in 1925. There had been a series of tragedies with the children. Polka's baby who was born soon after they arrived in Yugoslavia died at birth. Next year she gave birth to a son who died of dysentery when he was a week old. The third child, born a year later, was a son, Hinko; he too died a few days after his birth. The fourth child, a little girl called Zlatica, was born in 1923. She lived longer than any of the earlier children, but at the age of two she died of diphtheria, like Broz's brother and sister and so many other peasant children in the filthy villages of Croatia.

The loss of Zlatica hit her father very hard. He did not have the solace of religion to help him; the Marxist God of Historical Development, though he would ensure the ultimate triumph of the Elect over the reprobates, did not offer any consolation to bereaved parents. Tito briefly told Dedijer about the death of 'little Zlatica, a beautiful child with golden hair . . . I carried her coffin to the cemetery and buried her myself.'[11] As soon as he had the money available, he built a headstone over the graves of his children. A fifth child, a son named Žarko, was born in 1924. He was the only child of Broz and Polka who survived.

Perhaps, even if Broz had kept a good job, had had a happier marriage, and if all his children had survived, he would still have been dissatisfied with a quiet, uneventful life, and would have had an irresistible urge for more adventures, to run risks, and to exercise his qualities of leadership. But he now had little choice left open to him. His speech at his comrade's funeral and his eight days' imprisonment had marked him, in the eyes of the authorities, as a dangerous Communist agitator. The police came regularly to Veliko Trojstvo nearly every Saturday and searched his rooms.

The decisive event in Broz's life was the death of old Samuel Polak in the summer of 1925. His business was inherited by his son-in-law, another Jew named Oskar Rosenberg. Broz found him a hard man, very different from his father-in-law. Rosenberg was disturbed by what he had heard about Broz's political activities, and the visits of the police to his rooms on Saturdays. He gave Broz the choice: 'Either you go in for politics or you work.'[12]

Broz did not like this. When he was an acolyte in Kumrovec and the priest slapped his face, he decided never to go to church again; and when his master at Sisak boxed his ears for reading aloud *The Adventures of Sherlock Holmes*, he ran away from the workshop. Faced with the alternatives offered to him by Oskar Rosenberg, he decided to leave his job and become a professional revolutionary.

Nora Beloff's dislike of Tito and of his political doctrines has not prevented her from making a very shrewd assessment of his character. She tells a story of how in later years he said to some visiting Americans that he considered emigrating to the United States when he was a young man, and that if he had done so 'I would have become President of General Motors instead of Yugoslavia'. None of Tito's intimate acquaintances believe that he would have said this, and it is more likely that the American visitors put their own thoughts into Tito's mouth. Nora Beloff comments that Tito had 'many of the qualities of a successful tycoon: willingness to take risks, unscrupulousness in eliminating rivals, sharpness in negotiations, and an unusual capacity to inspire personal loyalty', as well as being 'highly acquisitive, coveting property and enjoying luxury'.[13]

There is a great deal of truth in this, but it is only a half-truth. Tito was also a devoted Communist, a sincere believer in the Marxist-Leninist faith. No one whose chief ambition was to acquire property and enjoy luxury would have become a full-time activist in the illegal Yugoslav Communist party in 1925. He was in many ways different from a president of General Motors. He was more like a medieval cardinal, combining a strong sense of his religious duty to the Church with his love of luxury and power. He was even closer to a conventional army general (and several peasants became generals in the Russian Tsarist army), risking his life in the service of his king or emperor, and not only enduring but also relishing the hardships and risks which his position entailed, as well as the privileges, the luxuries and above all the power which it brought him.

In the last resort, it was Oskar Rosenberg who made Broz a professional revolutionary at the age of thirty-three by giving him the choice either to give up his work for the Communist party or to lose his job. Rosenberg feared the Communists who derided his religion and threatened his property; but it was not the Communists who murdered him in the gas chambers in Poland in 1942.[14]

CHAPTER 9

❖

The Professional Revolutionary

T HE Law for the Protection of the State had almost destroyed the Communist party of Yugoslavia. When the law was passed in 1921 the party had 60,000 members; but now that membership had been made punishable by death, fewer than 3,000 remained.[1] Many of these zealots were in Montenegro, a land of poverty and violence with a centuries-old tradition of lawlessness and resistance to authority. Others were middle-class students at Belgrade University. Milovan Djilas, who was both a Montenegrin and a student in Belgrade, wrote many years later, long after he had repudiated Communism, that most of them were not themselves the victims of injustice but were idealists, who were outraged at the injustice of a society in which others were oppressed. 'The great majority of us young people became revolutionaries in the hope of realizing brotherhood and equality, of freeing our working people from exploitation, of giving them a happier life. In my early experience I didn't know a single man who had become a Communist out of ambition or hope of material gain.'[2] It was very different later on.

The Communist students at Belgrade University took part in violent demonstrations, like the revolutionary students in Germany in the years before the revolution of 1848 and the non-Communist 'New Left' after 1960. They demonstrated in the park and threw bricks at the police, and disrupted the lectures of the Conservative Professor Bartoš, who had criticized leftist students. 'Someone suggested that we beat him up,' wrote Djilas. 'I approved, but in a modified form; cause chaos at his lecture, but don't hurt him seriously.' So the Communist students merely surrounded him at the end of his lecture, and cursed him and spat at him. 'In the commotion

[86]

a few blows were dealt, but not on the head.' This was certainly 'a modified form' of violence by Balkan standards.

The students heard that some White Russian refugees from the Soviet Union were putting on a performance of Glinka's opera *A Life for the Tsar* in a theatre in Belgrade. The opera was based on the story of the heroism of a Russian peasant fighting for the Tsar against the Poles in the seventeenth century. The Communist students in the chemistry department obtained some tear gas, and the comrades released it in the middle of the performance. They were delighted to see the audience scatter, and even more delighted to read the indignant articles in the press condemning Communist hooliganism. They did not foresee that a few years later the opera would be performed in Moscow under the title *Ivan Susanin* and acclaimed by Stalin's journalists as a splendid tribute to the patriotism of the Russian soldier.[3]

In the more industrialized provinces of Slovenia and Croatia, the Communists concentrated on workers in factories, and tried to organize strikes. Although the Communist party was banned, the Communist-controlled trade unions were legal. The party told Broz to find work in important factories and become a shop steward of the Metalworkers Union. This task required far more skill and patience than organizing violent student demonstrations at universities, where the object had been to shock the university establishment and the bourgeoisie. Here Broz was expected to win the trust of the industrial workers by fighting for their interests and organizing strikes. If a strike led to confrontation with employers and police, so much the better, because even if the strike was ultimately unsuccessful it would increase the workers' resentment and their determination to overthrow the capitalists and the bourgeois state; but if the Communists repeatedly led the strikers to defeat and involved them in useless suffering, the workers would lose faith in the Communists and refuse to follow them.

Broz took a job as a metalworker in the shipyards at Kraljevica near Bakar on the north Adriatic coast, where ships had been built under the Austrian Empire since the beginning of the eighteenth century. The shipyards were now owned by a Hungarian combine in which both British and French armament companies held an interest. This Anglo-French involvement was important for the Communists because a strike in the shipyards could be portrayed as a struggle against the exploitation of the Yugoslavs by foreign imperialism.

Broz worked on repairing torpedo boats of the Yugoslav navy and building a pleasure yacht for the Conservative statesman Stojadinović while he strengthened the trade union organization in the shipyards and got himself elected as a shop steward.

He soon found an opportunity to organize a strike, because the company was seven weeks in arrears in paying the workforce's wages. The tradesmen at Kraljevica agreed to supply the workers with food and other necessaries on credit, but charged them more than if they had paid cash down. Broz summoned a meeting of the workers in the shipyard and told them that they were being cheated. The company was getting the bank interest on its money until the workers were paid, and the tradesmen were charging them higher prices for supplying goods on credit; but when the workers received their wages they would not get any interest for the weeks that they had to wait. This was perhaps an appeal more to capitalist than to Socialist principles of justice, but Broz was the last man to be dissuaded by such philosophical considerations from putting forward an effective argument. It impressed the workers, and they went on strike. After nine days the management gave in and paid the wages, but a few days later Broz was sacked.[4]

In October 1926 Broz got another job at a railway wagon-works at Smederevska Palanka, forty miles from Belgrade, which was owned by a company in which both Yugoslav and French capital was involved. The workers there had many complaints which he could exploit; it was bitterly cold in the workshops in winter, and the workers were often unfairly fined for alleged misconduct. In March 1927 he wrote an article in a trade union journal about conditions in the wagon-works. 'Workers are fined every day for no reason except that the manager so pleases. The provincial labour inspector turns a deaf ear to all our complaints ... Comrades, we must all join our militant trade union organization, and then carry out an energetic struggle against the cruel exploitation of the insatiable bourgeoisie.' Ten days after that article was published, Broz protested against an unreasonable fine imposed on a young Croat worker, and was sacked.[5]

Broz was now so well known as a troublemaker that no employer would offer him a job, while in the eyes of the Communist party he had shown himself worthy of promotion. The party decided to appoint him as a full-time trade union official, as secretary of the Zagreb branch of the Metalworkers Union. This was only a step to a further promotion, for a few weeks later he was appointed secretary of the union for the whole of Croatia. He would now receive a modest but sufficient wage and have the duty of directing the work of shop stewards throughout the country. 'I was then thirty-five,' he afterwards told Dedijer, 'and the event was a decisive point in my life, for it made me a full-time executive of the workers' movement.'[6] He could have put it another way and said: 'It made me a professional revolutionary.'

The police were watching him closely. They knew very well that he was a Communist, but they could not prove it, and in Yugoslavia in 1927 it was still necessary to prove that a man was guilty before he could be convicted of an offence. The judges believed in the rule of law; some of them even had liberal sympathies, and did not approve of the Law for the Protection of the State. But the law had been constitutionally enacted by a democratically elected National Assembly, and the judges believed that it was their duty to enforce it. They would not twist the law to please the government, but they would play their part in protecting the state from Communist subversion; and when there was a conflict between the evidence of a policeman and a Communist, they nearly always believed the policeman.

On a very hot day in July 1927 Broz was working alone in the Zagreb office of the Metalworkers Union when some plainclothes policemen walked in and told him that he was under arrest. When he asked them why, one of them replied: 'You have got into so much trouble, Broz, that we could arrest you at any time on anyone of a dozen charges.' As well as searching the office, the police also raided his flat and found fifty books there. Most of them were political left-wing books, including *Women and Socialism* by the German Socialist, August Bebel; *The Mother* by the Russian Soviet novelist, Maxim Gorky; and *The Iron Heel* by the American, Jack London. He had been one of Lenin's favourite authors, and his books were therefore read by Communists. None of Broz's books were banned in Yugoslavia, but the police thought it suspicious that a metalworker, even a trade union official, should possess fifty books.

He was taken in handcuffs to the town of Bakar, a few miles from the Kraljevica shipyards, where he found that six of his former workmates in the shipyard had also been arrested. The seven prisoners were taken to the local prison at Ogulin.[7] The prison was in an old fifteenth-century tower with several rooms. A number of prisoners were confined together in each room. But the authorities took care to separate Broz from his six companions from the ship-yards, and he found himself alone in a group of thieves and other non-political criminals.

Ever since the early part of the nineteenth century, it had been one of the grievances of left-wing intellectuals that when they were arrested for a political offence they were placed together with common criminals, who often ill-treated them. But Broz could cope with such a situation. He neither despised nor feared the criminals, who were not so very different from the men with whom he had worked in factories and whom he had led as an NCO in the Austrian army. He knew how to talk to them, how to explain his position as a trade union militant, and the kind of arguments which would make them sympathize with Communism. Having no illusions about them, he knew just how to handle them, and soon they were looking to him for guidance like the soldiers in his battalion had done in the Carpathians in 1915.

One Sunday afternoon an official ceremony was held in the market square under the prison windows and within earshot of the prisoners. The district prefect opened the proceedings and ended his speech: 'Long live His Majesty King Alexander!' One of the prisoners in Broz's room shouted out from the prison window: 'To hell with the king!' Broz immediately realized what the repercussions would be, and took charge of the situation. He told all the prisoners in the room to lie down and pretend to be asleep, and to say that they had heard nothing. It was not long before the prison warders burst into the room, indignantly demanding to know who had insulted the king. But all the prisoners followed Broz's instructions, and the authorities never identified the offender.

Broz was not ill-treated in Ogulin prison, but it was unbearably hot during the summer months. He also found the food very bad. He sent a formal protest to the district judge, but as the prison authorities illegally refused to pass it on, he went on hunger strike. He found, like many other hunger-strikers, that he was ravenously hungry on the second day, but by the third day his appetite had gone and he lapsed into a satisfied oblivion. The prison warders then became alarmed, and urged him to take food; so did his fellow-prisoners, the non-political criminals.

The district judge then visited Broz and urged him to drink the very palatable soup from his own kitchen. He told Broz that he himself was interested in Marxist theory and had Marxist books in his house, and that if Broz ended his hunger strike he could come to his house and read them. Broz remained adamant; he would continue his hunger strike until a date was fixed for his trial. On the fifth day the authorities gave in, and Broz took his first food.

At the request of the lawyers for the prosecution the trial of Broz and his colleagues was held in secret on the grounds of national security. They were charged under the Law for the Protection of the State with being members of an illegal organization, the Communist party. The prosecution had been unable to find any evidence of their party membership, but relied on the fact that their trade union had organized a strike at the Kraljevica shipyards, that Marxist and other left-wing books had been found in Broz's rooms, and that one of the other defendants had admitted that Broz had given him one of these Marxist books. The prosecuting lawyers admitted that it was not illegal to possess these books, which might quite properly be read by students of politics; but they argued that the possession of the books, not by scholars but by trade unionists, combined with their part in organizing strikes, proved that their trade union was a concealed Communist organization.

The court found the defendants guilty, but treated them leniently. Broz was sentenced to four months' imprisonment. He appealed against the conviction, and the prosecution appealed against the leniency of the sentence. He was released from prison pending the hearing of the appeal by the Court of Appeal in Zagreb.[8]

The Communist party told Broz not to surrender to the authorities for the hearing of his appeal, so that he could carry on underground work for the party. He went into hiding in Zagreb. He wore dark spectacles as a disguise and carried forged identity papers showing him to be a middle-class technician in the engineering industry. This meant wearing a smart suit and adopting a bourgeois lifestyle. He frequented the more expensive cafés and restaurants in Zagreb. This was a cover for the work that he was carrying out for the Communist party – contacting other party members whom he met in cafés or public parks, and co-ordinating their work in the trade unions and other organizations.

Broz enjoyed his new life. He had always liked wearing smart suits, and he liked the middle-class cafés and restaurants where he ate and drank at the expense of the Communist party. But in one respect he was in a different position from the other gentlemen in the cafés and restaurants. While they enjoyed the comfortable security of the middle-class bourgeois, Broz knew that at any time he might be arrested by the security police, tortured, and sentenced to long-term imprisonment, perhaps even death. The nervous stress would have been unbearable had he not adopted the attitude of other members of resistance and underground movements, and assumed that he would not be caught, just as a soldier in wartime assumes that he will not be killed. But if he had objectively weighed up his chances he would have realized that he would probably be caught one day.

The Communist movement for which he ran these risks was celebrating a great triumph – the tenth anniversary of the October Revolution in Russia. When the Bolsheviks had seized power on 7 November 1917 (25 October by the Old Style Russian calendar) Lenin had hoped that they would be able to equal the achievement of the Paris Commune of 1871 and survive for two months before being overthrown. They were still in power in November 1927, after defeating the White Russian armies and the expeditionary forces of Britain, France, Czechoslovakia, Poland, the United States and Japan. But the whole world was against them, and they were against the whole world. They did not keep to the rules, and nor did the international bourgeoisie keep to the rules when dealing with them.

The Soviet delegates who went to negotiate peace with the Poles were seized and murdered by the Poles. In many countries, like Yugo-slavia, the Communist party was illegal and its leaders were in prison. In Britain, France and the United States the party was legal, but Communist leaders were often arrested and sentenced to short terms of imprisonment for sedition, incitement to mutiny, or contempt of court. In British India, Communist leaders were serving long prison sentences. In the United States many Communists were arrested, and a fraudulent con-man was allowed to swindle the Soviet authorities out of a large sum of money because the courts ruled that the Soviet government, having no legal existence, could obtain no legal redress in the United States. Soviet ambassadors were assassinated by White Russian exiles in Switzerland and Poland, and the killers were either acquitted or sentenced to short terms of imprisonment by the Swiss and Polish courts. The Soviet government, unable to obtain bourgeois justice abroad, could inflict proletarian justice at home. In retaliation for the murder of their ambassador to Poland, twenty Russian aristo-crats, who had been imprisoned for counter-revolutionary activity, were shot.

The greatest anti-Communist among the British imperialists was

Winston Churchill. He told an audience in Edinburgh that 'the Soviet government of Russia is one of the worst tyrannies that has ever existed in the world', who aimed 'to poison the world, and so far as they can the British Empire, with their filthy propaganda'.[9]

In Italy Benito Mussolini, who had originally been a revolutionary left-wing agitator very close to the Anarchists, had founded a patriotic anti-Communist, anti-Socialist and anti-Liberal movement in 1919 which he called Fascism. He denounced the pacifist traitors who had opposed the First World War and the trade unions who disrupted the country with strikes. His Fascists beat up strikers and rioting peasants and forced them to drink quantities of castor oil. In 1922 they marched on Rome, and the king appointed Mussolini as his prime minister. The Liberals and Socialists joined with the Communists in condemning Mussolini's dictatorship; but the Comintern's call for a world-wide boycott of Italian goods was a failure. The British Conservative newspapers were more success-ful in organizing a boycott of Soviet goods. Many petrol stations in England in 1927 displayed notices: 'No Soviet petrol sold here.'

In January 1927 Churchill, who was chancellor of the exchequer in Baldwin's Conservative government, passed through Rome on his way home from a holiday abroad. He called on Mussolini, and afterwards held a press conference in Rome which was attended by press correspondents from all over the world. 'I could not help being charmed', he told them, 'by Signor Mussolini's gentle and simple bearing and by his cool, detached poise'; and he added: 'If I had been an Italian I am sure that I would have been wholeheartedly with you from start to finish in your triumphant struggle against the bestial appetites and passions of Leninism.' He said that Fascism 'has rendered a service to the whole world'. Italy 'has provided the necessary antidote to the Russian poison'.

There were protests from the Labour and Liberal parties in Eng-land; but the British ambassador in Rome, Sir Ronald Graham, wrote to Sir Austen Chamberlain, the British foreign secretary, that Chur-chill's press statement 'seemed to me extremely good . . . Mussolini was perfectly delighted with it, but I cannot say the same as regards the Russian press representative!'[10]

In Moscow, on the tenth anniversary of the Glorious October Revolution, the Bolshevik leaders were not worrying about the hostil-ity of the capitalist world. They were far too busy quarrelling among themselves. After Lenin's death Zinoviev* and Kamenev† ganged up with Stalin to oust Trotsky from power. Once this had been accomplished, Stalin joined with Bukharin‡ to destroy Zinoviev and Kamenev; so Zinoviev and Kamenev made an alliance with Trotsky. In the summer of 1927 they formed a secret organization within the Communist party, holding meetings and discussion groups. Stalin and Bukharin denounced this as an attempt to form a second party. In October Trotsky, Zinoviev and Kamenev and their supporters were expelled from the Communist party. Zinoviev and Kamenev recanted and were ultimately readmitted; Trotsky refused to recant and was banished from the Soviet Union.

At the meeting of the Fourth Plenum of the Executive Committee of the Comintern in February 1928, Bukharin denounced this attempt of the opposition to form a second party. 'There can be two parties in the USSR', he said, 'only in the sense that one rules and the other is in prison.'[11] In later years, Tito and the leaders of the Yugoslav Communist party at one time denounced Bukharin as a Fascist and afterwards praised him as the champion of Leninist freedom against Stalin; but Tito all his life accepted Bukharin's maxim that there could never be two parties in a Communist state unless one of them was in prison.

In October 1927 Chiang Kai-shek, who had been supported by the Communists in China, suddenly turned on his Communist allies and massacred 30,000 of them in Shanghai and Canton. At the same time the British Labour party and the trade unions, alarmed at the defeat of the general strike and under pressure from Conservative attacks, broke off relations with the Soviet trade unions and refused to accept 'Russian gold'. The Communists reacted by swinging to the left and launching their fiercest attacks on the Social-Democrats, who were denounced as agents of the bourgeoisie and the main

* Zinoviev, Grigory E. (1883–1936). Soviet Communist leader; close friend and collaborator of Lenin in Switzerland during the First World War; first secretary of the Communist International in 1919; expelled from the party, imprisoned, and a defendant in the first great Moscow trial during the purge of 1936–8; executed in August 1936.

† Kamenev, Lev B. (1883–1936). Soviet Communist leader; close collaborator with Zinoviev; a defendant in the Moscow trial and executed in August 1936.

‡ Bukharin, Nikolai (1888–1938). Soviet Communist leader; joined with Stalin to destroy Trotsky, Zinoviev and Kamenev in 1927; denounced and expelled from the party by Stalin in 1929; a defendant in the Moscow trial and executed in March 1938.

enemy of the working class. The Comintern called the Social-Democrats 'Social Fascists', and Stalin declared that 'Fascism and Social-Democracy are not antipodes but twins'. So Tito began his career as a professional revolutionary just at the time when the Communist parties throughout the world were adopting a Leftist line.

There were special problems in the Communist party of Yugoslavia. Ever since its formation in 1919 Sima Marković had been the leading figure in the party. He was a Serb, and believed in the union of all the nations of Yugoslavia in one state. But a united Yugoslavia has always meant Serb domination. The political, economic and financial administration was centred in the capital, Belgrade, in Serbia; and the Serbs, who constituted more than thirty per cent of the population of Yugoslavia and were the largest single national group, regarded the Croats, the Slovenes, the Bosnian Muslims and the other ethnic groups as inferior peoples in a Greater Serbia. The Croatian Peasant party, led by Stjepan Radić, demanded autonomy for Croatia, and were supported by many Croatian Communists who denounced the pro-Yugoslav policy of the Serb Marković.

The Comintern in Moscow also opposed a united Yugoslavia. King Alexander's 'Kingdom of Serbs, Croats and Slovenes' was a member of the Little Entente with Romania and Czechoslovakia and the ally of France against the Soviet Union. By encouraging separation in Yugoslavia, the Comintern would help to disrupt a French satellite state. So while Marković continued to call for a united Socialist Yugoslavia, Radić was fêted by the Soviet government when he visited Moscow in the summer of 1924.

On 25 February 1928 the Zagreb Communist party held a secret conference. The delegates had been elected during the previous weeks at secret meetings of the party cells and regional committees. As a security precaution the conference was held at night in an inn on the Pantovčak road leading up to the summit of a hill. In 1928 it was on the northern outskirts of Zagreb; today it is not far from the city centre. It was just across the road from the woodlands surrounding the mansion and park of Baron Nikolić. The inn was a very popular resort for holidaymakers, and no one would be surprised if many guests stayed there, drinking and carousing, all night long.

Broz was one of thirty-two delegates who walked up the hill through the snow on that February night. Another was Comrade Milković, sent from Moscow by the Comintern to try to knock some sense into the Zagreb Communist party and to persuade or bully it into repudiating Marković and Yugoslav unity, and to support Croat, Slovene and Macedonian separatism.

After Marković and the right wing had denounced ultra-leftism and national chauvinism, and the Croats and the left wing had branded Marković and the right wing as Greater-Serbian lackeys of French imperialism, Josip Broz addressed the delegates. He said that the rank-and-file of the party, fighting bravely in the illegal underground resistance against the Yugoslav bourgeoisie and their French imperialist masters, were disgusted at both right-wing and left-wing fractionalism. He proposed that the Executive Committee of the Comintern be asked to take charge of the Yugoslav Communist party, to cleanse it of all fractionalism. The man from Moscow said that he agreed with Comrade Broz. He proposed that the whole of the Central Committee of the Zagreb party be dismissed from office. The conference adopted his proposal, and a new Central Committee was elected with Broz as secretary.

After eight hours' discussion the meeting ended at five a.m., and the delegates left the inn one by one.[12] Soon afterwards, at the Fourth Congress of the Comintern in Moscow, Marković was expelled from the party, which would henceforth work first and foremost to destroy the united kingdom of Serbs, Croats and Slovenes.

The Communists planned a big political demonstration on May Day 1928, and Broz was given the task of organizing it. He knew that the police would ban the demonstration and take steps to prevent the demonstrators from assembling. Realizing that his secret plans would be leaked to the police by police spies inside the party and by careless talk, he instructed party workers to assemble at four different points, leading everyone to believe that the place to which he was told to go was the only assembly point. The police, hearing conflicting rumours as to where the demonstrators would meet, did not know which rumours were true and which were false.

The Social-Democrat party had announced that they would hold a May Day meeting on the evening of 1 May in a hall in Zagreb. The Communist party, following the new Comintern line of attacking the Social-Democrats as the worst enemy, decided to disrupt the meeting. Broz duly organized the attack on the hall. He did not worry unduly whether the party's strategy towards the Social-Democrats was right or wrong. He was still merely an efficient NCO in the Communist army, not yet a general and certainly not yet a

1. The house where Tito was born in Kumrovec. The statue of Tito is by Antun Augustinčić.

2. Tito's school at Kumrovec in 1900. The picture on the wall is of the Emperor Franz Joseph.

3. Tito's house at Veliko Trojstvo where he lived from 1922–5.

4. Tito with his first wife Pelagea Belousova
(Polka) and their son Žarko in 1927.

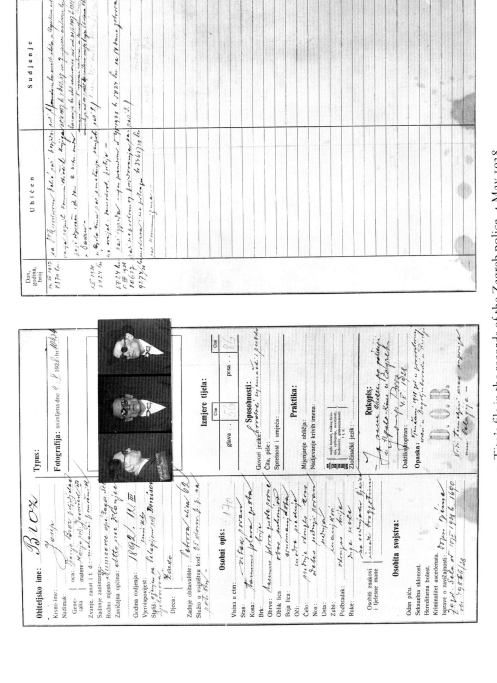

5. Tito's file in the records of the Zagreb police, 4 May 1928.

6. Tito at the time of his trial in Zagreb in November 1928.

7. Tito at the Seventh Congress of the Comintern in
Moscow in August 1935.

Detta pass innehåller 32 numrerade sidor.
Ce passeport contient 32 pages numérotées.
This passport contains 32 numbered pages.
Dieser Pass enthält 32 numerierte Seiten.

N:o  1086

SVERIGE

Suède Sweden Schweden

Pass   Passeport
Passport   Pass

Passinnehavarens fullständiga namn. Noms du porteur.
Full name of bearer.   Voller Namen des Inhabers.

John Alexander Karlsson

ledsagad av sin hustru   accompagné de sa femme
accompanied by his wife   begleitet von seiner Frau

och av .... barn under 15 år.
et de .... enfants au-dessous de 15 ans.
and by .... children under 15 years.
und von .... Kindern unter 15 Jahren.

Nationalitet: Svensk, Suédois, Swedish, Schwedische.

8. One of the false passports used by Tito in 1937–9.

clever politician. He just carried out the orders which the party gave him.

The police welcomed the opportunity to beat up Communists on an occasion when their provocative and thuggish behaviour had antagonized a large part of the Zagreb working class. Confronted with serried ranks of Communists determined to resist arrest, they adopted the usual police tactic of charging and grabbing any isolated demonstrator, pulling him out of the crowd and arresting him. The Communists, on their side, adopted the usual demonstrators' tactic of rescuing at once any arrested demonstrator from the hands of the police. When Broz saw a demonstrator being arrested, he and a group of comrades fought the police and rescued him. The arrested man escaped, but the police had noticed Broz's part in the incident, and when, a few minutes later, he was for a brief moment isolated from his supporters, they seized him and took him off to prison.

The police were so incompetent that they did not realize that the man they had arrested was Josip Broz who had failed to surrender for the hearing of his appeal after his trial at Ogulin and for whom they had been looking for many months. He produced his false papers and they charged him under his false name with a breach of the peace. He was sentenced to fourteen days' imprisonment, and then released.[13] He resumed his life as a middle-class engineer, put on once again his smart suits, and directed Communist activity from the fashionable cafés. The police continued to look for Josip Broz.

On 20 June 1928 a debate took place in the National Assembly in Belgrade. A Serbian MP who supported the government went to the rostrum to speak. Looking down on the other MPs he saw Radić and two other Croatian Opposition MPs sitting in their places. Suddenly, as he stood on the rostrum, he drew a revolver and fired at Radić and his two colleagues. The other two were killed instantly; Radić lingered for six weeks before he died of his wounds. No one made any attempt to arrest the murderer as he walked triumphantly out of the Chamber; but he voluntarily surrendered to the police later in the day, and was detained in custody, though no steps were taken to bring him to trial.

There was great indignation in Croatia at the assassination of Radić. The Communist party immediately proposed to Radić's Croatian Peasant party that they should take joint action against the government of murderers in Belgrade; but the Croatian Peasant party refused to collaborate with the Communists. The Communists then called for an armed uprising in Croatia, which was completely unrealistic and a typical example of the adventurist and ultra-leftist policy pursued by the Comintern during what they called 'the Third Period'. But the Communists succeeded in organizing several riots in Zagreb in August, in which a few policemen and many demonstrators were killed.

The police were searching everywhere for Broz. He had several lucky escapes. Once he was in the headquarters of a Communist trade union when the police raided it, asking all the people in the building where they could find Josip Broz. 'Can't you see he's not here?' said Broz, as he calmly walked out of the office.

He had a narrower shave on another occasion when the police burst into a house where he was sheltering, and he had to jump out of the window into the garden of a café and run for it. He always carried a revolver, and once, when he was being chased by the police, he turned and fired a shot at them, and escaped.[14]

He was eventually caught, like most underground and resistance activists are caught, not because he slipped up but through the activities of a police informer who had infiltrated the party. Broz had arranged to meet the informer at one of the houses where he sometimes spent the night, for he took the usual precaution of not sleeping more than a few nights in the same place. Broz turned up to keep the appointment at eleven p.m. on 4 August 1928. As he entered his room he was immediately seized and his arms were pinioned by two plainclothes policemen who had been hiding behind the door.

The policemen manacled Broz's hands and took him to the police station. His defiant manner angered one of the policemen, who struck him across the face so hard that he felt dizzy. At the station they questioned him and drafted a statement for him to sign admitting his Communist activities. When Broz refused to sign it, his interrogator seized one of the chairs and drove it twice into Broz's chest. Broz cried out scornfully: 'What a fine fellow you are, you can manage to beat a manacled man.' He spat blood, but the police refused his request to see a doctor.

He was held in prison for three months before he was brought to trial. He managed to write and smuggle out of prison an article which was published in the illegal Communist press and in the legal newspapers of the opposition Social-Democrat and Liberal parties. In this article he wrote that he had been tortured by the police. This was duly repeated after 1945 in several biographies of Tito; one of them described how the interrogators drove pins under his fingernails and toenails. This was often done to Communist prisoners under King Alexander's government, but not to Broz. Twenty years later, the British Labour MP, Konni Zilliacus, asked Tito if he had been tortured in 1928. He replied that he had received insults, blows and bruises, but nothing that could be called torture.[15]

Torture is a very pejorative and emotive word. If a terrorist, a Communist or a political dissident is punched, kicked and severely beaten during police interrogation and left with cuts and bruises, the victim's political sympathizers and the Opposition and foreign press will say that he has been tortured. The government spokesmen and the supporters of the regime will admit that he has been 'roughed up a little', 'knocked about a bit', or even 'beaten up', but will deny that he has been tortured. Broz played up the ill-treatment to which he had been subjected in his propaganda article at the time; he played it down in later years, for he knew that he had escaped the severe and prolonged torture which was inflicted a few years later, under King Alexander's dictatorship, on his comrades Djilas, Ranković and Kardelj.

He went on another hunger strike in prison as a protest against the delay in bringing him to trial and against the beatings inflicted on the other political prisoners.[16] Soon afterwards he was put on trial with five other men, charged under the Law for the Protection of the State with being members of an illegal organization, the Communist party, and working for the violent overthrow of the government.

The trial opened in Zagreb on 6 November 1928, before five High Court judges.[17] The public galleries of the small courtroom were so crowded that there was barely room to move. Most of the spectators were Communists or left-wing sympathizers; some were workers, others were students. A right-wing newspaper reported that 'they are young men with long curly hair or young girls with bobbed hair, perhaps followers of the new gospel, perhaps acquaintances of the six defendants. They never come to "bourgeois" trials, but only attend such propaganda, militant, international-messiah cases.'

After three of the defendants had been charged and examined on the first day, Broz was brought up on the second morning. In accordance with the usual Communist line in such circumstances, he intended to use the trial to make Communist propaganda, which he knew would be reported in the press, thus rendering one last service to the party before beginning the long prison sentence which he expected. But the judges were determined to stop Broz from using the trial to make Communist propaganda.

When asked to plead guilty or not guilty, Broz admitted that he was a member of the Communist party and therefore guilty under the Law for the Protection of the State, but said that he did not recognize that law, as it was only a temporary one. 'It is, however, still in force,' said the presiding judge, 'like any other law. That law takes you, and everyone who breaks it, to Lepoglava Prison. The law has been passed by the nation against you Communists, who, according to the people's view, are trying to corrupt them and they want to defend themselves against your destructive activity.' The judge added: 'You are pigheadedly sacrificing your young lives.' Broz replied: 'I am quite prepared to suffer.'

The police gave evidence that when they searched Broz's room they found Marxist-Leninist literature, with Stalin's *Problems of Leninism*, some notebooks in Broz's handwriting with passages in cipher, and two bombs. Broz admitted that he had been teaching the doctrines expounded in *Problems of Leninism*. He said that the passages in cipher in his notebooks contained the names of Communist party members and sympathizers with whom he was in contact, but he refused to reveal the names. He denied that he had had any bombs, and said that they had been planted by the police.

Broz's line about the bombs at his trial in 1928 was followed in the account of the trial in Dedijer's book *Josip Broz Tito* in 1953, in the English version *Tito Speaks*, and in all the official Yugoslav Communist histories. But Zilliacus wrote in his biography of Tito in 1952 that when he asked Tito about it, Tito laughed and said: 'They were my bombs all right.' Fitzroy Maclean says that Tito used exactly the same words to him. Djilas also believes that Tito had had two bombs in his possession and that his story at his trial that they had been planted by the police was a lie.[18]

If Zilliacus, Maclean and Djilas are right, it means that Tito and the Communist party of Yugoslavia in 1928 were diverging from the Comintern line and were planning to pursue an ultra-left line on individual terrorism. But Pero Damjanović, who was very close to Tito for many years, does not believe that Tito told Zilliacus and Maclean that they were his bombs. He believes that they misunderstood what Tito said, and that the confusion arose because Tito illegally carried a revolver when he was arrested in 1928, and that he meant that the revolver, not the bombs, was his.

The court ruled that the police witnesses were speaking the truth and that Broz was lying. When Broz said that he had been tortured in prison, the state prosecutor said that he was telling lies in order to portray himself as a martyr and to get money from Moscow. After the lawyer for the defence had made his final speech, the court asked the defendants if they had anything to say before judgment was given. Broz said that he wished to speak, and began to explain why he had become a Communist. The presiding judge told him that he would not allow Broz to use the courtroom as a platform from which to make Communist propaganda; and as Broz continued to speak, the judge ordered him to be silent and finally to be removed from the court. Broz was dragged out shouting: 'Long live the Communist party of Yugoslavia! Long live the Third International!'

The defendants were brought back to the court on 16 November to hear the verdict. Broz was found guilty and sentenced to five years' imprisonment. Two of the other defendants received shorter sentences, and the other three were acquitted. After sentence had been passed, Broz shouted three times: 'Long live the Communist party of Yugoslavia, long live the Third International!' before he was removed from the courtroom. 'Thus it was', wrote the local Conservative newspaper, 'that this unyielding Communist disappeared behind prison walls, just as the captain of a ship shouts when his ship is sinking.' The Communist paper *Borba* wrote that 'the trial of Josip Broz and his comrades has shown the bourgeois character of our judicial system'.

CHAPTER 10

✦

In King Alexander's Prisons

FOR a few weeks after Broz had been sentenced to his five-year prison term, he remained in the cells in the High Court of Justice in Zagreb. The party tried to arrange for his escape. One of the policemen, who was a secret Communist sympathizer, smuggled a file to Broz hidden in a loaf of bread. Broz filed through five of the six bars on the window of his cell without the prison authorities discovering his escape attempt; but before he had filed through the last remaining bar, he was moved to another cell, and a few days later he was taken to the prison at Lepoglava, not far from his native village of Kumrovec. The policeman who had sent him the file came under suspicion, so the party arranged for the policeman's escape to the Soviet Union. Some years later he was accused of being an agent of the Yugoslav police, and shot by the Soviet political police, the GPU.*[1]

After Broz was imprisoned, his wife Polka, with his four-year-old son Žarko, settled in Kumrovec. There was great sympathy for Broz in Kumrovec; not everyone in the village agreed with his politics, but he was very popular there. The villagers liked Polka too, although she had still not learned to speak more than a few words of Serbo-Croat, and they all wished to help and comfort her while her husband was in prison. Then one day they found that she had gone; she had left with Žarko without saying goodbye to anyone. A rumour spread in Kumrovec that she had been arrested and deported from Yugo-

* The Soviet political police has often changed its name, perhaps in the hope of deceiving the public into believing that a change of name meant a change in its methods. It has been called in succession the Cheka, the OGPU, the GPU, the NKVD, the MVD and the KGB.

slavia. Another story was that the Soviet government had ordered her to return to Russia; a third version was that the Comintern, thinking that she was in danger of being arrested, had organized her escape. She arrived in Moscow soon afterwards, and never told Žarko the reason why they had left Kumrovec so hurriedly.[2]

Djilas has written that Tito used his time in prison to study Marxism-Leninism properly for the first time.[3] This has misled some writers into believing that Communists in King Alexander's prisons were granted the privileges of 'fortress arrest', like the Socialist leaders in Bismarck's Germany, Rosa Luxemburg in Kaiser William II's time, Trotsky in Tsarist Russia, and Gandhi in the prisons of the British Raj in India, who were not obliged to do any work and were allowed, not only to read, but also to write books. But Tito and his colleagues were subjected to the usual discipline and rigours of criminals serving a prison sentence. On the other hand, they were not ill-treated like prisoners in a Nazi concentration camp or a labour camp in the Soviet Union. As in Nazi Germany, political prisoners were tortured during interrogation at police headquarters, but not while they were serving their sentences in an ordinary prison.

When Broz arrived at Lepoglava Prison in January 1929,[4] his head was shaved like a criminal's, and he was locked in a small cell which was very cold in the winter. He slept on a little folding bunk with a mattress and two blankets. The food was disgusting – turnip soup, a few beans, and a piece of bread twice a week. He was at first not allowed to have books; but books were permitted to prisoners serving longer sentences, and Broz was allowed to have them after the first three months.

He benefited from the fact that he was a skilled mechanic, for he was employed in Lepoglava carrying out repairs to the electrical system. This gave him the opportunity to move around the prison 'with my test bulb in one hand and a screwdriver in the other', and to speak to the other prisoners. The well-known Communist, Moša Pijade, was in Lepoglava. He was a middle-class Belgrade Jew, and a portrait-painter as well as a writer. He had been the editor of a Communist newspaper, and in 1925 was sentenced to twenty years' imprisonment for being a member of the Communist party; it was the longest prison sentence that had been imposed under the Law for the Protection of the State. Broz chose Pijade to help him in his electrical work. This made it possible for Pijade, too, to move around the prison, to contact the other Communist prisoners, and organize a Communist group. Pijade translated Marx's *Das Kapital* into Serbo-Croat while he was in prison. He also painted the portraits of several prisoners, including Broz, and of some of the warders.

Broz was occasionally sent out of the prison, accompanied by a warder, to do electrical repair work in houses in the town. There was a café in Lepoglava owned by a very kind-hearted and religious lady, Mrs Fidlerica. She and one of the prison warders agreed to help Broz to meet his friends, not realizing that these friends were in the Communist underground movement. Every two or three months Mrs Fidlerica would tell the prison authorities that there was a fault in her electrical wiring, and Broz and the warder would be sent to her café. She would then serve drinks to the warder in the café while Broz talked to his comrades in a room above.

A few weeks after Broz's trial, King Alexander carried out a *coup d'état* in Belgrade on the Christmas Eve of the Orthodox Church, 6 January 1929. He was determined to stamp out the Croatian nationalist movement and the rising discontent in Croatia following Radić's murder. He used as his excuse the stormy scenes in parliament which had culminated in the killing of Radić; but when the murderer was at last brought to trial, after the *coup d'état*, he served only a short term in prison and was then granted an estate in Macedonia where he lived quietly in retirement till his death.

On the day after the *coup*, the king broadcast a Christmas Day message to his people. 'Serbs, Croats, Slovenes! The highest interest of the nation and of the State . . . compels me, both as sovereign and as a son of my country, to address myself directly to my people . . . The hour has come when there can and may not be any intermediary between the King and his people.' He announced that parliament was dissolved. In due course elections would be held for a new parliament, but in the meantime the king would rule as a dictator and the country would remain under martial law. The name of the state would be changed from 'the Kingdom of Serbs, Croats and Slovenes' to 'the Kingdom of Yugoslavia'.[5] The country had informally been called 'Yugoslavia' ever since 1918 by the Serbs and by foreigners, but the Croatian nationalists resented the change of name, which to them emphasized the union with Serbia and Serb domination. The Communist party of Yugoslavia, following the anti-Yugoslav line of the Comintern and the Soviet government, duly condemned the change of name.[6]

In Britain and France the government and the Conservative press were not altogether happy about the *coup d'état*, but accepted it. 'It is difficult to suggest an alternative', wrote the leader-writer of *The Times* of London, 'or to find fault with King Alexander because he dared not wait until the confusion had become still more confounded and until the fissures in Yugoslav unity had widened into gaping chasms,' because 'the maintenance of Yugoslav unity is a European interest'.[7]

The *coup d'état* almost finished off the Yugoslav Communists. The Comintern reacted as it had done to Chiang Kai-shek's *coup* in China. They told the Communist leaders to escape abroad and to issue appeals to the rank-and-file party members and the Yugoslav workers and peasants to rise in armed revolt against the king's dictatorship. This irresponsible adventurism lost them more ground in the country, though after a few months they called off their appeals for armed revolt.

It was fortunate for Broz that he had been arrested five months earlier and was safely in jail when the *coup d'état* took place. After 6 January 1929, when Communists were arrested they were nearly always severely tortured, and sometimes murdered, by the police. Djilas, in his book *Memoir of a Revolutionary*, which he wrote many years after he had renounced Communism, has described the tortures that he suffered and witnessed at police headquarters in Belgrade, in Room Number 6 in the basement and in the interrogation room on the fourth floor. The Communist party had told its members that if they were unable to withstand torture they might confess their guilt, but that in no circumstances must they reveal the names of other comrades. Later the party line changed; the comrades were told that they must reveal nothing at all and must not admit their guilt, however severe the torture.

The chief of the Anti-Communist Branch of the Belgrade police, Vujković, was an expert in torturing Communists. After the first interrogation, he and his assistants would go to lunch, leaving the prisoner alone in the room for two hours looking at the metal whips on the table and thinking about what was going to happen to him. When they returned, the torture began. The prisoner was beaten not only on the buttocks but also on the ball of the foot, a form of torture which the Turkish police had adopted in the old days under the Ottoman Empire. Vujković's police also hammered nails into his feet, drove pins under his fingernails and toenails, and twisted his penis around a pencil. When a Communist who was being tortured protested, the police would reply that the Communists would do worse things to them if they ever came to power.[8]

Torture was applied only during police interrogation; but conditions worsened for all Communist prisoners after King Alexander established the dictatorship. A prisoner could ordinarily earn remission of part of his sentence for good conduct in prison, and might be released after serving half his term. But the Ministry of the Interior issued instructions to the prison governors that under no circumstances were Communists to be granted remission, but were always to serve their full sentence. The promise of remission was sometimes used to tempt the non-political convicts into spying on the Communist prisoners.[9]

After Broz had spent two and a half years in Lepoglava, he was suddenly accused of having attempted to escape, and as a punishment he was transferred to Maribor Prison in Slovenia in June 1931. Conditions at Maribor were worse than in any other prison in Yugoslavia. For the first few months after Broz arrived there, he was held in solitary confinement and forbidden to take any exercise or speak to the other prisoners. But the prison regulations were relaxed after some prisoners had gone on hunger strike and conditions in Maribor had been described in the legal press of the Social-Democrats and the Liberal Opposition parties. The prisoners were now allowed to have electric light in their rooms till midnight and to walk in the prison yard once a day and twice on Sundays. They were not allowed to speak to each other on these walks, but did so surreptitiously.

After a few months Broz's period of solitary confinement ended, and he was placed in a room with seven other prisoners. They were occasionally allowed to receive and write letters, which were censored by the prison authorities, and books and newspapers were sent to them. Broz regularly read the London journal *The Economist*, and many years later told his English friends that he thought it was an excellent magazine. At this time he could speak very little English, and did not begin to master the language until after 1950; but, someone who has a slight knowledge of a foreign language finds it easier to read it than to carry on a conversation in it.

Marxist-Leninist books were banned, even those that were being lawfully sold in left-wing bookshops in Zagreb. But friends outside removed the covers of Marxist books and sent them to the prisoners bound inside the covers of other books. The warders were so slack or ignorant that they did not notice the deception, although they had plenty of opportunities to inspect the books in the rooms while the prisoners were taking exercise in the prison yard. So Broz managed to read several Marxist works in Maribor, and especially studied Engels's *Anti-Dühring*.

Smoking was banned in Maribor. The members of the Socialist youth movement in Central Europe were urged by their leaders not to start smoking, so that they would not feel depressed when they were deprived of tobacco in prison;[10] but many Socialists and Communists were unable to follow this counsel of perfection. Broz was already a heavy smoker of the cheapest brand of Yugoslav cigarettes. Occasionally a cigarette was smuggled into the prison. Four of his seven cellmates were non-smokers, so Broz had to share the cigarette only with the three other prisoners. They marked the cigarette with a pencil, dividing it into four equal parts, and each of them smoked it as far as the next pencil mark before passing it on. The last of the four smokers got the stub, which was the heaviest in nicotine, so as cigarettes were smuggled in, they took it in turn to enjoy the privilege of smoking the stub.

The relaxation of the strictest regulations and the slackness and ignorance (and perhaps also the corruptibility) of the warders made life in Maribor bearable if hard. But the directive of the Ministry of the Interior that no Communist was to be granted remission was duly enforced in Broz's case. As the end of his five-year term approached, he was told that he was shortly to be released, and he was allowed to grow his hair to cover his shaven head. On 16 November 1933, five years to the day after he had been sentenced, he was given a new suit of civilian clothes and enough money to buy a packet of twenty of the cheapest cigarettes.

Dressed in his civilian suit, he walked out of the prison. But the police were waiting outside the gates, and as he stepped out into the street they arrested him. He was told that he would be taken to the prison at Ogulin to serve the four-month term to which he had been sentenced in 1927 and which he had avoided by going into hiding. After recovering from the initial shock, he decided that, after five years in prison, another four months would pass quickly; and it was encouraging that the policemen who escorted him from Maribor to Ogulin removed his handcuffs during the train journey.[11]

Again the prison sentence was enforced to the letter. Four months later, on 16 March 1934, Broz was released from the medieval fortress at Ogulin. He was immediately served with an order to go to his native village of Kumrovec, where he was to reside. He was to report to the police station at Kumrovec every day, and was not permitted to leave the village. He was told that if he disobeyed these orders he would be re-arrested and prosecuted under the appropriate police regulations. Apart from these restrictions, he was free to live as he pleased.

CHAPTER 11

❖

From Kumrovec to Moscow

ALARMING events had occurred in the world during the years that Broz had been in prison. The collapse of the New York Stock Exchange on Wall Street in October 1929 had been followed by the bankruptcy of the Austrian Kreditanstalt Bank in the summer of 1931 and the beginning of the most serious trade depression since the Industrial Revolution. By 1932 there was widespread unemployment in the United States, Britain and Germany, and in Yugoslavia the industrial regions of Croatia and Slovenia were also affected. For the Communists, this was the beginning of the final crisis of capitalism which Marx had predicted with mathematical precision in *Das Kapital*; $\frac{v}{c}$, the proportion of variable to constant capital, had inevitably fallen, thereby causing economic collapse, the 'increase in misery' of the proletariat, and the imminent approach of the international proletarian revolution when the expropriators would be expropriated.[1]

The Liberals were saddened at the failure to fulfil the hopes of 1918 and at the failure of the League of Nations to prevent the outbreak of wars. In September 1931 Japan invaded the Chinese province of Manchuria. China appealed to the League of Nations; but the League, which was dominated by Britain and France, did nothing. The Japanese army had intervened in Siberia against the Bolsheviks in 1918, and were an anti-Communist force who were to be encouraged, not restrained. Winston Churchill put this argument forcibly in February 1933 in a speech to the Anti-Socialist and Anti-Communist Union. 'I hope we should try in England to understand a little the position of Japan . . . On the one side they see the dark menace of Soviet Russia. On the other the chaos of China, four or five provinces of which are actually now being tortured under

Communist rule.'[2] Once again, as the Communists saw it, the British imperialists, led by Churchill, were taking the lead in inciting another invasion of the Soviet Union.

But a greater enemy than Churchill had now appeared. Cavaignac in Paris during the June Days of 1848, Galliffet the executioner of the Communards of 1871, Kolchak and Denikin in the Russian Civil War, Mannerheim, Horthy, Mussolini, all the villains in Communist historiography paled beside the figure of Adolf Hitler. He had formed his National Socialist German Workers' party with seven members in Munich in 1920; in the parliamentary elections throughout Germany in 1930 the party won 107 seats in the Reichstag.

He was followed by millions of Germans who shared his belief in the traditional values, his hatred of intellectuals, of sexual perverts, of women who did not confine their interests to 'church, kitchen and children', of trade unions, of foreigners. He hated Reds and he hated Jews. If he had lived in South Africa or in the southern states of the United States he would have hated blacks; but as he lived in Central Europe he hated Jews. He hated and envied the Jewish financiers whom he accused of dominating the German economy and exploiting the German workers. He hated and resented the small Jewish tradesmen who, he believed, cheated him by their hard bargains. He hated and despised the poverty-stricken Jews of Poland and Eastern Europe as dirty carriers of disease, 'sub-human' members of an inferior race who lusted to seduce and rape innocent, defenceless, blonde German girls. But most of all he hated the Marxist Jews, the traitors who had betrayed their country in wartime by calling the war in defence of Germany an 'imperialist war', and who outraged his patriotism by proclaiming that the workers had no fatherland and that a nation that oppresses another nation forges its own chains.

In 1932 he was invited to address a meeting of German industrialists in Düsseldorf. He told them that he and his party 'have formed the inexorable decision to destroy Marxism in Germany down to its very last root'.[3] After that the donations to the Nazi party funds poured in.

Heinz Neumann, one of the leaders of the German Communist party, launched the slogan 'Strike the Fascist wherever you meet him'. Groups of Communists sought out Nazis and killed them, as the Nazis killed Communists. But in the summer of 1931 Neumann visited Stalin at his holiday home in the Crimea. He began to tell Stalin about the Communist campaign against the Nazis in Germany, but Stalin interrupted him, and asked: 'Don't you think that if National Socialism came to power in Germany it would be so occupied in the West that the Soviet Union could develop in peace and build up Socialism?' Neumann was taken aback; but the Communists maintained their line that the greatest enemy of the proletariat was the Social-Democrats. Stalin thought that the British and French imperialists were the chief threat to the Soviet Union. If Hitler replaced a Liberal or Social-Democrat government in Germany, he would pursue an anti-French policy which would be to the advantage of the Soviet Union.[4]

On 30 January 1933 Hitler became chancellor of Germany. On the night of 27 February a fire broke out in the Reichstag, the parliament building in Berlin. It had been started by a Dutchman, van der Lubbe, who had once been a Communist. Hitler made it an excuse to suppress the Communist party. Communists were rounded up and imprisoned in concentration camps, and some non-Communist Jews were taken to concentration camps. In May the Social-Democratic party was also suppressed and its newspapers banned.

The Nazi atrocities were denounced abroad by Conservatives, Socialists and Liberals; but some right-wing Conservatives praised Hitler for having saved Germany from Communism. In Britain the Labour newspaper, the *Daily Herald*, published a front-page article on events in Germany under the headline: 'How Nazis are torturing Jews in Berlin'; but the Conservative *Daily Mail* believed that 'the sturdy young Nazis are Europe's guardians against the Communist danger'.[5]

The police in Berlin arrested three Bulgarian immigrants. They discovered that they were Communists and charged them with helping van der Lubbe burn the Reichstag, which by a retroactive law had been made punishable by death. They did not discover that one of them, Georgi Dimitrov,* was one of the most important officials of the Comintern. Dimitrov defended himself brilliantly at his trial, denouncing the Nazis and winning the admiration of Communists, Socialists and Liberals throughout the world.

The German judges still retained some degree of independence and

---

* Dimitrov, Georgi (1882–1949), Bulgarian Communist leader; escaped from Bulgaria after the failure of the Communist insurrection of 1923; a defendant in the Reichstag Fire Trial in Germany in 1933; went to the Soviet Union in 1934; general secretary of the Comintern 1935–43; prime minister of Bulgaria 1946–9.

impartiality. They found van der Lubbe guilty, and he was executed; but Dimitrov and his companions were acquitted. They remained in prison under the emergency powers, but a few weeks later were exchanged for some Germans in the Soviet Union and went to Moscow.

Hitler's triumph in Germany encouraged anti-Communist and anti-Socialist movements everywhere. A formidable Fascist movement developed in France; in Paris, the Fascists made an unsuccessful attempt to seize power in February 1934. A few days later, the right-wing Catholic government of Engelbert Dollfuss in Austria suppressed the Socialist party after a week's street fighting in Vienna. In every country in Europe the Fascists were advancing and the Communists were in retreat.

This was the situation which confronted Josip Broz when he was released from Ogulin prison on 16 March 1934. He complied with the police order and went to Kumrovec, where he was warmly welcomed by the villagers; many of them were his relations, and nearly all of them were his friends. He was surprised to find that even the police inspector was friendly. When Broz reported to the police station, the inspector hinted that the rule about reporting would not be too strictly enforced. According to Dedijer, Tito told him in 1952 that the only person in Kumrovec who was hostile to him was the village priest, who preached a sermon in which he said that Antichrist had returned to the village.[6]

This is one of many critical remarks about priests which appeared in Dedijer's biography of Tito, but it is perhaps a little misleading. Father Marcel Novak was as popular in Kumrovec as Josip Broz; he had recently taken up his duties in the parish and stayed there for thirty-five years. He was a tall, broad, jovial man, and was already putting on weight, though he had not yet reached his maximum of 144 kilos. He may have said in his sermon that Broz was Antichrist, but in the evenings he happily played cards (poker) with Broz at the village inn.

On the night of 30 April Father Marcel supervised the erection of the arch of flowers in honour of the Virgin Queen of the May which was put up every year on the eve of May Day, and remained there for the whole of the month of May. When Broz saw the arch on the morning of 1 May 1934 he said: 'You might have made some reference to the fact that it is May Day,' the day of the international proletariat.[7]

A few days later, Broz left Kumrovec, not because of the hostility of Father Marcel, but because the Communist party had told him to resume his underground revolutionary activities. He made his way to Zagreb, contacted his party comrades, and resumed his place on the Central Committee of the Croatian Communist party. The Croatian Communists were in a state of disarray, because the Executive Committee of the Communist party of Yugoslavia had escaped abroad and were directing the party from Vienna. Communications between Zagreb and Vienna were difficult, especially after Dollfuss had established his dictatorship and suppressed the Socialists. The Zagreb Communists told Broz to go to Vienna, find out what was happening there, and report back to Zagreb.

During the next six months Broz travelled several times between Zagreb, Vienna and Ljubljana. Sometimes he travelled on a forged passport provided by the Communist party of Yugoslavia or the Comintern. The usual practice was to find a passport which had been lawfully issued by some government to a man who was dead, and superimpose a photograph of Broz on the dead man's passport. But sometimes the forgeries were not very good and were easily detectable on a careful examination of the passport. Broz thought it was safer to walk across the frontier illegally without passing through immigration control. This involved bribing a mountain guide to show him an unguarded path. If the guide had no political principles and was merely doing it for the money, he might accept the bribe and then lead Broz straight to a frontier post and hand him over to the police; or he might blackmail Broz at a critical stage of the journey into paying more than the agreed sum.

Broz was the victim of a blackmailing guide on his first journey into Austria. He refused to pay any more, went on alone, and succeeded in crossing the frontier; but he had not gone far into Austria before he was stopped by the Home Guard (the *Heimwehr*). It was the night of 25 July 1934, the day on which the Austrian Nazis murdered Dollfuss in Vienna and tried to seize power in an unsuccessful *coup*; so the *Heimwehr* were very much on the alert. But Broz succeeded in persuading them that he was an Austrian mountaineer out for a walk; during his years in Vienna and in the Austrian army twenty years before he had learned to speak excellent German with an Austrian accent. They let him go on to Vienna. In view of his unfortunate experience with the mountain guide, Broz thought of a better way of crossing the frontier. He worked out a system by which the illegal

[113]

Communist immigrant could contact Austrian Communists who were doing their military service and were stationed on the frontier.[8]

Broz had been given the address in Vienna of a young woman who was a ballet dancer and a secret member of the Austrian Communist party. He stayed with her, and contacted the leaders in exile of the Communist party of Yugoslavia. The party was dominated by the general secretary, Milan Gorkić. His real name was Josip Cizinski. He was born in Ruthenia (Carpatho-Ukraine), which had been given to Czechoslovakia by the Allies in 1919; but when he was a child his father moved to Sarajevo, where Gorkić was brought up. He joined the Communist party and before he was thirty had become a fulltime agent of the Comintern. Like other agents, he was sent by the Comintern to work in various countries, including South Wales during the miners' strike and the General Strike of 1926. He was appointed in 1932 to replace Marković as the leader of the Communist party of Yugoslavia, though he had not been in Yugoslavia for many years.[9] His instructions were to make sure that the party repudiated the pro-Yugoslav policy of Marković and encouraged Croatian and Macedonian separatism.

Gorkić sent Broz to Ljubljana, where he stayed in the house of a theatrical producer and his wife, who was one of the best-known actresses in Yugoslavia. His host and hostess were not the only bourgeois intellectuals who were prepared to help the party. He had been told by Gorkić to organize a secret conference of the Communist party in Slovenia. The brother of the Roman Catholic Bishop of Ljubljana was a Communist sympathizer. The bishop kept his brother out of the limelight at his summer palace at Medvode, some eight miles north of Ljubljana. The brother invited Broz and thirty other Communist delegates to hold the conference in the bishop's summer palace during the weekend of 15–17 September 1934. The delegates slept in the palace, and dined in the bishop's banqueting hall, eating off plates marked with the bishop's coat-of-arms. While the bishop was indoctrinating the Slovenes with religion, 'the opium of the people', his brother was salving his conscience by personally waiting at table on the Communist delegates, 'constantly cursing his brother the bishop'.[10]

It was at this conference that Broz first met Edvard Kardelj, a twenty-four-year-old Slovene intellectual who had just qualified as a schoolmaster when he was arrested as a Communist, severely tortured, and sentenced to two years' imprisonment. Broz formed a very favourable opinion of Kardelj; he thought that 'he was an honest revolutionary at a time when many were corrupted by fractionalism'.[11] It was the beginning of a friendship and a collaboration which lasted for forty-five years.

As the police were looking for Josip Broz, who had failed to report to the police station in Kumrovec, Broz adopted various pseudonyms, like all Communists engaged in illegal underground work. He first called himself 'Rudi'; but when he found that another comrade had taken the name of Rudi, he decided to call himself 'Tito'. He wrote several articles for party journals in 1934, signing them 'Tito'. He had no particular reason for choosing the name, except that it was quite a common nickname for men in the Zagorje district around Kumrovec. In the Comintern apparatus he was known as 'Walter'.[12]

Gorkić and the Politburo in Vienna told Tito to write an article on 'The Duties of Communists in Prison' for the underground party press in Yugoslavia. A serious split had occurred between the Communists in prison. A new intake of prisoners had arrived in 1933 and 1934. They were journalists, lawyers, and students from Belgrade University; many of them were Serbs and Montenegrins, who combined the intemperate zeal and guilty conscience of middle-class intellectuals with the age-old Serbian and Montenegrin tradition of violent revolt, fighting hopeless battles against overwhelming odds. The twenty-three-year-old Montenegrin, Milovan Djilas, was one of their bravest and most reckless leaders.

Djilas and the 'leftists' told the Communist prisoners that it was their duty to carry on the class struggle within the prisons by refusing to obey the warders and provoking violent confrontations. This was opposed by the 'right-wing', especially by Pijade and the Croatian Communist leader, Andrija Hebrang. Pijade was happily working on his translation of *Das Kapital* and nearly half-way through his prison sentence, and did not wish to incur further punishment by engaging in a hopeless struggle. But Djilas and the leftists carried the day, and Pijade and Hebrang felt that they had no alternative except to go along with their comrades.

The Communist prisoners refused to assemble for roll-call, defied and insulted the warders, shouted Communist slogans, and sang revolutionary songs. For a time the warders did nothing, and allowed the prisoners to get away with it. Then one day they went in, and beat up the prisoners with rifle-butts, leaving many streaming with blood and several seriously wounded. The prisoners were punished

[115]

by increased sentences. Pijade had five years added to his twenty-year sentence, but in fact was released a few years later.[13]

Tito, in his article, came down on the side of Pijade, Hebrang and the right-wing. He outlined the duties of Communists in prison. They must stand firm under torture and must never reveal the names of their comrades or other vital information. They must not co-operate with the prison authorities, and in appropriate circumstances should go on hunger strike. But they must not provoke confrontations, which could lead only to defeat and unnecessary suffering for the comrades.

Tito also wrote articles on work in the trade unions and on anti-militarist activity. The Comintern and the Communist party of Yugoslavia still followed the Leninist policy of opposition to imperialist war, and did all they could to spread disaffection in the armies of Yugoslavia and the other states in the Little Entente, urging the Yugoslav, Czech and Romanian workers and peasants not to serve as cannon fodder in the imperialist wars of their masters, the French bourgeoisie, either against the Soviet Union or against other capitalist states like Italy, Germany, Bulgaria and Hungary.[14]

Tito was in Ljubljana on 9 October 1934 when he heard on the radio that King Alexander had been assassinated in Marseilles along with the French foreign minister, Louis Barthou, who had welcomed him on his state visit to France. The assassin was a member of the Croatian nationalist movement, the Ustasha; the leader of the Ustashas, Ante Pavelić, was a refugee in Rome, and his movement was subsidized by Mussolini. The League of Nations met hurriedly in an attempt to prevent a war between Yugoslavia and Italy which might develop into another world war. In Yugoslavia there was a new drive against the Ustashas and the Communists, who were lumped together by the Yugoslav government. The Communists and the Ustashas had indeed co-operated in prison. When the prison warders, who were nearly all Serbs, beat up Communist and Ustasha prisoners indiscriminately, the two groups, with their bloody noses and broken teeth, joined together in demonstrations of sympathy for each other.[15] But the Communists condemned the Ustashas for receiving subsidies from Fascist Italy, and the Ustashas criticized the Communists for being more concerned with the interests of the Soviet Union than with the independence of Croatia.

The police began a house-to-house search in Zagreb and Ljubljana, hoping to find Ustasha terrorists and Communists. The party decided that it was too dangerous for Tito to stay in Yugoslavia, and ordered him to leave at once for Vienna. He travelled on a forged Czech passport. He was worried, because he thought that it was a clumsy forgery which might be detected if there was a more thorough examination than usual of passports at the frontier after the king's assassination. But he had to take the risk, and with some misgivings boarded the train to Vienna in Ljubljana.

An Austrian woman with a six-month-old baby was travelling in the same compartment. Tito talked to her and played with the baby. When they reached the frontier, and the Yugoslav police entered the compartment, the woman asked Tito to hold the baby while she searched for her passport. Tito took the baby on his knee, and handed his passport to the policeman. At that moment the baby began to piddle, and Tito hastily lifted it off his knee and held it at arm's length. The policeman noticed what was happening and laughed, and amid the general amusement handed the passport back to Tito without examining it.[16]

On arriving in Vienna he stayed with a Jewish woman in a fourth-floor flat in the nineteenth district of the city. By law he was obliged, as a foreigner, to report his arrival to the police, but he did not wish to risk showing them the forged passport; so he paid his landlady an unusually high rent on the understanding that she did not tell the police that he was there. One day, when he was working in his room on a secret report to the Communist party in Yugoslavia, he noticed that there was a smell of gas. He went out on to the landing and discovered that the landlady's daughter had attempted suicide by gassing herself, because her employer had caught her stealing from the till to get money to go to the cinema. Tito was giving her the kiss of life, which he had been trained to do in the army, when the police and the ambulance arrived, for the neighbours, too, had smelt gas and had summoned them. The police asked Tito what he was doing there, and he said that he was a lodger in the house. They paid no more attention to him, and while the police and the ambulance men were reviving the girl, Tito coolly collected all the papers in his room and walked out of the building.[17]

The clerical-Fascist government of Schuschnigg in Austria was pursuing Communists and Socialists as well as Nazis, and Gorkić decided that the Politburo of the Communist party of Yugoslavia had better move to Brno in Czechoslovakia. Tito went with them. From Brno, Gorkić sent a comrade to Ljubljana to organize a secret

meeting of the Central Committee of the Communist Party of Yugoslavia on Christmas day, at which Tito was for the first time elected
a member of the Politburo; and the Politburo in Brno decided to
send him to Moscow to report to the Comintern on the situation in
Yugoslavia. At the beginning of February 1935 he arrived in Moscow, which he had never visited during his previous stay in the Soviet
Union. He had now become a full-time official of the Comintern.

CHAPTER 12

❖

The Hotel Lux

TITO arrived in Moscow at a critical time. Six weeks earlier, on 1 December 1934, Sergei Mironovich Kirov, the secretary of the Leningrad Communist party, was assassinated in his office by a young man. Within a few days the GPU had shot the assassin and over a hundred of his alleged accomplices after a summary trial at which it was 'proved' that the murder was a counter-revolutionary plot. Before his death Kirov had not been widely known outside Leningrad, but he was posthumously glorified as a paragon of proletarian Socialist virtue and Stalin's designated successor. Today most people believe that Stalin himself ordered the assassination, but the evidence for this is unreliable.

In January Zinoviev and Kamenev were put on trial charged with having objectively incited Kirov's murder by their anti-party and counter-revolutionary ideological deviations. Zinoviev was sentenced to ten years' imprisonment, and Kamenev to five years'. Many of their former supporters were arrested on similar charges. But within a few weeks of Tito's arrival in Moscow the arrests had subsided.

There were also signs of a new development in Soviet foreign policy. Stalin had at last realized that Hitler had become the greatest threat to the USSR. In September 1934 the Soviet Union joined the League of Nations, and a few months later signed a defence pact with France. For the first time since the October Revolution, even the British Conservatives were prepared to enter into friendly relations with the Soviet Union. In March 1935 the British foreign secretary, Sir John Simon, visited Hitler in Berlin, accompanied by his deputy at the Foreign Office, Anthony Eden. After their talks with Hitler, Eden went on to Moscow, though it was significant that the British foreign secretary himself visited Hitler, and only his deputy went to see Stalin.

Tito took up residence in the Hotel Lux in Gorki Street, which was reserved for officials of the Comintern. It was an old and out-of-date hotel, with small rooms and several annexes, and though comfortable was not luxurious by Western European standards. The residents had an apartment consisting of one room and a kitchenette with a primus stove and an electric cooker; but ordinarily they ate their meals in the communal restaurant on the ground floor. The security was very strict, and no one could enter the hotel without a pass. On one occasion a Yugoslav Communist who was staying in the hotel accompanied a guest to the hotel entrance and stepped out into the street for a moment to say goodbye to his friend. He had forgotten to take his pass with him, and the hotel porter, who had seen him walk out a few minutes earlier, refused to allow him to re-enter the hotel until he had telephoned another resident, who went to his room and brought his pass down to him.[1]

On arriving in Moscow Tito contacted Vladimir Čopić, who was one of the leading representatives of the Yugoslav Communist party with the Comintern. Gorkić had warmly recommended Tito to Čopić,[2] and Čopić introduced him to the leading personalities in the Comintern. He met Manuilsky, the representative of the Communist party of the Soviet Union; Dimitrov, the hero of the Reichstag Fire Trial; the Italian Palmiro Togliatti,* who was known as Ercole Ercoli in the Comintern; Otto Kuusinen of the Communist party of Finland; José Diaz of the Spanish Communist party; the American Communist, Earl Browder, whom Tito first met when they were going together to the cold shower-baths in the Hotel Lux;[3] and Wilhelm Pieck, the veteran German Communist. Pieck had been with Karl Liebknecht and Rosa Luxemburg when they were assassinated by military irregulars in Berlin in 1919; but the murderers had spared Pieck.

Tito was appointed a member of the secretariat of the Balkan section of the Comintern, which directed the activities of the Communist parties of Yugoslavia, Bulgaria, Romania and Greece. Pieck was

---

* Togliatti, Palmiro (1893–1964). Leader of the Italian Communist party; after Mussolini came to power went to Moscow, and under the name of Ercole Ercoli was one of the leading members of the Executive Committee of the Communist International; returned to Italy in 1943 and became a powerful figure in Italian politics and in the European Communist movement till his death.

in charge of the Balkan section; he had recently replaced Béla Kun, the leader of the Communist government of Hungary in 1919, who was in disgrace and soon afterwards was executed by the NKVD. Tito went every day to the offices of the Comintern in Mukhovaya Street, opposite the building which later became the Lenin Library. He sometimes lectured to foreign Communists who were taking a one-, two- or three-year course at the International Leninist School in Moscow. He was paid twenty roubles for each of his lectures, which usually dealt with work in the trade unions.[4]

He attended a course on military tactics at a Red Army school, where physical fitness and endurance were also tested. One of the endurance tests was to stand naked and motionless for two minutes submerged up to the neck in water at a temperature of one degree above freezing.[5] Apart from his daily journey between the Comintern office and the Hotel Lux, he did not travel around Moscow very much; but he occasionally went to the opera or ballet at the Bolshoi Theatre.

He contacted his wife Polka and his son Žarko; but he had fallen in love with an Austrian woman who worked in the Hotel Lux. She was Johanna Koenig, whose Party name was Lucia Bauer. Polka did not approve of this, and divorced Tito in April 1936. According to a recently discovered document, Tito married Lucia Bauer in Moscow on 13 October 1936, five days before he left Moscow for Vienna. We do not know why he married her. The story that it was in order to provide a home for Žarko, who was running wild in the streets, is untrue, for Žarko never met her.[6]

The Seventh Congress of the Comintern met in the Palace of the Trade Unions in Moscow on 25 July 1935. Tito was one of the 510 delegates from sixty-five Communist parties. Here for the first time he saw Stalin, who sat on the platform during the first session and joined in singing the 'International', but did not attend again. But his photograph was everywhere displayed, and in his absence he was praised by the delegates. Manuilsky declared that 'every pronouncement that Stalin makes is a landmark in the enrichment and deepening of Marxist-Leninist theory'; and the official report of the congress recorded that every mention of Stalin's name was greeted with 'stormy and prolonged applause, ovation, and shouts of hurrah'.

The congress lasted for nearly a month. Before the delegates dispersed on 20 August they endorsed the new line of the Executive Committee. Some of the old doctrines were reaffirmed. The congress declared that in no capitalist country would the standard of living of the working class ever return to the level it had reached before the economic crisis of 1929; and they emphasized that the victory of Communism would ultimately be achieved by violent revolution in every country of the world. But the Comintern reversed its previous policy of condemning the Social-Democrats as Social Fascists and the principal enemy of the working class. It proclaimed the need to defend bourgeois democracy against Fascism and called for a united front with the Social-Democrats. Manuilsky insisted that Stalin had not been wrong when he said that Fascism and Social-Democracy were not antipodes but twins; it was the situation that had changed.

Dimitrov was elected general secretary of the Comintern. He was assisted by a secretariat consisting of Manuilsky, Pieck, Togliatti, Kuusinen, Marty from France and Gottwald* from Czechoslovakia.[7]

After the congress Tito and the other Yugoslav delegates were taken on a tour of the Soviet Union, going as far as the Urals and into Siberia. Tito was able to tell his comrades how much things had improved in the backward areas since he was there in the first days after 1917.[8] Then he returned to carry on the party's underground work in Yugoslavia and explain the new Comintern line. The struggle against Fascism and war now meant defeating the reactionary bourgeoisie who wished to ally their countries with Hitler against the Soviet Union or to adopt a neutral attitude while Hitler invaded neighbouring countries and prepared to attack the Soviet Union. They must pressurize bourgeois governments to make a military alliance with the Soviet Union and thus deter Hitler and Mussolini from going to war. In the case of France's ally, Yugoslavia, they would no longer work to dismember the country in alliance with Croatian and Macedonian nationalists, but would unite with Social-Democrat, peasant and bourgeois parties to strengthen the national defence of Yugoslavia against Hitlerite and Italian Fascist aggression.

The party still carried on its work in the trade unions. Tito helped organize strikes in the Kraljevica shipyards and in the large coalfields at Trbovlje near Ljubljana, where several thousand workers were

---

* Gottwald, Klement (1896–1953). Czechoslovak Communist leader; member of Executive Committee of Comintern 1935–43; in Soviet Union during Second World War; prime minister of Czechoslovakia 1946–48; president of Czechoslovakia 1948–53; caught a chill attending Stalin's funeral in 1953 of which he died.

employed. His activities alarmed the employers, and rumours circulated that all the labour troubles in the country were instigated by the Comintern agent, Josip Broz. The manager of the large Trepča mines in Serbia was a Scotsman named A. S. Howie. He became very friendly with the British author Rebecca West when she visited Yugoslavia in 1937, and he featured in her book *Black Lamb and Grey Falcon* as 'Gospodie Mac'.[9] He told her about the nefarious activities of 'a Comintern agent called Brosz, son of a Czech Jew and a Hungarian mother, born near Novi Sad when it was Hungarian'. Howie got at least two things right; he knew that Broz had served in the Austrian army in the First World War and had been a prisoner-of-war in Russia. He told Rebecca West that Broz 'played a part in organising trouble – justified trouble – in Kragujovatz and in organising not so justified trouble in Trepča'.[10]

Tito had tried to persuade the Comintern that it would be better if the party leadership was inside Yugoslavia and not abroad. But Gorkić was determined that the Politburo should continue to direct the movement from abroad. The Comintern decided to compromise; Gorkić and the political leadership could stay abroad while Tito and the organizational administration worked within Yugoslavia.[11] Gorkić then decided to escape from the attentions of Schuschnigg's police in Vienna by moving the Politburo to Paris.

In 1936 and 1937 Tito travelled several times between Zagreb, Moscow and Paris, always using false passports. The Comintern was an efficient organization, but sometimes they slipped up. Once they gave Tito a Canadian passport which had been issued to some Croatian immigrant in Toronto or Alberta. When Tito arrived in Copenhagen on his way to Paris, the immigration officer who inspected his passport spoke to him in English. Tito could hardly speak a word of English and did not know what to do. But the immigration officer was a Communist sympathizer. He whispered to Tito that he had better learn a little English before he travelled on a Canadian passport.[12]

On another occasion Tito showed that he himself was not immune from human error. He was travelling from Prague to Paris through Nazi Germany on a forged passport which he had been given by his Comintern contact just before he left Prague. The German immigration officer to whom he handed the passport could not make out the name on the passport, and asked Tito what his name was. Tito's mind had suddenly gone blank; he had completely forgotten the name. But he had not lost his wits. He pretended that he could not speak German and did not understand what the officer was saying. After the officer had repeated the question several times, Tito remembered the name and told him. The officer was satisfied and allowed him to proceed on his journey.[13]

Tito returned to Moscow in August 1936. The Spanish Civil War had broken out a few weeks earlier. It was a continuation of the wars which had been fought in Spain during the nineteenth century, with a military *coup d'état* leading to a civil war of the right against the left, of the army, the Church hierarchy, and the landowning class against the Liberal government and the revolutionary workers in the towns. Both sides committed atrocities and executed their prisoners, and were ardently supported by their ideological sympathizers abroad. The Communists, Social-Democrats and Liberals throughout the world regarded it as a war between the 'government' and the 'rebels', between democracy and Fascism; the Conservatives and right-wing called it a war between the 'nationalists' and the 'Reds', between Christian civilization and Bolshevism.

From the first day Hitler, Mussolini and Dr Salazar, the Conservative dictator of Portugal, supported General Franco, the leader of the right-wing rebels. The French government of the Social-Democrat, Léon Blum,* which had just come to power after winning a general election with Communist support, wished to help the Spanish government; but the British Conservative government persuaded Blum to adopt a policy of non-intervention, which meant in practice that Britain and France did not send arms to the Spanish government although Germany, Italy and Portugal sent arms and troops to help Franco.

Winston Churchill, an elder statesman out of office, used his influence to persuade the French government to support the non-intervention policy. He told them that if France became involved in a conflict with Hitler and Mussolini over the Spanish Civil War, most British Conservatives would be on the side of Hitler and Mussolini. When he met the ambassador of the Spanish Liberal government he refused to shake his hand because the Spanish government side

---

* Blum, Léon (1872–1950); French Social-Democrat leader; prime minister 1936–7; imprisoned in Vichy France and in Germany during the Second World War; returning to France, he was again prime minister in December 1946; a respected figure in the European Socialist movement.

was stained with blood; and on 5 September 1936 he wrote to his wife: 'I am thankful the Spanish Nationalists are making progress'. The fighting in Spain was 'horrible! But better for the safety of all if the Communists are crushed.'[14]

But Churchill's attitude to Russia was changing. He had hated Bolshevism and admired Mussolini, but he was alarmed from the first by Hitler's policy and saw Nazi Germany as a menace to British interests. In order to defeat Hitler, he was ready to ally himself with Hitler's enemy, Stalin. On 6 May 1936 he wrote to Lord Londonderry: 'I fear very gravely however unless something happens to the Nazi regime in Germany there will be a devastating war in Europe ... British policy for four hundred years has been to oppose the strongest power in Europe by weaving together a combination of other countries strong enough to face the bully. Sometimes it is Spain, sometimes the French monarchy, sometimes the French Empire, sometimes Germany ... I have no doubt who it is now.'[15] In 1936 it was not Russia; it was Germany.

At the beginning of April 1936 he invited the Soviet ambassador, Ivan Maisky, to lunch at his country house at Chartwell near Westerham in Kent. Sir Maurice Hankey, the secretary to the Cabinet, who dined with Churchill at Chartwell a few days later, noted the change in Churchill's attitude. 'In view of the danger from Germany, he has buried his violent anti-Russian complex of former days and is apparently a bosom friend of M. Maisky.'[16]

But the British government, with the support of the great majority of the Conservative party, rejected Churchill's policy. The prime minister, Stanley Baldwin, told Churchill that he did not think that Hitler would attack Western Europe, 'and if he should move east I should not break my heart'. The only danger was that France would be drawn into a war with Germany 'owing to that appalling pact they made' with Russia. 'If there is any fighting in Europe to be done, I should like to see the Bolshies and the Nazis doing it.'[17]

An important development in Russia made it easier for Churchill to change his attitude. In August 1936 Zinoviev, Kamenev and other Communist leaders were executed after the first of the great show trials. It was the beginning of what became known as the 'Yezhov Purge', though Yezhov* himself was one of its last victims. In January

---

* Yezhov, Nikolai Ivanovich (1895–1939). Soviet Communist leader; succeeded Yagoda as head of the NKVD; chief organiser of the purge (the 'Yezhov Purge') of 1936–8; denounced, arrested and disappeared (probably executed) soon after January 1939.

1937 came the trial of Pyatakov and Radek; in June Marshal Tukhachevsky and other top generals were shot after a secret court-martial. Bukharin and other former leaders were condemned in another public trial in March 1938. A far greater number were executed all over the Soviet Union in secret trials or by the 'administrative action' of the NKVD; and many more were sent to forced labour camps and were never heard of again.

The first target of the terror were the Old Bolsheviks, though it soon spread far beyond them and engulfed large numbers of ordinary Soviet citizens, as the NKVD everywhere tried to supply their quotas of workers for the labour camps. The original Bolshevik leaders were mostly middle-class by birth, many of them were Jews, and they had lived in Western Europe and had been reared in Western European culture. Though they would strongly have denied it, they were in fact the last bourgeois revolutionaries, the political descendants of the French revolutionaries of 1793, of Marx and Engels, and of the men of 1848, whom they resembled in social origin, cultural background and political tactics. There was no place for them in the Soviet state which they had created. Stalin was relying on the far more popular forces of Russian patriotism, with its tradition of submission to a personal autocrat, the rejection of economic equality, and the suppression of all free criticism inside as well as outside the Communist party.

Churchill had always had a special hatred of 'Trotsky alias Bronstein' as he called him; he thought that he was the 'Ogre of Europe'.[18] Other anti-Communists in the West thought that Stalin and the Soviet government were still aiming at a Communist world revolution; but there was some reason to hope that the rule of fanatical internationalist revolutionaries was being replaced by a nationalist dictator who would be as willing as Churchill himself to make a military alliance with an ideological enemy if it was in the national interest of his country to do so.

On 24 September 1936 Churchill gave a lecture at the Théâtre des Ambassadeurs in Paris to a very distinguished audience and many representatives of the world press. It was a month after the Zinoviev trial in Moscow. Trotsky was living in Norway, but the Soviet government had asked the Norwegians to expel him, and the Norwegian Social-Democrat government had placed him under house arrest to please Stalin. The theme of Churchill's lecture was the duty of Britain and France to defend democracy against the 'two violent extremes', Nazism and Communism, which threatened it. 'Between the doctrines of Comrade Trotsky and those of Dr Goebbels there ought to be room for you and me, and a few others, to cultivate opinions of our own.'[19] This reference to 'Comrade Trotsky' and not to 'Comrade Stalin' was significant.

The foreign Communists in Moscow were particularly vulnerable. As foreigners they were regarded with suspicion, and had no popular support in Russia, apart from their friendship with a few influential Soviet Communists. Many of them had been condemned to death or to long terms of imprisonment in their own country, and neither would nor could ask their government to protect them in the Soviet Union. So the foreign Comintern officials suffered particularly from the purge.

One of the victims was the veteran Yugoslav Communist, Filip Filipović, who was known in the Comintern as 'Bošković'. When Tito returned to Moscow in August 1936 he was asked to report on Filipović. Although he knew that Filipović was under suspicion, he wrote a very favourable report.

Bošković is an old member of the Central Committee of the Communist Party of Yugoslavia and an old Socialist. He is very popular in the country, especially in Serbia. Comrade Bošković did not belong either to the Left or the Right fraction at the time of the fraction fights. But later, during 1932 and 1933, he did not adopt a regular line about the right method of preventing the formation of fractions, and because of this he himself became a part of this activity. Because of this, the ECCI [Executive Committee of the Communist International] removed him from his position. He is now in Moscow, where he works as a schoolteacher, and he is always included in our party activities.

I consider Comrade Bošković to be loyal to the leadership of the Central Committee of the Communist Party of Yugoslavia and devoted to the leadership of the Comintern. I am firmly convinced that this is true. I think it is absolutely essential that Comrade Bošković should be sent into the country as someone who can work legally. He can be of use in the movement of the Anti-Fascist People's Front.

31 August, 1936.   Walter.[20]

But Filipović was not sent back to Yugoslavia. He was sent to an NKVD prison, and shot.

The NKVD often came for the foreign Communists during the night in the Hotel Lux. The Comintern officials in their bedroom heard the footsteps in the passage and when there was no knock at their door, and the footsteps grew fainter, breathed again. They wondered which of their comrades had been taken, and found out next morning when they saw who was not there at breakfast. A few nights later they heard the steps again, and again noticed who was absent from breakfast. They never discussed the matter with their friends; even husbands and wives did not mention it to each other, or express any doubt about the guilt of their comrades who had been arrested.[21] They never confided to anyone that they were afraid that it might be their turn next. In many cases they refused to admit, even to themselves, that this was a possibility. What had they to fear? They knew that they were innocent and that all their comrades who had been arrested must have been guilty.

When Dedijer wrote his biography of Tito in 1953, after the injustices of the purges in the Soviet Union had been exposed in Yugoslavia, he asked Tito why he had supported the Soviet Union where such crimes were committed. Tito gave the reply which so many other foreign Communists could have given. For the little band of Communists, persecuted to a greater or lesser extent in every other country in the world, the Soviet Union was their only support and hope, the one good haven in a world of evil, a distant paradise of which they dreamed in their capitalist prisons. 'In the most trying hours', said Tito, 'through dismal nights and endless interrogations and maltreatment, during days of killing solitude in cells and close confinement, we were always sustained by the hope that all these agonies were not in vain, that there was a strong and mighty country, however far away, in which all the dreams for which we were fighting had been fulfilled. For us it was the homeland of the workers, in which labour was honoured, in which love, comradeship, and sincerity prevailed. With what joy I had felt the strength of that country as, emerging from prison in 1934, I listened in the dead of each night to Radio Moscow and heard the clock of the Kremlin tower striking the hours, and the stirring strains of the "International".'[22]

How could they have survived those endless interrogations, maltreatment and solitude in prison cells if they had known that more Communists would be killed under Stalin in the Soviet Union than by any other government in the world? When they realized that Communists were being shot in the Soviet Union, the only bearable explanation was that these Communists were in fact traitors and Fascist agents; for the only other explanation was that the Land of Socialism for which they had sacrificed so much was not Paradise but Hell.

But Tito had left Moscow before those terrible nights in the Hotel Lux. The purge of the Comintern officials did not really get underway until the spring of 1937, six months after Tito had been ordered to return to Yugoslavia and carry out an important duty. During August and September 1936 Franco's armies advanced everywhere in Spain, and it seemed as if they would soon capture Madrid and win the Civil War. While Mussolini sent bombers and other military equipment to Franco, Blum adhered strictly to the policy of non-intervention. Stalin was determined that the Soviet Union should not become involved; but he was quite prepared to agree to the suggestion of the French Communists that the Comintern should send Communist volunteers from all countries to fight for the Spanish government.[23] The volunteers not only risked their lives in Spain but also prosecution in the courts in their own countries, for the governments which supported non-intervention made it a criminal offence to fight in Spain. The volunteers went to France pretending to be going for a holiday, and from there the Communist party arranged their passage across the frontier into Spanish republican territory.

The Comintern told Tito to go to Yugoslavia and organize the recruitment of volunteers for the International Brigade in Spain. Gorkić supplied him with a forged passport, but Tito was learning to be suspicious. So many Communists travelling to Yugoslavia with forged passports had been spotted and arrested by the Yugoslav police on the frontier; and he noticed that on each occasion the passport had been supplied by Gorkić. He had no real reason to suspect Gorkić, but he knew that any member of a revolutionary organization might be an informer planted by the police; if Zinoviev and Kamenev were Fascist agents, why not Gorkić? He did not use the passport which Gorkić had given him, but privately obtained another forged passport under a different name.[24]

He reached Vienna in October 1936 and by December had safely crossed the Yugoslav frontier. He went to Split and discussed the best way of recruiting volunteers for the International Brigade and getting them to Spain. Travel overland was risky, as it meant passing through either Austria or Italy under the surveillance of Schuschnigg's or Mussolini's police; so Gorkić and the Politburo in Paris decided to charter a ship and send it to the Adriatic to transport the volunteers direct from Montenegro to the east coast of Spain, which was held by the Republican government.

While the chartered ship, *La Corse*, sailed from Marseilles to the Adriatic, 500 volunteers assembled on a hilltop near the coast of Montenegro. The Communist party had hired a considerable number of small boats to row the volunteers out to *La Corse*. Unfortunately the agreed embarkation point was not far from Milocer, the summer residence of King Peter's cousin and regent, Prince Paul, so the area was well guarded by the security police. They noticed that 500 young men who looked like Communists had assembled in the area, and wondered why they had hired so many rowing boats.

The embarkation had been fixed for the night of 2 March 1937, but a gale was blowing, making it impossible for the rowing boats to put to sea, and the boarding operation was postponed for twenty-four hours. The police used this delay to bring up reinforcements and cordon off the whole area. The embarkation began soon after nightfall. About half the volunteers were already on board when the police boarded the ship and arrested them. Their comrades were arrested on shore and on the hilltop. One Comintern agent who was on the ship jumped overboard and managed to escape; but the chief organizer of the project, Muk, who had come from Paris to direct the operation, was arrested. When questioned by the police, he told them everything. Five hundred Communists and fellow-travellers who had been prepared to fight Fascism in Spain were sentenced to many years' imprisonment for contravening the Law for the Protection of the State; and *La Corse*, which the Communist party had chartered for 750,000 French francs,* was confiscated by the Yugoslav government.[25]

Tito wrote next day from Split to the Politburo in Paris and told them the bad news. He at first suggested that they might try again, and charter another ship to take other Communist volunteers from Montenegro to Spain; but he soon realized that this would lead to a second disaster, as the police and the navy would be carefully watching the coast. They would have to send the volunteers overland, each one with a forged passport, and in sufficiently small groups so as not to arouse suspicion; for after the disaster of *La Corse*, the

---

* 750,000 French francs was worth £67,000 in 1937 – over £3,000,000 in terms of 1994 prices.

authorities knew that the Communists were sending Yugoslav volunteers to fight in Spain.

They were helped by the fact that an international exhibition was being held in Paris in 1937. It was the sequel to the great exhibitions of 1867 and 1900 and was named 'The Universal Exhibition of Peace'. The German and Soviet pavilions faced each other separated by an asphalt path some twenty feet wide. The German eagle and swastika were a few feet higher than the sickle and hammer raised in defiance against it by the statues of the male and female worker on the roof of the Soviet pavilion. Stalin easily beat Hitler in the cult of the personality. There were only one or two photographs and statues of Hitler in the German pavilion; but every photograph, statue and portrait in the Soviet pavilion included Stalin – Stalin talking to a worker, Stalin smoking a pipe with an old peasant, Stalin with children, Stalin with the party leaders, Stalin with his generals. Nearby was the Italian pavilion, in the modern functional style of the 1930s favoured by Mussolini, and the pavilion of the Spanish republican government; above the entrance were written the words of President Azaña: 'There are two million Spaniards under arms who will not allow anyone to walk over them.'[26]

People came to Paris from all over the world to see the exhibition, and this was a good excuse for Yugoslavs to come. Once they had arrived in Paris they could be sent secretly to the Pyrenees and across the Spanish frontier.

Soon after the disaster of *La Corse*, Tito went to Paris, and opened his office in a small hotel on the left bank. He organized the operation with his usual efficiency. He managed to send 1,192 Yugoslavs to fight in Spain. Most of them were refugees or other emigrants living in France and Belgium, in the United States and Canada, and in the Soviet Union; but 330 came from Yugoslavia. Five hundred and sixty-one were members of the Communist party; the other 631 were Social-Democrats or enthusiastic anti-Fascists who did not belong to any party. The largest contingent in the International Brigade were 10,000 French; apart from them, only Germany and Austria (combined), Italy, Great Britain and the United States sent more volunteers than the Yugoslavs. There were never more than 18,000 volunteers in the International Brigade at any one time. Against them were 50,000 Italian troops sent by Mussolini, 16,000 Germans sent by Hitler, and 20,000 Portuguese volunteers.

The casualty rate in the International Brigade was very high, for they fought with reckless courage and self-sacrifice against better-trained and better-equipped troops. In every national brigade about thirty per cent were killed and over fifty per cent wounded. The Yugoslavs suffered even higher casualties. Of their 1,200 men, 671 were killed, and another 300 wounded.[27]

Stalin sent less than 1,000 Russians to Spain, and ordered them to stay out of the firing line. They were mostly military technicians, journalists and members of the NKVD. The Soviet Union sent military equipment, including aircraft, to Spain, but made the Spanish government pay a good price in money for them and refused to send any supplies until the gold in the Bank of Spain had been deposited in Moscow as security for payment. When the Spanish Communists complained that the Soviet Union was not sending more aid, Togliatti, who had been sent to Spain with other prominent leaders of the Comintern, told them that the first duty of the Soviet Union was to safeguard its own security.[28]

The job of the NKVD in Spain was to arrest and murder Spanish and foreign Trotskyists, Anarchists, and anti-Stalinist Socialists. The Spanish Anarchists and the semi-Trotskyist POUM wished to carry through the social revolution during the war, to expropriate the landlords and the factory owners, and especially to burn the churches and monasteries of the hated Catholic Church. They also insisted that every army unit should decide by majority vote whether they should advance or retreat. The Communists required them to submit to military discipline, and wished to concentrate on winning the war, on defending bourgeois democracy against Fascism, and convincing the British and French governments that they had nothing to fear from the victory of the Republican government in Spain.

In May 1937 the Anarchists and the POUM rose in revolt in Barcelona against the Republican government. The rising was suppressed. The NKVD arrested, tortured and executed Anarchist and POUM supporters. After the NKVD agents had completed their work they were recalled to Moscow, where most of them were shot on Stalin's orders; he feared that they had come under Western influence in Spain.

After Tito came to prominence in 1943 it was widely reported that he had been in Spain during the Civil War. Some of his critics went further and said that he was sent there as an agent of the NKVD.[29] The Yugoslavs who had fought in Spain and survived formed the nucleus of the Partisan forces in Yugoslavia; so it was natural that people believed that the Partisans' commander-in-chief had also been there; and it is not surprising that volunteers from other countries who had fought in Spain and remembered a fleeting encounter there with a well-built Yugoslav, wondered if the man was Tito, and then persuaded themselves that it was he.

In fact, Tito never went to Spain. He always denied having been there, just as he denied having played a leading part in the Russian Civil War of 1918–20. There is no reliable evidence that he was there, and no reason to doubt his statement. If he had been in Spain he would have been much less likely to have survived the purges in the Soviet Union in 1938. Spain was one of the very few countries in the world where he never set foot during his life.

The story that Tito was in Spain has persisted partly because he was sometimes a little mysterious about his movements in 1937–8. At various times he gave different dates for his arrival and departure from Paris and Moscow. On several occasions, when he was asked where he had been on certain dates in 1938, he said that he could not remember.[30]

Peter Elstob was a young Englishman, a pilot officer in the Royal Air Force, who wished to fight Fascism in Spain. He contacted the Communist party, and in September 1936 went to Paris, and was sent on to Perpignan. Here he and his comrades were welcomed by a well-built man wearing a sort of battle-dress jacket, who was called 'the Yugoslav captain'. He spoke to them in French, and told them that they would be conducted across the frontier next morning.

Twenty-nine years later, Elstob was the press officer of the writers' organization, PEN, and attended a PEN literary congress in Yugoslavia. He and other prominent members attending the congress were presented to President Tito. As soon as Elstob saw Tito he thought that he recognized him as the man who had welcomed the volunteers at Perpignan in September 1936. When he and his colleagues were about to leave, he asked Tito: 'Forgive me, Your Excellency, but I went to Spain in 1936 as a British volunteer for the International Brigade. May I ask if you were in Perpignan in 1936?' Tito was not in the least offended by the question. He gave Elstob a most friendly smile, and replied: 'One goes to so many places at many different times.' This answer almost convinced Elstob that the man at Perpignan was Tito; but Tito was in fact in Moscow in September 1936.[31]

Tito travelled several times between Paris and Zagreb between May and August 1937. Apart from organizing the transport of the volunteers to Spain, he was also busy with preparation for the founding of a separate Croatian Communist party as distinct from the Communist party of Yugoslavia, for the Comintern had decided to make this concession to Croatian separatism. The founding conference took place at Samobor on 1 and 2 August 1937. In his speech to the conference, Tito said that it had been possible to form a Communist party of Croatia only because of the many years of struggle of the Communist party of Yugoslavia 'which defended not only the interests of the working class but also had always had the idea of national freedom, equality and brotherhood among the peoples written on its banners . . . We fight against national hatred and chauvinism, because we know that the true progress and freedom of the Croatian people are ensured in a brotherly harmony and co-operation with the other peoples of Yugoslavia.'[32]

During his months in Yugoslavia he never visited his friends in Kumrovec. He thought that this would be too dangerous, for the police might be keeping a watch on Kumrovec. It was a little safer to go to the nearby villages across the river Sutla in Slovenia, and some of his old associates came from Kumrovec to visit him there. But he longed to see his native village again. He told his friend Miroslav Krleža, the famous Croatian writer, how one night he went to the district and walked to the hills above Kumrovec. He looked down on the village and could clearly see in the moonlight the sloping vineyards on the hillsides and the houses in the valley, and hear the barking dogs. He sat and gazed for a while on the home that he loved before returning to Zagreb and his work for the Comintern.[33]

In July 1937 Gorkić was asked by the Comintern to come to Moscow. He was expecting to be asked to justify the fiasco of the voyage and capture of *La Corse*. He told his comrades in Paris that he would no doubt receive a 'headwashing' (carpeting) in Moscow. When he reached the Soviet Union he received, not a headwashing, but a bullet in the head, after months of interrogation, in the cellar of some NKVD prison. His Polish wife, Beti Glan, who was one of the directors of the Park of Culture and Rest in Moscow, was also arrested but was eventually released.[34]

Tito received a message from the Politburo of the Communist party of Yugoslavia to come at once to Paris. He arrived there on 17 August 1937. They told him the staggering news that Gorkić had been invited to go to Moscow and had been arrested on his arrival. But Tito knew this already, as he told the students at a party school in Kumrovec in March 1977, when he gave the fullest details yet of his whereabouts and actions in 1937 and 1938. 'I had already been informed about it by the Comintern, who gave me at the same time a mandate to take over the political secretariat. This is how I became general secretary and assumed the full responsibility for our Party.'[35] There has been much discussion about the date on which Tito became the general secretary of the Yugoslav Communist party; but there seems no doubt that he was the acting general secretary from August 1937, that he did not go to Moscow until August 1938, and that his appointment as general secretary was not finally ratified by the Comintern until 5 January 1939.[36]

In 1968 Tito granted an interview to the English author, Phyllis Auty, who was writing his biography. She asked him why he had survived when he was living in Moscow during the great purge: was it luck? Tito denied this. 'It was my own doing. I saw what it was all about and was careful to concern myself only with Yugoslav affairs, and that was why they had no holds to drag me in by. It was certainly not chance.'[37]

He minimized the risk by acting on one basic principle: as far as possible to stay out of the Soviet Union and out of Spain. When he first became secretary of the Communist party of Yugoslavia in August 1937 he told the Comintern that he could not go to Moscow immediately for he had to tidy up things in Paris. There were some comrades in the Communist party of Yugoslavia in Paris who were causing trouble by opposing his leadership, apparently more on personal grounds and out of a general resentment of authority than from any political disagreements with the party line. Tito told the Comintern that these troublemakers were making some headway among the students; and the Comintern appreciated that he had to stay in Paris until he had broken and disciplined them.

He then stressed the point which he had already made to Dimitrov before he became general secretary: the party leadership should be inside Yugoslavia and not in exile abroad. The party could win the confidence of the masses only if the leaders were on the spot, in contact with the workers and sharing the risks of illegal underground work under the dictatorship.[38] He did not add that it was not only desirable to share the risks of underground work in Yugoslavia, but also to avoid the risks of living in the Soviet Union. He had a better chance in Yugoslavia, on the run from Prince Paul's police, than as a sitting target for the NKVD in the Hotel Lux.

He had to impose strict discipline and stamp out any trace of 'fractionalism' to get the party in Yugoslavia to accept the complete change in the party line on war and its attitude to French imperialism. When the French foreign minister, Yvon Delbos, visited Belgrade in December 1937 Tito organized a great demonstration to greet him at the railway station. Thirty thousand Communist and anti-Fascist workers and students marched through the streets demanding solidarity with their French ally and resistance to German Fascism. The demonstration turned into a protest against the pro-German or neutralist policy of the Yugoslav government, and was broken up by the police. This led to violence; twenty demonstrators were injured, and many were arrested.[39]

Tito returned to Yugoslavia from Paris in March 1938. He heard a rumour that his opponents in the party in Paris had tipped off the Yugoslav police that he was coming to Zagreb and had told them the false name under which he would be travelling. He obtained another forged passport and left a week earlier than he had intended, travelling not to Zagreb but to Belgrade.[40] He arrived safely and stayed in the flat of a young intellectual, Vladimir Dedijer, who had been a refugee in England as a child during the First World War and later became the London correspondent of the Liberal Belgrade newspaper, *Politika*. Dedijer had not yet joined the Communist party, but he was a friend of Djilas and a very devoted fellow-traveller.

Tito arrived in Belgrade a few days before Hitler marched into Austria. Again Britain and France and the League of Nations did nothing to stop him. The annexation of Austria caused alarm in Yugoslavia, for it brought the German Nazis to the country's borders. There was a good response to the Communist party of Yugoslavia's appeal condemning the annexation of Austria and calling for united resistance to Hitler. In April the Social-Democrat and trade union congress in Zagreb agreed to collaborate with the Communists in a People's Front against Fascism, and stopped their campaigns against the Communist party and the Soviet Union.[41]

In June Tito thought it wise to write to Dimitrov and Pieck and suggest that he should come to Moscow to report; if he was to retain the confidence of the Comintern, he must show that he was willing to go to Moscow, and it was better to go there at his own suggestion than to wait until he was summoned. He travelled by Paris to Copenhagen. He had to wait two months in Paris for his Soviet visa, apparently because of some bureaucratic incompetence, and reached Moscow on 24 August 1938. He found that the situation in Moscow was more dangerous than he had expected. More than a hundred Yugoslav Communists were arrested by the NKVD and executed, or disappeared and were never seen again. They included nearly all the most prominent leaders of the Communist party of Yugoslavia and over twenty members of the Central Committee – more than all the members of the Central Committee killed by the Yugoslav government before 1941 and by the Germans, Italians and their allies during the Second World War. Many of them were arrested while Tito was in Moscow in November 1938.[42]

All the Yugoslav Communists were under suspicion, and word had got around that they were dangerous to know. There were rumours that the Comintern was about to dissolve the Yugoslav Communist party. Tito and his friend Veljko Vlahović, who had lost a leg fighting in Spain, noticed that none of the Communists in the Hotel Lux would sit at their table at breakfast. Tito told Vlahović not to worry. 'One day they'll be grabbing chairs from each other to sit with us.'[43]

The position was particularly difficult for Tito because when he reached Moscow he found that both Polka and Lucia Bauer had been arrested and accused of being imperialist spies. On 27 September 1938 Tito wrote to Dimitrov and Manuilsky, expressing his sense of guilt that, through lack of vigilance, he had not noticed any treasonable activities in either of his two wives.[44] Polka was not sent to a labour camp, but she was held in prison for twenty-seven months. Lucia Bauer was under more suspicion as a foreign Communist in the Hotel Lux, but she too was eventually released. There was also the problem of what to do about Žarko. Tito liked his son, but was obviously not in a position to take care of him, and he could not be sure how long he himself would be alive and free. So he spent thirty roubles in buying Žarko a pair of skates, and placed him in a boarding school just outside Kharkov.

But Žarko had some of his father's daring and spirit of adventure. While Polka was in prison, he was transferred to a school at Penza; he did not like it, and ran away. He was returned to the school, but ran away again with a school friend. Polka, who by this time had been released from prison, was prepared to look after him; but he preferred to stay with his friend's mother, Vladimirovna Varesco, who came from Bosnia and had married an Italian. In 1941, when he was seventeen, he joined the Soviet Army to fight the Germans.[45]

According to Tito, he never denounced anyone as a Trotskyist to the Comintern or the NKVD, but on several occasions he was asked for information about Yugoslav Communists who had been arrested or had already been accused. He usually managed to avoid having to denounce them by saying that he did not know them; but he was unable to avoid writing a report on Horvatin, the Croatian Communist leader who had been arrested as a Trotskyist. Tito wrote ambiguously, saying that he did not know whether or not Horvatin was a Trotskyist. Horvatin was never heard of again, and was probably executed by the NKVD.[46]

Some of Tito's critics do not believe that his own account and the published documents give a true picture of his activities in Moscow during the great purge. They ask why Tito was one of the very few Yugoslavs to survive, and think that it must have been because he proved his loyalty to Stalin by denouncing his comrades who were under suspicion, especially those who were his rivals for the party leadership. But Tito was too shrewd to do this. Denunciation of rivals was not a good way to survive, for anyone who did so ran the risk of being denounced himself if his rivals came out on top in the power struggle. It was safer to keep as quiet as possible and stay out of the limelight. Tito also took the obvious precautions; realizing that his room in the Hotel Lux was certain to be bugged, he took care not to discuss politics there. Once his son Žarko, now aged fourteen, came to visit him in the hotel. Žarko ran into the room and excitedly reported that another comrade had been arrested by the NKVD. Tito quickly seized Žarko's arm, led him out of the room and the hotel, and took him for a walk in the park.[47] He knew that they could talk freely in the park.

While he was in Moscow, Tito was given the task of helping Čopić translate from Russian into Serbo-Croat the *History of the Communist Party of the Soviet Union (Bolsheviks)*, which had recently been published in the Soviet Union. It was intended, for all except the most advanced students, to replace the Marxist classics of Marx, Engels and Lenin. The greatest importance was attached to the book in every Communist party in the world. When it was first published it was said to have been inspired and approved by Stalin. Later, it was announced that Stalin himself had written the chapter on dialectical materialism; and eventually that Stalin was the author of the whole book.

The *History of the CPSU(B)* began with a brief survey of the situation in Russia at the end of the nineteenth century, the foundation of the Bolshevik party by Lenin, and the Revolution of 1917, before turning into a violent tirade against Trotsky and Bukharin and a fulsome eulogy of Stalin. Stylistically it is a bad and boring book. It contains none of the brilliance and humour of Marx, the vigour of Engels, the clarity of thought of Lenin, or the sarcasm of Trotsky. There is only repetitive abuse of Stalin's opponents in the Communist party.

The work of translation was entrusted by the Comintern to Čopić, assisted by Tito and Jovanović, another Yugoslav Communist. Čopić had edited the Serbo-Croat edition of Lenin's *Collected Works*. Since he had welcomed Tito to Moscow in 1935 he had fought in Spain where he had been wounded and promoted to the rank of Lieutenant-General in the Republican army. Čopić, Tito and Jovanović had only got as far as Chapter 2, dealing with the events of 1901–4, when Čopić was arrested as a Trotskyist; in due course he was executed. Tito continued working on the translation with Jovanović, wondering how long it would be before he shared the fate of his fellow-translator. He was well paid for his work, for a new policy had recently been introduced in the Soviet Union of paying financial rewards to workers who worked harder than their colleagues. Tito bought himself a diamond ring with the money that he received for his translation.[48]

He had translated the account of the plots against Lenin in 1918 by the 'counter-revolutionary conspiracy of the Bukharinites, Trotskyites and "Left" Socialist Revolutionaries'; of how 'Lenin had branded Bukharin as a champion of the profiteers, Nepmen and kulaks'; of the 'degeneration of the Bukharinites into political double-dealers' and the 'degeneration of the Trotskyite double-dealers into a White-Guard gang of assassins and spies'. Then Ozren Miler, a young Communist who came from the German minority in Yugoslavia, drew the attention of the Comintern to an inaccurate translation of one passage in the book which showed that Tito was a Trotskyist. According to Djilas, there were a number of inaccuracies in the translation, as Tito cheerfully admitted when Djilas drew his attention to them; but none of them had any political significance.[49]

Tito was a good friend of the German Communist, Florin, who was the chairman of the Control Commission of the Comintern. As soon as Tito was denounced, Florin told him not to worry, as the investigation would turn out all right for him. Other influential Communists spoke in his favour, and he was exonerated.[50]

Tito had an unpleasant shock one day when he was travelling on a Moscow bus and happened to see Miletić, who had caused Tito a great deal of trouble by his leftist attitude in prison in Yugoslavia. Tito had not realized that Miletić had come to Moscow. His fears were justified, because a few days later Miletić denounced Tito to the Comintern as a Trotskyist. But again Tito was cleared. Miletić was arrested next day, and disappeared.[51]

So Tito survived. If 'it was certainly not chance', there is no doubt that in Moscow during the Great Purge, as on several other occasions, Tito was very lucky. A leading Yugoslav Communist for whom he had written a favourable reference had been shot as a traitor; both his wives had been arrested as traitors; his fellow-translator had been shot as a traitor; and he himself had been denounced by two people as a traitor. Yet Tito survived.

There were various factors working in his favour. He was working class by origin, and had never been inclined to take part in theoretical arguments about Marxism and Leninism; so he was not regarded as one of the Socialist intellectuals who were viewed with so much suspicion. He had an attractive personality and a capacity for making friends. The new men who had replaced and purged the old Bolsheviks felt that he was 'one of us'. Some of his friends were influential and helped him in difficult times. He was always grateful to Dimitrov; forty years later he said: 'I have Dimitrov to thank for not having been arrested.'[52] Pieck was another useful friend.

Perhaps the most helpful friend of all was Ivan Karaivanov. He was a member of the NKVD, and could use his influence to save Tito as long as he himself was not a victim of the purge. Tito was sufficiently close to Karaivanov to tell him what he thought about Stalin. Once when Tito was complaining to Karaivanov that he had not been able to persuade the Comintern to send him abroad, Karaivanov suggested to Tito that he should write to Stalin about it. 'Oh no,' said Tito. 'It is better that he should not know about me.'[53]

But Tito thought that it was events in Yugoslavia which had helped him most. When he went to Moscow in August 1938 the German threat to Czechoslovakia was fast developing. Hitler announced his determination to liberate the German population in the Sudetenland and compel the Czech government to cede the province to Germany.

The right-wing governments in Poland and Hungary supported Germany, hoping to get their share of the spoils when Czechoslovakia was dismembered. The Czechs expected France to honour her treaty obligations to assist Czechoslovakia against an attack by another power. The Soviet Union supported the Czechs, and offered to go to war to prevent a German attack provided that France did the same.

But from the beginning of the crisis the British government had been on Hitler's side, doing their best to prevent the French from fulfilling their treaty obligations to defend Czechoslovakia. They were strongly opposed to the policy which Churchill favoured of a military alliance of Britain, France and the Soviet Union, and rejected the proposal which the Soviet ambassador, Maisky, made to Churchill, that the League of Nations should take action.[54]

The Communists everywhere took the lead in the campaign to prevent this new Fascist aggression. In Yugoslavia they called for volunteers to fight for the Czechs. There was a great response, and thousands of volunteers wishing to enlist came to the Czech embassy in Belgrade. Not all of them were Communists or left-wing sympathizers; some were Serbian nationalists and ex-servicemen who had fought in the Serbian army in the First World War. But the Communists had played the chief part in organizing the call for volunteers, and Tito claimed the credit for it with the Comintern.[55]

At two a.m. on 21 September the British and French ambassadors in Prague called on President Beneš* and urged him to agree immediately to the cession of the Sudetenland to Germany. Under this pressure Beneš surrendered. The dismemberment of Czechoslovakia was agreed at Munich by Hitler, Mussolini, and the British and French prime ministers, Neville Chamberlain and Edouard Daladier, while the Czech foreign minister, Jan Masaryk, waited in the anteroom to be informed of the fate of his country. The Soviet Union was not consulted; it was in effect an alliance of Britain and France with Nazi Germany and Fascist Italy against the Soviet Union. 'What happened at Munich was simply colossal,' said Mussolini. 'What

---

* Beneš, Edvard (1884–1948), Czechoslovak Liberal politician; as Masaryk's chief lieutenant, organised the anti-Austrian resistance movement in Bohemia during the First World War; foreign minister of Czechoslovakia 1919–35; succeeded Masaryk as president of Czechoslovakia in 1935; resigned and took refuge abroad after the Munich Agreement in 1938; head of the Czechoslovak government in London during the Second World War; president of Czechoslovakia 1945–8.

happened at Munich spelt the end of Bolshevism in Europe, the end of all Russian influence on our continent.'[56]

As Beneš accepted the Munich Agreement, the Czech embassy in Belgrade had to turn down the offer of help from the Yugoslav volunteers. But the reaction in Yugoslavia to the campaign to aid the Czechs had made a favourable impression in Moscow. Tito was now sure that the Comintern would not dissolve the Yugoslav party and that his own position had been strengthened.[57]

By this time, Tito had lost most of his illusions about the Soviet Union. 'I knew that many things were wrong,' he told Dedijer in 1952. 'I witnessed a great many injustices.' He knew of a Yugoslav factory worker in the Soviet Union who was sent to eight years' exile in northern Siberia and his wife to five years' in southern Siberia although they had done nothing wrong. He knew that Dimitrov's brother-in-law was hiding from the NKVD in Dimitrov's flat. 'But it was my revolutionary duty at the time not to criticize and not to help alien propaganda against that country, for at that time it was the only country where a revolution had been carried out and where Socialism had to be built. I considered that propaganda should not be made against that country; that my duty was to make propaganda in my own country for Socialism.'[58] He said much the same to his friend Fitzroy Maclean, who had himself been in Moscow in 1938 and had been shocked by the great purge. Maclean noted that Tito, like other Communists at that time, 'though appalled at what was happening there, they still saw Soviet Russia as the Country of the Revolution, and as such, at that time, the only hope for the World Communist Movement in which they firmly believed.'.[59]

In any case, what other choice had Tito except to continue to work for his Communist cause and hope that the blemishes which stained it would be removed one day? If he returned to Yugoslavia and gave himself up to the authorities, he would probably be imprisoned for the offences which he had committed against the Law for the Protection of the State. If he asked for political asylum in Britain, France or the United States, was it likely to be granted to him? And if he renounced his loyalty to the Soviet Union, where would he end up? In political impotence and virtual inactivity, like Trotsky and the Yugoslav Communist, Ciliga? Or would he go over completely to the enemy, like Doriot, who became a Fascist leader in France after he had been expelled from the Communist party as a Trotskyist; like other former Communists whose disillusionment with Stalin led them to support Hitler; or like the ex-Communists of a later period who became assistants to Senator McCarthy in his anti-Communist drive in the United States?

Tito was too deeply committed to the Communist cause to draw back now. If he did, the best he could hope for would be to live in obscurity. This did not appeal to a man of his temperament. He preferred to gamble, as he did when he played poker, on being almost the sole survivor among the Yugoslav Communists in Moscow.

Perhaps the chief reason why he did not denounce the Soviet Union and Stalin was simply that he did not wish to 'let the side down'. Fitzroy Maclean called Tito a 'soldier of the revolution',[60] and the analogy applies better to him than to many Communists. He served the Communist party and the Soviet Union in much the same spirit as a soldier serves his country. Apart from all rational arguments, he felt a strong loyalty to the Soviet Union. Many other Communists, when they discovered the truth about Stalin's regime, felt that their conscience compelled them to expose what was happening there; and many of them ended by going over to the enemy. The conscience of Sergeant-Major Broz was not so sensitive as theirs. He regretted, but was not unduly surprised, to find that 'our side' too sometimes committed atrocities; and this would not make him desert to the enemy. Tito was not the only soldier who has said 'My country right or wrong'; and his country in 1938 was the Soviet Union.

CHAPTER 13

The Hitler-Stalin Pact

O N 5 January 1939 a meeting of the Comintern secretariat was held, with Dimitrov in the chair, at which it was agreed that Tito's position as general secretary of the Communist party of Yugoslavia should be confirmed.[1] Immediately after the meeting Tito returned to Yugoslavia with instructions to destroy all splinter groups in the party and to press on with the policy of the People's Front and anti-Fascist unity.

The Communists tried to work not only with the Social-Democrats and Liberals but also with patriotic groups who were opposed to Germany and Italy. The policy of weakening Yugoslav unity was abandoned, for Yugoslavia had to be strengthened as a potential member of an anti-German alliance. The Communists joined in the national celebrations on 1 December, the anniversary of the foundation of the Yugoslav state in 1918. They sang patriotic songs and issued the slogan 'We shall defend the Fatherland'. In March 1939, at an illegal student demonstration in Belgrade, the Communists shouted 'Long live Yugoslavia!' and 'Long live our army!' as they faced the baton charges of the police.[2] But the Yugoslav government, noticing how their ally France always gave way to Hitler, were turning towards Germany. The British ambassador reported that the Regent, Prince Paul, 'looks upon the Nazi regime as the bulwark against Bolshevism' and would 'prefer to see Yugoslavia dominated by Germany than overrun by Italy via Albania or delivered over to the tender mercies of the Communists'.[3]

Pursuing the policy of the People's Front, the Communists tried to attract eminent intellectuals to the party, if not as party members at least as 'fellow-travellers'. Tito and Krleža had been friends for many years. Krleža had left-wing opinions and sympathized with the

Soviet Union, and Tito liked Krleža's books; but it was the duty of 'Agitprop' (the Agitation and Propaganda Department of the Communist party) to draw Krleža into the party, and the relations between Krleža and Djilas, who was in charge of Agitprop, were less satisfactory. One day Djilas asked Krleža what he thought of the Soviet poet, Mayakovsky. Krleža said that he did not like Mayakovsky's work. Djilas pointed out that Stalin had called Mayakovsky 'the greatest poet of the Soviet epoch'. 'That's Stalin's opinion,' replied Krleža. Djilas was shocked at this remark. He reported it to the other party comrades, who said that Krleža was 'impudent'; but Djilas thought that it was merely 'the caprice of a great and conceited writer'. Worse was to come; they discovered that Krleža had grave doubts about the Moscow trials, though he had not criticized them publicly because he did not wish to break with the Communist party.

Djilas and his comrades sadly decided that there was no place for Krleža in the party, and Djilas asked permission to denounce Krleža in the party's literary journal. Tito agreed, but he did not break off his personal friendship with Krleža.[4]

In August 1939 Tito left for Moscow; he went to Paris, and then from Le Havre to Leningrad on the Soviet ship *Sibir*. While he was at sea he heard about the German-Soviet Pact that Molotov and the German foreign minister von Ribbentrop had signed in Moscow on 23 August.[5] It was hailed in the Communist press as a great victory for peace and a defeat for the plans of the French and British imperialists to embroil the Soviet Union in war with Germany. Many Communists in Western Europe were shocked, and left the party; but nearly all the Yugoslav Communists accepted the pact quite happily, and were pleased that Stalin had beaten the Western bourgeoisie at their own game.[6] Hitler now felt that he could safely invade Poland. By the time that Tito reached Moscow at the beginning of September, Britain and France were at war with Germany and the Soviet Union was neutral.

The Communist parties had to consider what attitude they would adopt towards the war. In France the Daladier government suppressed the Communist newspapers a few days after the German-Soviet Pact, even before the outbreak of war; but the French Communist party issued a statement that 'should Hitler declare war on France, he will have against him the entire French people with the Communists in the front rank . . . they will be the best defenders of democracy and the independence of France'.[7] The British

Communist party followed suit, as did most other Communist parties. But the Communist leaders in Yugoslavia took a different attitude. In 1914 Lenin had proclaimed that a war between two capitalist states in Europe would always be an imperialist war on both sides, and that the workers in both the belligerent camps must oppose the war and work to transform the imperialist war into civil war. The Communists had abandoned this policy in 1935, declaring that in capitalist countries allied to the Soviet Union the workers must support the war. But would they be justified in supporting a war waged by a capitalist government if the Soviet Union were not its ally? If the Soviet Union were neutral, should not the Leninist principle apply once again?

The Communists in Yugoslavia immediately began to discuss the nature of the war. Djilas and his comrades in Belgrade had no doubt that it was an imperialist war which must be opposed by Communists everywhere. At the beginning of September he met Kardelj at the railway station in Zagreb. 'Just or unjust?' asked Djilas. Kardelj knew at once that Djilas was referring to the war, and replied without hesitation: 'Unjust, of course.'[8] The Communists in Zagreb and Ljubljana had reached the same conclusion as their comrades in Belgrade.

The Yugoslav Communists had acted on their own initiative before they had been able to contact Tito in Moscow. The Comintern did not decide so quickly, and was unusually slow in giving a clear directive to the world Communist movement. They did not realize at once that the Communist party of Yugoslavia was out of step with the French Communist party, and they had not yet received a directive from Stalin and the Communist party of the Soviet Union.

A few days after the outbreak of war, Manuilsky called a meeting of the leaders in Moscow of the other parties of the Comintern. He asked them all to draft a proclamation which they thought should be issued by the Communist party to the workers in their countries and to bring their drafts to a meeting next morning. Tito spent the evening writing out his manifesto. It called on the Yugoslav people to stand ready to defend their country against an attack by the German or Italian Fascists.

When he went to the meeting next morning, he found that no one else had drafted a manifesto. They made various excuses, but Tito knew the real reason: they had all been afraid that they would get into trouble if they put over the wrong line. They 'were afraid of making a mistake,' said Tito many years later, 'and a mistake meant the Lubianka.' When Tito read out his draft, Manuilsky was very pleased with it. He had given his colleagues a strong hint about the line that they were expected to adopt, but Tito was the only one who had the courage to take the hint.[9]

Djilas and the Yugoslav Communists were taken aback when they heard that the French Communist party was supporting the war,[10] and they wanted to hear from Tito in Moscow; but it was a few weeks before Tito sent word to them that their line was quite correct. Soon after Manuilsky had approved his draft manifesto on the war, Stalin told the Comintern to order the Communist parties in all the belligerent countries to pursue the correct Leninist line and oppose the imperialist war that their bourgeois governments were waging. The Comintern promptly changed the party line, and Tito changed his line. Many years later he said that in September 1939 Stalin reverted to his old policy that it was essential 'not to fight Fascism but to go back to the so-called class confrontation, the struggle of "class against class" between the proletariat and the bourgeoisie'.[11]

The French Communist party veered around, and denounced the imperialist war. Their deputies were expelled from the National Assembly and their councillors from all local government bodies. Communist propaganda was made punishable by death. The general secretary of the French Communist party, Thorez, was called up for the army; he deserted, and was smuggled through Belgium and Switzerland to Moscow. The other Communist leaders and many thousands of their followers were sentenced to long terms of imprisonment or interned in concentration camps in very harsh conditions.

The survivors among the Yugoslav Communists who had fought in Spain made their way across the Pyrenees after Franco's victory, and with the other refugees from Spain were imprisoned in the concentration camp at Le Vernet. There they were at the mercy of a sadistic camp commandant who on the slightest excuse used his whip on the prisoners.[12] Many of them were handed over to the Nazis after the fall of France in 1940 and were executed or sent to forced labour in concentration camps in Germany, but some escaped and joined the French Resistance.[13] Eventually the last survivors of the Yugoslavs in the International Brigade reached their homeland. The party hid them in various houses until the time arrived for them to join the Partisans in the mountains in the Second World War.

On 16 September 1939 the Red Army invaded eastern Poland as a result of a secret agreement between Stalin and Hitler. Public opinion in Western Europe, particularly among the Socialists, was shocked at this flagrant case of Soviet imperialism. The Yugoslav Communists welcomed it;[14] the Soviet Union had extended the frontiers of Socialism and had saved the people of eastern Poland from German occupation. Churchill did not condemn it. In a radio broadcast soon after the invasion, he said that it was regrettable that the Russian army had entered Poland as an invader and not as an ally of the Poles, but much better that they should be there instead of the Germans.[15]

On 30 November 1939 the Red Army invaded Finland, after the Finnish Social-Democrat government had refused Stalin's request to cede territory near Leningrad to the Soviet Union in return for larger but valueless Russian territory further north. Again public opinion abroad was shocked, particularly at the air raids launched by the Soviet Air Force against the civilian population in Helsinki. Ever since the Italian and German air raids on civilian targets in Abyssinia and Spain, the bombing of civilians had been denounced as an atrocity which only Fascists would commit. Churchill took the same attitude when he called for better anti-aircraft defences and a more efficient air force to meet the German threat. 'I do not believe in reprisals upon the enemy civilian population,' he wrote in the *News of the World* on 1 May 1938. 'On the contrary, the more they try to kill our women and children, the more we should devote ourselves to killing their fighting men.'[16] On the outbreak of war the British government announced that the Royal Air Force would drop leaflets, not bombs, on German cities. Yet here was the Soviet Air Force, like the Nazi *Luftwaffe* and the Italians, killing women and children during the night in Helsinki.

Even the Yugoslav Communists were taken aback by the Soviet attack on Finland; but their sense of discipline and their devotion to the Soviet Union soon dispelled all their doubts, especially when they saw how the French and British bourgeoisie were using the war in Finland as an opportunity to start hostilities against the USSR. A recruiting office for Finland was opened in Piccadilly in London, and even soldiers in the British army, in wartime, were allowed to volunteer. The British government sent a hundred aircraft to help the Finns.

The Red Army seriously bungled the campaign, and the Finns repulsed repeated Soviet attacks. This encouraged the British and French governments to consider sending troops to fight for Finland.

But the Red Army managed to win just in time to stop the Anglo-French intervention. They broke through the Finnish defences and imposed a peace treaty by which the Finns ceded a small area of territory near Leningrad.

On 14 December 1939, while Tito was in Moscow, the Communist party of Yugoslavia organized a great illegal demonstration in Belgrade. It was called to protest against the attempts of the bourgeois governments of Britain and France to involve Yugoslavia in the imperialist war, and also against the rising cost of living. It was organized by Aleksandar Ranković, a young Serbian Communist who had been imprisoned and tortured under King Alexander's dictatorship. He was dark, silent, cool, very efficient, utterly devoted to the Communist cause, and, as he was later to show, quite ruthless to the agents of the class enemy. Ranković's friend Djilas helped him organize the demonstration.

A new Yugoslav government had been formed in August 1939 as a result of some hard political bargaining. Vlatko Maček, the leader of the Croatian Peasant party, was a moderate Liberal, but he agreed to enter a coalition government headed by the Serbian Conservative, Cvetković, and to support Cvetković's anti-Communist policy at home and his pro-German foreign policy, in return for a considerable degree of autonomy which for the first time was now granted to Croatia. One result of this policy of devolution was that Croatian Communists imprisoned in Belgrade were sent to Croatia and released there, though the police drive against Communists was soon to become more severe in Croatia than in Serbia.

The Cvetković-Maček government banned the demonstration of 14 December. But the Communists assembled at various points in Belgrade at eight p.m., and fought the police for several hours through the dark winter evening. When the police baton-charged them, the demonstrators pelted the police with stones and bottles. Then the police opened fire in Aleksandar Street. The unarmed demonstrators in other parts of the city, hearing the gunfire, ran eagerly towards it, determined to help their comrades. Four of the demonstrators were killed.[17] Two days later, the government announced that a concentration camp would be opened at Lepoglava for Communist troublemakers, and several leading Communists were arrested, including Pijade and the youth leader, Lola Ribar.

In January 1940 the Comintern told Tito to return to Yugoslavia.

The war had made travelling more difficult. Tito sailed from Odessa to Istanbul on a forged Canadian passport; but not for the first time the Comintern had slipped up, and had not realized that British subjects now required a visa for Yugoslavia. Tito found someone in Istanbul who could forge the visa, but he was not happy about the forgery. He thought that the Yugoslav immigration authorities would inspect his passport less closely if he said that he was merely travelling through Yugoslavia on his way to the United States. He sent a message to the party in Zagreb telling them to forge a passport for him in another name and with a Yugoslav transit visa and to send a comrade to bring it to him in Istanbul. The Zagreb party sent a young man, Vladimir Velebit. He was the son of a general in the old Austro-Hungarian imperial army, and had become a barrister practising in Zagreb. For some years he had been close to the Communist party, though he had only recently become a secret party member. The police had no idea that he had any links with the Communists.

Tito did not like the passport which Velebit brought, and asked the party in Zagreb to send him another forged passport. This time they sent a young Slovene girl student to take it to Tito in Istanbul. Tito was equally dissatisfied with this third passport. In the end he decided to travel on the original passport in the name of the Canadian which had been issued to him by the Comintern, after a forged transit visa for Yugoslavia had been added by a forger in Istanbul.

Tito waited for three months in Istanbul till he was satisfied with the passport. Playing the part of the Canadian businessman, he stayed at the luxury Park Hotel, bought fashionable clothes, and frequented expensive cafés and restaurants. He was not short of money, which was provided by the Comintern. He went to an Italian shipping office in Istanbul and bought a through ticket by train to Zagreb, by sea to Italy, and from Italy on the liner *Conte di Savoia* to New York.

He started on his journey at the beginning of April 1940. When he crossed the frontier from Turkey to Greece in the train the authorities hardly looked at the passport; but the Yugoslav immigration officers on the frontier with Greece were suspicious when they saw that the passport had been issued at the British consulate in Moscow, and asked Tito to explain this. He said that he was a Canadian who had been in the Soviet Union on business, that his Canadian passport had expired while he was there, and that he had been issued with a new one in Moscow. The immigration officers were satisfied. Tito overheard one of them say to his colleague that they had better not cause any trouble to a British subject.[18]

When he reached Zagreb, he contacted the party, moved into a safe flat, and destroyed his Canadian passport and his ticket to New York. A few days later he was sitting in the Café Korzo in Zagreb. Calling for a newspaper, he read a short item which reported that the Italian liner *Conte di Savoia* had been stopped by the British navy off Gibraltar. Italy was still neutral in the war, but before allowing the ship to proceed, the British searched her, for they had been informed that there was a dangerous spy on board who was travelling to London. 'And there was I sitting in Zagreb,' said Tito.[19]

In Zagreb, Tito lived as husband and wife with Herta Haas, a young, middle-class Slovene Communist girl who had first met him when she was working for the party as a courier between Zagreb and Paris. She was very popular with her party comrades, and Tito was very attached to her. He took her with him when he travelled around the country attending party conferences and meetings, though none of the other Communist leaders brought their wives, and occasionally allowed her to attend the meetings of the Central Committee.[20]

It was just at this time that the British government, despite the protests of the Norwegian government, announced that the British navy would lay mines in Norwegian territorial waters to prevent German U-boats from taking refuge there. Germany thereupon invaded Denmark and Norway. Tito's newspaper *Komunist* in Zagreb followed the correct Comintern line. 'The fire of the imperialist war has spread to Scandinavia, to Norway,' it commented on 2 May 1940. 'Who is responsible for all the misfortunes, for all the horrors which the peace-loving Norwegian people have to endure? . . . The imperialists of London and Paris are mainly responsible.'[21]

A week later, Hitler attacked in France, Belgium and Holland, and Churchill became prime minister, with Labour ministers in his government. 'This is the worst government that has ever ruled Britain,' wrote the Comintern journal *World News and Views* in Moscow.[22] Within six weeks France had surrendered and the Germans were in Paris. The leaders of the illegal French Communist party went to the German governor of Paris and asked permission to publish the party newspaper *l'Humanité*, because it would 'denounce the efforts of the agents of British imperialism who want to drag the French colonies into the war'.[23] The Germans refused permission and arrested the Communists who had come to see them.

Tito may well have had his private misgivings over the party line, but he dutifully carried it out throughout the summer of 1940. He was always more interested in party organization than party policy. He wished to build up an efficient and united party, purged of troublemakers and fractionalists and composed of members who could be relied on to obey orders and, when the time came, to carry through the proletarian revolution in Yugoslavia. Between May and September 1940 he organized and attended illegal party conferences in Slovenia, Dalmatia, Montenegro and Croatia.[24] He vigorously carried out the instructions which Dimitrov and the Comintern secretariat had given him to purge the Yugoslav party of all dissidents and splinter groups; there were more of them in Dalmatia than in any other part of Yugoslavia. He denounced them in the violent language that the Comintern required, and called on all party members to boycott them, to break off social relations with them, and not to greet them in the street;[25] but his action against the dissidents stopped far short of a Moscow-style purge. Tito once said, in later years, that dissidents in the party deserved to be hit over the head but not beheaded.[26]

Tito had not enjoyed living in Moscow, with the constant prospect that he might be the next Yugoslav Communist to be arrested; but one aspect of life in the Soviet Union appealed to him. He had found that in the higher ranks of the party it was possible to combine loyal service to the Communist cause with good living. The leading party officials indulged in heavy eating and drinking and loud parties, though Djilas may well be right in thinking that they drank as much as they did in order to forget their fears of the NKVD. He has said that in Stalin's circle of friends they all enjoyed wine and song, but were not interested in women.[27] Tito wanted women as well as wine and song.

The Communists in the Soviet Union had not only accepted but had also actively encouraged economic inequality. They introduced the Stakhanovite system of payment by results, enabling one worker to earn a far higher wage than his fellow-workers. In the government and the party, there was a system of privileges for the élite which resembled the Sumptuary Laws of the Middle Ages. They insisted that a government and party official should have a larger desk and a more expensive carpet in his office than his assistant officials, and that he should eat more and better food than his inferiors in the communal office restaurant.[28] Tito, unlike the old Bolsheviks and many Socialists, had no objection to this system.

When he returned from Moscow in 1940 the Politburo of the Communist Party of Yugoslavia discussed what salaries should be paid to party officials. Until this time, each official, whatever his standing in the party, was paid 2,000 dinars per month, which was about the salary of a schoolmaster. Tito now proposed that the salary of the members of the Politburo should be increased to 3,000 dinars per month. They then discussed what salary Tito should receive as general secretary of the party, and agreed that Tito himself should be asked to name the figure that he considered suitable. Tito said that he thought that he should be paid 6,000 dinars per month. His chief motive in suggesting this larger sum was probably not personal gain so much as a desire to show the Comintern that the Yugoslav party was following the principle of inequality which had been approved by the Communist Party of the Soviet Union. The Politburo also decided to buy a vineyard in the vicinity of Zagreb and present it as a gift to Tito, who was able to supplement his income by selling the produce of the vineyard.[29] He also had a chauffeur-driven car, which was a privilege granted to high officials of the Communist party in every country. This privilege was not always appreciated, because the chauffeur was usually an agent of the Soviet NKVD; but Tito chose as chauffeur Branko Malešević, who was completely loyal to him.

The reorganization of the party was progressing very satisfactorily. In eighteen months party membership had almost doubled, despite the loss of the comrades who had died in Spain. The Communist party of Yugoslavia now had 6,500 members, and the Communist Youth, the SKOJ, had 18,000.[30]

The Fifth National Conference of the party was held in October 1940. It was very efficiently organized by Tito and four other members of the organizing committee, which included the Croatian party secretary, Rade Končar, and Tito's chauffeur Malešević. They arranged for 101 delegates to assemble for this illegal meeting without the police knowing anything about it. A suitable house was chosen some time in advance; it was a villa at Dubrava on the outskirts of Zagreb. Communist building workers were employed to knock down an interior wall so as to convert several rooms into a hall big enough for a conference. Chairs for the delegates, made by Communist carpenters, and food prepared by women comrades, were brought to the house some time in advance. Large posters with photographs of Marx, Engels, Lenin and Stalin were hung in the hall.

Very few of the delegates were told in advance where the conference was to be held. They came to Zagreb in small groups at staggered times during the previous three days, and were met at different places by their contacts. There were only a very few hitches in the travelling arrangements, and none of these led to any arrests. On 18 October, the evening before the conference began, their contacts brought them to the villa. They all had to fill in a form giving their name, class background, length of party membership, and prison experience; all the forms were destroyed as soon as the party secretariat had analysed the statistics. Fifty-three of the delegates were workers, fourteen peasants, and twenty-nine intellectuals. More than two-thirds of them had been in prison and half of them had been tortured.

The conference lasted for five days. No one was allowed to leave the house until it was over, except for Tito and Herta, who arrived and left every day by car. At the end of the conference, the delegates left in small, staggered groups and found their own way home. All arrived back safely.[31]

Tito's long report to the conference, and the resolutions passed unanimously by the delegates, all followed the Comintern line. This had shifted a little since the summer. At the outbreak of war Stalin, like many other observers, had thought that the Allied armies on the Western front would prove to be stronger than the Germans, and would at least hold Hitler's armies at bay in a long war; and Britain and France were adopting a much more hostile attitude than Germany towards the Soviet Union during the war in Finland. By the autumn the position was very different; Germany now looked a greater threat than the Western powers.

Tito was therefore able to adopt a policy which was more in line with his own feelings and the manifesto which he had drafted for Manuilsky in September 1939. He condemned the British and French imperialists and their war aims, and their supporters 'the faithful servants of capitalism, the reactionary Social-Democrats headed by Blum, Citrine,* Sanderson† and others'; but he was even more severe

* Citrine, Walter, Lord (1887–1983), British right-wing trade union and Labour leader; strongly criticised by the Communists and left-wing Socialists, especially after he had accepted a knighthood in 1935.

† There was no prominent Social-Democratic or right-wing trade union leader named Sanderson. Tito was perhaps referring to Arthur Henderson (1863–1935), one of the founders of the British Labour party and foreign secretary in the Labour government of 1929–31. Henderson had been denounced by Lenin for supporting the 'imperialist war' of 1914–18.

on the Cvetković-Maček government which was failing to resist the threat from the German and Italian imperialists. 'The peoples of Yugoslavia do not want Fascism,' said Tito. 'They do not want a totalitarian regime, they do not want to become slaves of the German and Italian financial oligarchy as they never wanted to become reconciled to the semi-colonial dependence imposed on them by the so-called Western democracies after the first imperialist war.' He referred to their efforts in distributing illegally the *History of the Communist Party of the Soviet Union (Bolsheviks)*, 'this magnificent book which was written with the co-operation of our great teacher and leader, Comrade Stalin himself', and praised 'the most revolutionary and heroic Communist Party of the Soviet Union'.

He warned the delegates against the Trotskyists, who were secretly infiltrating the party, in disguise, 'because they know that the majority of people hate the very name of Trotskyism, which is no longer an ideological movement but a conspiracy of traitors' who had united with the 'Social-Democratic traitors'. He said that party members must not get drunk, because they might reveal party secrets while they were drunk, and to get drunk was unworthy of a Communist. He had intended to tell them that they must not behave like the Communist in Zagreb in 1933, who invited young women comrades to his flat on the pretext of instructing them in Marxism, and then seduced them to the music of the 'International'; but he omitted this passage when he delivered the speech.

He introduced a novelty at the close of his speech. After saying 'Long live our great leader and teacher, Comrade Stalin', he added: 'Long live his faithful disciple and fellow-worker, Comrade Dimitrov, pilot of the Comintern'.[32] His speech was received in silence by the delegates, for they had been instructed not to attract the attention of the neighbours by applauding the speakers.[33]

The party programme had been summed up in a message sent to Stalin by the Croatian Communist party: 'These dear words, "Comrade Stalin" are a programme for us.'[34] Many years later, long after he had repudiated Stalinism, Communism and Marxism-Leninism, Djilas said that the Yugoslav Communists had loved fanatically the Soviet Union and Stalin, because if they had been less fanatical they could never have fought and defeated the Fascists.[35] The Soviet Union and Comrade Stalin meant much to Tito too; but he loved them not with the hysterical love of the fanatic and the recent convert, but as a soldier and a conventional citizen loves his country and the leader to whom he has pledged his loyalty. He knew all their faults and weaknesses, but he would not betray them.

CHAPTER 14

❖

The German Invasion

HE British imperialists, like all belligerents in wartime, were naturally trying to draw the neutrals into the war on their side; but their machinations would have had a better chance of success if they had been winning the war. In the spring of 1941 nearly everyone except the British public thought that they were losing the war. Prince Paul loved England; he liked his cousin King George VI, London society, his London tailor, and Ascot, Wimbledon and Henley; but he thought that the interests of Yugoslavia demanded that he remain on good terms with Hitler.[1] He decided to take even firmer action against Communists and other anti-Nazis.

In December 1940 General Nedić, the minister of war, drafted a secret order, which was dated and was to be issued on 7 January 1941. It provided for the opening of six concentration camps at various places in Serbia where Communists could be interned without trial, and laid down the number of guards and other officials who were to be employed in each of the camps. A young officer in the War Office in Belgrade, Živadin Simić, found out about the order and informed the Communist party, who told him to try and obtain a copy of it.

Simić waited until Nedić and his ADC went out to attend a meeting, and then went into his office and removed the draft order. It was a two-page document. In the days before photocopying, it had to be copied by hand; but Simić asked another Communist who worked in the War Office to help him. They each of them copied out one page, and managed to do this and return the document to Nedić's office before he returned from the meeting.

When Simić showed his copy of the draft order to his party comrades, they told him that he must deliver it to a Very Important

Comrade. Simić met the Very Important Comrade in one of the Communist party's 'safe houses' belonging to a party sympathizer who was unknown to the police. The Very Important Comrade took the document and briefly thanked Simić for his services to the party. It was only some years later that Simić discovered that the Very Important Comrade was Tito. The Communists waited until 7 January and then printed thousands of copies of the order on a secret printing press, and distributed them at night from house to house in Belgrade, to the anger and embarrassment of the government. The authorities tried to find out the source of the leak, but they did not suspect Simić.[2]

Hitler had decided to attack the Soviet Union; he believed that Britain would never make peace with him as long as she had a strong potential ally in his rear in the East.[3] But Mussolini had attacked Greece from Albania, and was getting the worse of the fighting there against Greek and British forces; so Hitler had to rescue Mussolini from his difficulties before he could invade the Soviet Union. He moved seven divisions into Bulgaria with the consent of King Boris, and asked Prince Paul for permission to send six more divisions into Yugoslavia so that they could pass on from there into Greece. Tito and the Communists opposed the entry of German troops into Yugoslavia, but they also opposed the attempts of the British and French bourgeoisie to involve Yugoslavia in the imperialist war. They organized strikes in munitions factories. One of them lasted for three months, and was the longest strike that had ever taken place in Yugoslavia. The government retaliated by banning the Social-Democratic trade unions, which had come under Communist influence. Their assets were given to a non-political trade union.[4]

The Communists told the members of the Communist Youth that they must not evade the call-up; they were to join the army and make Communist propaganda to the other soldiers. The War Office then weeded out all known Communists in the army and formed them into four special companies of 500 men each; a member of the political police was appointed commanding officer of these companies. The party made an exception in the case of the Communist youth leader, Lola Ribar, and other prominent Communists: they were told to evade the call-up and go underground; they would have been marked men if they had joined a battalion of Communist soldiers under an officer of the political police. Two mutinies broke out in the army, and several Communist soldiers were shot.[5]

On 1 March 1941 Prince Paul visited Hitler at Berchtesgaden. Hitler told him that the German army would invade Russia in the summer as soon as they had driven the Allies out of Greece, and would destroy Bolshevism. He knew that this would please Paul. He hinted that after the fall of the Bolshevik regime Russia should be ruled by a Tsar, who might very suitably be a member of the Karadjordjević family.[6] On 25 March Yugoslavia signed the Tripartite Pact with Germany and Bulgaria, and agreed that German troops could pass through Yugoslavia on their way to Greece.

A group of Serbian officers was opposed to the pro-Axis policy of the Prince Regent and his government. They wished to adhere to the traditional pro-Allied and anti-German policy which Serbia had pursued since before the First World War. One of the most able members of this group was Colonel Draža Mihailović. He had fought as a boy in the Balkan Wars of 1912–13 and with the Allies on the Salonika front in the First World War. He had more recently been the Yugoslav military attaché in Prague. He was a Serbian patriot, and a loyal servant of the Karadjordjević dynasty. He believed in a Greater Serbia, as did nearly all Serbs except for the small minority who believed in a Greater Soviet Union.

Mihailović had made a favourable impression on British diplomats and agents in Belgrade. He had also impressed Rebecca West, who met him when she visited the military college at Niš in 1937.[7] She later described him as 'a typical Serb officer – and by great effort I did once make myself realise imaginatively what that meant. It is to live in a world where 2 + 2 = 5, and a blend of lawlessness and discipline and impiety and piety and cruelty and universal love work out to something that in the end harmonises pretty well with the English world where 2 + 2 = 4 and either/or is the operative principle.'[8]

As soon as the news came over the radio that Yugoslavia had adhered to the Tripartite Pact, protest demonstrations broke out spontaneously in Belgrade. The students at the university took the lead, and the population joined them in the streets. To the surprise of the demonstrators, the police made very little attempt to stop them. Someone in the crowd shouted out: 'Better war than the Pact!' and the crowd took up the slogan.[9]

The Communist students at the university went out on to the campus, and from the campus into the streets, with all the other students and the people. Slavenka Petnički was one of them. She was

a Croat from Dalmatia. Her father was a businessman in Split, a
Conservative and a loyal supporter of the Karadjordjević regime; but
she had married a prominent Communist, who was a member of the
Central Committee of the Communist Party of Yugoslavia. She herself had not joined the party, though she was painstakingly reading
Engels's *Anti-Dühring* while taking her course in medicine at Belgrade University. On the afternoon of 26 March she did not bother
her head with what her husband thought or what the party line
might be. 'We just wanted to fight the Fascists,' she said in later
years, 'it was as simple as that'.[10]

It was not quite as simple as that for Djilas and Ranković and the
Serbian party leadership in Belgrade. They too felt the pull of public
opinion, and instinctively wished to join in the popular demand to
fight Fascism. But what was the correct party line? What would the
Comintern say? And – perhaps even more important – what would
Tito in Zagreb say? But after a short discussion they decided that it
was permissible to support the demonstrations against the pact provided that it was made clear at the same time that they were not
supporting the efforts of the British bourgeoisie to drag Yugoslavia
into the imperialist war.

They called a demonstration for eight p.m. that evening. They
were disappointed that only 1,000 people turned up; but the rest of
the population had already demonstrated that afternoon before the
party had got around to calling on them to do so. The party had
decided that the slogan should be: 'Only an alliance with the Soviet
Union can save us from war.' But hardly anyone repeated this slogan;
they were all shouting: 'Better war than the Pact!' and 'Better the
grave than be a slave!' Djilas and Ranković were surprised that again
the police made very little effort to stop them.[11]

Next morning the radio announced that General Simović had made
a *coup d'état*, removed Prince Paul from the regency, and proclaimed
the personal rule of the seventeen-year-old King Peter II. The new
government did not publicly repudiate the Tripartite Pact, but that
did not deceive Hitler. 'Even if Yugoslavia should at first make dec-
larations of loyalty', he declared, 'she must be considered as an enemy
and therefore must be destroyed as quickly as possible.'[12]

The people were out in the streets again in the afternoon, shouting
'Better war than the Pact!' and cheering the king and Simović. This
time the Communists were more perplexed about what they should
do. The Simović government was a bourgeois government; it had

not released the Communists in prison or removed the ban on the Communist party, and it had not yet made a military alliance with the Soviet Union. Many party militants urged the party to call a demonstration against the government in Belgrade; but after a long discussion, Djilas and Ranković decided that any demonstration against the government would weaken the national solidarity against the Fascist menace. The Communist party did not call for a demonstration on 27 March. Many of them joined the people in the streets. The demonstrators attacked the German Tourist Office and burned the German swastika flag.[13]

Two days later Tito arrived from Zagreb. When the Belgrade comrades told him what they had done on 26 and 27 March, he laughed. 'I was not in the least surprised when I heard what you had done,' he said, 'for the Belgrade party was always sectarian. Of course, you were quite right.' But he considered that the attack on the German Tourist Office and the burning of the swastika was a provocation likely to cause the Germans to invade. He thought that it was the act of *agents provocateurs* who were in the pay of the British imperialists who hoped that it would draw Yugoslavia into the imperialist war.[14] He must have realized that it was much more likely to have been the act of some hothead in the crowd; but he was right in thinking that it was a foolhardy provocation, and was following the Comintern line in showing that in this respect at least the Communist party of Yugoslavia still opposed the imperialist war.

Djilas and Ranković were very proud that they had pleased '*Stari*', 'the Old Man', as they called Tito. He was now aged forty-nine, and nearly twenty years older than most of his closest collaborators; but the name 'the Old Man' showed not only the difference in age but also the veneration with which they regarded him. Both Djilas and Ranković were members of the Politburo of the Communist party of Yugoslavia; but the Politburo very rarely met. The Old Man decided everything himself.

Tito had returned to Zagreb before 6 April, when the German army invaded Yugoslavia and the Luftwaffe bombed Belgrade. The air attack, which the Germans named 'Operation Punishment', was directed at the city centre, and the object was to kill and terrorize the civilian population. Estimates of the casualties vary from 5,000 to 17,000. Members of the Politburo who were in Belgrade managed to meet in the evening and decided that they themselves and all party members should leave Belgrade for the south with all the other evacuees who were fleeing in a state bordering on panic from German bombers and German and Hungarian troops advancing on Belgrade from the north. Only 30,000 of the 300,000 inhabitants of Belgrade remained in the city.[15]

Many Communists joined the army, as the party had ordered. But many others, believing that it was still an imperialist war, deserted. In some areas the officers of the Royal Yugoslav Army did not seem to know what to do. To Churchill's disappointment, the king and government did not remain in the country to direct the national resistance from the mountains, but flew to Athens and Cairo only eight days after the Germans invaded, and from there to Jerusalem. In some cases local Communists approached the army commanding officers in the district and asked permission to fight the Germans or Bulgarians; but the offers were usually refused.[16] Within eleven days the Yugoslav resistance had collapsed, and the whole country was occupied by German, Hungarian, Bulgarian and Italian troops.

The Germans entered Zagreb on 10 April. They were welcomed by many sections of the population, for they were supported by Pavelić's Ustashas, and had promised to create an independent Croatian state. Maček's Croatian Peasant party, which at the last election before the war had the support of the majority of the electorate in Croatia, adopted a neutral attitude. Maček had been a member of the Cvetković government which had joined the Tripartite Pact, and most Croats regarded Simović's *coup d'état* in Belgrade as a Serbian nationalist movement directed not against the Germans but against the Cvetković government's concessions to the Croatian demand for autonomy.

After the revolution of 27 March the Ministry of the Interior and the police authorities in Serbia released the Communist political prisoners, though no amnesty was officially proclaimed. But the Maček government in Croatia refused to release the Communists in Lepoglava concentration camp. Tito launched a campaign to free the prisoners, but the speed of the German advance and the Ustasha seizure of power gave him very little time to achieve his aim. The Communists were still in prison when the Germans and Ustashas took over, and they were all executed.

The Comintern's May Day manifesto showed that there was no change in the party line. 'The capitalist miscreants are dragging the peoples into a new world imperialist carnage,' but 'facing the capitalist world ... stands the great Land of Socialism. The British and

French warmongers and their Social-Democratic lickspittles are furious at the fact that the Soviet Union occupies a position of neutrality towards their imperialist war.'[17] But Tito, while not publicly repudiating the Comintern line, was bypassing it. He gave orders that the Communists and the Communist Youth should undergo military training in preparation for the moment, which might come quite soon, when they would be called on to rise in revolt and fight against Fascism. In his report to the Comintern at the end of May he barely paid lip-service to the party's opposition to imperialist war. He wrote about it in the past tense. 'During the entire period of the imperialist war' the first aim of the Communist party of Yugoslavia was 'to struggle against Yugoslavia's being drawn into the imperialist war on the side of Britain and France, for such a danger did exist', as it was the aim of one section of the Serbian bourgeoisie. But the rest of the report dealt with the party's struggle against the Tripartite Pact and the courage with which the Communists had fought in the army against the Fascist invaders.[18]

The Germans altered the map of Yugoslavia. Croatia became an independent state under the Ustashas. They offered the crown of Croatia to an Italian prince who accepted and became King Tomislav II (Tomislav I had reigned in the tenth century), but he never set foot in his kingdom, which was ruled by Pavelić as regent and Poglavnik (the Leader). Pavelić ceded part of Dalmatia to Italy, but in compensation was allowed to annex Bosnia-Herzegovina to Croatia. Germany annexed the northern, and Italy the southern, part of Slovenia. Hungary, Bulgaria and Mussolini's puppet state of Albania annexed parts of Serbia. Bulgaria also annexed Yugoslav Macedonia. Montenegro became an independent kingdom under another Italian prince. Like King Tomislav II he never visited his kingdom, which was occupied by Italian troops.

In Croatia the Ustashas immediately began killing Serbs, Jews and gipsies. Many thousands were rounded up in the cafés and in the street and taken to Jasenovac concentration camp, some sixty miles south of Zagreb. Jasenovac, like the concentration and labour camps in Nazi Germany and the Soviet Union, was largely run by the prisoners themselves. Some of them were chosen by the camp guards to run the camp and received certain privileges in return. The internees worked in the fields from dawn till dusk, and had to eat, surreptitiously, the berries in the fields in order to survive. They were punished for breaches of camp discipline by being sent to the camp prison, and were often hanged, but many of them who had committed no offence were taken away and shot, hanged or drowned. Many were shot by the camp commandant, Luburić, who would stroll through the camp and amuse himself by placing his revolver up against the heads of the prisoners; sometimes he pulled the trigger, sometimes he did not. The other prisoners only knew that their friends had been killed when their names were left out at the daily roll-call.[19]

Many more were killed outside the camps by bands of Ustashas, who went into the villages slaughtering Serbs, Jews and gipsies. By far the greatest number of the victims were Serbs, because there were many more of them; whole districts like Lika, Kordun and Banija, where the Serbs were a majority of the population, were virtually exterminated. In the Jadovno district, the salt mines provided the Ustashas with a good method of ethnically cleansing the area: they threw the Serbs down the deep holes into the salt mines and left them there to die. After a few days the Ustashas returned and sent the dogs down the mines to kill any survivors. One woman gave birth to a baby down the mine. The baby died, but she survived for forty-two days by feeding on the body and blood of the other victims, and in the end managed to climb out, and lived.[20]

The Ustashas regarded themselves as waging a religious war for the Roman Catholic Church against Eastern Orthodox Serbs, Jews, and Bolshevik atheists. They made it a criminal offence to use the Cyrillic alphabet. In Zagreb no Jew or Serb was allowed to live in the area north of Ilica Street and Vlasko Street.[21] All Serbs were required to wear a blue band on their right arm bearing the letter P for Pravoslavac (Orthodox). They were offered the choice of becoming Roman Catholics or being put to death. The Ustashas justified forcible conversion because they claimed that many Croats had been forced to convert from Roman Catholicism to Orthodox Christianity on pain of death in the days of Tsar Dušan's Greater Serbia in the fourteenth century; the Ustashas were merely using force to cancel out the force used six hundred years before. They sometimes went into the villages and asked the children there to make the sign of the cross. If they crossed themselves from left to right, the Ustashas knew that they were Roman Catholics. If they crossed themselves from right to left, they were Orthodox, and were promptly killed.

The extermination of whole populations was nothing new. It had been practised throughout the centuries long before someone invented the word 'genocide'. Within the past seventy years Turks had massacred Bulgarians, Armenians, Herzegovinians and Greeks; Greeks had massacred Turks; and Ukrainians had massacred Jews. But their enemies are justified in accusing the Ustashas of having inaugurated the policy of genocide in the Second World War. Nearly a quarter of a million Serbs, Jews and gipsies had been murdered in Croatia before the Wahnsee Conference in January 1942 when Heydrich* first proposed that Jews should be killed in gas chambers in German-occupied Poland. In the conditions of invasion, resistance and civil war which reigned in Croatia in 1941–5 it was impossible to compile the figures of the numbers killed; it has been placed as high as 700,000 by Serb, and as low as 60,000 by Croat, writers. But recent research by conscientious historians suggests that 330,000 is the correct figure.

The political parties who for so long had demanded autonomy for Croatia knew the nationalist feeling among Croats and their resentment of the Serbian domination from which they had suffered under the Karadjordjević monarchy. They did not venture to oppose the creation of the independent Ustasha state. Maček accepted the situation for a few months. Then he was arrested and sent to Jasenovac; but in 1942 he was released, and confined under house arrest for the rest of the war.

The head of the Roman Catholic Church in Croatia, Aloysius Stepinac, Archbishop of Zagreb, officiated at a Te Deum in his cathedral to give thanks for the foundation of the Ustasha state. He praised the Ustashas in his sermon. Other Roman Catholic bishops were more active supporters of the Ustashas. They hailed the triumph of the Virgin Mother of God who had visited her Croats, and raised the slogan: 'For Christ and the Ustashas!' A Franciscan monk, Father Filipović Majstorović, went around with the Ustashas, and several Catholic priests baptized the terrified Orthodox Serbs who were brought to them by armed Ustashas. After some months, diplomatic pressure from King Peter's government and the Allies in Rome persuaded the Vatican to intervene. Pope Pius XII ordered the clergy in Croatia to refuse to assist at forcible baptisms. Then it was pointed

---

* Heydrich, Reinhard (1904–42). German Nazi leader; proposed the adoption of the policy of the mass-extermination of the Jews at the Wahnsee Conference in January 1942; governor of Bohemia and Moravia 1941–2; assassinated by Czechoslovak agents sent from London in June 1942.

out to them that if forcible baptism was banned, this closed one of the few loopholes for survival which were open to the Serbs; and the Catholic clergy resumed the baptisms. Eventually in May 1942 Pavelić granted religious toleration to the Orthodox Serbs; but the killing continued.

Many Jews escaped to the Italian occupation zone in Dalmatia. The Italian army in many cases protected them from the Ustashas. Many were transported to Italy, and the great majority of them survived till 1945. But only 1,000 of the 40,000 gipsies in Croatia survived. The young and able-bodied Serbs and gipsies went to the mountains and joined resistance groups. In the Serbian enclaves many Serbs formed bands and massacred Croats.[22]

When the Ustasha terror started, Tito was in Zagreb. As a Communist, he was, of course, in great danger; but he knew that the efficiency of the party underground organization gave him an excellent chance of survival, and he was not the worrying type. The party had a number of safe houses and couriers who carried messages to and from the party leadership and Tito. There were Communists or Communist sympathizers in every walk of life who helped the party; the authorities did not suspect them because of their social position. There were Communist doctors and nurses who cared for the wounded and the sick. There were Communists in the police force who protected the comrades in the underground. There were Communists in the civil service who leaked information to the party of the plans of the Germans and the Ustashas. There was that very respectable lawyer, Dr Vladimir Velebit, who operated a secret radio transmitter in his house which enabled Tito to keep in touch with the Comintern and was the only secret radio transmitter in Yugoslavia which was never discovered by the occupation authorities.[23] There were Communist rescue squads who were trained to organize the escape of captured Communists if the prisoner was sufficiently important for it to be worth while risking lives to save him. In Jasenovac and the other concentration camps the Communists had a very efficient network; Communists managed to be appointed to the group of prisoners who administered the camp. They could then see to it that Communists were not placed on the lists of those prisoners who were to be executed.

Tito decided that he would have to move to Belgrade. In later years he said that Communists were in much greater danger in Belgrade than in Zagreb, because the German Gestapo and the other security services were better organized in Belgrade, but that he never-theless decided to move the party headquarters to Belgrade because the resistance had to be an all-Yugoslav affair and the leadership had to be in the Federal capital to emphasize this.[24] But according to Djilas, Zagreb was more dangerous than Belgrade,[25] which is not surprising in view of the zeal of the Ustashas in the spring and summer of 1941.

Tito's wife, Herta Haas, was in the ninth month of her pregnancy; but Tito dared not wait to see the birth of his child. He was warned that the police were on his trail, and not to return to his flat. When the Ustashas came to power they ordered that all cars should be temporarily surrendered to the police. Tito hid his car in a shed, where it was seen some weeks later by a workman. The workman informed the police, who were now making inquiries about the car. So Tito moved to another address.[26] He also received a tip-off that, following on the creation of the independent state of Croatia, the frontier controls would be tightened in two days' time, and passports and identity documents would be more closely inspected. He asked Velebit to take care of Herta, and left for Belgrade by train with a forged identity card on Thursday 22 May. Herta came with him to the railway station, where they said goodbye; they were to meet again in very different circumstances. Tito had no trouble at the frontier, and reached Belgrade safely.

Herta went into labour next day. Velebit took her to the hospital in Zagreb which the Communists regularly used; the doctor in charge was a secret Communist sympathizer. She gave birth to a son, Miša on 24 May. Velebit took flowers to her in the hospital, and a few days later brought her and Miša home.[27]

The German preparations were well under way for Operation Barbarossa, the invasion of the Soviet Union. British spies had found out about it, and told the British government. Churchill warned Maisky, and instructed Sir Stafford Cripps, the British ambassador in Moscow, to convey the warning to Molotov and to Stalin personally. Stalin refused to believe it; he thought that it was a provocation intended to damage relations between the Soviet Union and Germany, and draw the Soviet Union into the war. He had perhaps some justifi-cation for his suspicion, because it is a well-known ploy for belligerents in wartime to pass disinformation with the object of drawing neutrals into the war; but it was an extraordinary blunder to take no steps to prepare for the attack in case the British report was true.

At the end of May a German officer in Belgrade was talking to a Serbian official, and casually mentioned that the Germans would attack Russia next month. The official was a secret Communist. He told Tito, who sent a radio message to Dimitrov in Moscow, passing on the warning. But Stalin refused to believe any of the reports.[28]

He still refused to believe them at three a.m. on 22 June, when the Germans invaded the Soviet Union along a 2,000-mile front. When he was informed that German aircraft were bombing Sevastopol, he was sure that some mistake had occurred, and gave orders that the anti-aircraft defences were not to open fire on them. A few hours later the German ambassador in Moscow called on Molotov and handed him the declaration of war. Molotov said to him: 'Do you think we deserved this?'[29] The Soviet government had given the Nazis everything they wanted; they had delivered oil, munitions and other war supplies, and had handed over German Communist refugees in the Soviet Union to the Gestapo, who sent them to concentration camps.

Later on 22 June Tito and the members of the Politburo held a meeting in Belgrade. They issued a statement announcing that 'the frenzied German Fascist bandits' had attacked the Soviet Union. It carried no appeal to Yugoslav patriotism or to any section of the population except to the 'proletarians from all parts of Yugoslavia' and the 'Communists of Yugoslavia' to whom it was addressed. 'Do not stand idly by while the precious blood of the heroic people of Soviet Russia is shed . . . long live the great and invincible land of Socialism, the Soviet Union . . . long live the leader and organizer of past and future victories of the great and mighty Soviet Union, Comrade Stalin . . . long live the international solidarity of all oppressed and exploited peoples!'[30]

On the same day the Comintern sent a message to the Yugoslav Communists, urging them to form a united national front for the defeat of the German and Italian Fascist bandits and the defence of the Soviet Union. 'Bear in mind that, at this present stage, what you are concerned with is liberation from Fascist oppression, and not Socialist revolution.'[31]

On the following night some Communists in Croatia committed an act of sabotage on the Zagreb–Belgrade railway,[32] thus enabling the government of Croatia in 1993 to claim that the Yugoslav struggle against the German invader began in Croatia. On 1 July the Comintern sent an order to the Yugoslav Communists: 'Without wasting a moment ... start a partisan war behind the enemy's lines.'[33] Without waiting for the Comintern, Tito had already taken steps to do just that. At a meeting on 27 June the Politburo appointed Tito commander-in-chief of the National Liberation Forces.[34]

Tito knew that there was a better chance of starting a rising in Serbia than in any other part of Yugoslavia. Many thousands of Serbs were already going into the mountains for fear of being murdered by the Hungarians in the Voyvodina and by the Ustashas in Croatia and Bosnia-Herzegovina. The Croats, if they were not all active supporters of the Ustashas, were on the whole still passive, apart from the Communists and their sympathizers.

Life in Belgrade for Tito and the Communists had become much more dangerous after 22 June. The Germans immediately realized that as they had invaded the Soviet Union the Yugoslav Communists would now become troublesome, and they increased security precautions in Belgrade. They stopped passers-by at random in the street and demanded to see their identity papers. From time to time they sealed off some part of the city and conducted house-to-house searches there. Tito and the other Communist leaders decided to go out as little as possible. A Communist builder built a secret room in the house where he was staying in Drajzerova Street; he could hide there if the house was raided by the police. He had a small store of hand grenades in the secret room; if the police did find him, he would use them, and fight and die rather than be captured alive. On the rare occasions when he did go out, he carried a loaded revolver and some hand grenades.[35]

He usually communicated with the other Communist leaders by couriers who were not known to the authorities as Communists and had more chance than many other comrades of passing safely through the streets. Communist girl students were often chosen for this duty. They knew that if they were caught they would almost certainly be tortured, and probably shot or hanged after the torture; but with the idealism, the certainties and the confidence of youth, they were happy to take the risk.

One girl courier was Davorjanka Paunović, who was known in the Communist party as Zdenka. As soon as Tito saw her, he fell in love with her, and she soon became his mistress. The new morality which had been introduced into party life since Tito became secretary, the taboo on sexual promiscuity on which Djilas had insisted, the code of sexual conduct which laid down that a comrade must be loyal to his partner until he divorced or separated from her: all went completely by the board where Tito and Zdenka were concerned. By the rules, he should have been faithful to his comrade Herta with her baby in Zagreb. But he was very attractive to women, with his blue eyes, his dominant but gentle personality, his knack of making them feel that he was interested in them, and the streak of kindness in his character which was genuine, whatever he might sometimes do in politics. He loved women. When a woman offered herself to him, he could not resist her; and he knew, every day in Belgrade in the summer of 1941, that this might be his last opportunity ever to have a woman. Tomorrow he might be dead, killed in his last battle with the Fascists who came to arrest him, or else alive in the prison torture chambers.

On 4 July he took the risk of going to a meeting of the Politburo at Ribnikar's villa in a residential district of Belgrade, which is today the Museum of 4 July. To minimize the risk, the members arrived separately one by one at intervals of twenty minutes. They made their plans for the uprising. Djilas was to go to his native Montenegro, and other leaders to Bosnia and Slovenia, to organize the insurrection.[36]

They were all optimistic, and convinced that the Red Army would soon sweep through Europe and arrive in Yugoslavia. In fact the Red Army had completely failed to meet the German invasion. Stalin's air force, the largest in Europe, had been almost destroyed on the ground in sudden attacks from the Luftwaffe. The German army had advanced on a wide front, often without encountering any resistance, and in the first week had advanced more than a hundred miles into the Soviet Union. Even the Soviet radio broadcasts admitted this; but the Yugoslav Communist leaders ignored the truth. At their meeting on 4 July, Djilas, Ranković, Kardelj, one after another said that the Red Army would roll back the Germans and would be marching into Yugoslavia to liberate them within a few weeks. Only Tito said nothing about this; he did not contradict their optimistic forecasts, but kept his doubts to himself.[37]

The Germans appointed General Nedić, who was a right-wing Conservative, to be ruler of Serbia. He formed a coalition government of right-wing parties, including the followers of Ljotić.* The

---

* Ljotić, Dimitrije (1891–1945); Serbian right-wing nationalist leader; minister of justice under King Alexander; formed the Serbian Volunteer Corps which fought for the Germans in the Second World War; killed in a motor accident while attempting to escape from Yugoslavia to Austria in April 1945.

first objective in Ljotić's political programme was to destroy Communists and Jews, but he did not agree with certain aspects of Italian Fascist or German Nazi policies – especially their belief that the State should to some extent direct economic policy. He was a Serbian nationalist, and opposed the German policy of supporting the Croatian Ustashas. He himself refused to join Nedić's government, but allowed some of his party leaders to do so.[38]

The Germans themselves were worried about the anti-Serbian excesses of the Ustashas. Why could not Croatian Ustashas and Ljotić's Serbs unite to exterminate Bolsheviks and Jews? They were disturbed when their Serbian collaborators complained to them that the Ustashas were treating the Serbs as if they were Jews.[39] Only Hitler supported the Ustasha policy. When Pavelić visited him at Berchtesgaden on 7 June 1941, Hitler told him that the Ustashas were dealing correctly with the large minority of Serbs in Croatia. The methods that Pavelić was adopting might be painful, but he would have to pursue an intolerant national policy for fifty years if an independent Croatia was to survive.[40]

Resistance was spreading in Serbia. As early as 22 July 1941 the German Foreign Office representative with the army, Felix Benzler, reported to Berlin that there was widespread Communist sabotage in Serbia, and asked for the help of experts in counter-terrorism. He sent four more telegrams in August, emphasizing the danger. 'The Communist movement is spreading,' he wrote on 27 August, 'and is operating with nationalist slogans which are beginning to meet with a response'. The terrorists were attacking the railways, municipal offices, and mining installations, and German troops could not travel safely by road or rail except in convoy. On 11 September he reported that the people, 'under the influence of nationalistically camouflaged Communist slogans', were attacking German troops. As the Nedić government seemed unable to deal with the situation, 'we must now prepare for having to crush the insurrectionary movement by ourselves'.[41]

Within a week Hitler ordered Field-Marshal F. M. List, his commander-in-chief in south-east Europe, to suppress the revolt. Field-Marshal Keitel in Berlin instructed List that between fifty and a hundred 'Communists' should be shot as hostages for every German soldier killed.[42] This made many Serbs feel that even if they took no active part in the resistance, they might be shot as hostages by the Germans; so more of them fled from their homes to join the resistance fighters in south-west Serbia.[43]

In the area around Užice, to the south of Belgrade, local Communists began a social revolution, ignoring Stalin's instructions, passed on to the Communist party of Yugoslavia by the Comintern, to fight only for national liberation. Stalin and the Comintern opposed a social revolution in Yugoslavia in the Second World War as strongly as they had opposed it in Spain during the Civil War. In both cases their chief motive was the same: they did not wish to antagonize the British government whose support they desperately needed in the face of the Fascist danger. But was there also another reason? Did Stalin actually wish to prevent a Socialist revolution and the establishment of a Communist government in any other country except in areas which had already been occupied by the Red Army?[44] The Communists and fellow-travellers throughout the world might be less devoted to the Soviet Union, the land of Socialism, if there were also other Socialist lands in the world.

The Communists raised their flag, the sickle and hammer, over the public buildings in Užice. They dressed the Partisans in a uniform which included a cap with the five-pointed red star, the 'Soviet star' worn by the Red Guards in Russia during the Russian Civil War. Stalin was angry when he heard about the red Soviet star in Užice.[45] The Yugoslav Communists were trying to carry out a Communist revolution, which was exactly what he had told them not to do.

Some of the peasants seized the land of the richer peasants, who were labelled 'kulaks' by the Communists; for if they were kulaks, any action against them was as justified as it had been in the Soviet Union during the collectivization campaign. Some of the 'kulaks' murdered Communists. The Communists also accused them of being in secret communication with the German army to the north and the Italian army to the south-west. So the Communists executed several of these rich peasants as traitors.

They also killed a few dissident Communists whom they called 'Trotskyists'. This was not their general policy. If any of the dissidents who had been expelled from the party for fractionalism now volunteered to join the Partisans, Tito was ready to welcome them and in due course to readmit them to the party; but in some cases Partisan commanders refused to accept them, or even shot them.

The Communists were particularly hostile to the followers of Petko Miletić, who were known as the Petkovac. Miletić had carried his dispute with Pijade about how Communists should behave in prison to the lengths of instigating his followers to assault and even murder

Pijade and his supporters, and Miletić would have had Tito shot as a Trotskyist in the Soviet Union if he himself had not been purged there. Djilas refused to accept a suspected Petkovac into the Partisan forces, and the man went away, wandering through the country till he was arrested and interned in a concentration camp, where Vujković, the police chief of Belgrade, recognized him as a Communist and had him shot. In the autumn of 1941 the Partisans shot thirty-four Petkovac dissidents in a railway siding near Užice.[46]

The Partisans could not forgive their former comrade, Zivojin Pavlović, who had once been the distribution manager of the leading Communist party newspaper, *Proleter*. Pavlović had been outraged by the execution in the Soviet Union of so many of the leading Yugoslav Communists, and had denounced it in his book *The Balance-sheet of the Soviet Thermidor*, which was highly praised and subsidized by Prince Paul's government. The Partisans accused him of having become a police informer. When they found him in a village near Užice in November 1941 they tortured him to make him disclose the names of his contacts in the Communist party, and then shot him.[47]

Tito thought that it was time for him to take command of the Partisan forces in the Užice area. On 17 September 1941 he set out on his dangerous journey, leaving Belgrade by train for the south with his forged identity papers. He travelled in a party of five, with a priest of the Orthodox Church, an ethnic German from the German minority in Hungarian-occupied Vojvodina, and Zdenka and another young woman. All his four travelling companions were secret Communists. The presence of an Orthodox priest and one of Hitler's beloved '*Auslandsdeutsche*', a German liberated from Yugoslav oppression, would allay suspicion; and it was useful to have two pretty girls in the party, as the soldiers, policemen and officials whom they met on the journey would be more likely to look at the pretty girls than at the men travelling with them. Tito and the German from Vojvodina spoke German on the train.

After they had travelled south from Belgrade for about fifty miles, they were told that the train could not proceed any further because the bridge across the River Morava had been blown up by Communists. Tito and his party got out and walked for about twenty miles, turning north-west and going back on their route till they reached the town of Čačak. Here Zdenka saw a policeman who knew her by sight, but he did not notice them. They went on to Pozega where they hired a horsecab and told the driver to go to Krupanj near the Partisan headquarters at Robaje. The driver was suspicious; he knew that the Communist Partisans controlled the country beyond Krupanj. He said that he hoped that they were not going to join the Partisans. Tito laughed, and said that he would hardly be wearing a smart lounge suit if he was intending to join the Partisans. The driver was satisfied, and took them to Krupanj.

From there they walked on into Partisan country. Soon they were stopped by the Partisan sentries, but Tito succeeded, with some difficulty, in proving his identity to the sentries, and after he had congratulated them on their vigilance, he and his party reached the Partisan headquarters at Robaje. He changed out of his city suit, into a plain dark uniform, and assumed his duties as commander-in-chief of the Partisan forces.[48]

CHAPTER 15

❖

From Užice to Bihać

COLONEL Draža Mihailović was only twenty miles away at Ravna Gora. He had raised a force of guerrillas who called themselves 'Chetniks', after the Chetniks who had fought against the Turks in the Balkan Wars of 1912–13. His plan was for his Chetniks to take part in a few minor actions against the Germans if they had the opportunity to do so, but their main function would be to wait until a British invasion force landed in Yugoslavia; then the Chetniks would rise and attack the Germans at the decisive moment.

Mihailović managed with some difficulty to enter into radio communication with the exiled Yugoslav government, who had now moved from Jerusalem to London. King Peter and his prime minister, General Simović, approved of Mihailović's policy of conserving his forces till the Allies landed.[1] They informed the British government about Mihailović's activities and policy in Yugoslavia.

In July 1940, after the fall of France, Churchill had set up the Special Operations Executive (SOE) to organize'subversion and sabotage against the enemy overseas';[2] they were to incite acts of sabotage, and attacks on German soldiers, in every country of occupied Europe. The Germans, of course, called this 'terrorism'. The SOE was placed under the Ministry of Economic Warfare. In August 1941 Hugh Dalton, the Socialist minister of economic warfare, discussed the situation in Yugoslavia with members of the Yugoslav government and officers of the British War Office. They agreed, as Dalton reported to Churchill, that the guerrillas in Yugoslavia should for the time being do enough to embarrass the Germans 'and prevent any reduction in their numbers', but that they should not start an insurrection 'which could only result at present in severe repression and the loss of our key men'. They should prepare to rise 'when we give the signal'.[3]

But the Yugoslav Communists were not prepared to wait until the British government gave the signal. They had answered the Comintern's call to give all possible assistance to the Soviet Union by immediately attacking the Germans; and the Communists in Užice wished to seize the land from the kulaks and carry through the social revolution. The Partisans attacked the Germans wherever they came across them, without waiting for a signal from the British and orders from Mihailović. Apart from the main body of the Partisans around Užice, they carried out acts of sabotage in Croatia and Slovenia, and killed notorious Fascist collaborators in the cities. They repeatedly blew up the Zagreb to Belgrade railway and other important rail links. In a town in Herzegovina a group of Communists coolly walked into an expensive restaurant, shot dead the Italian Fascist chief of police who was dining there, and quickly walked out again. In Belgrade they shot Vujković, the chief of police who had tortured Djilas and the other Communists, as he was riding his bicycle through the city. He was seriously wounded, but survived. They lured his deputy chief of police into the flat of a woman with whom he was in love, and strangled him.[4]

Many Chetniks also wished to kill Germans at once, and took part in joint operations with the Communist Partisans. This angered Mihailović. It was not only a breach of discipline by his men, but it also helped the Communists, whom he bitterly hated. He thought that they had always been a subversive element in the Kingdom of Yugoslavia, the enemies of the lawful Karadjordjević dynasty, who were aiming at social revolution and the victory of Bolshevism and who had rightly been suppressed and imprisoned. Mihailović had one word to describe the Communists: 'jailbirds'.[5]

But while Mihailović pursued his Fabian military strategy and did not engage the enemy, he could not resist the temptation of claiming the credit for the attacks on the Germans by the Partisans and the undisciplined Chetniks who collaborated with them. This impressed the British government. On 28 August 1941 Churchill wrote to Dalton that King Peter's government had reported that 'there is widespread guerrilla activity in Yugoslavia' and that he thought that the British should try to send them help.[6] The Yugoslave government in London announced that Mihailović's guerrilla activities were pinning down thirty or forty German divisions who were stationed in Yugoslavia to deal with them. This, as we now know, was an exaggeration. The Germans in fact had only five German divisions in Yugoslavia, with another fourteen Italian, three Bulgarian and three Croatian divisions; and many of these divisions were not at full strength.[7] The error is not surprising. Throughout history generals have often exaggerated the strength of enemy forces, either because of faulty intelligence or from a desire to emphasize the dangers that they were facing. This figure of thirty German divisions implanted itself in the minds of the British military and political leaders, and the myth invented by King Peter's government afterwards persisted to the benefit of Tito.

As soon as Tito joined the Partisans at Robaje, he contacted Mihailović and suggested that they should discuss joint action against the Germans and Italians. They met next day on 19 September in a house at Struganik, between Robaje and Mihailović's headquarters at Ravna Gora.[8] Tito was escorted by fifteen Partisans. Mihailović and all the Chetnik officers with him wore long beards, for, in traditional Serbian fashion, they had sworn an oath not to shave until they had driven the foreign enemy from the soil of the Fatherland. All the Partisans were clean-shaven, except for an occasional moustache. This was one of many differences between the two groups. There were no women among the Chetnik fighters, who honoured women (except for the enemy's women, whom they sometimes raped), but kept them in their place. Many women were serving with the Partisans. All the Chetniks were Serbs. The Partisans included Serbs, Montenegrins, Croats, Slovenes and Muslims, though in September 1941 they were mostly Serbs, because the Serbs had more reason than members of the other nationalities to leave their homes and take to the hills.

Mihailović knew that he was meeting the leader of the Communist Partisans, but he did not know his name. When Tito arrived, he introduced himself by saying 'I am Tito'. 'Is that your only name?' asked Mihailović. 'It will do for the moment,' said Tito. 'Where do you come from?' asked Mihailović. 'From up there,' said Tito, meaning from the north, from Croatia. Mihailović interpreted this as meaning that Tito had come from Russia. He also believed that Tito spoke Serbo-Croat with a Russian accent, as did other people who did not realize that it was Tito's half-Croat half-Slovene accent.

Mihailović tried to persuade Tito that the time was not ripe for action against the Germans; if they attempted anything, they would be defeated with heavy losses, and many Serbs would be executed as hostages. He was right about the hostages. Keitel had ordered that fifty or a hundred hostages should be shot for every German soldier killed. General Franz Böhme, the commander in Serbia, was more specific. On 10 October he ordered that in every case where a German soldier was killed, a hundred Serbs would be shot. He soon showed that he meant what he said. On 21 October 2,300 young Serbs, many of them sixth-form schoolboys, were rounded up at random in Kragujevac, some forty miles south of Belgrade, and shot in reprisal for the twenty-three German soldiers who had recently been killed by resistance groups.[9]

By this time a British officer had been sent to Yugoslavia. Colonel Hudson, who before the war had worked as a mining engineer in Yugoslavia and had acted as an intelligence agent for the British, accompanied two Yugoslav officers sent to Mihailović by the Yugoslav government in London. They were landed from a submarine on the coast of Montenegro, but could not find their way to Mihailović's headquarters and arrived instead at Užice, where Hudson met Tito before going on to Mihailović at Ravna Gora.[10] He told Tito that the British government wished to help all resistance groups who were fighting against the Germans. But Hudson found that the Partisans whom he met were not particularly interested in receiving help from the British, for they were convinced that the Russians would very shortly arrive and liberate Yugoslavia.[11] Their self-deception was extraordinary. By the end of October the Germans on the Russian front were besieging Leningrad in the north; in the centre they were less than forty miles from Moscow, and their officers could see the towers of the Kremlin through their field glasses; and in the south they had advanced more than 1,000 miles, capturing Kiev, Kharkov and Odessa and more than 700,000 prisoners.

Tito and Mihailović met again on 27 October in a house in the village of Brajići, not far from Mihailović's headquarters.[12] Tito brought thirty Partisans with him in two trucks; they were all armed with tommy-guns. Hudson came to Brajići with Mihailović, but Mihailović turned down Tito's suggestion that Hudson should be present at their talk. Perhaps he did not wish the British to know that he was hardening his attitude towards Tito; at the meeting, he demanded that the Partisans should surrender the towns of Užice and Čačak to the Chetniks.

Tito refused to agree to this. He offered to serve with his Partisans under Mihailović, who would be appointed commander-in-chief of the joint Chetnik and Partisan forces; but he admitted in later years to his British biographer Phyllis Auty that if Mihailović had accepted this offer, he personally would not have served under him.[13] Mihailović and Tito did agree that the Partisans would allow the Chetniks to have half the munitions produced by their armaments factory in Užice in return for Mihailović giving the Partisans half the supplies which the British dropped to them by parachute. This was an arrangement which in the immediate future would benefit the Chetniks more than the Partisans, because so far the British, despite their promises of support, had managed to drop only one consignment of arms to the Chetniks.

After their talk, Mihailović asked Tito if he would like a glass of sweet Sumadija tea. Tito accepted, but when he took a deep swig at the beverage he half-choked and spluttered, for the tea was in fact a strong variety of plum brandy. Mihailović laughed heartily as Tito dried the places on his uniform where he had spat out the plum brandy. This was a typical example of a hearty, good-natured Chetnik joke.

Tito and his party spent the night at Brajići. Tito wondered if the Chetniks would attack them during the night, and took care to sleep with his revolver under his pillow. When they left next day, they were stopped at a bridge outside the village by an armed band of Chetniks, who refused to let them pass without 'the colonel's' permission. They had to return to Mihailović's headquarters where they waited for half an hour until an officer came to them, apologized for the delay, and said that Mihailović would allow them to leave. The delay had been caused because the bridge was mined and had to be defused.

Five days later, on the night of 1–2 November, the Chetniks suddenly attacked Užice. They were routed and driven off by the Partisans. Mihailović afterwards said that it was the Partisans, not the Chetniks, who had begun hostilities by attacking the Chetniks' smelting works at Zajača on 28 October, the day after the meeting between Tito and Mihailović. Most impartial historians reject this allegation; but in any case Mihailović had decided, before the night of 1 November and within a few days of his talk with Tito, that as Tito had refused to surrender Užice and Čačak, he would try to capture Užice by force. He sent a radio message to his government in London that he 'feared' that he would have to occupy Užice in order to prevent the spread of Communism in the area.[14]

After the Chetnik defeat at Užice, Mihailović asked Hudson to arrange for more arms to be sent to him from Cairo, as soon as possible. But Hudson knew that the British government did not wish to risk the loss of their aircraft and personnel by dropping arms in Yugoslavia if the arms would be used, not against the Germans, but in a civil war between rival Yugoslav factions. He reported to Cairo that he believed that the dropping of the first consignment of arms to the Chetniks had made the situation worse: Mihailović had attacked Užice because he knew that the British were supporting him and that no one outside Yugoslavia had ever heard of the Partisans. Hudson therefore radioed Cairo not to drop any more supplies to the Chetniks for the time being, and he told Mihailović what he had done.[15] Mihailović was very angry.

The Partisans completely misunderstood what had happened. They were convinced that Hudson was responsible for the Chetnik attack on Užice. Dedijer firmly believed it. Before the war he had been the correspondent in London of the Liberal *Politika*, but his friend Djilas had persuaded him to join the Communist party. He was serving with the Partisans, and with Tito's encouragement he was keeping a diary; it was to be a record of the Partisan struggle against Fascism. He wrote in the diary that the British imperialists had incited Mihailović to attack the Partisans because they wished to ensure that the resistance movements in enemy-occupied countries did not fall under Communist leadership. Nearly forty years later Kardelj repeated this in his memoirs.[16] It was the explanation which fitted in best with Marxist-Leninist theory. The Communists remembered that the British imperialists had sent their armies to support the Whites against the Bolsheviks in Russia, that they had consistently refused to resist Fascist aggression before the Second World War, and that they had been ready to go to war with the Soviet Union over Finland. Of course they were inciting the Chetniks to attack the Partisans, for Winston Churchill, now British prime minister, had always been the most violent anti-Communist of all the British bourgeoisie.

The Partisans were right on one point. The British government had decided to support Mihailović against the Partisans. On 16 November Hudson received a message from London: 'His Majesty's Government now consider fight should be Yugoslavs for Yugoslavia and not revolt led by Communists for Russia.'[17]

Meanwhile the Germans had launched an offensive to crush the Serbian insurrection. They were advancing rapidly from the north on both Užice and Ravna Gora.

Keitel had issued an order to the German army to regard all resistance in Serbia as being 'Communist inspired', whether the rebels were using Communist or nationalist slogans. The orders for the offensive issued to Field-Marshal List instructed him to destroy the 'Communist bands'; but he was also told to crush any Chetniks whom he encountered.[18]

The chief of German Intelligence in Serbia, Captain Matl, had heard that the Chetniks had attacked the Partisans at Užice, and hoped that he could persuade Mihailović to abandon his resistance to the Germans. He arranged a meeting between Mihailović and officers of the German High Command in the village of Divci on 11 November. Mihailović told the Germans that if they left him alone and did not attack him at Ravna Gora, he would do nothing to hamper their campaign against the Partisans. The Germans replied that if he wished to be left in peace he must formally submit to the authority of Nedić's government. Mihailović refused to agree to this, so the peace talks broke down.[19]

Tito did not know of Mihailović's meeting with the Germans when he proposed that he and Mihailović should meet for the third time to discuss united action against the Germans. Mihailović agreed to further talks, but neither he nor Tito attended the meeting at Čačak on 20 November when Ranković and the youth leader Lola Ribar met Mihailović's representatives. After a long discussion the talks were adjourned to 27 November, when they met again at Čačak; but next day they hastily moved to Pranjani, as the Germans were rapidly approaching Čačak. At the talks the Chetniks and the Partisans agreed to unite against the Germans; to appoint a joint commission of inquiry to discover who had been responsible for the outbreak of fighting between them and to court-martial the people responsible; and to release the prisoners captured on both sides. But though Tito sent a radio message to Mihailović on 28 November again offering to serve under him in joint operations against the Germans, the Partisans insisted on retaining their own military units. Hudson reported to Cairo that the negotiations had broken down on this point.[20]

The Communists had made enemies in Užice. Some of the population who did not like their social revolution were prepared to help the Germans. One of them succeeded in planting a bomb in the armaments factory, which exploded on 21 November and did very great damage, because it detonated a series of other explosions in the underground passages of the factory, killing hundreds of Partisan workers. The Nedić collaborationist newspapers in Serbia claimed that more than 650 Communists had been killed in the explosion. Tito, who regularly visited the factory, was only twenty-five yards away from the bomb, but he was unhurt.[21]

On 1 December the Germans entered Užice, a few hours after Tito and the Partisans had evacuated the town and retreated south, bombed by German aircraft and suffering heavy casualties. On 3 December Benzler reported to Berlin that the operations against the Communists in Serbia had been successfully accomplished; but he added that Mihailović at Ravna Gora remained 'a rallying point for all insurgents with nationalist leanings' and a potential threat, though he was no danger for the moment because he was fighting the Communists. The Germans decided to wipe him out, and having dealt with the Partisans they marched against the Chetniks at Ravna Gora. Mihailović disbanded his men, and took to the mountains with only five followers. Once he was nearly caught when he lay hidden in a ditch while the German soldiers walked all around him. He made his way to Montenegro, where his followers regrouped and joined him in the mountains.[22]

The Partisans too retreated south into Montenegro. The Germans and Italians had agreed that Montenegro was in the Italian zone of operations, and the Italian army went into action against the Partisans. The Italians were much more willing than the Germans to enlist the support of the Chetniks. Several local Chetnik commanders fought with the Italians against the Partisans in Montenegro, though it is doubtful how far Mihailović himself approved of their action. In Montenegro, as at Užice, many local inhabitants who did not like Communism remained passive as the Italians advanced, and some of them actively helped the Italians.[23]

On 4 December the first snow of the winter fell, but the Partisans pressed on, covering between fifteen and twenty miles a day. Their morale remained high, and only the hired guides showed any reluctance to keep on; they sometimes had to be forced at revolver point to continue on the journey. Once the Partisans were nearly trapped by the Italians, who approached the village in which they were resting without being spotted by the Partisan sentries. The Partisans who were in the house where Tito was lodging looked out of the window and saw the Italians 250 yards away. They rushed out of the house, and Tito, taking charge, ordered them to lie down and open fire on the advancing Italians. The Italians fired mortars at them, but overshot their target, and the Partisans succeeded in retreating from the village and escaping. The Italians burned the house where Tito had stayed after they had killed the owner's daughter-in-law, who had given birth to twins ten days before. They also killed a pregnant woman.[24]

At Rudo, on 21 December, Stalin's birthday, Tito formed the best of his Partisan fighters into a crack unit which he named the First Proletarian Brigade. Stalin disapproved of the name, just as he disapproved of the red star on the Partisans' uniforms.[25] The Partisans followed the Soviet example in appointing a 'political commissar' alongside the commanding officer in every army unit. The respective duties of the commanding officer and the political commissar were clearly defined. The commanding officer was responsible for military tactics, the political commissar for maintaining the morale, discipline and ideological loyalty of the soldiers in his unit.

The Partisans had reached Bosnia by 24 December. It had now turned very cold, the temperature falling to twenty-six degrees centigrade below freezing point by 30 December. Sometimes they had to march through snow several feet deep. But the snow had one advantage: it grounded the German planes and gave them a respite from air attacks.[26]

They celebrated the arrival of the New Year, convinced that it would bring a change in their fortunes. 'Farewell 1941! Don't ever come back!' wrote Dedijer in his diary. 'Long live 1942! Long live victory! Long live our Party!'[27]

In the middle of January the Germans and the Ustashas launched another offensive against the Partisans. Their attacks were hampered by the cold and the snow, and the Partisans were able to slip away to the south, and then, evading the enemy, to return to their positions in Bosnia.

On 25 January they reached Foča. Tito decided to make Foča his headquarters and to stay there for some time. It was in the heart of Bosnia, and in the town and the surrounding district they came across both Muslims and Serbs and the fury of the fighting between the three ethnic groups in Bosnia. By this time the Ustashas had killed at least 100,000 Serbs in Croatia and Bosnia. They also killed

Muslims who, like the Orthodox Serbs, were enemies of the Roman Catholic Church and of the Virgin Mother of God and her Croats. Mihailović announced that he would kill a Croat for every Serb that they had killed,[28] and when his Chetniks captured a village they massacred the Croats.

Haji Amin Husseini, the Grand Mufti of Jerusalem in the British protectorate of Palestine, had fled abroad after he had incited an armed uprising of Arabs against the British in protest against the British policy of allowing a limited number of Jews to settle in Palestine. He visited Hitler and congratulated him on his war against the British imperialists and the Jews. Hitler sent him to Bosnia to recruit Muslims into the Waffen SS, the international legion of Fascists of all countries who volunteered to fight against the Bolsheviks in Russia. The Mufti had a limited success, and a number of Muslims enlisted in units under German command.[29] They did not find many Jews to kill in Bosnia, for most Jews had either been killed already by the Ustashas or had escaped to the protection of the Italians in Dalmatia or to Italy. So they took the opportunity to kill Serbs, as they had been told that the Serbs were fighting with the Chetniks against the Germans. The Chetniks retaliated by killing Muslims, without pausing to inquire if their victims were for, or against, the Germans.

When the Partisans entered a Muslim village in Bosnia, the inhabitants fled, thinking that the Partisans were Chetniks who would kill them. The Partisans set out to win the Muslims' confidence; they told them that they had no hatred for Muslims, but believed in the fraternal union and love of all the peoples of Yugoslavia. They promised to protect the Muslims against both the Chetniks and the Ustashas. They also offered to protect the Bosnian Serbs who told them of the atrocities committed against them by Muslims in Sarajevo. Dedijer came across a young Serbian girl who told him that Muslims had raped and killed three of her cousins and their mother in Sarajevo. She wanted to kill every Muslim, man, woman and child. Dedijer asked her how it could ever be justifiable to kill either a Muslim or a Serbian child; but she found it difficult to understand his point of view.[30]

The Partisans, too, sometimes killed people; but Tito ordered them, as a general rule, not to kill their prisoners. He decided from the beginning of his campaign that he would spare the lives of the enemy soldiers whom he captured in the hope of exchanging them for Communist prisoners in Jasenovac and the other concentration camps and in the prisons in Zagreb and Belgrade. This involved the trouble of guarding and feeding the prisoners, but they could be made to do useful work as carriers of the luggage on the march and as stretcher-bearers for the wounded Partisans. At Užice and in Montenegro in the autumn of 1941 the Partisans had sometimes killed rich peasants; but Tito, complying with the Comintern directive, had put a stop to this. Captured Ustashas and Chetniks who had murdered or tortured Partisans were executed; so were enemy agents who were discovered spying or committing sabotage in areas occupied by the Partisans. Sometimes, when a band of Chetniks were captured, the officers were shot, but the rank-and-file were spared. Some of them volunteered to join the Partisans, and were allowed to do so.

Volunteers from all ethnic and religious groups were joining the Partisans. Very few of them were Communists, but they believed that the Partisans were fighting not only for an independent but also for a freer Yugoslavia and above all for a united Yugoslavia in which they would be protected from the violence of their fellow-countrymen. They were also deeply impressed by the charisma of this Partisan leader who called himself 'Tito' whoever he might be, and by his extraordinary optimism. On one occasion Tito was addressing a batch of newly enlisted volunteers in the square in Foča when the Chetniks in the mountains above the town opened fire on the assembled Partisans. Tito remained completely calm and unmoved. 'Those Chetniks up there who are now firing on us', he said, 'will have joined us within a year.' His optimism was so infectious that his audience actually believed him; and most of those Chetniks had in fact become Partisans within a year.[31]

Tito was tireless and efficient, intervening not only in the details of the guerrilla military operations but also in the administration of the region under Partisan control and in the steps that should be taken to increase the yield of milk from the cows. He appointed Djilas to be the head of the Agitprop department, and Djilas chose Dedijer as his assistant. They produced a regular edition of *Borba*, the Communist party newspaper which had first begun as a legal newspaper in 1919 and had continued to be published illegally throughout all the period that the party was banned. *Borba* put over the party line.

The Communists found that many of the inhabitants of the Foča area had mistaken ideas about the Soviet Union. They had believed the lies told them by the Chetniks that in the Soviet Union the people were oppressed by the Bolsheviks and women were owned in common. *Borba* and the propagandists in Agitprop told the people about the glorious victories of the Red Army in Russia, and how the soldiers of the Soviet Union would soon arrive to liberate them; and they told them, too, that they could not trust the British imperialists who were supporting Mihailović and the Chetniks, despite the fact that the Chetniks were fighting on the side of the Germans and Italians. They told them about the heroic resistance workers in Serbia who had been shot as hostages by the Germans, and about the metalworker at Kragujevac who had called out as he faced the firing squad: 'You may drink Serb blood, you Fascist curs, but the Red Army and our Partisans will soon destroy you. Long live free Serbia! Long live the Partisans! Long live the Communist Party! Long live the Soviet Union! Long live Comrade Stalin!'[32]

Above all, Agitprop told the people that the Partisans and the Communist party believed in the brotherly union of all the peoples of Yugoslavia. They would protect the Muslims against Croatian and Serbian Fascists, the Serbs against Croatian and Muslim Fascists, and the Croats against Muslim and Serbian Fascists. There was no reason why the three ethnic groups in Bosnia should not live peaceably together, for 170 different races and nationalities lived in peace and friendship in the Soviet Union, the land of Socialism.[33]

Agitprop organized demonstrations and public meetings on 7 November, the anniversary of the Great October Revolution, and on the international workers' holiday on May Day. They organized study groups at which the people could ask questions and could be told the truth about the Soviet Union and Communism. At one meeting a woman asked if there would be running water in the cottages after the war. Yes, under Socialism there will be running water in the peasants' homes as well as brotherly love between all the peoples of Yugoslavia.[34]

The Communists regularly held party meetings at which they were expected to indulge in self-criticism, to admit their shortcomings, how they had not performed their military duties as efficiently as they should have done, or how they had failed to make the people realize the extent of the achievements of the Soviet Union and of the glorious Red Army. But Comrade Tito hardly ever attended a party meeting. The Old Man showed himself to his soldiers and Party comrades from time to time, and occasionally let them see that he was sharing their hardships and dangers. But he knew that familiarity may breed contempt, and that a touch of aloofness and mystery, and the feeling among his men that a sight of him was a rare privilege, could help surround him with an aura of leadership.[35]

When the Partisans entered a village or a town, they normally requisitioned the château, or the largest mansion in the town. Tito then moved in with Zdenka.[36] The members of the Politburo – Djilas, Kardelj, Ranković, Pijade and Sreten Žujović (Crni) either lived with Tito in the château or went there every day. These were the only people whom he saw regularly, apart from his headquarters staff. One of the staff was his secretary Olga Humo. She had been born Olga Ninčić, the daughter of the foreign minister in King Alexander's government, who was now with King Peter in London. Like several other upper-class girls she had become a Communist, and married a Bosnian Muslim, Avdo Humo, one of Tito's commanders. Apart from Zdenka and Olga, Tito had two other women secretaries. They dealt with all his correspondence, except for his letters to Dimitrov and the Comintern. He always wrote these letters himself.[37]

The chief cause of friction at Tito's headquarters was Zdenka – tall and slim, with dark hair, olive-skinned but pale, for her health was not good. She was exuberant and loud, but became frightened and almost hysterical in air raids; there were other women Partisans who were frightened in air raids, although, like Zdenka, they had calmly run greater risks as Communist couriers under the nose of the Gestapo in Belgrade. Being conscious that Tito was completely infatuated with her, she made herself very unpopular by trying to order everyone around. She was disliked by all the members of Tito's headquarters staff, particularly because they knew that in any dispute Tito would always come down on Zdenka's side. She once insulted Djilas, who became so angry that he threatened to seize her by her hair and throw her over a cliff. On another occasion she quarrelled with Ranković, and scolded him at the top of her voice in the presence of the other members of the Politburo and Tito's staff. Ranković never forgave her for this, and never spoke to her again. Sometimes she stormed at Tito, who always put up with her taunts in silence.[38] Perhaps he realized that she was slowly dying of tuberculosis.

On Saturday 21 February 1942 a rare event took place in the Communist party in Foča. Tito turned up at a meeting of the headquarters party cell. After various party members had spoken, and indulged in self-criticism, the Old Man spoke. He referred to the role of the British working class in forcing the British government to co-operate with the Soviet Union, to the conflict of policy in the Pacific and the Far East between the British imperialists, who were retreating before the Japanese, and the American imperialists who were fighting them. Then he turned to the situation in Yugoslavia. The Serbian bourgeoisie, instead of fighting against the occupation forces, had begun a class war against the Serbian proletariat; but although the Communist party would fight the bourgeoisie in this class war, the main enemy for the moment were the armies of occupation. 'We will liquidate the kulak, but not because he is a kulak but because he is a fifth columnist . . . The present struggle is national liberation in form, but class war in essence.' Thus Tito skilfully combined the Soviet and Comintern line with the wish of the leftist members of the Communist party of Yugoslavia to carry through the social revolution.

There was no self-criticism in Tito's speech, and the party members were delighted with his 'splendid report'.[39] Self-criticism stopped short at the Old Man.

Contrary to what Dedijer and Kardelj believed, the British government wished to stop the fighting between Chetniks and Partisans. They asked the Soviet government to use their influence with the Partisans to achieve this, just as the British government would use its influence with the Yugoslav government in exile and with Mihailović. King Peter's government had a minister accredited to Moscow; he had left Moscow for Kuibishev in the Urals when all the Soviet government, except Stalin himself, moved there in December 1941 at a time when the German army was less than forty miles from the Kremlin. The Yugoslav minister in Kuibishev also asked the Soviet deputy foreign minister, Vyshinsky,* to use Soviet influence with the Partisans to make peace with the Chetniks. The Soviet government declined, taking their usual line that the Comintern and foreign Communist parties had nothing to do with them. Vyshinsky said that he agreed that it would be desirable if the civil war in Yugoslavia could be ended, but that the Soviet government could do nothing to help bring this about as they had no representative with the Yugoslav

---

* Vyshinsky, Andrei Y. (1883–1954); Soviet Communist leader; counsel for the prosecution at the great Moscow trials during the purge of 1936–8; assistant foreign minister 1940–9; foreign minister 1949–53.

Partisans. The British military mission in Moscow made the same request to the Soviet Ministry of Defence in Moscow, but added that 'the British government regards Colonel Mihailović as the only possible leader' and thought that 'all parties should obey his orders'.[40]

In December 1941, during the retreat from Užice, Tito radioed to the Comintern that he and his men were being attacked by Chetniks who were fighting together with the Italians. He also asked the Comintern to send him help as soon as possible. He did not receive an immediate reply to either point. The Partisans tuned in on their radios to the BBC in London and heard them praising Mihailović and the Chetniks for their valour against the Germans. This made them very angry; they were risking their lives and suffering heavy casualties fighting against the German and Italian Fascists, and the BBC were giving the credit for their achievements to Mihailović and the Chetniks, who were fighting on the side of the Germans and Italians. They were even more distressed to hear the same line put over not only by the broadcasting station of the British imperialists but also by Radio Free Yugoslavia broadcasting from Ufa in the Soviet Union. A Yugoslav Communist was officially in charge of these broadcasts from Ufa, but it was controlled by the Comintern, and of course put over the propaganda line of the Soviet government. Radio Free Yugoslavia praised the struggle of the Yugoslav people against the Fascist invaders under the valiant leadership of Colonel Mihailović.

In December 1941 King Peter promoted Mihailović to the rank of brigadier-general, and appointed him commander-in-chief of the Yugoslav Army in the Homeland. A month later, Mihailović was appointed minister of the army, navy and air force in the Yugoslav government in exile.

In February 1942 Tito at last received a radio message from the Comintern. It said that the Soviet military authorities would try to send aid to the Partisans, and asked what form of assistance Tito required, and what arrangements could be made for a plane to land with the supplies. Tito asked them to send medicines, ammunition for their rifles, boots, and material for making uniforms; the uniforms were important, so that the Partisans could claim, if they were captured, that they were belligerents entitled to be treated as prisoners-of-war. Tito told the Comintern where a plane carrying the supplies could land near Foča.

The Partisans cleared away the snow from the agreed landing place, and waited all night in the bitter cold for the Soviet plane to arrive. As no plane came, they waited there again the next day, and every night for thirty-seven days; but still no Soviet plane arrived, nor did they receive any explanation from the Comintern.[41] Instead, the Comintern sent a radio message on 5 March criticizing the Partisans for allowing their resistance movement to 'acquire a Communist character' and for calling one of their brigades a 'proletarian brigade'. The message also dealt with Tito's complaint that Mihailović and the Chetniks were helping the Germans. 'It is difficult to agree that London and the Yugoslav government are siding with the invaders. There must be some great misunderstanding here.'[42]

It was not until 29 March that Tito received an explanation of why the Soviet plane had not arrived. The Comintern said that it had proved to be more difficult to send the plane than they had realized, and they regretted that the Partisans could not expect any help in the immediate future.[43]

Tito had heard that Molotov would be going to London in May for talks with Churchill and Eden. He radioed to the Comintern the full facts about the Chetnik attacks on the Partisans and their collaboration with the Italians, so that Molotov could raise the matter with the British government in London. He received no acknowledgement from the Comintern. During Molotov's six days of talks in London, which resulted in the signature of the twenty years' friendship treaty between Britain and the USSR, many international issues were discussed; but neither Molotov nor Churchill and Eden made any reference to the situation in Yugoslavia.[44]

In February an English officer, Major Atherton, and his Irish radio operator landed by parachute in Partisan territory in Montenegro. For some reason the Partisans who encountered Atherton were suspicious of him, and sent word to Tito asking him what they should do. Tito told them to escort Atherton to him in Foča, where Atherton arrived on 19 March. Tito, too, was suspicious, despite the fact that Dedijer recognized Atherton, whom he had met briefly when he was in England as the correspondent of *Politika* before the war. On 6 April Tito wrote to Pijade that he felt that there was something 'not right' about Atherton; and two days later, hearing that the British might be sending another liaison officer to contact the Partisans in Croatia, he warned the Croatian Partisans to be on their guard against any British officer who might arrive in their midst, and against any plots of the British imperialist agents.[45] His suspicions increased when Atherton and his radio operator left Foča on the night of 15 April without having told anyone of their impending departure and leaving their radio transmitter behind in Foča.

Atherton had intended to make his way to Mihailović's head-quarters. He never arrived, and he and his radio operator were never seen again. There is no doubt that Atherton was murdered some-where on his journey and robbed of the large sum in gold that he carried in his money-belt. The Chetniks accused the Partisans of murdering him; the Partisans said that he was killed by the Chetniks. It remains an unsolved murder mystery, but the weight of evidence suggests that he was killed for the gold by an independent bandit chief who sometimes fought on the side of the Chetniks but was not under Mihailović's command.[46]

In April the Germans launched their Third Offensive against the Partisans. In the spring weather they could use their aircraft, and the Partisans could not hold Foča. On 10 May they withdrew from Foča after they had held it for 110 days, which Dedijer proudly noted was longer than the Paris Commune had lasted in 1871 or the Hungarian Soviet Republic in 1919.[47] They set out on a march which eventually took them by a roundabout route to Bihać, 150 miles to the north-west in Bosnia and near the former border with Croatia.

Life was very hard for the Partisans on the march, particularly in the winter, when they had to endure the cold in the mountains. The women shared the hardships with the men. They refused any offer of help from their male comrades, and would not let them carry their packs. 'I am a Partisan,' they insisted.[48]

Sometimes the Partisans went short of food for several weeks. Then they would come to a part of the country where food was plentiful, and would eat large meals.

From time to time, supporters would come from the towns in occupied territory to join them. A troop of actors came; some of them were well-known. They performed plays in a clearance in the forest, with the audience sitting on the ground. Agitprop was a little worried about the actors, because intellectuals were often ultra-leftists and undisciplined fractionalists.[49]

The Partisans' most important acquisition was the Croatian poet, Vladimir Nazor, who joined them in December 1942. He was sixty-seven, and a strange, romantic-looking individual; unlike all the other Partisans, he wore a beard, but it was a pointed white beard, not the full bushy beard of the Chetniks. He caused some problems for the Partisans. He sat on a horse and advanced very slowly along the roads and paths, accompanied by a devoted servant (a former Italian prisoner-of-war) and a cow which provided him with milk. It was a problem for the Partisans how to hurry him up when the Germans were attacking them. But Tito was very glad to have a famous poet with them, and all the Partisans admired his courage and his readiness to endure hardships. When they came to a village, Nazor usually stayed in the château with Tito and Zdenka.[50]

For recreation, the Partisans swam in the rivers, played volleyball, and competed in athletic sports. They organized volleyball championships between their various battalions. At headquarters Tito fished in the streams, and played chess and dominoes with the members of the Politburo. He preferred dominoes, as it was less of a mental effort. Dedijer once watched a game of chess between Tito and Djilas, and recorded in his diary that though Djilas attacked at first and appeared to be winning, Tito defended doggedly and won in the end. According to Djilas, he and Tito were about equally good; sometimes he won, and sometimes he lost, against Tito. Then Ranković suggested to Djilas that he ought to allow Tito to win, so as not to upset the Old Man and cause him to have a sleepless night which would impair his efficiency as a leader next day. Djilas said that in future Ranković, and not he, should play Tito at chess. Ranković was always inclined to draw his games, and when he found that he was beating Tito he always offered him a draw.[51]

As the Partisans marched from Foča to Bihać in the summer of 1942, being attacked continually by Germans and from time to time by Chetniks, they heard on the radio from the BBC of the actions which Mihailović was supposed to be conducting against the Germans, and not a word about the Partisans. In June King Peter and his prime minister went to Washington and met President Roosevelt. On 24 July the White House spokesman at a press conference referred to the meeting with King Peter and to 'the fine achievements of General Mihailović and his daring men' which were 'an example of spontaneous and unselfish will to victory'.[52]

But at last there was good news. On 6 July 1942 Radio Free Yugoslavia, which had now moved from Ufa to Moscow, broadcast a resolution which had been passed by what they called 'patriots of Montenegro, Sandzak and Bosnia', which Tito had sent to the Comintern a fortnight earlier. It denounced Mihailović as a traitor

9. The house in Zagreb, where the illegal conference of the Communist Party was held in October 1940.

10. Ribnikar's villa in Belgrade, where the decision to launch the insurrection was taken on 4 July 1941.

POTJERNICA ZA DRUGOM TITOM

11. The German proclamation of July 1943
offering a reward of 100,000 Reichsmarks for the capture of Tito.

12. Milka Kufrin during her Partisan years, 1941–5.

13. Tito with Davorjanka Paunović (Zdenka) in 1942.

14. Tito and his comrades at Jajce in 1943.
Left to right: Lola Ribar, Djilas, Sreten Djurović, Ranković, Tito, Hebrang, Moša Pijade, Kardelj.

15. A meeting of the Politburo of the CPY in the cave on *Vis* in June 1944.

16. Tito and Churchill at Naples, August 1944.

and a collaborator with the Germans. It was the signal for the Comintern to launch a campaign against Mihailović. While King Peter's minister in Kuibishev was protesting to the Soviet government against the broadcast by Radio Free Yugoslavia, the Communist newspaper in New York, the *Daily Worker*, reported that Radio Free Yugoslavia had denounced Mihailović as a traitor. The influential American journalist, Louis Adamic, started a campaign against him in the United States. In October the BBC referred for the first time to the Partisans. But the Soviet press and Radio Moscow, as distinct from Radio Free Yugoslavia, said nothing about the Partisans and continued to praise Mihailović. To Tito's annoyance, the Soviet government agreed that the Yugoslav legation in Kuibishev should be raised to the status of an embassy. When the Yugoslav ambassador there suggested to the Soviet government that they should send a military mission to Mihailović's headquarters, Vyshinsky replied that they would like to do so if it proved possible to arrange for a high-ranking Soviet officer to arrive there.[53]

As people in Britain and the United States heard for the first time about the existence of the Partisans, they also heard that the leader of the Partisans was a man named Tito. Mihailović, after his meetings with Tito in the autumn of 1941, had radioed to his government in London that the Partisan leader was a Communist who used the false name Tito. The government officials, the intelligence services, and the press in Britain and the United States speculated about who this Tito might be. At first it was widely believed that he was Lebedev, who had been the Soviet military attaché in Belgrade before the German invasion;[54] but soon wilder stories were circulating. It was sometimes suggested that there was no such person as Tito and that the name stood for the collective leadership, the Third International Terrorist Organization, which in Serbo-Croat, as in English, would have the initials TITO. Another theory was that Tito was a woman.

Even in the Communist party of Yugoslavia there were many members who did not at first know who Tito was. They thought that the party had probably appointed as commander-in-chief of the Partisans a comrade who had gained military experience in the Spanish Civil War. They thought that Tito was probably Kosta Nadj, who had fought in Spain.[55]

The Germans were the first to identify Tito correctly. They looked through the police files in Zagreb and discovered that he was Josip Broz, who had been born in Kumrovec in May 1892, had served in the Austrian army in the First World War, had lived for five years in Russia during the Russian Revolution and Civil War, and had served six years in prison in Croatia from 1928 to 1934. This was published in the German press in April 1942, and in the press in Spain and other neutral countries in Europe. It was only several months later that the press in Britain and the United States revealed that Tito was Josip Broz.

Mihailović was very scornful. On 27 March 1943 he radioed King Peter's government in London: 'Can a convict like Josip Broz, who is listed with the Zagreb police under No.10434, alias leader of the Communists under the name of Tito, be compared with the Yugoslav army as a national fighter? . . . The plunderer of churches and convict Josip Broz, a locksmith's assistant?'[56]

Soon after the Partisans reached Bihać, Tito called a conference to discuss the future government of Yugoslavia. He invited seventy-one 'prominent fighters and patriots' to a conference in Bihać, signing the invitation 'Commandant Tito'. Tito had not consulted the Comintern before issuing the invitations for the meeting. When the Comintern heard about it, they warned Tito that while there was nothing wrong in convening a conference it must not make any claim to be the government of Yugoslavia in opposition to King Peter's government; nor must the conference discuss the future of the monarchy in Yugoslavia.[57]

When the conference met on 26 November, Tito opened the proceedings with a presidential address to the fifty-four delegates who had managed to reach Bihać. He was careful, on the one hand, to show his willingness to submit to the orders of the Comintern, but he also dropped a strong hint that he was planning to go against their wishes. He said that when he issued the invitations to the conference he had intended to propose to them that they should set up 'something like a government', but that he had been asked not to do so by the Comintern and would comply with their wishes. 'Comrades, we have no possibility of setting up a legal government, because international relations and conditions do not permit it as yet.' If he felt any resentment for the failure of the Russians to send aid to the Partisans or to denounce Mihailović, he did not show it in his speech; but he did not eulogize the Soviet Union in the usual manner of Communist speakers, and he did not mention Stalin. He said that all that they had achieved in their struggle in Yugoslavia was 'in some measure due to our great Slav brothers, the Russians, and all the peoples of the Soviet Union', and ended his speech: 'Long live our great ally the Soviet Union! Long live the heroic Red Army! Long live our allies, Britain and America! Death to Fascism, freedom to the people!'

The conference voted to set up the Anti-Fascist Council of National Liberation of Yugoslavia, which became known from the initials of its name as AVNOJ. It adopted a six-point programme which was very moderate, and was intended to show that the Partisans were not planning to make Yugoslavia a Communist state. They stood for national liberation from the invaders, the independence of the country, and true democratic rights; the inviolability of private property; for a free market economy and individual initiative in industry, trade and agriculture; no radical transformation of society; free elections would be held after the war; they would not adopt a policy of coercion and would not encourage lawlessness; and they would stand for equal rights for the Serbs, Croats, Slovenes, Macedonians and Montenegrins and all the peoples of Yugoslavia.[58]

Some of the best fighters among the Partisans were selected as delegates to the Bihać conference. One of them was Milka Kufrin, a student from Zagreb who had joined the Partisans in Croatia and first went into action in sabotage operations against the Zagreb-Belgrade railway. She did so well that it was not long before she was appointed political commissar of her unit of a hundred men. In recognition of her achievements, Lola Ribar, the Youth Leader, chose her to make the speech of welcome to Tito when he attended the session of the Youth Congress.

Milka had never made a public speech and was very nervous. When she went to the rostrum and looked at the audience, with Tito sitting facing her in the front row, she became quite terrified and could not think of a word to say. After standing there silent for a moment, she called out: 'Death to Fascism!' and ran out of the hall in tears. Tito saw what had happened; he came after her, took her gently by the hand, and led her back into the hall. After the end of the session he said jokingly to Lola Ribar: 'Our young people know better how to fight than how to speak.'[59]

———— ❖ ————

CHAPTER 16

The March Negotiations and the Sutjeska

THE Special Operations Executive of the Ministry of Economic Warfare in London had set up a headquarters in Cairo to deal with problems in the Middle East and the Balkans. In the autumn of 1942 information reached SOE Cairo which showed that the Germans in Yugoslavia were using more of their manpower to fight against the Partisans than against the Chetniks. We do not know how SOE Cairo obtained this information, and there has been a good deal of controversy about this. It was contained in a report written by Brigadier Keble, the chief of staff to Lord Glenconner, who was the head of SOE Cairo. One theory is that the information came from the German radio messages intercepted and decoded by the British 'Ultra' machine at Bletchley in Buckinghamshire in England, and that Keble, who in his previous post had been on the very restricted list of persons who were entitled to receive the intercepts, continued to receive them in Cairo, though he was not entitled to do so. But it is possible that he obtained the information from other sources.[1]

Keble's two chief assistants at SOE Cairo were Captain William Deakin and Captain Basil Davidson. Deakin, a history Fellow at an Oxford college, had helped Churchill as a research assistant when Churchill was writing his biography of the great Duke of Marlborough in the early 1930s. Davidson had been a journalist, had been recruited into British intelligence at the beginning of the war, and had worked as an agent in the Balkans. A great deal has been made of the fact that James Klugmann, a Communist, was also working in Keble's department in SOE Cairo. Everyone recruited into SOE had to sign a statement that he was neither a Fascist nor a Communist, and steps were taken to prevent any Communist from joining SOE; but Klugmann's record had been destroyed by an incendiary bomb during an air raid in London.[2]

This has been the basis of a farfetched theory to explain why the British government decided in 1943 to switch its support from Mihailović to Tito. The Communist agent Klugmann somehow falsified the intercepts which Keble received and thus misled Keble into thinking that the Partisans in Yugoslavia were fighting the Germans more effectively than the Chetniks were doing. Keble thereupon wrote a report to this effect, and arranged for Deakin, as a personal friend of Churchill, to present this report to him when Churchill passed through Cairo in January 1943. The report persuaded Churchill to send first Deakin and later Fitzroy Maclean to Tito's headquarters, and Deakin and Maclean then persuaded Churchill to abandon Mihailović and support Tito. This theory is quite wrong. In fact, Klugmann was never in a position to juggle with the intercepts.[3] When Deakin met Churchill in Cairo in January 1943 it was a purely social meeting at Churchill's invitation because of their personal friendship, and Deakin did not play any part in bringing Keble's report to Churchill's attention.[4]

Klugmann's membership of the Communist party and Basil Davidson's left-wing sympathies were much less important in influencing British policy towards Tito than the general leftist mood in Britain in 1943. The Soviet Union was Britain's ally, not her enemy; there were Labour ministers in the coalition government; the Labour movement and the trade unions, except for a small number of Trotskyists and Pacifists, enthusiastically supported the war. The Conservatives were discredited because the Conservative government of Baldwin and Neville Chamberlain had pursued a policy of appeasing Hitler and Mussolini against the strong opposition of the Labour party but with the support of the large majority of Conservative MPs, one of whom was now in prison, detained under Defence Regulation 18B as a Nazi sympathizer. In France and other European countries the right wing had welcomed the Germans, preferring them to the Communists, and were collaborating with the occupation forces. At a time when Hitler was calling on all the anti-Communists in Europe to follow him in a crusade against Bolshevism, Hitler's enemies naturally tended to sympathize with Communism.

It was not a question of a few corrupted fellow-travellers, but of a strong leftward swing of public opinion. Mildly left-wing sympathizers were to be found in SOE, in the BBC, and in many other institutions, including the wartime civil service. These people were not Communists, and would never have contemplated betraying their country by giving military information to the Soviet Union; but they were receptive to pro-Communist propaganda, they were inclined to believe what the Communists told them, they were ready to give the Communists the benefit of the doubt. It was different in the Foreign Office; there the diplomats carried on the old tradition of British foreign policy, and were hostile to Communists and the Soviet Union. Many of them sympathized with the policy of the Vatican under Pope Pius XII and with General Franco in Spain, though it would be a great exaggeration to say that they had pro-Fascist sympathies.

When the Germans invaded Norway and Denmark, and Belgium and Holland, and the Italians invaded Greece, Britain had immediately welcomed these countries as allies; but the Foreign Office did not wish to welcome the Soviet Union as an ally on 22 June 1941, when they heard of the German invasion of Russia, partly because of their anti-Communist prejudices, and partly because they did not wish to alienate anti-Bolshevik opinion in the neutral countries. The right-wing throughout Europe had welcomed the attack on the Soviet Union. In Madrid thousands of demonstrators had pledged their support for Hitler's crusade, and the government had called for volunteers to enlist in the Blue Division to fight in the German army on the Russian front.

On the evening of 22 June Churchill broadcast to the nation. He did not consult any of his ministers about his speech, or tell them in advance what he was intending to say. His secretary, John Colville, noted in his diary that Eden was worried because he 'wanted to vet the text, and couldn't'.[5] When he and the Foreign Office heard the broadcast, they were taken aback by Churchill's unequivocal support for the Soviet Union. 'No one has been a more consistent opponent of Communism than I have for the last twenty-five years. I will unsay no word that I have spoken about it. But all this fades away before the spectacle which is now unfolding. The past, with its crimes, its follies and its tragedies flashes away . . . We are resolved to destroy Hitler and every vestige of the Nazi regime . . . It follows therefore that we shall give whatever help we can to Russia and to the Russian people.'[6]

Eden and his under-secretary Viscount Cranborne (a Cecil and a true-blue Tory) were staying with Churchill at Chequers, and discussed the broadcast with Churchill later that same evening. They pointed out to Churchill that 'politically Russia was as bad as Germany and half the country would object to being associated with her too closely'. But Churchill took the view that 'Russia was now at war, innocent peasants were being slaughtered, and we should forget about Soviet systems or the Comintern and extend our hand to fellow human-beings in distress'. Colville recorded that 'the argument was brilliant and extremely vehement'.[7]

In Britain there was a spontaneous outburst of enthusiasm for the Soviet Union. Although the Red Army was in full retreat, they were acclaimed as heroes by the press and the BBC. Lord Beaverbrook's Conservative *Daily Express* was as enthusiastic as the left-wing Liberal *News Chronicle*. The commander-in-chief of the Red Army, Marshal Timoshenko, became the popular hero 'Timo', and Stalin was portrayed as a lovable 'Uncle Joe'. Russian clothes, Russian films and Russian music became fashionable; the radio constantly played Red Army marches and pop-songs about Uncle Joe. Department stores in Oxford Street in London flew the red flag with the sickle and hammer above the shop until the Soviet embassy indignantly protested that the stores had no right to fly the national flag of the Soviet Union. The diplomats in the Foreign Office, the red-tabbed generals in Whitehall and other members of the Establishment might believe that the Red Army would soon collapse and that Hitler would be in Moscow in no time; but they only whispered it in their clubs.

It was perhaps because Churchill was worried about the anti-Soviet feeling in these circles that he thought it necessary to give official encouragement to the enthusiasm for the Soviet Union. In November 1941 he invited John Platts-Mills to meet him in his room at the House of Commons. Platts-Mills was a left-wing barrister who did not hold a Communist party card, but invariably followed the party line. Churchill was in jovial mood. He said to Platts-Mills: 'For twenty-five years I have been telling the British people how terrible the Russians are, and I have no doubt I shall have to tell it to them again after the war; but now I want you to tell them how wonderful the Russians are.' He asked Platts-Mills to organize a great pro-Russian campaign in Britain. The government would provide him with all the money that he needed, and Mrs Churchill would be closely associated with the campaign. Churchill suggested that Dr Hewlett Johnson, the dean of Canterbury, should also take part; the dean, who had been labelled 'the Red Dean' in the Conservative press, was as close to the Communist party as Platts-Mills. Churchill told Platts-Mills not to be afraid that the press would denounce him as a Communist if he undertook this task; Churchill and the government would protect him from any criticism, and Mrs Churchill's participation would be enough to prevent this.[8]

Platts-Mills agreed to run the 'Aid for Russia' campaign with the Dean of Canterbury and Mrs Churchill, and it was a great success. The highlight of the campaign was when workers in the armaments factories were persuaded to work overtime to make a Spitfire fighter plane for Russia, and Mrs Churchill was photographed receiving the gift of the Spitfires in the factories. Lord Beaverbrook, whose newspapers had always denounced Communism, spoke at great pro-Soviet demonstrations organized by the Aid to Russia campaign, and warmly praised the Red Army, the Soviet Union and Stalin. At one of these demonstrations General Gough was on the platform. He had been a hate-figure to the leftists ever since he organized the 'Curragh Mutiny' in 1914 when army officers threatened to resign their commissions if they were ordered to suppress a right-wing rebellion in Ulster. But in 1942 the leftists in the audience in London cheered him loudly when he began his speech: 'Ladies and gentlemen, and may I say comrades?'[9]

In this climate of opinion it was easy to persuade the British public, the press, the BBC and even the civil servants that there were pro-Communist Partisans in Yugoslavia who were fighting the Germans more effectively than right-wing army officers and Chetniks. For a year after the Soviet Union entered the war the British, like the American, public believed that Mihailović and his Chetniks were great guerrilla fighters; but as soon as Radio Free Yugoslavia in Moscow denounced Mihailović as a traitor, the British public were prepared to believe this and to switch their affections to Tito. In October 1942 there was a noticeable change in the line put over in BBC broadcasts; they referred less and less to the Chetniks and more and more to the Partisans, giving Tito and the Partisans the credit for actions against the Germans.[10]

The report on the situation in Yugoslavia that Brigadier Keble wrote for Churchill on 30 January 1943 was very misleading. He wrote that Mihailović was holding down three German and six Bulgarian divisions, but that there were Partisan groups in Slovenia and Croatia who were engaging three German, nineteen Italian, six Croatian and three Hungarian divisions. Altogether, the guerrilla resistance was forcing the Germans to keep half a million men in

Yugoslavia.[11] Not only were these figures wildly wrong, but Keble did not know that the main force of the Partisans was with Tito in Bosnia. But the report was right in one respect: there were other resistance groups in Yugoslavia apart from Mihailović's Chetniks, and they were a bigger cause of worry to the Germans.

In September 1942 General Alexander, the supreme commander of the British forces in Egypt, sent a message to Mihailović asking him to blow up a bridge on the railway from Yugoslavia to Greece which the Germans were using to send supplies to Rommel's army in Africa. This would have been a help to the Allied cause in the days just before the Battle of El Alamein; but Mihailović did not blow up the bridge. He afterwards said that this was because the British had not sent him the explosives which he needed to do it.[12] He did start fighting against the Serbian Fascist supporters of the Germans, attacking both the followers of Ljotić and the Serbian regular army of the Nedić government. The Germans responded by executing Chetnik supporters in Belgrade and elsewhere;[13] but the German radio messages intercepted by British intelligence showed clearly that these minor actions by Mihailović did not compare with the preparations that the Germans had made for their Third Offensive against the Partisans in the summer of 1942.

SOE Cairo would have had even more reason to believe that the Partisans were doing more damage to the Germans than were the Chetniks if the British codebreakers had succeeded in breaking the Italian as well as the German ciphers; but as far as codes were concerned, the Italians were more efficient than the Germans, and their higher codes were almost unbreakable.[14] So SOE did not know what the Italian field commanders in Montenegro were reporting to their High Command during their campaign against the Partisans when the Chetniks were fighting on the Italian side.

Yugoslavia was not yet a major issue for the Allies. Churchill and Roosevelt did not discuss Yugoslavia at their meeting at Casablanca in January 1943. But when Churchill went on to Turkey to meet the Turkish prime minister at Adana to try to persuade him to enter the war on the Allied side, he told him about 'the highly hopeful resistance maintained both by General Mihailović in Serbia and the Partisans in Croatia and Slovenia'. He added that he was not afraid of Communism, and that Communism was being modified in Russia.[15]

After leaving Adana, Churchill spent a few days in Cairo, where he met his friend Deakin for a lunch.[16] He also met Keble, and read his report on Yugoslavia. He decided to send a British liaison officer to the Partisans in Croatia. There was to be no question of withdrawing British aid from Mihailović, let alone denouncing him as a traitor and a collaborator with the Germans and Italians; but a mission was to be sent to these other resistance groups in Croatia to see if they were worth helping.

Colonel Bailey had already been sent to Mihailović; he landed by parachute on Christmas Day 1942. He was not impressed by what he saw at Chetnik headquarters, for it was obvious to him that Mihailović was not prepared to take any action against the Germans for the time being. On 28 February 1943 Mihailović took Bailey to a typically Serbian christening party in the village of Donje Lipovo in Montenegro. After a great deal of plum brandy had been drunk, Mihailović made a speech to his Chetniks. He violently denounced the British for failing to send him arms and other supplies, and for abandoning the Serbs to their fate; the British were hoping to win the war at the expense of others, and to buy Serbian blood at the cost of a trivial supply of munitions. But nothing would divert the Serbs from their sworn and sacred duty to annihilate the Partisans. He ended by telling the guests his order of priorities. His enemies were the Ustashas, the Partisans, the Croats and the Muslims; when he had dealt with these, he would deal with the Germans and the Italians. Bailey was not pleased, and sent a report on the speech to Cairo.[17]

Mihailović had not engaged in any negotiations with the Germans since his first meeting with Matl in November 1941; but his subordinate commanders in Montenegro were constantly in touch with the Italians and sometimes combined with them in joint actions against the Partisans. In April 1942 the Italian governor of Montenegro attended the funeral in Cetinje of a Chetnik commander who had been killed fighting with the Italians against the Partisans. An Orthodox priest preached the sermon; he called on the spirit of St Sava, the patron saint of Serbia, to help the youth of Montenegro to 'shake off the poison of the most hellish social infection, Communism'.[18]

Mihailović sometimes reprimanded the Chetnik commanders who collaborated with the Italians; but he did not take any steps to stop this collaboration. He had received only one consignment of arms from the British, and nothing further since Hudson had advised Cairo to stop the deliveries in November 1941; so he felt quite justified in accepting arms from the Italians. He had no objection if, in order to obtain Italian arms, he had to help them fight the Partisans; he would use the arms against the Italians one day, when the Allies landed in Yugoslavia.

Hitler was annoyed that the Italians were helping the Chetniks, and in February 1943 raised the matter with Mussolini. He argued that although at present the Chetniks might be less of a menace than the Communists to the Axis forces in Yugoslavia, Mihailović and the Serbian nationalists were just as much their enemy, and were only waiting for an Allied landing to fight against the German and Italian troops with the weapons that Mussolini was sending them. 'If a landing takes place tomorrow, Duce, anywhere in the Balkans, then Communists, followers of Mihailović and all the other irregulars will be in accord on one thing: launching an immediate attack on the German or Italian armed forces (as the case may be) in support of the enemy landings. I consider it disastrous, Duce, that after we have conquered the whole area in battle, there should still exist armed and politically organized persons ready to turn against us in any emergency.'[19]

Mussolini reluctantly agreed to comply with Hitler's wishes, and in April 1943 the Italian High Command ordered their commanders in Montenegro to stop supplying the Chetniks with any more arms, and to take active steps to disarm them 'as soon as the Partisans have ceased to be a dangerous armed movement'.[20] This meant that the Italians would do nothing against the Chetniks for the time being, and local commanders continued unofficially to co-operate with them against the Partisans.

Tito from time to time entered into negotiations with the Germans to try to arrange an exchange of prisoners. In the summer of 1942 the Partisans captured Dr Ott, a German mining engineer who had been sent from Germany to help develop the mines in Yugoslavia for the benefit of the German war effort. Ott was very well treated by the Partisans, and at Tito's suggestion he wrote to the Germans and arranged a series of meetings between comparatively junior German commanders and Tito's envoys. On several occasions an exchange was agreed.[21] The Germans were usually prepared to release several Partisans in exchange for a German officer held by the Partisans; but occasionally a prominent Communist was set free in exchange for several German prisoners.

Tito managed to persuade the Germans and the Ustashas to free Andrija Hebrang as part of an exchange. Hebrang had come to the fore in the Croatian Communist party in the years before the war, and when the Germans invaded, he stayed behind in Zagreb to organize the underground resistance. He unwisely lived in the same villa just outside Zagreb as a Russian spy and his wife. The Russian had been sent by the Soviet government to obtain military information and transmit it to Moscow. It was a breach of the security precautions of the Communist underground movement for Hebrang to stay in the Russian's house, and it had consequences which Hebrang should have foreseen. When Pavelić's secret police tracked down the Russian spy and raided his home, they caught Hebrang too. Hebrang was shot in the face when the police broke in. According to the Communists, he resisted arrest by firing at the police, who fired back and wounded him; the police version was that Hebrang shot himself in a suicide attempt. He was rushed to a prison hospital and after he had recovered he was imprisoned in a concentration camp, though the Communists had expected that he would be executed. He was exchanged for Ustasha and German prisoners of the Partisans in 1942.[22]

On 17 January 1943 the British intercepted and decoded a message sent by the German army in Yugoslavia which showed that the Germans were preparing to launch Operation *Weiss* (White).[23] This was the code name for the operation which the Partisans called the Fourth Offensive. Two German, four Italian and two Ustasha divisions were to attack the Partisans at Bihać from the north. The Partisans would only be able to escape by crossing the River Neretva; but across the Neretva were the Chetniks, who would certainly take the opportunity to attack the retreating Partisans, although there was no collaboration between the Germans and the Chetniks. Mihailović was preparing to attack the Partisans. He had recently told his Chetniks: 'Now is the time to beat the Communists to their knees.'[24]

Tito was worried. Typhus had broken out among the Partisans; hundreds of them had caught it. There would also be the wounded, for casualties were sure to be heavy when the German planes began bombing them. He was alarmed at the prospect of evacuating his sick and wounded across the Neretva under the fire of the Germans behind them and the Chetniks in front of them.[25] He decided to try to arrange a truce with the Germans which would leave him free to cross the Neretva and attack the Chetniks without being attacked by the Germans.

Tito did not consult anyone before reaching his decision. Early in March 1943 he revealed his plan to Djilas, Ranković and Pijade. A German officer who had been captured by the Partisans would be sent back to the Germans with a letter proposing a meeting to arrange for the exchange of prisoners; then, when Tito's representatives met the Germans, they would propose another meeting with higher-ranking German officers and offer the truce. Tito would send Djilas, Koča Popović and Velebit to meet the Germans. Djilas was a member of the Politburo; Koča Popović was the commander of the élite unit of the Partisans, the First Proletarian Brigade; and Velebit would go as the interpreter, because he spoke perfect German. He was also a lawyer, with a knowledge of international law, and would be useful in drafting a treaty.

Tito's colleagues were a little taken aback at his proposal. Djilas asked: 'What will the Russians say?' 'Well, *they* think first of their own people,' said Tito.[26]

After contact had been made with the Germans by couriers with white flags passing between the lines, Djilas, Koča Popović and Velebit met the German Lieutenant-General Dippold on 11 March in a cottage in the village of Gornji Vakuf.[27] Dippold did not shake hands with them, but with formal courtesy invited them to be seated on the other side of a simple wooden table. When he had heard their proposals, he said that he had no power to negotiate with them, but sent them on to Sarajevo and from there to Zagreb. In Zagreb they met General Glaise von Horstenau, an Austrian general whose ancestors had fought in the Seven Years' War, under Radetzky, and at Solferino. He himself had served in the First World War and had been in the Austrian delegation that negotiated with Trotsky at the peace talks at Brest-Litovsk in 1918. He later joined the Austrian Nazis, and welcomed the Germans when they marched into Austria; but he remained in essence an aristocratic officer of the old Austrian army, and did not approve of the policy of shooting hostages in Yugoslavia. He was favourably impressed when Velebit told him, in excellent German with an Austrian accent, that his father had been a general in the 'k.*und k.*' (imperial and royal Austro-Hungarian) army. Velebit explained that he had joined the Partisans only because he was afraid of being arrested if he remained in Zagreb; but here Velebit was misleading the Nazi general.

The two sides reached agreement on the exchange of prisoners: nine German soldiers would be released in exchange for seventeen

Partisan prisoners in Ustasha concentration camps. Herta Haas was to be one of the Partisans to be exchanged; Tito had told his envoys to do everything possible to obtain her release. Ott wondered why the Partisans were so insistent that Herta should be included in the list; but he understood when Djilas told him that she was the girl friend of one of the Partisan generals.[28]

They then discussed the Partisans' proposal for a truce. The Partisans said that they regarded the Chetniks as their main enemy, and did not wish to fight against the Germans unless the Germans attacked them, as they thought that there was no reason why the Germans and the Partisans should fight each other.[29] They offered to suspend the sabotage operations against the Zagreb–Belgrade railway which were being carried out by the Partisans in Croatia, if the Germans would call off the Fourth Offensive and not attack them along the Neretva. Horstenau asked them what the Partisans would do if the British and American forces landed in Yugoslavia. The Partisan envoys said that if the British landed without first having reached an agreement with them, they would fight against any British attempt to impose a government on them. Horstenau then asked if they would issue a public declaration repudiating their alliance with Britain, the United States and the Soviet Union; but the Partisans would not agree to this.

At the end of the talks, the Germans said that they would consider the Partisans' proposals. It is not surprising that there was a certain amount of misunderstanding between the two sides, especially as the Partisans were obviously happy that there should be a misunderstanding. They seem to have misled the Germans to some extent. The Germans believed that the Partisans were less hostile to them than they really were, and even thought that the Partisans would agree to fight on their side against the Allies; but the Partisans did not go as far as this.

After the talks had finished, the Germans allowed the Partisan envoys to wander around Zagreb. Koča Popović went back to the Partisan army, but Djilas and Velebit spent a few days visiting their friends in Zagreb, going to the cinema, and noticing that the women were wearing their skirts five centimetres (two inches) shorter than before the war.[30] They had rejoined Tito by 30 March. The greatest hazard which they encountered on their mission was returning to their own lines without being shot by the Partisan sentries.[31]

Horstenau wished to accept the Partisans' proposals. So did the

German ambassador to Pavelić's government, Siegfried Kasche, although he was a Nazi and a member of the SS. He believed that they could trust the Partisans, because they had always waged war honourably and had not ill-treated their prisoners. He pointed out to Berlin that it would be a great blow to the morale of the Allies and all resistance groups in Yugoslavia if Tito and his Partisans gave up the struggle against the Germans.[32] But Hitler flatly rejected the proposal. 'One does not negotiate with rebels,' he said. 'Rebels are to be shot.'[33]

On 21 April Ribbentrop wrote to Kasche explaining why the Partisans' proposals for a truce must be rejected. It would be impossible for the Germans to come to an agreement with the Partisans just after they had persuaded Mussolini to abandon his policy of making agreements with the Chetniks. 'I must point out that it is not for us to play off the Chetniks and the Partisans against each other by clever tactics, but to destroy them both.'[34]

But the exchange of prisoners duly went ahead. When the exchanged Partisans reached Tito's camp, they were warmly welcomed by their comrades; but Herta Haas was very put out to find Zdenka living with Tito. She avoided seeing Tito as much as possible, and spent much of her time with her old friend Velebit. She served with the main force of the Partisans throughout the arduous campaigns of the summer of 1943, but in November arranged to be transferred to the Partisan units in Slovenia. She did this in order to get away from Tito and Zdenka.[35]

Tito informed the Comintern that he had sent representatives to meet the Germans. He probably realized that they would find out about it; British intelligence discovered it in April through the German intercepts.[36] But he told the Comintern only that there had been an agreement with the Germans for an exchange of prisoners. He did not mention that he had offered to make a truce and to call off sabotage operations against the Zagreb–Belgrade railway.

The agreement for an exchange of prisoners was enough to annoy the Comintern. They sent a message to Tito expressing surprise that he was prepared to enter into negotiations on any matter with the German Fascists. Tito resented the criticism, after the Comintern had failed to send him any material help. He radioed to Moscow: 'If you cannot help us, then at least do not hinder us.'[37]

The Partisans, having crossed the Neretva under heavy German attacks, could now concentrate on fighting against the Chetniks in Montenegro. Tito ordered them to fight the Chetniks, not the Germans. 'On your way, do not fight the Germans,' he told them. 'Your most important task at this moment is to ... annihilate the Chetniks of Draža Mihailović' because they were the greatest danger to the development of the national liberation struggle.[38] The Chetniks retreated before the Partisan advance; but they captured some of the wounded stragglers in the Partisan army, and tortured them before they killed them. Some of the Partisans were slaughtered in the tra-ditional Chetnik way. Each was forced to lie on the ground with his head on a stone like a pig being prepared for slaughter. Then one of the Chetniks cut his throat.[39]

The British decided to send a military mission to the Partisans to find out what they were doing against the Germans. They suggested to the Soviet government that a joint Anglo-Soviet mission should be sent; but as the Russians showed no interest in the idea, the British decided to act on their own.[40] Captain Jones was sent to the Partisans in Croatia, accompanied by a number of Canadian Croats, most of whom were Communists. Captain Stuart, Captain Deakin and four other men were to be dropped by parachute near Tito's headquarters in Montenegro.

Before they arrived, the Germans had launched another offensive, Operation *Schwarz* (Black) against the Partisans. The Fifth Offensive began on 15 May 1943. More than 100,000 German and other Axis troops took part, for the German High Command were determined to carry out Hitler's orders and destroy once and for all the 20,000 Partisans who had now joined Tito's main army in Bosnia. Their plan was to surround the Partisans, and having prevented their escape, to exterminate them, taking no prisoners but killing them all. As the Germans advanced and the attacks from the air began, Tito realized that his only chance of escape was to cross the River Sutjeska and to escape to the south before the net closed. But he did not wish to leave before the British mission arrived. It was important that the British should see for themselves how he was fighting the Germans.

The greatest problem was the wounded and the typhus patients. Tito issued the order: 'Do not leave any wounded comrade behind.'[41] But it was difficult to move the seriously wounded, though this task was given first priority. Tito ordered the Agitprop personnel to stop their propaganda activities for the time being, and to help the medical staff to care for and transport the wounded and the sick. There were not enough carts in which to carry the patients, and it was often impossible to drive carts up and down the steep mountain paths through the forests along the Sutjeska. The Partisans placed the wounded on horses; one comrade led the horse and another held the patient in position on the horse's back.

But there was a shortage of horses, for the Germans, knowing that the Partisans needed them, had slaughtered the horses in the neighbourhood. So a wounded Partisan had to be carried by two of his comrades, one holding his feet and the other his shoulders, as they moved forward very slowly through the forests and across the mountains being bombed continually from the air by more than twenty aircraft. The Partisans had no defences against air attack except the trees in the forests which hid them from the view of the bomber crews.[42]

Tito was in a cheerful mood, or at least maintained the morale of his men by appearing to be cheerful. He was confident that the Partisans would survive the Fifth Offensive, and was making his plans for the future. On 24 May he met Dedijer, who was helping move the wounded. Tito told him that as the Partisans were now becoming a regular army, he had decided to introduce military ranks among them; and he told him that the English were sending a military mission which would land by parachute next day. He then discussed with Dedijer the news which had been received from Moscow by radio a few days before: the Comintern had been dissolved without any warning or any consultation with the Communist parties who belonged to it, by a decision of the twelve members of the Presidium of the Executive Committee in Moscow. Tito said that he was pleased at the decision. It would deprive Hitler of the argument that the Comintern was instigating revolution everywhere. 'Besides, the Communist parties themselves will now show more initiative.'[43]

Even at the height of the fighting on the Sutjeska, Tito had not forgotten the struggle with the fractionalists in the party in pre-war days, and was as careful not to run unnecessary risks as he had been when he waited so long in Istanbul till he was satisfied with his forged passport. He discovered that Mladen Čaldarović, who had been expelled from the party as a dissident in 1937, had joined the Partisans and was working under Djilas with Agitprop on the headquarters battalion. Tito was prepared to let Čaldarović join the Partisans, but would not run the risk of having him so near his headquarters, and moved him to other duties.[44]

Dedijer prepared to welcome the British mission. He wrote in his diary on 24 May: 'The Old Man says we must set off for the Piva as soon as possible, but the arrival of the English mission is holding us back. If it were not for this we would have left several days ago.' The British mission did not arrive next day. Bad weather made it necessary for them to postpone their flight from North Africa to Montenegro. 'We haven't had any luck,' wrote Dedijer on 25 May, 'when we needed sunshine, it rained. Consequently the English did not come tonight.' Nor did they come on 26 May, when Dedijer wrote: 'We must abandon the Piva as soon as possible. Every hour wasted costs us dearly. But we cannot leave here until the English mission arrives.'[45] They arrived on the night of 27–28 May, landing in a small field not far from Tito's headquarters in the early hours of the morning, and were taken by the welcoming party to Tito.[46]

Twenty-four years later, after some Yugoslav writers had blamed the British mission for delaying the Partisans' retreat by their late arrival, Tito assured Deakin that this was untrue, and that he had not been forced to alter his plans because the British did not arrive until 28 May.[47] But there is no doubt that Tito delayed his own departure and was the last to leave the area with his headquarters staff because he waited for the arrival of the British, and that he was prepared to take the additional risk of being captured by the Germans in order to make sure that British officers were present during the Fifth Offensive and saw with their own eyes how he was fighting the Germans. He realized how important this was to his cause and to the future course of events in Yugoslavia. Arguments about whether the intercepts proved that Partisans or Chetniks were the more valuable ally for the British would count for very little after Deakin had reported that he had himself seen the Partisans in action against 100,000 German soldiers and aircraft.

The five weeks of the Battle of the Sutjeska and the Fifth Offensive were the greatest ordeal that the Partisans had to endure during the Second World War. Every day the German attacks and air raids continued, and the Partisans' casualties increased. As always in their campaigns, the women played their part at the side of the men. Many of them were university students from wealthy middle-class families, the daughters of King Alexander's Cabinet ministers, of higher civil servants and of leading figures in Belgrade and Zagreb society. Some of them had visited these same forests and mountains a few years earlier on happy summer holidays with their parents or boy friends.[48]

Dedijer's wife Olga, the daughter of a very wealthy family in Zemun, had just qualified as a surgeon. She worked incessantly with the medical teams during the Fifth Offensive, but was herself wounded by a bomb during an air attack. She carried on with the others for nine days, sometimes riding on horseback and sometimes walking. Then her colleagues realized that they would have to amputate her arm, but the operation came too late. Dedijer was with her when she died on a forest path. They buried her there in an unmarked grave, like so many other Partisans.[49]

On 9 June Tito was with Stuart and Deakin and his headquarters staff, emerging from the trees into a clearing in the forest, when some German planes flew low overhead and released their bombs. A fragment struck Stuart in the head and killed him. The commander of Tito's bodyguard, who had fought for two years in Spain, was also killed. Deakin was wounded in the leg. Tito had thrown himself on the ground, like a trained soldier, at the approach of the bomber plane, and his Alsatian dog, Luks, threw himself across Tito's body to protect him. A bomb splinter wounded Tito in his left arm just above the elbow. Another splinter struck and killed Luks. It would have struck Tito in the neck had not Luks been lying on him, so the dog saved Tito's life.[50]

Ranković took charge, and impressed Deakin by his coolness and efficiency in the emergency.[51] At first the doctors were worried about Tito's wound, for he developed a high temperature; but he was able to continue directing operations throughout. For some days he had his arm in a sling, but soon recovered from the wound.

The majority of the Partisans escaped from the German encirclement. One night Deakin and his party passed through a gap between the Germans who were just over half a mile from them on one side and 500 yards on the other, and the ring closed fifteen minutes later.[52] The Germans were convinced that they had trapped Tito. On 10 June General Lüters, who was in command of the Fifth Offensive, radioed: 'Strong enemy forces hemmed into very narrow area in Sutjeska-Piva, among them the presence of Tito is for certain confirmed . . . The hour of the complete destruction of the Tito army has come.'[53] But Tito had got away. Some of the Partisan rearguard and many of the wounded were trapped. They were shot by the Germans, who sent patrols to find and kill all the Partisans who were hiding in villages, forests and caves in the area, and burned fifty villages in the district.[54]

The Germans soon realized that they had not caught Tito in the ring around the Sutjeska. In July 1943 they issued a reward of 100,000 German Reichsmarks for his capture. They printed posters, with his photograph, in Serbo-Croat, in the Latin alphabet for Croatia and the Cyrillic for Serbia, and fixed the posters to the walls in cities, towns and villages. The people were informed about the wickedness of Josip Broz, who called himself Tito. 'In the Spanish Civil War and in Soviet Russia he was trained in the manner of the GPU in all matters of terror, and bestial destruction of people, and in every kind of desecration of every sense of decency.'[55] A similar reward of 100,000 Reichsmarks was issued for Mihailović.[56]

In the summer of 1943 King Victor Emanuel of Italy arrested Mussolini and signed an armistice with the Allies. As Italian resistance ceased, there was a rush by the Allies and the Germans, in Italy and in the Italian-occupied territories, to seize the Italian arms and to occupy the strong-points that their armies had held. In Dalmatia and Montenegro the Partisans managed to get hold of most of the arms. The Italian surrender led to an uprising in Dalmatia, which became one of the strongest centres of Partisan activity. But the Germans immediately launched their Sixth Offensive against the Partisans, for they were determined to control the coast before the British and American armies could land there. They succeeded in recapturing Split, Dubrovnik and the coastal area, and all the Yugoslav islands in the Adriatic except Vis.

Some of the Italian soldiers deserted to the Partisans. They were not the only foreigners serving with Tito, for a number of Czech, Polish, Hungarian, Bulgarian and Austrian Communists and leftists had somehow managed to escape from German-occupied Europe and reach the territory which he held. But after 1943 there were more Italians than foreigners of any other nationality with the Partisans.[57] They called their unit the 'Garibaldi Brigade'. Those who were captured by the Germans were invariably shot. Some were imprisoned in a barn on the island of Hvar during the night before their execution. One of them wrote on the wall of their prison: 'Mussolini, the traitor of Europe, will one day meet with justice at the hands of the people.'[58]

In the autumn, Tito attended the second congress of the Croatian Anti-Fascist Youth. Milka Kufrin had become the president of the organization. She chose a member of the Executive Committee to make the speech welcoming Tito; but when he arrived, he recognized her, and insisted that she make the welcoming speech. 'I want to find out if you have learned how to speak,' he told her. He discovered that she could now speak as well as fight.[59]

❖

CHAPTER 17

Fitzroy Maclean

AFTER Deakin's reports on the Fifth Offensive had reached Cairo and London, the Allies could have no doubt that it was worth their while to send military aid to Tito, though they had not yet decided to stop aid to Mihailović. Churchill decided to send Fitzroy Maclean to Tito. Maclean was the perfect choice for the mission. The son of a Highland military family, he had joined the diplomatic corps and had served at the British embassy in Moscow during Stalin's Great Purge. He had attended Bukharin's trial, and had tried unsuccessfully to raise with the Soviet Foreign Office the case of British subjects who had gone to the Soviet Union as enthusiastic Communists and were then arrested and shot as Trotskyists and spies. One evening he took an attractive Russian girl out to dinner in Moscow. A few days later she was arrested for having been in contact with a foreign spy, and disappeared. These experiences left Maclean very hostile to the Soviet regime. After the Hitler–Stalin Pact he wrote a memorandum for the Foreign Office in which he suggested that the British Air Force should bomb the Soviet oilfields in the Caucasus in order to check the Soviet threat to the British Empire in Asia.[1]

In 1941 Maclean wished to volunteer for the army. As the Foreign Office would not release him he resigned from the diplomatic service to stand for the House of Commons at one of the uncontested by-elections which took place in wartime under the party political truce. Having been elected an MP, he joined the army and after being posted to Cairo took part in several daring Commando raids behind enemy lines. Churchill knew that he would have the necessary physical stamina and courage for a military mission in enemy-occupied territory, and the political knowledge required to assess the situation in Yugoslavia. He had the prestige of being an MP; and as he was very anti-Communist, there was no danger of his being duped into supporting the Communists in Yugoslavia.

Churchill insisted that Maclean, who was a captain in the army, should be rapidly promoted in the course of a few weeks to the rank of brigadier to give him the proper military status for his mission. He invited Maclean to Chequers on 29 July 1943 to receive his instructions. Maclean said to Churchill that he understood that Tito and his Partisans were Communists and that if they were successful they would probably make Yugoslavia a Communist state; and he asked Churchill how the British government would view such a development. Churchill said that as long as the threat of Nazi Germany remained, we could not afford to consider questions of long-term policy. Maclean's only duty in Yugoslavia would be to discover who was killing most Germans and to suggest how we could help them to kill more.[2]

Maclean landed by parachute in Bosnia on 17 September and was taken to Tito's headquarters. The moment he saw Tito he formed a favourable impression of him, for he was different from the Communist officials whom Maclean had met in Moscow. Tito was prepared to speak frankly and to take decisions, unlike the Moscow Communists who were always referring to higher authority; and unlike them, he had a sense of humour. Like so many other people who met Tito, Maclean was impressed by his powerful personality and by his blue eyes; and though Maclean found him a little quiet and shy when they began their conversation, he thought this an endearing quality. He was obviously impressed by Tito, because he at once thought of Napoleon's maxim: 'In war, it is not men but the man who counts.'[3]

They spoke to each other in German. Maclean and Tito both spoke German and Russian, but Maclean thought that he spoke better German than Tito did, while Tito spoke better Russian than he did, so Maclean chose German as their language.[4] Tito told him about his early life and his meetings with Mihailović in 1941. They talked about King Peter, and Tito said that the question of the future of the monarch would have to be decided by the people after the war. Maclean said that he thought that the Partisans were rather hard on King Peter, and asked if they would accept King Peter if he wished to come and fight for the Partisans. This idea amused Tito. He said that King Peter's presence might help the Partisan cause in Serbia, but not in Croatia, where the Karadjordjević dynasty was unpopular.

Maclean then turned the conversation to politics. He said that he was a Conservative, and Tito said that he was a Communist. Maclean asked Tito if he wished to make Yugoslavia Communist after the war. Tito said that he did, but that it might have to be a gradual process; for the moment, the movement he was leading was a People's Front, not a one-party Communist movement. Maclean asked if the new Yugoslavia which the Partisans would establish would be an independent state or part of the Soviet Union. 'You must remember', said Tito, 'the sacrifices which we are making in this struggle for our independence. Hundreds of thousands of Yugoslavs have suffered torture and death, men, women and children . . . You need not suppose that we shall lightly cast aside a prize which has been won at such cost.'[5]

Less than three weeks after this conversation between Maclean and Tito, another conversation took place between Deakin and Velebit. They discussed the future of Yugoslavia after the war. 'The Partisan leadership', said Velebit, 'has no plan or intention of immediate social revolution. The prime object is the reconstruction of the country after the war, and it is realized that a revolutionary programme would cause an internal struggle which would fatally weaken the country.'[6] This statement was very much stronger than what Tito said to Maclean, and it is interesting that Tito should have been more revealing than Velebit was to Deakin about the Communists' intentions in Yugoslavia after the war. But Velebit believed that he was speaking the truth. He was a member of the Communist party, but was not in any position of authority in the party. He did not know what Tito's political intentions really were, and repeated what he personally thought was the party line.[7] Tito was intelligent enough to realize that he could not get away with this when he talked to Maclean. A frank admission that he, as a Communist, aimed eventually at a Communist Yugoslavia was more likely to make a favourable impression on Maclean. His qualification that it might not be possible to introduce Communism immediately was the most that Maclean would be prepared to believe.

This was the beginning of a lifelong friendship between Tito and Maclean, between these two men with their very different backgrounds and opinions. They established a link which has often existed between *Realpolitiker* of opposite viewpoints, between Communist and Conservative, ever since Engels went foxhunting with the Tory squires in Lancashire and told them how much he admired the Duke of Wellington. Maclean regarded Tito as a 'soldier of the revolution';[8] and as an army officer, a Conservative MP, and a member of a Highland clan, he could understand much better than a Social-Democratic journalist or a Liberal university professor how Tito could serve his country, the Soviet Union, and his leader Stalin even when he did not approve of what they were doing.

After Maclean had spent seven weeks with Tito, he wrote a report to Churchill.[9] He recommended that Britain should send as much military aid as possible to Tito and stop all aid to Mihailović. This was going further than anyone had so far suggested, and conflicted with Foreign Office policy. Mihailović was the minister for defence in King Peter's government which Britain recognized as the government of Yugoslavia; to repudiate Mihailović would embarrass British relations with King Peter as well as conflicting with the anti-Communist feelings of many officials in the British Foreign Office.

Maclean's memorandum of 6 November 1943 has been criticized in recent years by sympathizers with Mihailović, who blame the British government for switching support from Mihailović to Tito, thus making it possible for Tito to introduce Communism into Yugoslavia. They consider that Maclean's memorandum was responsible for this, and that Maclean was deceived by Tito into believing that the Partisans were killing many more Germans than they really were. It is true that the figures which Maclean gave in the report greatly exaggerated the number of German divisions which were engaged in fighting the Partisans; like all members of British intelligence, Maclean accepted the figure of thirty divisions engaged in Yugoslavia which had first been given by King Peter's government. But Maclean was certainly right in stating that the Partisans were fighting and killing more Germans than Mihailović. The Chetniks' occasional skirmishes with the followers of Ljotić and Nedić could not compare with the Partisans' battles against the Germans during the six German offensives.

But there was another reason why Maclean urged the British government to abandon Mihailović. The Partisans were so strong 'that nothing short of armed intervention will prevent them from taking power in Yugoslavia as soon as the Germans are finally driven out. Furthermore, they can count on the powerful backing of our Soviet allies.' If Britain supported Mihailović, who was 'Pan-Serb, anti-Croat, and violently reactionary', this would drive the Partisans to the conclusion 'that the Soviet Union is their only friend'; but by abandoning Mihailović, 'we should establish Anglo-Yugoslav relations on a firm basis which would do much to consolidate our position in the Balkans after the war'.

Churchill had probably already decided to abandon Mihailović before he read Maclean's memorandum. He took the opposite line about Greece, although the situations in Greece and in Yugoslavia were very similar. King George of Greece, like King Alexander of Yugoslavia, had established a dictatorship before the war; he appointed General Metaxas to be military dictator of Greece in 1936. Under Metaxas, Communists were arrested and tortured as they were under King Alexander in Yugoslavia. When Mussolini invaded Greece in 1940, and Greece entered the war on the side of Britain, the Greek Communists denounced it as an imperialist war; but after the Soviet Union was invaded, the Communists organized a resistance movement against the Germans.

In Greece, like in Yugoslavia, there were two resistance movements, one royalist and one Communist. General Zervas organized the EDES guerrillas in support of King George's government in exile in Cairo. The Communists formed a National Democratic Front (EAM), which was controlled by the Communists; and Communist partisans, the ELAS, carried on guerrilla warfare in the mountains of northern Greece. In the autumn of 1942 the British dropped a military mission in Greece and invited EDES and ELAS to unite under the command of the British officers. ELAS agreed to do so, and helped a British military unit to blow up an important railway bridge in northern Greece on the line which the Germans used to send supplies to North Africa.[10]

The peace settlement of 1919 had divided Macedonia between Yugoslavia, Greece and Bulgaria; but Hitler gave all Macedonia to Bulgaria, and Bulgarian troops occupied the country. After Germany invaded the Soviet Union, the Macedonian Communists organized a resistance movement against the Bulgarian forces. Tito sent his General Tempo to lead the revolt in Macedonia. The Macedonian Communists drove the Bulgarian army units over the frontier into Greece, and Tempo, pursuing them, linked up with the ELAS guerrillas before returning to Yugoslavia and rejoining Tito in Bosnia, after fighting the Italians in Montenegro.[11]

Tito advised the Greek Communists to refuse to place the ELAS forces under British command; they should operate independently against the Germans in Greece, and should work closely together with his Yugoslav Partisans.[12] ELAS continued to serve under the British, but the EAM political leaders denounced King George and his government in Cairo. The British invited representatives of ELAS to Cairo to hold talks with the Greek government; but the talks broke down because the British insisted on ELAS agreeing to obey the king and his government.[13]

The commander of the British units working with ELAS in Greece, Colonel Myers, was sympathetic to ELAS because he was favourably impressed by their fighting qualities. In the summer of 1943 he was recalled to London to report on the situation, and saw Eden at the Foreign Office and King George VI.[14] On 2 October he was invited to visit Churchill at Chequers. There was an informal gathering at Chequers: Churchill's brother was there; he had never played any part in politics or in public life.

After lunch Churchill discussed the situation in Greece with Myers. He listened courteously as Myers argued the case in favour of ELAS, but he refused to make any concessions to them. He said that he would not be imposed upon by the 'Wintringhams', and would not give in to the Greek Communists.[15] He was referring to the prominent English Communist leader, Tom Wintringham, who had been sentenced to six months' imprisonment at the Old Bailey in London in 1925 for inciting soldiers to mutiny, and later commanded the British battalion in the International Brigade in the Spanish Civil War. Wintringham became an expert in Spain in street fighting against tanks. In 1940 he was not allowed to join the British army or the Home Guard because he was a Communist; so he wrote articles for the press and a paperback book on street fighting, and army officers bought the book so that they could pass on Wintringham's experience to their men.

In Churchill's eyes, there were good and bad revolutionaries. Tom Wintringham, like the 'ogre of Europe', Trotsky, was a bad revolutionary. But Churchill had always admired Garibaldi; when he was a young man he had thought of writing a biography of Garibaldi, but instead wrote a novel, *Savrola*, in which the hero is a romantic revolutionary leader. He became very friendly with Michael Collins, the founder of the IRA, when Collins came to London to negotiate the Irish treaty in 1921, at a time when Conservative politicians and army generals were saying that negotiating with Collins was 'shaking hands with murder'. He had also enjoyed meeting the Russian terrorist, Boris Savinkov.[16] In the summer of 1943 he was adding Tom

Wintringham and the Greek Communists to his list of bad revolutionaries; but he was beginning to regard Tito as a good, romantic revolutionary.

But Churchill's policy towards Greece and Yugoslavia was decided not by his likes and dislikes for revolutionary heroes and villains but by his assessment of British national interests. He wished to collaborate with the Soviet Union against Germany and hoped he could do a satisfactory deal with Stalin. When he met Stalin in Moscow in 1942 he liked him, and thought that they could reach an agreement about Europe based on a recognition of British and Russian national interests. In the summer of 1943 he was already thinking of a settlement along the lines which he proposed to Stalin in October 1944 – that the Soviet Union should control Romania, that Britain should control Greece, and that they share influence in Yugoslavia on a fifty-fifty basis.[17]

When Churchill met Stalin and Roosevelt in Teheran in November 1943 he was full of enthusiasm for Tito, and proposed that the Allies should give Tito wholehearted support. Roosevelt was not very interested, and Stalin minimized the importance of Tito's achievements. When Churchill said that Tito's 'stalwarts' were holding down thirty German divisions in Yugoslavia, Stalin said that his information was that there were only seven German divisions in Yugoslavia. Stalin's figures were accurate. Churchill again got on well with Stalin at Teheran. When he proposed Stalin's health at a dinner, he said that Stalin should be ranked with the great heroes of Russian history and had earned the title of 'Stalin the Great'. He also proposed a toast to 'the proletarian masses'. Stalin replied by proposing a toast to the Conservative party.[18]

While the 'Big Three' were meeting in Teheran, Tito was addressing the second national conference of AVNOJ at Jajce in Bosnia, a year almost to the day after he had spoken at the conference at Bihać when AVNOJ was formed. At Jajce he took the step that the Comintern had dissuaded him from taking at Bihać, and called on AVNOJ to form a provisional government of Yugoslavia. The Comintern was no longer in existence and events had moved on a long way in the past twelve months.

In his opening speech at the conference on 29 November 1943 Tito began by asking why the Germans had been able to overrun Yugoslavia so quickly in 1941. It was because of 'the twenty years of oppression of the nations of Yugoslavia, such as the Croats, Macedonians, Slovenes and others by a handful of Pan-Serbian hegemonists', plus the corruption of the ruling class. 'The German and Italian conquerors brought to power the bloody Ustasha beasts in Croatia and the despicable traitor Nedić in Serbia,' and the massacres of the entire Serbian population in Croatia and Bosnia took place. In this difficult situation 'there was only one organization in our country that had for twenty years been outlawed and persecuted by all the regimes in Yugoslavia which placed all its experience and organizing abilities, all its tried fighters, at the service of its enslaved peoples. The Communist Party alone led the people to armed uprising.'

Now victory over Hitler, 'this greatest enemy of mankind', was not far off, thanks to the glorious Red Army and the victory of Great Britain and the United States in North Africa, Sicily and Italy. It was therefore time for the people of Yugoslavia to consider the question of the future government of their country. They did not want the monarchy back, because 'the monarchy has been the sponsor of Pan-Serbian hegemony and the oppression of other nations'. King Alexander had introduced a military dictatorship in 1929, and King Peter was still supporting 'that most contemptible traitor Draža Mihailović' who was fighting on the side of the Germans and Italians. So AVNOJ must declare itself to be the provisional government of Yugoslavia after the war.

Having opened his speech by claiming that only the Communist party had led the armed uprising against the invaders, he afterwards warned his audience that the invaders, the Ustashas and the Chetniks were saying 'that the struggle for national liberation in Yugoslavia has been a purely Communist affair' and 'is an attempt by the Communists to seize power, to abolish private ownership, and to destroy the Church and religion and culture'. But this was a lie propagated by Goebbels. The aim of the Partisans was 'to realize the national aspirations of the Yugoslav people for a free, genuinely democratic, fraternal and federal Yugoslavia'.[19]

The conference proclaimed that AVNOJ was the provisional government of Yugoslavia under the presidency of Dr Ivan Ribar, who had for many years been a prominent liberal politician in Croatia; his son, Lola Ribar, was the leader of the Communist Youth. The conference also promoted Josip Broz Tito to the rank of Marshal of Yugoslavia.

Tito developed his ideas about postwar Yugoslavia in an article which he wrote for a Partisan periodical *New Yugoslavia* which was published on 1 March 1944.[20] He wrote about the terrible housing conditions in Yugoslavia which were due not only to the great destruction of houses during the war but also to the neglect of the housing problem by the monarchy and the prewar governments. After the war rehousing the people would be a first priority for the government of the new Yugoslavia. He appealed to all Yugoslavs who were fighting on the side of the invader to join the Partisans. This was their last chance. Those who continued to serve in the invader's armies would be punished. There was still much to be discussed about the future government of Yugoslavia. 'The issue of federation at present is only a word to many citizens of our country'; but this was a strong enough hint to win the support of the nations in Yugoslavia who resented Serbian domination.

Some of the Partisans resented Tito's offer of an amnesty to the traitors who joined him now before it was too late. The Partisans in Bosnia remembered that the Serbian Chetniks had murdered thousands of Muslim men, women and children, throwing their corpses into the River Drina; how could they accept the killers as their allies? But Tito, as always, was a realist; it would cost a great deal in effort and lives to exterminate all the Chetniks, and it would be advantageous if many of them came over to his side. The Bosnian Partisan, Zulsikarpašić, told Tito that his mind boggled at the thought of welcoming the Chetniks who had committed such crimes; but shrugged off his objections.[21]

Captain Deakin and the members of the British mission had been in the visitors' gallery at the Jajce conference, and a report of Tito's speech was sent to Churchill; but although the British government, and especially the Foreign Office, did not approve of Tito's criticism of King Peter, this did not deter Churchill from following Maclean's advice to send all possible aid to Tito and none to Mihailović. In January 1944 Churchill passed through Cairo on his way home from Teheran, and met Maclean, who reported to him on his mission to Tito. Maclean found Churchill in a villa near the Pyramids, in bed, and smoking a cigar.

Maclean repeated his advice to help Tito and not Mihailović, but said that he thought that the prime minister should clearly understand that Tito was a Communist, and that however much he might talk at the moment about democracy and a People's Front, he intended to establish a Communist state in Yugoslavia as soon as he could. Churchill asked Maclean: 'Do you intend to make Yugoslavia your home after the war?' 'No, sir' replied Maclean. 'Neither do I,' said Churchill, 'and that being so, the less you and I worry about the form of government they set up, the better. That is for them to decide. What interests us is, which of them is doing most harm to the Germans.'[22]

When Eden went to Moscow in October 1943 for talks with Stalin and Molotov, he told Molotov that the British government intended to send arms on the largest possible scale to Tito and might perhaps cut off aid from Mihailović. Molotov was very put out. He said that this would be very inadvisable, and would upset the whole balance of power in Yugoslavia and could cause serious difficulties there. He thought it would be better if the Soviet Union sent supplies to Tito, while Britain continued to supply Mihailović. Eden was adamant that whatever the Soviet Union might do, Britain would send arms to Tito. Eden had had some doubts about whether it was advisable to pursue this policy, for his officials at the Foreign Office did not like it, but Churchill had won him over.

Molotov continued all day to argue that the British government should back Mihailović and not Tito; but when the discussion resumed next morning, he had changed his mind. He now said that the Soviet government welcomed the British decision to support Tito. The Soviet Union would send a military mission to Tito, but they would also send one to Mihailović; and he said that he hoped that the British, too, would continue to keep a liaison officer with Mihailović.[23]

It is not surprising that Stalin was annoyed to hear that the British were transferring their support to Tito. Stalin's first objective in the postwar settlement was to get Poland. He wanted to incorporate eastern Poland into the Soviet Union and to install in western Poland a Communist or Communist-dominated government which would be friendly to the Soviet Union. For 150 years Tsarist Russia had held eastern Poland, and Stalin wanted to have it again and was prepared to make concessions in order to get it. He had no interest in Yugoslavia, and was willing to give it to the British and their ally King Peter in return for Poland. It seemed likely that Churchill would be prepared to agree to the bargain; but now Tito and the Communist party of Yugoslavia were upsetting Stalin's plans. The Yugoslav Communists had always been a little troublesome, with their left and right-wing fractions. They had decided in September 1939 that the war of Britain and France against Germany was an imperialist war

[223]

a whole month before Stalin had told them to do so; and there had been those red stars and proletarian brigades and other signs of ultra-leftism at Užice. And here were the British trying to ingratiate themselves with Tito by sending him military aid when the Soviet Union had not sent him any at all. If Tito received a large amount of military aid from the British and established friendly relations with the Western allies independently of the Soviet Union, the Yugoslav Communists would become even more rebellious and insufferable.

At last the Soviet Union sent a military mission to Tito. It was headed by General Korneyev. Stalin did not have a high opinion of Korneyev, and complained that he was an incurable drunkard.[24] Korneyev's arrival was delayed because, as he had lost a leg at Stalingrad, he could not land by parachute, and arrangements had to be made for the plane carrying him to land on some suitable airstrip. Korneyev eventually arrived at Tito's headquarters on 23 February 1944. He was warmly welcomed by the Partisans, and Tito entertained him at a sumptuous banquet next day. But Korneyev told Maclean that he would have preferred it if he had been sent on a mission to Washington.[25]

On 22 February 1944 Churchill made a statement on Yugoslavia in the House of Commons. He sent the draft of his speech to Eden. 'The Chetniks, as General Mihailović's followers are called, joined with the Germans and Italians to strike at those patriotic defenders of their native soil whom they thought sufficient to dismiss as "Communists". At the present time the followers of Marshal Tito outnumber tenfold those of General Mihailović who acts in the name of the Royal Yugoslav Government, and of course the Partisans are the only people who are doing any fighting against the Germans. For a long time I have taken particular interest in Marshal Tito's movement, and have tried and am trying by every means to bring him help ... We intend to back him with every scrap of strength we can draw.'

Eden was not happy about Churchill's draft. 'I am doubtful whether this is the right moment to present Tito with so big a bouquet in public. We hope to persuade him to go further towards meeting our wishes in regard to his co-operation with King Peter. I am afraid that if Tito gained the impression that you are already so much pleased with him it would be difficult to get anything more out of him.' Eden advised Churchill to cut out his references to Mihailović, and reminded him that there were many MPs in the House who supported Mihailović.[26]

Churchill made one change in his draft to please Eden. Instead of saying that Mihailović and the Chetniks had fought on the side of the Germans and Italians, he said, in Eden's words, that Mihailović 'drifted into a position in which some of his commanders made accommodations with the Italian and German troops'; but he did not modify any of his praise of Tito. He clearly told the House that the Partisans had far more popular support than the Chetniks and that Tito, whom he warmly praised, would receive aid from Britain.[27]

King Peter and his government were now really alarmed. They were in a stronger position in the United States than in Britain. Roosevelt was less enthusiastic than Churchill about Tito. He was strongly pro-Serb, but did not seem to be aware of the problems of the other nations of Yugoslavia.[28] King Peter's ambassador in Washington, Konstantin Fotić, was a Serb, a strong supporter of the monarchy, and an enemy of Communism. He organized demonstrations and protests among Americans of Serbian ethnic origin, and formed the Central National Committee to support Mihailović. But leftist sympathizers gained control of the United Committee of Americans of South Slav Origin; they arranged anti-royalist and pro-Tito demonstrations, and a boycott of the film *The Chetniks*, a Hollywood thriller which glorified the exploits of Mihailović's men against the Germans. A propaganda campaign publicized the atrocities committed by the Chetniks on their Partisan prisoners.[29]

In England the opposition to the new pro-Tito policy was quieter, but the members of the Establishment who supported Mihailović and hated Communism used their influence in the Foreign Office. Rebecca West was considered to be something of an expert on Yugoslavia since the publication of her best-selling book *Black Lamb and Grey Falcon* in 1942. She wrote to her friend Sir Orme Sargent at the Foreign Office to urge him to support Mihailović, 'a typical Serb officer', and not Tito 'the professional revolutionary' who would bring 'nothing but death and damnation'. 'I can understand your feelings about the Yugoslav situation,' replied Sir Orme, 'but however sad the results we are bound by military necessity.'[30] Another correspondent warned the Foreign Office of the 'lust for blood' of 'Tito Broz' and the 'Belgrade anarchist' Moša Pijade, and the other Yugoslav Communist leaders, all of whom had fought in Spain. Many of the allegations about Tito concerned the atrocities which he was supposed to have committed in Spain, where he had been sent by the Comintern to run a prison ship in Barcelona harbour; in this ship he terrorized people 'who refused to submit to the GPU Dictatorship set up in Spain'. The Foreign Office had heard this story before, for it had been raised on several occasions in the educational lectures for soldiers in the army.[31]

Mihailović realized that he must do something to impress the British if they were to be prevented from abandoning him. With the help of the British liaison officer with him, Captain Michael Lees, and his team, he blew up an important railway bridge which the Germans used to transport men and munitions to Greece. He and Lees were incensed when they heard the BBC announce that the bridge had been blown up by Tito's Partisans.[32] Eighteen months before, the BBC had repeatedly given Mihailović the credit for the Partisans' achievements.

Mihailović also thought it advisable to gain some political support. He called a conference at Ba near Valjevo in Serbia on 25 January 1944. It was attended by 274 moderate politicians, of whom the most prominent was Topalović, the leader of the small Serbian Social-Democratic party. The delegates at the conference expressed their opposition to Communism, their support for democratic Socialism, Liberalism and free elections, and their intention of establishing after the war a loose federation in which Serbia, Croatia and Slovenia would have a large degree of autonomy; but they pledged their loyalty to King Peter and his government in London. They sent a copy of their resolutions to Churchill; but Churchill did not reply.[33]

The British High Command in Cairo gave Mihailović one last chance. They asked him to blow up a bridge on the Belgrade–Salonika railway line. Mihailović did not blow it up. The British officers who were with him afterwards claimed that this was because of a misunderstanding with the British authorities in Cairo. In May 1944 the British recalled their military mission with Mihailović.[34]

Mihailović reacted to the withdrawal of the British mission by drawing closer to the Germans. On 8 May 1944 he wrote to his commander in central and south-east Serbia and pointed out that the Germans had not attacked the Chetniks during their Sixth Offensive against the Partisans. 'On the contrary, many of our comrades were helped and enabled to avoid attacks made by the Communists . . . As we have not sufficient munitions and forces, we cannot carry on fighting on two fronts. At present our most dangerous enemies are the Communists. Therefore I order that every kind of armed action against the occupier's forces cease.'[35]

The British stepped up the supply of arms to Tito. Up to the autumn of 1943 they had sent him 800 tons of supplies. In the next eighteen months they sent him 60,000 tons.[36] As long as all the supplies were dropped from aircraft only a very limited amount could be sent. But in the autumn of 1943 the Allies began sending in supplies from Bari in Italy to Dalmatia by sea. The British captured the island of Vis in the Adriatic, and held it as a base for sending supplies to Tito and for attacking the other islands in the Adriatic which the Germans had captured during the Sixth Offensive in the autumn of 1943. The Partisans also had a navy operating among the islands. It was placed under the command of Admiral Černi. He was one of several officers of the pre-war Royal Yugoslav Navy who joined the Partisans.

The Allied soldiers and sailors stationed on Vis were of course interested in the women Partisans, and were surprised to find that their male comrades did not make love to them. The story went around among the Allied troops that Partisan women who became pregnant were shot; another version was that any of them found having sex with a man was shot.[37] These stories were quite untrue. It was merely that the extreme physical fatigue and the privations which the women suffered left them with no energy or inclination for sex. There were many cases of young women who stopped menstruating after a few months' service with the Partisans.[38]

The Communist code of sexual conduct also restricted sex between the comrades. It caused the downfall of Petar Radović, the chief political commissar of the Partisan navy on Vis. Radović had been at Belgrade University with Djilas, and had taken the lead in breaking up lectures by Conservative professors; but he had a weakness for women. He was expelled from the party before the war for political unreliability, but he joined the Partisans in 1941 and fought so bravely that he was readmitted to the party.

He had not rid himself of his old weakness. Tall and strong, with a flashing smile which revealed a row of brass teeth, he was popular with women and could not resist them. He fell in love with the daughter of a Czech poet; she lived with her father on the island of Hvar. Another woman found out and denounced Radović to the party. He was told that he would be expelled if he continued his affair with the poet's daughter. The prospect of being expelled from the party for a second time so appalled him that he committed suicide, shooting himself with his revolver. At least his comrades gave him a good funeral.[39]

In view of the party's moral code and the severity with which it was enforced against comrades as useful as Radović, it is surprising that there was not more disapproving comment among the Partisans about Tito's relations with Zdenka. It was not generally known outside Tito's headquarters that Zdenka was Tito's mistress, though everyone on his headquarters staff knew about it. They did not approve, but they all blamed Zdenka, not Tito. The Old Man was a law unto himself. The Partisans were beginning to talk about him in the same way that they talked about Stalin. Tito was regarded 'as a sort of demi-god', says his secretary, Olga Humo.[40]

The Partisans were helped by British and American aircraft which operated from Bari and Foggia and raided German military and industrial targets on the Yugoslav mainland. Between October and December 1943 they made very heavy air raids on the Germans in the Croatian port of Zadar, and on Split, Skopje, Šibenik and Niš. There were heavy casualties among the civilian population. The Allies had not informed Tito, who first heard about the raid on Zadar from the BBC broadcasts. He made a strong protest to the Allied governments.[41] After this the British and American authorities always asked Tito's permission before bombing targets in Yugoslavia. He gave them permission to make more air raids on Zadar and on other towns.

In April 1944, with Tito's consent, American planes bombed Belgrade on the Easter Sunday of the Orthodox Church. It was not, like the German air raid of 1941, aimed at the civilian population in the city centre. The targets of the American air raid were the armament factories in the suburbs. But there were very heavy casualties among the civilian population; according to some estimates, the American planes killed more Serbian civilians in Belgrade on 16 April 1944 than the German Luftwaffe had killed on 6 April 1941. In Serbia today some people say that Tito, being a Croat, asked his friend Fitzroy Maclean to arrange for the RAF to bomb Belgrade in order to kill as many Serbs as possible; they actually assert that no Croatian town was bombed by Allied aircraft. In fact the Croatian and Dalmatian ports were a prime target for the Allied bombers, and Zadar was flattened.

Slavenka Petnički acted as an interpreter during one of the air raids on Split. She had enlisted in the Partisan forces as a nurse. There was an acute shortage of nurses among the Partisans. One day when she was particularly busy in the hospital ward, her superior officer came in and told her that because of her excellent English she was being transferred from the hospital to headquarters staff to act as an interpreter with the British liaison officers. She said that she was badly needed in the hospital and refused to leave it. Her commanding officer told her that this was not merely an order which he was giving her as her superior officer; it was a decision of the party. She argued no longer, although she had never actually joined the party, despite her husband's position in it and her own sympathies for the Communist cause.

She was both pleased and worried as the reports came in about the air raid on Split. The main target of the attack was the bishop's palace, because it had been requisitioned by the Germans and reports had been received that a large quantity of munitions and gunpowder had been stored there. When the bombs hit the palace the gunpowder blew up and caused very great damage in Split. The casualties among the civilian population were very heavy, and the gutters in the city ran with blood.[42]

Slavenka believed that her parents were in Split. She did not know that her mother and her little sister Vasja had left Split a few weeks before in an attempt to escape to Egypt. Her father, a business man, Mr Kekez, had always been loyal to the monarchy and now supported Mihailović and the Chetniks. One evening he and his seventeen-year-old son were walking on the sea-front in Split when they were attacked and hacked to death with choppers and their bodies thrown into the sea. Their family never knew whether it was the Partisans or the Ustashas who killed them; both factions often murdered Chetniks. It was probably the Partisans, because Kekez had occasionally worked as a translator for the German army of occupation, and his son had been unjustly accused of having collaborated with the occupation authorities.[43]

The British government invited Tito to send a military mission to Cairo. Tito chose Velebit to lead the delegation. Dedijer, who was suffering from a head wound that he had received during the Fifth Offensive, went with them, for Deakin had arranged that he was to be cared for at a British military hospital in Cairo. Deakin and other members of the British mission were in the travelling party. They went to an airstrip in a field about a hundred miles from Tito's headquarters at Jajce. As they were boarding the aircraft a German plane appeared, dropped its bombs, and machine-gunned the Partisans. Several members of the party were killed, including the Communist Youth leader, Lola Ribar, and the plane was wrecked.[44] The loss of Lola Ribar was a heavy blow to Tito and the Partisans. The news was broken to his father as he was presiding at the conference of AVNOJ in Jajce.

Velebit and his colleagues made another attempt to leave for Cairo. This time they boarded the plane safely and reached Bari, where they stayed for a short time before proceeding to Cairo. Dedijer became involved in a certain amount of friction with the British military authorities in Bari and Cairo. He was very suspicious of the British imperialists, and saw a sinister motive in everything that any British officer or soldier did. When they visited him in hospital in Cairo, he thought that it was an imperialist trick; and he was even more suspicious when a South African soldier with left-wing sympathies offered to come to Yugoslavia and fight in the Partisan army.[45]

Velebit was not, like Dedijer, a member of Agitprop, and coming from an old military family he could talk to the British generals in Cairo as easily as he had talked to General Glaise von Horstenau. Someone in Cairo invented the story that General Sir Maitland Wilson, the commander-in-chief in the Middle East under the supreme command of General Alexander, was rude to Velebit, that Velebit resented this, and that it caused ill-will between Tito and the British government. This was untrue. Velebit insists today that he had a high regard for General Wilson, and that Wilson always treated him in a correct and friendly way.[46]

Velebit encountered greater difficulties when Tito sent him on a mission to London in the spring of 1944, but they were political, not personal, difficulties. The Foreign Office did not wish any action to be taken which would imply that the British government were recognizing Tito's AVNOJ Council in Jajce as the government of Yugoslavia. But the British government recognized the Partisans as a military body allied to the British forces; so it would be in order for them to receive a military, but not a political, mission from the Partisans. Velebit could meet any general in London, but not Churchill, Eden or a member of the British government.

Before he left for London, Velebit was contacted by one of the Russian officers on General Korneyev's staff at Partisan headquarters, and asked to act as an agent of Soviet intelligence in

London. Velebit said that he would have to consult his leaders about this. Ranković told him that he must do all he could to help the Soviet Union when he was in London, and pass on to Soviet intelligence any information which they wished to know; and he was given a code word which would be used by the Soviet agent who would contact him in London.

Velebit flew to London by Algiers and Gibraltar. He arrived in London on 1 May 1944. Everyone knew that the Second Front, which Stalin and the Communist parties throughout the world had been demanding for the last three years, was about to be opened and that the Allied invasion of France was imminent, though the place of landing and the exact date of D-day were kept secret.

Velebit stayed at the Savoy Hotel in London. He was duly contacted by the Soviet intelligence agent in London, who turned out to be a representative of the Soviet news agency TASS. The TASS man arranged to meet Velebit on a bench in Kensington Gardens near the Albert Memorial. Velebit did not take any of the precautions which he took to throw the Gestapo off his trail when he was working for the Communist underground in Zagreb; he quite openly took a taxi from the Savoy Hotel to the Albert Memorial, and met the TASS man. There were only two things which Soviet intelligence wished to find out from Velebit: were the British and Americans planning to land troops in Yugoslavia or anywhere on the eastern coast of the Adriatic; and what were the plans of King Peter's government? Velebit told the TASS man that he had heard nothing which led him to believe that the Western Allies were planning a landing on the Adriatic coast; and he told him about his political talks with the ministers in King Peter's government.[47]

Velebit met the generals and colonels at the War Office, and General Dwight D. Eisenhower, the American commander-in-chief of the invasion army, at the American embassy in Grosvenor Square in London. But his chief object was to meet Churchill; he knew that Tito attached great importance to this, as it would be interpreted as unofficial political recognition by the British government of the AVNOJ provisional government at Jajce. Eden, following the advice of his officials, wished to prevent the meeting with Churchill.

The London Socialist and left-wing intellectuals welcomed Velebit, for they were very pleased to meet one of Tito's Partisans. Kingsley Martin, editor of the influential left-wing journal the *New Statesman*, became friendly with him and used his influence with the Labour ministers in the government to arrange for Velebit to see Churchill. The left-wing Socialist Sir Stafford Cripps, who had been sent to Moscow as ambassador by Churchill and on his return had been appointed minister of aircraft production, ignored the wishes of the Foreign Office that Velebit should not meet a member of the British government, and invited Velebit to breakfast. Kingsley Martin also asked Harold Laski, chairman of the National Executive of the Labour party, to help, and Laski wrote to Churchill on behalf of the Labour party asking him to meet Velebit. Laski, a brilliant but rather didactic university professor who had never been an MP, was the last man likely to have a favourable influence on Churchill; but Kingsley Martin also mentioned the matter to Beaverbrook, who knew better than most people how to achieve results.

Martin was spending the weekend at his country cottage on the South Downs. The telephone rang; Beaverbrook was on the line. 'How did you know that I was here?' asked Martin. 'Because I have a secretary who would find you even if you were in hell,' said Beaverbrook. He told Martin that he would see what he could do about Velebit.

Some days later, Fitzroy Maclean, who had returned to England to report to Churchill, called on Velebit at the Savoy Hotel and told him that Churchill would receive him. Velebit saw Churchill on 21 May. Churchill was very friendly, and though no important business was transacted at the meeting, Velebit had achieved what he and Tito wanted: a press report that Churchill had met Tito's representative, and the defeat of the Foreign Office plan to prevent this step towards political recognition. Velebit assumed that it was Laski's approach on behalf of the Labour party which had persuaded Churchill to agree to see him. It was only many years later that he discovered that Beaverbrook's intervention had been decisive.[48]

CHAPTER 18

❖

From Drvar to Belgrade

I N Yugoslavia the Germans had launched the Seventh Offensive
in May 1944. They gave it the code name *Rösselsprung* (Knight's
Move). Their objective was to attack Tito's headquarters at
Drvar in Bosnia with paratroopers and capture Tito, if possible alive.
The Partisans realized that the Germans might try to do this, for
there had been loose talk in Zagreb in November 1943 about the
possibility of an attack on Jajce at the time of the AVNOJ conference.
In March 1944 Tito warned his commanders to expect an attack
by paratroopers on Drvar and to concentrate their forces there;
but as the weeks passed by and no attack came, the Partisan
forces were dispersed so that they could take part in operations
elsewhere.[1]

Hitler took a personal interest in the operation to capture Tito. It
was to be carried out on 25 May, which was Tito's official birthday,
by 2,000 troops of the crack airborne Prinz Eugen division. The
operation was planned in the strictest secrecy. Only a handful of
people knew about it in advance; the paratroopers were briefed on
the object of their mission only two hours before they left Zagreb
airport.[2] The Germans afterwards believed that the Partisans were
ready waiting for the attack, and that this showed that some traitor
in the German camp had warned them. In fact the Partisans were
taken completely by surprise.

The Partisans had established a small hut, which was rather
inaccurately called a cave, on the mountainside at the edge of the
forest, with the valley below and a plateau above. It was used as an
office by the Partisan High Command, and their archives were
housed there. Tito often came there during the day, but he usually
worked and slept in another cave in the village of Bastasi a few miles

away, and on the days when he came to Drvar he returned in the evening to Bastasi in his jeep.

The Germans cannot have known that Tito slept at Bastasi, because if he had been there at dawn on 25 May he would have incurred no danger at all from the German attack. But on 24 May he and Kardelj decided to stay the night in Drvar, so that they would be there early next morning for his birthday celebrations. Tito, after going to the cinema in Drvar and enjoying the Soviet film *Soya Kosmodemyaskaya*, stayed the night in a ramshackle building very near the cave in Drvar.[3]

The Germans began the operation by bombing Drvar at six a.m. on 25 May.[4] General Jovanić, who commanded a division in Koča Popović's corps, had been ordered to send one of his brigades to reinforce the defenders of Drvar, and they had arrived there the previous day;[5] but he himself and the rest of his men were between ten and thirty kilometres away when they heard the noise of the bombing. They immediately ran towards Drvar; but they had not yet arrived there when the first German paratroopers attacked at ten a.m.[6] The men and women Partisans who were stationed in Drvar were ready, and immediately counter-attacked as the German paratroopers landed. The first wave of paratroopers were all killed; they were 'mercilessly massacred by the Partisans', wrote General Glaise von Horstenau.[7] But more paratroopers arrived, and overwhelmed the Partisans.

When the attack began, Tito went to the cave with Zdenka, his dog Tigar, and a few members of his staff and bodyguard. Soon afterwards he was joined there by Kardelj, his secretary Olga Humo, and by other leading Partisans, until twelve men and eight women were crowded into the cave. They heard the firing very close, and looking out, saw the paratroopers two hundred yards away in the valley below. Tito saw that the paratroopers had captured his jeep and were driving about in it. He saw a paratrooper shoot a Partisan fighter, and was so angry that he called for a rifle to shoot the paratrooper; but Crni Žujović told him that it would be very foolish to betray their position by firing at the Germans.

The bullets were flying across the entrance to the cave. One of Tito's bodyguard ventured out and was immediately shot dead. Zdenka became very excited, and shouted, 'They'll kill us, they'll kill us!'[8]; and his dog Tigar, too, was frightened, as he always was in air raids.[9]

Tito realized that they would have to leave the cave by the emergency exit. This involved removing one of the floorboards and climbing down a rope to a stream lower down the hillside, which at this point was obscured from view by trees and bushes. By following a track along the stream and through a sawmill, it was possible to climb up to the plateau above the cave.

They divided into several groups. They would all leave by climbing down the rope; but once they reached the stream below, each group would make its own way to safety as best it could. They climbed down the rope one by one. Tito went first, followed by Zdenka; but Tigar was the first to reach the stream at the bottom. He had somehow managed to scramble down. When he saw Tito descending on the rope, he began to bark. Tito realized that the barking dog might betray their position to the Germans and cost the lives of the whole party. For a moment he thought that he would have to shoot Tigar with his revolver; but he could not bring himself to do it. Instead he gently closed Tigar's mouth with his hands, and Tigar stopped barking.

Tito, Zdenka, and two other comrades set off with Tigar to climb up to the plateau. At one point they were spotted by the Germans, who fired at them; but the bullets did not come very near. The paratroopers were only a ten-minute walk away, but they ignored the plateau. They were running around in the valley brandishing photographs of Tito and asking everyone they met where he was to be found. No one, not even the children, told them the location of the cave, and they never reached it. They killed several civilians, particularly the young people.

They succeeded in capturing one trophy. Tito had asked a local tailor to make a new marshal's uniform for him. The tailor had just finished it, but it was still in his workshop. It was badly gashed when a German bomb hit the shop. The paratroopers found the uniform, and the German newspapers duly boasted of this great success; but Tito and his companions, after reaching the plateau, hurried away through the forest and escaped.

Hitler was very put out at the failure to capture Tito. 'It seems that the Führer is very angry, and shouts "Treason!"' wrote Glaise von Horstenau.[10] But Tito laughed about his escape. 'The Germans always make one mistake,' he said, 'if they had landed on the plateau, instead of in the valley, no one would have got away.'[11]

It had been agreed that if the escaping Partisans became separated, they would all head for Potoci, some ten miles east of Drvar. Tito and his party duly reached Potoci, and the other Partisan groups and the British and Soviet liaison officers also made their way there.[12] Both the Partisan and the British radio transmitters had been put out of action in the attack on Drvar; but the British signals officer, Captain Hilary King, and his colleagues managed to save one set, with the essential ancillary equipment, and were thus able to maintain radio contact with the British headquarters in Bari.

Tito had escaped from the immediate danger, but the Germans were all around; so Tito and his party moved on from Potoci, travelling a few miles by train on a little forest railway before abandoning the train and continuing on horseback and on foot. They were often under fire. Once an enemy shell landed just behind Tito's horse and wounded a member of the Russian mission.

German land forces, following up behind the paratroopers, encircled the whole area, and it was clear that having prevented Tito's escape from the ring, they would hunt him down and perhaps eventually catch him. Even if he managed to avoid capture, he would be unable to remain in contact with the Partisan units and direct operations in other parts of Yugoslavia. General Korneyev believed that the Soviet mission could not usefully function in their present circumstances, and on 31 May he asked King to get into radio contact with Bari and arrange for a Soviet plane to fly to the area and take him and the members of his mission to Italy. Korneyev strongly advised Tito to come with him. At first Tito refused to go, for he was very reluctant to leave Yugoslavia; but Colonel Vivian Street, the head of the British mission, joined Korneyev in urging him to leave, and pointed out that if Tito flew to Italy he could at once go on to the island of Vis, which had been occupied by British forces. Here he would again be on Yugoslav soil.

Eventually, at noon on 3 June, the ninth day after he had left Drvar, Tito told Street that he was willing to go to Bari. As soon as the British in Bari received the radio message from Street, they hastily made preparations for the evacuation to take place that same night. They arranged for six American planes to take part in the operation, and a Soviet pilot was to make the journey twice on the same night. The planes would land on a hastily improvised airstrip in a field in the valley at Kupreško Polje at nine p.m. on 3 June.

Tito was at the airstrip at nine p.m., with Kardelj, Korneyev, Street, the other members of the Soviet and British missions, the headquarters staff, Zdenka and the dog. They lit fires to show their position, but there was thick cloud and the pilots could not see them. Tito and his party heard the sound of a plane overhead, but as the noise grew fainter they realized that the plane had flown past them and that they had failed to make contact. But then there was a break in the cloud, and the Soviet pilot, who was flying the first plane, saw the fires and landed on the airstrip. Tito, Zdenka and Tigar got into the plane with other members of the party; and the six American planes, which also brought supplies of arms and equipment to the Partisans, arrived soon afterwards before the Soviet pilot returned on his second trip. They had all reached Bari before the night was out.

Several British generals and Velebit were at the airfield in Bari in the middle of the night to welcome Tito. But the Soviet pilot landed in a distant part of the airfield, where they were met by a car from the Soviet mission in Bari, and Tito was driven away without having contacted the British welcoming party; for he did not wish the press to find out that he had left Yugoslavia. It was some hours before Tito made contact with his British hosts.[13]

The British authorities housed Tito in a comfortable villa on the outskirts of Bari, but he stayed there only two nights before leaving for Vis. While he was in Bari he heard on 5 June that the Allied armies had captured Rome, and next morning the news came of the Allied landing in Normandy. Tito left for Vis in a British warship in the evening of 6 June. The journey took six hours, because the British were holding manoeuvres in the Adriatic, and the ship carrying Tito altered her course to avoid interfering with the manoeuvres. The whole sky was lit up with flashes of gunfire, and Tito spent the night on the bridge with the British captain, watching the manoeuvres. They landed on Vis at dawn on 7 June.

Tito set up his headquarters in a cottage in a village, but the Partisans were worried that it might be a target for a German attack, because a solitary German reconnaissance plane, flying very high, out of range of the anti-aircraft defences, was often seen over Vis. So next day Tito moved to a bombproof shelter in a cave on Mount Hum on the western side of the island. The Partisans fitted out the cave as a comfortable residence for Tito and Zdenka. It was divided up into rooms, with bedrooms, offices, and a conference room, as well as a bunk for the dog.[14]

The day after Tito reached Vis, General Korneyev and the Soviet mission also arrived from Bari. Among Korneyev's officers was Lieutenant Žarko Broz. Žarko had joined the Red Army at the time of the German invasion and had taken part in the successful Soviet counter-offensive in the snow in front of Moscow in December 1941, where he was wounded and lost his right arm. He was thereupon discharged from the army; but when the Free Yugoslav Legion was formed on the Russian front, Žarko was allowed to join it, and in the summer of 1944 he was sent to join Korneyev's mission to Tito.

When Korneyev met Tito on Vis and introduced his staff, Žarko saluted smartly. Tito smiled, and said to Korneyev: 'You have trained him well.' Afterwards Tito and his son had their first private meeting since Tito had last seen Žarko as a child in Moscow, and they had much to say to each other.[15]

Churchill now set out to find a satisfactory political solution for Yugoslavia. He told the House of Commons that in Greece he supported a king and in Yugoslavia a Communist;[16] but he did not wish to see Yugoslavia become a Communist state if he could help it, or to hand it over completely to the Soviet Union. 'There is little doubt', he wrote to Eden on 1 April 1944, 'that the Russians will drive straight ahead for a Communist Tito-governed Yugoslavia, and will denounce everything done to the contrary as "undemocratic"'. But he thought that 'we may have a forlorn hope' of preventing this if they could bring about a reconciliation between Tito and King Peter 'in the next five or six weeks'.[17] This should be easier now while Tito 'lies under our protection on the island of Vis'.[18]

Churchill's plan was that King Peter should disown and dismiss Mihailović and recognize Tito as commander-in-chief of the Royal Army in Yugoslavia. The King's Conservative Serbian prime minister should resign, and a coalition government should be formed under Šubašić. He was a Croat Liberal who had held the ancient office of Ban (governor) of Croatia under King Alexander and Prince Paul before the war. This ought to reconcile the Croats and the other nationalist groups in Yugoslavia, and convince them that in future King Peter's government would not be an instrument of Serbian domination. Tito would agree to serve under the king and Šubašić's government, and the provisional government established by AVNOJ would be disbanded. Some of its members could enter Šubašić's coalition government. Tito would renounce any intention of establishing Communism in Yugoslavia. After the war free elections would be held, and a parliamentary democracy would be established there.[19]

This put Tito in a very difficult position, and he had to manoeuvre with great skill. He and his comrades in the Communist party wished to carry through the social revolution and establish a Communist state in Yugoslavia after the war. They had not fought the Fascists for three years, endured so many hardships, made such heavy sacrifices, and seen so many of their comrades killed, in order to re-establish a regime like the royal dictatorship of King Alexander or a bourgeois parliamentary democracy where every man and woman would have one vote, irrespective of whether they had spent the war safe and inactive in their homes or risking death and torture with the Partisans in the mountains or in the underground resistance groups in the towns, but where the most devoted Communists would be unable to vote because they had been killed in battle or executed by Fascist firing squads.

But he realized the weakness of his position. He relied on the British imperialists to supply him with arms, to transport his wounded Partisans to hospitals in Italy, and to send a plane to rescue him and Zdenka from the German paratroopers; and it was useful to have the British liaison officers at his headquarters, the British troops guarding Vis, and the British naval forces operating there. But he did not want to see a British army land in Yugoslavia. From time to time Churchill suggested to his generals and to Roosevelt and Stalin that an Allied expeditionary force should be diverted from the campaign in Italy to land on the Dalmatian coast and to march across Croatia and Slovenia to link up with the Russian army in Hungary.[20] Fortunately for Tito, neither the British and American generals, nor Roosevelt and Stalin, were in favour of Churchill's proposal, for they thought that it would have a detrimental effect on the campaign in Italy and Normandy.[21] If Yugoslavia were occupied by a British army, it would be impossible to carry through a Communist revolution there. Tito realized how justified his fears had been when he saw the British army in Greece suppress a Communist revolution in December 1944.

Four days after Tito arrived in Vis, he received a telegram from Churchill announcing that Šubašić would be coming to Vis accompanied by Sir George Stevenson, the British ambassador to King Peter's government in London. Šubašić would be bringing Churchill's proposals for a reconciliation between King Peter and the AVNOJ Council. Tito summoned a meeting of the Politburo in the cave. His colleagues were very suspicious of the British proposals, but agreed to Tito's suggestion that he, Kardelj, Bakarić and old Josip Smodlaka should discuss the proposals with Šubašić and Stevenson.[22]

Šubašić and Stevenson arrived in Vis on 14 June and were entertained by Tito at a dinner that evening in a cottage in a village on the island.[23] When the Partisans entertained their guests at a banquet, the hospitality was lavish. A British officer who attended these banquets on Vis said many years later that the amount of food and drink consumed at an official banquet in the City of London was meagre compared with the quantities eaten and drunk at the Partisans' functions on Vis and in the mountains during the Second World War. The Partisans served ten or eleven courses to their guests, and the dinners usually lasted for more than five hours.[24]

On 15 June the discussions between the Partisan leaders and Šubašić and Stevenson began in the conference room in Tito's cave. There was hard bargaining between the two sides, which continued throughout a second day, but on the morning of 17 June Tito and Šubašić signed an agreement. It provided that King Peter's government would consist of progressive and democratic ministers who had never fought against the Partisans. This government and the National Council of AVNOJ would collaborate to form a national front to fight against the Germans. AVNOJ would not raise the question of the future of the monarchy, as this could be left in abeyance without hindering the common fight against the invader, and should be decided by the people after the war. The king's government would recognize the achievements of AVNOJ and the Partisans, and would help AVNOJ to punish traitors who had collaborated with the enemy. Tito would declare his willingness to cooperate with the king's government, and AVNOJ would not claim to be the government of Yugoslavia.[25]

When the agreement was published, many Partisans opposed it, and believed that their leaders had submitted to the wishes of the British bourgeoisie. At the meeting of the Communist Youth, the members would chant in unison 'We will not have King Peter'.[26] On 15 July Tito received an invitation from Sir Henry Maitland Wilson to come to Italy for further discussions. The Politburo objected to the Allies interfering in matters concerning the government of Yugoslavia, and at their meeting on 20 July decided that Tito should refuse the invitation. Velebit was instructed to make it known that invitations to hold political discussions must come from the British government and not from its military commanders. The British thereupon began to make difficulties for the Partisans. They obstructed the discussions about sending Tito sixty-eight Yugoslav ships which had been captured by the Germans earlier in the war and had been liberated by the Allied armies in Italy; and they ordered the AVNOJ military mission in London to suspend its activities on the grounds that these could now be conducted by Šubašić's government.[27]

Tito then agreed to accept Wilson's invitation, and flew to Italy. On 6 August he met Wilson in Caserta, and next day he was taken to the Allied front line, where he had discussions with General Alexander, the Allied commander-in-chief in Italy.[28] He had already guessed the closely guarded secret that he had been invited to Italy to meet Churchill.[29] They met in the villa where Churchill was staying in Naples.

Tito brought Žarko with him to meet Churchill. But while they were waiting for Churchill to arrive they had drinks on the terrace. Tigar lay under the table on which were the wine glasses and coffee cups. Suddenly Tigar saw a cat, and jumped up, upsetting the table and breaking the glasses and cups. Tito told Žarko to take Tigar away, and so Žarko missed Churchill.[30]

Tito's talks with Churchill lasted two days, on 12 and 13 August. Fitzroy Maclean and Eden's private secretary, Pierson Dixon, were present with Major Clissold as Churchill's interpreter and Olga Humo as Tito's. On the second day they were joined by Šubašić and his minister of the interior.[31]

The weather was very hot. Churchill wore a white cotton siren suit with an open-necked shirt, as he often did on informal occasions. Tito was dressed in a field-marshal's uniform which had been specially fitted out for him in Moscow, with golden leaves on his collar and cuffs, and with decorations. He was sweating in the heat, and Churchill afterwards joked with his doctor, Lord Moran, about the way that Tito several times put his finger under his collar to loosen it, as it was obviously too tight for him.[32] Tito had always liked wearing smart clothes; and correctness in dress was a sign of self-respect and good discipline.[33] A hundred and fifty years before, the British aristocracy had adopted the same attitude; but by the twentieth century it had become fashionable among them to wear informal clothes on informal occasions. The dress worn by Churchill and Tito at the Naples conference reflected their relationship. Tito wished to impress Churchill, but Churchill had no need to impress Tito.

Churchill and Tito agreed to carry out the agreement that Tito had signed with Šubašić. Churchill suggested that Tito should meet King Peter, but Tito did not think that this was feasible in the immediate future. Churchill asked Tito if he intended to make Yugoslavia a Communist state. Tito said that he had already made it clear that he would not do so. Churchill pressed Tito to say this publicly. Tito was reluctant to do this, but eventually agreed to Churchill's demand. Tito told Churchill that he thought that Yugoslavia was entitled to have Trieste after the war; but Churchill said that this was impossible, because as the Italians were now fighting on the side of the Allies, they should not be deprived of Trieste.[34]

The meeting ended on the most friendly note, with a dinner at which Churchill and Tito proposed each other's health and made speeches proclaiming their friendship.[35] Churchill presented Olga Humo with a gold pendant as a tribute to her work as interpreter. Next day Tito returned to Vis and two days later, on 17 August, issued the statement that Churchill wanted. He declared that the liberation movement in Yugoslavia was 'national and democratic'; its only aim was to conduct the struggle against the occupying forces and their lackeys, and to create a democratic Yugoslavia, 'not the establishment of Communism, which our enemies attribute to us'.[36] Tito was not speaking the truth. He did aim at establishing Communism in Yugoslavia, and he knew that Churchill intended to stop him from doing this.

Tito maintained excellent personal relations with the British officers on Vis. Lieutenant-Colonel Tom Churchill, who was in command of the British commando force on Vis, visited Tito in his cave on several occasions. He noted that Tito's face looked stern when it was in repose, but that 'he had a brilliant smile which lit up his face and brought a pronounced twinkle into his eyes'. Tito's dog Tigar was always present at their talks, watching every move that Tom Churchill made. When they had finished their discussions, small plates of fish were usually handed round, with bread, and served with excellent *prošek* wine which had been brought from Hvar. Tito would give pieces of the fish to Tigar while he talked to his guests.[37]

Nearly all the British officers who met Tito were impressed, like other people who knew him, by his powerful personality, his 'charisma' as so many of them called it. One of the exceptions was the author, Evelyn Waugh, who served as an officer in the British army on Vis and elsewhere in Yugoslavia. He soon accepted that he had been wrong in believing that Tito was a woman, but did not change his conviction that he was an enemy of the Catholic Church. Waugh got into contact with Roman Catholic abbots and priests who told him how the Communists were persecuting the Catholic Church in areas under their control, and that the persecution would be even worse if they took over the government of Yugoslavia after the war. Waugh wrote a report about this to his superior officers, and when he realized that his report would be shelved, he sent a copy of it to the Pope. The British authorities considered prosecuting Waugh under the Official Secrets Act, but decided that it would be wiser to take no action.[38]

The underlying tension in the relations between the Allies and the Partisans was shown in what superficially was a light-hearted incident. Admiral Morgan, who commanded the British navy in the Adriatic, arrived at Vis and was entertained to lunch by Tito at another lavish banquet. The Russian General Korneyev was among the guests. Admiral Morgan asked Tito if he would like to come on board a British ship to watch the bombardment of a neighbouring island which was in German hands. Tito said that he would like to accept, but thought that General Korneyev should come too. Morgan said that this was a purely personal invitation and that he was inviting Tito, not Korneyev. Tito tried to turn the whole thing into a joke. He asked whether the British bombardment of the island would be a formal or an informal bombardment. Morgan said that it would be quite an informal bombardment, and Tito said that in that case he thought it would be in order for him to come without Korneyev. But next morning, after Tito had gone on board the British ship, two Russian naval officers ran up and at the last moment jumped on to the ship. Korneyev later explained to a British officer that he had sent his two officers to observe what was happening on the voyage, because he suspected that the British were taking Tito to a secret rendezvous with King Peter.[39]

Many Yugoslav Communists had misgivings about Tito's agreement with Šubašić, and were taken aback at his public declaration that the national liberation movement did not intend to make Yugoslavia a Communist state. On 12 September Tito addressed a meeting on Vis to commemorate the second anniversary of the formation of the First Dalmatian Brigade of the Partisan army. Tito paid tribute to the heroism of the soldiers of the brigade and to their many comrades who had fallen in the struggle; and he praised Dalmatia for having been the first part of Croatia to rise up against the occupying forces and the Ustashas. He staked his claim to Rijeka (Fiume) which Yugoslavia had granted Mussolini in 1924, saying that Fascism was an international phenomenon which must be destroyed everywhere. The people of Yugoslavia had fought not only to free their country but also to liberate their brothers in Istria. 'We seek no foreign territory, but we will not give up what is ours.' Yugoslavia was only a small nation compared to her great allies, but she must not be ignored.

He ended by referring to the Vis Agreement with Šubašić. He realized that this agreement had 'been received with a definite misapprehension, not only among our fighting men but also by other parts of the population'. They thought it was unnecessary to make the agreement because the Partisans had achieved so much by their own unaided efforts that they did not need to compromise their principles in order to obtain assistance from anyone else. But they were mistaken. 'No, comrades, this agreement was necessary,' and it had helped the movement politically. But he promised that he would go no further without the consent of the people, and that he still stood fully by the decisions of the second AVNOJ conference at Jajce in November 1943. He ended his speech: 'Long live our new and happy Yugoslavia, a democratic and federal Yugoslavia! Long live our great allies, the USSR, England and America! Long live our brothers of the glorious Red Army which today stands on our frontiers! Death to Fascism! Freedom to the people!'[40]

The ardent Communists – the leftists who had always been active in the Communist party of Yugoslavia, and the comrades who had insisted on carrying through the ultra-leftist policy at Užice – were discontented. There might have been serious disaffection in the Partisan ranks had it not been for their personal devotion to Tito, to the Old Man. But Tito knew that he had to tread cautiously in dealing with Churchill. He thoroughly appreciated the power relationship between the British Empire and the Yugoslav Partisans. Churchill had given him a great deal of help, but he would not help him to make Yugoslavia Communist. If a British army landed in Yugoslavia, Churchill would certainly prevent the establishment of a Communist state. The only person who could prevent Churchill from doing this was Stalin, if Stalin could be persuaded to overcome his usual caution, to interest himself in the Communist revolution in Yugoslavia, and to realize that he could do better for the Soviet Union than a fifty-fifty division of Yugoslavia with Churchill.

Not for the first or last time, Tito took an important decision without consulting anyone, not even the Politburo. The Soviet air attaché at Allied headquarters in Italy explained that it was necessary for Soviet pilots under training to practise night landing on a narrow air strip; would the British authorities permit them to practise on the air strip on Vis? The permission was granted, and for three or four nights in succession the British troops guarding the air strip saw a Soviet plane land, wait for a few minutes, and then take off again. On the last night, after the Soviet plane had landed, Tito suddenly appeared, climbed quickly on board, and flew off in the aircraft.[41]

He was accompanied only by General Korneyev, Žarko, another officer, and Tigar. He had not intended taking Tigar, but the dog made so much difficulty about being separated from Tito that he was allowed to come. A Partisan put a sack over his head as they approached the plane to prevent him from barking.[42] At least there was no problem about Zdenka. Her health had completely broken down, and she was suffering so badly from tuberculosis that she had been flown from Vis to a sanatorium in Russia some weeks earlier.[43]

Next day, the Partisan sentries in front of Tito's cave stood on guard, and told anyone who came that Tito was busy and could not be disturbed. But the sentries on the air strip had recognized Tito, and immediately reported to Lieutenant-Commander Morgan-Giles that he had flown away in a Soviet plane.[44] When the news reached Churchill, he commented: 'Tito has levanted';[45] but the British could only guess where he had gone. He had in fact been flown to Cralova in Romania, which had been occupied by the advancing Red Army a few weeks before. From there he flew on to Moscow. When Churchill and Eden visited Moscow a month later, Molotov told them that Tito had been there. Eden said that it was most discourteous of Tito to leave Vis in this way without telling the British that he was going to Moscow. Molotov replied that one could not expect good manners from a Yugoslav peasant.[46]

Tito now met Stalin for the first time, though he had briefly seen him on the platform at the seventh congress of the Comintern in 1935. Their relationship was very different now. Stalin greeted him warmly, addressing him as 'Walter', the name by which Tito had been known in the Comintern when he was in Moscow before the war. Stalin tried to persuade Tito to take no step towards establishing

Communism in Yugoslavia and to agree to the return of King Peter; he said jovially that if King Peter proved to be troublesome, Tito could always 'slip a knife in his back' at some future date.[47] Tito argued with Stalin, telling him that the situation in Yugoslavia was ripe for the Communists to take power, and pointing out how this would strengthen the position of the Soviet Union against British and American imperialism.[48]

By the middle of September 1944 the Red Army had liberated Romania and Bulgaria and was only a few miles from the borders of Yugoslavia. Tito urged Stalin to order the Red Army to enter Yugoslavia as soon as possible, after asking his permission as the representative of AVNOJ, the provisional government of the Yugoslav people. A week earlier, Fitzroy Maclean had told the American representative at Caserta that he believed that Tito would try to stop the Russians from entering Yugoslavia, as he would prefer Yugoslavia to be liberated by his Partisans than by the Red Army.[49] Maclean did not realize that Tito preferred Yugoslavia to be liberated by the Red Army than the British army. Above all Tito wanted Belgrade to be liberated by the Red Army and the Partisans together, and quickly.

He asked Stalin to send tanks to help the advance on Belgrade. Stalin lifted the telephone receiver and asked to be put through immediately to Marshal Tolbukhin in Sofia. 'Tito's here with me,' he said to Tolbukhin, 'he wants us to give him a tank brigade. Have you got any tanks there?' Tito heard Tolbukhin say yes. 'Give him a corps,' said Stalin.[50]

The Red Army entered Yugoslavia on 1 October. The first armed Yugoslavs whom they encountered were Mihailović's bearded Chetniks, for they had crossed the frontier in a part of Serbia which was under Chetnik control. The Chetniks did not resist them, and greeted them as allies, and the Russians drove on north towards Belgrade without bothering about the Chetniks.[51]

The Free Yugoslav Legion entered Yugoslavia with the Red Army. Like 'free legions' of other nationalities, it consisted of prisoners-of-war who had been captured when fighting for the Germans and had been persuaded to change sides, and join the Red Army. The commander of the Yugoslav Legion was Marko Mesić, a Croat. He had two medals on his chest. One of them, the Order of St Sava, had been given to him by King Alexander when he was an officer in the Royal Yugoslav Army; but in 1941 he had joined the Ustashas, and had volunteered for service on the Russian front, where he was awarded the Iron Cross by Hitler. After he was taken prisoner by the Russians, he had enlisted in the Free Yugoslav Legion, and at Stalin's insistence had been appointed commander of the Legion.

Tito met the Free Yugoslav Legion in Romania on his journey home from Moscow. He spoke to Mesić and told him that his past record as an Ustasha would be forgiven if, from now on, he was a loyal officer in the Yugoslav national army. Perhaps Tito thought that a soldier who had won two military medals and was so highly regarded by Stalin was worth having on his side, even if the medals had been awarded by King Alexander and Hitler. Mesić was loyal to Tito, and served him well, and soon afterwards Tito awarded him his third medal.[52]

Tito did not bear any resentment against individuals who had done him some personal injury in the past. Another officer in the Free Yugoslav Legion was the Yugoslav Communist, Ozren Miler, who in Moscow in 1938 had accused Tito of being a Trotskyist because of some passage in his translation of the *History of the Communist Party of the Soviet Union (Bolsheviks)*. When the other Yugoslavs in the Legion heard that Miler had denounced Tito, they objected to Miler being one of their officers; but the Russians refused to remove Miler. As soon as the Legion entered Yugoslavia and was free of Russian control, the Yugoslavs again demanded that Miler be dismissed; but Tito insisted that he should continue to serve.[53]

After fighting for three years against the Germans, Tito was now on the verge of victory; but the Nazis still hoped to catch and kill him. On 21 September 1944 Heinrich Himmler, the Reichsführer of the SS, addressed a meeting of officers at Jägerhöhe. 'I would like to give another example of steadfastness, that of Marshal Tito,' said Himmler. 'I must really say that he is a veteran Communist, this Herr Josip Broz, a consistent man. Unfortunately he is our enemy. He really has properly earned his title of Marshal. When we catch him we shall do him in at once; you can be sure of that; he is our enemy. But I wish we had a dozen Titos in Germany . . . The man had nothing at all. He was between the Russians, the British and Americans, and had the nerve actually to take the British and Americans for a ride and to shit on them in the most comical way. He is a Moscow man . . . He has never capitulated.'[54]

The Red Army advanced rapidly on Belgrade. Tito ordered units of the Partisans to go with them; he felt that the Yugoslav National

Army, as the Partisans were now called, as well as the Red Army must liberate Belgrade. There was also a Bulgarian division serving with the Red Army, for Bulgaria had changed sides and declared war on Germany when the Red Army captured Sofia. In later years, when Yugoslav-Bulgarian relations were a little tense, Tito said that he had agreed only reluctantly to the entry of the Bulgarian soldiers into Yugoslavia;[55] but the Russians and the Bulgarians asked his permission first, and he granted it.

The Germans put up a fairly serious resistance, and there was some fighting before they retreated to the north and the Red Army and the Partisans entered the city in triumph on 23 October. On 24 October Tito addressed his soldiers and the people from the balcony of King Alexander's palace, and took up his residence in the palace. Whatever the legal position might be, and despite his Vis Agreement with Šubašić, he acted henceforth as the head of the Yugoslav government in the federal capital, Belgrade.

Fitzroy Maclean met him again in Belgrade. He told Tito how offended Churchill had been that Tito had left Vis and gone to Moscow without informing the British authorities. Tito replied that Churchill had not informed him that he was going to Quebec to meet President Roosevelt. Maclean and Churchill considered that Tito's remark was impertinent;[56] but that only showed how necessary it was for Tito to have Stalin's support and the Red Army on hand.

The British knew that Tito had outwitted them, but there was little that they could do about it. The South African prime minister, Field-Marshal Smuts, an elder statesman of the Empire, feared the worst, for he had always been a strong opponent of Communism. On 26 September 1944 he wrote to Churchill: 'In spite of all the help Tito has obtained only from us, he has not behaved loyally to us. I fear that our interests will suffer by his supremacy in Yugoslavia.'[57] Churchill agreed; in his eyes, Tito was no longer a good revolutionary, but a bad one. On 3 December he telegraphed to Smuts: 'Tito has turned very nasty and is of course thinking now only of grabbing Trieste, Istria, Fiume etc. for a virtually Communist Yugoslavia.'[58]

Harold Macmillan, who held the novel position of a Cabinet minister attached to Allied headquarters in Italy, had always been more suspicious than Churchill of Tito; but he accepted the situation realistically. On 6 October 1944 he wrote to the Foreign Office from Caserta: 'Of course Tito's behaviour is not very satisfactory. It has always been my view . . . that Marshal Tito intends to make himself master of Yugoslavia at the end of the war. It is for that reason he wishes to eliminate the Chetniks . . . and of course the Russians will support the Marshal wholeheartedly. I am not sure therefore how strong are the threats about dealing with Tito at the peace settlement.' Macmillan thought that by concentrating all their military effort in Western Europe they had lost the chance to influence events in the Balkans. 'We must certainly do all we can by bluff but it is no good using bluff so transparently that it is easily called.'[59]

The Germans had decided to make a stand before Budapest. The Red Army's advance was held up for six weeks in the suburbs as fierce fighting continued for the Hungarian capital. Meanwhile British forces had landed in Greece and liberated Athens, and the Germans were withdrawing their forces from Greece to reinforce the defence of Budapest. The British High Command decided, after consultation with the Russians, to cut off the German retreat from Greece. This could be done if British troops with artillery could seize control of Cetinje in Montenegro. A British force, which was given the code name of 'Floydforce', occupied the pass and installed eight guns there; but the British thought it necessary to ask Tito's permission before opening fire on the Germans.

Tito granted permission to the British to land at Dubrovnik, but he would not agree to Floydforce preventing the German retreat from Greece. If the Germans could not retreat, they would remain in occupation of Yugoslav territory in Macedonia south of the pass, and might vent their spite on the civilian population there. Tito wished to liberate Yugoslav soil from the Germans as soon as possible, and to claim the credit for doing so. The political value of liberating Yugoslavia from the Germans was more important to Tito than the effect on the Allied war effort in Hungary, even if it meant that more Russian lives would be lost before Budapest. He refused to allow the British to move more guns inland from Dubrovnik, and the plan for Floydforce to prevent the German retreat was abandoned.[60]

This was only one of a series of incidents which caused friction between the British and the Partisans in November 1944. A British soldier was so indignant when he saw a Partisan officer kick a wounded German prisoner that he struck the officer; but a British captain intervened to defuse the situation, and the Partisan general agreed that it had been very wrong of his officer to kick the wounded prisoner.[61]

The British were exasperated by the attitude of some Partisan commanders, particularly by the political commissars.[62] Sometimes the local Partisan officers apologized to the British and explained that they were forced to follow the instructions which they received from Belgrade;[63] sometimes the higher Partisan authorities claimed that the fault lay with insubordinate local commanders.[64] At the summit, Tito and Maclean still got on very well. According to Maclean, whenever a little local difficulty arose, he could always smooth things out after raising the matter with Tito.[65]

Events in Greece caused further tension with the British. After liberating Athens, the British brought back King George and his Conservative government. EAM called a protest demonstration in Athens on 3 December and the police fired on the demonstrators, killing eleven and wounding sixty people, including women and young children. The Greek government accused the Communists of having deliberately put the women and children in the front row of the demonstrators in order to make martyrs of them. The ELAS guerrillas began an armed uprising against the government, and the British army intervened on the government side. For a month they fought the Communists in the streets of Athens before driving them out of the city and suppressing the revolt.

When Churchill went to Moscow in October 1944, Stalin agreed to his proposal that Russia should have a ninety to ten preponderant influence in Romania, that Britain and Russia should be fifty-fifty in Yugoslavia, and that Britain should have a ninety to ten influence in Greece.[66] He therefore decided to give no support to ELAS, but did not trouble to tell the Greek Communists about this,[67] any more than Churchill told the British agents in Romania.[68] When ELAS rose in rebellion in December 1944, they expected to receive some aid from the Soviet Union, even if it stopped short of military intervention. But none came, and at the Yalta conference in February 1945 Churchill thanked Stalin for the attitude that he had adopted about Greece.[69]

There were strong protests in Britain against Churchill's policy in Greece, and the left-wing Socialists and Liberals denounced the government in the House of Commons, in the press, and at public demonstrations. Tito never mentioned Greece in his talks with Maclean,[70] or made any public statement about it; but Djilas and Agitprop launched a strong anti-British campaign in Yugoslavia, and warned the Partisans and the people against the British imperialists.[71]

Churchill was unimpressed by all the protests, and adhered to his policy of supporting a king in Greece and a Communist in Yugoslavia. As King Peter was still prevaricating and refusing to dismiss the Conservative ministers from his government, Churchill lost patience with him, and in January 1945 told him bluntly that if he did not agree to the reconstruction of the Yugoslav government and the implementation of the Tito–Šubašić agreement, the British government would simply announce that it was imposing this situation on Yugoslavia. The king gave way.[72]

The United States, a little reluctantly, followed the British lead; they withdrew their mission from Mihailović and sent an envoy to Tito in Belgrade. In February 1945 Field-Marshal Alexander went there and agreed to supply Tito with a large quantity of arms. Tito now called up men of military age for service in his armed forces. This changed the character of the National Liberation Army, for only a small proportion of the 800,000 conscripted men were devoted Communists. The relationship between the men and women in the army changed; they now wanted to have sex together. This caused problems, and the women were in most places withdrawn from service in the front line and sent to perform duties in the rear.[73]

Mihailović and his Chetniks were concentrated in southern Serbia. Tito ordered Koča Popović to lead three divisions against the Chetniks, and some fighting took place. Not far away, a German force was holding out in the town of Leskovac in southern Serbia. With Tito's approval, the British asked the American Air Force to bomb the town, which was virtually flattened. Many Serbian civilians were killed in the air raid. It had a very demoralizing effect on the Chetniks in the vicinity, and seems to have induced some of them to surrender to the Partisans. If the Allied air force was on Tito's side, what chance did the Chetniks have against him?[74] But in the summer of 1945 Mihailović was still holding out in Serbia.

Budapest fell to the Russians on 18 January, and the Germans retreated further to the north. When they evacuated the Vojvodina the majority of the German inhabitants there went with them; many of them had enlisted in the German *Waffen* SS. In Slovenia, the anti-Communist White Guards joined the retreating Germans. Ljotić's Serbian Fascists also joined them, marching north to Slovenia and linking up with the White Guards.[75] All these groups decided to retreat into Austria and surrender to the British or American forces, who, they hoped, would protect them from the vengeance of the Red Army and the Yugoslav Partisans.

By now the Red Army had launched the final attack on Berlin. In northern Italy large areas of the country were controlled by Italian Partisans under Communist leadership. On 28 April they caught Mussolini as he tried to escape into Switzerland. He and his mistress were tried by a drum-head court-martial which sentenced them to death after a trial which lasted only a few minutes, and they were shot. Two days later, the German radio stations interrupted their programmes to make a solemn announcement: 'Today in Berlin the leader of the Greater German Reich, Adolf Hitler, fell in the fight against Bolshevism.'[76]

The Yugoslav National Liberation Army was marching on Trieste. Tito ordered them to press on as fast as possible, although they were suffering heavy casualties; he wanted them to take Trieste before the Allied armies captured it. The Partisans just won the race. They entered Trieste at nine a.m. on 1 May. A New Zealand regiment, the vanguard of the Allied army, arrived at five that afternoon, and the main force of the British Army on 3 May. On 1 May Berlin surrendered to the Russians and a week later Tito broadcast to the nation from Belgrade. 'Today, 9 May, exactly forty-nine months and three days after the Fascist attack on Yugoslavia, the most powerful aggressive force in Europe, Germany, has capitulated.'[77]

CHAPTER 19

❖

Victory and Revenge

THE war in Europe was officially over, but, as Tito pointed out to his army, there was still some fighting to be done in Yugoslavia.[1] Mihailović and his Chetniks were holding out in Serbia; and in the north-west the German army, accompanied by Ustashas, by Pavelić's regular Croatian army, by the Slovene White Guards, by Ljotić's Serbian Fascists, and by a few Chetniks, were trying to escape into Austria, where they hoped the British army would protect them from the Russians and Tito's Partisans.

Tito ordered his forces to encircle them and prevent their escape; but his local commander, General Basta, had not waited for orders, and had moved rapidly to cut off their retreat.[2] Tito believed that if they reached Austria, they would be protected by the British and American imperialists and probably be used at some future date to attack Communist Yugoslavia and the Soviet Union. Not long ago the British had been supporting the Chetniks; they had once helped White Russian armies to fight against the Bolsheviks in Russia; now that the common enemy, Nazi Germany, had been defeated, they would probably again pursue the same policy.

Some of the British authorities were in fact already thinking along these lines. Sir Orme Sargent at the Foreign Office, who in February 1944 had told Rebecca West how deeply he regretted that military necessity had obliged the British to help Tito, wrote to Churchill on 28 April 1945: 'We had hoped that these anti-Partisan forces in north-west Yugoslavia might, without any assistance from us, prevent Tito from entering Venezia Giulia and Trieste in advance of our troops.' But he admitted that it would be difficult to 'justify collaboration with those troops who hitherto had openly collaborated with the Germans'; so 'I am afraid we must agree' to the suggestion of Sir George Stevenson, who was now the ambassador in Belgrade, that the Yugoslav anti-Partisan forces who escaped to Austria should be disarmed and interned.[3]

Churchill had turned strongly against Tito. He realized that Tito had outwitted him, but there was nothing that he could do except express his anger and instruct his intelligence services to probe into Tito's Communist past and sex life to obtain information which could if necessary be used against him in future. 'Ask the Foreign Office for the fullest possible dossier about Tito,' he wrote on 20 May 1945. 'Is it true that he was educated for four years at a Communist college?' Was it true that he had organized strikes on the Dalmatian coast and 'did not move to fight for Yugoslavia when it was attacked by Germany, but waited till June 22, 1941 when the Comintern gave instructions to all its minions to help Russia? Has he ever been married, and how many times?' The Foreign Office duly supplied Churchill with Tito's dossier. It was compiled by an SOE agent who had been stationed at the British consulate in Zagreb from 1939 to 1941, and was described by the Foreign Office as 'a bit of an expert on Tito'; but it was wildly inaccurate. It stated that Tito had been sent by the Comintern to Australia and Iran in 1923 and had been arrested by the Yugoslav police in Split in 1937 for organising strikes.[4]

But Churchill knew that Tito had won in Yugoslavia. He realized 'how vain it is to throw away our substance in a losing game with Soviet Russia in Titoland . . . Nothing will wrest Yugoslavia from the Russian grip. In this particular theatre the policy is "dis-engage". On the contrary in Greece it is "hold fast".'[5]

The Partisans had another motive for wishing to prevent their enemies' escape into Allied-occupied territory: revenge. Their losses and their sufferings had been terrible, and they did not forget or forgive. Of the 12,000 members of the Communist Party of Yugo-slavia in 1941, 9,000 had been killed in the war,[6] some by the Germans and Italians, but many by the Ustashas and the Chetniks. Most of the 3,000 survivors had lost a dear friend, a wife or a husband. They knew from the handful of survivors who had escaped from enemy captivity of the tortures which in so many cases had been inflicted on their comrades before they were killed. They would have wanted revenge even if they had not been inhabitants of the Balkans.

The Partisans succeeded in surrounding and capturing many of their retreating enemies, including Kasche, and some German and

Ustasha generals who had ordered the shooting of hostages and had committed other war crimes. One of them was General Tomašević, who as Captain Tomašević had been Tito's commander in the Austro-Hungarian army in the First World War. Tito had then thought that he was too severe a disciplinarian; but he was a good deal more severe as an Ustasha general in the Second World War.[7] Kasche, Tomašević and the others were tried as war criminals and executed. The former police chief in Belgrade, Vujković, who had tortured the Communists in police headquarters under King Alexander's dictatorship and had collaborated with the Germans, was shot by the Partisans. But about 200,000 of the anti-Partisan forces succeeded in reaching the British zone of Austria.

The Great Powers had agreed that Austria was to be treated not as a conquered enemy country but as the first victim of German aggression which had now been liberated. It was divided into British, American, French and Soviet occupation zones. On 2 April 1945 Tito officially asked the British, American and Soviet governments that Yugoslavia should be given an occupation zone in Austria; and early in May the Partisan army entered the Austrian province of Carinthia, where some of the population were Slavs by origin. They claimed that they had come to liberate their Slav brethren in Carinthia, which should be incorporated into Yugoslavia. On 13 May Tito wrote to the British ambassador in Belgrade, Stevenson, and complained that only the Soviet Union had replied to the Yugoslav note of 2 April demanding to have an occupation zone in Austria.[8]

The British were determined that the Partisan army should not remain in either Trieste or Carinthia. There were already signs that relations with the Soviet Union might not be as friendly in the future as they had been during the war, and the British government did not want to see Tito, Stalin's ally, holding Trieste and part of Austria.

Some 75,000 Soviet citizens, many of whom were Cossacks, had served in the German army. They had fought for Hitler not only on the Russian front but also against the Communist Partisans in northern Italy and against Tito's Partisans in Yugoslavia. At the Yalta Conference in February, Churchill and Roosevelt had agreed with Stalin that any of them who were captured by the British or American forces should be extradited to the Soviet Union. An exception had been made in the case of the citizens of the three Baltic republics of Lithuania, Latvia and Estonia, because as Britain and the United States had not recognized their annexation by the Soviet Union in

1940, they could not admit that the inhabitants were Soviet citizens, as the Soviet authorities insisted. Nothing was expressly agreed at Yalta about the position of Tsarist White Russians who had escaped from Russia after the revolution of 1917 and had enthusiastically supported Hitler's anti-Bolshevik crusade; but many of them were handed over to the Red Army by the British military authorities in Austria, and were executed as traitors in the Soviet Union.

The Yalta agreement had not referred to the position of Yugoslavs; but when the British military authorities, in May 1945, found themselves confronted with the problem of guarding and feeding 200,000 anti-Communist Yugoslavs in Austria, they were not at all averse to the idea of surrendering them to the Partisans. They were eager to induce the Partisans to agree to withdraw from Trieste and Carinthia; and if they could persuade the Partisans to agree to this on condition that the anti-Communist refugees were delivered up, it would be a very satisfactory solution from the British point of view. The British statesmen and army officers who were involved in the negotiations with the Partisans, and the Partisans themselves, have always strongly denied that any such bargain was made, and they are undoubtedly right; but the British felt that if they were going to get involved in a confrontation with Tito, it should be over Trieste and Carinthia, about which they cared, and not over the fate of the anti-Communist Yugoslavs, about which they did not care. They agreed to surrender the 200,000 refugees to the Partisans, and the Partisans agreed to withdraw from the city of Trieste and from Austria. Between 24 and 29 May 23,000 refugees were delivered to the Partisans.[9]

Orders had been given that they were not to be told of their destination, because if they knew where they were going they might try a mass escape, and they were given to understand that they were being transferred to other camps in Italy. They only realized the truth when they saw that the train was not following the line to Italy, but had branched off to the left on another line which led to the Yugoslav frontier. Then one of them saw that there were guards on the train with the red Partisan star in their caps. When it dawned on the refugees that they were being delivered to the Partisans they were reduced to utter despair. No wonder; they knew what their side had done to the Partisans.

Rade Končar, the general secretary of the Communist party of Croatia, had warned them what to expect when, after enduring prolonged torture, he stood waiting to be hanged on a Fascist gallows: 'I ask for no mercy, and we will show no mercy to you.'[10]

If the survivors are to be believed, nearly all the 23,000 Ustashas, White Guards and Ljotić followers who were delivered to the Partisans were marched to Kočevje and shot beside trenches which had been dug in the woods. A few escaped, and have since told their story. They have described the fury of a woman Partisan who walked among them brandishing a whip with which she flogged an old priest when she found him kneeling in prayer; and how Colonel Penezić, the chief of Tito's political police in Serbia, the OZNA, arrived from Belgrade in his highly polished boots and ordered a massacre of all the prisoners. But they admit that Penezić spared the lives of the young boys among the prisoners. He said that the youth must be cherished and re-educated to be good and useful Communists.[11] They were luckier than all the young boys who were slaughtered by the Ustashas and the Chetniks for being Orthodox or Muslim or for helping the Partisans.

A few British officers, feeling sympathy with the anti-Communist Yugoslavs and guessing what was likely to happen to them if they were returned to Tito, allowed them to escape. One British soldier was so won over by the prisoners that he assaulted and wounded a Yugoslav Partisan who came to take them away.[12] For the Partisans, no further proof was needed that the British were on the side of the Fascists.

Tito had realized that, after all that they had suffered, it would not be easy to prevent the Partisans from bloody retaliation on the Ustashas and Chetniks. In March 1944 he had called on all the Ustashas and other Fascists collaborating with the enemy to join his Partisans at once, for if they ignored this appeal and continued serving in the armed forces of the invader, they would be punished as traitors.[13] But he gave them another chance after the liberation of Belgrade, and on 21 November 1944 he granted an amnesty to anyone who surrendered before 15 January 1945 unless they had committed war crimes.

On 12 January 1945 he issued an order to all the commanders of his armies 'to apply the amnesty immediately to all persons who are included in it', and that capital punishment could be carried out only after proper legal process, as laid down in Article 29 of the Military Regulations, had shown the persons concerned to have been guilty of murder, arson, looting or rape. 'On other persons sentenced to capital punishment, such as operators, organizers and intellectual progenitors of crimes and treacherous activities, capital punishment can be carried out only and exclusively after prior permission of the Council of Higher Military Courts at General Headquarters.' Another order of 11 February 1945 set up military courts, each consisting of three army officers, in every army division, with a Court of Appeal in every corps, and again insisted that capital punishment could only be carried out after the case had been tried in these courts.[14]

After the Partisans entered Zagreb, all officers who had served in Pavelić's army were ordered to surrender to the Partisan authorities within forty-eight hours. Those who did so were sifted into officers and men; the rank-and-file were allowed to go home, but the officers were interned in camps. Most of these officers were released after a few weeks, and only a small number were tried and executed for treason and collaboration with the enemy.[15]

When the Partisan army had marched towards the Austrian frontier and into Carinthia, and was capturing the thousands of prisoners surrendered by the British, Tito issued an order on 14 May 1945 to the Supreme Headquarters of the Slovenian Army:

Take the most energetic measures to prevent at all costs the killing of prisoners-of-war and captives by units, organizations or individuals. If there are among the prisoners-of-war and the women who have been arrested, any persons who should be held responsible for having committed war crimes, they are to be handed over to the military courts, who shall sign a statement in writing that they have taken charge of them.

Death to Fascism! Freedom to the People!

Tito. 14 May, 1945. Belgrade.[16]

General Basta, the commander-in-chief in Slovenia, insists that he scrupulously obeyed Tito's order, and refrained from taking vengeance on the Ustashas and Chetniks who had murdered so many members of his family. But he does not accept responsibility for anything that happened outside the area of his command; and generals who were even higher in rank than Basta have admitted, as Djilas has done, that many people who were labelled by the Communists as 'Fascists' were summarily executed in the summer of 1945 without any form of trial.[17] Most of the Germans and Hungarians in the Vojvodina had collaborated with the invader, and many of them were killed by the Partisans in the winter of 1944–45. Those who survived, and had not fled with the retreating German and Hungarian armies, were deported after the war. The Partisans had announced that only those who had fought on the side of the invaders would be punished, and that no one would suffer for any of his political actions before the war; but this rule was not always followed.[18]

The fate of the refugees, and the part which the British army had played in bringing it about, was not generally known in Britain and the United States at the time. The story was told by anti-Tito Yugoslavs in America about fifteen years later. It took almost forty years for it to become generally known in Britain. The Partisans' massacre of their political opponents, and Britain's part in it, was then widely publicized and condemned by people who viewed it from the standpoint of 1984 not 1945. In 1984 many could feel sympathy for Croats, Slovenes and Serbs (as well as Russians) who found themselves in a world dominated by two dictators, Hitler and Stalin, and decided to fight for Hitler against Stalin. Very few people in Britain saw the situation in this light in 1945.

The association of names illustrates, and also helps to formulate, public opinion. Today people speak and write about 'Hitler and Stalin'; but hardly anyone spoke of 'Hitler and Stalin' during the Second World War. At that time people spoke about 'Hitler and Mussolini' and 'Churchill, Roosevelt and Stalin'. Hitler was Britain's enemy and Stalin was Britain's ally. Any Russian or Yugoslav who fought for Hitler against Stalin and Tito was a traitor to his country, and it was right to hand him over to Stalin and Tito to be punished as he deserved, just as it would have been right for the Russians and Yugoslavs to have extradited William Joyce, 'Lord Haw-Haw', to Britain to be tried and executed as a traitor for having broadcast propaganda on the German radio.

If some of the victims killed by the Partisans in the pits at Kočevje had not murdered Partisans or committed war crimes, and had not even fought for the Fascist invaders, then they were innocent victims of war; but they were no more innocent than the two-year-old child killed in the British air raid on Dresden whose photograph was plastered by Goebbels on the front page of the German newspapers under the caption: 'He died for Germany'.[19] The British public in 1945, having accepted the killing of 90,000 civilians in one night in Dresden in February and of 300,000 by one bomb in Hiroshima in August, would not have been unduly distressed had they known that Tito had killed 23,000 in May, even if they had not been prepared to agree with General Glaise von Horstenau that there is no moral distinction between horizontal and vertical terror – between being massacred horizontally by the bullets of a firing squad or vertically by bombs dropped from the air.

By the standards of the Second World War the number of the Partisans' victims was relatively small. Today in Britain Tito is condemned for killing the 23,000 refugees handed over to him; but many people in Serbia condemn him for having killed so few. They say that only 'the Croat Broz' could have been satisfied with the death of some 30,000 Croats as sufficient atonement for the 700,000 Serbs murdered by the Ustashas, though the figure of 700,000 is almost certainly as exaggerated as the figure of 300,000 said to have been killed by the Partisans in 1945.[20]

Some of the worst war criminals succeeded in reaching Austria, and escaped. Before the end of May 1945, the British authorities had changed their policy of handing over the anti-Communist refugees to the Partisans; henceforth they were detained in internment camps, and in due course they were released. Many Ustashas made use of their connection with their fellow Roman Catholics, who helped obtain their release from the British internment camps and then organized their escape from Austria and Italy to Franco's Spain or to South America.[21] Pavelić himself escaped, and remained free despite all the efforts of Tito's government to obtain his extradition, until he died in Madrid in 1959, having survived an assassination attempt in Argentina two years before. Dinko Sakić, who had succeeded Luburić as commandant of the Jasenovac camp, also reached South America, and returned to Austria in 1991 to take part in a reunion at Bleiburg of survivors among the German SS and Croatian Ustashas.

Tito received welcome news from the south. On 13 May 1945 Koča Popović's army succeeded in cornering and defeating Mihailović and the Chetniks on the Sutjeska, near the site of the great battle of 1943. The Chetniks fled in all directions. Mihailović escaped into the mountains with a small band of followers, and foiled every attempt by the Partisans to catch him; but every day more Chetniks surrendered to the Partisans. Some were killed or ill-treated, but most were welcomed and pardoned. Louise Rayner, an Englishwoman who had married a Serb and spent the war enduring the shortages and hardships of life in a Serbian village, saw a Chetnik prisoner who had had both his thumbs cut off by the Partisans;[22] but most of the young men who had left a few years earlier to join the Chetniks returned proudly wearing Partisan uniform, boasting that they had won the war.

Tito announced that free democratic elections would be held for a Constituent Assembly to decide the future government of Yugoslavia. He invited the United Nations and political parties in Western Europe to send observers to make sure that the elections were free and fair. Before the election Djilas and Agitprop organized an intensive propaganda campaign vilifying not only the Fascist and right-wing groups who had collaborated with the invader, but also Liberal, Social-Democratic and left-wing parties which at various times had joined in a united front with the Communists and were prepared to do so now. These parties were not allowed access to the radio, and had no national newspapers in which they could reply to the Communist attacks.

The most powerful of these parties was Maček's Peasant party in Croatia. Maček denied that he had collaborated with the Germans or Ustashas; he had spent most of the war imprisoned by the Ustashas either in a concentration camp or under house arrest. But it was not very difficult for the Communists to portray him as a collaborator; he had joined Cvetković's pro-Nazi government before the war, and had never called on the people of Croatia to join the resistance movement against the Germans and the Ustashas after 1941.

The Communists persuaded some members of the Croat Peasant party to found a new Peasant party which would be free of the taint of collaboration which clung to Maček and his party. This new party did well in the election and succeeded in splitting Maček's party and destroying its political influence in Croatia. After the election the new Peasant party dissolved itself, and advised its members to support the Communist party. Maček's Peasant party was unostentatiously suppressed.[23]

As a victorious war hero Tito was a popular figure in Yugoslavia, and undoubtedly had the support of the majority of the electors, even in Serbia, where the Chetniks had most support. The pressure of public opinion and Djilas's efficient propaganda succeeded in overpowering the political opposition to the Communists. Rumours circulated that the elections were not really free and that people who voted against Tito would be victimized. The electors voted by dropping a metal counter into either the government or the Opposition candidates' boxes. It was said that if the counter was dropped into the Opposition candidate's box, it would make a ringing noise which would be heard by the officials in the polling station who would thus know that the voter had voted for the Opposition and would make him suffer for having done so;[24] but in fact the boxes were lined with rubber, and no sound was heard when counters were dropped into them.[25]

By the time that the foreign observers arrived, everything was set for a big government majority. Many of the observers were politically sympathetic to Tito. The left-wing Labour MP, Konni Zilliacus, came from Britain with a group of other Labour MPs; some of them were well-known pro-Communist fellow-travellers. They were all delighted when they were presented to Tito, and all agreed that the election was fair.[26] Tito's candidates obtained ninety-six per cent of the votes.

With this majority in the Constituent Assembly, Tito proceeded step by step to set aside the agreement which he had signed with Šubašić on Vis in June 1944. The Constituent Assembly abolished the monarchy, declared a republic, and chose Ivan Ribar as president, with Tito as prime minister. Šubašić was persuaded to resign as King Peter's prime minister and took office in Tito's government as foreign minister. He was gradually ousted from influence in his ministry and some time later resigned from the government, and withdrew into private life. By the summer of 1946 Yugoslavia had become a full-dress Communist state, a one-party dictatorship with Tito as the dictator.

Yugoslavia adopted a constitution which was almost an exact replica of the 1937 'Stalin Constitution' of the Soviet Union. It granted all the citizens of Yugoslavia the fundamental freedoms of speech and the press, and exemption from arbitrary arrest and imprisonment; but these rights could if necessary be suspended in the interests of state security. In practice there was no opposition in parliament and no free press, and no right to demonstrate against the government.

On 7 July 1945 Tito addressed a meeting at Mladenovac on Mount Kosmaj in Serbia on the anniversary and in the area of the first outbreak of armed resistance against the German army of occupation in 1941. He knew that there was more opposition to his government, and more support for the Chetniks, in Serbia than in any other part of Yugoslavia, and he went out of his way to praise the Serbian uprising of 7 July 1941. 'It was the Serbian people, the flower of Serbian youth, who set the example to the other peoples of Yugoslavia and showed them how to fight the common enemy.'

He then replied to those critics in foreign countries who asserted that there was no democracy in Yugoslavia, and that it was a land where people went in fear. 'The vast majority lived in fear before the war, fear of that gendarmerie which was everywhere and at everybody's heels ... But those who live in fear today are those formerly accustomed to terrorizing the people.' There was a small group of people in Yugoslavia, and all the critics abroad, who wanted to see the OZNA disbanded. 'I remember the time when I wanted the gendarmerie disbanded'; but the royal government had not disbanded the gendarmerie, and he would not disband the OZNA. 'If the OZNA strikes fear into the bones of those who do not like the new Yugoslavia, that is to the advantage of our people.' Everyone would be free to criticize the authorities provided that it was 'positive criticism'. 'Of course, unhealthy criticism, carping, malicious criticism intended to make things out even worse than they are, should be suppressed, but healthy criticism should be valued, for it is of help to us.'

He asked the audience to reflect on what would have happened in Yugoslavia had the Partisans not won their struggle against their enemies. 'Think well about this, dear brothers and sisters, and you will see that we should have been in a state of terrible chaos, in a fratricidal war, in a country which would no longer be Yugoslavia, but would be only a group of petty little states fighting among themselves and destroying each other. But our people do not want that to happen.'[27]

CHAPTER 20

❖

The Cold War

I N foreign policy Tito intended to pursue a tough attitude towards
Britain and the United States. Now that German Fascism had
been defeated, the worst enemy was British imperialism, which
had recently been the ally, but was normally the enemy, of international Communism. Tito wished to give all the help and encouragement which he could to left-wing movements in Europe and
throughout the world. The nearest revolutionaries were in a neighbouring country, Greece, with its hundred-mile frontier with the
Yugoslav province of Macedonia. The ELAS forces, having been
driven out of Athens by British troops in January 1945, were continuing spasmodic guerrilla resistance in the mountains of northern
Greece.

Tito gave ELAS all the support short of war which a friendly
neighbouring state can give to rebel guerrillas. He sent them arms
from Yugoslavia; he sent General Dapčević and other military
experts to help train their fighters;[1] he allowed them to retreat into
Yugoslavia when they were hard pressed by the Greek government
forces, and re-enter Greece to continue the struggle at an opportune
time. He allowed their wounded to receive medical treatment in
Yugoslavia. Similar aid was given to ELAS by Greece's other two
Communist neighbours, Albania and Bulgaria, but it was not on the
same scale as the aid which they received from Yugoslavia.

Many Greek children were evacuated across the frontier from
northern Greece. Some went to Bulgaria, Albania and the Soviet
Union, but most went to Yugoslavia. The government of Greece,
and official propaganda in Britain and the United States, accused
Yugoslavia and the other Communist governments of kidnapping
these children so that they could be indoctrinated with Communist

propaganda, and declared that it was a crime against humanity. Tito and the Communists said that they were rescuing the children from the horrors of civil war to which they were being subjected by the Greek agents of British imperialism.

At the end of the war, movements for independence from the colonial powers developed in British Malaya, in Dutch Indonesia, and in French Indo-China; in Malaya and Indo-China they were under Communist leadership. The Chinese Communists, who had made a united front with Chiang Kai-shek against the Japanese, resumed their war against him after the defeat of Japan. Tito gave moral support to all these revolutionary movements.

Stalin had a different perspective. He had won the war, and wanted to rule the world jointly with Britain and the United States. He would safeguard his frontiers by installing Communist governments, or governments under Communist influence, in the states bordering on the Soviet Union, and would exact complete obedience from these governments; but he wished to avoid conflict with Britain and the United States outside his sphere of interest. When he attended a summit conference in July 1945 at Potsdam with Churchill and Harry S. Truman, who had become president of the United States when Roosevelt died, Truman told him that the United States had developed and tested a nuclear bomb which it was intending to use against Japan. Stalin realized that this formidable new weapon gave the United States an overwhelming military advantage over the Soviet Union, and he was determined to avoid war with the United States until the Soviet Union had developed its own nuclear weapons, which it succeeded in doing by 1949.

At the Potsdam Conference, the United States secretary of state, James Byrnes, congratulated Stalin on the achievement of the Red Army which had fought its way for nearly 2,000 miles from Stalingrad to Berlin. Stalin modestly declined the compliment, and said wistfully: 'Tsar Alexander got to Paris.'[2] By 1945 Stalin saw himself as the successor to Alexander I, the conqueror of Napoleon in 1814, not to Lenin in 1917. He would have liked to create, like Tsar Alexander, a Holy Alliance of the superpowers to divide up and rule the world. He would then be able to extract the maximum amount of reparations from defeated Germany and extend Soviet influence elsewhere. He proposed to Britain and the United States that the Soviet Union should be granted a trusteeship over the Italian colony of Tripolitania in North Africa, which meant in practice that

Tripolitania should be ceded to the Soviet Union. Britain and the United States rejected the proposal, and Tripolitania was made part of an independent Libya.

Stalin told the Italian Communist party to disarm the Partisans in northern Italy, to avoid calling strikes or engaging in other disruptive activity, and to join a coalition government with the Italian Christian Democrats and right-wing parties. He told the French Communist party to pursue the same policy and to enter a coalition government with de Gaulle. He told the Chinese Communists not to begin a civil war against Chiang Kai-shek, but to continue supporting him. He told Tito that he would not support his claim to Trieste, and urged him to stop aiding the Communist guerrillas in Greece.

But even before the war against Germany was finally ended, friction arose between the Soviet Union and the Western Allies. President Truman, a typical American small businessman from Missouri, was strongly opposed to Communism. When Germany attacked the Soviet Union in 1941, he had publicly declared that he hoped the Nazis and the Communists would kill each other off. At the end of April 1945 he had a stormy interview with Molotov in Washington, when he took Molotov to task because the Soviet Union was violating those clauses of the Yalta agreement by which they promised to hold free democratic elections in Poland.[3] The American belief in democratic institutions, and the pressure exerted on senators and congressmen by immigrants from Poland and other countries of Eastern Europe, made the government of the United States unwilling to give Stalin a free hand to enforce his form of Communist dictatorship over the peoples of Eastern Europe.

In Britain the Labour party came to power because of the leftward swing of public opinion. Many voters believed that Britain would be able to establish better relations with the Soviet Union than a Conservative government could do, because 'Left speaks to Left';[4] but in fact precisely the opposite occurred. Attlee appointed Ernest Bevin as his foreign secretary. Bevin throughout his political life had fought Communists in the trade union movement, and his hatred of the Soviet Union fitted in well with the policy of the Foreign Office, who had not liked the pro-Soviet policy that Churchill had been pursuing during the Second World War. The traditional British foreign policy of preserving the balance of power in Europe meant that Britain must oppose and thwart the policy of the Soviet Union, which since the defeat of Hitler had become the dominant power in

Europe. The Foreign Office were delighted to find that the new Labour foreign secretary was as anti-Russian as they were. British diplomats became aware of a noticeable change in British foreign policy and a hardening of attitude towards the Soviet Union after Bevin took over from Eden as foreign secretary.[5]

Stalin strongly resented Truman's concern over the absence of free elections and democratic freedoms in Soviet-occupied territory. It had probably never occurred to him that anyone would expect him to take seriously the clauses in the Yalta agreement which promised democratic rights to the Poles, and he believed that the attitude of Truman and Bevin could be explained only by their desire to meddle in the Soviet sphere of influence and to create a breach between their countries and the Soviet Union. In September 1945 the foreign ministers of the Soviet Union, Britain and the United States met in London to discuss the peace treaty with Germany and the problems of the postwar world. Bevin and Byrnes proposed that France be invited to join them in their discussions. Molotov strongly opposed this. The admission of France would be the thin end of the wedge which would lead to the admission of all the small nations. He thought that Bevin and Byrnes were adopting this attitude because they did not wish to reach agreement with the Soviet Union but to outvote the Soviet Union in the discussions. Molotov was forced to give way, and the French foreign minister, Bidault,* joined them in what would become a series of Four-Power meetings.

In 1941 Britain and the Soviet Union decided on a joint British-Soviet occupation of Iran to thwart the Shah's pro-German policy; the British army marched in from the south and west and the Red Army from the north. Now Bevin proposed that Britain and the Soviet Union should both withdraw their troops from Iran. But the Soviet Union had encouraged the growth of a left-wing movement in their zone of occupation, and divided the large estates among the peasants. Bevin insisted that the Red Army withdraw from Iran, and the Soviet Union eventually agreed to do so. Tito took the lead in denouncing the British government, who had insisted on over-throwing the land reform in northern Iran and in returning to the

---

* Bidault, Georges (1899–1983). French liberal politician; a prominent leader of the Resistance in France during the Second World War; foreign minister 1945–51 and 1953–4; leader of the terrorist campaign against the granting of independence to Algeria in 1961–2; went into exile, but was pardoned and returned to France in 1968.

landlords the land that had been divided among the peasants.

The Soviet Union retaliated for this hostile British policy by supporting for the first time the ELAS guerrillas in Greece. At the meeting of the United Nations Security Council in London in January 1946 Vyshinsky denounced British policy in Greece, and the meeting developed into a slanging match between him and Bevin. In March Churchill, now leader of the Opposition, in a speech at Fulton in Missouri, criticized the Soviet Union for erecting an iron curtain in Europe, and warned the United States and Western Europe against the Soviet threat.

It was the beginning of the Cold War. Tito came out enthusiastically on the side of the Soviet Union, and was seen in Britain and the United States as the most hostile and pro-Soviet of all the Communist dictators in Eastern Europe. But he was already causing some problems for Stalin. For the first time, another Communist party had emulated the Communist Party of the Soviet Union and had come to power by carrying through a successful Communist revolution. Tito's prestige stood very high among Communists and left-wing sympathizers in Yugoslavia and throughout the world. The Yugoslavs were acclaimed as the only people who had liberated themselves instead of being liberated either by the Red Army or by the British and the Americans.

Tito's critics, both in the Soviet Union and in Western Europe and the United States, have often pointed out that this is a myth. They argue that Tito and the Partisans could never have driven out Hitler's armies by their own efforts if the Germans had not been defeated by the Soviet, British and United States forces. But the Yugoslav Partisans had played a much more important part in liberating their country than the resistance movements elsewhere in Europe; and if the Yugoslav Partisans had not liberated themselves from the Germans, they had certainly carried through their own Communist revolution. Stalin and the Comintern had told them to fight only for national liberation and not for a Communist Yugoslavia; Stalin had made an agreement with Churchill for a fifty-fifty British and Soviet control of Yugoslavia;[6] and he had agreed to the return of King Peter. Tito and the Yugoslav Communists, by themselves, had upset this agreement and had made Yugoslavia a hundred per cent Communist.

The atmosphere in Yugoslavia was very different from Poland, Czechoslovakia, Hungary, Bulgaria or Romania. In Czechoslovakia civil servants in dark suits and starched collars governed the country from offices hung with photographs of Masaryk, Beneš and Stalin, and the civil servants attended functions and frequented expensive restaurants with Russian officers in their splendid uniforms. In Yugoslavia young revolutionaries with tommy-guns on their shoulders and fervour in their eyes patrolled the frontier posts and internal checkpoints, singing revolutionary songs about Tito, and the other Communist anthems, the 'Varshavianka', 'Soviet Land', the 'Bandiera Rossa', and the 'International'. They were joined by equally enthusiastic young Communists and Leftists from foreign countries who came to work long hours as volunteers in building a new railway in Yugoslavia or in the fields to help bring in the harvest. As they marched through the streets, and at their social gatherings in the evenings, they chanted the slogan 'Tito, Stalin, Dimitrov!' Stalin would have preferred this slogan if the words 'Tito' and 'Dimitrov' had been left out.

The adulation of Tito in Yugoslavia almost equalled the adulation of Stalin in the Soviet Union. Photographs of Tito, usually in his marshal's uniform, were everywhere displayed in government offices, banks, shops and cafés. There was a 'Titograd' or some other city named after Tito in every republic, and a 'Tito Street' as well as a 'Red Army Street' in every town and in many villages. The word 'Tito' was painted up on walls; in some places it was carved out of the rock, in enormous letters, on mountainsides, and on islands in the harbours of the Adriatic.[7] In the schools, the young children, the seven-year-olds in the youth organization 'Tito's Pioneers', lined up in the school playground, standing with their clenched fists raised to touch the red stars in their school caps, while the teacher called out 'For the Fatherland with Tito!', and the children made the prescribed response: 'Onward!'[8]

All this worried Stalin; a Communist leader who was so popular might become difficult to control. He dealt with the problem by alternately flattering Tito and cutting him down to size.

The first signs of tension between the Soviet Union and Communist Yugoslavia arose as early as the autumn of 1944 after the liberation of Belgrade. The Red Army in Yugoslavia, as in all the other countries which they occupied, looted and raped. During the battle for Belgrade, a Partisan girl was sent as a courier from a Partisan unit to link up with the nearest Red Army regiment. She was raped at the regimental headquarters by a Red Army officer. There were other cases where Partisan girls working as nurses were raped by Red Army NCOs. This was not the comradely assistance which the Yugoslav Partisans had expected to receive from the glorious Red Army.

Djilas mentioned the incidents to General Korneyev. He told him that Partisans who had encountered the British army on Vis and elsewhere were saying that British officers had higher morals than Red Army officers. Korneyev became very angry. He accused Djilas of insulting the Soviet Army, and reported to Moscow that Djilas was a Trotskyist.[9]

Tito and Djilas tried to calm things down when they went to Moscow in April 1945 to sign a treaty of friendship with the Soviet Union. Tito was treated with great honour, and seated next to Stalin at the banquets. Stalin raised the question of Djilas's remarks to Korneyev about the Red Army rapes. He complained that Djilas had offended an army which was shedding its blood to help them to get rid of the Germans. 'There are black sheep in every family, but it would be strange to condemn the whole family because of one black sheep.' Djilas went out of his way in Moscow to emphasize his devotion to the Soviet Union, and said that 'there is no force on earth which could break the fraternal alliance of the peoples of Yugoslavia with the peoples of the Soviet Union'.[10]

On 21 May 1945 Tito visited Zagreb soon after the city had been liberated. In his speech he referred to the friendship between Yugoslavia and the Soviet Union. It was 'a brotherhood affirmed and hardened through all the common battles in which we fought side by side with our great Slav brothers, our great and mighty ally the Soviet Union under the leadership and genius of Stalin'.[11]

But six days later he made a speech in Ljubljana. He complained that the Partisans had been forced by the Allies to withdraw from Carinthia. 'Our brothers in Istria and the Slovene littoral are free, but our brothers in Carinthia are not yet liberated ... Only a few days have passed since the Yugoslav Army have had to leave Carinthia, and we already hear the laments and cries for help of our brothers in Carinthia.' If the war had been a just war, 'we demand also a just termination of this war, we demand that everyone be master in his own house ... We will not be mixed up in the politics of spheres of interest.' Yugoslavia today was not the Yugoslavia of 1919. 'There is a new Yugoslavia today ... We demand nothing more than that they should regard it as such. This Yugoslavia is not an object for barter and bargaining.'[12]

The Soviet government was so sensitive to criticism, and so determined to take every opportunity to assert its domination over its satellite states, that it chose to interpret Tito's words as an attack on the Soviet Union. The Soviet ambassador in Belgrade, Sadchikov, raised the matter with Kardelj, who had been appointed foreign minister. Kardelj assured Sadchikov that Tito had been referring only to Britain and the United States who were obstructing Yugoslavia's just claims to Trieste and Carinthia. The Soviet government were not satisfied with this explanation. Molotov instructed Sadchikov to raise the matter again. 'We regard Comrade Tito's speech as an unfriendly attack on the Soviet Union, and the explanation by Comrade Kardelj as unsatisfactory . . . Tell Comrade Tito that if he should once again permit such an attack on the Soviet Union, we shall be forced to reply with open criticism in the press, and disavow him.'[13]

When Sadchikov spoke to Kardelj on 5 June, Kardelj behaved not as the foreign minister of an independent state, but as a good Communist indulging in self-criticism at a party meeting. 'He said that he thought our opinion of Tito's speech was correct,' wrote Sadchikov. 'He also agreed that the Soviet Union could no longer tolerate similar statements . . . Kardelj asked me to convey to you his gratitude for this well-timed criticism.' Kardelj went on to say that Tito had done good work 'in liquidating fractionalism in the Communist party of Yugoslavia and in organizing the people's liberation struggle, but he was inclined to regard Yugoslavia as a self-sufficient unit outside the general development of the proletarian revolution and Socialism'. Kardelj also complained that Tito did not convene regular meetings of the party Central Committee. He told Sadchikov that he hoped that the Soviet government would regard Yugoslavia as a future part of the Soviet Union, and the Communist party of Yugoslavia as a future branch of the Communist party of the Soviet Union. Sadchikov had no instructions to go as far as this, and replied that whatever situation might arise in the future, at present he would regard Yugoslavia as an independent state and the Communist party of Yugoslavia as an independent party.[14]

Either from careless talk, or from a calculated desire to cause mischief, the Soviet government leaked news of what Kardelj had said to Sadchikov, and it was reported to Tito. He raised it with Kardelj, who protested to Tito that he had no intention of being disloyal to him. Tito cheerfully accepted this; even Djilas, after he had become a severe critic of Tito and of the Communist regime, admitted that Tito never bore a personal grudge against individuals who had done him a bad turn.[15]

The Yugoslav army hunted down Mihailović. For ten months they searched for him unsuccessfully in the mountains of southern Serbia, as one by one his supporters surrendered to the Partisans. He did not consider the possibility of escaping abroad. He would remain in Yugoslavia until his supporters flocked to him again, and the Serbian people rose in revolt against Communist tyranny.

Then one of his followers betrayed him and revealed his where-abouts to the OZNA, who captured him in March 1946.[16] The news reached Ranković, who was minister of the interior, just as Tito was leaving Belgrade on a visit to Warsaw. Ranković sent a message to Tito: 'The plan is fulfilled.' When Tito reached Warsaw he tele-phoned Stalin and told him the news.

Stalin said that he was pleased, but his next reaction was annoy-ance; why had he heard the news from Tito and not from the NKVD representative in Belgrade? Was it because the Yugoslav authorities had not told the NKVD representative? The NKVD man first heard of Mihailović's capture when he read it in the Yugoslav newspapers next day. He protested to Ranković, and told him how he had been reprimanded by Stalin. Ranković thought the complaint was absurd, and said: 'Surely the main thing is that Draža has been caught.'[17]

Mihailović was brought to Belgrade. The government decided to bring him to trial, and searched for damning evidence against him. They had captured his files of correspondence, which showed how he had been in contact with the occupation authorities; but they wanted more evidence, particularly of his collaboration with the Germans. This evidence was hard to find, because the Germans, unlike the Italians, had not often worked together with Mihailović. Ranković's OZNA questioned German prisoners-of-war and fifth columnists who were awaiting trial as traitors.

Dr Gert Feine, a career diplomat who had never been an enthusi-astic Nazi, was first secretary at the German embassy in Belgrade until he hurriedly left after the demonstrations against the Tripartite Pact on 27 March 1941. He spent the rest of the war in the Foreign Office in Berlin. He was perturbed when he was informed in the spring of 1946 that the Yugoslav authorities wished to interrogate him; surely no one could accuse him of war crimes? His anxieties disappeared as soon as he reached Belgrade. He was entertained at ten-course dinners, which were a welcome change from the meagre rations allocated to German civilians in 1946, and realized that all they wanted from him was that he should give evidence against Mihailović; had Mihailović been in contact with the German embassy before the outbreak of war? They accepted his assurances that he had never had any dealings with Mihailović and could give no evidence about him, and Feine returned to Germany after a few pleasant weeks in Yugoslavia.[18]

The trial of Mihailović opened on 10 June 1946 in the great guard room at Topčider, the former headquarters of the Royal Guard on the outskirts of Belgrade.[19] It was not a fair trial, but neither was it a stage-managed trial on the Soviet model, with the defendant confessing to every crime in the calendar, vilifying himself, and asking the court to impose the death sentence. It was more like an old-fashioned revolutionary trial, like the trials of Charles I, of Louis XVI, of the Emperor Maximilian in Mexico, and the trials before the French revolutionary tribunal of 1794. Mihailović admitted that he had at various times negotiated with the Germans, but denied that he had ever been a traitor to his country.

There was some sympathy for him in Britain, and a good deal more in the United States. Several British and American officers, who had been stationed at his headquarters during the war, wished to give evidence for the defence; but the court refused to allow them to be called as witnesses, on the grounds that as they only stayed for a short time with Mihailović, they would not be in a position to know whether he had had contacts with the Germans. Mihailović was interrogated at great length by the court, and was repeatedly asked whether he had met representatives of the German High Command. The implication of these questions was that such meetings would themselves have been acts of treason. No one said anything about the meetings between Tito's delegates and General Glaise von Horstenau. Very few people in Yugoslavia knew anything about this in 1946.

Mihailović made a final plea in his defence, and was allowed to speak for four and a half hours without interruption from the court, though only a small part of his speech was published in the official report of the trial. He explained the position which he had adopted throughout the war, but said that 'the whirlwind, the world whirlwind, carried me and my work away'.[20] His attitude impressed the foreign journalists who were present in court, and they praised his courage and dignity, which won him great sympathy abroad, though he was virulently abused by press and radio in Yugoslavia. He was sentenced to death. His friends persuaded him to send a petition for clemency to Tito, but Tito refused to commute the death sentence, and he was executed by a firing squad on 17 July 1946.

The United States government made an official protest to Yugoslavia against the way in which the trial was conducted. Congress in Washington appointed a congressional committee to investigate the conduct of the trial, and the committee reported that the trial was a frame-up and that Mihailović was innocent. He was posthumously awarded an American decoration by President Truman.[21]

Relations between Yugoslavia and the United States were now very bad. Roosevelt and the United States government had never been as enthusiastic as Churchill was for Tito, but after the liberation of Belgrade the United States agreed, rather reluctantly, to recognize Tito's government. The American advisers disagreed in their assessment of Tito and his future policy. The US envoy, Robert D. Murphy, who visited Tito on Vis in August 1944, thought that he 'was more of a national patriot than an international Communist';[22] but Alexander C. Kirk, the representative of the OSS in Caserta, wrote in December 1944 that Tito's regime was potentially a serious threat to American interests, because the leaders were 'apostles of a faith inspired not least by envy or who have been made vindictive by repression ... Given this background, their very asceticism can make these men dangerous.'[23] By the summer of 1946 Truman and the US State Department were quite convinced that Kirk had been right and Murphy wrong; and they refused to deliver to Tito the gold that King Peter's government had deposited in Washington in 1941.

In the last months of the war, the United Nations had set up its Relief and Rehabilitation Agency (UNRRA) to bring relief to the countries and peoples suffering from the war. Few countries had suffered as much as Yugoslavia, and UNRRA officials were working there by the winter of 1944–5. One of them was the British Communist James Klugmann, who had been transferred there from SOE Cairo; but most of the officials were Americans. They had difficulties with Tito from the very beginning. UNRRA insisted that their aid should be distributed without political discrimination and wished to verify this; the Yugoslav government accused the UNRRA officials of being American spies, and would not allow them to travel anywhere. After the deterioration in United States-Yugoslav relations, UNRRA aid was suspended.[24]

After this, Yugoslavia came to depend increasingly on the Soviet Union for economic aid as well as for political support. The Soviet Union signed commercial treaties with all the Communist states of Eastern Europe, and offered to sign a similar treaty with Yugoslavia. Velebit, as assistant foreign minister, was given the duty of negotiating the commercial treaty. He began by asking the Yugoslav ambassadors in Bucharest and Sofia to send him copies of the commercial treaties which Romania and Bulgaria had recently signed with the Soviet Union. When he studied them, he was surprised to see how one-sided they were, giving all the advantages to the Soviet Union and none to Romania or Bulgaria. He was well prepared for argument when the Soviet ambassador called at the Foreign Office in Belgrade to discuss the question.

Velebit opened the discussion by saying that he thought that before going into details they should discuss the underlying principles on which the treaty should be based. The Soviet ambassador looked surprised. 'But there is nothing to discuss,' he said. 'I have got the draft of the treaty here with me.' He took the draft treaty from his dispatch case and proposed that he and Velebit should initial it without further discussion. When Velebit refused, the ambassador walked out and made a very adverse report to Moscow about Velebit. A few weeks later, Tito, Kardelj and the Politburo of the Yugoslav Communist party decided to accept and sign the Soviet ambassador's draft of the treaty.[25]

American military planes often flew on scheduled flights over Yugoslavia. Tito complained that they sometimes violated Yugoslav air space. If American-Yugoslav relations had been friendly, the matter could have been straightened out without difficulty; but in the political atmosphere of the summer of 1946, it was almost bound to lead to an incident. The Yugoslav government sent a strong protest to the United States against the violation of its air space. The United States government denied that any violation had occurred, and assured the Yugoslavs that United States planes never flew over the territory of a friendly state without permission; but we now know that this was untrue, and that the United States and its NATO allies sent many planes on secret spying missions over the territory of the Soviet Union. Tito alleged that the flights continued, and denounced the United States publicly in the Yugoslav National Assembly.

In August 1946 Yugoslav fighters shot down two United States military planes flying between Vienna and Udine in Italy; one of them passed very near Tito's hunting lodge at Bled, where Tito was in residence. Five United States airmen were killed.[26] The State Department sent a strong protest to Yugoslavia, and there was a great outcry in the American press. Kardelj and Molotov were attending a conference in Paris at the time. Molotov said to Kardelj: 'Congratulations, but don't do it again.'[27]

Tito followed this advice and did not do it again; and when the United States threatened to take the case to the Security Council of the United Nations, he gave way, apologized, and agreed to pay 150,000 US dollars compensation to the United States government and the families of the dead airmen. According to the Yugoslavs, there were several other violations of Yugoslav air space by American planes during August; but the Yugoslavs this time pretended not to notice.

Tito's government also came into conflict with the Church. The Orthodox and Muslim religious leaders were prepared to submit to the authority of his government, but the Roman Catholic Church in Croatia was his biggest problem. The Roman Catholic clergy and the Communist Party of Yugoslavia carried on the war between the Church and 'the Revolution' which had been raging ever since Pope Pius VI issued his encyclical against the French Revolution in 1791; it had been fought out with great savagery on both sides over 150 years in the Vendée in France, in Italy, in Spain, and in Mexico, and most cruelly of all in Croatia and Bosnia during the Second World War.

When Tito first came to power he tried to win over the Roman Catholic Church and persuade them to collaborate with the new Communist regime. On 2 June 1945 he met a deputation of leading Catholic clergy; but the Archbishop of Zagreb, Aloysius Stepinac, did not attend. Tito thanked them for coming to meet him, and for their willingness to cooperate with the Yugoslav federal government. 'I must tell you, as a Catholic myself, that I have not been satisfied with the attitude of a certain part of the Croatian clergy during these difficult historic times . . . But that does not mean . . . that I condemn the clergy as a whole.' There would have to be a new type of Catholic Church which would cooperate with the state in building up a Federal Yugoslavia in which the Orthodox Church, representing the largest number of Yugoslavs, would play a predominant role. 'For my part, I would say that our Church shall be a National Church more suited to the nation.' He said that he would not condemn the papacy. 'No, that I will not do. Yet I must say that I take a critical view of it, for that supreme body has always leaned rather towards Italy than towards our people . . . I should like to see the Catholic Church in Croatia more independent.'[28]

Djilas and Agitprop were unhappy that Tito should have told the delegation that he was a Catholic. He had, of course, been brought up a Roman Catholic, and he was at this moment trying to woo the Catholic Church; but the hatred of the Yugoslav Communists for Roman Catholicism, and their devotion to militant atheism, was so strong that they could not allow Tito to call himself a Catholic. So when his statement was printed, they altered his words 'as a Catholic myself' to 'as a Croat myself'.[29]

Tito was proposing that the Roman Catholic Church of Croatia should repudiate its obedience to Rome and cooperate with the Communist government in return for being granted not only toleration but also privileges by the state. Archbishop Stepinac rejected Tito's proposal. He opposed the government's policy of nationalizing the Church lands, for the agrarian reform, which forbade anyone to own more than ten hectares of land, had been applied to the Church. The government had abolished the teaching of religion in the state schools, though the Catholic Church was free to teach it in their own private schools. Hebrang, as a Croat, was in closer touch with public opinion in Croatia than were some of the other Communist leaders; he proposed that no attempt should be made to interfere with the compulsory teaching of the Roman Catholic religion in state schools.[30] But this was a matter of principle for the Communist Party of Yugoslavia, and he was overruled by the Politburo.

In October 1945 Archbishop Stepinac issued a pastoral letter to the clergy in Croatia. He strongly condemned the government's policy and did not mince his words. He criticized the nationalization of Church lands and the persecution of priests, for many priests had been arrested on a charge of collaboration with the invader during the war, and some of them had been killed or sentenced to terms of imprisonment.

Tito hit back by publishing an open letter to the Roman Catholic clergy. If they had accepted his offer to create a Croatian Church independent of Rome he would have forgiven the Church for having collaborated with the Germans and the Ustashas during the war; but now he harped vigorously on this theme. He claimed that the so-called persecution of the clergy, to which Stepinac had referred in his pastoral letter, was the arrest and punishment of priests who had helped the Germans and the Ustashas. 'The bishops play the hero and say they are ready for the fight, even if it costs them their lives. The fight against whom? Against the people's government, of course, against our new democratic Yugoslavia . . . But how is it that the bishops did not issue this kind of pastoral letter, to be read in all the churches, in the days of Pavelić and the Germans, against those terrible massacres of Serbs in Croatia in which hundreds of thousands of women, children and menfolk lost their lives?' Why did they not issue a pastoral letter against 'that most terrible slaughter-house, the Jasenovac concentration camp, where Ustashas slaughtered Serb and Croat without distinction?'[31]

Stepinac remained at liberty for a year after issuing this pastoral letter, and continued to attack the government in his sermons, though he was under close surveillance by Ranković's secret police, the OZNA. Deakin, who was now a diplomat at the British embassy in Belgrade, went to see Stepinac; he wished to find out his attitude so that he could inform the British government. Soon afterwards he met Tito at an official reception. Tito came up to him in his usual jovial mood. 'I hear you have been to see Stepinac,' said Tito. Deakin admitted that he had visited the archbishop. Tito laughed and said: 'I can guess what he said to you,' and then proceeded to repeat, almost word for word, what Stepinac had in fact told Deakin.[32]

On 30 September 1946 Stepinac was arrested, and charged with treason for having collaborated with the enemy during the war. He was tried together with Colonel Lisak, a notorious Ustasha war criminal. Stepinac was ably defended by the lawyer who had defended Tito at his trial in the same court in Zagreb in 1928.[33] The trial, like Mihailović's, was not fair or impartial, but it was not a stage-managed Soviet-type trial. Stepinac did not confess or cringe; he vigorously justified himself and denounced the Communist government from the dock.[34]

He was found guilty; but the judges, in passing sentence, recognized that he was less guilty than Lisak, who was condemned to death, and executed. Stepinac was sentenced to sixteen years' imprisonment. The sentence was strongly criticized abroad by the Roman Catholic Church, by the governments of Britain, the United States and other countries, and generally by anti-Communist public opinion. In the United States, Congress passed a resolution condemning the trials of both Mihailović and Stepinac.

In the midst of his troubles at home and the challenges to him from abroad, Tito suffered a great personal tragedy. On 1 May 1946 Zdenka died of tuberculosis at the age of twenty-seven. Tito took her loss very much to heart. He erected a monument to her in the garden of his presidential mansion in Belgrade, and saw that fresh flowers were placed on it every day.

Zdenka's cousin, Vera Miletić, had a daughter by one of Tito's Partisan commanders, Moma Marković, at the beginning of the war. Soon afterwards she was arrested by the Gestapo. It was reported to the party that she had faltered under torture and revealed the names of several comrades who, as a result, were arrested and executed. Her family refused to believe this; and even if she had failed in this most important of all Communist duties, who had the right to blame her except those who had endured similar tortures in silence? But she was afterwards shot as a traitor by the Partisans.

Zdenka's parents adopted Vera Miletić's baby, Mirjana. They lived in Požarevac in Serbia, some fifty miles east of Belgrade. There was an impressive fifteenth-century house in Požarevac, the home of a member of the Karadjordjević family who was a distant relative of King Peter. He disappeared in 1945, and the house was nationalized. The authorities decided that it should be preserved as a historical museum, being a fine example of medieval Serbian architecture; but Tito intervened, and insisted that it should be given as a home to Zdenka's parents. They lived there for the rest of their lives with Mirjana, and when they died they left the house to Mirjana in their will. Mirjana married Slobodan Milošević, and is now the wife of the Serbian president. She still owns the house where she spent her childhood, and it is Milošević's country residence.[35]

CHAPTER 21

❖

The Break with Stalin

THE international situation took a turn for the worse in 1947. The meeting in Moscow of the four foreign ministers, Molotov, Bevin, Byrnes and Bidault, ended in the usual recriminations; and no agreement could be reached on the future of Germany. At the same time the British government handed over its responsibilities in Greece to the United States. President Truman announced his new policy, which became known as the 'Truman doctrine', that the United States would 'support free peoples who are resisting attempted subjugation by armed minorities or by outside pressure', and that this doctrine would be enforced in Greece.[1]

Tito reacted by intensifying the political repression in Yugoslavia. A number of left-wing politicians were accused of being counter-revolutionaries and sentenced to imprisonment. A group of Serbian anti-Communists were convicted of plotting to assassinate Tito on the instructions of Western intelligence services, and the leader was hanged. In foreign policy, Yugoslavia became even more violently anti-American, and stepped up aid to Markos's ELAS guerrillas in Greece; but the Truman doctrine had made Stalin still more cautious about Greece. He wished at all costs to avoid war with the United States, at least until the Soviet Union, like the United States, had a nuclear bomb.

In June 1947 the United States secretary of state, General Marshall, offered economic aid from the United States to countries which were still suffering from the economic difficulties caused by the Second World War. The British and other governments of Western Europe gratefully welcomed 'Marshall Aid', and praised American generosity; the Soviet Union, and the Communists throughout the world, denounced it as an imperialist plot to subject the economy of the countries that received it to the domination of Wall Street and American imperialism.

Marshall Aid would undoubtedly have helped the Yugoslavs, who were suffering many hardships, to develop a rehousing programme and to achieve economic growth; these hardships became acute when the harvest failed, as it did in 1947. If Tito had had a free hand, he would probably have accepted Marshall Aid and given the Americans nothing in return; it was a policy which he had successfully adopted with British military aid during the war, and would adopt again, equally successfully, with American financial aid after 1949. But the Soviet Union insisted that all its Communist satellite states reject Marshall Aid, for it was unacceptable to Stalin that the peoples of Eastern Europe should have their standard of living raised by aid from the American imperialists. Tito's policy of friendship with the Soviet Union left him with no choice in the matter, and he violently and immediately rejected the offer of Marshall Aid.

The meeting of the General Assembly of the United Nations in New York in September 1947 was another occasion for a slanging match between East and West. Vyshinsky, in his speech, made a violent attack on the United States; but he was eclipsed by Aleš Bebler, the Yugoslav assistant foreign minister, whose speech was so bitter that it went beyond the bounds of normal diplomatic behaviour. But Tito remained on friendly terms with his old British acquaintances. He was relaxed and jovial when he met Deakin at official receptions in Belgrade, and with Fitzroy Maclean, who visited him in Zagreb in the summer of 1947. Maclean, who was now an Opposition MP, told him frankly that he was now 'deeply distrusted and disliked by almost all British opinion'; but after their talk had 'opened rather stormily', the rest of Maclean's visit to Zagreb 'was given up to merry-making with the Marshal and some of his intimates, all old friends of mine'.[2]

In November 1947 the General Assembly of the United Nations voted to divide Palestine between the Arabs and the Jews, and thus created the state of Israel. The voting in the Assembly cut right across the alliances of the Cold War, because every state had its own reasons for adopting a line on this issue. The United States and most of its Western European allies voted for Israel, and so did the Soviet Union and the Communist governments of Eastern Europe; but Yugoslavia abstained, along with Great Britain, and several other countries. The Arab states voted against, and Greece voted with them because of her economic ties with Egypt. Tito decided to abstain because of the Muslims in Bosnia. Stalin accepted this, and the abstention did not weaken the unity of the Soviet bloc.

In October 1947 the Communist parties of nine countries formed a new international organization, the Communist Information Bureau. In the West the name of the new organization was usually shortened to 'Cominform'; but the Communists in the organization called it the 'Informbureau', probably because the name sounded less like the 'Comintern'. Unlike the Comintern, membership of the Cominform was limited to the nine Communist parties. Seven of the nine were parties who had come to power and formed the government of their countries: the Soviet Union, Poland, Czechoslovakia, Hungary, Yugoslavia, Bulgaria and Romania. The other two were the French and Italian parties, the strongest Communist parties in Western Europe.

The inaugural meeting of the Cominform was held at Szklarska Poreba in Poland from 22–27 September. Kardelj and Djilas, who represented the Communist Party of Yugoslavia, launched an attack on the policy of the French and Italian Communist parties, condemning them for entering coalition governments with the bourgeois parties in 1944 and for calling off the revolutionary movements among the workers in northern Italy and France, who could have carried through a Communist revolution if Togliatti and Thorez had not restrained them. The error of their policy, argued Kardelj and Djilas, had been exposed by the fact that they had been unceremoniously thrown out of their coalition governments as soon as the American imperialists gave the order to the French and Italian bourgeoisie. The French and Italian parties had in fact, of course, pursued their policy on Stalin's instructions; but the Yugoslav delegates did not mention this, and Zhdanov, who represented the Communist Party of the Soviet Union at the meeting, seemed to agree with Kardelj and Djilas.[3]

Zhdanov proposed that the secretariat of the Cominform should be established in Belgrade. This was an innovation, for the most fundamental feature of the Comintern had been that its headquarters were in Moscow. The suggestion that the headquarters of the Cominform should be in Belgrade had probably first been made by Stalin himself. But Stalin, while flattering Tito by this proposal, was becoming more suspicious of him. According to later revelations by Russians with inside information, his attitude to Tito was influenced by a conflict of policy and a power struggle in the Kremlin.[4] The Soviet leaders were divided as to whether to adopt a belligerent or a conciliatory policy towards the United States and its allies. Zhdanov and Molotov were the leaders of the belligerent group, while Malenkov headed the conciliatory faction.

Stalin, with his usual caution, supported Malenkov's position. He was often away from Moscow at his residences in the Crimea, and on these occasions the Zhdanov-Molotov faction was able to gain control; but in the winter of 1947–8, Stalin reasserted his authority and ensured the victory of Malenkov's group. Tito and the Communist party of Yugoslavia, with their aggressive revolutionary attitude towards the West, were regarded as supporters of Zhdanov and Molotov; so Malenkov and Stalin wished to weaken Tito as a means of striking at Zhdanov and Molotov. If this version of events is correct, the leaders of the Communist party of Yugoslavia knew nothing about it. Djilas had never heard of any division between Stalin and Zhdanov on foreign policy until I put the suggestion to him in 1993.

Stalin sometimes raised with Tito the unsatisfactory relationship between him and Enver Hoxha, the Communist president of Albania. The antagonism between the Serbs and the Albanians over Kosovo went back for several centuries. Kosovo was sacred to the Serbs as the birthplace of the Serbian Orthodox Church and the site of their last heroic struggle against the Turks in 1389; but the majority of the population were Albanian Muslims as the Muslim birthrate was eight times higher than the Serbs'. Mussolini annexed Albania to Italy in 1939 and gave Kosovo to Albania in 1941.

When Hitler invaded the Soviet Union, the tiny Albanian Communist party did its duty and began a resistance movement against the Italian occupation forces. Enver Hoxha, who was party secretary, was an intellectual who became a schoolmaster in Albania and a professional revolutionary directing the party's illegal operations from Paris; but the great majority of Albanians were shepherds, and too isolated from each other to unite in a strong Communist party or an effective resistance movement. Tito's Partisans worked closely with the Albanian Communists during the Second World War; but the Yugoslavs were very conscious that their Albanian comrades were much less effective than they were, and the Albanians resented the attitude of the Yugoslavs, who seemed to them to be arrogant and patronizing.

In the summer of 1946 Tito sent two divisions of Yugoslav troops into Albania to protect the country against the danger of an invasion from Greece if the Greek government decided to retaliate for Albanian assistance to the ELAS forces. Enver Hoxha was not altogether pleased to see the troops there, especially as Tito had sent them in without consulting Stalin.[5]

Stalin's mistrust of Tito came to a head over the thorny question of Balkan federation, which since the 1920s had been a distant objective of the Yugoslav, Bulgarian and Greek Communists. After the victory of Communism in the Balkans, a federation between Yugoslavia, Bulgaria and Albania became a practical possibility. In August 1947, when Tito was on holiday at Bled in Slovenia, he was visited by Dimitrov, who was now prime minister of Bulgaria. They discussed the possibility of forming a federal union between Yugoslavia and Bulgaria. They approved the idea, but though Tito would have been happy to go ahead at once, Dimitrov saw the difficulties. The Bulgarian people would think that their country was being absorbed into Yugoslavia and was becoming another Yugoslav republic like Slovenia, Croatia, Bosnia, Serbia, Montenegro and Macedonia. The discussions continued at a lower level after Dimitrov had returned home, and in November 1947 a joint declaration was issued by the Yugoslav and Bulgarian governments. They declared that a federation between Yugoslavia and Bulgaria was a goal to be achieved one day, but not immediately. Neither Tito nor Dimitrov had consulted Stalin before issuing the declaration.

Stalin was very angry. He summoned Tito and Dimitrov to Moscow to explain their conduct. Dimitrov went, but Tito sent Djilas, Kardelj and Ranković with a message that he could not come himself because he was ill. The Bulgarian and Yugoslav delegates had long discussions with Stalin and the Politburo of the Communist party of the Soviet Union in February 1948. Stalin did not object in principle to the idea of a Balkan federation, but he objected to the form in which it had been proposed by Tito and Dimitrov; but what annoyed him most was that they should have issued a statement on the subject without having first consulted the Soviet Union.

He then turned to Greece. He advised Tito and Dimitrov to discontinue their aid to the ELAS guerrillas. He admitted that in 1946 he had advised the Chinese Communists to abandon their struggle against Chiang Kai-shek, that Mao Tse-tung had disregarded his advice, and that the Chinese Communists were now rapidly advancing against Chiang Kai-shek's armies in North China; but Stalin said that the situation in Greece was very different from the situation in China, and that though he had been wrong about China in 1946 he was right about Greece now, for the United States had become involved in Greece, and the United States was very strong.[6]

Stalin again referred to Djilas's offence in accusing Red Army officers of rape, though it was more than three years since Djilas had made the remark. Stalin said that he could not blame any Russian soldier who had marched and fought all the way from Stalingrad to Belgrade if he wanted to have some fun with a girl and help himself to a few trinkets. He told Djilas about a Red Army major who had shot and killed a civilian who was trying to prevent him from raping a girl. The major was court-martialled and sentenced to death, but Stalin, as commander-in-chief, had pardoned him. Stalin said that his decision had been vindicated, because after the major returned to his unit he performed great deeds of valour.[7] Djilas, who thought that rape was the most heinous of crimes, began to wonder if the great Stalin was really the father of the workers and peasants and the leader of all progressive mankind.

Dimitrov admitted his error about Balkan federation, and thanked Stalin for reprimanding him. Djilas and Kardelj at first refused to indulge in self-criticism, but after Stalin had applied more pressure, Kardelj signed a document in which he promised that Yugoslavia would not take any step in foreign policy without first consulting the Soviet Union.[8] Stalin expected that after Kardelj and Djilas arrived back in Belgrade, Tito would write to him confirming Kardelj's undertaking. A few days after the talks in Moscow ended, Gottwald and the Czechoslovak Communists carried through a *coup d'état* in Prague, ousting most of the non-Communist ministers from the coalition government and establishing a Communist dictatorship. The *coup* in Czechoslovakia aroused great indignation in Western Europe and the United States. Tito and the Communist party of Yugoslavia congratulated Gottwald and the Czechoslovak Communists on the *coup*; but they did not confirm Kardelj's promise to Stalin that Yugoslavia would take no step in foreign policy without consulting the Soviet Union.

Since the end of the war a number of Soviet military experts and civilian technicians had been working in Yugoslavia. On 18 March 1948 the Soviet defence minister, Marshal Bulganin, informed the Yugoslav government that the Soviet Union was withdrawing all the military experts from Yugoslavia; and next day the Soviet chargé d'affaires told Tito that all the Soviet economic advisers would also be withdrawn because they were 'surrounded by absence of comradeship'. Tito thereupon wrote to Molotov, stating that Soviet personnel had always been treated in a most friendly way in Yugoslavia and asking for the true explanation of their withdrawal.[9]

On 27 March a letter signed by Stalin and Molotov was sent to Tito and the leaders of the CPY, accusing them of a series of offences. Stalin and Molotov brought up again Djilas's statement that Soviet officers were more immoral than British officers. They accused the Yugoslav secret police of spying on Soviet intelligence officers and other Soviet citizens in Yugoslavia. They wrote that Tito and the Yugoslav Communists had merged the Communist party in the National Front and were not pursuing a specifically Communist policy of class struggle, that they allowed capitalism to continue in the villages, and that they had adopted 'the rotten opportunist theory ... that capitalist elements will grow peacefully into Socialism, a theory taken from Bernstein, Folmar and Bukharin'. This was a brazen accusation to make, seeing that it was Stalin and the Comintern in Moscow who had consistently criticized the Yugoslav Communists for pursuing a revolutionary policy of class struggle. Stalin and Molotov complained that 'quite dubious Marxists of the type of Djilas, Vukmanović (Tempo), Kidrič, Ranković and others' had been saying that Socialism in the Soviet Union was no longer revolutionary, that only the Yugoslav Communist party was revolutionary, and that the Soviet Union was guilty of Great-Power chauvinism; and they pointed out that Trotsky had made the same accusation against the Communist party of the Soviet Union before he became an agent of the foreign imperialists. They wrote that they could not understand why Velebit was still the assistant foreign minister, for 'the Yugoslav comrades know that Velebit is an English spy'.[10]

The Russians had been suspicious of Velebit for some time. He had visited England during the war, and he had made difficulties about signing the Soviet-Yugoslav commercial treaty. Not long before the Stalin-Molotov note, Velebit had been approached by a Soviet representative in Belgrade who asked him to supply secret intelligence reports about Yugoslav foreign policy to Soviet agents. He refused. The Soviet agent then reminded him that in 1944 he had agreed to act as an agent for Soviet intelligence in London. Velebit said that it was one thing to spy for the Soviet Union in London at the orders of his own government, and a very different thing to spy on his own government in Yugoslavia at the orders of the Soviet Union. The Soviet agent seemed quite unable to appreciate the distinction, and reported to Moscow that Velebit was an English spy.

When Tito received Stalin and Molotov's letter, he showed it to Velebit, who immediately offered to resign as assistant foreign minister. Tito reluctantly accepted his resignation.[11] On 13 April Tito and Kardelj wrote to Stalin and Molotov that although there was no evidence that Velebit was a British spy, and despite his excellent record in the wartime resistance movement, they were nevertheless removing him from his post as assistant foreign minister. Soon afterwards Velebit was transferred to the Ministry of Foreign Trade, which particularly interested him, and gave him the opportunity of negotiating several important trade and financial agreements with foreign governments.

In their letter Tito and Kardelj rebutted all the accusations of Stalin and Molotov, and stressed their loyalty to the Soviet Union.[12] The Soviet Communist party continued the correspondence with another letter on 4 May in which they repeated all the old accusations. They now asserted that 'Velebit is not the only spy in the offices of the Ministry of Foreign Affairs' in Belgrade. They accused the Yugoslav Communist leaders of acting like Trotsky, and of exaggerating the achievements of the Partisans during the war; 'the French and Italian Communist parties in matters of revolution have not less, but greater, merits than the Yugoslav Communist party'.[13]

On 17 May Tito and Kardelj sent a very brief reply. They wrote that the letter of the CPSU of 4 May 'convinces us that it is futile to make any explanations', but they assured the Russians that they would continue to build Socialism and 'to be truly loyal to the Soviet Union' and 'to the teachings of Marx, Engels, Lenin and Stalin'.[14]

Stalin was right in thinking that Ranković's OZNA was spying on the Soviet technicians in Yugoslavia and their Yugoslav sympathizers. Tito wished to find out how Stalin and Molotov had discovered what the Yugoslav leaders had been saying in private about the Soviet Union. Ranković was able to tell him that two important Communist leaders, Hebrang and Žujović (who was nicknamed 'Crni' (black)) had been in secret contact with the Soviet embassy. Hebrang and Žujović were arrested. The Soviet ambassador protested against their arrest, and declared that if any harm came to the two comrades the Soviet Union would denounce the leaders of the CPY as 'criminal murderers'. He asked that representatives of the CPSU should attend the interrogation of Hebrang and Žjujović. The CPY rejected 'the very thought of our Party leaders being described as "criminal murderers"', and informed the CPSU that their participation in the interrogation of Hebrang and Žujović 'cannot even be considered'.[15]

The other parties in the Cominform joined in. The Hungarian prime minister and veteran Communist, Rákosi, launched a fierce attack on the CPY at a private meeting of the Hungarian Communist party; but so far no hint of the dispute had appeared in public. The Bulgarian Communist party followed the Soviet party line; but in April Dimitrov passed through Belgrade on his way from Sofia to Czechoslovakia. His train stopped for a while in Belgrade railway station, and Djilas took the opportunity to have a short talk with him in the train. As Djilas was leaving, Dimitrov pressed his hand and whispered: 'Stand firm.'[16]

Tito and Kardelj suggested that the CPSU should send one of its leading members to Belgrade to discuss their disagreements with the CPY. The Soviet Communist party declined and suggested instead that the whole dispute should be discussed at the next meeting of the Cominform in Bucharest.[17] The CPY did not send a representative to the meeting. The Cominform then decided to expel the CPY. It was on 28 June, a date which has meant so much in Serbian history – the day of the destruction of the Serbian kingdom by the Turks at Kosovo in 1389, of the burning of the bones of St Sava, the patron saint of Serbia, by the Turks in 1594, and of the assassination of the Archduke Franz Ferdinand of Austria at Sarajevo in 1914 which led to the First World War.

The Cominform resolution stated that 'the Information Bureau declares that the leadership of the Yugoslav Communist party is pursuing an unfriendly policy towards the Soviet Union'. It could therefore no longer remain a member of the Cominform. It was the duty of the members of the CPY to 'compel their present leaders to ... break with nationalism, to return to internationalism'. If the leaders failed to do so, it would be 'their duty to replace them and to choose a new internationalist leadership of the party'.[18]

The news was first published in the Czechoslovak Communist newspaper *Rude Pravo*, and immediately the press in every Communist country began to attack Tito and the Yugoslav Communists. Everywhere, both in the Communist states and in the Western world, the news came as a complete surprise; but it ought not to have surprised anyone who had studied the history of the Communist movement and the different perspectives of Stalin and Tito.

Tito and the Yugoslav Communists insisted that the responsibility for the break with the Cominform did not rest with them, and that the Soviet Union alone was responsible for it. Tito's right-wing critics abroad, particularly in the United States, agree with them; they argue that Tito remained a Communist and a loyal supporter of the Soviet Union, and that he deserves no credit for the break with Stalin, which came about only because Stalin forced a rupture, against Tito's will.[19] But this is not quite true. The split occurred because Stalin demanded absolute obedience from Tito and the CPY, and Tito and the Yugoslav Communists refused to submit to Stalin's demands. If Tito had wished to avoid the split with the Soviet Union he could have done so by adopting a completely submissive attitude, by indulging in the self-criticism which was required of him. Every other Communist party would have submitted, as Tito and the CPY would have done at any time before 1941.

By refusing to admit that he was wrong, by arresting Hebrang and Žujović, and by refusing to attend the meeting of the Cominform in Bucharest, Tito defied Stalin, knowing very well what the consequences would be. He had realized for some time that Stalin and the CPSU were not working for the victory of international Socialism, but for Russian domination, and that they were treating all foreign Communists as their agents and vassals. He had had enough of it, and now, unlike in the years when he was living in the Hotel Lux in Moscow, he was in a position where he could defy Stalin, and he intended to do so.

CHAPTER 22

❖

Defying the Lightning

YUGOSLAVIA'S expulsion from the Cominform had a shock effect on the Communist parties of Eastern Europe. Tito cannot have been surprised that his Polish, East German, Czechoslovak, Hungarian, Romanian and Bulgarian comrades – even Dimitrov, whatever he may have whispered to Djilas – publicly supported Stalin and ritually denounced the CPY and the 'Titoists'. But in the rank-and-file of their parties, there was strong sympathy for Yugoslavia. All the Communist party members who were disgusted by the privileges of the party leaders and the tyranny of the secret police, but still believed in the principle of Communism, saw Tito's Yugoslavia as the centre of their hopes, as proof that a Communist party could defy Stalin, and that it was possible to have Communism without Stalinism.

News of the expulsion came at a time when an international youth congress was taking place in Prague under the auspices of the Czechoslovak Sokol organization. The Yugoslav team who had gone to Prague to take part in the sports and gymnastic display were suddenly informed by their hosts that Tito was not a great Communist but a traitor. They reacted with defiant patriotism and Titoist solidarity. They hung banners with 'Tito' inscribed on them from the windows of their barracks until the banners were confiscated by the Czechoslovak police. On the last day of the festival, when the Yugoslavs gave a gymnastic display, they ended their performance by lining up on the sports ground in lines and a circle which formed the letters 'TITO'. Many of the spectators cheered them loudly.[1]

But could Tito rely on the loyalty of the members of the CPY?

For years he himself, like Djilas and Agitprop, had told them to be loyal to the Soviet Union and the great Stalin; would they now follow Stalin when he called on the Yugoslav rank-and-file to overthrow Tito? Ranković had already arrested two prominent Yugoslav party leaders, Hebrang and Žujović, who had been close to Tito during the war. Soon after the Cominform resolution, Tito's ambassador in Bucharest defected, asked Romania for asylum, and issued a statement denouncing Tito. In October the Yugoslav chargé d'affaires in Budapest, Brankov, similarly defected to Hungary and declared that Tito was a traitor. Several of the Yugoslavs who were working or studying in the Soviet Union pledged their support for Stalin and the Soviet Union against Tito, and joined committees working for the liberation of Yugoslavia from Tito's regime. How many more of the rank-and-file of the party inside Yugoslavia would follow suit? Apart from Communist loyalty to the Soviet Union, would the traditional Slav sympathies for Russia, which had always been strong in Serbia and even stronger in Montenegro, draw many of the people to support Stalin against Tito?

It is not surprising that Tito was worried in the summer of 1948. He knew that if, in the last resort, it came to war against the Soviet Union and its satellite states, Yugoslavia would stand no chance; and he could not rely on the support of the Western powers. The United States and Britain and their allies might perhaps decide to go to war, or to threaten war and the use of nuclear weapons, in order to prevent their enemy, the Soviet Union, from overrunning Yugoslavia and gaining access to the Adriatic; but Truman and Bevin did not like Tito and his Communist regime, and they might well decide to let him stew in his own juice if he fell out with his Russian friends.

Tito afterwards told Maclean that the rupture with the Soviet Union was the most traumatic experience of his life. Djilas believes that the gallstones from which Tito suffered soon afterwards were largely due to his anxieties about the quarrel with Stalin.[2] But Tito remained calm and resolute in the crisis. None of his intimate colleagues had any doubt that it was he, and he alone, who took the decision to resist Stalin in 1948.

Three weeks after Yugoslavia was expelled from the Cominform, the Fifth Congress of the CPY was held on 21 July at Topčider, where the trial of Mihailović had been held two years before. It was the first party congress since the Fourth Congress, which had been held abroad at Dresden in 1928.* Tito, as general secretary of the party, delivered his report to the 2,300 delegates. His speech lasted for eight hours; there were short intervals for rest and refreshments. He surveyed the history of the Socialist and workers' movement in all the countries of Yugoslavia, beginning with the strike of the typesetters in Zagreb against the sixteen-hour working day in 1865, and dealing with the foundation of the CPY, and its support in the years after 1918 for the national resistance of the Slovenes, Croats and Muslims in Bosnia against 'the Pan-Serbian bourgeoisie led by the King'. He reminded the delegates of how the Communist party, after he became general secretary in 1937, had purged itself of fractionalists and Trotskyists. He spoke at length about the Partisans' achievement during the Second World War, and of the heroic acts of individual comrades who had cried out 'Long live the Soviet Union and Comrade Stalin!' as they died. 'Hundreds of workers', said Tito, 'died with these words on their lips.'

After he had been speaking for seven and a half hours, he turned, in the last half-hour of his speech, to 'the resolution of the Informbureau . . . to the monstrous accusations against our Party and its leadership', and to the 'insults to our country'. He strongly repudiated the 'painful' accusation that 'we have turned our backs on the Soviet Union and the countries of people's democracies'. He made no attack on any of his critics by name, except to say that the Yugoslav Communist leaders were 'being shamelessly slandered and smeared by the leaders of the Communist Party of Bulgaria'. He indignantly denied that he and his colleagues were Trotskyists. 'Did we enter the life and death struggle on the side of the Soviet Union in 1941 on the basis of Trotskyist conceptions, or because of loyalty to Marxism-Leninism, a theory that . . . is being realized in the Soviet Union under the leadership of Comrade Stalin?' He ended by assuring the delegates that, having got rid of 'unsound, irresolute, hostile elements' like Žujović and Hebrang, 'we shall remain inexorable, consistent, as we have learned to be from Lenin and Stalin'. But the pictures of Lenin and Stalin, and of Marx and Engels, behind the platform were completely dwarfed by the enormous portrait of Tito.

---

* The party conference in Zagreb in October 1940 (see supra, Chapter 13, pp. 153–5) was technically a conference, not a congress, though it had most of the characteristics of a congress. A congress was a more important gathering than a conference.

His speech was greeted with the greatest enthusiasm by the congress. It was periodically interrupted by shouts of 'Hero Tito!' At the end he received a standing ovation, with all the delegates shouting 'Stalin, Tito!' and 'Tito, Party!'[3]

Tito had uttered no word of criticism of Stalin in his speech. When he published the correspondence between the CPSU and the CPY, in response to a challenge from the CPSU that he did not dare to do so, he deleted Stalin's signature from the letters addressed to him by Stalin and Molotov. When the CPSU published the correspondence, they also deleted Stalin's signature, presumably because they did not wish it to be known that Stalin's personal intervention had been unsuccessful. In later years, Tito told a friend why he had not criticized Stalin in his speech in July 1948. 'I had to give Stalin time to behave in such a way that people in Yugoslavia would say "Down with Stalin!" of their own accord without my having to suggest it to them.'[4]

A week after the Fifth Congress, on 30 July 1948, the International Danube Commission met in Belgrade. The Commission had been set up by Britain and France under the Treaty of Versailles in 1919 to control navigation on the Danube, and was dominated by Britain and France; but now the Soviet Union was determined to exclude Britain and France from having any say about the Danube. The Soviet Union was represented at the conference by Vyshinsky; Romania by the veteran Communist, Ana Pauker,* and Yugoslavia by the foreign minister and assistant foreign minister, Stanoye Simić and Bebler. Tito left Belgrade and went to Slovenia for his August holiday, thus avoiding the embarrassment of having to preside at a banquet for Vyshinsky, Ana Pauker, and the other delegates from the Cominform countries.

Vyshinsky took a tough line against Britain and France at the conference. The Yugoslav delegates supported him and voted with the Soviet Union and the other Cominform countries. Britain and France refused to accept the legality of the conference decisions, but could do nothing to prevent the Soviet Union from controlling the Danube.

---

* Pauker, Ana (1893–1960). Romanian Communist leader; imprisoned in Romania, she escaped to Moscow, and returned to Romania with the Red Army in 1944 to become the most powerful figure in the country; foreign minister 1947–52; disgraced in 1952, she lived in retirement till her death.

The Yugoslavs afterwards said that while Ana Pauker was in Belgrade for the Danube Conference, she secretly contacted General Arso Jovanović and other important Yugoslavs. Jovanović had been an officer in the Royal Yugoslav Army but he joined the Partisans at the beginning of the war. Tito, partly in recognition of his abilities and partly in order to encourage other regular army officers to join him, appointed Jovanović to be his chief of staff. After the war, Tito sent him to Moscow, where he had a love affair with the daughter of a Soviet general. According to the Yugoslavs, she persuaded him to become an agent of the NKVD.

On 12 August 1948, the last day of the Danube Conference, Jovanović left Belgrade with Colonel Branko Petričević and Colonel Vlado Dapčević, who was the brother of Tito's leading general Peko Dapčević. They said that they were going on a boar-hunting expedition in the forests near the Romanian frontier. When they arrived in the district they visited a local army commander to suggest to him that they should all commandeer a tank, drive over the frontier, and defect to Romania. The local commander was not at home, so they changed their plan and decided to walk over the frontier during the night. They set out after dark, but ran into a group of forest wardens who were looking for poachers. When the wardens challenged them, Jovanović fired at a warden with his revolver, and the warden fired back and killed Jovanović. Vlado Dapčević and Petričević ran off into the forest. Petričević was arrested next day, and Dapčević three weeks later. They were both court-martialled for desertion and treason, and each of them was sentenced to twenty years' imprisonment;[5] but they were released from prison in 1955.

The Soviet Union and the Cominform countries accused the Yugoslav secret police of murdering Jovanović in cold blood; but for nearly a year their propaganda campaign against Yugoslavia and Tito was restrained. This was apparently thanks to Stalin. At the beginning of September 1948 Gottwald visited Stalin in the Crimea. He suggested to Stalin that the Red Army might march into Yugoslavia and destroy Tito. Stalin rejected this plan. He told Gottwald that he did not wish to destroy Tito, who was a valuable man; he wanted to see Tito recant and humble himself before the Soviet Union, and then return to the fold as a good and loyal Communist.[6]

The Western governments did not at first know what to make of the split between Stalin and Tito. Some observers in the West thought that it was an elaborate Communist plot to trick the Western powers into thinking that Tito was no longer a Communist, so that they would give him Marshall Aid and military equipment and secrets which he could then pass on surreptitiously to the Soviet Union. This farfetched idea was naturally encouraged by anti-Tito Yugoslav refugees in the United States, who feared that if the American government and people thought that Tito had abandoned Communism, they would support his regime and prevent any plans to overthrow him and restore the old regime or establish a liberal democracy in Yugoslavia.

Such ideas were even to be found in the British Foreign Office. The French ambassador in London reported that 'they do not even exclude the possibility that the whole thing is a manoeuvre'.[7] On 2 July 1948 the Foreign Office noted that 'Tito may be leading a schism, but he remains a convinced Communist.'[8] Cecil King, at the British embassy in Belgrade, was more far-sighted than some of his diplomatic colleagues in London. Two days after Yugoslavia was expelled from the Cominform, King wrote to the Foreign Office: 'Trotzky's heresy had no territorial basis larger than a villa in Mexico and even then it was necessary to axe him in the most literal sense of the term. The effect of a heresy firmly established in a whole European country must be incomparably greater and raise at once the parallel of the opposition of Constantinople to Rome.'[9]

The United States ambassador in Belgrade, Cavendish Cannon, was more eager to help Tito than most of the Western diplomats. On 29 June 1948, the day after Yugoslavia was expelled from the Cominform, he advised the United States government to make a public declaration that it would intervene to defend the territorial integrity of small nations, including Yugoslavia.[10] But Bevin, with his deep hatred of all Communists, was very reluctant to do anything to help Tito; and he was conscious that a declaration of Western support might embarrass Tito. He wished to 'let the Communists quarrel among themselves'.[11] He immediately urged the United States government to make no move to support Tito, and was relieved when he was informed that the United States had no intention of following the advice of its ambassador in Belgrade. As late as February 1949 Bevin still believed that Tito's policy was 'in the nature . . . of a put-up job designed to pave the way for Yugoslavia's return to the Stalinist fold'.[12]

The French government, like Bevin, were very suspicious of Tito. They were worried that the United States might relax its economic measures against the Yugoslavs, and believed that 'for the moment we should let them stew in their own juice'.[13]

Truman had announced that the policy of the United States would be one of 'containment' – to contain Communism and prevent its spread to 'free' countries. But this was not good enough for ardent anti-Communists in the United States and elsewhere, certainly not for the refugees from Communist states. They wanted the United States and its allies to pursue a 'roll-back' policy, of liberating Communist countries by organizing counter-revolutions against the Communist governments. In March 1948 the American OSS was renamed the Central Intelligence Agency (CIA) and entrusted with the duty of fighting Communism. The United States government, while officially pursuing a policy only of containment, authorized the CIA to support subversive movements in Communist countries; but it instructed the CIA that in present circumstances it was not to work for the overthrow of Tito's government.

Someone in the CIA disregarded these instructions, and thought that this was the time, when Tito could no longer rely on Soviet assistance, to encourage a revolution and install a Chetnik government in Yugoslavia. In January 1949 a number of Chetnik refugees in the United States were dropped by parachute in Yugoslavia from American planes with instructions to start a resistance movement and armed risings against Tito's government. The Chetniks were all rounded up quite quickly by Ranković's OZNA, and sentenced to many years in prison for counter-revolutionary activities. The French ambassador in Belgrade was the first to hear of it, and told Cannon, who had not been informed of this CIA project. He urged the State Department to stop the CIA plots to overthrow Tito. 'In Yugo', he wrote on 31 January 1949, 'there are not three choices but two: Tito or a Moscow tool.'[14] Even Bevin now agreed with this view. 'I entirely agree with Mr Cannon,' he wrote to the State Department on 21 February 1949, 'that any backing of anti-Tito elements, for instance by attempts to use ex-Ustasi or Chetnik elements in the country for any purpose whatsoever, would be playing straight into the Soviet hand.'[15]

Tito's chief anxiety was not the Chetniks or the CIA, but the Cominform supporters in the CPY. It is not surprising that Tito, having been for years an important agent in a Stalinist party, decided to fight Stalin with Stalinist methods. Ranković and his secret police searched tirelessly for Cominform supporters among party members.

They found that there were enough of them to cause alarm, although the majority of party members were loyal to Tito. The secret police reported that only one out of twenty party members in Croatia supported the Cominform; and although it was as high as one in six in Montenegro, even here more than eighty per cent of party members supported Tito.[16]

Not every Communist who supported the Cominform did so out of devotion to the Soviet Union. Some were disgusted with Tito's regime because of the privileges enjoyed by the party leaders or the petty tyranny of state and party officials and the secret police. Whereas in Czechoslovakia, Hungary, Poland and Bulgaria, Communists who were disillusioned with the Communist governments under which they lived believed that Tito's regime in Yugoslavia was true Communism without the Stalinist blemishes; so Yugoslav Communists who disliked the realities of Tito's rule now had an explanation of what had gone wrong. Tito had perverted Communism; the Communist cause for which they had suffered and for which so many of their comrades had died was not this unsavoury regime in Yugoslavia, but the Communism of the Soviet Union and of all the other Communist countries who had denounced Tito as a traitor.

Tito ordered Ranković to open an internment camp for political suspects; under an emergency law, the minister of the interior could order anyone to be confined there without trial for a maximum of three years. The camp was opened on Goli Otok (Bare Island), an island in the Adriatic off the coast of northern Croatia. According to Djilas, Tito did not consult either the government or the Politburo before deciding to open the camp on Goli Otok;[17] but he discussed it with Kardelj, who agreed with the proposal. It had first been suggested to Tito by his close friend, Stevo Krajačić, who had formerly been a member of the Russian NKVD.[18] The camp was run on the usual model of Nazi and Soviet concentration and labour camps, with selected prisoners running the camp for the guards.

Between 1949 and 1952 more than 12,000 people were sent to Goli Otok. Most of them were arrested after being denounced by neighbours or by colleagues in their place of work for having made some remark against Tito or in praise of the Cominform resolution. Many were arrested because it was reported that they had listened to Radio Moscow or Radio Prague, though there was no law which forbade Yugoslav citizens to listen to foreign radio stations. One woman who admitted that she had tuned in to Radio Moscow because she enjoyed listening to Russian music was sent to Goli Otok. Husbands and wives of prisoners on Goli Otok were encouraged to denounce and divorce their spouses; but children were not expected to repudiate their parents, or held responsible for their parents' offences, as they were in the Soviet Union and Czechoslovakia.

The guards, and the prisoners chosen to help them run the camp, treated the internees on Goli Otok with great brutality. All new arrivals at the camp had to run the gauntlet between two rows of other prisoners who beat and kicked them as they passed along the line. Apart from the new arrivals, internees who had been on Goli Otok for several months were sometimes chosen, quite arbitrarily, to run the gauntlet. There seemed to be no particular reason why some prisoners were selected to do the punching and kicking and others to be punched and kicked. Some of the prisoners standing in the line struck softly, or intentionally missed the victim running past them; but others tried to impress the guards by hitting and kicking hard. Sometimes the victim running the gauntlet collapsed and fainted before reaching the end of the line.

The internees were made to work from dawn till dusk in the quarries on Goli Otok. They had to carry the stones from one place to another, and if they did not move fast enough they were beaten by the guards. They had to work all day without water, even in the summer heat, unless they drank the salt water of the sea at the edge of the quarry.

Most of the internees were members of the Communist party, and many of them had fought with the Partisans during the war. Some had been imprisoned in King Alexander's jails, and some were survivors from the Ustasha camp at Jasenovac. They found the conditions on Goli Otok in Tito's Yugoslavia worse than anything they had encountered in their earlier prisons, and worse even than Jasenovac. In Jasenovac they had been able to assuage their hunger by eating berries while they worked for long hours in the fields, though this was against the regulations; but there were no berries in the stone quarries on Goli Otok. In Jasenovac prisoners were normally not beaten by the guards, except in the inner punishment prison where they were sent if they had broken the prison regulations; on Goli Otok prisoners were often beaten if they carried the stones too slowly in the quarries. But at least on Goli Otok the commandant did not stroll through the camp shooting the prisoners at random, as Luburić had done in Jasenovac.[19]

[298]

Tito and the leaders in Belgrade did not know what was going on at Goli Otok, and did not want to know. Once, Djilas said to Ranković: 'Now we are treating Stalin's followers as he treated his enemies.' 'Don't say that! Don't talk about it!' said Ranković. When Ranković visited Goli Otok, he found that the internees seemed contented and were loyal to Tito and the regime; but he only met those who had recanted their Stalinist opinions and were receiving better treatment. Then in September 1953 Djilas happened to meet the author Dobrica Ćosić, who had visited Goli Otok. 'He told me', wrote Djilas, 'that the security service, the UDBA,* had devised and applied corrective methods that were possibly the most diabolical in history.'

Djilas reported this to Ranković and Kardelj. 'I knew something vile was going on there!' shouted Kardelj angrily. Ranković at last ordered an investigation into conditions on Goli Otok, and the prisoners were then treated a little less harshly.[20]

Like other dictators throughout history, Tito sometimes intervened to protect individuals from his secret police in special cases which had been brought to his attention. At Lepoglava old Mrs Fidlerica still ran her café, as she had done twenty years before when Tito was a prisoner at Lepoglava and she had pretended that electrical repairs had to be carried out in her flat, so as to give Tito an excuse to meet his friends there. The UDBA discovered that she was still helping the prisoners in Lepoglava; they arrested her, and decided to prosecute her for counter-revolutionary activity. Tito ordered them to release her. 'Leave the old woman alone,' he said, 'she is very religious. She used to help us, and now she is helping the reactionaries. She sees no difference at all, and believes that she is doing a good deed.'[21]

In the spring of 1949 Stalin stepped up the campaign against Tito. The criticism of Tito on the Cominformist radio and in their press became much more violent. In every Communist country of Eastern Europe a drive was launched against Titoist agents. In Albania the minister of the interior, Xoxe, was arrested in December 1948 and accused of working at Tito's orders to overthrow the Communist government of Albania; he was executed in June 1949. László Rajk, the Hungarian foreign minister, was the chief defendant in a big

---

* The OZNA, following the example of the GPU, had changed its name to UDBA.

show trial in Budapest in September. He had fought in Spain and had been imprisoned by the Nazis during the Second World War, and since the expulsion of Yugoslavia from the Cominform he had zealously denounced Tito and the CPY.

Rajk confessed at his trial that he had worked inside the illegal Hungarian Communist party as a police informer for Admiral Horthy's government since 1931, that he had been a Fascist agent in the International Brigade in Spain, and that he had been recruited by Ranković to take part in a conspiracy to carry out a *coup d'état* in Hungary and overthrow Rákosi's Communist government. One of the co-defendants at his trial was the former Yugoslav chargé d'affaires in Budapest, Brankov, who had issued his statement denouncing Tito in October 1948. He now confessed that he had done this on Ranković's instructions in order to win the confidence of the Hungarian Communist leaders and help organize Rajk's Titoist *coup d'état*. Rajk was sentenced to death, and executed. Brankov was sentenced to imprisonment for life.

In Bulgaria the deputy prime minister, Trajko Kostov, who had regularly denounced Tito since the Cominform resolution, was put on trial in December 1949 charged with having plotted with Tito and Ranković to assassinate Dimitrov, who had died a natural death in July, and to destroy the independence of Bulgaria by incorporating it into 'Fascist Yugoslavia, which had been converted into a colony of American and British imperialism'. He had hoped to 'open the gates of Bulgaria to Ranković's janissaries' on the orders of 'butcher Tito'.[22] He confessed, and was executed.

In the summer of 1949 the Soviet Union and the Communist countries of Eastern Europe imposed economic sanctions against Yugoslavia. This hit Yugoslavia hard, for since 1945 Yugoslav trade had been largely with the Soviet Union, and made it necessary for Tito to seek economic aid from the West. The West was prepared to help him. Even Bevin had been converted to the policy of 'keeping Tito afloat';[23] and the United States National Security Council believed that 'much as we dislike him, Tito is presently performing brilliantly in our interests in leading successfully and effectively the attack from within the Communist family on Soviet imperialism'.[24]

But Britain and the United States expected something in return from Tito; they wanted him to stop supporting the ELAS guerrillas in Greece. Tito was already considering doing this. In January 1949 General Markos, the leader of the ELAS guerrillas, who had closely collaborated with Tito's generals, was dismissed from the leadership of ELAS and criticized as a Titoist. He was replaced by the Greek Communist leader Zachariades, who denounced Tito and supported the Cominform accusations against him. In January Bebler told Sir Charles Peake, the British ambassador, that the Yugoslav government 'was sick and tired of supporting a rabble of Greek refugees of whom they were only too anxious to be rid'.[25]

In March 1949 Tito made secret contact with the Greek prime minister, General Tsaldaris; but Tsaldaris talked too freely to the correspondent of the British *Daily Mail*, and news of his contacts with Yugoslavia leaked out. The Cominform used it in their propaganda against Tito, and Tito broke off negotiations with Tsaldaris.

In April 1949 Maclean told the British Foreign Office that he was intending to pay a private visit to Tito. On 26 April Bevin telegraphed to the British ambassador in Belgrade that while he realized that it would be very unwise for Maclean to try to pressurize Tito, he hoped that he would drop a 'hint' to Tito that Britain would not continue giving him economic aid unless he stopped supporting ELAS in Greece. Bevin thought that Maclean should 'lose no opportunity which may occur of making it clear to Tito that he cannot expect to make capital indefinitely out of our desire to keep him afloat without giving us something in return. The return which he can most easily make to us without losing internal prestige is unobtrusively to withdraw support from the Greek rebels. If the Greek Government forces could be relieved from pressure on their Yugoslav front, this might make all the difference between victory and defeat.'[26]

The British embassy in Belgrade were sceptical. Britain had recently signed a trade agreement with Communist Poland without attaching political strings, and the embassy feared that Tito would resent that a different criterion was being applied to him.[27]

Maclean lunched with Tito on 5 May. There were only two other people present at the lunch, and Maclean and Tito were alone together during their talk. Maclean has never written about this meeting in any of his books, or given any information about it to any other author who has interviewed him; but his report to the Foreign Office is now in the Public Record Office. He found that Tito 'was as usual very friendly', and he was impressed by his self-confidence and cheerfulness in face of the threat from Stalin. He thought that Tito 'perhaps rather fancies himself in the role of Ajax defying the lightning, especially as the lightning has so far proved singularly ineffective'.[28]

Maclean approached the question of Greece very tactfully. He assured Tito that the British government had no wish to interfere in the internal affairs of Yugoslavia or to draw Tito into the Western camp, but that they hoped that he would stop helping ELAS in Greece. Tito admitted that he had helped ELAS in the past, but said that the situation had now changed. He could not refuse to grant political asylum to Greeks who escaped across the frontier into Yugoslavia, but he would not in future allow them to return to Greece to continue the fight. He asked Maclean to keep this very secret, as it would embarrass him politically if it were known. Maclean assured him that he could rely on Bevin to keep the secret.[29]

Peake did not believe that Tito would keep his promise to stop helping ELAS; even if he wished to do so, he would be prevented by 'his Left Wing, and notably Rankovic and Djilas, both of whom seem to be in the ascendant for the time being'.[30] But on 10 July Tito announced in a speech at the Military Academy at Pula in Istria that the frontier between Yugoslavia and Greece had been closed.[31]

As relations between Yugoslavia and the Soviet Union worsened during 1949, the British and United States governments suggested to Tito that he should follow up his abandonment of ELAS by establishing friendly relations with the Greek government; and they offered to act as mediators between Yugoslavia and Greece. Tito was cautious about agreeing to this suggestion, and wished to postpone any decision until after the Greek election in April 1950; he felt that it would be easier for him to improve relations with Greece if Tsaldaris was succeeded as Greek prime minister by the more moderate General Plastiras.[32]

In March 1950 George Allen, who had succeeded Cannon as United States ambassador in Belgrade, went to Athens for talks with Tsaldaris's government. The Soviet government guessed correctly that he was mediating between Yugoslavia and Greece. The official Soviet newspaper *Pravda* wrote on 26 March that there were plans for 'a military-political alliance between Tito's police-Gestapo Yugoslavia and monarcho-Fascist Greece'; and the Albanian Communist newspaper *Zeri i Popullit* wrote that 'the clique of Tito, committing the foulest treachery ever heard of in history against the heroic struggle of the Greek people', had plunged 'a dagger into the back of the Greek democratic army'.[33]

On 13 April Tito made a confidential approach to Plastiras, who became prime minister of Greece on 20 April; and on 22 April Tito proposed a resumption of diplomatic relations with Greece. It was widely believed in Greece that Britain and the United States had used their influence to secure Plastiras's appointment as prime minister in order to please Tito. The French government, who were as hostile as ever to Tito, thought that Grady, the United States ambassador in Athens, was an 'occult viceroy' in Greece.[34]

At the meeting of the United Nations General Assembly in September 1949 the election was held for the Security Council, which alone could decide to go to war or impose economic sanctions against a state which was condemned as an aggressor. There were five permanent members of the Security Council who could veto a resolution – the United States, Britain, the Soviet Union, France and China. The Chinese Communists had driven Chiang Kai-shek out of mainland China, and he was holding out only in the island of Formosa (Taiwan); but he still represented China at the United Nations. The other six members of the Security Council were elected to serve for two years.

It had been unofficially agreed between the Great Powers that the elected members should include some states from the Western world, some from Eastern Europe, and some from the British Commonwealth. Since the foundation of the United Nations in 1945, the two Eastern European states had of course always been members of the Soviet bloc; but in 1949 Yugoslavia announced that she would stand for election to the Security Council. Bebler explained to the British ambassador that Tito believed that if Yugoslavia were elected to the Security Council it would be regarded as a gesture of world support for Yugoslavia which would deter the Soviet Union and its satellites from invading.[35]

The Soviet Union reacted angrily; the election of Yugoslavia would be a breach of the informal agreement about the distribution of seats in the Security Council between the Great Powers. They nominated Czechoslovakia for the Eastern European seat.

The United States announced that it would support Yugoslavia. Nearly all the British diplomats in Belgrade and in the Foreign Office wanted Britain to follow the American lead; but Bevin was determined to vote for Czechoslovakia.[36] He did not wish to provoke the Soviet Union and upset the existing arrangements for the sake of giving a Security Council seat to a Communist like Tito. He feared that it would lead the Soviet Union to oppose the election of two Commonwealth states to the Security Council; and 'if we voted for the Yugoslavs this might have the effect of making them think that we would give them more support in the event of a Russian attack then we would in fact be able to give them'.[37] All the British Cabinet except the left-wing Aneurin Bevan agreed with him'[38] and the Foreign Office noted sadly that 'the Secretary of State has now telegraphed to say that he has decided against supporting the Yugoslav candidature, and there is nothing more we can really do'.[39]

Vyshinsky summoned a large press conference at the United Nations, and declared that the election of Yugoslavia to the Security Council would be illegal under the United Nations Charter, and might cause the Soviet Union to cease to support the United Nations; but the United States lobbied strongly for Yugoslavia. When the voting took place on 20 October, Yugoslavia received thirty-seven votes and Czechoslovakia twenty.[40] Yugoslavia was one vote short of the two-thirds majority which it needed to be elected; but on the same day Bevin telegraphed to the British delegation at the United Nations that if Yugoslavia was not elected on the first ballot and Czechoslovakia did not get more than twenty or twenty-five votes, 'you have authority to switch your vote to Yugoslavia at your discretion'.[41] They probably did so, because on the second ballot Yugoslavia was elected by thirty-nine votes against Czechoslovakia's nineteen; but the way in which the British delegate voted was never made public.

Yugoslavia seemed to have thrown in her lot with the United States and the West; but Tito was determined to preserve his freedom of action, and also his principles, as far as this was practicable. The revolutionary movement in French Indo-China, under the leadership of the Communist Ho Chi Minh, had gained control of the north of the country and had established a government in Hanoi; in the south, the French had set up a puppet government under Bao Dai in Saigon. On 31 January 1950 the Soviet Union recognized Ho Chi Minh's government as the government of the independent state of Vietnam. Tito informed the foreign diplomats in Belgrade that he intended to recognize Ho Chi Minh.

The French government were angry, and decided to oppose the grant of any economic aid to Tito. The United States secretary of state, Dean Acheson, was also outraged. He sent a telegram to the United States ambassador in Belgrade pointing out that 'Sov recognition of Ho' would 'further Commie expansionist aims. Recognition by Yugo wld strengthen very forces against which it is fighting for its own independence . . . We do not wish make direct threats Yugo Govt but you shld ensure they clearly understand seriousness of obstacles which Yugo recognition of Ho wld create.'[42]

As Acheson's argument had no effect on the Yugoslav government, he instructed the first secretary at the United States embassy, Fowler, to tell Tito 'that recognition Ho would not fail to affect attitude of many Americans toward economic assistance to Yugoslavia'.[43] Tito reacted very adversely to this threat. Fowler reported to Acheson that 'Tito clearly interpreted this to be pressure on Yugoslav government and he took occasion to let us know that he would not countenance pressure from U.S. . . . . It is obvious that Tito has been angered by implication that U.S. attitude toward economic assistance will be affected by Yugoslav action re recognition Ho Chi Minh. He has taken this occasion to let us and Cominform know forcefully that he will not allow interference from any quarter.'[44] Tito followed up his stand against Fowler in private with a public statement of his independence. On 18 February 1950, in a speech at Užice, he said that no one could buy Yugoslav independence with economic aid.

On 25 June 1950 the armies of North Korea crossed the 38th Parallel and invaded South Korea. The idea had apparently first been suggested to Stalin by the Communist president of North Korea, Kim il Sung, and Stalin agreed after Mao Tse-tung had assured him that the United States would not intervene in a Korean civil war; but Stalin took the precaution of withdrawing Soviet military advisers from North Korea before the attack was launched, because he did not wish the Soviet Union to be associated with the attack.[45] The United States immediately raised the matter in the Security Council of the United Nations. The Soviet delegate had for some months refused to attend any meeting of the United Nations as a protest against the refusal of the United Nations to admit Communist China in place of Chiang Kai-shek's Taiwan as the representative of China in the Security Council; he did not attend the meeting of the Security Council on 26 June to use the Soviet veto against the proposal to send troops to repel North Korean aggression, which was carried by nine votes against nil; but Yugoslavia abstained.

Tito could thus claim to be neutral between the Soviet Union and American imperialism. The United States told Tito that they were disappointed that after Yugoslavia had been successfully elected to the Security Council she had not voted against North Korean aggression. Tito said that he feared that if he had done so, it would have been interpreted by the Soviet Union as a sign that Yugoslavia had joined the Western alliance and might have provoked an invasion of Yugoslavia by the Soviet Union and its allies.[46]

The North Koreans swept rapidly through South Korea and by August had overrun the whole country except for a small area on the south-east coast, where General MacArthur had concentrated the American forces. In September he counter-attacked, and the North Koreans retreated as fast as they had advanced to the 38th Parallel from where they had started. The United Nations discussed whether their armies should halt on the 38th Parallel or invade North Korea and overthrow the Communist regime there. They voted to invade North Korea; Yugoslavia again abstained. Within a few weeks the American forces had occupied the northern capital of Pyongyang and reached the Yalu River, the frontier between North Korea and Communist China. The Communist press throughout the world was full of reports of the atrocities committed in the north by the South Koreans who were fighting by the side of the American and United Nations troops.

When the United Nations troops reached the Yalu, Mao Tse-tung proposed to Stalin that the Chinese Communist armies should enter North Korea and go to the assistance of the North Koreans. Stalin advised Mao Tse-tung not to intervene, for intervention might provoke a world war; but Mao nevertheless decided to act. Chinese Communist troops crossed the Yalu and drove the American and United Nations forces back to the 38th Parallel. The United Nations General Assembly then passed a resolution condemning Communist China as the aggressor. The Soviet Union and its allies voted against the resolution, and Yugoslavia abstained. Yugoslavia displeased the United States by supporting the efforts of the Indian prime minister, Jawaharlal Nehru, to mediate between the United Nations and Communist China.[47]

However the Yugoslav delegate might vote at the United Nations, the Korean War brought Tito closer to the Western powers than he had ever been or would ever be in the future. The United States and its allies believed that it was Stalin who had ordered Kim il Sung to invade South Korea. This convinced them that Stalin was now ready to order his satellite states to begin local wars against their neighbours, that what he had done in Asia he could do in Europe, and that he might tell Romania, Bulgaria, Hungary and Albania to invade Yugoslavia. They were right. The Soviet Union now had the nuclear bomb. The United States and NATO had announced a large-scale rearmament programme, and statements by American politicians, and the Anglo-American attempt to start a civil war in Albania, suggested that the United States had abandoned containment and would now pursue a roll-back policy and would try to overthrow Communist regimes everywhere, including the Soviet Union. Stalin and the Red Army High Command seem to have decided that they would be better placed to win a Third World War in 1950 than in three or four years' time. They were also encouraged by the speed with which the North Koreans had advanced in South Korea and the delayed American response.

So in the summer of 1950 the Red Army High Command were instructed to draw up plans for the invasion of Yugoslavia in the spring or summer of 1951, in the first place by the armies of Hungary, Romania, Bulgaria and Albania, and if necessary by the Red Army itself. But in the autumn of 1950 Stalin countermanded the order. He was apparently impressed by the success of MacArthur's counter-attack in Korea.

As early as July 1950, within a fortnight of the outbreak of the Korean War, the United States military authorities were discussing how Yugoslavia could be drawn into the Western defence plans. Tito was very ready to take part in these military talks, but he still did not wish to join NATO, just as the Western foreign ministers did not wish to have NATO's democratic image spoilt by admitting a Communist country. The French complained that Yugoslavia was having all the advantages of belonging to NATO without the burdens and obligations of membership.[48] As always, France was more anti-Tito, and the United States more pro-Tito, than any of the other NATO allies.

In January 1951 Stalin summoned the defence ministers in the Communist governments of Eastern Europe to a conference in the Kremlin. He told them that he was again considering launching an attack on Yugoslavia in the spring. He had apparently been encouraged by the Chinese Communists' success against MacArthur's army in Korea. He believed that if Hungary, Romania, Bulgaria and Albania simultaneously invaded Yugoslavia, while the Red Army marched in through Czechoslovakia and Hungary and through the Ljubljana gap, they could overrun Yugoslavia before the United

States would have time to intervene; and once they were there, the United States and NATO would not start a Third World War in order to reinstate Tito in power. Marshal Zhukov was told to resurrect the invasion plan which had first been drawn up in the summer of 1950 and then shelved in the autumn. The Red Army believed that in order to win a swift success they would have to outnumber Tito's forces by at least three to one; but even if Tito was able, as he claimed, to put 400,000 soldiers into the field immediately, the satellite states could assemble nearly three times that number without the Red Army being obliged to intervene.[49]

The United States was ready to go to war with the Soviet Union. On 15 January 1951 the American joint chiefs of staff urged Truman to pursue 'a co-ordinated and integrated crusade against Kremlin-dominated Communism everywhere', explaining that by 'crusade' they meant 'a vigorous and aggressive movement for the advancement of an idea or cause'.[50] The last man who had led a crusade against Communism was Adolf Hitler, and then events had forced the supreme anti-Communist, Winston Churchill, to order the British army to fight on the Communist side; now that the United States was leading another anti-Communist crusade, events were forcing the Communist Tito to join the crusaders, though it was entirely thanks to him that the crusade was directed only against 'Kremlin-dominated Communism'.

The American generals were more eager than anyone else to help Tito. The British Labour government thought that the dictator Tito, like the dictator Franco, was an undesirable ally; but the American chiefs of staff were as happy to have the one as the other, and equally happy to have anti-Soviet refugees from the Baltic states, including those who had murdered Jews under the Nazis, along with members of the Nazi intelligence service who had experience in catching Communists, and the Russian Cossacks and Croat Ustashas who had fought for Hitler in the Second World War and had not been handed over to the Red Army or to Tito in May 1945.

At the end of January 1951 Djilas paid a secret visit to London and met Attlee. He asked him to supply arms to Yugoslavia, which faced an imminent attack from the Cominform states. Djilas said that it would be better if the arms were supplied neither through NATO, nor officially by Western governments, but were sent as unobtrusively as possible. Tito made the same request to the French ambassador in Belgrade, and Velebit asked the United States government in Washington. The French did not respond. The British government was in favour of sending the arms, but decided that it could do nothing until it had discussed the matter with the Americans. The United States government granted Velebit's request without consulting any of its allies; in less than six weeks all the formalities had been completed and the dispatch of the arms was authorized by Truman on 12 March 1951.[51] While Tito was waiting for the American reply, he promised on 22 February that if the Red Army attacked Greece or West Germany, or Italy through Austria, Yugoslavia would enter the war on the side of NATO.[52]

Tito and Koča Popović, his chief of staff, drew up their plans for the defence of the country. They could put thirty-eight divisions in the field, but they expected to be attacked by eighty-five divisions from the Soviet satellite states who would have air support from the Soviet Air Force. They thought that the main attack would come from the north. They should be able to hold the line along the Danube, and Belgrade, for fifteen days; but after twenty days Belgrade would have been captured, and by the thirty-fifth day after the invasion they would have retreated to a line along the River Sava from Zagreb to Kraljevo. In the south, their armies based on Skopje would defend the frontier against the Albanians, but they did not plan to counter-attack and invade Albania. Ultimately they might have to resort to guerrilla warfare in the Bosnian mountains.[53] Tito and Koča Popović considered the possibility of impeding the advance of the invading Cominform armies by flooding parts of Serbia as far south as the northern approaches to Belgrade by destroying the cliffs and rocks along the banks of the Danube at the Djerdap Gorge; but several Serbian generals opposed the proposal.[54]

The American chiefs of staff had a different plan. They believed that the United States should reply to an attack by the Soviet satellite states on Yugoslavia by using the atomic bomb against the satellites.[55] They thought that as the Soviet Union still possessed only a small arsenal of atomic bombs, the Russians would be unlikely to use them in retaliation for an American nuclear attack on the satellite states; they would use them only in retaliation for the atomic bombing of the Soviet Union.[56]

In March 1951 the American and British chiefs of staff had discussions about the American proposal. The British were reluctant to use the atomic bomb; but on 7 April the American chiefs of staff proposed that 'Final decision should not be made now on the employment of atomic weapons against the satellite states. However, in view of the existence of suitable and highly profitable target complexes, and for the psychological advantages that would be obtained thereby, the United States should, after an attack occurs and in the light of the conditions then existing, give serious consideration to the use of atomic weapons against the satellite states. Plans for such use should be prepared.'[57] The American General Omar Bradley believed 'that in practice effect of use of atom bomb would not be disappointing'.[58]

The British were not happy about this proposal, and the United States government were less keen on it than their chiefs of staff. On 23 May 1951 the State Department's policy planning staff recommended that if the Soviet satellite states attacked Yugoslavia, 'we would probably not make atomic or other attacks on Soviet territory. Although there would be appropriate atomic targets in Czechoslovakia and Rumania, we might, but probably would not, use atomic weapons against them.' But if the Soviet Union as well as its satellite states took part in an attack on Yugoslavia, 'we would use atomic weapons on Soviet, and possibly satellite, targets'. But they thought that the United States would have more moral justification for doing this if the Soviet Union or its satellites attacked Greece than in the case of Yugoslavia, because Greece, though not a member of NATO, was a non-Communist country.[59]

There is no record that the United States government consulted Tito about this plan; his chief of the cabinet of the Supreme Command of the Yugoslav armed forces, General Petar Babić, first heard about it from me in 1993. Tito would hardly have relished the idea of the United States protecting Yugoslavia by using atomic bombs against Czechoslovakia and Romania; because although the Soviet Union would probably not have retaliated by using atomic bombs against the United States, they might well have used them against Yugoslavia. Tito would not have welcomed a war in which the United States and the Soviet Union dropped atomic bombs on their enemy's allies but not on each other.

As for Britain, the Labour government showed a marked reluctance to help Communist Yugoslavia. They agreed that if there was an attack on Yugoslavia, NATO should give the Yugoslavs strategic and tactical air support; but they were opposed to sending even a token land force to Yugoslavia, and insisted that if the war spread from Yugoslavia and became a global war, no troops should be withdrawn from the defence of any NATO state in order to help the Yugoslavs. This contrasted strikingly with the eagerness with which Attlee had sent British troops to defend the right-wing dictatorship of Syngman Rhee in South Korea from a Soviet-satellite attack. The British chiefs of staff also opposed the proposal that Tito's generals should be informed about the Anglo-American discussions as to what they should do in the event of an attack on Yugoslavia.[60]

But the year 1951 passed away without any invasion of Yugoslavia or any use of atomic bombs by the United States. In October the Conservatives won a general election in Britain, and Churchill became prime minister and Eden foreign secretary. Churchill had declared that he wished to attend a summit conference with Truman and Stalin, and hoped that he might be able to persuade Stalin to end the Cold War; and with his great prestige, particularly in the United States, he was able to exercise a greater restraining influence on Truman than Attlee or Bevin could or wished to do.

In February 1952 King George VI died, and old Ivan Ribar, the President of the Presidium of the National Assembly, went to London for the funeral. He made a very favourable impression on the British Foreign Office, who were convinced that he was not a Communist and that he appreciated the advantages of constitutional monarchy. In the funeral procession he walked side by side with the sixteen-year-old king of Iraq, who told him proudly about his successes at his English public school.[61] The description of Ribar in the official programme as 'the President of the Presidium of the Yugoslav Republic'[62] seems to have deceived several persons, including even Fitzroy Maclean, into thinking that it was Tito who was walking in the funeral procession;[63] but Tito did not come to London for George VI's funeral.

By the beginning of 1952 times were changing in Yugoslavia. The press had become freer and more critical; censorship of books had become much less strict; most important of all, people felt that they could speak more freely in the streets. A new code of law was introduced, which restricted the powers of the police to carry out arbitrary arrests, and they were less frequent. Kardelj even spoke in the National Assembly on 1 April 1952 about the Marxist-Leninist doctrine of the withering away of the state.[64] Criticism of Stalin and the Soviet Union became more outspoken. It was now possible to publish books like Weissberg's *Conspiracy of Silence*,[65] which exposed the trials and the methods of interrogation adopted by the NKVD in the

Soviet Union, the horrors of the Great Purge, and the silence of Communists who knew what was happening but kept quiet and justified it. Dedijer published his biography of Tito, in which he quoted long passages in Tito's own words; one section of the book dealt with Tito's years in Moscow and why he continued to believe in the Soviet Union.[66]

Economic controls were also relaxed. The regulations that gave privileges to party officials were modified, and a free market was allowed to operate to a limited degree. American and British economic aid had helped relieve the greatest economic hardships, though the people were still poor. A joke was going round in 1952. Why does Marshal Tito hold so many offices in the state? Because none of us can make ends meet if we have only one job.[67]

The British ambassador in Belgrade, Sir Ivo Mallett, was encouraged. 'It is by drawing Tito into our councils and our camp', he wrote to Eden on 26 September 1952, 'that we shall best advance the liberalisation of the regime.'[68] But Tito did not intend it to become too liberal. Prisoners were still being held on Goli Otok and treated harshly there; but conditions were a little less harsh, and fewer people were being arrested and more released. Crni Žujović was released from prison. The prison authorities had allowed him to read the official Hungarian report of Rajk's trial, which so disgusted him that he recanted his pro-Cominform opinions and expressed his full support for Tito.[69]

The case of his fellow-prisoner Hebrang ended more tragically and is much more mysterious. The official story published by Tito and Ranković at the time of his arrest was that after he was arrested by Pavelić's police in Zagreb in February 1942 he gave way under torture and agreed to become an agent of the Gestapo. He was released in an exchange of prisoners with the Partisans in October 1942. The Gestapo reports which proved his guilt were sent to Berlin, where the Russians found them when they captured Berlin in 1945; but instead of informing Tito that Hebrang had been an agent of the Gestapo, the Russians used the information to blackmail Hebrang into becoming a Russian spy. He agreed to work for them, and sent his reports to the Soviet embassy in Belgrade until he was detected by Ranković's police agents and arrested in May 1948, just before the Cominform resolution which expelled Yugoslavia.[70]

The Chetniks in Serbia today tell a different story. They say that Tito knew in 1945 that Hebrang had been a spy for the Gestapo, but that he nevertheless appointed Hebrang to govern Croatia after the liberation. It was not until Hebrang sided with the Cominform that Tito revealed that he had worked for the Germans during the war.[71]

Today Hebrang is a national hero in Croatia. Both the Titoist and the Chetnik stories about him are rejected on all sides. The Croats say that he never worked for the Gestapo, and that there is no evidence against him apart from the fact that after he was arrested he was sent to Jasenovac instead of being executed and that he was later released under an exchange of prisoners. They say that he was an honest and democratic Croat and Communist who wished to introduce a more democratic form of Communism without a secret police and a centralized tyranny in Belgrade. When they are asked to explain why, if he held these democratic views, he supported the Cominform against Tito and why Stalin so warmly supported him, they say that Stalin was merely mischief-making. Stalin plotted secretly to get rid of Tito and to replace him by Hebrang because he knew that Hebrang was more popular than Tito in Yugoslavia and that he could therefore use Hebrang to weaken Tito.

The most incriminating evidence against Hebrang was published by Milatović, who conducted the investigation into Hebrang's case. It is a telegram sent in May 1942 from the Gestapo in Zagreb to the Gestapo in Vienna; the original document is in the Yugoslav government secret archives, having allegedly been sent to Belgrade by the KGB after the rapprochement between Khrushchev and Tito in 1955. Hebrang's supporters say that it is a forgery, and that this is proved by the fact that it is typed on a typewriter which was first manufactured in Czechoslovakia in 1946.[72]

Ko/PY   Agram [Zagreb] 4 May, 1942.
To the Secret State Police, State Police Office, Vienna.
Concerning: Zugelj Milan, Communist, Croat, now in Vienna.
Police record: None.
According to information given to the Croatian police by the arrested Communist Hebrang, he is receiving reports about the situation in the Reich from the Communist Zugelj, a manual worker now in Vienna. H. did not wish to give any further details during his interrogation.
In this connection it should be pointed out that H. was a member of the CC of the Croatian CP.
Signed: Hübner, SS Obersturmführer.[73]

[313]

Even if this document is not a forgery, it does not prove that Hebrang was an agent of the Gestapo in any ordinary meaning of the term, but only that while he was being interrogated, almost certainly under torture, he gave the name but not the address of his contact in Vienna. Nor should we forget what was meant by that wonderful understatement by the Gestapo that Hebrang 'did not wish to give any further details during his interrogation'.

In 1952 it was announced that Hebrang had committed suicide in prison by hanging himself with his tie. Hardly anyone in Yugoslavia believes this today. Even people who supported Tito against Hebrang and the Cominform in 1948, including some of Tito's close collaborators and personal friends, are convinced that Hebrang was murdered by the prison warders and that they would not have killed him unless Tito had ordered them to do it. They say that the murder of Hebrang was shameful and the one unforgivable act of Tito's career. This version of events does not explain why Hebrang so steadfastly refused to condemn the Cominform, as Žujović did, and why, if Tito was prepared to release Žujović, he murdered Hebrang. If Hebrang was murdered, this surely does not necessarily mean that the crime was committed on Tito's orders. In a dictatorship as well as in a democratic country, policemen and prison warders can kill prisoners in custody without orders from the prime minister or the dictator.

Tito was still in conflict with the Roman Catholic Church. He was on much better terms with the Orthodox Church, and in 1950 returned to the Church part of their property which had been nationalized. But Stepinac was still in prison. Tito offered to release him if he would resign his post as archbishop and go abroad; but Stepinac refused, for he was determined to be a martyr for the Catholic Church. In the autumn of 1952 Pope Pius XII created Stepinac a cardinal. Tito indignantly broke off diplomatic relations with the Vatican.

In May 1952 Tito celebrated his sixtieth birthday. After an operation for gallstones that year he had been nursed by Jovanka Budisavljević. Jovanka came from a Serbian peasant family in Lika, one of the Serbian enclaves in Croatia, and had escaped being massacred by the Ustashas by joining the Partisans. After the enigmatic Polka, the intellectuals Lucia Bauer and Herta Haas, and the flamboyant Zdenka, this simple, homely and not very well educated peasant woman, who was some thirty years younger than he, became Tito's new wife.

In the summer of 1952 Velebit, who was ambassador in Rome, was asked to invite Jovanka to stay for a few weeks in the embassy so that his wife could teach her deportment and the correct etiquette in the drawing room and at the dinner table. He had heard rumours about Jovanka and Tito, and guessed the reason why he had been asked to teach her how to behave in society. He did not reveal the reason to Mrs Velebit, but she, too, guessed. They both enjoyed having Jovanka in the embassy in Rome, and she and Vera Velebit became close friends. She learned the correct etiquette very quickly.[74]

In September 1952 Tito invited Eden, as British foreign secretary, to come to Belgrade on an official visit.[75] It was a gesture of Anglo-Yugoslav solidarity designed to impress Stalin.

Tito sprang a surprise on his English guests, on his household, and on the world. Jovanka appeared as hostess at his receptions and dinners, and was introduced for the first time as the president's wife. Eden was annoyed. He had just married again after divorcing his first wife, and he would have brought the new Mrs Eden with him had he known that Tito had remarried and that there would be a hostess at the banquets and receptions.[76]

Tito no longer expected an immediate invasion from the Soviet Union, but the Cominform's hate campaign continued. In November 1952 there was another great show trial, this time in Czechoslovakia. The general secretary of the Communist party, Rudolf Slánský,* the former foreign minister Vladimir Clementis,† and a number of other leading Communists were charged with having been traitors for many years. Several of the defendants were Jews, and were accused of being Zionist agents, but also of having committed their crimes at Tito's orders. They all confessed, vilified themselves, and were sentenced to death or long terms of imprisonment. Slánský, Clementis and several others were executed.

On 1 March 1953 Stalin had a stroke. Four days later he died at the age of seventy-three to the grief and consternation of the members of his Politburo and of many millions of Soviet citizens.

---

* Slánský, Rudolf (1901–52); general secretary of the Czechoslovak Communist party; was the chief defendant in the Slánský trial in 1952, and executed.

† Clementis, Vladimir (1902–52). Czechoslovak Communist leader; foreign minister 1948–50; a defendant in the Slánský trial in 1952, and executed.

— ❖ —

CHAPTER 23

The Triumphant Tito

T ITO had survived Stalin, just as he had survived Hitler; but the worry for the Special Branch of Scotland Yard in London was whether he would survive his state visit to Britain, for they suspected that there were former Ustasha and Chetnik refugees in the country who might try to assassinate him, to say nothing of the harmless but annoying Roman Catholic enthusiasts who would surround him shouting 'Freedom for Cardinal Stepinac!'

During Eden's visit to Belgrade he had invited Tito to come to London in the following spring on a state visit to Queen Elizabeth II, but warned Tito that there might be opposition from Roman Catholics, who objected to Tito's measures against the Catholic Church in Yugoslavia and particularly to the continued imprisonment of Stepinac. Tito accepted the invitation, and said that his Roman Catholic critics were misinformed about his policy and about Stepinac. Neither Tito nor the British knew that the Soviet KGB had planned to assassinate Tito during his visit to London; but the plan was cancelled after Stalin's death.

Tito travelled to London by sea in the training ship *Galeb*, which he much preferred to air travel. He arrived on 16 March 1953, eleven days after Stalin's death. He sailed to Greenwich, where he transferred to a British launch and went on up the Thames amid tight security. He landed near Westminster Bridge and was welcomed by the Duke of Edinburgh, Churchill and Eden. The whole area had been sealed off by the police. All the bridges over that stretch of the river had been closed, and the large crowds who had gathered on the Embankment to see him were moved away by the police an hour before he arrived. As a security precaution, the programme for his visit was not disclosed in advance to the public.

The chief purpose of the visit was to show the world, and especially Stalin's successors in the Soviet Union, that Tito was now closely allied to the West. There was the usual programme arranged for visiting heads of state. He lunched with the Queen at Buckingham Palace and dined with Churchill at 10 Downing Street. He met the leaders of the Labour party and the London County Council, and gave a reception for over 800 guests at the Yugoslav embassy. It was a hurried and hectic five days, as he was driven, flanked everywhere by a police motorcycle escort, from White Lodge in Richmond Park, where he was staying, to Cambridge University, Windsor Castle, the British Museum, the Tower of London and Hampton Court, where he stayed for exactly fifteen minutes. There was an unfortunate incident when he attended the air display at Duxford airfield in Cambridgeshire, for two British airmen were killed in a plane accident.[1]

He received three London schoolchildren at the Yugoslav embassy, when they presented him with a gift of £112 which had been collected by London schoolchildren for a school in Yugoslavia.[2] He was equally charming to more hostile visitors. A dozen Conservative MPs tried to persuade him that now that he had firmly joined the Free World of the West he ought to realize how much the Free World was concerned about the treatment of Christians in Yugoslavia. He made a very good impression on them. They reported that 'his reply was very courteous and considerate', and that he had said that 'there was perhaps a certain amount of misconception as to the true state of affairs in his country'.[3]

His talks with Churchill and Eden about international affairs dealt with the thorny problem of Trieste. Yugoslav forces had been in occupation of the Slav hinterland at Trieste, which was called 'Zone B', while the British and American forces were in the city of Trieste and Zone A. The final decision on the frontiers at Trieste had been postponed; but in the summer of 1953 the United States and British governments announced that they proposed to hand over the administration of Zone A to Italy. Tito reacted strongly; he declared that Yugoslavia would not agree to Italy having Zone A.

On 6 September 1953 he addressed a crowd of 300,000 at Okroglica in Zone B. After attacking Italian policy in Trieste in Mussolini's time, he said that the present Italian government still wished to enslave the Slav peoples of the area. 'So far as the Italian people are concerned, we have nothing but respect for them, and we regret that their leaders are taking them along such a wrong path as they have adopted lately.' The Italians must understand that they could not seize Yugoslav territory. 'There stands on this side of the border today a nation that is capable and proud; a nation with a fighting spirit; peace-loving, but determined to defend every inch of its land, no matter who might attack it.'[4]

Tito ordered his army to be ready to enter Zone A with their tanks if the Allied forces handed it over to the Italians; but he knew that in the last resort he would have to give in to the United States and Britain. Djilas was with Tito in the White Palace in Belgrade when he gave the order to General Kosta Nadj to be ready to send the tanks into Zone A. 'How are we going to fire at the Italians', asked Djilas, 'when they are protected by the Americans and the English? Are we going to fire on them as well?' 'We'll go in if the Italians go in,' said Tito, 'then we'll see.' He then explained why he was adopting such a belligerent attitude about Zone A. 'If we are not decisive, they will ask for Zone B too. That's what I am afraid of.'[5]

In view of Tito's stand, the Western powers postponed the immediate hand-over of Zone A to Italy; but after further negotiations the final settlement was reached in London in October 1954. Italy obtained Zone A and Yugoslavia Zone B.

Soon after Stalin's death Nikita Khrushchev became general secretary of the Communist party of the Soviet Union, and directed the policy of the Soviet government. He had been one of Stalin's loyal officials for the last fifteen years. At the time of the festivities to mark Stalin's seventieth birthday in December 1949, he had equalled all the other Soviet spokesmen in glorification of the leader, whom he praised for his 'mortal combat with the enemies of the people – Mensheviks, SRs, Trotskyites, Zinovievites, Bukharinites, bourgeois nationalists' and 'the Tito-Ranković band of murderers and spies'.[6]

But he now initiated a policy of conciliation in international affairs and a gradual relaxation of the Stalinist repression in the Soviet Union. In the autumn of 1953 Beria was arrested, tried in secret, and shot. He was the third consecutive chief of the NKVD to be executed, but he was also the last. By executing Stalin's last executioner, his successors ended the terrible Stalinist years. Henceforth the leaders of the CPSU, like Tito in Yugoslavia, would adopt somewhat milder methods of getting rid of their political rivals.

There was a relaxation of international tension. In the summer of 1954 the Geneva Agreement ended the war in Vietnam; pending the holding of elections, the country was divided between the Communist North and the South under the French puppet ruler Bao Dai. Next year the leaders of the United States and the Soviet Union held a friendly summit meeting for the first time for ten years when President Eisenhower, Eden (who had succeeded Churchill as prime minister) and the French prime minister met Khrushchev and Marshal Bulganin in Geneva.

Tito could at last look forward to a quieter life, and he intended to enjoy it to the full. He had undergone many hardships since his birth at Kumrovec in Franz Joseph's empire sixty-one years before – the poverty of a young worker who was often unemployed; the mutilation of his finger by unfenced machinery in the factories of pre-1914 Vienna; the winter campaign in the Carpathians in 1915; the flogging by the Cossacks in Russia two years later; the dangers of underground work for the Communist party and prison life in King Alexander's Yugoslavia; the Hotel Lux in Moscow during the purges; the Gestapo in Belgrade in 1941; the Sutjeska, the raid on his cave at Drvar, and the hardships of life in the mountains of Bosnia during the Partisans' campaigns. He had endured much more than Franklin D. Roosevelt in New York society, than Truman amid the comforts of Middle America, than Churchill, who had always had the services of a valet or a batman even at Omdurman and in the trenches during the First World War, or than Lenin in the cafés of Zurich and Montparnasse. Now Tito could enjoy the rewards of power as compensation for his years of struggle and suffering.

Fifty years earlier, when he was working in a Sisak sweatshop and tramping the roads between Zagreb and Trieste in search of work, Austrian archdukes lived in palaces and hunting lodges where they chased wild boars in the forests and ate gargantuan meals when they returned from a day's shooting. Now Tito had palaces in Belgrade, Zagreb and Ljubljana, a hunting lodge near Bled in Slovenia and a holiday home on the island of Brioni off the Croatian coast. Some people did not approve of this. In the housing shortage in Yugoslavia, which was still acute after the war, no one was allowed to have a second home; but people said that Tito had seventy-six palaces. This was a grotesque exaggeration. In every part of the country there was some government residence, and the people, or at least the officials, of the district expected Tito to stay there overnight from time to time. It was a great distortion of language to call them Tito's palaces. 'You might as well say', says his son Miša Broz, 'that the Waldorf-Astoria Hotel in New York was one of Tito's palaces because he once stayed the night there.'[7]

He had a suite of rooms in the White Palace in Belgrade, but he hardly ever stayed there, and used the White Palace only as offices. Soon after the liberation, the government gave him for his private residence a house at 15 Užička Street, very close to the house where he had lived secretly during the dangerous summer months of 1941. It had been built shortly before the Second World War for the wealthy engineer, Acović. From time to time new buildings were added in the grounds, and by the 1970s there were a total of eight buildings there.

The main building, although much too small to be called a palace, was rather like a palace in style, with no passages but with one large room leading out of another, all built in an impressive modern style which had nothing in the least vulgar or ostentatious. The dining room contained one large and one small table, the small one where he and Jovanka ate alone or with the family and a few friends, and the larger one where they dined when they had guests. Tito's study was a large impressive room. At one end there was a large desk at which Tito sat looking across the room. On the desk he had a small coloured photograph of Lenin. Behind him was a big mural showing the defeat of Gubec and the peasants in the battle of Donja Stubica near Kumrovec during the revolt of 1573. Also behind him was a little bust of Gubec, which was a replica of the statue which had been unveiled in Tito's presence on the battlefield on the 400th anniversary in 1973, and a small bust of Lenin.[8]

In 1964 the government of Croatia built an enormous palace for him in Zagreb. It was much larger than the old palace in the town centre where the Habsburg emperors had stayed when they came to Zagreb and where Tito lived during the first years after 1945. The new palace was on the hill of Pantovčak, in the beautiful park and woodlands which had belonged to the family of Baron Nikolić who had been prominent at the court in Vienna. Across the road in front of the grounds was the inn where the secret Communist party conference had been held on that snowy night in February 1928. The last Baroness Nikolić had lived till 1962 in the old manor house in the grounds, and had allowed the inhabitants of Zagreb to walk in her woods on Sundays.

After the property was nationalized in 1962, the Communist authorities decided to build the super-palace for Tito in the grounds.

17. Tito on Vis in 1944.

18. Tito and Nazor in Zagreb in May 1945.

Третье. Нам непонятно, почему английский шпион Велебит продолжает оставаться в системе министерства иностранных дел Югославии в качестве первого помощника министра. Югославские товарищи знают, что Велебит является английским шпионом. Они знают и то, что представители Советского правительства также считают Велебита шпионом. И все же, несмотря на это, Велебит остается первым помощником министра иностранных дел Югославии. Возможно, что Югославское правительство хочет использовать Велебита именно как шпиона Англии. Как известно, буржуазные правительства считают вполне допустимым иметь в своем составе шпионов военных империалистических держав, милость которых они хотят себе обеспечить, и согласны, таким образом, поставить себя под контроль этих держав. Мы считаем такую практику абсолютно недопустимой для марксистов. Как бы то ни было, Советское правительство не может поставить свою переписку с Югославским правительством под контроль английского шпиона. Понятно, что поскольку Велебит все еще остается в составе руководства иностранными делами Югославии, Советское правительство считает себя поставленным в затруднительное положение и лишено возможности вести откровенную переписку с Югославским правительством через систему министерства иностранных дел Югославии.

Таковы факты, вызвавшие недовольство Советского правительства и ЦК ВКП(б) и ведущие к ухудшению в отношениях между СССР и Югославией.

Эти факты, как уже сказано выше, не связаны с вопросом об отзыве военных и гражданских специалистов, тем не менее они играют не малую роль в деле ухудшения отношений между нашими странами.

27 марта
1948 года.
Москва.

По поручению Цека
В. Молотов
И. Сталин

19. The last page of the letter to the Central Committee of the CPY of 27 March 1948 signed by Molotov and Stalin.

20. The Fifth Congress of the CPY in Belgrade in July 1948. The delegates vote unanimously in support of Tito's decision to break with Stalin.

21. (*Above*) The Fifth Conference of the CPY in Zagreb in 1952. The photographs of Marx, Engels and Lenin on the wall look lopsided, because the fourth photograph (of Stalin) has been removed.

22. (*Below*) Tito with Queen Elizabeth II, Queen Elizabeth the Queen Mother, the Duke of Edinburgh and Princess Margaret in London in March 1953.

23. Tito at a supper with the schoolteachers in his native village of Kumrovec in December 1953.

24. Tito welcomes Khrushchev at Belgrade airport in May 1955.

25. Tito at the Acropolis in Athens in June 1954.

26. Tito on a hunting expedition.

27. Tito and Churchill in Split in 1960.

28. Tito and his wife Jovanka Budisavlj at the home of his cousin Martin Broz i Kumrovec in 1962.

29. (*Above*) Left to right: Kardelj, Tito, Ranković.
30. (*Below*) Tito (dressed in native Serb costume) with his wife
Jovanka at a New Year's Eve party in her native village of Lički Osik
in the Serb enclave of Lika in Croatia on 31 December 1967.

31. Statue of Tito by Antun Augustinčić.

They commissioned a leading architect to build this twentieth-century Versailles. Any admirer of modern architecture will find it impressive, but Tito's taste in architecture, as in music, had not changed since his days as a young metalworker in Vienna, and he did not like the palace, even after he had furnished the large state rooms with eighteenth-century rococo furniture which, surprisingly, blends very well with the building. The public was no longer allowed to walk in the woods, which were surrounded with high electrified fences for Tito's protection. The UDBA wished to take further security measures by demolishing the houses on the other side of the street and evacuating the residents in Pantovčak, but Tito would not allow this.[9] He stayed in the palace as little as possible. When he came to Zagreb he usually stayed there for one or two nights and then moved to his native village of Kumrovec, which was only twenty miles away.[10] He could commute from there to Zagreb.

In later years he became more exasperated when he was given another residence by a grateful nation, perhaps because he knew how unpopular it made him in some quarters. He used to go regularly to Igalo in Montenegro every summer for the annual army manoeuvres; it gave him the opportunity to see the latest military developments and to spend some happy hours with his generals. In 1976 the authorities built a new luxury villa for him at Igalo; they kept it as a surprise, and when he arrived there, they invited him in and proudly presented it to him. He was furious; he struck with his stick so hard on one of the glass-topped tables that it cracked, and he declared that the people who had built the house could live in it, because he never would. He became so angry that his staff made themselves scarce; but eventually they sent a pretty young cook to bring him some pastry, which restored his good temper. He did, in fact, agree to live in the new villa when he went to Igalo for the manoeuvres; but he continued to be annoyed about it.[11]

In contrast to Tito's many houses and the luxury in which he and Jovanka lived at the State's expense, people noted how his sons Žarko and Miša led hard-working, frugal lives and did not share in any of their father's luxuries. Tito's Socialist principles led him to take the attitude that though he had earned his privileges by his services to the country and the party, his sons were not entitled to enjoy unearned privileges merely because they were his sons. When Žarko first settled in Belgrade after the liberation and his discharge from the army, there were adverse comments in some circles that he was enjoying a *jeunesse dorée* lifestyle, though one might have hoped that after all that he had suffered in the Soviet Union and in the war, he was entitled to a little luxury; but Tito was determined that neither Žarko nor Miša should obtain any privileges because of his position.

In this matter, Tito was in a no-win situation with one section of public opinion. If he had obtained privileges for his sons, he would certainly have been accused of being a hypocritical Socialist who was building up a dynasty of plutocrats; as it was, he was accused of harshness and meanness towards his family, of indulging in every luxury himself and denying it to his sons. But no such criticism came from the sons themselves. Žarko and Miša fully accepted their position, agreed with Tito's attitude, and remained on excellent terms with him.[12] Both of them obtained a good position in industry by their own merits.

The house where Tito was born in Kumrovec had been turned into a national museum, and when he went to Kumrovec he stayed in a new hotel which had been built a little way up the mountain side on the outskirts of the village. A suite in the hotel was permanently reserved for him, until the hotel was closed and converted into his private residence. He had always loved Kumrovec, and when he was president of Yugoslavia he went there whenever he could.

In December 1953 he visited the village school at Kumrovec where he had been a schoolboy fifty years before. The headmaster was his cousin Martin Broz.[13] Like many other Croats, Martin had stayed on in his teaching job under Pavelić's regime. He was not an Ustasha supporter, but as a good Catholic he did not like the Communists and never considered joining the Partisans. He had therefore lost his job as the headmaster in 1945 and was appointed to a smaller school, but afterwards the authorities forgave him sufficiently to allow him to return to his post as headmaster of Kumrovec.

Tito had heard about the wartime activities of his Broz cousins. Martin was told that once after the war Tito asked about Martin's mother: 'How are Pepa and her Ustasha sons?' But if Tito did in fact say this, he was half-joking. He had in any case decided by this time that if any Ustasha had escaped his well-deserved fate and survived the massacres in 1945, it was now necessary to forgive him and draw a veil over the past.[14]

During his visit to Kumrovec, Tito showed great interest in the school and the welfare of the teachers. He was surprised that they still lived in such little old cottages. He was told that plans had been drawn up to build better houses for the teachers, but the project had been stopped by some government officials who thought that it would spoil the old-world charm of Kumrovec. Tito had lost too many of his brothers and sisters and his own children from diphtheria in their infancy to appreciate the charm of rural slums. He ordered that the new houses should be built.

In the evening he had supper with the teachers. It was an informal, carefree occasion, with no security men in evidence except for one policeman at the door of the house. Tito was in very cheerful mood. He laughed when the French teacher told him her favourite story of how, after Stalin died, the Politburo in the Kremlin discussed where he should be buried, and decided that he could be buried anywhere except in Jerusalem, because there had once been a resurrection in Jerusalem, and they did not want to risk a second resurrection in Stalin's case. As always, Tito enjoyed a joke at his own expense. He told them how a little boy in Split had asked him for his autograph, and after obtaining it had asked him for the autograph a second time. When Tito asked why the boy wanted to have two copies of his autograph, the boy said that he had agreed with a friend to swop two autographs of Tito for one autograph of Beara, the goalkeeper of the Hajduk football team in Split.

The teachers asked Tito how he had enjoyed his visit to London and his meeting with the Queen of England, and which member of the royal family he had preferred. He said that he had enjoyed meeting them all, but particularly Princess Margaret, who had delighted him with her charm and her informal manners. They asked him which of the world statesmen he had met had most impressed him. 'Churchill,' he replied, 'he is a great man. He is, of course, our enemy and has always been the enemy of Communism, but he is an enemy whom one must respect, an enemy one likes to have.'

He was interested to hear that the local hunting club still went hare-shooting in the hills around Kumrovec, and said that he would like to join their shooting party from time to time. He duly came on the appointed day accompanied by two of his generals, dressed in the local hunting club's uniform of fur jacket, green trousers, black boots, and a green hat with a pheasant's feather. But the other members of the party ran into difficulties with the UDBA policemen whose duty was to protect Tito; the UDBA would not allow them to approach Tito with loaded guns, and they removed all their ammunition. It was not a very successful shoot. Tito shot two hares, but his generals missed everything they shot at, and no one else had any ammunition.

Tito came again some time later for another day's shooting. This time the UDBA would not allow the members of the party even to have unloaded guns. When they met Tito, as arranged, at the nearby railway station, he was very surprised to see that they had not brought their guns, and he was annoyed when they told him the reason. He insisted that they should bring their guns next time. But on the next occasion the UDBA again prevented them from bringing their guns. They explained that Tito had said that he wanted them to bring their guns. 'He may want it, but we don't,' said the UDBA men. Eventually, Tito reached a compromise with his bodyguard. No one who came within three hundred yards of Tito would be allowed to bring his gun, but those who remained on the perimeter of the shooting party would be allowed to have them.

Tito, with his shooting expeditions, his palaces, and hunting lodges, ruled Yugoslavia like a sixteenth-century monarch, spending a great deal of time in his country residences and leaving his ministers to undertake the day-to-day administration of the government, but always taking the final decision himself on really important matters. He was not interested in economics, and did not pretend to know anything about the subject; he left it to Kardelj, and to Boris Kidrič at the Treasury and Velebit at the Department of Foreign Trade, to decide whether to have more or less centralized controls, more or less devolution, and more or less of a free market economy. Their decisions on these matters varied from time to time as the financial and economic situation changed, and as rival economists with their different theories gained and lost influence in the ministries. Tito was not interested and did not intervene. But he took a keen personal interest in foreign policy, in questions concerning the army and defence, and in political control of the Communist party. At least once a month he had a long discussion with his foreign minister on the international situation; and having laid down the general guidelines of foreign policy, he left the minister free to implement it without interference.[15]

He rose early, and was working in his study by six a.m. He took at least an hour's exercise every day, walking in his gardens and parks. He was usually in bed by midnight. He had a hearty appetite, but still preferred peasant food, particularly thick soups and cheese dishes. He was himself an excellent cook, and whenever he had the time he would cook a meal for his family, who particularly enjoyed his dishes of sausages, salami and garlic. He was not a heavy drinker, but at meals drank several glasses of dry white wine, or occasionally red wine, often mixed with water. He hardly ever drank *šljivovica*, the plum brandy so popular in Yugoslavia, and much preferred whisky, or whisky mixed with Coca-Cola. He was a heavy smoker, smoking 100 or 120 cigarettes a day in a wooden pipe-shaped cigarette-holder, like other inhabitants of Kumrovec.

In the evening, he sometimes played the piano as a relaxation, usually choosing pieces from Chopin. He sometimes played duets with the American ambassador, Cannon, who had been an amateur concert pianist. But Tito gave up playing the piano after he reached the age of seventy because his fingers became too stiff. He played billiards with the members of his household. He enjoyed films, and saw more than 300 films a year in his private cinema in his house at Užicka Street. He, Jovanka, and the members of his staff who were on duty that day would watch films most evenings after supper. When they watched films with dialogue in foreign languages, Tito would translate it into Serbo-Croat for the benefit of the staff. He enjoyed unashamedly watching films about himself, particularly the film in which Richard Burton played him; and he and Jovanka entertained Richard Burton and Elizabeth Taylor at his holiday home on the island of Brioni in Istria.

Tito was himself a keen photographer. He took photographs of Jovanka and the family, and when he travelled abroad on his state visits he took his own snapshots to supplement the photographs taken by his official photographer and the pressmen who travelled with him. He developed the photographs himself. He also did metal-work as a hobby; it reminded him of his youth. He occasionally did a little gardening. To the end of his life he enjoyed playing poker, as he had always done.[16]

He enjoyed state occasions, the public receptions and the banquets, with the guests in evening dress, with white tie and tails being obligatory on the more important occasions, unless uniform was worn with many military decorations. The story of his hundreds of smart suits and uniforms, on which many visitors, including Enver Hoxha, made adverse comments,[17] were exaggerated. They were partly due to the fact that Jovanka refused to allow the staff to throw out any of his clothes; at the end of his life his 538 ties included many which he had not worn since 1953.[18] But he had always liked dressing well. He enjoyed every aspect of the pomp and glitter of power.

The intellectuals and the former upper classes secretly laughed at him as a *parvenu* and a vulgarian. They ridiculed his old-fashioned low-brow tastes, his liking for nineteenth-century Viennese waltzes, and his lack of interest in modern art.[19] He sometimes made derogatory remarks about surrealist paintings, but did not ban them or require artists and writers to produce 'proletarian art' in the style that was compulsory in the Soviet Union during Zhdanov's cultural purges. Some intellectuals have suggested that he was quite uncultured and knew nothing at all about literature, but this has been exaggerated. He renewed his pre-war friendship with Krleža, though he was disappointed that Krleža had not joined the Partisans in the war, like Nazor had done. When Velebit's father-in-law, the famous painter Becić, painted Tito's portrait, he was surprised to find that Tito was not only a patient sitter and a charming man, but also showed a real interest in art. Becić had always been opposed to Communism and to Tito's political activities, but by the end of the sittings he had a much more favourable opinion of Tito as a man.[20] Tito was friendly with the sculptor Antun Augustinčić, but their friendship was chiefly based on the fact that they both enjoyed playing poker.

He was still interested in women, and was still attractive to them. Today a visitor to Serbia will often meet many men who denounce Tito as a tyrant, but their tirades against him are often interrupted by their wives who point out that whatever faults Tito may have had, he was a very attractive man, with his charisma, his perfect manners, and his kind blue eyes. There were naturally many stories about his love affairs. There was the story of the opera singer who had married one of Tito's generals; Tito was said to have pursued her so ardently that she eventually emigrated to escape his attentions. There were stories about an actress and a film star who were said to be his mistresses. Most of these stories seem to have been simply gossip.

Tito's chief lieutenants were Pijade, Kardelj, Ranković and Djilas, the leading members of the former Politburo; at the Sixth Party Congress in 1952 the name of the Politburo was changed to the Executive Committee, and the Communist party was renamed the 'League of Communists', after Marx's organization in 1848. Tito himself had never claimed to be a Marxist theoretician like Stalin, who wrote books about Marxism-Leninism and from time to time made pronouncements about linguistics and genetics which were then accepted as unchallengeable truths. Tito left Marxist theory to Pijade, and above all to Kardelj.

Ranković, the minister of the interior, concentrated on state security. He and his secret agents in the UDBA had defeated all Stalin's attempts to incite a revolt in the CPY and had sent all the subversive elements to Goli Otok, as well as catching the Chetniks parachuted into Yugoslavia by the CIA to commit sabotage and assassination. Many people feared Ranković, but most of them respected him for his integrity, his incorruptibility and his loyal devotion to Communist Yugoslavia and to Tito personally.

Djilas was still in charge of Agitprop and directing the propaganda line in the party daily newspaper, *Borba*. He had always seemed to be the most devoted, the most self-sacrificing, the most fanatical and the most uncompromising of all the Communist leaders. He was a Montenegrin, from one of the poorest parts of Yugoslavia, a 'land without justice' as he called it, where the people of his generation had been brought up to hate the Turkish oppressor but also to hate the other clans with whom their family had been at war as long as anyone could remember. 'My father's grandfather, my own two grandfathers, my father and my uncle were killed,' he wrote, 'it seems to me that I was born with blood in my eyes. My first sight was of blood. My first words were blood and bathed in blood.'[21]

He endured imprisonment and torture under King Alexander. He applied a simple test to decide whether a party member was to be respected: had he withstood torture without revealing anything to the interrogators?[22] He had been one of the leftists among the Communists in the prisons in 1934 who had provoked confrontation with the prison warders, knowing very well the brutalities and suffering which he and his comrades would have to endure as a result. During the war he was one of the most ruthless of the Partisan leaders. On one occasion he ordered a young Partisan to prove his loyalty by killing his father, who was fighting for the Chetniks. When the son, instead, warned his father that the Partisans were coming to kill him, Djilas ordered that the son should be shot.[23]

When he went to Moscow in 1944 and met Stalin, he was disgusted. At dinner on cold winter evenings, Stalin, instead of discussing Socialist theories, insisted on his guests playing a game. They were all to guess what the temperature was outside, and for every degree that they were wrong they had to drink a glass of vodka. Djilas was even more disgusted when Molotov went with him to the loo, and proceeded to piss into the urinal in full view of Djilas, who quickly retreated into a locked cubicle to piss. It reminded Djilas of King Alexander's prisons, where the prisoners were forced to piss in each other's presence. If Churchill and Eden had the same experience in the loo with Molotov when they attended banquets in the Kremlin, they cannot have been in the least surprised; but in this, as in other matters, the leaders of the Soviet Union had more in common with the British ruling class than with their ardent disciples in other countries.[24] When the split with the Cominform occurred, Djilas became the leading propagandist against the Soviet Union, and by 1952 his Agitprop was exposing all the horrors of Stalin's Great Purge.

But by 1953 Djilas's articles in *Borba* were annoying many leading party members, for he attacked their privileges and the selfishness and corruption of the party hierarchy. They complained about Djilas. Eventually his articles were brought to Tito's attention. Tito glanced at them, and said that they seemed harmless enough to him. Djilas, hearing that he was being criticized, asked Tito what he thought about the articles. 'Well,' said Tito, 'the line you are taking seems alright, and you write well. But you should write more against the bourgeoisie. It is still strong, psychologically in particular. And you should write more for our young people; the young are the most important. They are not ready for democracy yet; the dictatorship has to go on.'[25] Djilas continued his campaign against the party bureaucrats and their privileges.

One of Tito's leading generals, Peko Dapčević, married a beautiful actress. Most of the Communist leaders had married wives who had fought with the Partisans during the war; but the actress had never shown any interest in Communism or the resistance movement, and had spent the war in safety in Zagreb. She was resented by many of the other wives, and the wife of General Tempo was particularly hostile to her. Djilas was a friend of Dapčević, and malicious gossipers spread the story that he was even more friendly with Dapčević's actress-wife. He published a story in *Borba* which clearly referred to Mrs Tempo's hostility to Mrs Dapčević.

This very much annoyed the leading party members. They would have expected Djilas, the rigid puritan and ascetic, to denounce leading figures in the party who fell for a bourgeois actress instead of marrying a loyal Communist; but instead he was adopting exactly the opposite attitude. This seemed to them to prove that Djilas was just out to cause trouble. They resented what seemed to them to be Djilas's intellectual snobbery when he wrote about 'all the exalted women from semi-peasant backgrounds' who were 'semi-educated' and who believed that their service as Partisans during the war entitled them to 'grab and hoard *de luxe* furniture and works of art, tasteless, of course, but by means of which they satisfied their primitive instincts of greed and imagined and puffed-up notions of their social status, with all the pretentiousness and omniscience of the ignorant'.[26]

At last the protests within the party grew so strong that Tito was forced to take action. He was spending Christmas in Slovenia when the latest complaints reached him, and he became very angry with Djilas for causing so much trouble. When he returned to Belgrade he ordered that Djilas's case should be considered at a special meeting of the Central Committee of the party. Before the meeting, Djilas asked to see Tito, who received him in the White Palace in Belgrade. Kardelj and Ranković were present, and Kardelj accused Djilas of having become a 'revisionist', like the German Social-Democrat Bernstein, who in 1898 had been accused of revisionism by Lenin and other left-wing members of the Second International. During the conversation, Djilas asked if he could have some coffee, as he had not been able to sleep at night recently because of his anxiety about the case. 'Others are not sleeping either,' said Tito drily.[27]

The meeting of the Central Committee was held on 16 January 1954, in the presence of 108 delegates in Belgrade, and the proceedings were broadcast live on television.[28] Tito presided, and opened the proceedings. He blamed himself for not having acted sooner against Djilas, who had become separated from his comrades. 'The influence of the West, his journeys abroad, and all sorts of other influences from abroad counteracted the influence of our reality, our revolutionary past and of all revolutionary experience.' He accused Djilas of 'advocating democracy at any price'.[29] He was followed by Kardelj, who accused Djilas of holding opinions which were a mixture of Anarchism and bourgeois Liberalism.

Then Djilas spoke in his defence. He claimed that he was still a Marxist, but no longer a Leninist. Pijade strongly attacked Djilas, and expressed a view which was prevalent in some quarters in Belgrade: 'He has a villa and two cars and so forth; he has far more than those whom he has described as a repulsive caste.'[30] One by one the members of the Central Committee criticized Djilas. Only his wife and Dedijer spoke in his defence. That night Djilas decided to recant his opinions, and did so at the second session next day. The Central Committee decided that he should be expelled from the Central Committee and given a final warning before being expelled from the party. Djilas himself voted in favour of the resolution.

Tito closed the proceedings by saying that they had shown the unity of the party, and that Yugoslavia would pursue her own path towards Socialism and Socialist democracy without veering either to the East or to the West. He hoped that Djilas would now rectify his errors. 'We shall then see how genuine his self-criticism has been.'[31]

Aneurin Bevan had met Djilas when Djilas attended the coronation of Queen Elizabeth II in June 1953, and they found themselves in agreement on many points. It has often been said that Bevan's influence persuaded Djilas to write his controversial articles in *Borba* in the autumn of 1953; but Djilas denies this.[32] After the condemnation of Djilas by the Central Committee, Bevan wrote to Tito and urged him to take no steps against either Djilas or Dedijer. In his reply, Tito wrote that no action would be taken against Dedijer, and that Djilas would continue to receive his state pension for his past services, and had not been expelled from the party. 'Dear friend,' he wrote to Bevan, 'the case has affected you owing to your personal and friendly relations with Dedijer and Djilas, but believe me that Djilas's case has hurt us twice as much, both as friends and collaborators of long standing in a revolutionary cause.'[33]

Six weeks after his expulsion from the Central Committee, Djilas wrote to his local branch of the Communist party returning his party card and resigning from the party because he no longer considered himself to be a Communist.[34]

---　❖　---

CHAPTER 24

Khrushchev: The Crisis of 1956

I N later years Djilas stated that Tito took action against him
because after Stalin's death Tito wished to improve relations with
the Soviet Union;[1] as Djilas represented the liberating force in
the Yugoslav Communist party, Tito thought that by striking at
Djilas he would show the Soviet Union that he was not moving closer
to the West. But there had been no signs of a rapprochement between
Yugoslavia and the Soviet Union in January 1954, and soon after
the censure of Djilas Tito drew closer than ever before to the Western
Powers. At their suggestion he agreed to make a military defence
pact with Turkey and Greece. In April 1954 he visited Istanbul,
where he had last been in 1940 when he had waited there for a
satisfactory forged passport; and in July he visited Athens. In August
the Balkan Pact between Yugoslavia, Greece and Turkey was signed
in Bled; and next year Tito received the king and queen of Greece
when they paid a state visit to Belgrade.

After his visits to Istanbul and Athens, Tito went further afield. In
the winter of 1954–55 he went to India and Burma. In India he
established excellent relations with the prime minister, Jawaharlal
Nehru. Both Tito and Nehru had passed through prisons on their
way to power, though they had taken different roads – Tito's by
illegal underground work and armed resistance, Nehru's by passive
resistance; and largely because of this they had established different
kinds of regimes in their countries. But both of them were now
opposed to Western imperialism and to Stalinism, and both were
ideologically neutral in the Cold War between the United States and
the Soviet Union.

On his way home from India Tito met the Egyptian president,
Colonel Nasser, in Cairo. Nasser was one of a group of army officers

who had overthrown the Egyptian monarchy in 1952, driving the drunken playboy King Farouk into exile and establishing a nationalist regime with vaguely Socialist doctrines and fiercely opposed to British and American imperialism. Nasser was equally hostile to the state of Israel, which in his view had deprived the Arabs of their land in Palestine and had become a puppet state of the United States and a bastion of American imperialism in the Middle East. Tito was sympathetic to Nasser's objectives, for it had always been Marxist-Leninist policy to support bourgeois nationalist movements against the great imperialist powers in Asia and Africa. It was true that Nasser suppressed the Communist party in Egypt; so did every other left-wing dictator in the Middle East, for the American puppet state of Israel was the only country in the area where the Communist party was legal. But Tito could understand that a dictator might find it advisable to suppress the Communist party and arrest Communists; he himself had imprisoned 12,000 Communists on Goli Otok.

Kardelj had been appointed acting president during Tito's absence in India, and he was confronted with more trouble from Djilas. Tito, as he had written to Aneurin Bevan, was eager for a reconciliation with Djilas and Dedijer, and Ranković made this clear in several talks with Dedijer during 1954. But Djilas was suffering from a fever caused partly by his old wartime head wound, but chiefly by his guilty conscience at having recanted at the hearing before the Central Committee in January. Dedijer was the only one of his old comrades, apart from his loyal wife, who visited Djilas during his illness; but when Dedijer told him about Ranković's offer, Djilas became convinced that Dedijer was an agent of Tito and Ranković. The Executive Committee of the party then invited Djilas to put his ideas into writing so that his differences with the party could be hammered out; but Djilas refused, being convinced that it was a trick to trap him. He was as determined now to make trouble for Tito as he had been to defy King Alexander's prison warders twenty years before.

Djilas's staunchness stiffened Dedijer. When the Control Commission of the Communist party questioned him about his association with Djilas, he refused to answer their questions, walked out of the meeting, and told the Belgrade correspondent of *The Times* of London. On 25 December Djilas gave an interview to the *New York Times* in which he demanded that a second legal party should be formed in Yugoslavia to replace the one-party system. Kardelj denounced Djilas and Dedijer; he said that they had conspired with reactionary circles abroad to prevent the advance of Yugoslavia towards the establishment of true Socialism. They were both charged with propaganda against Yugoslavia and prosecuted in the local district court.

The trial took place in January 1955. Foreign press correspondents were not admitted on the grounds that they would not give a fair and impartial report of the proceedings. Both defendants were found guilty; Djilas was sentenced to eighteen months', and Dedijer to six months', imprisonment; but in both cases the sentences were suspended, and the two men were set free. The editorial in *Borba* insisted that they had been convicted not for expressing their views but for publishing statements in foreign newspapers with the intention of causing foreign intervention in Yugoslavia's internal affairs. Their most ardent admirers could hardly deny the truth of this statement.[2]

Khrushchev had decided to pursue a policy of reconciliation with Tito. He publicly admitted that Stalin's policy towards Yugoslavia had been wrong, and suggested that he should have a meeting with Tito. Some members of the Soviet Politburo, led by Suslov and Molotov, opposed this policy, but submitted to Khrushchev's wishes.[3] Instead of inviting Tito to come to Moscow, Khrushchev suggested that he and Bulganin should go to Belgrade, which would be a more striking demonstration of Soviet repentance for their past policy. Tito agreed, and Khrushchev and Bulganin arrived in Belgrade on 26 May 1955.

When Tito welcomed them at the airport, Khrushchev immediately made a public apology for Soviet policy towards Yugoslavia in 1948. 'We sincerely regret . . . and resolutely sweep aside all the bitterness of that period . . . We have thoroughly investigated the materials upon which the grave accusations and insults to the leaders of Yugoslavia were based at that time . . . these materials were fabricated by Beria and Abakumov, the contemptible agents of imperialism who had fraudulently wormed their way into the ranks of our party.'[4]

In the course of their very friendly conversations, Khrushchev said to Tito that there was now a good basis for Soviet-Yugoslav friendship because 'we have got rid of Beria and you have got rid of Djilas'.[5] His point was that Beria had been responsible for the hardline anti-Tito policy which the Soviet Union had adopted in 1948, and Djilas had wished to install bourgeois democracy in Yugoslavia; having got rid of both these extremes, they could now cooperate on the basis of a moderate Communist dictatorship. Tito said that he and his colleagues could not accept that Beria alone had been responsible for Soviet policy towards Yugoslavia in 1948, and said that Stalin was responsible. He told Khrushchev that it would be easier to convince the Yugoslavs that Soviet policy had really changed, and to build up friendly cooperation between all the Communist states of Eastern Europe, if Khrushchev were publicly to repudiate Stalin and expose the Stalinist policy during the Great Purge.[6]

It was partly because of Yugoslav pressure that Khrushchev made his speech to the Twentieth Congress of the Communist party of the Soviet Union in February 1956 in which he informed the astounded delegates that although Stalin had done some good service to the party and the Soviet Union, he had committed grave blunders and crimes. Khrushchev said that Stalin had encouraged the 'cult of the personality' and popular adulation of himself; he had committed some serious errors as a military commander during the Second World War; and during the Purges, thanks to Stalin, many loyal comrades had been unjustly accused and executed as Trotskyists and spies.[7]

In June 1956 Tito paid a state visit to the Soviet Union which lasted for nearly three weeks.[8] He travelled with Jovanka, Kardelj, Koča Popović and other leaders by train through Romania. There were speeches of welcome and demonstrations by large crowds wherever he went. In Moscow, Tito and Khrushchev went on a walk-about among the welcoming crowds; they went into a confectioner's shop and ordered ice-cream, but then found that neither Khrushchev nor Tito had any money to pay for the ice-cream. Tito gave a dinner for the Soviet leaders at the Yugoslav embassy. His speech at the banquet was followed by speeches from Khrushchev, Voroshilov, Bulganin, Mikoyan, Kaganovich and Molotov. The Yugoslav ambassador, Veljko Mićunović, noted in his diary: 'All the Soviet leaders seemed to be competing among themselves to see who could condemn Stalin's policy against Yugoslavia in the sharpest tones.'[9]

After several days of receptions, banquets and sightseeing in Moscow, Tito visited Leningrad, where he had a tremendous reception; it was estimated that more than a million people came out into the streets to cheer him. He then went to the Crimea, and from there to Stalingrad and Novorossiysk. At Stalingrad 100,000 people welcomed him. He and Khrushchev went on a walk- about surrounded by enthusiastic crowds who pressed in so closely around them that they became separated from their bodyguard, to the great alarm of the NKVD men who were protecting them; but Tito and Khrushchev were quite unperturbed. They returned to Moscow, where they attended a great rally in the Dynamo Sports Stadium, and both of them made speeches about the new friendship between the Soviet Union and Yugoslavia.

After spending nineteen days in the Soviet Union, Tito left Moscow on 21 June by train for Romania. Here, too, he had a great reception; he and the Romanian Communist leader, Gheorghe Gheorghiu-Dej, addressed a meeting in Bucharest which was attended by 200,000 people.[10]

But behind the façade of friendship there were tensions in Soviet-Yugoslav relations. These were due chiefly to Khrushchev's touchiness, for he was always liable to change from ostentatious displays of warm affection to rudeness and hostility. His blunt speaking and very coarse sense of humour could be useful in breaking down barriers and introducing a relaxed atmosphere between the diplomats in Moscow, but they could also cause some ruffled feathers and stir up resentment.

He had the habit of telling a good joke so often that it palled. He was always telling the diplomats that to understand the German problem they must persuade Chancellor Adenauer to strip naked and then look at him both from the back and the front. If they looked at him from the back they would see that there was a divided Germany; if they looked at him from the front they would see that his policy did not stand up and never could stand up.[11] Most of the diplomats did not think that this was very funny after they had heard it half a dozen times.

Hardly had Tito returned to Belgrade before Khrushchev was bitterly complaining to Mićunović that the Yugoslav press had given less coverage to Tito's visit to the Soviet Union and to the speeches of the Soviet leaders than the Soviet press had given to Tito's speeches. On the other hand, Mićunović found that the United States ambassador in Moscow was noticeably less friendly towards him. 'They seem to have been upset by the three weeks of Yugoslav-Soviet celebrations,' he wrote. 'The atmosphere at my meetings with the Americans in Moscow is less agreeable than at any time in the last few years.'[12]

In his talks with Khrushchev, Tito spoke well of Nasser, and urged Khrushchev to give him the full support of the Soviet Union. Khrushchev was doubtful about this, for Nasser was not a Communist, and had not pursued a policy of large-scale nationalization. Tito told Khrushchev that they must be patient with Nasser; they could not expect him to move too quickly towards Socialism.[13]

Since 1875 the Suez Canal had been controlled by a private international company in which the British government held a majority of the shares. In July 1956 Nasser announced that the Egyptian government had taken control of the canal. The British government refused to recognize the nationalization of the canal. An international conference was held in London in August to resolve the problem, but failed to find a solution. Tito defended Egypt's right to take control of a canal which crossed her territory, and saw Nasser's action as a justifiable step in the struggle against Western imperialism.

In the summer of 1956 anti-Russian demonstrations took place in Poland; at Poznan they led to riots and the police fired on the demonstrators. After some weeks of tension, Khrushchev used his influence to secure the appointment of Gomulka* as leader of the Polish Communist party and prime minister. Gomulka had been imprisoned at Stalin's insistence in 1949 charged with nationalist deviation, Titoism and anti-Soviet doctrines, and had served seven years before being released just before he took office.

Trouble was also brewing in Hungary, where a conflict had developed between Imre Nagy, who favoured a more Liberal policy, and the prime minister, Rákosi, who insisted on pursuing a hard Stalinist line. Tito urged Khrushchev to get rid of Rákosi and appoint a more moderate leader in Hungary. In July 1956 Rákosi resigned and was succeeded by Gerö. Tito was not very keen on Gerö, who had always supported a hardline policy, but he preferred him to Rákosi, and invited Gerö to Belgrade to show his solidarity with Communist Hungary. The most liberal sections of the Hungarian Communist party would have liked to see Nagy as prime minister; but Khrushchev and the Soviet leaders were not prepared to accept Nagy; they thought he was anti-Soviet.

---

* Gomulka, Wladislav (1905–82); Polish Communist leader; imprisoned in 1949 as a Titoist sympathiser; released in 1955 and became head of the Polish Communist government; played a prominent part in the Soviet invasion of Czechoslovakia in 1968.

Under pressure from the liberals in the Hungarian Communist party and from Tito, Gerö announced that Rajk had been wrongly convicted and executed in 1949; he was not a Titoist spy, but a patriot who had been framed by Stalin and Rákosi. On 23 October the government held a memorial meeting in Budapest in honour of Rajk, and thousands of demonstrators came into the streets. The demonstration turned into an anti-Russian and anti-Communist riot. Hostile crowds demonstrated before the Soviet embassy, and the statue of Stalin in Budapest was demolished. Gerö resigned, and Nagy became prime minister, but the anti-Communist demonstrations continued. The crowds attacked the barracks of the secret police and lynched several policemen. They also attacked Communists in the streets.

In Britain Eden's Conservative government had decided to resort to force against Nasser, and the French government under the Social-Democrat prime minister, Guy Mollet, agreed to join in. Eden and Mollet decided to enlist the support of Israel. On 19 October 1956 a very secret meeting was held at Sèvres near Paris between the British, French and Israeli foreign ministers, at which it was agreed that Israel would invade Egypt, giving a pretext to Britain and France to send troops to seize the Suez Canal to prevent it from being damaged in the fighting between Israel and Egypt. The crises in Hungary and Egypt came to the boil at the same time. On 26 October the British and French air forces bombed Port Said, and next day their troops landed and occupied the town. On 26 October the Red Army entered Hungary; the Soviet government announced that they had come to help the Nagy government restore order in the country.

Khrushchev protested against the British and French attack on Port Said, and the United States government also disapproved of this intervention by their British and French allies. Khrushchev proposed to Eisenhower that the Soviet Union and the United States should jointly intervene to protect Egypt and drive out the British and French troops. The United States government indignantly rejected this proposal, as Khrushchev knew they would, thus making it possible for Khrushchev to claim that the United States was supporting the British and French aggressors and that only the Soviet Union protected small nations against the imperialists. Khrushchev reminded the British government that the Soviet Union had long-distance rockets which were capable of bombing British cities in the same way that the British air force was bombing Port Said, while the United States

privately told the British that economic aid from the United States
would cease unless the British withdrew from Egypt. The British
and French evacuated Port Said, having achieved nothing by their
intervention except that they had diverted against themselves some
of the world's moral indignation at the Russian invasion of Hungary.

In Hungary the entry of the Red Army had aroused the fury of
the people. In Budapest the people threw home-made petrol bombs
at the tanks, and fought the Red Army as best they could. Nagy
protested against Russian intervention, and asked the Soviet Union
to withdraw its troops. Tito joined in the protests against Soviet
intervention, but he was in a difficult position. He could not support
the use of force by the Soviet Union against another Communist
state; but he was worried about the developments in Hungary. The
demonstrations which had begun as a tribute to the Communist
Rajk, the innocent victim of Stalin and Rákosi, were developing
into an attack on all Communists. The crowds who were lynching
Communists in Budapest would also have lynched Rajk had he still
been alive and had fallen into their hands.

On 28 October Khrushchev announced that Soviet troops were
withdrawing from Hungary. Next day Tito sent a note to Nagy,
expressing his support for him, but warning him not to allow the
situation in Hungary to be exploited by 'international reaction'
and to develop into counter-revolution.[14] On 30 October Nagy
announced that Hungary would withdraw from the Warsaw Pact
and adopt a policy of neutrality between the Soviet Union and the
Western Powers.

Khrushchev believed that if Hungary went, all the satellite states
in Eastern Europe might go. On 2 November he decided to send the
Red Army back into Hungary with orders to suppress the counter-
revolution. He realized that this would lead to a storm of protest
throughout the world, and he was eager to have Tito's moral support.
His attitude is a tribute to the position which Tito had attained as
the leader of Communist opposition to Soviet domination and of the
movement for an independent national Communism in the countries
of Eastern Europe. He contacted Tito and asked if he could visit him
secretly that very day. Tito was in his palace on the island of Brioni
in Istria, and hurriedly made preparations to receive Khrushchev
there.

The Red Army began to move towards the Hungarian frontier in
the early afternoon of 2 November. At the same time Khrushchev

and Malenkov set off from an airport near Moscow in a military plane which landed in the early evening at the Yugoslav airport at Pula, not far from Brioni.[15] The weather was very bad for flying, and the passengers had a rough ride; Malenkov had to lie down in the plane. From Pula they were taken in a motorboat to Brioni. In order to reduce the chances of being seen, they were taken the long way round and approached the island from the side of the open sea. The water was choppy, and Malenkov felt seasick. On the most critical day of a great international crisis, the head of the government of the Soviet Union, one of the two most powerful men in the world, found himself at sea in a motorboat on a dark and stormy night feeling rather sick. But they reached Brioni safely and found Tito, Kardelj and Ranković waiting to receive them on the jetty.

They went to Tito's palace and began their talks at seven p.m. Only six men were present – Tito, Kardelj, Ranković and Mićunović, the ambassador in Moscow, on the Yugoslav side, and Khrushchev and Malenkov on the Soviet side. There were no interpreters, for all four Yugoslavs spoke fluent Russian. No minutes of the meeting were taken, but the participants occasionally made a note for their own convenience. They discussed the situation till ten p.m., when they went to another room for a buffet supper; but after supper they resumed their talks, which did not end till five o'clock in the morning.

Khrushchev was very agitated and upset about the situation. 'Communists are being killed in Hungary,' he told Tito. He said that the Soviet Union could not allow this state of affairs to continue. If Hungary withdrew from the Warsaw Pact and the Socialist alliance, she would join NATO and the allies of the United States; and this would bring the American armed forces to the frontiers of the Soviet Union. But he always returned to the same theme, that Communists were being killed in Hungary. Tito said that the Soviet Union was to blame for the situation in Hungary, which would never have arisen if Stalin and Rákosi had handled the situation more skilfully and less brutally; but he agreed that what was happening in Hungary was a counter-revolution which would destroy Socialism not only in Hungary but throughout Eastern Europe, and that in the circumstances the Soviet Union had no choice but to intervene, and were right to send in the Red Army.

Khrushchev said that as Nagy had denounced the Soviet intervention, and would certainly condemn the return of the Red Army, he would have to be removed as prime minister. Khrushchev said that he was proposing to install Ferenc Munnich as prime minister in Nagy's place. Tito did not think that this was desirable. Munnich had been the Hungarian ambassador in Moscow when Rákosi was in power, and would be particularly associated with the Soviet Union in the minds of the Hungarians. Tito suggested that János Kadar would be a better choice than Munnich. Kadar was a loyal Communist but he had been denounced as a Titoist by Rákosi, and had spent three years in prison from 1952 to 1955. Khrushchev said that he would have preferred Munnich, whom he had got to know when Munnich was ambassador in Moscow. But he agreed to invite Kadar to become prime minister of Hungary.

Khrushchev and Malenkov flew back to Moscow from Pula early in the morning of 3 November, after Tito had driven them himself in his car to the jetty at Brioni. Khrushchev was very satisfied with the result of his hurried visit to Tito. He had expected that Tito would oppose Soviet intervention in Hungary as strongly as Gomulka and the Polish Communists had done. 'But we were pleasantly surprised. Tito said we were absolutely right and that we should send our soldiers into action as quickly as possible. He said we had an obligation to help Hungary crush the counter-revolution . . . We had been ready for resistance, but instead we received his whole-hearted support. I would even say he went further than we did in urging a speedy and decisive resolution of the problem.' Tito had always been a political realist. He knew that the rising in Hungary would not stop at the overthrow of Stalinism, or even with the achievement of bourgeois democracy, but might well go as far as a right-wing military dictatorship or some form of Fascism.

As soon as Khrushchev reached Moscow, he gave the order to invade Hungary. The Red Army drove straight for Budapest, and entered the city during the night of 3 November. Fighting went on throughout the night and next day, but the Red Army was in control of Budapest within twenty-four hours. On 4 November Nagy and forty-one other prominent Hungarians came to the Yugoslav embassy in Budapest and asked for asylum, and the ambassador agreed to shelter them in the embassy.

Soon afterwards Red Army tanks and troops arrived and surrounded the embassy. Russian officers inspected the documents of everyone arriving at the embassy and refused to allow anyone except Yugoslav diplomats to enter the building. Then the soldiers in one of the tanks opened fire with machine-guns at the ground floor of the embassy, breaking the windows and killing a Yugoslav diplomat as he sat working at his desk.[16]

Yugoslavia made a strong protest to the Soviet Union about the killing of the diplomat, and the Soviet Union protested to Yugoslavia against the granting of asylum to Nagy. On 7 November Mićunović attended a reception in the Kremlin on the anniversary of the October Revolution; it was boycotted by the British and American diplomats. Khrushchev indignantly complained that Nagy, the leader of the counter-revolution, should have been granted asylum in the Yugoslav embassy. Then he tried to reduce the tension and win Yugoslav goodwill, as he often did, by telling derogatory jokes about Stalin.[17]

The suppression of the rising in Hungary caused more indignation in Western Europe than anything the Soviet Union had ever done. It led to mass resignations from the Communist parties in many parts of the world. The resistance in Hungary had been almost crushed, but anger abroad was at its height, when Tito made a speech about the international situation at the Military College at Pula on 11 November.[18]

He said that the tragic situation which had arisen was the result of the policy pursued by Stalin and the leadership of the Communist Party of the Soviet Union. It was not merely that they had adopted the cult of the personality; they had pursued an incorrect policy towards the other Socialist countries, and even today these errors were sometimes committed by the leaders of the Communist party of the Soviet Union. They had blamed Yugoslavia for the demonstrations of the Polish workers in Poznan; 'yes, we are to blame, because we are in the world, because we are what we are, because we have built the kind of Yugoslavia which exists today, because our development is stretching across frontiers'.

He said that Rákosi was responsible for the situation in Hungary, and Gerö, too, had made a mistake when he called in a foreign army – the Soviet army – to suppress the popular movement against 'the Stalinist elements which were still in power'. This so enraged the people that the supporters of the prewar dictatorship of Horthy* were able to take advantage of the situation. 'The justified revolt and

---

* Horthy, Admiral Niklós (1868–1957), commander-in-chief of Austro-Hungarian navy in First World War; victor of Battle of Otranto in 1917; overthrew Bela Kun's Communist government in 1919; dictator of Hungary 1919–44; after first supporting Germany in Second World War, disagreed with Hitler's policy and resigned in 1944; lived in exile in Portugal until his death.

uprising against the Rákosi clique turned into an insurrection against Socialism and the Soviet Union, and the Communists who found themselves in the ranks of the rebels saw that their objective, whether they wanted it or not, was no longer the fight for Socialism but for a return to the old order after the reaction had taken things in hand.'

The leadership of the revolt was taken over by Horthy supporters. It was unsafe to speak the word 'comrade' or to be seen wearing a red star; and many Communists were hanged. 'They attacked and killed in the streets people who were wearing yellow shoes just because the police also wore yellow shoes. They went into houses and killed the Communists in their homes. This was what the unchecked Fascist and reactionary mob accomplished.'

The first intervention of the Soviet army was absolutely unjustified. But what about the second Soviet intervention? 'We have said, and we will always say again, that we are opposed to the intervention of foreign military forces. But which was the lesser evil? Chaos, civil war, counter-revolution, and a new world war, or an intervention by Soviet troops? . . . I say clearly that the first alternative was the worst thing that could have occurred, and the second, the intervention of Soviet troops, was a necessary evil.' The whole episode was a tragedy. Socialism had suffered a great blow.

He then gave a warning to the reactionaries in Yugoslavia. 'They are thinking "It has reached this point in Hungary, the followers of Horthy and the Vatican have achieved things there, now is the chance for us". There are such elements in Yugoslavia, but I will tell them that they are making a dreadful mistake,' for they would face 600,000 party members steeled by struggle and revolution.

He ended by referring more briefly to the situation in Egypt, and his friendship for Nasser, who was of course perfectly entitled to nationalize the Suez Canal. Egypt was then attacked, first by Israel and then by Britain and France; this joint aggression was probably secretly prepared in advance (and we now know that Tito was right on this point). But the intervention failed. 'The Egyptian people did not overthrow Nasser, as Eden expected. But in England the Labour party strongly opposed the aggression of the government party.' Yugoslavia would support Nasser's policy towards Israel and his support for the Arab independence movement against France in Algeria.

Tito's speech at Pula angered both Khrushchev and Djilas. Khrushchev hardly seemed to notice that Tito had approved of the final and decisive Soviet intervention in Hungary as he had promised to do a week before at their all-night talks in Brioni. He noticed only that Tito had referred to the Stalinist elements which still existed in the Communist party of the Soviet Union, that he had condemned the first Soviet intervention, and that he had not uncritically supported Soviet policy. Relations between the Soviet Union and Yugoslavia remained strained for some time, and though they later improved, and waxed hot and cold throughout Khrushchev's years in power, he and Tito never again attained the degree of friendship that had existed between them from May 1955 to November 1956.

The events in Hungary led to the final rift between Tito and Djilas. Eight days after Tito's speech at Pula, the *New Leader* in New York published an article by Djilas. 'With the Hungarian people's revolution,' wrote Djilas, 'a new chapter began in the history of humanity.' But the Yugoslav government had adopted an ambiguous attitude towards this inspiring event; it had been 'unable in its foreign policy to depart from its narrow ideological and bureaucratic class interests', and had betrayed the principle of 'equality and non-interference in internal affairs'.[19]

Tito and Ranković had taken no action against Djilas on several occasions recently when he had published articles in the foreign press which were critical of Yugoslav government policy. But that Djilas, at this juncture, could publish an article in the press in the United States which ignored the danger of counter-revolution in Hungary and criticized Tito's policy, seemed to Tito to indicate that Djilas had joined the ranks of the Western imperialists. Of course, if Yugoslavia had been a bourgeois democracy no action would have been taken against Djilas; but Tito had never intended Yugoslavia to become a bourgeois democracy.

The day after Djilas's article was published, he was arrested. On 12 December 1956 he was tried in secret on the charge of violating the conditions of his suspended prison sentence of January 1955 that he would not in future make 'hostile propaganda' against Yugoslavia. He was sentenced to three years' imprisonment, and this time the sentence was not suspended. He was taken to the prison at Sremska Mitrovica where he had been imprisoned in the days of King Alexander.[20]

The rapprochement between the Soviet Union and Yugoslavia brought welcome relief to Polka. She had been released from prison after serving twenty-seven months at the time of the Great Purge, and she had watched the development of the careers of her former husband and her son. She often thought of the possibility of going to Yugoslavia where she had lived for eight years in the 1920s, but never actually went there.

After Tito's split with Stalin and the Cominform, Polka was approached by the KGB. They asked her to go to Yugoslavia and work there as an agent for the Soviet Union. She refused, and soon afterwards was arrested and imprisoned for some years. After Stalin's death and the improvement of relations with Yugoslavia, she lived unmolested in the Soviet Union. She knew that Tito did not wish to renew their acquaintanceship, but she kept in touch with Žarko.

In 1965 Žarko visited her in the Soviet Union and suggested that she should at last fulfil her wish to visit Yugoslavia. She agreed, but then Žarko had to go into hospital for an operation and her trip was again postponed until after he came out of hospital. They had left it too late. Polka died in 1967 at the age of sixty-three without ever having revisited Yugoslavia.[21]

Lucia Bauer, too, survived the Great Purge, and in due course was released from prison. She gave up politics, and lived quietly in the Soviet Union for the rest of her life. She was still living there in 1990.[22]

❖

CHAPTER 25

Non-Alignment

ITO had been placed in a difficulty by the request of Nagy and his followers for asylum in the Yugoslav embassy. In his speech at Pula he had criticized Nagy for his handling of the situation during the uprising in Hungary; but he did not believe that Nagy should be punished as a counter-revolutionary, even if he had allowed the counter-revolutionaries to capture the leadership of the popular movement. Tito was therefore pleased when the Yugoslav ambassador in Budapest on 22 November 1956 reached an agreement with Kadar's government. The Hungarians agreed that neither Nagy nor any of his forty-one supporters in the Yugoslav embassy would be arrested or charged with any offence which they had committed before 4 November. At the request of the Yugoslavs, the Hungarians put this undertaking into writing. Nagy and his companions therefore left the Yugoslav embassy on the evening of 22 November. Several of them, including Nagy, were immediately arrested by the Red Army. They were put on a plane to Bucharest and held prisoners in Romania.[1]

Yugoslavia made a strong protest both to the Hungarian and Soviet governments, and the Yugoslav foreign minister, Koča Popović, threatened to raise the matter at the United Nations. Khrushchev said that the Soviet Union had not been party to any agreement with Yugoslavia about Nagy, and that they had removed him to Romania because his presence in Hungary was a threat to the security of the country. This led to a sharp deterioration in relations between Yugoslavia and the Soviet Union.[2]

Both Tito and Khrushchev wished to restore their old friendship, but always some incident arose which caused new friction. From time to time the Soviet or Yugoslav press published an article which was slightly critical of the other country, and the offending issue of *Borba* or *Pravda* was confiscated in the Soviet Union or Yugoslavia. When Pijade died in May 1957 the Yugoslavs were offended that *Pravda* devoted only a few lines to his obituary. There was controversy about the position of the Yugoslavs who had supported the Cominform in 1948 and had taken refuge in the Soviet Union. Tito refused Khrushchev's request that he should grant them an amnesty, though he did pardon a few individuals and allow them to return to Yugoslavia. There was indignation in the Soviet Union that Tito, though he had granted an amnesty to Ustashas and Chetniks, was still imprisoning Yugoslav Communists who had supported the Cominform.[3]

In July 1957 there was an attempt to overthrow Khrushchev by the hardline Stalinist group in the Politburo, which was led by Molotov, Kaganovich and Malenkov – the 'MKM group'. Their main argument was that Khrushchev's more liberal policy in the Soviet Union, and particularly his denunciation of Stalin, had been responsible for the unrest in Poland and the rising in Hungary. Molotov's faction obtained a majority in the Politburo, but Khrushchev appealed to the Central Committee, which outvoted the MKM group. At the decisive moment Zhukov and the Red Army leadership used their influence in support of Khrushchev.

Three months later, Khrushchev got rid of Zhukov, immediately after Zhukov returned from a visit to Yugoslavia. Khrushchev seems to have thought that if Zhukov could use his influence to overturn a decision of the Politburo, he might one day use it against Khrushchev himself. Neither Molotov nor Zhukov were arrested, sent to a labour camp, or held for long years in prison. Molotov was sent as ambassador to Mongolia, and Zhukov retired into private life. In the Soviet Union, if not in Hungary, the Stalin era was a thing of the past.

Immediately after Khrushchev's victory over Molotov, he and Tito met in Romania. On 29 July Tito left Belgrade with Kardelj, Ranković and Mićunović. They travelled by ship down the Danube, and met Khrushchev at the town of Snagov near Bucharest. Khrushchev was accompanied by several leading Soviet Communists, including Mikoyan, Andropov, and the old Finnish Communist, Kuusinen, who had been a member of the secretariat of the Comintern when Tito was living in the Hotel Lux in Moscow nearly twenty years before. There was every prospect of better relations with the Soviet Union now that the MKM group had been defeated.[4]

Djilas has always believed that whenever Tito drew closer to the

Soviet Union he treated Djilas more harshly.[5] This theory is not always borne out by the facts, and it may or may not have been coincidence that fresh measures were taken against Djilas soon after Tito's meeting with Khrushchev at Snagov. In August 1957 Djilas's book *The New Class* was published in New York and London. It was a Marxist analysis of the development of a ruling class under a Communist system, and the most important contribution since Trotsky to Marxist theory. But by the time that the book was published, Djilas had rejected Marxism — something which he had said at the hearing before the Central Committee in January 1954 that he would never do. If Djilas had confined himself to this analysis of a new class, his book might have been accepted by Kardelj, who was also developing new forms of Marxism. But it contained a direct attack on the Communist state. 'Its method of control is one of the most shameful pages in human history,' and it will end in 'failure and shameful ruin ... The totalitarian tyranny and control of the New Class which came into being during the Revolution has been the yoke under which the blood and sweat of all members of society flow.'[6]

Djilas was brought from prison to face a new charge of having attempted 'to compromise the idea of Socialism and the international workers' movement'. When he declared 'I wrote the truth from the first word to the last', the judge ordered the trial to proceed in secret. He was convicted, and sentenced to a further six years in addition to the three-year term which he was serving.[7]

Tito seemed again to be moving closer to the Soviet Union. Soon after his meeting with Khrushchev in Romania, he recognized the Communist government which had been established in East Germany. The West German government angrily broke off diplomatic relations with Yugoslavia.

But Tito had quite decided to pursue his policy of independence from both the great superpowers. In November 1957 there were celebrations in the Soviet Union of the fortieth anniversary of the October Revolution, and to mark the occasion a meeting was held in Moscow of the leaders of the twelve most important Communist parties in the world.[8] All the heads of state of the Communist countries of Eastern Europe attended, and Mao Tse-tung came from China. Tito sent Kardelj and Ranković and two other leading Yugoslav Communists, but he did not go himself, apologizing for his absence on the grounds of ill-health.

Khrushchev and Mao and the other Communist leaders welcomed Kardelj and Ranković, but they thought that Tito's ill-health was only an excuse, and they were disappointed that the Yugoslav delegates refused to sign the joint declaration of the other twelve Communist parties which referred to the 'Socialist camp headed by the Soviet Union', though Khrushchev told them that it was Mao who had insisted on including this phrase. By the end of the Moscow Conference relations between the Yugoslavs and the other delegates were strained, and the Yugoslavs encountered signs of hostility from Soviet officials. 'Why is Tito sitting on two stools?' asked a high-ranking Red Army officer. 'Is he for the Soviet Union or the United States?' Another Soviet official asked: 'What is this Yugoslav Socialism? There cannot be any other Socialism apart from the one being built in the Soviet Union.'[9]

In April 1958 the Seventh Congress of the League of Communists of Yugoslavia was held in Ljubljana. The draft programme of the Congress adopted a firm middle-of-the-road position. It condemned 'bourgeois revisionism', but also 'dogmatism', 'bureaucratism' and 'Stalinism', which led to 'pseudo-revolutionary sectarianism'. The draft programme admitted the possibility of cooperation between Communist parties and 'progressive elements' in the West. The Yugoslavs invited the foreign Communist and Social-Democratic parties to send delegates to the congress, but the invitation was accepted only by the two small Communist parties of Denmark and Norway and by a few Socialist parties from Asia, Africa and Latin America. The congress was boycotted by the Social-Democratic parties of Western Europe because of Tito's support for the Soviet intervention in Hungary and the imprisonment of Djilas, and by the Communist parties because they condemned the draft programme as 'revisionist'.[10]

There was further tension with the Soviet Union when Khrushchev went to Bulgaria and in a speech in Sofia on 3 June 1958 criticized Yugoslavia for receiving aid from the United States. Tito replied sharply in a speech at Labin in Istria on 15 June. 'Comrade Khrushchev often repeats that Socialism cannot be built with American wheat. I think it can be done by anyone who knows how to do it, while a person who doesn't know how to do it cannot build Socialism even with his own wheat. Khrushchev says we live on charity received from the imperialist countries . . . What moral right have those who attack us to rebuke us about American aid or credits when Khrushchev himself has just tried to conclude an economic agreement with America?'[11]

Three days later it was announced that Nagy had been brought back from Romania to Hungary and executed with three other members of his government. Mićunović in Moscow made a strong protest to Khrushchev, who said that Tito must raise the matter with the Hungarian government, not the Soviet Union. On 28 June, the tenth anniversary of the expulsion of Yugoslavia from the Cominform, *Pravda* published an attack on Yugoslavia by Gomulka, who had once been imprisoned for being a Titoist; and the Soviet Union refused to renew economic aid to Yugoslavia.[12]

But Tito was unperturbed when he addressed a meeting in Belgrade on 19 April 1959 to celebrate the fortieth anniversary of the foundation of the Communist party of Yugoslavia in 1919. He surveyed the history of the struggle from the beginning, when it was decided to form 'a revolutionary Marxist party'; of its struggles in King Alexander's Yugoslavia in 'more than twenty years of illegal work and the thousands of Communists and Young Communists who were thrown into prison for long terms of hard labour'; of the mistakes which the party leadership had made under Marković and Gorkić, and the struggle against fractionalism which he had had to wage when he became general secretary.

He paid tribute to Filipović, Cvijić-Štefek, Čopić, Vujović and Horvatin, 'who together with a hundred or so other leading Communists from our country met their death in Stalin's prisons and concentration camps ... We are under an obligation to remember these comrades today and to pay a debt of gratitude to them, notwithstanding all the mistakes and weaknesses some of them may have shown in Party work, for they have suffered a hard fate, the hardest that can befall a revolutionary, and that is to die innocent from bullets fired by his own people, falsely accused of betraying ideas for which he fought and to which he devoted his whole life. Such a method of destruction of men, of revolutionaries, is sharply condemned by us Yugoslav Communists.' He had written very differently about these comrades and their fate in his articles in *Proleter* in 1939.

He said that the Communist party of Yugoslavia had always been an internationalist party. It had proved this when it helped Dimitrov and 2,000 Bulgarian refugees in 1923, when it prevented troops from being sent to crush the Hungarian Soviet government in 1919 and waged its campaign to save Rákosi from the death sentence, when it sent more than 1,300* volunteers to fight in Spain and raised 200,000 volunteers to fight for Czechoslovakia at the time of Munich. 'However, since the Czechoslovak government did not decide to offer resistance, and the Czechoslovak Communist leadership, which today denounces us so loudly, did not find it necessary or did not have the courage to step forward in defence of the independence of its country, our action remained only an expression of sympathy for our brotherly Czech and Slovak peoples.'

During the Second World War the Communist party of Yugoslavia had helped to form the Communist resistance movement in Albania, and Italian, Bulgarian, Hungarian, Czechoslovak, Polish and Austrian units had served with the Yugoslav Partisans. 'The graves of our Communists are scattered all over Europe,' from Madrid to Marseilles, where some comrades fell fighting with the French resistance, to the Arctic Circle in Norway, where 3,000 Partisan prisoners of war are buried. They all 'laid down their lives for a better future not only for their own people but for other people as well. It would not be immodest to say that there are few parties which can face the international proletariat with such a record in carrying out its international obligations in the last forty years . . . We can . . . show to all that we have always carried high the banner of Marx, Engels and Lenin.'[13]

In the autumn of 1958 a Third World War seemed imminent as the Chinese Communists bombarded the off-shore islands still held by Chiang Kai-shek's government in Taiwan and the United States threatened to begin a nuclear war if the attacks continued. Khrushchev, knowing that he had rockets which had reached the moon and could also carry the hydrogen bomb to the cities of the United States, demanded a German peace treaty which would compel the Western allies to withdraw from West Berlin; and in Cuba Fidel Castro led a revolution which in January 1959 overthrew the dictatorship of the American puppet, Batista, destroyed American influence in Cuba, and established a Communist government in the American hemisphere within ninety miles of the United States. By the summer of 1959 the danger seemed to have passed, and hopes for peace rose throughout the world. The British prime minister, Harold Macmillan, went to Moscow, and Khrushchev visited Eisenhower in the

* Tito was slightly exaggerating. In fact, 1,192 Yugoslav volunteers fought in Spain (see supra, Chapter 12, p. 131).

White House, and received a friendly reception in many cities of the United States.

These hopes were dashed in May 1960. An unauthorized flight by a United States reconnaissance plane over the Soviet Union gave Khrushchev the excuse to walk out of a summit conference in Paris and to boast about his rockets. When he was asked at a press conference if he intended to use them to launch a rocket attack with H-bombs on the United States, he replied: 'That is for us to decide.'

As the United States and the Soviet Union resumed the Cold War and prepared for what might easily become a third World War, Tito was ideologically neutral between them. So were millions of Socialists, radicals, pacifists and other leftists in Western Europe and still more in Asia, Africa and Latin America, which were becoming known as the 'Third World'. They did not like American imperialism, and felt that Khrushchev's Soviet Union was only marginally better; and they were afraid of the rigid Stalinist orthodoxy and aggressive policies of Communist China. But they believed in Socialism, and they opposed capitalist exploitation, which in the countries of the Third World kept the proletariat and the peasantry in greater poverty than the worst which had been endured by the workers in Western Europe when Marx and Engels were writing that the proletariat had nothing to lose but their chains.[14] They supported the struggles against national and racial oppression in South Africa, the Congo, and Vietnam, and noticed that the most reactionary and brutal oppressors, like the Ku Klux Klan in Mississippi, the Apartheid regime in Pretoria, the puppet rulers in Saigon, and the black warlords in the Congo, all denounced their opponents as 'Communists' and were supported by the governments of the United States, Britain and France.

They were also disturbed by the aggressive language of the government and press in the United States, though it was now sometimes equalled by Khrushchev's talk, and at the repeated rejections by the United States and its allies of all peace proposals put forward by the Soviet Union. They were worried about the NATO policy of rearming Western Germany and employing former Nazi officers in their armed forces and former Gestapo agents in their counter-espionage services. Worst of all, they were alarmed by the declared intention of the United States and NATO to use nuclear weapons in case of war. The Soviet government, with its large land armies, repeatedly declared that they would not be the first to use the

H-bomb or the A-bomb, but would resort to it only in retaliation for its use against them by NATO; the United States and the NATO powers refused to give any such undertaking, and said, on the contrary, that they would use the A-bomb as soon as war broke out. The slogan which had become so popular in the United States 'Better dead than Red' alarmed the Socialists throughout the world and particularly Tito and his old Partisans, who had seen so many of their comrades die in order to make Yugoslavia Red.

Tito had relied on the United States and NATO to protect Yugoslavia from a Soviet invasion in 1951, and he still relied on economic aid from the United States and Western Europe to revive his battered economy; but he could not support them ideologically in the Cold War in 1960. His principles here coincided with his interests. His principles prevented him from supporting either side and required him to pursue a policy of neutralism; but by doing so he could not only remain on the fence, ready to play off the Soviet Union and the United States against each other, but he could also become the leader of a world movement, the association of 'Non-aligned States'.

Tito's past achievements, his personality, and his prestige made it possible for him to stand out as one of the leaders of a movement which included such dominant statesmen as Nehru, Nasser, the Emperor Haile Selassie of Ethiopia, Nyerere of Tanzania, and Sukarno of Indonesia. Tito was too much of a realist to imagine that the speeches and resolutions of the non-aligned statesmen could deter the United States and the Soviet Union if they were really determined to plunge the world into a nuclear holocaust; but even in the age of the H-bomb the force of world public opinion is not entirely negligible, and if a Third World War did not break out, the Non-aligned movement could at least enhance the position of Tito and Yugoslavia in the world.

Tito established a particularly friendly relationship with President Ceauşescu* of Romania. Ceauşescu's rigid Communist dictatorship in Romania was almost Stalinist in its severity; it was certainly more oppressive than the post-Stalinist regime in the Soviet Union. But the Romanian Communists pursued an independent policy towards the Soviet Union and refused to continue to be a Soviet satellite. Commu-

---

* Ceauşescu, Nicolai (1918–89), Romanian Communist leader; became leader of the party in 1965; president of Romania 1967–89; overthrown by a revolution in 1989 and executed after a drumhead court-martial.

nist Romania was therefore just what Tito approved of: it was an independent national Communist regime which was not subservient to the Soviet Union.

Tito did not like Ceauşescu personally, because when they went hunting wild boars together, Ceauşescu cheated and broke the rules. He once took a shot at a boar, and having missed it, fired at it a second time after the boar had moved out of Ceauşescu's and into Tito's field of fire. Tito then killed the boar with his first shot, but Ceauşescu falsely claimed that he too had hit the boar with his shot. 'In that case, your shot must have gone up the hole under the boar's tail,' said Tito sarcastically. When they went hunting together again a few years later, Ceauşescu again claimed to have killed a boar when it was in fact Tito who had shot it.[15] But Tito did not allow his personal resentment at Ceauşescu's hunting ethics to weaken their political alliance.

The annual meeting of the General Assembly of the United Nations in September 1960 was even stormier than usual. Tito decided to attend in person, and so did Khrushchev and Castro. It was Tito's first visit to the United States. The Act of Congress of 1952 which prohibited the entry into the United States of anyone who was or had ever been a member of the Communist party of any country, did not apply to those travelling on a diplomatic passport, and Tito, Khrushchev and Castro all arrived in New York.

Khrushchev made a very violent speech. When Harold Macmillan was speaking, Khrushchev interrupted and heckled Macmillan, and to emphasize his disagreement he took off his shoe and banged it on his desk. Castro went to the rostrum wearing his guerrilla's battle-dress, and his beard was as full as the beards of Mihailović and his Chetniks; he too launched a bitter attack on the United States. But President Tito was a most distinguished figure, an elder statesman, aged sixty-eight, wearing spectacles, and impeccably dressed in a well-tailored dark suit.

The peasant boy from Kumrovec, the Communist shop steward at the Kraljevica shipyards, the political prisoner of Lepoglava, the Comintern official of the Hotel Lux, the Partisan leader on the Sutjeska, now not only looked but also spoke like a wise and responsible world leader. 'We have not come here, of course, to heap more oil upon the fire or to side with any of the extreme attitudes that may reflect present tense international relations. We have come with a desire, above all, to contribute as much as possible to the easing of world tensions.' He dealt with the disturbing situation which had arisen all over the world, and with the situation in Germany. 'Although our people have, in the recent past, suffered severely at the hands of German militarism and Fascism, we harbour no feelings of hatred towards the German people. We are, however, deeply concerned by the revival of militarism in the Federal Republic of Germany.'

He referred to the continuing five-year struggle of the people of Algeria against French colonial domination, and to the Congo, where the United Nations peace-keeping force had stood by and allowed the Radical prime minister, Patrice Lumumba, to be clubbed to death by the troops of the dissident right-wing leader, Tshombe. But his language was restrained. 'The war in Algeria continues endlessly, and conflicts and crises arise, as in the case of the Congo, of Cuba, Laos and West Irian, and seriously imperil world peace. We cannot, as members of the United Nations, reconcile ourselves to such a state of affairs.' He did not forget Latin America. 'A solution to the problems of Latin America is to be sought, in our view, primarily through an accelerated industrialization.'

But the most important problem was disarmament. 'The fact that the cost of a single B 70 super-bomber is equal to the total assistance extended through the United Nations for the development of underdeveloped countries in the course of one year, points clearly to the urgent need of abandoning the course now pursued.' The most important first step would be to stop nuclear tests.

Gone was the old Leninist doctrine of the Comintern, of the inevitability of imperialist wars between capitalist states and the older doctrine of a war to emancipate oppressed peoples which had been advocated by revolutionaries since the days of the Jacobins and the young General Napoleon Bonaparte. Yugoslavia believed in 'the obligation of non-interference in the internal affairs of other peoples and states and the right of every people to organize its own internal development and its own life . . . We believe and maintain that there is no alternative to active peaceful co-existence in the world of today and tomorrow . . . We believe and maintain that war is no longer inevitable, or rather that there exist real prospects for its permanent elimination as an instrument of policy and means of settling international disputes.'[16]

The hopes of the Liberals and leftwingers rose when the Democratic candidate, John F. Kennedy, defeated the right-wing and very anti-Communist Republican Richard M. Nixon to become president of the United States in January 1961. But the international situation became even more dangerous. Kennedy was a Liberal and a progressive. In the Soviet Union Khrushchev pursued an increasingly Liberal policy. He allowed Soviet authors like Solzhenitsyn to publish novels exposing the horrors of conditions in labour camps, though no one had yet published a book in Yugoslavia about the camp on Goli Otok. But the more liberal the policies which Kennedy and Khrushchev pursued at home, the more they thought it necessary to impress their critics by adopting a tough policy abroad. There was also a clash of personalities between them. Kennedy was a playboy and a show-off. Khrushchev was a rude and boorish show-off. Their meeting in Vienna in April 1961 was a disaster; Khrushchev tried to browbeat Kennedy, who returned to Washington determined to teach Khrushchev a lesson.

Khrushchev again demanded a German peace settlement which would mean that American, British and French troops would have to withdraw from West Berlin and leave it to the mercy of the Russians. In August, to the dismay of the Campaign for Nuclear Disarmament and leftists throughout the world and Tito's Non-aligned movement, the Soviet Union resumed nuclear testing and detonated a fifty-seven-megaton H-bomb in the Arctic; it was the biggest nuclear bomb that had so far been tested. The right-wing press in Britain and America now published the stories and statistics showing the effects of nuclear fall-out on present and future generations throughout the world which had hitherto been published only in left-wing newspapers. At the same time the East German government built the Berlin Wall on the boundary of the Soviet and Western zones, and ordered border guards to shoot anyone who tried to escape from the East to the West and who did not stop when challenged. Several young men were shot while escaping, and demonstrations took place on the western side of the wall.

Kennedy was determined to overthrow Castro's Communist government in Cuba, and ordered the CIA to achieve this. When an invasion of Cuba by Cuban anti-Communist refugees was defeated, Kennedy authorized the CIA to assassinate Castro and do the maximum damage to the Cuban economy. The CIA persuaded Castro's discarded mistress to poison him, but she changed her mind at the last moment and warned him. Other Cuban anti-Communist CIA agents poured petrol over the tails of cats and set fire to them, so that the suffering and terrorized animals ran through the sugar plantations setting fire to them and ruining the Cuban sugar crop.[17] Tito could not be an ally of a nation which adopted such methods against a Communist state.

The United States accepted this Yugoslav neutrality. In the summer of 1961 the French Socialist, André Philip, visited Kennedy in Washington. He told Kennedy that European Socialists were shocked that the United States government was working to bring down the Castro regime in Cuba (he did not know about the assassination attempt) merely because Castro was a Communist. Kennedy denied this. He said that the United States were working against Castro not because he was a Communist but because he was a Soviet puppet, and the national interests of the United States were threatened by having a Soviet satellite state in the American hemisphere. Kennedy pointed out the different policy that the United States was pursuing towards Yugoslavia. Tito was as much a Communist as Castro, but as he was no threat to the national interests of the United States, Kennedy was making no attempt to overthrow his regime, but was, on the contrary, giving him economic aid.[18]

The 'peace camp headed by the Soviet Union' was very displeased with Tito. Relations between the Soviet Union and Communist China were becoming strained. Tito had been disappointed by the Chinese Communists. He had always hoped that as they, like the Yugoslavs, had made their own revolution in defiance of Stalin's advice, they too would develop their own national Communism independently of the Soviet Union. They did so, but not in the direction that Tito had wished; as the Soviet leaders saw it, Tito deviated to the right and Mao deviated to the left. Communist China split with the Soviet Union after Khrushchev had denounced Stalin, and Mao stepped forward as the standard-bearer of true Stalinism.

By 1961 the photographs of Stalin had been rather belatedly removed from the government offices in the Soviet Union; the name of the heroic wartime city of Stalingrad had been changed to Volgograd; and Stalin's embalmed body had been removed from its place beside Lenin's in the mausoleum in the Kremlin and reburied by the side of lesser Soviet leaders near the Kremlin wall. In Communist China the four pictures of Marx, Engels, Lenin and Stalin were still everywhere displayed.

By the summer of 1960 the Soviet Union and Communist China were on the verge of an irrevocable split. The Soviet Union withdrew its economic aid from China, and the Chinese Communists publicly condemned Khrushchev and the Communist party of the Soviet Union for repudiating Stalin. In November 1960 Khrushchev and Mao made a last attempt to avert a breach when a meeting of the leaders of the twelve Communist parties was held in Moscow. The obvious basis on which they could achieve a fragile unity was anti-Titoism. They passed a resolution condemning the Yugoslav doctrine of peaceful co-existence between capitalist and Communist states as 'revisionist'.[19]

Despite the Soviet acceptance of the anti-Tito resolution, the Chinese Communists continued to denounce Khrushchev and the Soviet party for their deviation from Stalinism. The final break came in the summer of 1961. Before leaving Moscow, Chou En-lai ostentatiously placed a wreath of flowers on Stalin's more modest grave. By 1969 the High Command of the Red Army were drawing up plans for launching a nuclear war against Communist China.

Djilas believes that it was because of this new rift between Tito and the Soviet Union that he was released from prison in January 1961. But Djilas has been a little misleading in his later accounts of his release, and has somewhat obscured the extent to which he was prepared to compromise with the regime. He had long discussions in his prison with Slobodan Penezić, a high-ranking UDBA officer, whom Djilas had known well when they were fighting side by side with the Partisans at Užice in 1941. Djilas told Penezić that he did not renounce any of his doctrines or repent anything which he had done; but he agreed to sign the petition for clemency which Penezić drafted for him. 'I am determined to preserve my integrity and to adhere to any solution you propose which is acceptable according to my moral principles . . . After release from jail I will not undertake any political activity contrary to the laws of the Federal People's Republic of Yugoslavia which would put me in a position of criminal responsibility, nor will I seek to do my country any damage, and in the future I will permit no one to reprint the book The New Class.'[20]

In the Soviet Union in Stalin's time, this would have been indignantly rejected as an utterly insufficient recantation; but Tito's government accepted it, and were probably glad to be able to do so. Now that Tito was the leader of the Non-aligned States, with many democratic parties among his allies, it was much better if Djilas was out of jail. Djilas was released on 20 January 1961, having served just under half of his nine-year sentence.[21]

In September 1961 the world seemed very close to a Third World War. In London the CND and the Committee of 100 called for demonstrations against nuclear war and the policy of the United States and NATO in Berlin. When the British government banned the demonstration, over 100,000 people flocked into Trafalgar Square in London; several prominent persons were arrested, including the ninety-year-old philosopher, Bertrand Russell, who had always been a strong opponent of Communism and the Soviet Union. At this critical time, Tito convened a conference of the Non-aligned States in Belgrade. It was attended by representatives of twenty-five countries, including Nasser, Nehru, Haile Selassie, Sukarno of Indonesia, Nyerere of Tanzania and Nkrumah of Ghana.

Tito of course presided, and opened the conference on 3 September with a speech in which he laid down the principles which were later accepted in the resolutions adopted by the conference. They condemned all blocs of states, including NATO and the Warsaw Pact, and stated that for this reason they would not form themselves into a Non-aligned bloc. They called for peaceful co-existence, for the immediate grant of independence to colonial countries, and for an immediate treaty for 'general and complete disarmament'. They opposed all military bases on the territories of other states; the policy of Apartheid in South Africa; the 'imperialist' policies being pursued in the Middle East; and any recourse to force in solving the problems of Germany and Berlin. They supported the 'struggle of the people of Palestine', the admission of Communist China to the United Nations, the evacuation of United States bases in Cuba, the immediate ban on all nuclear tests, and the creation of a United Nations capital development fund to help underdeveloped nations. They also supported the struggle of the people of Algeria against French imperialism, and recognized their illegal revolutionary organization, the FLN, as the lawful government in Algeria.[22]

The decisions of the conference were criticized by the United States and the Western powers, who claimed that Tito and the Non-aligned States were drawing close to the Soviet Union; for neutrals who are really neutral are always accused by both belligerents of supporting the other side. General de Gaulle, who had never liked Tito and during the Second World War had much preferred Mihailović,[23] was now the president of France, and after the recognition of the FLN he withdrew his ambassador from Belgrade.[24]

The United States and NATO called Khrushchev's bluff over

Berlin, and war was averted. In Washington, senators and congressmen were reminded by their Ustasha and Chetnik constituents that Tito was a Communist, that he was friendly with Khrushchev, and that he had supported the Soviet position on most points during the Berlin crisis.[25] They asked why the American taxpayer should pay for subsidies to Tito. Under pressure from Congress, Kennedy ordered an investigation into the desirability of suspending economic aid to Yugoslavia.

Tito, as usual, reacted strongly. In a speech at Skopje on 13 November 1961 he declared that Yugoslavia would never allow her foreign policy to be influenced by the grant or withdrawal of economic aid.[26] Once again he got away with it. After months of investigation, the United States government announced that it would not, for the time being, suspend economic aid to Yugoslavia.

As usual, Djilas was the victim of the shifts in Tito's foreign policy, and as usual he bravely courted trouble which he could have avoided. He wrote a book, *Conversations with Stalin*, in which he described how he had become disillusioned with Stalin when he was sent to negotiate with him in Moscow in March 1944 and April 1945. He submitted the manuscript to Yugoslav publishers, but after consulting the government they all refused to publish it. So Djilas sent the manuscript to an American publisher, who announced at the beginning of April 1962 that it would be published in New York in May. The American newspapers began serializing it at the beginning of April, a few days before the Soviet foreign minister, Andrei Gromyko, was due to arrive in Belgrade on an official visit.

On 7 April Djilas was arrested. Tito immediately received letters and telegrams of protest from sixteen British Labour MPs, from ninety-nine well-known British writers, and from authors in India and the United States; but they had no effect.[27]

If anyone except Djilas had been the author of *Conversations with Stalin*, and if he had deleted the last five of the 173 pages of the book, the Yugoslav government would probably have had no objection to its publication. Djilas denounced Stalin as 'the greatest criminal in history – and, let us hope, for all time to come', as a Caligula, a Borgia, and a Tsar Ivan the Terrible; for 'history does not know a despot as brutal and as cynical as Stalin'. His language was as unrestrained as it had been in the days when, as director of Agitprop in the Second World War, he wrote adulatory praise of 'the great Stalin'.

The denunciation of Stalin had reached its peak in the Soviet Union in the autumn of 1961 and things had been written about him, and openly published there, which were nearly as harsh as Djilas's statements. But in his final chapter Djilas accused 'Stalin's present critics – I mean his successors' of being responsible for Stalinism. Stalin had now been dethroned in the Soviet Union, but this had been done 'in cheap theatrical style'; and Djilas pointed out that it was this 'monster' who, second only to Lenin, had built Socialism in the Soviet Union.[28] Djilas clearly implied that Socialism was therefore a discreditable system.

It is not surprising that Tito was exasperated by Djilas's action in publishing his book in the United States. At this time Khrushchev had gone further than ever before in exposing Stalin's crimes and destroying his system. He was allowing Solzhenitsyn to publish legally *One Day in the Life of Ivan Denisovich*. Many of the victims of Stalin's purges, if not yet Trotsky and Bukharin themselves, were being posthumously rehabilitated. He was trying, and apparently succeeding, in building in the Soviet Union the more tolerant kind of Socialism which was favoured by Tito and his many supporters in Western Europe and the Third World. This was the time, in Tito's view, to encourage Khrushchev, and to help him resist both the pressure from the Stalinist factions in the Soviet Union and from Mao Tse-tung, and also the threat of nuclear war from the United States and NATO. Yet Djilas chose this time to publish what was clearly an attack on Khrushchev and on all forms of Socialism, and to publish it in the United States. Djilas had written that Stalin 'was one of those rare and terrible dogmatists capable of destroying nine-tenths of the human race to "make happy" the remaining tenth'.[29] Tito and his friends in the Non-aligned nations believed that this was a perfect description, not only of Stalin, but also of those people in the United States who were clamouring for the first use of the atomic bomb against the Soviet Union because 'Better dead than Red'.

On 14 May 1962 Djilas was put on trial[30] charged with disclosing state secrets contrary to Section 320 of the Yugoslav Criminal Code. The trial was held in public and many foreign journalists were in court. The prosecutor admitted that many of the 'secrets' which Djilas had disclosed in his book had already been published elsewhere, but this was no defence to a charge under this section of the statute. He said that Djilas had added comments, and had published the book in circumstances, which assisted reactionary circles abroad who wished to wage the Cold War and to discredit Yugoslavia's social system, foreign policy, and links with the Non-aligned countries.

Djilas interrupted the proceedings, protesting against the prosecutor's statement. He was behaving very differently from his conduct at the first hearing before the Party Central Committee eight years before; now he was challenging the authority of the Communist court, and behaving as Tito had done when charged before a court in King Alexander's days. Djilas did not behave – and the judge, the prosecutor and Tito did not expect or wish him to behave – as Zinoviev, Bukharin, Rajk and Slánský had behaved at their trials in Stalinist Russia, Hungary and Czechoslovakia.

The judge cleared the court and ordered that the trial should continue *in camera*. Djilas's wife and family were the only spectators allowed to remain in court. The public were readmitted six hours later to hear the verdict and sentence. Djilas had been found guilty and was sentenced to five years' imprisonment which was to run in addition to the three years and eight months which had been suspended from his previous sentence. There were renewed protests from the West and the Third World as Djilas returned to Sremska Mitrovica prison to serve nearly nine more years in prison. The *New York Times* wrote that the trial was 'a blatant relapse into Stalinism'.[31] The writer of this article did not realize what Stalinism was.

Stefica Djilas lodged an appeal on her husband's behalf; but in July it was announced that the Serbian Supreme Court had dismissed the appeal. Again, as with the trials of Mihailović, Stepinac, and Djilas's earlier trials, the hearing was unfair, but not Stalinist. In a bourgeois democracy, Djilas would have been allowed to publish his book. The foreign secretary would have arranged for a question to be asked in Parliament, and he would have replied that the government deplored the publication of the book, particularly at so inopportune a time immediately before the visit of Mr Gromyko to Belgrade. But Tito had shown again that he would not allow bourgeois democracy to be established in Yugoslavia during his lifetime.

In October 1962 the CIA discovered that Khrushchev had established secret nuclear missile bases in Cuba, which placed many cities of the United States within range of these Soviet rockets. Kennedy did not privately ask Khrushchev to withdraw them, but seized the opportunity to announce his discovery on television, and publicly to demand their removal in a manner which enabled him to gain a great diplomatic victory over the Soviet Union, to avenge the humiliating way in which Khrushchev had treated him in Vienna, to enhance his prestige in the United States, and to lower Khrushchev's prestige in the Soviet Union. In return Kennedy promised that the United States would not invade Cuba; but this *quid pro quo*, though it angered the military leaders in Washington, did not prevent the world from regarding the crisis as a great defeat for the Soviet Union. While the United States and the Soviet Union were busy with the Cuba missile crisis, the Chinese Communists invaded India to obtain a small rectification of the frontier between India and Chinese-occupied Tibet. Kennedy had compelled Khrushchev to retreat, but no one forced Mao to retreat. The events of October 1962 were a victory for the United States and Communist China, and a defeat for India and Tito's Non-aligned States, and for Khrushchev's more liberal brand of Communism.

In December 1962 Tito visited the Soviet Union and addressed a session of the Supreme Soviet in Moscow. He warmly praised Khrushchev's statesmanship in withdrawing the missiles from Cuba and saving the whole world, including Yugoslavia, from the Third World War.[32] In July 1963 he welcomed Khrushchev to Yugoslavia and toured the country with him. But the Cuba crisis had reduced Khrushchev's prestige in the Kremlin. In October 1964 he fell from power, being ousted by his successor, Leonid Brezhnev, in a very similar way to the manner in which Khrushchev had got rid first of Molotov and Malenkov and then of Zhukov in 1957. The advent of Brezhnev ended the development towards greater freedom, but did not lead to a return to full-blooded Stalinism. Khrushchev was not shot or sent to a labour camp, but was allowed to end his days under virtual house arrest.

From 1944 to 1948, Tito had been close to Stalin's Soviet Union; from 1949 to 1955 he had been close to the United States; from 1955 to 1964, despite all the strains in their relationship, he had been closer to Khrushchev's Soviet Union; but just as his attitude during the Berlin crisis of 1961 had permanently alienated him, at least to some extent, from the United States, so the fall of Khrushchev and the advent of Brezhnev alienated him to some extent from the Soviet Union. For the last sixteen years of Tito's life and rule he moved sometimes a little closer to the East and sometimes a little closer to the West; but he was now a really neutral neutralist, and never even contemplated getting off his fence and coming down firmly on one side or the other.

CHAPTER 26

❖

Liberals and Hardliners

THE Old Man really was an old man now. In 1962 his seventieth birthday was celebrated throughout the country; but next year he was re-elected president of Yugoslavia for a further term. He was still in good health, physically active and mentally alert. He could still walk energetically through the forests of Slovenia and Vojvodina in pursuit of stags and wild boars, and on the hillside near Kumrovec chasing hares with the local shooting club; and he travelled frequently by plane or ship throughout the world.

During his first four years as ruler of Yugoslavia, he had visited only the Soviet Union and its satellite 'People's Democracies' of Eastern Europe. After the split with Stalin and the Cominform, he did not go abroad for several years; but beginning with his visit to London in March 1953 he travelled all over the world, to the countries of the Western Alliance, to the Soviet Union and its allies, and to the Non-aligned states. In the twenty-eight years from 1952 to 1979 he made fifty-six foreign tours, visiting fifty-five different countries in every continent except Australia.[1] He went several times to Egypt, to the states of the Middle East, and to India and Burma. He visited North Africa, West Africa and East Africa. In the Sudan and Ethiopia he shot lions, elephants, buffalo and antelopes; but he stopped the hunt in Ethiopia when he discovered, to his indignation, that a member of his retinue had shot a giraffe, which is a protected species and a sacred animal to the Ethiopians.[2]

On three occasions he visited the Emperor Haile Selassie of Ethiopia. Haile Selassie had been a rather surprising hero of the European leftists, including the Communists, in 1935, because of his resistance to Mussolini's invasion of Ethiopia; and although he could

[364]

by no stretch of the imagination be called a Socialist, he was a benev-olent dictator of whom Tito would justifiably approve. Haile Selassie gave Tito a great reception in Addis Ababa. He also endeared himself to Tito's staff by his charm and courtesy, and the lengths to which he went to ensure their comforts and to meet their convenience.[3]

The staff had a more difficult time when Tito went to India; for however satisfactory his political relations with the Indian govern-ment may have been, Tito did not like Indian food. Once, before a state banquet in Delhi, he asked his social secretary to arrange for him to have a dish of Croatian peasant food in his room at the embassy to quench his appetite before the banquet began, so that he could merely eat a few mouthfuls of the Indian dishes which would be served to him at the banquet.[4]

His most controversial foreign tour was his visit to South America in 1963. The Catholic hierarchy in Yugoslavia expressed their satis-faction that the president of the Catholic country of Brazil had invited Tito to visit him; but the Cardinal Archbishop of Rio de Janeiro denounced Tito as an atheist, and both the governor of the Guana-bara province where Rio is situated, and the governor of São Paulo province, refused to receive him. So Tito visited only Brasilia, and neither Rio de Janeiro nor São Paulo. The coalition government of Chile welcomed him, but two right-wing ministers resigned in protest.[5]

After a brief stop in Bolivia he went on to Mexico, and was natur-ally more at home in that Radical revolutionary country. The Mexi-can president and Tito both made speeches at the state banquet in support of peaceful co-existence between Socialist and capitalist states.[6] After his death a statue of Tito was erected in the park at Chapultepec in Mexico City.

When he reached the United States he visited President Kennedy at the White House in Washington, arriving by helicopter and miss-ing Jackie Kennedy, who came home shortly after he had left. He then addressed the General Assembly of the United Nations in New York. His appeal for peaceful co-existence and for banning the use and testing of nuclear weapons won even greater approval than his speech in 1960, and he was given a standing ovation by the delegates.[7]

But the Croatian and Serbian refugees organized protest demon-strations against his visit and against the policy of Kennedy's govern-ment in granting economic aid to Yugoslavia. They published pamphlets about the killing of the Ustashas and Chetniks by the Partisans in May 1945, and put pressure on their representatives in Congress. On the day when Tito arrived in Washington Senator Dodd, the Democrat from Connecticut, said in the Senate that Tito was an evil man with blood on his hands. A Republican in the House of Representatives called him 'the butcher of Belgrade'; and the extreme right-wing Republican Senator Barry Goldwater, who next year was the Republican candidate for president of the United States, declared in the Senate that Tito would surreptitiously pass on to Moscow every dollar that was paid to him by the United States.[8]

Tito was closely guarded by the American police wherever he went; but when he stayed at the Waldorf-Astoria Hotel in New York two Ustashas succeeded in getting into the hotel, climbing the fire escape, and reaching the eighth floor before being arrested two floors below Tito's suite. The Yugoslav security officers in New York complained that the American police guarding Tito had been slack, and Kennedy ordered an investigation. Some Albanians demonstrated outside the United Nations building when Tito arrived; they were protesting against the oppression of the Albanians in Kosovo.[9]

Before Tito left New York for England, his ship was thoroughly searched for bombs. A crowd of about 200 spectators cheered him when he arrived with his police escort at the jetty to board the ship. The police held back demonstrators who carried banners with the inscriptions 'Tito pig', 'Tito murderer', and 'Hang Tito'; they were not allowed to reach the pier.[10]

The people of Yugoslavia, like the people of other nations in similar situations, were both proud of Tito's foreign visits and irritated by them. They were proud that their president was playing the part of a major statesman on the international stage, but some muttered that he was paying more attention to foreign countries than to the problems at home, and complained in whispers about the cost to the Yugoslav taxpayer of his foreign travels. 'Is there a man in the moon?' they asked in Belgrade. 'No, because if there were, Tito would have visited him.'[11]

Now that the danger of invasion had passed, Tito knew that he could safely go abroad, leaving the nation's problems to be dealt with by his capable ministers and civil servants. The most important problems were economic, and he had always left economics to the experts.[12] But the experts were at loggerheads with each other.

The Yugoslav economy faced great difficulties in the early years after 1945, with the enormous devastation caused by the Second World War, the freezing of Yugoslav assets by the United States, and Stalin's blockade after 1948; and a series of bad harvests made matters worse. As soon as Belgrade had been liberated from the Germans, Tito announced that Yugoslavia had a Five Year Plan. The opponents of the regime, and economists in the West, condemned the Five Year Plan as a piece of Communist bombast, inspired by Tito's desire to copy the Soviet Union; while Stalin was annoyed that Tito should have the effrontery to imagine that Yugoslavia, like the Soviet Union, could have a Five Year Plan.[13] Stalin was right in believing that Tito's Five Year Plan was over-ambitious, and it did in fact run into difficulties.

Both before and after the split with Stalin in 1948 the government in Belgrade exercised the strictest controls over the economy.[14] There were quotas, rationing, currency restrictions, a ban on foreign travel by Yugoslav citizens, and a reluctance to grant visas to foreigners apart from visiting delegations. The anxieties of Ranković's UDBA that foreign visitors might be imperialist or Soviet spies prevented the development of a tourist trade in Yugoslavia.

There was not much scope for the economists to try out their conflicting theories during the difficult years before 1960. All they could do was to try to keep the country afloat with the economic aid from the United States, and to try to feed the people as adequately as possible. In the years when the harvest failed, the peasants killed off the cattle because there was no feed for them, and the people ate enormous meals of beef and pork during the autumn, wondering if there would be any food at all in the spring. As well as suffering from bad harvests, some part of the country was from time to time severely damaged by earthquakes.

Tito's aim was to modernize and industrialize Yugoslavia in order to raise the living standards of the people, and despite all the difficulties he succeeded in making some progress. Industrial production more than doubled between 1952 and 1959; and the proportion of the population engaged in agriculture fell as the government succeeded in transferring agricultural workers into industry.

In 1949 a number of leading Yugoslav Communists, with Kardelj at their head, put forward the idea of 'Workers' Self-Management'. It was a political reaction to the split with Stalin and the alternative to the domination of a centralized bureaucracy. Tito was at first rather sceptical; he was not sure that workers' self-management would work in practice. But Kardelj and Djilas won him over,[15] the scheme was put into operation, and by 1960 everyone in Yugoslavia paid lip-service to the idea, and no one ventured to criticize it. There was also a great drive during the 1950s to relax bureaucratic controls, to have the economy managed by much smaller units, to encourage competition between enterprises, and to move a long way towards establishing a free market economy.

But there were critics of this development. Smaller units were in many ways more efficient, but in other respects they were less efficient. They increased production costs, and made large-scale planning more difficult. The critics claimed that they increased bureaucracy, because now, instead of a number of bureaucrats in Belgrade, there were bureaucrats in every town and village in Yugoslavia, finding office jobs for themselves in every small working unit. The free market economy increased the number of consumer goods available to the people, but it was also leading to inflation.

At the root of the dispute about the advantages of central planning against the free market economy lay the conflict of interests between the different republics in the Federation, between the prosperous industrialized north and the agricultural and impoverished south. The average income of the population in Croatia was nearly twice as high as in Bosnia, Montenegro and Macedonia; in Slovenia it was two and a half times higher. Serbia occupied a midway position, thanks to its prosperous northern province in the Vojvodina (an autonomous province which was part of Serbia) and the poor south in Kosovo and Metohija.[16] The differences increased under the free market economy; every year Croatia, Slovenia and the Vojvodina became richer and Bosnia, Herzegovina, Montenegro, Macedonia, Kosovo and Metohija became poorer. Tito was very conscious of this problem, as he told Dedijer. 'I have for many years fought on the international field to put a stop to the pauperisation of the greater part of the world. The rich countries are getting richer and richer and the poor ones are getting poorer at full speed. I am sorry to see that this same process is developing in Yugoslavia too.' Since 1945 'the industrial regions in Yugoslavia are getting richer and richer at the expense of economically underdeveloped regions of our country.[17]

Tito was determined to raise the standard of living in the south, and bring jobs to the area. This could be done much better by central planning than by a free market economy. The critics of planning said that planning went wrong. They were always citing the case of the government's decision to open a steel mill in Nikšić in the poorest and remotest part of Montenegro. The mill was built in 1953, but the railway to Nikšić was not completed till 1961, a paved road was only constructed in 1963, and it was not until 1975 that a standard-gauge railway made it possible to connect the steel mill with the more distant parts of Yugoslavia.[18] The planners said it was unfair of their opponents to refer always to this one exceptional case; the free marketeers said that if the Nikšić mill was exceptionally bad, there were many other cases which were nearly as bad.

As long as the arguments were confined to the purely economic level, Tito was content to deal with foreign policy and army efficiency from his office in the White Palace in Belgrade, or to go to Brioni or on another foreign tour, and leave the economists to argue the merits of the free market economy and planning; but he became alarmed when he realized that the economic arguments were a cloak for deep political disagreements. The comrades who favoured a free market economy also supported more autonomy for the six republics and more political freedom. Those who supported more centralized planning wanted more political as well as more economic control from Belgrade and no relaxation of the dictatorship.

The divisions reached the highest level. In the Executive Committee of the League of Communists (which everyone still called, unofficially, 'the Politburo') Kardelj led the liberal faction. He was the only one among the leaders of the Yugoslav Communists who could be called a Marxist theoretician. Writing in Marxist language and in Marxist style, and taking care to safeguard himself against any charge of 'revisionism', he argued that events in the Soviet Union had shown that true Socialism must take the path of workers' selfmanagement, and a partial relaxation – though not a complete abolition – of the political dictatorship. Ranković led the hardliners. He, too, said that he favoured a gradual liberalization of the regime, but he feared that it had been developing too fast. He wished to adhere to more centralized planning and tighter economic controls.

In November 1961 Tito made a speech at Skopje[19] shortly before he left for a long visit to Africa. He spoke a little vaguely about the need to correct the prevailing errors in the economy; there was too much competition for the export market between many small enterprises; grants were still being given for unnecessary new factories, and prices were still rising. When Tito returned from Africa in

February he found that there was talk on all sides about an economic breakdown.

Tito called a meeting of the 'enlarged Executive Committee' of the League of Communists, which was held in Belgrade on 14 March 1962. It was attended by the fourteen members of the Executive Committee, the fourteen other members of the Central Committee, and twenty-three representatives of the League in the republics.* Tito opened the meeting by saying that they faced not merely an economic crisis but also a political crisis. Stefanović agreed, and commented that if they did not solve the crisis they would all be in the devil of a mess. 'In two devils of a mess', interjected Tito, who added that if they could not pull themselves together, unite, and solve their differences, they might as well hand over everything to the devil's mother. Kardelj and Ranković put their opposing points of view. Tito, as always, adopted a midway position, trying to find a compromise which would satisfy both sides and which would provide the basis for a reconciliation. But by the end of the meeting he seemed to be inclining to Ranković's side.[20]

On 6 May Tito spoke at a public meeting in Split. He clearly indicated that there would be a return to tighter controls, and that restrictions would be imposed on the market economy. He criticized the managers of enterprises as a class. There was too great a differential between their salaries and those of the workers. The managers travelled abroad too much and bought too many cars for themselves. Some of them were corrupt, and sold industrial secrets to foreign competitors. New laws must be introduced against 'economic criminals' and 'the little private groups' of directors of enterprises and the chairmen of the council committees. New import controls must be imposed to prevent the purchase by the managers of so many foreign cars, and price controls to counter the effects of inflation. The managers thought that these attacks were unfair, and that the criticism of excessive foreign travel did not come well from Tito.[21]

---

* Stefanović suggested, and Tito and Ranković agreed, that the proceedings at the meeting should be recorded, but that only two copies of the minutes should be made from the recording. One copy was given to Tito and the other to Ranković. Tito's copy is in his archives, which are still closed. Ranković's copy was placed in the archives of the Central Committee, where Živadin Simić, as a member of the organizational board of the Central Committee, obtained possession of it. He made photocopies of part of the minutes for the members of the Central Committee, and was good enough to show his copy to me.

In his speech at Split, Tito had expressed the opinion of the planners and of Ranković, who had temporarily won the day, and Kardelj had to accept defeat. In the summer Kardelj had the misfortune to be shot and slightly wounded when he was on a hunting expedition. The shot had been fired by another member of the shooting party, Jovan Veselinov, who was a minister in the Serbian government; and although it was a typical and not uncommon hunting accident, the rumourmongers said that the Serb Veselinov had deliberately tried to murder the Slovene Kardelj.[22]

In December 1962 Kardelj suddenly went to London without telling Tito or anyone else that he was going. He travelled secretly on a diplomatic passport, and stayed at a private hotel in Kensington which was used exclusively by the Yugoslav embassy and was run by a manager appointed by the embassy. The British journalists did not find out that he was in England, and no report of his visit appeared in any newspaper in any country.

When Tito first heard that Kardelj had gone to London, he said to Tempo: 'Kardelj has deserted me.' Tempo urged him not to jump to conclusions. Tempo went to see Ranković, who as Kardelj's leading opponent was the best person to intercede for Kardelj with Tito; and Ranković, who as always was honest, incorruptible and devoted, agreed to do so. He pointed out to Tito that there were three possible explanations of what Kardelj had done. He might have defected to the West; he might have gone to see an English doctor about his hunting accident; or he might just have gone to London for a holiday.

There had been some trouble at the Yugoslav embassy in London. The ambassador, Prica, had asked to see the intelligence officers' reports and their list of informants in England; the intelligence officers had refused to show them to the ambassador, because it was an accepted rule in the Yugoslav diplomatic service that ambassadors did not see the intelligence reports. Tito sent Živadin Simić to tell the ambassador that he was in the wrong. Simić was now working in the Foreign Office in Belgrade, and was the secretary of the diplomatic branch of the League of Communists, with the duty of vetting the party loyalty of the diplomats. He had been ambassador in Khartoum when Tito went there in 1959 and 1962, and had helped organize a big game hunt in the southern Sudan when Tito had killed a lioness with his first shot.

Tito told Simić that while he was in London he should see Kardelj and find out what was happening. When Simić reached the embassy in London he telephoned Kardelj at the private hotel and asked to see him; but Kardelj refused to meet him or to come to the telephone.

Simić returned to Belgrade and reported on his failure to contact Kardelj; but Kardelj's friend Bakarić, who was a prominent liberal in the League of Communists, offered to go to London and persuade Kardelj to return. Bakarić returned to Belgrade with Kardelj, who explained that he had merely exercised his right to go to London for a holiday without asking anyone's permission. Tito was delighted to see him and quickly forgave him. Simić thought that the whole thing was a put-up job between Kardelj and Bakarić to show their independence and boost Bakarić's reputation.[23] It certainly showed the difference between Tito's regime and Stalin's.

Tito continued to rely first and foremost on Ranković. When the new Constitution was adopted in 1963 it was at Tito's suggestion that a new post of vice-president of Yugoslavia was created so that Ranković could be appointed vice-president.[24] After his promotion Ranković ceased to be minister of the interior and in charge of the UDBA. The new minister of the interior, Svetislav Stefanović, took over the UDBA, but Ranković gave him the benefit of his advice and championed the interests of the UDBA in the government.

But the forces of liberalism were strong. They had the support of public opinion in Croatia and Slovenia, for the Croats and Slovenes wanted more freedom to trade with Western Europe, particularly with Western Germany, and to continue to raise their standard of living by buying more Yugoslav and foreign consumer goods. They did not wish their taxes to be spent in starting enterprises in Montenegro and Macedonia in order to alleviate the poverty in the south.[25]

Milka Kufrin was no longer the shy young heroine that she had been in 1942. She was now not only an experienced public speaker but also assistant minister of foreign trade. She was one of the very few women to play a leading part in the government of Yugoslavia; for although so many women had fought with the Partisans, very few had reached the higher ranks of the State or the party.

Milka Kufrin thought of a way of helping to overcome the adverse balance of Yugoslavia's foreign trade. Why not attract foreign tourists to Yugoslavia, to the sunny beaches of Dalmatia, Montenegro and the islands during the heat of the summer? There had been some modification in recent years in the rigid visa restrictions of the early post-war period, but far more could be done in this respect.

In 1960 she wrote a memorandum on the subject which she sent to Tito personally. She pointed out to him that Yugoslavia earned only 18 million dollars per annum from foreign tourists; but she believed that this could be increased to over 100 million if the requirement for visas was abolished, if foreign tourists were offered Yugoslav dinars at a more favourable rate of exchange, and if money was invested in improving the hotels and other tourist facilities. It was some time before Tito or any member of the government reacted to her proposal, but a year or so later she was appointed chairman of the Federal Council for Tourism, and told to go ahead and put her ideas into practice.

There was considerable opposition to her proposals. Some of the more rigid party stalwarts were hostile. There was nothing about tourism in any work by Marx or Lenin. The beaches of Yugoslavia should be used not by foreign tourists but by Yugoslav workers to go there on excursions and holidays organized by their trade unions so that they could return refreshed after the holiday to their work in the factories. The strongest opposition came from the UDBA, supported by Ranković. They were convinced that foreign spies would arrive disguised as tourists.

Despite all the opposition, Tito encouraged her to go ahead. In 1963 he expanded the Council of Tourism into the Ministry of Tourism, and appointed Milka Kufrin as the minister of tourism in the government of Croatia. After much argument and against the opposition of Ranković, Stefanović and the Ministry of Foreign Affairs, she persuaded Tito to allow foreigners from all countries to come to Yugoslavia without visas. Several foreign countries then abolished the need for Yugoslav visitors to have visas, but not all countries gave reciprocal treatment to Yugoslavs. The Yugoslav Foreign Ministry thought that this placed Yugoslavia in an inferior position as compared with these foreign countries, and despite Milka Kufrin's opposition the regulations were changed in 1967. Henceforth foreigners could come to Yugoslavia without visas only if their country allowed Yugoslav visitors to dispense with visas; but this did not do great damage to the tourist industry. Milka Kufrin's proposal for a favourable rate of exchange for tourists was adopted; the tourists obtained 300 dinars for one dollar, at a time when the usual rate of exchange was 50 dinars to the dollar.

Tourism proved to be as successful as Milka Kufrin had forecast.

Thousands of tourists came every year, mostly from West Germany, but many from Britain and other Western countries. There was constant friction with the UDBA. Many of the tourists wished to take holiday snapshots, but the police were very suspicious of cameras. The Ministry of Tourism succeeded in abolishing some of the restrictions on taking photographs, but the police sometimes ignored the regulations, and confiscated the photographs and the cameras.

The disputes between the Ministry of Tourism and the UDBA became part of the struggle between the planners and the free marketeers. If tourism was to be encouraged, then hotel-keepers and shop-keepers in the holiday districts had to be granted freedom from rationing and trading restrictions; and government funds had to be allocated to building hotels on the Adriatic coast in preference to new factories in Macedonia and southern Serbia. It may have been coincidence that Kardelj was a Slovene and Ranković a Serb, because these two Communist veterans, despite their differences, were loyal only to the idea of a united Communist Yugoslavia, to the international proletarian revolution, and to Tito personally; but in the divisions within the government, there was a tendency for ministers and officials who represented the coastal areas, with tourist facilities, to favour a free market economy, while those from the inland countries, where there was no tourist trade, preferred centralized planning. Slovenia, Croatia and Montenegro were more likely to support, and Serbia, Bosnia and Macedonia to oppose, the free market economy.[26]

Apart from the foreigners on holiday in Yugoslavia, foreign currency was also brought into the country by Yugoslavs working abroad. Many Yugoslavs went to work in Germany and Austria. Most of them came from Slovenia and Croatia, which were nearer than the other republics to the Austrian frontier. This emigration helped to ease the unemployment problem in Yugoslavia. In the first years of Tito's regime, foreign travel was restricted, as in other Communist countries; but the restrictions were gradually relaxed, and by 1962 any Yugoslav could leave the country without an exit permit.[27] Tito's Yugoslavia was the only Communist country in the world which allowed its citizens to travel freely abroad, and was a striking contrast to the Soviet Union, East Germany, and the other countries of the 'Socialist camp' with their electrified wires along the frontier and their Berlin Wall to prevent the people from emigrating.

The Czechoslovak Communist leader, Husák,* once declared that a frontier is not a boulevard that anyone may freely cross at will; but the Yugoslav frontier was as much a boulevard as the frontier of any democratic state of Western Europe.

But there was no unlimited freedom for writers and artists in Yugoslavia. Tito and his government did not enforce the rigid conformity and the insistence on 'proletarian literature', 'proletarian art' and 'Socialist realism' which Stalin and Zhdanov had imposed in the Soviet Union. But there was sporadic censorship, with periods of great freedom followed by a tightening of the control, as in the nineteenth-century dictatorships of Metternich and Napoleon III.

Tito did not like *art nouveau*, surrealism and the more bizarre examples of modern experimental art. The film producer Makavejev whose films were discouraged and sometimes banned, called Tito's taste in art '*kitsch*', and said that his whole regime and personality, with his love of fine uniforms and show, was *kitsch*;[28] but this is surely unfair. In his house at 15 Užička Street in Belgrade, the walls in every room are covered with paintings, mostly by impressionist artists, and all in excellent taste.

Some people thought that Tito had been influenced by the views on modern art which his friend Khrushchev expressed at the Manège exhibition in Moscow. When Tito addressed the Seventh Congress of Yugoslav Youth in Belgrade on 25 January 1963 he warned them not to be influenced by intellectuals who find everything banal and ordinary, who become enthusiastic about decadent art from abroad, and think Marxism is out of date. 'There is no question here of administrative intervention, but public opinion cannot afford to be passive when faced with such problems.' He said that too much public money was being spent on 'certain so-called modernistic works which have no connection with artistic creativeness, much less with the realities of our time'.[29] Whatever this may have meant, it did not place any restrictions on the work of surrealist painters.

The Belgrade literary magazine *Delo* was not afraid to publish in its issue of January 1965 an article by Mihajlo Mihajlov, the son of

---

* Husák, Gustav (1913–91), Czechoslovak Communist leader; prime minister of Slovakia 1946–50; imprisoned for nationalist deviation 1954–60; supported the national movement for independence from the Soviet Union in 1968, but after the Soviet invasion he headed the pro-Soviet puppet government in Czechoslovakia and suppressed freedom; president of Czechoslovakia 1973–89; resigned after the revolution of 1989 and lived in retirement till his death.

a Russian Tsarist refugee who had become a lecturer in the Faculty of Philosophy of the University of Zagreb at Zadar. Mihajlov described his talks with Soviet writers during his recent visit to Moscow, and how they now had far more freedom to express their views under Khrushchev than they had had under Stalin. But he criticized Lenin, and accused him of introducing the system of forced labour camps in the Soviet Union. Mihajlov developed this theme in a second article in the February issue of *Delo*; but the government ordered the seizure of all copies of the February issue, and on 4 March Mihajlov was arrested and charged with disseminating hostile propaganda. Everyone believed that it was the Soviet ambassador who had asked Tito to arrest Mihajlov, and that Tito had agreed in order to establish good relations with Brezhnev, who four months before had replaced Khrushchev as leader of the Soviet Union.

On 27 March Mihajlov was dismissed from his post at the university. When his trial began in Zadar on 29 April he was charged with distributing banned material and bringing a foreign state into contempt. He was sentenced to nine months' imprisonment, but the sentence was suspended. Lenin was still a sacred figure to Tito and the Yugoslav Communists. Mihajlov was treated more leniently for attacking Lenin in Yugoslavia than he would have been if he had attacked the Prophet Mohammed in Saudi Arabia or Iran.

Mihajlov was as unwilling as Djilas to keep quiet. In July 1966 he announced that he intended to start a new journal which he hoped would lead to the foundation of a new political party. He was arrested, and sentenced to twelve months' imprisonment. This time the sentence was not suspended.[30]

The disagreements between the liberals and the hardliners divided the Council of Ministers. Tito, as president of Yugoslavia, did not attend the meetings, which were presided over by the prime minister, Petar Stambolić. Tito had appointed the ministers so as to maintain an even balance between the liberals and the hardliners. When proposals in the Council of Ministers were put to the vote, there was usually an equal number of votes for and against. This left the decision to Stambolić's casting vote; but he very often refused to give his casting vote, and declared that it was impossible to reach a decision. He would then go to Brioni to see Tito, and other ministers also went there. In due course the dispute would be decided by Tito, who would come down on one side or the other.[31]

One day in 1964 Milka Kufrin was suddenly informed that she

was guilty of political and moral deviation and anti-party activity. She was completely taken aback by this quite unexpected accusation. She went to Ranković and demanded to know the reason for these charges, and to see the evidence against her. Ranković showed her the accusation, although he would not allow her to take a copy of it. She was accused of having demanded the abolition of visas for foreign tourists because she wished to make it easier for foreign governments to send spies into the country. She was also accused of immoral conduct with the chauffeur who was assigned to her as minister of tourism; the chauffeur had stated that she had tried to force him to have sex with her by threatening to punish him if he refused.

She told Ranković that these accusations were false, and demanded that her case be investigated by the party so that she could prove her innocence. Ranković said that she had no right to demand an investigation. He told her that she would hear more in due course when she was summoned by the party to answer the charges against her. Meanwhile she must continue to perform her duties as minister of tourism and must not discuss the case with anyone.

Milka Kufrin waited for more than a year without hearing anything further, but always with this cloud hanging over her. She was appalled at the prospect of being expelled from the party, and thought of committing suicide; every morning she wondered if she would be arrested before the day was out. She went to see Tito at Brioni and explained to him what had happened. He was very sympathetic, and told her not to worry. She did not tell anybody except Tito, but she noticed that her party comrades, and even her friends, avoided her and cut her when she passed them in the street. She went again to Brioni. Tito again told her not to worry, and said that as he was about to return to Belgrade she must travel with him in his famous Blue Train which had been specially designed for him as president. Tongues wagged when they were seen arriving together at the railway station in Belgrade. Next day she noticed that her friends were greeting her in the street.[32]

Tito seems to have made up his mind in February 1966 to get rid of Ranković; conscious of the swell of public opinion in favour of liberalism, he decided to come down firmly on their side. In February 1966 the Third Plenum of the Central Committee of the League of Communists of Yugoslavia was held in Belgrade. Before the opening of the plenum, Tito had a frank talk with Ranković,[33] and when he spoke at the plenum he made it clear that trouble was brewing.

He said that 'the conflict of opinion in the Communist ranks' was 'entangled with petty bourgeois and who knows what other conflicts of opinion ... The question is, how has it come to pass that the development of Socialism in our country is being rendered imposs- ible. This has been the aim of the class enemy.' Nowadays party work 'is carried on in cafés and all sorts of schemes are hatched for pushing people into this or that responsible post. Not only that: certain Communists, or more accurately certain members of the League of Communists of Yugoslavia are falling under the influence of petty bourgeois ideology from the West and of reactionaries inside the country who have remained from before the war.'[34]

Tito's words were far from clear, but as his speech was made in public and reported in the press, everyone knew that something was afoot. Soon after the Third Plenum Ranković visited the Soviet Union. While he was there, Bakarić made a series of speeches in which he criticized the manner in which the party organization was operating. He was not more specific, but his words were interpreted as a criticism of Ranković.[35]

The minister of the interior, Stefanović, was officially responsible for the activities of the UDBA. His second-in-command was Vojslav Lukić. It was widely believed that Lukić was chiefly responsible for the oppressive actions of the UDBA. Both Stefanović and Lukić were Serbs, like Ranković. Tito was not sure that he could trust the other Serbs in UDBA to conduct an impartial investigation into the conduct of Lukić, Stefanović and Ranković; so he ordered that they should be investigated by Croatian officers of UDBA in Zagreb, and by the Army counter-intelligence, for he knew that he could trust the Army, who were devoted to him personally.[36] The inquiries continued for nearly two months. Then on 9 June it was announced that the investi- gators had discovered that UDBA had bugged Tito's telephone in his palace in Belgrade.[37]

It was time for the party to step in, to curb this spying on leading party members and the anti-party activities of UDBA. The Executive Committee of the League of Communists appointed a commission to investigate UDBA. Tito was careful, as he always was, to avoid inflaming national hatreds between the various republics. He arranged for Krsto Crvenkovski, a Macedonian, to be appointed chairman of the commission; but it included Serbs and representa- tives of the other nationalities, including the rising young Croat leader, Mika Tripalo.

All their inquiries seemed to indicate that Lukić was chiefly responsible for the excesses committed by UDBA. Lukić admitted to Tripalo that UDBA had files on over a million people in Croatia alone. He explained that as every man and woman had some vice or weakness which foreign agents might exploit to blackmail them into spying against Yugoslavia, it was essential that UDBA should discover what these vices and weaknesses were by spying on as many people as possible.[38] Milka Kufrin's chauffeur confessed that there was no word of truth in his statement accusing her of having tried to force him to become her lover. He said that the statement had been dictated to him by an UDBA agent in Lukić's office. The commission exonerated Milka Kufrin from all the charges against her.[39]

Stefanović indignantly denied that he had authorized the bugging of Tito's telephone; he said that if anyone had done this, it was not UDBA. All Ranković's colleagues still maintain this attitude today.[40] Several impartial observers, including his British acquaintance Sir Fitzroy Maclean, have doubted whether Ranković would have bugged Tito's telephone, in view of his personal loyalty to Tito.[41] But the members of the investigating commission are certain that it was the work of UDBA, and think that Ranković probably knew about it. They admit that Ranković would never have plotted to overthrow Tito. Some believe that he was working to ensure that, as vice-president of Yugoslavia, he would take over the leadership of the State and the party when Tito died; but above all they believe that Ranković, like Stefanović and Lukić, was spying for the sake of spying; they were bugging everybody because they found it intolerable that there was anyone whom they had not bugged.[42]

Ranković was in the unusual position of being a chief of the secret police whom nearly everyone esteemed. Even the liberals who brought him down, and his intended victim, Milka Kufrin, were ready to exonerate him from most of the blame; they thought that his subordinates Stefanović and Lukić were far guiltier than he.[43] But he had been so closely associated with UDBA he could not possibly survive its exposure and the purge of the purgers.

The commission's report was considered at a meeting of the Central Committee of the Communist League of Yugoslavia at Brioni in July 1966. Simić, who for the last ten months had been ambassador in Canada, was recalled from Ottawa to explain his conduct in Belgrade when he had been the secretary of the diplomatic branch of the party; for he had always been very close to Ranković. On 15 July he wrote to Tito, alleging that the accusations against him and Ranković and their supporters were lies told by Kardelj's faction. Tito did not reply. Simić afterwards discovered that he had never received the letter.

Ranković, Stefanović, Lukić, Simić, and other leading party members who had been linked in people's minds with UDBA, were expelled from the League of Communists, and in due course were deprived of all their offices in the government. It was announced that they and fourteen others would be prosecuted for corruption, oppression and other offences; but in December Tito announced that, in view of their past services to the country and the party, no further action would be taken against them.[44]

As usual, Tito acted in a far less ruthless way than Stalin. In the Soviet Union, Yagoda, Yezhov and Beria had all been shot; in Yugoslavia, Ranković was allowed to retire into private life on a pension. Simić, who was also allowed to retire on a pension, became so disgusted with politics that he devoted his time to writing delightful books about fish and about hunting animals, for he thought that fish and animals were nicer and more interesting than human beings.

Some of Djilas's friends objected to the leniency which had been shown to Ranković, and compared it with the repeated persecution to which Djilas had been subjected;[45] but this is not a fair comparison. For his first offence, Djilas was merely expelled from the Central Committee, not even from the party as Ranković was. After his expulsion, Ranković was prepared to live quietly in retirement, whereas Djilas, rightly or wrongly, offended again and again, and eventually was sent to prison after his third offence. From Tito's viewpoint, there was a fundamental difference between the attitudes of his two former comrades. Djilas had clearly repudiated both Socialism and Non-alignment, and had associated himself with the cause of bourgeois democracy and the Western Powers, whereas Ranković had always since 1948 been equally opposed to the West and the Soviet Union.

But Djilas benefited from Ranković's downfall. Tito followed his pardon of Ranković with a general amnesty, under which Djilas was released from prison on 31 December 1966 on the sole condition that he took no part in politics for the next five years. He had served four years and seven months of his nine-year sentence. He was not the only one to benefit from the liberals' victory. The year 1966 ushered in the least oppressive period of Tito's rule in Yugoslavia.

CHAPTER 27

❖

The Prague Spring and the Crisis of 1968

AMID all his other anxieties, there was one subject on which Tito felt reasonably happy. 'We have solved the national question', he said in 1962.[1] The peoples of Yugoslavia remembered the horrors of the Second World War, when Croatian Ustashas, Serbian Chetniks and Muslim Fascists had slaughtered nearly a million Croats, Serbs and Muslims, until the Communists arrived and united all the peoples in fraternal solidarity in a Federal Communist Yugoslavia. The people would never wish to see a return to those terrible days. This was the guarantee that they would all embrace 'the Yugoslav idea', and the official propaganda line which taught them that they were not Slovenes, Croats, Serbs or Muslims but Yugoslavs.

Yet there were disturbing signs that the Yugoslav Idea was not being accepted everywhere. Many Slovenes, Croats and Muslims feared that it would again mean Serbian domination, as it had done under King Alexander and Prince Paul between the wars. A united Yugoslavia was always dominated by the Serbs; it was a new name for a Greater Serbia. The federal capital, Belgrade, was in Serbia, and the head offices of the central government, of the nationalized enterprises, of the banks, and of the trade unions were all in Belgrade. So Tito passed a constitution for the Federal Republic of Yugoslavia which provided a complicated series of checks and balances to safeguard the autonomy of the republics. From time to time a new constitution was drawn up with new guarantees for autonomy and further checks on the central power. All the constitutions since 1946 gave the republics the right to secede unilaterally from Yugoslavia. Tito was confident that this right would not be exercised as long as all the republics were one-party republics ruled by the Communist party.

As usual it was the intellectuals and the youth, the writers and the students, who caused the trouble. Writers like Djilas who put forward unorthodox ideas about a new class and new ways to Socialism – unless the new way coincided with Tito's and Kardelj's new way – ran a very good chance of being sent to prison; but it was not so easy to deal with writers who fought on the nationalist issue on which they would have widespread popular support. In 1967 Croatian intellectuals revived the organization Matica Hrvatska (Croatian Cultural Centre) which had originally been formed during the Croatian intellectual renaissance of the 1840s.

As in so many other countries, the movement came to a head over the language question, though the difference between Croat and Serb is no greater than the variations in the English spoken in England and the United States or in the German of north and south Germany. For more than 150 years Croatian and Serbian intellectuals had been arguing about whether Serb and Croat were the same or two different languages. It seemed as if the question had been settled back in 1850 when the great Serbian lexicographer Vuk Karadžić met leading Croatian intellectuals in Vienna and decided that Serb and Croat were one Serbo-Croat language with two different alphabets, and that Serbo-Croat should be written in the Latin alphabet in Croatia and in the Cyrillic alphabet in Serbia. The question arose again in Communist Yugoslavia 104 years later, when the agreement reached in Vienna was confirmed at Novi Sad in 1954. The Communist daily newspaper *Borba* was published with the pages printed alternately in the Latin and Cyrillic alphabets and the front page being in Latin and Cyrillic on alternate days.

On 17 March 1967 the important Zagreb journal *Globus* published a declaration signed by thirteen leading Croatian writers. Most of them were members of the Croatian Communist party, and they included Tito's friend, Krleža, who was on the Central Committee of the party. They demanded that a new clause should be inserted into the Yugoslav Constitution recognizing that Croat was a separate language from Serb and not merely a Serbo-Croat dialect.

There was an immediate response from forty-five Serbian writers, most of whom were leading members of the Serbian Communist party. They demanded that the children of the 700,000 Serbs living in Croatia should be taught to speak Serb, not Croat, in school, and that they should do their lessons in the Cyrillic alphabet. They also demanded that only the Cyrillic alphabet be used in the captions on Belgrade television.

Tito clamped down on both groups. With his agreement, the Croatian Communist party forced Krleža to resign from the Central Committee, and the forty-five Serbian writers received a warning to behave themselves.[2] In February 1967 Tito spoke at the Fourth Plenum of the Central Committee of the League of Communists. He said that too much freedom had hitherto been granted to writers. 'We have shrugged our shoulders and thought that it would not hurt anyone if we allowed everybody to talk and write as they please. But we have gone too far. Certainly we will not brainwash anyone and prescribe what he shall write, but nor shall we allow anyone to write against our social way of life. We shall not permit the spreading of divisive slogans, of national intolerance and chauvinism which sometimes happens now in our schools and other cases of our social life. Communists must smash this sort of thing and make it imposs-ible. Hitherto they have not always been capable of doing this.'[3]

Tito was also having difficulties with his foreign policy. In 1961 the United States took over from France the task of fighting Commu-nism in Vietnam and maintaining in power the right-wing dictator-ship in the South against the Communist Vietcong in the North. Three years later President Johnson announced that the United States would send ground troops to fight the Communists in Vietnam. Left-wing opinion throughout the world condemned American inter-vention, and the campaign of protest led to demonstrating students in the United States being shot dead by the National Guard. Tito sympathized strongly with the Vietcong. For many years Ho Chi Minh had supported Mao Tse-tung's line of condemning the revisionism of the Yugoslav Communists; but though Tito, at the Eighth Congress of the League of Communists in Belgrade in December 1964, strongly condemned the Chinese Communists for resuming nuclear tests and for building up a new power bloc which was a threat to world peace,[4] he nevertheless supported Ho Chi Minh's struggle against American imperialism.

Since the Arab-Israeli War and the Anglo-French intervention in Egypt in 1956, a United Nations peace-keeping force had been sta-tioned in Egypt, separating the Egyptians from the Israeli forces. In the spring of 1967 Nasser ordered the United Nations forces to leave Egypt, and after they had complied he made open and flamboyant preparations to invade Israel. Tito had always sympathized with the

Arab cause against Israel, but he strongly advised Nasser not to begin hostilities, and Brezhnev and the Soviet government concurred in this advice. Nasser reluctantly agreed not to start the war; but the Israelis, seeing his preparations and expecting an imminent attack, decided to launch a preemptive strike. On 5 June 1967 they swooped on Nasser's forces, destroyed nearly all his air force, and routed his army in the Six Day War. Tito and Brezhnev blamed the United States for this Israeli aggression. They felt very aggrieved that while they had prevented Egypt from attacking Israel, the United States had not prevented Israel from attacking Egypt.

As soon as the war began, Tito urged Brezhnev to give all possible assistance, short of war, to Nasser. Brezhnev agreed to fly military supplies to Egypt, and Tito offered to give the Soviet aircraft landing facilities in Yugoslavia on their journey. A certain amount of aid was sent in this way, but it could not prevent the Israelis from seizing substantial tracts of Egyptian and other Arab territory and more than doubling the size of the state of Israel. Tito could do nothing except break off diplomatic relations with Israel.[5]

On the last day of the Six Day War, there was a secret meeting in Moscow of the leaders of the Communist parties of the Soviet Union and of Eastern Europe. Tito flew to Moscow with his foreign minister, Koča Popović, and General Jovanić. As soon as they arrived they went straight to a meeting in the Kremlin, which began at midnight, at which they discussed the situation caused by the Arab defeat. Brezhnev and Kadar turned to Tito and asked him to report on the war in which 'your Non-aligned Bloc' was involved. During the meeting Brezhnev received a telephone call from the Soviet ambassador in Cairo; he reported that Nasser was in despair and was threatening to commit suicide.

Tito urged the others to remain calm. He said that he knew the Arabs; they were very excitable, and the Communist leaders should take no hasty decisions until he had talked to Nasser on the telephone. At two a.m. they went to another room for drinks, and Tito telephoned Nasser and succeeded in calming him down. The meeting resumed and continued till three in the morning.[6] The other leaders urged Tito to use his influence to restrain Nasser, but Tito was not eager to do this. 'Why should I influence Nasser?' he said. 'He knows what he is doing.'[7]

Tito had drawn closer to the Soviet Union over Vietnam and the Six Day War, but Yugoslav-Soviet friendship suffered a severe setback in the year of revolutions, 1968. Czechoslovakia was one of the last of the Communist countries to feel the effects of de-Stalinization, but in 1965 the thaw slowly began when the hardline Stalinist Novotný was ousted from the leadership. Communists who had been executed as Titoists after the Slánský and other trials were posthumously rehabilitated, and a certain very limited amount of freedom was permitted.

On 5 January 1968 Alexander Dubček was appointed general secretary of the Czechoslovak Communist party, and launched the movement which became known as the 'Prague Spring'. A wave of enthusiasm spread through the whole country. Dubček and his leading colleagues were Communists, and made no attacks on the Soviet Union; but in the new atmosphere of freedom some writers went as far as Djilas in criticizing the Soviet Union and Socialism, and published articles for which they would have been arrested and prosecuted in Yugoslavia. By March the Soviet press was sharply attacking Dubček and the new government in Czechoslovakia.

Tito at once realized the importance and the dangers of events in Czechoslovakia. In April he flew to Moscow to discuss the situation with Brezhnev. He strongly advised him not to use force to crush Dubček and the Prague Spring. He pointed out that the situation was very different from the crisis in Hungary in 1956. No Communists were being lynched in Prague, and the movement there was not a counter-revolution. Brezhnev assured Tito that he was not contemplating any invasion of Czechoslovakia,[8] and he took no drastic action for another four months.

But 1968, like 1848, was a year of revolutions, and the revolutionary mood among the students spread from Prague to Paris and from Paris to Belgrade. In May trouble erupted at Belgrade University. The students demonstrated against rising prices, and demanded higher student grants and a removal of the rigid and conservative professors. They extended their demands to general political questions which had nothing to do with the university, protesting against the privileges of the bureaucracy and party leaders and calling for more political freedom.

One evening some students clashed with young proletarians from a Workers' Youth Brigade about which group was entitled to admission to an entertainment at a dance hall. The police charged the rioters, beating them with their truncheons. Next day 4,000 students demonstrated in the streets, and were again charged by the police.

This time 169 students were badly injured and required hospital treatment.

Next day the students occupied the university premises and held a sit-in. They were supported by the Communist Students Union. They paraded with slogans 'For a better and freer University', and 'Down with the Princes of Socialism'. The Communist students managed to persuade the others to withdraw this last slogan.[9]

On 9 June Tito broadcast to the nation on television. He addressed the students in the tone of a patient and loving father. He said that every one of their demands was justified, and promised to see that they were granted; if he could not do this, he would not continue as president, because no Communist should cling to office for its own sake. But as the demonstrations were making it more difficult for him to achieve the desired results, he asked the students to stop them, to abandon their sit-in, and to go home. The magic worked. The students of the Law Faculty who were watching him on television broke into loud applause; they shouted 'We are Tito's, and Tito is ours!' The sit-in and the demonstrations ended next day.[10]

Things were not going so well in Czechoslovakia. On 15 July the representatives of the Communist parties of the Soviet Union, Bulgaria, Hungary, Poland and East Germany met in Warsaw and sent a letter to Dubček and the Czechoslovak Communist party. It was signed, among others, by Kadar for Hungary, Gomulka for Poland, Ulbricht for East Germany, and Brezhnev, Kosygin and Podgorny for the Soviet Union. 'We are not interfering . . . in your measures which are aiming at improving . . . the development of Socialist democracy,' but 'we cannot consent to hostile forces compelling your country to leave the Socialist path and threatening to tear Czechoslovakia away from the Socialist commonwealth. This is no longer your concern alone.' At a time when American imperialism was waging 'its criminal war in Vietnam' and supporting 'the Israeli aggressors in the Middle East', they called on the Czechoslovak Communist party to defeat the 'forces of the counter-revolution' in Czechoslovakia.[11] Tito did not disagree with these statements, but he did not accept that the Prague Spring was the counter-revolution.

On 29 July Brezhnev and Dubček met in Brezhnev's train at Cierna-nad-Tisou on the Czechoslovak-Soviet frontier. It seemed as if the threat of Soviet invasion had receded. On 9 August Tito arrived in Prague. He received a great ovation from the large crowds who assembled in the streets to welcome him. He gave them a pledge of wholehearted Yugoslav support for their new democratic form of Socialism.[12] He was followed by President Ceauşescu of Romania, who came to Prague on 13 August. Ceauşescu, too, spoke in support of Dubček and the Prague Spring.

On the night of 20 August the Soviet army invaded Czechoslovakia; a token force of Polish, Hungarian and Bulgarian troops marched in with them. The people of Czechoslovakia came out on to the streets, in their thousands, but they could not stop the Soviet tanks. Dubček and the Communist leaders were taken to Moscow, and were not allowed to return to Prague until they had submitted to all the Soviet demands. The Western Powers protested, but took no action. Nearly every Communist party in the world, outside the Soviet bloc, even the usually docile French and Italian parties, denounced the invasion.[13] Ho Chi Minh could not afford to antagonize the Soviet Union who were supplying him with anti-aircraft missiles to defend Hanoi from American air raids; but Mao Tse-tung and Ceauşescu strongly condemned the Soviet action.

None of them reacted as strongly as Tito. On the evening of 21 August, the Executive Committee of the Yugoslav League of Communists condemned the Soviet invasion of Czechoslovakia, and next day Tito flew to Bucharest to discuss the situation with Ceauseşcu. As soon as he returned to Belgrade he broadcast to the Yugoslav people on television. He denounced the Soviet invasion of Czechoslovakia and their destruction of Dubček's 'progressive revolution', and compared it to Stalin's action against Yugoslavia in 1948. He warned the people that Yugoslavia too was threatened by a Soviet invasion; but 'we shall know how to defend and protect Yugoslav independence with all our means against whatever side the threat comes from'.[14]

The Western governments thought that he was exaggerating the danger, for Brezhnev had given no sign of hostility towards Tito, and the Soviet Union did not have a common frontier with Yugoslavia. But Tito believed, or professed to believe, that the Soviet Union might invade Yugoslavia through Romania, and crush first Ceauşescu and then himself.[15] He appealed to all Yugoslav men and women between the ages of eighteen and sixty-five to enlist in Partisan detachments. There was a great response from the people, and anti-Russian demonstrations were held all over Yugoslavia.[16] Some people believed that Tito reacted so strongly not because he feared a Soviet invasion of Yugoslavia but in order to make more than a verbal protest against Brezhnev's policy in Czechoslovakia. Others thought that he hoped that the awareness of the Soviet threat to the nation's independence would put an end to the student unrest in Yugoslavia.

The Soviet Union reacted angrily to the protests in Yugoslavia and Romania. The Soviet ambassadors in Bucharest and Belgrade used threatening language to Ceauşescu and Tito. It worked with Ceau-şescu, and the Romanian press toned down its criticism of the invasion of Czechoslovakia.[17] It did not work with Tito. He told the ambassador that he would not listen to threats, and ordered him out of the room.[18]

The Soviet action of 21 August 1968 was a fatal blow to Tito's hopes. It destroyed what was perhaps the last chance of building the more tolerant kind of Socialism in which Tito believed and of avoiding the triumph of the counter-revolution in Eastern Europe and the Soviet Union and at least a temporary return to capitalism there after the events of 1989–91. But progress was made towards achieving Tito's other great objective of peaceful co-existence between Socialist and capitalist states. In 1969 Richard Nixon became president of the United States. Nixon had made his reputation as a young senator by his vicious attacks on Communists; but as president he embarked on a policy of rapprochement with both the Soviet Union and Communist China. He visited Mao Tse-tung and Brezhnev, and received Brezhnev in Washington. He also visited Tito in Belgrade in September 1970. He tried for three years to win the war in Vietnam, but in 1972 agreed to withdraw United States' troops. After this the Vietcong overran the South without much difficulty, and by 1975 the whole of Vietnam was a Communist state.

Nasser died in 1970, but Tito continued his policy of support for Egypt. In 1973 another war broke out between Israel and the neighbouring Arab states. This time Israel only just won. During the war, Tito again supported Egypt and the Arab states, and granted landing rights in Yugoslavia to Soviet planes which flew in military supplies to Egypt and Syria.[19] After a few weeks of international tension, the détente in the Cold War continued.

Tito pursued his policy of friendship with both the Soviet Union and the United States and their allies. After Mao Tse-tung's death in 1976 he also became friendly with Communist China. He continued his foreign travels to every part of the world, and received heads of state and other distinguished visitors in Belgrade and at

Brioni. In February 1970 the Queen of England's sister, Princess Margaret, who had so charmed him when he met her in London in 1953, visited him at Brioni with her husband the Earl of Snowdon; and in October 1972 Queen Elizabeth II and the Duke of Edinburgh came to Belgrade. His closest links were with the statesmen of the Non-aligned countries. The conference of the Non-aligned states in Belgrade in 1961 was followed by conferences in Cairo in 1964, in Lusaka in 1970, in Algiers in 1973, in Colombo in 1976 and in Havana in 1979. Twenty-five Non-aligned States sent delegates to Belgrade, but eighteen years later in Havana the number of states had risen to ninety-two.[20]

At all these conferences, Tito called for international détente, an end to the Cold War, the banning and destruction of nuclear weapons, an end to colonialism and racism, and economic aid to the developing countries of the Third World. Above all he wished to prevent war, especially nuclear war. 'I have always been against war,' he said in an interview in Colombo in 1976, 'and for a peaceful settlement of all problems . . . Just as I have supported, as a Communist, what I have been struggling for all my life, so here too I have been determined that mankind should reorganize itself in a different way.'[21]

He was an inspiration to the leaders of the national liberation movements in Africa. In the last year of Tito's life, Robert Mugabe came to power in Zimbabwe after many years of guerrilla warfare against Ian Smith's government of the white settlers. 'It was from Tito', said Mugabe, 'that I drew inspiration while searching for the best road to take and when making crucial decisions during our liberation struggle. I often thought, what would Tito do at that moment?'[22] And Tito, on his side, thought that Europe should turn to Africa and the underdeveloped world for inspiration.

On 31 July 1975 Tito addressed the conference of European powers in Helsinki when East and West seemed closer together than they had been for many years, with even Brezhnev's Soviet Union promising to guarantee some basic civil rights to its citizens. 'It was in Europe', said Tito, 'that this colonialism was born which still today has not been completely eradicated. It was unfortunately here that Fascism, too, first saw the light – Fascism, that most evil ideology that the world has ever known. It was in Europe that two catastrophic world wars began, and Europe was the first to suffer the harmful effects of the Cold War.' Today it was in Vietnam,

Cambodia and Africa that men were making the greatest sacrifices to win their national freedom. On the thirtieth anniversary of the defeat of Fascism, its horrors were still remembered, especially by those who had experienced 'this horrible Calvary'. The crimes of the past should be forgiven, but never forgotten.[23]

CHAPTER 28

❖

Curbing the Croats

A T home, the nationalists continued to make trouble. In 1969, after long debates in the Federal National Assembly, the government decided, in order to save money, not to proceed with the plan to build a motorway in Slovenia from Ljubljana to Nova Gorica. The Communist prime minister of Slovenia protested, and was supported by thousands of demonstrators who paraded in the streets of Ljubljana denouncing the central government's decision.[1] The people in the north continued to resent the spending of the Slovenian and Croatian taxpayer's money in projects to modernize and develop the south. The Croatian economist, Šime Djodan, said in February 1971 that in the Austro-Hungarian Empire fifty-five per cent of the Croats' income was spent outside Croatia, under King Alexander and Prince Paul forty-six per cent, but that now under Tito it was sixty-three per cent. 'Thus for the Croats the Socialist Federal Republic of Yugoslavia is a greater exploiter, and therefore less acceptable, than Austria-Hungary or the old Yugoslavia.'[2]

To add to Tito's difficulties, his health was causing problems. He was overweight, and had an occasional slight heart attack. His liver was affected, and his doctors had ordered him not to eat rich and fatty foods; but he sometimes disregarded these orders. He suffered from sciatica, and walked with the help of a black walking stick. He also seemed to be going blind. His doctors told him that he was suffering from a disease of the eyes which was caused by his excessive smoking, with his 120 cigarettes a day. They told him that he must stop smoking at once. He reluctantly complied, and became bad-tempered and a little absentminded. It seemed to affect his powers of concentration. It was not very noticeable, but his son Miša was conscious of it, and wondered if the Old Man was beginning to lose his mental faculties at the age of seventy-seven. But the mental deterioration did not develop. After giving up smoking completely for more than a year, Tito began to smoke occasional cigars, and this made him happier without causing any further deterioration of his eyesight. His lack of concentration disappeared, and he was as mentally alert as he had ever been.[3]

He needed all his capacities to deal with the situation which developed in Croatia in 1971. Again the trouble came chiefly from the intellectuals and the students; they demanded more intellectual and political freedom. Tito's Yugoslavia had never been as free as in the period since the fall of Ranković in 1966. Censorship was considerably relaxed. Foreign books which had previously been banned, or at least not translated into Serbo-Croat, could now be published. George Orwell's *Animal Farm* and *1984* were translated and widely read by the intellectuals. But a little freedom whetted their appetite for more, and by 1971 the students at both Zagreb and Belgrade universities were taking part in demonstrations for a better and freer country.

In Croatia the liberal movement coincided with a revival of Croatian nationalism. A few of the nationalists were Ustashas who wistfully looked back to the days of Pavelić's Independent State of Croatia; but most of them were too young to remember the Ustashas and the horrors of the Second World War, and could dream of an independent Croatia which was not associated in their minds with the Ustashas. They were inspired, not by Pavelić, but more by Jelačić, the hero (or to Marx and Engels the villain) of 1849. General Franjo Tudjman, who had fought under Tito with the Partisans, supported the nationalist movement.

The alliance of liberals and Croatian nationalists was supported by the Croatian Communist party, not merely by a handful of dissidents and demonstrating students but by the party leadership, who rebelled against the domination of Tito and Belgrade, just as Tito had rebelled against Stalin and Moscow, and Dubček against Brezhnev and Moscow. Tito was in two minds as to how to deal with the situation. He did not wish the people to think of him as a Stalin or a Brezhnev suppressing a move towards an independent national Communism, or as an agent, like King Alexander, of the Pan-Serbian hegemony which he and the Communist party of Yugoslavia had always denounced. But too much freedom could be dangerous; and a revival of Croatian nationalism and a rejection of the Yugoslav Idea could be very dangerous. Would the movement in Croatia be transformed into a 'counter-revolution' as had happened in Hungary in 1956, or was it a 'progressive revolution' like the Prague Spring of 1968? Tito was very reluctant to label the movement in Croatia as counter-revolutionary and to clamp down on it, and he tolerated it for more than a year.

The Federal Constitution of 1963 had gone a long way towards granting autonomy to the national republics; but in 1970 Tito, now aged seventy-eight, told his constitutional experts to draft a new federal constitution which would grant even more autonomy to the republics and would establish a stable Yugoslavia after his death. A committee was set up under the chairmanship of Kardelj, who was chiefly responsible for drafting the new constitution; Tito himself only occasionally intervened in the committee's discussions.[4] The committee recommended that Tito should remain president for life, but that after his death the president of Yugoslavia would be elected for one year from each of the national republics in rotation. He would be advised by a federal presidential council consisting of three representatives from each republic and two from each of the autonomous regions of Vojvodina and Kosovo. In the Federal Assembly each republic would have a veto on all proposed legislation. The residuary clause, which always plays so important a part in every federal constitution, provided that all matters not expressly stated in the constitution to be reserved for the federal government should be dealt with by the national republics. National defence and the call-up for the army and the militia was almost the only matter which was placed exclusively under the federal government. Each republic would have the right to secede from the Yugoslav confederation.[5]

Tito approved the recommendations. He showed the draft of the new constitution to Fitzroy Maclean. 'Do you think it will work?' asked Tito. 'I hope so,' said Maclean. 'So do I,' said Tito.[*]

Tito was reminded that there was still an Ustasha threat when aged Ustashas, including some concentration camp guards in Jasenovac

---

[*] This is the version of his conversation with Tito which Sir Fitzroy Maclean told to me in 1990. He gave a slightly different account in his book *Josip Broz Tito*, p. 108. which he published in 1980 soon after Tito's death. There he wrote that Tito said to him: 'Do you think it will work?', that he replied 'I don't see why not,' and that Tito 'cheerfully' said, 'Nor do I.' The later version, though spoken with the hindsight of 1990, is very plausible.

and other war criminals from South America, attended an Ustasha rally in Munich in 1971 to commemorate the thirtieth anniversary of the proclamation of Pavelić's Ustasha state. Worse, two young men who had not yet been born in 1941, assassinated the Yugoslav ambassador in Stockholm. At their trial they proudly claimed to be Ustashas and to have killed the ambassador because he was the representative of a Communist government which was oppressing the people of Croatia.[6]

In April 1971 the students of Zagreb University made a little revolution in the university. They met and announced that they had deposed the rector and appointed one of the student leaders to be rector in his place. This caused great excitement throughout Yugoslavia. The Croatian Communist prime minister, Savka Dabčević-Kučar, was a forceful young woman, and she sympathized with the nationalist cause. So did the party leaders Pero Pirker and Tripalo, who had investigated the charges against Ranković. They were on the side of the students and took no action against them.

On 15 April Tito, in a speech at Priština, gave a warning about the gravity of the situation. 'Behaviour in the League of Communists is not good ... You know that I have been for a long time at the head of the Communist Party and the League of Communists of Yugoslavia. But I think that we have never had such a situation as we have today.'[7]

On 15 June 1971 a meeting of the Executive Bureau of the Presidency of the CPY was held in Belgrade, and the Croatian representatives, including Tripalo, attended it. Tito had his private room in the building, but he hardly ever went there. On this occasion he did go there, and he asked Tripalo to come to his room. He appealed to Tripalo to help him deal with the problems in Croatia, and told him that if Tripalo agreed to help him he would advance him higher than he could imagine. Tripalo said that he could not abandon the principles which had led him to become a Communist and that he could not abandon his country. Tito said that the problem in Croatia was that they had a Serb minority in Lika and other parts of the country who could not be ignored. Tripalo said that the problem to be dealt with in Croatia was not the Serbs in Croatia but the Croats in Croatia.[8] It was a discouraging conversation for Tito.

Brezhnev stepped in. After his invasion of Czechoslovakia in 1968 he had put forward a policy which became known as the 'Brezhnev doctrine'; the Soviet Union would intervene by force to suppress any counter-revolution in the Communist countries to prevent them from going over to the West. He knew how Tito had condemned his 'fraternal assistance' to Czechoslovakia in August 1968; so he may well have been speaking maliciously when he told Tito that if the situation in Croatia got out of hand, he would be willing to send the Soviet Army to give Tito fraternal assistance in suppressing the disturbances.[9] Tito did not welcome this offer of assistance, but he managed to turn Brezhnev's statement to his own advantage.

On 4 and 5 July Tito attended a meeting of the Croatian Communist party at Brežice, some twenty miles west of Zagreb. The proceedings were kept secret at the time, but Tito's speech was published in May 1972. Today it reads like a prophecy. 'Under the cover of "national interest" all Hell is assembling ... It may go as far as counter-revolution ... In some villages the Serbs, out of fear, are drilling and arming themselves ... Do we want to have 1941 again?' He then told the audience about Brezhnev's offer of 'fraternal assistance' to suppress the disturbances in Croatia. 'Do you realize that if disorders take place, others will at once be there? ... I would prefer to restore order with our own army than allow others to do it. We have lost prestige abroad and it will be hard to retrieve it. They are speculating that "when Tito goes, the whole thing will collapse", and some are seriously waiting for that ... The Great Powers will use any devil who will work for them, even if he is a Communist.'[10]

He could use Brezhnev's kind offer of help to warn the Yugoslav people that if they allowed their differences to go to the point of civil war, a Great Power was standing in the wings ready to intervene. But when Tito's worst fears had been realized, the Soviet Union no longer existed, and the threat of foreign intervention came from a different quarter.

The meeting adjourned to enable the delegates to attend a lavish lunch. After the lunch Tito came up between Tripalo and Savka Dabčević-Kučar and put an arm around each of them. 'You two are applauded more than I am in Croatia these days', he said genially.[11] They would have preferred not to have received the compliment.

In September Tito came on an official visit to Zagreb. He was welcomed at the airport by the Croatian party leaders and a military band, which played the unofficial Yugoslav national anthem, the song of the Slavs, 'Hej Slaveni'. When it ended, Tito began to move off, but the band then played the Croatian national song 'Lijepa naša domovina' which dated from Jelačić's time; very few Croats realized that the words had been written by a poet who was Eastern Orthodox by religion and closely linked to the royal Obrenović family of Serbia. Tito was surprised, but stood to attention during the playing of the anthem. When it was over, General Ljubičić, the minister of defence, who had come with Tito from Belgrade and who was a Serb, told the military band that they must not play the Croatian anthem again.

Tito and his party were driven from the airport to the centre of Zagreb. When they reached the Square of the Republic (today Jelačić Square) the crowds were so thick that it was almost impossible for the cars to pass through, and Tripalo, who had come with Tito from the airport, suggested that they had better get out and walk. Tito agreed, and the party walked slowly along Ilica Street from the Square of the Republic to Britannia Square. Tito was very pensive as he looked at the crowds in the streets and at the windows of the houses along the route.[12]

General Ljubičić and the Serbs in the government in Belgrade and in the army urged him to take firmer action against the Croatian nationalist movement. They were supported by Bakarić's group in the Croatian Communist leadership. But Tito was determined to win over Tripalo and Savka and the Croatian Communist leaders who were flirting with nationalism and to avoid a confrontation and the use of force. Before leaving Zagreb he issued a statement that he was satisfied with the situation in Croatia and realized that the fears of a dangerous growth of nationalism had been much exaggerated.

He returned to Belgrade to welcome Brezhnev, who came on a state visit. Brezhnev, too, urged Tito to take a firm line in Croatia. But in October Tito went off to Teheran to attend the celebration of four thousand years of the Iranian monarchy. Ljubičić and Bakarić began to wonder if he was losing his grip.

Tito went on from Teheran to India, Cairo and Washington, where he discussed the international situation with Nixon before visiting Canada and London. After lunching with the Queen at Buckingham Palace he returned to Belgrade[13] to find that the situation in Croatia had deteriorated. While he was in Canada, Savka had made a speech on 5 November at the meeting of the Central Committee of the Croatian Communist party. She applauded the 'mass movement' in Croatia, and criticized those who rejected 'mass support' on the grounds of 'some abstract revolutionary purity'; that was 'sectarianism and fear of the mobilization of the masses'. But 'we, as a League of Communists' were not 'a closed sect who think that society and the working people exist for us and not we for them.'[14]

The government in Belgrade became seriously alarmed, and again urged Tito to take drastic action; but Tito went off to Bucharest to visit Ceauşescu. A few hours before he left, on 22 November, the Croatian Student Federation issued a statement protesting against a law which compelled Croatian workers returning from abroad to hand over the foreign currency that they had earned to the federal government in Belgrade and not to the Croatian authorities in Zagreb. The Student Federation called for a general strike of students and a mass occupation of Zagreb University and other schools and colleges throughout Croatia.[15] But this did not stop Tito from leaving for Bucharest.

When Tito returned from Bucharest he was confronted with insistent demands from General Ljubičić for action against the Croatian nationalists. As Tito was still reluctant, Ljubičić produced his trump card: he told Tito that the organization of the Old Partisan Fighters, which included Croats as well as Serbs and men and women from all the other republics, were very distressed at Tito's failure to act.[16] Tito then decided that he had no choice but to suppress the Croatian movement. He called a meeting of the Party Presidium of the League of Communists to be held on 2 December at Karadjordjevo, a former hunting lodge of the royal family in Serbia a few miles north of Belgrade, and invited the Croatian members of the Party Presidium and fourteen other Croatian Communist leaders to meet him there the day before the meeting began. In Croatia the people resented the fact that their leaders had been ordered to attend a meeting in Serbia, and thought that the date, the anniversary of the foundation of King Alexander's kingdom of Yugoslavia on 1 December 1918, had been deliberately chosen to affront their feelings as Croats. Before the Croatian Communist leaders left Zagreb, Savka Dabčević-Kučar spoke on television on 29 November and called on the students to end the strike;[17] but this came too late to change Tito's decision.

Tito's meeting with the nineteen members of the Croatian delegation opened at Karadjordjevo at one p.m. on 1 December.[18] Tito tried to persuade them to repudiate the nationalist movement in Croatia, which was developing into a counter-revolution. He did not confront them with a declaration which they were required to sign, as Dubček and his colleagues had been compelled to do by the Soviet Politburo in the Kremlin in August 1968; nor were they asked to vote for any specific resolution, though this had been the regular practice in the Communist Party of the Soviet Union. He merely wanted them to repudiate Croatian nationalism in general terms. Eight of them, including Bakarić and Josip Vrhovec, agreed to do so; the other eleven, led by Tripalo, Savka and Pirker refused.

The discussion continued for sixteen hours, and did not end till five o'clock next morning. During one of the short intervals in the discussion, Tito took Savka and Pirker aside. He said that he realized that they were good and loyal comrades who had been led astray by Tripalo. He urged them to repudiate Tripalo and nationalism; but they refused to abandon their colleague and the mass movement.

The exhausted Croats had six hours in which to get some sleep before Tripalo, Savka and three others had to attend the meeting of the Party Presidium which began at eleven a.m. on 2 December. It was usual for important official meetings to be recorded on video, and the cameras were in place when Tito opened the proceedings. He said that the Croatian Communist leadership had been 'rather liberal' when confronted with what he now openly called 'a counter-revolution'. He admitted that some of the Croatian complaints about the economic system might be justified, but that did not justify their unconstitutional action. He traced the trouble to the lack of 'Marxist education' in the schools and universities and to the fact that the professors and teachers had tolerated 'anti-Marxist' and 'pro-Western' ideas. He called on the leaders of the Croatian Communist party to mend their ways and remedy the situation immediately.[19]

Tito's speech was followed by a general discussion in which Tripalo and Savka denied that the student and national movement in Croatia was counter-revolutionary, and claimed that it was a mass movement of the Croatian people and that the Communists must place themselves at the head of it. After some hours' discussion the meeting was adjourned till the evening. During the afternoon it was announced that Tito would broadcast to the nation on television at five p.m. When Tripalo and Savka turned on their television sets at five o'clock they realized that Tito's broadcast was a recording of his speech that morning in the Party Presidium which had been filmed on video. Their own speeches at the meeting had also been recorded, but were not broadcast. They felt that they had been tricked, because they had not been warned that Tito's speech would be shown on television. When the meeting of the Party Presidium resumed in the evening, Tripalo and Savka said that in view of Tito's television broadcast there was no point in continuing the argument, as the issue had obviously been settled, and they left at once for Zagreb.[20]

Tito made a final attempt to divide his leading opponents. During the meeting at Karadjordjevo he had said to Pirker and Savka that he considered them to be good comrades who had been misled by Tripalo; but a week later, on 8 December, he telephoned Pirker and Savka and asked them to resign from the Central Committee of the Croatian Communist party and from the Croatian government. He also telephoned Tripalo and said that there was no reason why he should resign with his two colleagues and that he hoped that Tripalo would not resign but would continue to serve in the government and on the Executive Committee of the League of Communists.[21] Early in the morning of 12 December the student leaders in Zagreb were arrested, and Savka, Pirker and Tripalo all resigned.

The students called a protest demonstration in Zagreb which was broken up by the police, who arrested hundreds of demonstrators. Most of them were taken to a police station, beaten, and then released. A few were held in prison for several months, and in January 1972 the most prominent leaders and some writers who had supported Croatian nationalism and the Matica Hrvatska were sentenced to five years' imprisonment.[22] The Matica Hrvatska was suppressed.

Tripalo, Savka and Pirker were not arrested, though they were followed everywhere by UDBA men. When they protested, UDBA said that they were trailing them for their own protection.[23] Tudjman was arrested. Some years before, Tito had prevented Ranković from arresting him for nationalist counter-revolutionary activities, and Tito now intervened again to help him. Krleža went to see Tito and made a plea for Tudjman, who was released soon afterwards.[24]

Bakarić, Vrhovec and the new leadership in Croatia were unhappy about their position. They did not wish to be considered enemies of the Croatian people and of their legitimate aspirations; but they were convinced that Tripalo and Savka had been playing with fire by encouraging the nationalist movement, and they wished to help Tito defeat chauvinism and the counter-revolution in Croatia and preserve the Yugoslav Idea. They were very distressed at the police violence against the student demonstrators, and issued instructions that it must not be repeated;[25] but Tito knew that violence is inevitable when student demonstrators and police come into conflict. He had delayed taking action against the Croatian nationalists for a long time, but once he decided to act he did not stop at half-measures and allowed the police their head. During the remaining years of Tito's life UDBA acted nearly as ruthlessly as they had done under Ranković, though Goli Otok was now run on comparatively humane lines as a prison for non-political criminals.

The liberal elements had gained control of the Serbian Communist party. They sympathized with the Croatian Communists whom Tito was suppressing, and although anti-Croat feeling in Serbia made it politically impossible for the Serbian liberals to coordinate their opposition with the Croatian Communist resistance, at least they did not take advantage of the troubles in Croatia to stir up anti-Croat feeling in the Serbian Communist party; and they made their protest against the repression in Croatia in January 1972. Later that year, Tito ordered a purge of the Serbian Communist party. It was carried out much more quietly than in Croatia, but the liberals were ousted from office in the party leadership.[26]

Tito also had to deal with the problem of Kosovo. Ranković had received the blame, perhaps unfairly, for the severe repression by the government of the independence movement of the Albanians in Kosovo, and after his fall Tito pursued a conciliatory policy towards them. Both in Kosovo and Bosnia he encouraged the Muslims.[27] He created a new nationality of Muslims, to rank beside Croats, Serbs, Slovenes, Montenegrins and Macedonians, although hitherto the word 'Muslim' indicated only a religion, not a nationality.

Since the recent events in Bosnia, Tito has sometimes been criticized for creating a Muslim nation. He had three reasons for doing so. It fitted in with his policy of checks and balances to strengthen the Muslims against the stronger power of the Serbs; it went well with his foreign policy of alliance with the Non-aligned Muslim countries of the Middle East and North Africa; and he hoped he could weaken Muslim fundamentalism if it became accepted that it was possible for a Muslim not to be a fundamentalist or indeed any kind of Muslim in religion, but a Communist atheist by doctrine and a Muslim by nationality. He knew that he would get no support from Muslim fundamentalism, even before the Ayatollah Khomeini denounced him as an atheist persecutor of Islam.[28]

The draft constitution was duly adopted in 1974. It gave almost complete autonomy to the national republics, including the right to secede from the Yugoslav Federation which they had always had under Tito. Tripalo and Savka Dabčević-Kučar thought that Tito had stolen and implemented their programme after he had suppressed them; but behind the façade of the constitution the centre of political power remained in the hands of the central government in Belgrade, and especially of UDBA.

Intellectuals were frustrated, but not regimented in a Stalinist way. When the film director Makavejev made an ironic film which treated with scant respect a character named Vladimir Ilyich, Brezhnev and the Russians were annoyed at this affront to Lenin. The film was praised at the Cannes Film Festival in 1971. Tito allowed it to be entered for the Pula Film Festival, but arranged for UDBA to put all sorts of obstructions in the way to prevent the film being shown in Yugoslavia, though Tito himself saw the film privately and apparently enjoyed it.[29]

Nor were the activities of UDBA impeded by the international Declaration of Human Rights signed by nearly every country in the world, including Yugoslavia and the Soviet Union, at the international conference in Helsinki in 1975 where Tito played such a prominent part. Whatever Tito may have done in Helsinki, the liberals and intellectuals in Yugoslavia thought sadly about their lost freedoms and looked back nostalgically at the five liberal years from 1966 to 1971 – the only five years during Tito's thirty-five years in power when writers in Yugoslavia were relatively free.

At least UDBA now left Djilas in peace, for they were too busy searching for Croatian nationalists. The authorities no longer arrested and persecuted him when he published his books in the United States, but merely banned their importation into Yugoslavia. They took no further action when Djilas in 1977 published his book *Wartime* in the United States and Britain. It contained the fullest account which had so far been given of the secret negotiations which he, Koča Popović and Velebit had conducted with the Germans in March 1943. Djilas wrote in the book that he would not have revealed these official secrets if they had not already been published by foreign writers abroad. He took a risk here, for when he was sentenced to imprisonment in 1962 for publishing *Conversations with Stalin* in the United States, the court had ruled that it was no defence to a prosecution for revealing official secrets to show that the secrets had already been disclosed by others.

The story of the 'March negotiations' was arousing a good deal of interest among Yugoslavs from whom it had been kept for so long as a closely guarded secret. Not a word had been written or spoken about the negotiations in any of the official Yugoslav histories of the

Partisans' operations during the Second World War, or in the speeches made on all the anniversary celebrations of the Fourth Offensive on the Neretva. Dedijer had recorded in his wartime diary that Djilas had told him that he had been in Zagreb in March 1943, but this passage had been deleted when the diary was published in Belgrade in 1945.

The Soviet spies and the agents of the Cominform countries did not find out about the March negotiations. They had discovered that Tito had prevented the British Floydforce from cutting off the German retreat from Greece in November 1944, and used this in their propaganda after the Rajk and Kostov trials in 1949;[30] but though they talked vaguely about the Fascist Tito having secretly plotted with the Germans during the Second World War, they said nothing about the March negotiations till it was revealed by the former German intelligence officer, Walter Hoettl, in his book *The Secret Front* in 1950.[31] As Hoettl's book included some rather improbable revelations about German wartime espionage, and was written in a somewhat sensational style, his story about the March negotiations was not widely believed until Walter Roberts, the United States cultural attaché in Belgrade, published in the United States in 1973 his scholarly history of the Second World War in Yugoslavia.[32] Roberts had discovered the official German account of the talks among the captured German documents. His book was not published in Yugoslavia.

Some years after the publication of Hoettl's book in 1950, Velebit, who was then the ambassador in London, was approached by his friend, the Polish Marxist writer Isaac Deutscher, who suggested to Velebit that it would be in the interests of Yugoslavia, as well as of historians, if the Yugoslav government published the truth about the March negotiations.[33] When Velebit returned to Belgrade he suggested this to Tito, who agreed with him; but after a year nothing had been published. Velebit then again raised the matter with Tito, and again Tito agreed that the story should be officially published in Yugoslavia; but still nothing happened.

In 1968, during the liberal period in Yugoslavia, the editor of the Belgrade journal *Politika* informed Velebit that they wished to publish an account of the March negotiations and asked Velebit to write it. Velebit did so, and sent his typescript to *Politika*, but they did not publish it. In October of the same year, 1968, Tito granted an interview to the British author, Phyllis Auty, who was writing his biography. When she asked him about the March negotiations he told her that they had dealt with the exchange of prisoners and nothing else.[34]

In 1972 a new edition of Dedijer's wartime diary was published in Yugoslavia. For the first time it contained the reference to Djilas's visit to Zagreb in March 1943; but this remained the only mention of the March negotiations to be published in Yugoslavia until Tito spoke in 1978 at the thirty-fifth anniversary celebrations of the Battle of the Neretva. Tito told his audience that in the very difficult situation which the Partisans faced during the Fourth Offensive, he sent his envoys to negotiate with the Germans about an exchange of prisoners and other matters, but that the envoys exceeded their instructions when they offered to make a truce with the Germans. Velebit was angry, and so was Koča Popović, because they remembered that they had reported to Tito and had acted on his express instructions at every stage of the negotiations.[35]

Although UDBA left Djilas alone, they were still interested in Yugoslavs who had supported the Cominform. Tito would not forgive the Cominform supporters. He had consistently refused Khrushchev's requests to allow those who had fled to the Soviet Union to return to Yugoslavia[36]; and Cominformists in Yugoslavia who had been released from Goli Otok were still kept under observation by the UDBA nearly thirty years later.[37] Like every other dictator throughout history, Tito was strangely frightened of his dissenters who had escaped abroad, even if their only activity there was to denounce him in obscure little newspapers which circulated among a few hundred other exiles.

Vlado Dapčević* had escaped to the Soviet Union in 1955 after his release from prison; but in 1968 he left the Soviet Union and went to Brussels, where he wrote against Tito in obscure newspapers. In 1975 the Yugoslav and Romanian authorities agreed that Ceauşescu's secret police should lure Dapčević to Romania and hand him over to UDBA. According to Ion Pacepa, the head of the Romanian secret police who defected to the United States in 1978, the matter was discussed and arranged between Tito and Ceauşescu over drinks when Ceauşescu visited Tito at Brioni.[38] The stories of defecting secret police agents have to be received with a certain amount of scepticism. If Pacepa's story is true, it is surprising; arrangements for

* See supra, Chapter 22, p. 294.

the kidnapping of refugees are usually made between intelligence agents at secret rendezvous, not by heads of state when they visit each other.

But Dapčević was certainly persuaded to come to Romania by the Romanian secret police. With their knowledge he was forcibly seized by UDBA in Bucharest and brought to Yugoslavia, after the UDBA agents had killed two of his friends who tried to prevent them from seizing him. When he was put on trial in Belgrade the story of the kidnapping was suppressed, and he was accused of having illegally entered Yugoslavia in order to engage in subversive opposition against the regime.

But Dapčević was defended by a lawyer, Jovan Barović, who believed in the traditional western idea that a defendant was entitled to a fair trial whatever his political beliefs and that the truth should not be distorted in a court of law. Barović was a Montenegrin who had fought with Tito's Partisans in the war and was an old friend of Djilas's. In the last years of Tito's rule, Barović appeared for the defence in a number of political trials and conducted the case in the best traditions of great eighteenth-century political defence lawyers like Thomas Erskine and John Philpot Curran. He was not often able to obtain an acquittal against the determination of a prejudiced court to convict, but he frequently exposed the activities of UDBA and other authorities. He naturally made himself very unpopular with the secret police and the government; but the fact that he was able to carry out his duties as a defence lawyer shows that Tito's regime, for all its faults and the many misdeeds of UDBA, was very different from the Soviet Union under Stalin.

At Dapčević's trial Barović argued that Dapčević was not guilty of illegal entry into Yugoslavia because he had not entered the country of his own free will, but had been kidnapped in Romania by UDBA. The allegation was indignantly denied by the prosecution and was not accepted by the court, but the story was widely believed in Yugoslavia. Dapčević was sentenced to death, but the sentence was commuted to twenty years' imprisonment.[39]

In September 1975 Tito went to Zagreb to open the international trade fair, and in the evening attended a gala performance at the Opera House. That morning, about seven hours before Tito was due to arrive at the Opera House, a small bomb exploded on the other side of the park about 300 yards from the Opera House. The police said that it was a plot to assassinate Tito, although the bomb was much too small to do any damage at the Opera House even if it had not exploded seven hours before Tito arrived.

After two months of inquiries, the police arrested five young Croats and charged them with attempting to assassinate Tito. One of the five had served a prison sentence after the disturbances of 1971 for nationalist and counter-revolutionary activities; the other four claimed that they had no connection with any political organization. They were tortured by the police in order to induce them to confess, and were held in prison for three years before being brought to trial in Zagreb in November 1978.

Barović appeared for the defence. Using the knowledge that he had acquired during his service with the Partisans in the war and his acquaintance with army officers, he called witnesses who proved that the bomb which was produced in evidence by the prosecution could not have exploded. He told the prisoners to remove their shirts in court in order to show the scars of the tortures that they had suffered in prison, and argued that they had been framed.

The trial continued for several weeks, and was reported in the Yugoslav and foreign press. The court found the defendants not guilty of the attempt to assassinate Tito, but guilty of membership of a counter-revolutionary organization, for which one of them was sentenced to nine years' imprisonment and the others to shorter terms. It was said that Tito was very angry about the way in which UDBA had mishandled the case.

Two months later, on 6 February 1979, Barović was driving himself in his car from his home in Belgrade to a nearby town where he was to appear for one of the parties in an unimportant non-political case. He was driving along a two-way road at a steady forty miles per hour when his car suddenly spun round on to the other side of the road right into the path of an oncoming lorry. Barović's car was crushed by the lorry and he was killed instantly. The authorities issued a statement that he had suffered a sudden heart attack, but the medical evidence at the inquest disproved this. His family and friends and many members of the public were convinced that he had been murdered by UDBA, who had not forgiven him for having exposed them at the Zagreb trial.

It is difficult to explain why a car which was being driven at forty miles per hour by a careful driver like Barović should suddenly spin round in front of an oncoming lorry; but it is equally difficult to explain how UDBA could have deliberately planned his death. The lorry was not following Barović's car, but was coming in the opposite direction, and no one could have arranged for Barović to lose control of his car and for it to spin round just at the moment when the lorry was coming on. Barović's family do not believe that the lorry-driver was an UDBA agent or that he deliberately killed Barović. If UDBA murdered Barović, they could only have done so by tampering with the steering of his car in the hope that it would get out of control at a moment when it would involve Barović in an accident, as in fact occurred. Whatever the truth, many people in Yugoslavia believed that Tito's secret police would have been perfectly capable of murdering a defence lawyer who had exposed their methods in court.[40]

Tito no longer had the assistance of the old guard who had been his closest collaborators in the early days. Pijade and Kidrič had died before 1960. Djilas and Ranković had been expelled from the party and were living in retirement. Only Kardelj still remained as active as ever, writing his memoirs and other books in which he developed new theories about the Yugoslav road to Socialism, and explaining current developments in Marxist terms, as well as continuing to play his part in governing the country; but in February 1979 Kardelj died of cancer at the age of sixty-nine.

So Tito had to find new and younger men, and after 1974 he relied chiefly on General Ljubičić and Stane Dolanc. Ljubičić was a Serb, and though Dolanc himself was a Slovene, both he and Ljubičić were generally considered by every nation, except the Serbs, to be instruments of the Serbian domination of Yugoslavia. In all the other republics the people resented the influence of the Serbian officials in Ljubičić and Dolanc's administration, though the Serbs complained that there was a majority of Croats and Slovenes on every governmental committee. Dolanc rose very rapidly in the party and government. In 1975 he was appointed to the key position of secretary to the party Presidium, and though the appointment was originally only for one year, his term was afterwards extended to four years.

Tito had always tended to leave the day-to-day administration to subordinates, while he dealt only with important policy decisions in the White Palace in Belgrade or on Brioni. But it had always been possible for ministers, and for anyone else with a good reason, to see him and appeal to him about important issues. Increasingly now, people who asked for an audience with Tito were told that they could not see him and that Ljubičić or Dolanc would deal with them.

Rumours began to circulate that Tito was becoming senile and that this was why Ljubičić and Dolanc were keeping him away from the public.

Some people who had known Tito slightly, when they saw him now on television attending receptions or other functions, thought that he looked and moved so differently that he must have had some kind of stroke, and that this was being concealed from the public. But any slowness of movement by Tito was in fact solely due to his sciatica. His son Miša, who could see him whenever he wished, says that these stories were quite untrue, and that Tito, as he advanced into his eighties, was in excellent shape.[41] Other rumours gave a different explanation as to why it was so difficult these days to gain access to Tito: Dolanc was using Tito's old age as an excuse to prevent anyone from seeing him so that all business had to be transacted through Dolanc and Ljubičić. This would make them alone the real rulers of the country and would ensure that no one else would be able to destroy their influence over Tito.

These allegations were exaggerated. Dolanc, like many other efficient secretaries and high executives, had a tendency to try to take everything into his own hands and run the whole show; but Tito's other ministers say that even if Dolanc had wished to control Tito, he could never have succeeded because Tito would not have permitted this. The ministers themselves had no difficulty in gaining access to Tito whenever they wished to see him, and always found that he discussed the affairs of their department with great clarity and good sense.[42]

But he spent less time dealing with state affairs, and more in hunting. He adopted a more relaxed and leisurely lifestyle. When the international writers' organization, PEN, held their congress in Yugoslavia in 1974, Tito invited the distinguished German and English writers, Heinrich Böll and V. S. Pritchett, to visit him at one of his country residences. His secretary had told them that the president would see them for half an hour; but Tito spent four hours with them. 'Like any country gentleman', wrote Pritchett, 'he was determined on taking us round his estate – not a garden path, not a wooded *allée* did we miss.' After entertaining them at an open-air supper in his woods, he made sure that they caught their plane from Belgrade by sending a police escort to clear the roads for them as his driver drove them 120 miles to the airport in fifty minutes.[43]

Miodrag Zečević was not only a distinguished lawyer who had

played an important part in drafting the Constitution of 1974; he was also an officer of the Federation of Hunters. He often hunted with Tito. Zečević and two other officers of the federation called to see Tito at his residence at 15 Užička Street in Belgrade, having been told that Tito could see them for only fifteen minutes because General Ljubičić was then due to call on Tito, and after him the Saudi Arabian ambassador. Tito talked to Zečević and his colleagues about hunting for an hour and a half while Ljubičić and the ambassador waited. Tito took them into the hunting pavilion in the garden where about 250 of his hunting trophies were on view. He took them round the pavilion, and was able to tell them when and where he had shot every one of the trophies.[44]

Perhaps it was not only his obsession with hunting, and the tendency of Dolanc and Ljubičić to handle everything themselves, which made it difficult for anyone except his family and his ministers to gain access to him. Perhaps he made this an excuse for not seeing people whom he did not wish to see. The Bosnian Muslim and veteran Communist leader, General Avdo Humo, who had been a prominent Partisan commander during the Second World War, protested against the suppression of the opposition in the Serbian Communist party in 1972, and was removed from his offices in the party and in the army. His wife Olga Humo, remembering the kindness which Tito had always shown her when she was his secretary and interpreter in Jajce, Drvar, Vis and Naples in 1943–44, wrote to him on her husband's behalf. Tito did not reply to her letter, or even send an acknowledgement.[45]

General Bulat and his wife, Milka Kufrin, had a similar experience. The force of Croatian nationalism remained very strong after the purge of 1971, even in official government circles. When Bulat, who was an old Partisan fighter, said in the Croatian parliament in 1972 that the government must safeguard not only the rights of the Croats in Croatia but also those of the Serbian minority in the Lika enclave, he was violently denounced by other deputies in the parliament, who claimed that, being a Serb, he had no right to take any part in politics in Croatia. But in the army, which was increasingly coming under Serbian control, Bulat was regarded with suspicion as being pro-Croatian, because he lived in Zagreb and Milka Kufrin was a Croat. Bulat wrote to Tito and asked for his help. He received a reply from the Ministry of Defence stating that his letter would be placed before the commander-in-chief (Tito), but he heard nothing more.

Milka Kufrin was a friend of Dara Janeković, a journalist who worked for the Zagreb chain of newspapers, *Vjesnik*. Tito agreed to give an interview for publication in *Vjesnik*, and in February 1973 the editor sent Dara to interview him in Brioni. She took the opportunity to tell him that Milka Kufrin was worried about her husband's position in Croatia and in the army, and that Bulat had never received a reply from Tito to his letter. Tito told Dara that he had not been shown the letter, and asked her to send Milka to visit him in Brioni. When Milka came, he promised her that he would allow no one to harm Bulat, and would protect him and Milka against both Croatian and Serbian nationalists.[46]

In 1978 Tito invited Tempo to Brioni. Tempo found him 'absentminded'. Tempo asked him: 'What's wrong with Yugoslavia?' 'There is no Yugoslavia,' said Tito. 'What's wrong with the party?' asked Tempo. Tito replied: 'There is no party any more'. Tito then complained that people were saying that his son was an American spy. When Tempo told Tito that he had written to him about the ills of the country and the party, Tito said that he had never received the letter.[47]

CHAPTER 29

❖

The Last Days

O N 25 May 1977 Tito's eighty-fifth birthday was celebrated throughout Yugoslavia, and the country also celebrated the fortieth anniversary of his appointment as general secretary of the Communist party of Yugoslavia in 1937. Tito attended many public functions and his wife Jovanka was always with him. But later in the year, when he went on a state visit to Moscow, North Korea and China, Jovanka did not go with him; nor did she go with him to the United States when he visited President Carter in 1978. By this time the rumours were spreading, and soon everyone knew that Tito and Jovanka had separated and were living apart. They never met.

No official explanation was ever given, and all the rumours were contradictory. One story was that Tito at eighty-five had acquired a new young mistress. Another was that Jovanka was having an affair with General Jovanić, who was nearly thirty years younger than Tito and only a few years older than Jovanka. Others thought that there were political reasons for the separation, but here too there were three entirely different stories. One was that Tito suddenly discovered in 1977 that Jovanka had for many years been an agent of the KGB and had been spying on him for the Russians. Another story was that, as a Serb from the Lika enclave in Croatia, she had used her influence over Tito on behalf of the Serbs, and that Tito had foiled her Serbian plot and had freed himself from her influence and sent her away. A third version was that, far from being an agent of the Serbs, she opposed the Serbian domination of the government by the Ljubičić-Dolanc group, and that it was the Serbian faction who drove her away from Tito's court.

There was no truth in any of these stories; but the truth was sad. Tito and Jovanka had been happily married for more than twenty years. She had gracefully accompanied him on his state visits all over the world and acted as his hostess to the international statesmen who came to Belgrade and Brioni, for Vlatko and Vera Velebit had found her a very eager pupil when they taught her etiquette at their embassy in Rome.[1] There had also been the happy informal occasions at Kumrovec, and at Lički Osik, when she took Tito in 1967 to her native village in Lika and they had celebrated New Year's Eve with the traditional ritual of the Serbs in Croatia.[2]

But by the early 1970s, when Jovanka was nearly fifty, she began to show other aspects of her character. She incurred lavish expenditure in connection with the household, all of which was paid for by the state, ordering furniture, decorations and clothes one day, and then suddenly changing her mind and ordering something else instead.[3] She combined this lavish expenditure with stinginess. One evening she sent a woman secretary to visit the well-known painter Milan Jovanović. When she and Tito had visited the King and Queen of Sweden, she had noticed how the Queen's silver spoons contained the intertwined initials of the royal couple; and she wished Jovanović to design similar spoons with her and Tito's initials intertwined. Jovanović asked to see her to discuss the design, but the secretary said that this was impossible.

Jovanović was busily engaged in work for another patron, but the secretary said that Jovanka insisted that Jovanović drop this work and design her spoons within a few days. He tried to discuss with the secretary the question of his fee, but the secretary told him not to worry about this, as Jovanka would reward him generously. He finished the work on time, but it was many months before he was paid his fee. When it was eventually paid, he received a far lower sum that he expected; it was below the accepted economic payment for this kind of work.[4]

She became involved in endless quarrels with the staff. They were all devoted to Tito. 'A good employer?' says his secretary Ranko Bugarčić. 'He was the best employer anyone could have,' always asking after the health of the servants and ensuring that they were contented.[5] But the staff had a very different opinion about Jovanka. She often sacked one of them for some trivial offence. One day she sacked all the staff, and Tito had to put the matter right. Her vagaries put Tito under considerable strain.[6]

She was also at loggerheads with Tito's ministers, General Ljubičić and Dolanc. She became convinced that they were trying to murder

Tito. She trusted only General Jovanić, who had been her commanding officer in the Partisans during the war. She gazed adoringly up at him when they danced together,[7] and behaved in such a way that the rumour spread, quite wrongly, that they were lovers. Tito sent a friend to see her and to calm her down. The friend reported to Tito that she was seriously disturbed, and Tito agreed.[8]

A member of Tito's household has disclosed details of several matrimonial quarrels between Tito and Jovanka in the two years before their separation. These stories have been published, but their authenticity has been questioned by some of Jovanka's friends. According to these stories, by 1975 the situation had reached such a pitch that the family doctor recommended that she should see a psychiatrist. When Tito told her, she protested indignantly and accused Tito of having an affair with one of the women on his staff. There was a violent altercation, during which Tito's nerves snapped. He struck the table with his stick and damaged the tip of the stick, before collapsing in exhaustion and requiring medical attention.[9] But Tito defended Jovanka from all the criticisms of his staff. He apologized to them for her conduct, and asked them to remember that she was upset because he was so much older than she was, and because she had been unable to have children.[10]

After this incident there were some months of peace and quiet. In August 1976 they went to Colombo for the conference of Non-Aligned States. They stayed at the Intercontinental Hotel, but were not satisfied with it, for the lift was very crowded and did not always work; so they decided to move to Tito's yacht, the *Galeb*, which was lying in the harbour. Tito and some of his staff went to the *Galeb* while Jovanka stayed behind in the Intercontinental Hotel for an hour or so to supervise the move. When she came on to the *Galeb* she happened to catch sight of the woman whom she thought was Tito's mistress. She made a dreadful scene, which deeply upset Tito.[11]

They spent New Year's Eve in 1976 in Zagreb. Tito decided to make her happy by conferring on her the Order of the Yugoslav Star, with sash, for her services to the nation. It was to be presented to her, in the usual way, by the Croatian prime minister, Bakarić, and preparations were made for the ceremony to take place at seven p.m. on 31 December. At six p.m. Jovanka suddenly refused to receive the decoration as a protest against the way in which she was being treated; she was apparently indignant that it was to be presented to her by Bakarić and not by Tito himself. Tito sadly gave orders that the ceremony was to be cancelled, and tried to give her a happy New Year's Eve.[12]

All this time the difficulties with Jovanka had been successfully concealed from the public; but matters came to a head in the summer of 1977 when Tito was planning to go with Jovanka on his state visit to Moscow, Pyongyang and Peking. He was taking his foreign minister, Miloš Minić, and Dolanc in his entourage, and the woman on his staff whom Jovanka imagined was his mistress. Jovanka demanded that Dolanc and the woman should not go on the journey. Tito would not agree to this. He did not think it right that Jovanka, who held no official position in the state or the League of Communists, should try to dictate which of his ministers he took with him on a state visit. So Jovanka refused to go. Tito then decided to separate from Jovanka. On 14 June 1977 he moved out of 15 Užička Street, and took up his residence in the White Palace. Jovanka remained at Užička Street.[13]

Tito was sad, and often thought about Jovanka. One day he was walking in the garden of the White Palace with his assistant General Tihomir-Tice Stanojević. He asked Stanojević if he had seen Jovanka recently. When Stanojević said that he had, Tito picked some flowers. He handed them to Stanojević and said: 'Give these to Jovanka from me.'[14]

He had a successful visit to Moscow, Pyongyang and Peking, and then went off on another journey to France, Portugal and Algiers. After the official visit to Paris he was able to spend four days recuperating at a luxury hotel at Mont de Moussan in south-west France. His party of forty, including four ministers, the Yugoslav ambassador, his doctor, his cook and his bodyguard, took over the whole hotel, though there were only thirty-seven rooms for the forty of them. The hotel proprietor was duly impressed to see Tito eat a breakfast of cabbage soup, sausage, boiled meat and roast chicken at six a.m., an eight-course lunch at midday, a large tea of cheesecake, and a variety of thick soups for supper; but he was a little dismayed when Tito and his party left without paying the bill, though it was of course settled later.[15]

Tito was back in Belgrade in December 1977 to receive Margaret Thatcher, the leader of the Conservative Opposition in Britain,[16] and in the spring of 1978 went to the United States. He met Jimmy Carter, the fourth president of the United States with whom he established very friendly relations, and, returning to Yugoslavia by London, had dinner with the Queen at Buckingham Palace.[17]

He was still reasonably fit at eighty-six, but was not happy at the development of events. Like other great statesmen, he had become conscious of how little he could really do to control events. How could he stop the brutality of human nature, the cruelty of the brutal corporal in the barrack room in Zagreb who had reduced a young recruit to tears in 1913, of the Cossacks in Russia in 1917, of the police in King Alexander's Yugoslavia, of the party officials and the NKVD in the land of Socialism, the workers' paradise, of the Ustashas, Chetniks and Fascist Muslims in the Second World War, of his Partisans who had killed Ustashas and Chetniks without trial despite all those orders of the day that he had signed about trial before military courts, of his guards on Goli Otok of which he only pretended to be ignorant? He knew all about the brutality of UDBA, and that once he had belatedly and reluctantly agreed to let them loose on the Croatian national movement there was very little that he could do to control them.

He also knew that he could do very little to control the future. He persuaded the Federal Assembly to turn his favourite hunting ground of Belje to the north of Belgrade, which was partly in Vojvodina and partly in Croatia, into a federal park outside all the national republics. One day in 1978 he went hunting there with a shooting party which included Zečević. During the lunch interval he said to Zečević that he hoped that after he himself was dead, Zečević would do all he could to prevent the federal park from being divided up again between the republics. 'If they get half a chance, they will tear it apart after my death.' And he added: 'And they will tear apart a lot of other things too.'[18]

In August 1979 he left for the sixth conference of Non-Aligned States in Havana. He was worried about the tendency of their host, Fidel Castro, to become involved in military adventures in Angola and to draw the Non-Aligned movement into an alliance with the Soviet Union against Communist China. A clash had arisen between Communist Vietnam and Communist Cambodia after they had together defeated the United States. The Soviet Union supported Vietnam, and China supported Cambodia. The wholesale massacres perpetrated by Pol Pot's regime in Cambodia gave Vietnam an excuse to invade the country, overthrow Pol Pot, and in effect annex Cambodia; whereupon China invaded Vietnam. Tito, who had established friendly relations with Communist China after many years of hostility, wished the Non-Aligned movement to remain neutral in the dispute and to act as mediators between the two hostile Communist power blocs. On the day after he arrived in Cuba, Castro visited him in his villa on the outskirts of Havana, and Tito tried to persuade Castro to adopt a more neutral position; but there was no serious public disagreement at the conference.[19]

He returned to Belgrade, and at the beginning of December left for Karadjordjevo, where he saw in the new year. On 1 January 1980 he presided at the usual New Year lunch for the members of the Central Committee of the League of Communists,[20] and made his annual television broadcast to the nation. He seemed in excellent health and spirits; but two days later he entered the best clinic in the country in Ljubljana for a check-up on the inflammation in his left leg. He was released from the clinic after forty-eight hours, but the doctors were not happy about his condition, and decided to operate on his leg. On 12 January he presided at a meeting in the morning, and then entered the clinic, which he was never to leave during his life.

The operation was performed next day, but as it was not effective the doctors decided that it was necessary to amputate his leg to prevent the development of gangrene. The left leg was amputated on 20 January. He seemed to be recovering from the operation and on 23 January he got out of bed, and was in a cheerful mood. He was visited by his sons Žarko and Miša, and also by Jovanka, for after initial hesitation and opposition from the doctors she was allowed to come.[21]

By the middle of February he had developed trouble with his kidney, and by the end of the month he was connected every day to an artificial kidney machine, and had also developed pneumonia, internal bleeding, and trouble with his heart. By April his liver was failing; his general condition grew worse, and he was permanently in intensive care. On 3 May there was a slight improvement; but next day, at five p.m., on 4 May 1980, three days before his eighty-eighth birthday, it was announced on television that the Central Committee of the League of Communists of Yugoslavia informed the people of the death at 15.05 hours of Comrade Josip Broz Tito.*

---

* Those who are determined that there should be a mystery about Tito's death, as well as about his true identiy, have stated that Tito died on 13 February 1980 and that the news of his death was suppressed for nearly three months. This would mean that for these three months the daily bulletins on his health were a complete invention, which seems very unlikely, as there was no good reason to postpone for three months the announcement of his death. The story is denied by those who were members of his government in 1980.

CHAPTER 30

❖

Yugoslavia after Tito

T HE wars which have raged for the last three years in the former Yugoslavia are outside the scope of a biography of Tito; for they did not happen, and could not have happened, during his lifetime. But no sooner had he died, and his magnificent funeral was over, than the world began to wonder whether Yugoslavia would survive him. Many people thought that the Soviet Union would soon take over the country.

In little ways, the changes began at once. Under the Constitution, Vice-President Koliševski became president when Tito died, and delivered the funeral oration. Many people believed that this meant that he would be chosen as Tito's successor; but Koliševski's term of office expired only a fortnight after his moment of glory. On 10 July 1980, just sixty-seven days after Tito's death, Jovanka was abruptly ordered to leave within three days the house at 15 Užička Street where she had lived for twenty-five years with Tito and for the last three years by herself.[1] Although the house had been Tito's private residence, it had always belonged to the state; and all the furniture, paintings, jewels, clothes and other objects that Tito and Jovanka had acquired were also state property. She became involved in bitter arguments with the government, which lasted for years; she accused them of stealing her private property.

Žarko and Miša were more ready to accept the fact that Tito, like a good Socialist, had not acquired any private fortune either at home or abroad from his position as President of Yugoslavia. Even the diamond ring which he always wore on his finger turned out to be the property of the state. His sons inherited nothing except one or two suits of his clothes, and Jovanka inherited nothing at all.[2]

In other respects things seemed to continue as before. Yugoslavia

[416]

remained a dictatorship with many restraints on freedom but not a totalitarian state like Nazi Germany or the Soviet Union under Stalin. It experienced economic difficulties, including unemployment and inflation, but pulled through with the help of foreign loans. Djilas was again arrested for criticizing the government at illegal lectures. Yugoslavia continued to pursue its policy of non-alignment as the Cold War intensified after the Soviet Union invaded Afghanistan and Reagan and Margaret Thatcher became President of the United States and prime minister of Great Britain.

Tito's Yugoslavia survived his death; but it could not survive the advent of Gorbachev, the Louis XVI of the twentieth century. Gorbachev allowed the first free elections for more than seventy years to be held in the Soviet Union at a time of great economic hardship, just as Louis XVI called the first meeting of the States-General in France for 175 years immediately after the cold and hungry winter of 1788–9. As a result, both of them toppled the regimes in many neighbouring countries as well as destroying themselves, though Gorbachov has fortunately escaped Louis XVI's ultimate fate.

Slobodan Milošević had become the leader of the government and League of Communists of Yugoslavia. He continued Tito's Communist regime and imprisoned Šešelj, the extremist leader of Serbian Chetnik nationalism. But in the post-Gorbachev world, with all the neighbouring countries turning to democracy, Milošević felt it necessary to hold free elections in Yugoslavia; and there was no surer way of winning a free election than by advocating an extreme nationalist policy and posing as the champion of a Greater Serbia. In 1987 he went to Kosovo and enflamed Serbian nationalist hatred. The forces of Croatian nationalism, never far below the surface, broke out, and Slovenian nationalists demanded independence from a Serbian-dominated Yugoslavia.

The Serbs, after an initial attempt to crush the Slovenes, were prepared to let Slovenia go, but they feared that Slovenian independence would lead to Croatian independence, and there was a Serbian minority in Croatia. After Slovenia came Croatia, and after Croatia Bosnia. The Serbian Chetniks, who are chiefly responsible for the wars, began their policy of 'ethnic cleansing' of Croats and Muslims. They say that they remember the massacres of 700,000* Serbs by the Ustasha Croats in 1941–5, and that this time they themselves

---

* For the true figure, see *supra*, p. 165.

will start the killing and will exterminate the Croats before the Croats exterminate them.[3] The result was what Djilas has called a return to the civil war of 1941–5 without the Communists.[4] Serbs, Croats and Bosnian Muslims massacre each other, and Bosnia is again the principal battleground; but no Partisans have come along to offer to protect every ethnic group from being slaughtered by the others. The killing continues, with the high proportion of deaths and the heavy casualties which are so usual in small wars in which small forces are involved; and the peoples of the former Yugoslavia can agree on nothing except that there is no language called Serbo-Croat, and in their hatred and contempt for the United Nations. In 1878 the Great Powers drew a new map of the Balkans and compelled the inhabitants of the area to accept it. In 1912–13 they allowed the people of the Balkans to fight it out among themselves without any foreign intervention. In 1991–4 the Great Powers (who now call themselves 'the international community') did neither the one thing nor the other, and their policy has prolonged the wars, and increased the casualties and the suffering.

In Serbia, Tito is discredited. The guard of honour has been withdrawn from his grave, though the Hall of Flowers, where the grave lies, has now been reopened after having been closed for many months. The street which was once called 'King Milan Street' and after 1945 'Marshal Tito Avenue' is now the Avenue of the Rulers of Serbia. Marx-Engels Square is now Pašić Square after the Serbian statesman of the early twentieth century. A monument has been erected to Mihailović, and Serbian patriots speak with hatred about 'the Croat Broz'. But some of the poorer people regret that wage differentials between rich and poor are higher now than they were under Tito.

In Britain, it was fashionable a few years ago to blame Fitzroy Maclean and Deakin and the Communist agent Klugmann for supporting Tito and not Mihailović in 1943, for the critics hesitate to blame Churchill, who was really responsible for this decision. Today this line is not so popular, as people wonder if backing the Chetniks in 1943 would have caused the horrors of 1991–4 to take place forty-five years earlier. A few years ago people were saying that Tito was a Communist butcher; now many of them are saying that he was the only man who could hold together a country like Yugoslavia and give her peoples forty-five years of peace between two holocausts.

In Croatia they began the struggle against Greater Serbian chauvinism by claiming to be the champions of democracy and the free market economy, and calling on Western Europe and the United States, and above all on Germany, to help them in their fight against 'Serbian Panzer-Communism'.[5] In Zagreb, like in Belgrade, there is no longer a Marshal Tito Street, but only an Andrija Hebrang Street; and the Square of the Victims of Fascism has been renamed 'the Square of Distinguished Croats'. But Tito, the local Croat boy, is less unpopular in Croatia than he is in Serbia. His birthplace in Kumrovec is preserved and open to visitors more readily than his tomb in Belgrade. President Tudjman expresses a high regard for Tito. Apart from his gratitude for the protection which Tito extended to him personally, he believes that as long as Tito lived, Yugoslavia was slowly evolving towards a confederation of independent states in which Croats could have lived, and that it was only after Tito's death that the government of Yugoslavia adopted the Greater Serbian policy which made it necessary for Croatia to follow a different path.[6]

So Tito's regime did not survive him, but, like Oliver Cromwell's, dissolved in anarchy after his death. Tito greatly admired Cromwell,[7] and in some ways resembled him politically, although in his private life he was closer to Charles II. Like Cromwell, he was a relatively mild dictator, balancing against each other the opposing factions among his supporters and relying above all on the loyalty of the army to him personally. Cromwell lived to the age of fifty-nine and ruled Britain for five years. Tito, with the benefit of twentieth-century medicine and hygiene, lived to be eighty-eight and ruled Yugoslavia for thirty-five years.

No student of history should be surprised that the collapse of the Soviet empire in Eastern Europe led to the same results as the collapse of the Spanish Empire in Latin America, the British Empire in India, the Belgian rule in the Congo and the Roman Empire in Europe 1,600 years ago: to massacres and wars among peoples who had hitherto lived in peace under a despotism which was perhaps resented more by the politicians and the intellectuals and the rebellious youth than by the mass of the people. Perhaps the Yugoslavs, like the former subjects of the King of Spain and the British Raj in South America and India, will eventually find a way of living in peace in independent states. If not, the people will demand to be governed by a strong king or dictator, as they did in Tudor England after the

Wars of the Roses. They will say, in the words which Marx put into the mouths of the French bourgeoisie after the revolution of 1848: 'Better end with a terror than terror without end.'[8]

Today the people of the country that was once Yugoslavia think of Tito more sympathetically than they did a few years ago. In Sarajevo and Mostar many people are saying that it was better to live under a system where the political leaders might be arbitrarily imprisoned than in a country where 300,000 people have been slaughtered in two years and the survivors dare not emerge from their houses to look for food without running the risk of being killed by snipers or in a largely pointless bombardment. In Belgrade, on the days when they have to queue for five hours for bread, the word passes along the line: 'We didn't have to do this in Tito's time.' Tito's statues have been removed in many places in Bosnia; but the graffiti on the empty base reads: 'Come back, Tito'. On 15 September 1993 a Muslim from Bihać wrote in the visitors' book at the house in Kumrovec where Tito was born: 'When you were around I walked on two legs, and now I walk on one leg.'[9]

The people appreciate in retrospect more than they did at the time the days when they were ruled from Belgrade by Josip Broz Tito and people said that Yugoslavia had six republics, five nations, four languages, three religions, two alphabets and one party.

References

Chapter 1: Funeral of a Communist

1. For the announcement of Tito's death, the bringing of his body to Belgrade, the lying-in-state, the funeral and funeral orations, see *Hronologija*, ii. 481–520; *Bilo je časno živjeti s Titom*, 154–5, 163, 170, 176–7, 179, 182–3, 185, 187, 276–7; *Socialist Thought and Practice*, xx (v). 27–40; Kljakić, 'Utakmica se odlaže' (in *Politika*, 24 Oct. 1993); information from Duška Jovanović; BBC television recording of the funeral, 8 May 1980; *The Times*, 5, 6, 7, 8 and 9 May 1980; *Josip Broz Tito Memorial Centre*, 64–67 (unpag.).
2. *The Times*, 7 May 1980.
3. *Ibid.*, 5 May 1980.
4. *Ibid.*, 8 May 1980.
5. Information from R. Bugarčić (Tito's secretary).
6. *Socialist Thought and Practice*, v. 36.
7. Information from Ž. Simić.
8. *The Times*, 18 Dec. 1991; 6 Aug. 1992.

Chapter 2: The Yugoslavs

1. Minns, 'Slavs' (in *Encyclopaedia Britannica*, 10th edn. xxv. 230); Wilkes, *The Illyricans*, 268–70.
2. Minns (in *op. cit.*, xxv. 231).
3. Dedijer, *Tito Speaks*, 4; Auty, *Tito*, 8–9.
4. Temperly, *History of Serbia*, 111.

Chapter 3: The Marxists

1. Marx and Engels, *Communist Manifesto*, 40–60.
2. *Ibid.*, 71 (my translation from the German).
3. Marx to the Franco-Swiss Federal Council of the International (Nov. 1869) (*Marx's Political Writings*, iii. 118).
4. Marx, *The Eighteenth Brumaire of Louis Bonaparte*, 23.
5. Marx and Engels, *Communist Manifesto*, 71 (my translation from the German).
6. Engels, 'Hungary and Panslavism' (in Marx and Engels, *The Russian Menace to Europe*, 63–66); Marx, *Revolution and Counter-revolution in Germany*, 61, 64–65.
7. For the nationalist policy of Marx and Engels in Germany and their opposition to Pan-Slavism in 1848–9, see Meyer, 'Karl Marx und die deutsche Revolution von 1848' (in *Historische Zeitschrift*, clxxii. 522, 528); Marx, *Revolution and Counter-revolution in Germany in 1848*, 61–62, 64–65, 83–85, 88–89; Marx and Engels, *The Russian Menace to Europe*, 25, 27, 57, 61–66, 68–72, 76, 78–81.
8. Engels's Preface to the first English edition of *Das Kapital* (in 1886) (in *Capital*, i. 30).
9. General Council of the International Working Men's Association to Abraham Lincoln, 29 Nov. 1864 (*General Council of First International, Minutes*, 51–54).
10. Marx, *The Civil War in France*, 21–63, especially p. 35.
11. Duff to Crown Princess Victoria 1 Feb. 1879 (*Times Literary Supplement*, 15 July 1949).

Chapter 4: Young Josip Broz

1. Information from Martin Broz; Dedijer, *Novi priloži*, 18.
2. Information from Martin Broz; Auty. 4, 295; Vinterhalter, *In the path of Tito*, 43; M. Djilas, *Wartime*, 370; M. Djilas, *Tito*, 20; P. Simić, *Tito Agent Kominterne*, 107.
3. Information from Martin Broz. The first birth of a Broz child in Kumrovec to be recorded in the Church register was in 1843.
4. For Tito's ancestors, grandfather and father, see Auty, 9–11, 13–15; Vinterhalter, 43–44; Dedijer, *Tito Speaks*, 4–6.
5. Dedijer, *Tito Speaks*, 6.
6. Dedijer, *Josip Broz Tito*. This passage is omitted in *Tito Speaks* and the other foreign translations.
7. Dedijer, *Tito Speaks*, 10.
8. *Ibid.*, 6.

9. Information from Josip and Martin Broz.
10. Dedijer, *Tito Speaks*, 5.
11. *Ibid.*, 8.
12. Information from Slavenka Oughtred (Petnički).
13. Dedijer, *Josip Broz Tito*, 8 (this passage is omitted from *Tito Speaks*); Maclean, *Disputed Barricade*, 16; Auty, 17.
14. Dedijer, *Tito Speaks*, 9.
15. The school in Kumrovec is preserved today as a musuem, and was seen by me in September 1993.
16. Dedijer, *Tito Speaks*, 10.
17. *Ibid.*, 11–12.
18. *Ibid.*, 9.
19. Auty, 3.
20. Dedijer, *Tito Speaks*, 3–4, 11.
21. *Ibid.*, 7–8.
22. *Ibid.*, 11.
23. *Ibid.*, 12.
24. *Ibid.*, 12–13.
25. *Ibid.*, 13–15.

Chapter 5: The Metalworker

1. Engels's Preface to 1895 edition of Marx, *The Class Struggles in France (1848–1850)*, 19–27.
2. Avakumović, *History of the Communist Party of Yugoslavia*, 2; Dedijer, *Tito Speaks*, 16.
3. Dedijer, *Tito Speaks*, 15.
4. *Ibid.*, 18, 21.
5. *Ibid.*, 19.
6. Information from Slavenka Oughtred (Petnički).
7. Dedijer, *Tito Speaks*, 20.
8. *Ibid.*, 20.
9. For Tito's travels in Slovenia, Bohemia and Germany, see *ibid.*, 22–23; *Hronologija*, i. 10.
10. Vlahović and Kačarević, *Velika obmana*, 68–69.
11. For Tito's stay in Wiener-Neustadt, and Vienna, see Dedijer, *Tito Speaks*, 23–24.
12. Djilas, *Tito*, 8.
13. Hitler, *Mein Kampf*, 60, 61, 67; Fest, *Hitler*, 39.
14. Vlahović and Kačarević, 69–70.
15. For the anti-war policy of the Second International in 1907 and 1912, see Joll, *The Second International*, 133–9, 152–7.

16. Nettl, *Rosa Luxemburg*, 481.
17. Information from Vera Ridley.
18. Dedijer, *Tito Speaks*, 24–25.
19. *Ibid.*, 25.
20. Information from Miša Broz.
21. For the reaction of the Socialist parties to the outbreak of the First World War, see Joll, 159–81.
22. Lenin, *The War and the Second International*, 62; Zinoviev and Lenin, *Socialism and War*, 24.
23. Joll, 163.
24. Lenin, *What is to be Done?* (in Lenin, *Collected Works*, iv (ii). 187, 196–201.

Chapter 6: Sergeant-Major Broz

1. For the conflicting accounts of Tito's imprisonment in Peterwardein, see Dedijer, *Tito Speaks*, 26; M. Djilas, *Tito*, 16–17. See also *Hronologija*, i. 10.
2. For Tito's experiences in the Austro-Hungarian army and in Russia, referred to in this chapter, see Dedijer, *Tito Speaks*, 26–34.
3. Lockhart, *Memoirs of a British Agent*, 172.
4. Zeman and Scharlau, *The Merchant of Revolution*, 145–8, 157–8, 209–29; Shub, *Lenin*, 243–7.

Chapter 7: The Russian Civil War

1. M. Djilas, *Tito*, 129–30.
2. Dedijer, *Tito Speaks*, 34.
3. Lenin's theses for the foundation meeting of the Comintern, 4 Mar. 1919 (in Degras, *The Communist International*, i. 8–9).
4. Trotsky, *My Life*, 338.
5. For Tito's activities in Siberia during the Russian Civil War described in this chapter, see Zilliacus, *Tito of Yugoslavia*, 51–53; Auty, 36–38; Vinterhalter, 68.
6. Silverlight, *The Victors' Dilemma*, 233; Serge, *Memoirs of a Revolutionary*, 83.
7. Dedijer, *Tito Speaks*, 35 (the passage is omitted in the Serbo-Croat edition *Josip Broz Tito*).
8. Lenin to the Hungarian Communists, 27 May 1919 (Degras, i. 48).
9. *Ibid.*, i. 52.
10. Taylor, *The Future of the Southern Slavs*, 243–8; Temperly, 326.

11. Comintern's appeal to workers and soldiers in all countries to save the Hungarian revolution, 28 Mar. 1919 (Degras. i. 48–50); Tito, *Forty Years of Struggle of the Communist Party of Yugoslavia*, 43–44; Dedijer, *Tito Speaks*, 39; Avakumović, 32, 34–35.
12. Churchill's speeches at the Aldwych Club, 11 Apr. 1919, and in Sunderland, 3 Jan. 1920 (Ullman, *Britain and the Russian Civil War*, 153; *Morning Post*, 5 Jan. 1920).
13. Silverlight, 191–6; Ullman, 141–2.
14. Churchill, *Great Contemporaries*, 125–33.
15. Hansard, 29 May 1919 (col. 1521); Ullman, 181–2.
16. Auty, 38, 297; Vinterhalter, 68.

Chapter 8: Return to Yugoslavia

1. Auty, 44, 298; M. Djilas, *Tito*, 17; Avakumović, 123.
2. Auty, 38; Dedijer, *Tito Speaks*, 40.
3. For Tito's life at Veliko Trojstvo, see Auty, 51; Dedijer, *Tito Speaks*, 42, 47–48.
4. For the events in Yugoslavia in 1919–21, see Dedijer, *Tito Speaks*, 39–42; Avakumović, 27–56; Auty, 45–49.
5. Dedijer, *Tito Speaks*, 38.
6. Avakumović, 6.
7. *Ibid.*, 178.
8. *Ibid.*
9. Dedijer, *Tito Speaks*, 45–46.
10. *Ibid.*, 44–45.
11. *Ibid.*, 48.
12. *Ibid.*, 47.
13. Nora Beloff, *Tito's Flawed Legacy*, 34.
14. Dedijer, *Tito Speaks*, 47.

Chapter 9: The Professional Revolutionary

1. Avakumović, 41, 89.
2. M. Djilas, *Memoir of a Revolutionary*, 92–93.
3. *Ibid.*, 102.
4. Dedijer, *Tito Speaks*, 49–51; *Organizovani Radnik*, 26 Aug. 1926.
5. Dedijer, *Tito Speaks*, 51–52; Stanojević, *Tito u Palanci*, 11–35.
6. Dedijer, *Tito Speaks*, 53.
7. *Ibid.*, where Tito said he was arrested in June 1927. *Hronologija*, i. 11, gives the date as 14 July 1927.

8. Dedijer, *Tito Speaks*, 54–56.
9. Gilbert, *Winston S. Churchill*, v. 48.
10. *The Times*, 21 Jan. 1927; Graham to Austen Chamberlain, 21 Jan. 1927 (Gilbert, v. 916).
11. Degras, ii. 424.
12. Dedijer, *Tito Speaks*, 58–59; Avakumović, 89; Tito, *Struggle of CPY between the Two Wars*, 25–28.
13. Dedijer, *Tito Speaks*, 59–60; Avakumović, 123.
14. Dedijer, *Tito Speaks*, 61; Dedijer, *Josip Broz Tito*, 152–3 (this passage is omitted in *Tito Speaks*); Avakumović, 96–97.
15. Dedijer, *Tito Speaks*, 61; Zilliacus, 78.
16. Dedijer, *Tito Speaks*, 62.
17. For Tito's trial and the quotations from *Novosti* and *Borba*, see *ibid.*, 62–69.
18. Zilliacus, 78; Sir Fitzroy Maclean's statement to me, Nov. 1990; M. Djilas, *Tito*, 18.

Chapter 10: In King Alexander's Prisons

1. Dedijer, *Tito Speaks*, 73–74; Avakumović, 124.
2. Information from Josip Broz of Kumrovec and Žarko Broz.
3. M. Djilas, *Tito*, 9, 19.
4. For Tito's experiences in prison in Lepoglava and Maribor, see Dedijer, *Tito Speaks*, 74–78.
5. *The Times*, 7 Jan. 1929.
6. A. Djilas, *The Contested Country*, 87
7. *The Times*, 8 Jan. 1929.
8. M. Djilas, *Memoir of a Revolutionary*, 70, 74, 110, 116–21; Dedijer, *Tito Speaks*, 70–73.
9. M. Djilas, *Memoir of a Revolutionary*, 157.
10. Information from Vera Ridley.
11. Dedijer, *Tito Speaks*, 78.

Chapter 11: From Kumrovec to Moscow

1. Marx, *Capital*, i. 837; iii. 247–71.
2. Gilbert, v. 457.
3. Hitler's speech on 27 Jan. 1932 (in *Penguin Book of Twentieth-Century Speeches*, 115).
4. Margarete Buber (Neumann), *Under Two Dictators*, p. xi.

5. Daily Herald, 10 Mar. 1933; Griffiths, *Fellow Travellers of the Right*, 164.
6. Dedijer, *Tito Speaks*, 80.
7. Information from Josip Broz of Kumrovec.
8. Dedijer, *Tito Speaks*, 82–84, 89.
9. Avakumović, 98–99; Auty, 82–83.
10. Dedijer, *Tito Speaks*, 87.
11. *Ibid.*, 71–73, 87–88.
12. *Ibid.*, 80–81. See also Maclean, *Disputed Barricade*, 103. Some inhabitants of the Zagorje district question Dedijer's statement (ascribed to Tito) that 'Tito' is a common nickname in the district (information from Martin Broz).
13. M. Djilas, *Memoir of a Revolutionary*, 191–3, 206–13.
14. Dedijer, *Tito Speaks*, 88–89.
15. M. Djilas, *Memoir of a Revolutionary*, 206–19.
16. Dedijer, *Tito Speaks*, 90.
17. *Ibid.*, 91.

Chapter 12: The Hotel Lux

1. Dedijer, *Tito Speaks*, 96; Auty, 94, 97.
2. Gorkić to Čopić, 16 Jan. 1935 (in P. Simić, *Tito Agent Kominterne*, 201).
3. Dedijer, *Tito Speaks*, 98.
4. *Ibid.*, 97–99; M. Djilas, *Tito*, 11.
5. Information from Margarete Buber-Neumann.
6. P. Simić, 112; information from Žarko Broz.
7. Degras, iii. 346–78, 485; Auty, 102–4.
8. Dedijer, *Tito Speaks*, 100.
9. Rebecca West, *Black Lamb and Grey Falcon*, ii. 305; information from Victoria Glendinning.
10. Cicely Adams (Rebecca West) to Sir Orme Sargent, 20 Feb. 1944 (PRO/ FO 371/44269).
11. Dedijer, *Tito Speaks*, 103.
12. *Ibid.*, 110–11.
13. *Ibid.*, 107.
14. Churchill to Corbin, 31 July 1936; Churchill to Eden, 7 and 10 Aug. 1936; Churchill to Mrs Churchill, 5 Sept. 1936 (Gilbert, v. 781–2, 785); Thomas, *The Spanish Civil War*, 220.
15. Churchill to Londonderry, 6 May 1936 (Gilbert, v. 732–3).
16. Gilbert, v. 723.
17. *Ibid.*, v. 777.

18. Churchill's article 'The Ogre of Europe', in *John o' London's Weekly*, reprinted as 'Leon Trotsky alias Bronstein' in Churchill, *Great Contemporaries*, 197–205; see Deutscher, *The Prophet Outcast*, 19.
19. Gilbert, v. 788.
20. Tito to the Comintern, 31 Aug. 1936 (Filipović, *Sabrana dela*, xiv. 306).
21. Information from Margarete Buber-Neumann.
22. Dedijer, *Tito Speaks*, 95–96.
23. Thomas, 295–6.
24. Dedijer, *Tito Speaks*, 95–96.
25. For the incident of *La Corse*, see *ibid.*, 107–8; Auty, 113–14; Avakumović, 120; M. Djilas, *Memoir of a Revolutionary*, 266–7; Tito, *Struggle of CPY between the Two Wars*, 48.
26. My personal observation in 1937.
27. Avakumović, 120–1; Thomas, 298, 634–5, 637–9; Dedijer, *Tito Speaks*, 109.
28. Thomas, 232.
29. See, for example, the cases cited *infra*, in note 31 to Chapter 17. There is no evidence whatever to support Hugh Thomas's statement (in *The Spanish Civil War*, 298) that 'it seems probable' that Tito went to Spain and that he suppressed the fact because of 'some aspect of the Gorkić murder'. The execution of Gorkić, in which Tito was not involved, took place (not in 1936, but in November 1937) in the Soviet Union, and had nothing to do with Spain.
30. Information from Slavenka Oughtred (Petnički).
31. Information from Peter Elstob.
32. Tito, *Struggle of CPY between the Two Wars*, 49; *Hronologija*, vol. i. 1 and 2 Aug. 1937.
33. Dedijer, *Tito Speaks*, 249–50; Auty, 117–18; information from Josip Broz of Kumrovec.
34. Dedijer, *Tito Speaks*, 109; Avakumović, 121.
35. Tito, *Struggle of CPY between the Two Wars*, 50.
36. For the best account of the fall of Gorkić, Tito's appointment as general secretary, and the dates, see Auty, 118–31; Vinterhalter, 208. Both these books were published before Tito's speech at Kumrovec in March 1977 (see Tito, *Struggle of CPY between the Two Wars*).
37. Auty, 127, 305; and see Tito's statement to Djilas on the reason why he survived the purge, in M. Djilas, *Tito*, 26.
38. Dedijer, *Tito Speaks*, 103, 111.
39. *Hronologija*, vol. i., 22 Nov., 12 Dec. 1937.
40. Auty, 123.
41. Dedijer, *Tito Speaks*, 117–18; Avakumović, 171.
42. Avakumović, 128–34; Auty, 126.

43. Dedijer, *Tito Speaks*, 125–6.
44. Vaksberg, *Hôtel Lux*, 225.
45. Information from Žarko Broz.
46. Auty, 109, 126; Avakumović, 130–1; but see P. Simić, 106–7.
47. Information from Žarko Broz; Auty, 127.
48. Tito, *Struggle of CPY between the Two Wars*, 55; Maclean, *Tito*, 48; Auty, 125, 147; but see M. Djilas, *Tito*, 130.
49. *History of CPSU (B)*, 204, 241, 297; Tito, *Struggle of CPY between the Two Wars*, 55; information from Milovan Djilas.
50. Tito, *Struggle of CPY between the Two Wars*, 55.
51. Avakumović, 134; Auty, 130.
52. Tito, *Struggle of CPY between the Two Wars*, 55.
53. *Ibid.*, 57.
54. Gilbert, v. 968.
55. Tito, *Struggle of CPY between the Two Wars*, 56–57; Tito, *Forty Years of Struggle of CPY*, 44; Avakumović, 171–2; Dimitrov, *After Munich*, 15.
56. Deakin, *The Brutal Friendship*, 8.
57. Tito, *Struggle of CPY between the Two Wars*, 57.
58. Dedijer, *Tito Speaks*, 100–1.
59. Maclean, *Disputed Barricade*, 42.
60. *Ibid.*, 28.

Chapter 13: The Hitler–Stalin Pact

1. *Hronologija*, vol. i, 5 Jan. 1939; Vinterhalter, 215; Auty, 130; Tito, *Struggle of CPY between the Two Wars*, 57.
2. Avakumović, 172–3; Draskovich, *Tito, Moscow's Trojan horse*, 73.
3. Balfour to Eden, 31 July 1936 (PRO/FO 371/20436, R.4727, p. 77).
4. M. Djilas, *Memoir of a Revolutionary*, 343–5.
5. Tito, *Struggle of CPY between the Two Wars*, 62.
6. M. Djilas, *Memoir of a Revolutionary*, 329.
7. Degras, iii. 439.
8. M. Djilas, *Memoir of a Revolutionary*, 332.
9. Tito, *Struggle of CPY between the Two Wars*, 62–63.
10. M. Djilas, *Memoir of a Revolutionary*, 331.
11. Tito, *Struggle of CPY between the Two Wars*, 63.
12. Koestler, *Scum of the Earth*, 125–6.
13. Tito, *Forty Years of Struggle of CPY*, 45.
14. M. Djilas, *Memoir of a Revolutionary*, 333.
15. Gilbert, vi. 49–50.
16. *Ibid.*, v. 937–8.

17. Dedijer, *War Diaries*, ii. 20–21; M. Djilas, *Memoir of a Revolutionary*, 335; *Hronologija*, vol. i., 14 Dec. 1939; Avakumović, 180.
18. Dedijer, *Tito Speaks*, 126–7; Auty, 147–8; Maclean, *Disputed Barricade*, 108–10; M. Djilas, *Memoir of a Revolutionary*, 351–2.
19. Tito, *Struggle of CPY between the Two Wars*, 64.
20. M. Djilas, *Tito*, 119; information from Olga Humo (Tito's wartime secretary).
21. Avakumović, 176.
22. Degras, iii. 464.
23. *Ibid.*, iii. 463.
24. *Hronologija*, vol. i, 29 June, 19 July, 2–4, 11, 16–18 , 25 Aug. 1940.
25. Avakumović, 134–7; M. Djilas, *Tito*, 29.
26. M. Djilas, *Tito*, 32.
27. Urban, 'Conversations with Djilas' (*Encounter*, Dec. 1979, 30).
28. Leonhard, *Child of the revolution*, 376–9.
29. M. Djilas, *Tito*, 9.
30. Avakumović, 185–6.
31. Auty, 150–1; A. Djilas, 93; Dedijer, *Tito Speaks*, 127–8; M. Djilas, *Memoir of a Revolutionary*, 354; Tito to Begić (Oct. 1970) (Damjanović Archives).
32. *Peta zemaljska konferencija KPJ*, 3–45, esp. pp. 36, 39, 43–45; see also Vinterhalter, 240–2; Clissold, *Yugoslavia and the Soviet Union*, 117–21.
33. M. Djilas, *Memoir of a Revolutionary*, 354.
34. A. Djilas, 92.
35. Urban (in *Encounter*, Dec. 1979, 28).

Chapter 14: The German Invasion

1. *Jugoslovensko-Britanski Odnosi*, 231–3.
2. Information from Živadin Simić.
3. Fest, 642–7.
4. Avakumović, 179–80.
5. *Ibid.*, 112, 180–1.
6. Dedijer, *Tito Speaks*, 130.
7. Rebecca West, letter in *TLS*, 21 Apr. 1972.
8. Cicely Adams, (Rebecca West) to Sir Orme Sargent, 20 Feb. 1944 (PRO/FO 371/44269).
9. Hoptner, *Yugoslavia in crisis*, 258–9.
10. Information from Slavenka Oughtred (Petnički).
11. M. Djilas, *Memoir of a Revolutionary*, 369; Dedijer, *Tito Speaks*, 133–7.

12. Roberts, *Tito, Mihailović and the Allies*, 15.
13. M. Djilas, *Memoir of a Revolutionary*, 369–72; Dedijer, *Tito Speaks*, 130–1.
14. M. Djilas, *Memoir of a Revolutionary*, 373.
15. *Ibid.*, 381–3.
16. *Ibid.*, 384.
17. Degras, iii. 466.
18. Clissold, *Yugoslavia and the Soviet Union*, 125–6.
19. Information from a former prisoner in Jasenovac who does not wish to be identified.
20. See the film *Masakr* (Belgrade, 1990); *Crime without Punishment*, 17.
21. Information from Dr Vladimir Velebit.
22. For the Ustasha massacres and persecution of Serbs, Jews and gipsies, and for objective estimates of the numbers killed, see Hory and Broszat, *Der kroatische Ustascha-Staat*, 84–106; A. Djilas, 118–27, 210 (n. 38), 212 (n. 58) and the sources cited there. See also *France*, 13 Oct. 1941. For the Serbian allegations, see *Never Again, passim*; *Crime without Punishment*, 17–23.
23. Information from Dr Velebit.
24. Tito, *Struggle of CPY, between the Two Wars*, 107–8.
25. M. Djilas, *Memoir of a Revolutionary*, 373.
26. Dedijer, *Tito Speaks*, 142–3.
27. Information from Herta Haas, Vladimir Velebit, and Miša Broz. The statement in various publications that Tito came from Zagreb to Belgrade earlier in May seem to be based on a misleading statement by Dedijer. Tito visited Zemun early in May 1941, but returned to Zagreb. He only finally left Zagreb on 22 May.
28. Dedijer, *Tito Speaks*, 143.
29. Werth, *Russia at War*, 127.
30. Clissold, *Yugoslavia and the Soviet Union*, 127.
31. Comintern to CPY, 22 June 1941 (*ibid.*, 128).
32. Dedijer, *Tito Speaks*, 147.
33. Clissold, *Yugoslavia and the Soviet Union*, 129.
34. Dedijer, *Tito Speaks*, 147.
35. *Ibid.*, 149.
36. *Ibid.*, 149–50; Dedijer, *War Diaries*, i. 11.
37. Clissold, *Yugoslavia and the Soviet Union*, 10.
38. Hory and Broszat, 105, 113.
39. Ačimović to Förster, 4 May 1941 (*ibid.*, 96).
40. *Ibid.*, 97.
41. Roberts, 24–25.
42. *Ibid.*, 31; Auty, 188.
43. Roberts, 25–31.

44. See Urban (in *Encounter*, Dec. 1979, 17).

45. Comintern to Tito, 5 Mar. 1942 (Clissold, *Yugoslavia and the Soviet Union*, 145–6); Djilas, *Wartime*, 120.

46. Information from Mladen Čaldarović. He was informed about the executions in the railway siding by an eye-witness who gave him the names of the executed dissidents.

47. Djilas, *Wartime*, 101; Clissold, *Whirlwind*, 69; Avakumović, 121. See Pavlović, *Bilans Sovjetskog Termidora* (reprinted in *Intervju*, 14 July 1989); P. Simić, 130–2.

48. Auty, 175–6; Dedijer, *J. B. Tito*, 157 (the passage is greatly shortened in *Tito Speaks*, 157); *Hronologija*, vol. i., 17 and 18 Sept. 1941; Roberts, 25.

Chapter 15: From Užice to Bihać

1. Roberts, 26.

2. M. R. D. Foot, *SOE*, 19–21. The words 'subversion and sabotage against the enemy overseas' are in Neville Chamberlain's memorandum of 19 July 1940.

3. Ehrman, *Grand Strategy*, v. 77.

4. Dedijer, *War Diaries*, i. 192; Djilas, *Wartime*, 10.

5. Roberts, 114.

6. Deakin, *Embattled Mountain*, 126.

7. Roberts, 69, 131.

8. For the first meeting between Tito and Mihailović, see *ibid.*, 40; Dedijer, *Tito Speaks*, 158–9; Minić, *Oslobodilački ili Gratanski Rat u Jugoslaviji*, 88.

9. Roberts, 31.

10. Deakin, *Embattled Mountain*, 126–36.

11. *Ibid.*, 135; information from Sir W. Deakin.

12. For the second meeting between Tito and Mihailović, see Dedijer, *Tito Speaks*, 161–4; Auty, 189–91; Minić, *Oslobodilački ili Gratanski Rat*, 91.

13. Auty, 191.

14. Roberts, 34.

15. *Ibid.*, 35.

16. Dedijer, *War Diaries*, i. 41; Kardelj, *Reminiscences*, 22.

17. Deakin, *Embattled Mountain*, 140; and see Lord Glenconner to Dixon, 15 Nov. 1941 (PRO/FO371/30220/R9874); Sweet-Escott, in *British Policy Towards Wartime Resistance in Yugoslavia and Greece*, 23.

18. Roberts, 25, 31, 35.

19. *Ibid.*, 35.

20. *Ibid.*, 36–37.
21. Dedijer, *War Diaries*, i. 55–56.
22. Roberts, 37–39.
23. Clissold, *Whirlwind*, 83.
24. Dedijer, *War Diaries*, i. 61, 65.
25. *Ibid.*, 70; Roberts, 58; Clissold, *Yugoslavia and the Soviet Union*, 145–6.
26. Dedijer, *War Diaries*, i. 71–75.
27. *Ibid.*, 73.
28. Martin, *Web of Disinformation*, 49–52.
29. Hoettl, *The Secret Front*, 157–8.
30. Dedijer, *War Diaries*, i. 80.
31. Information from Dr Branko Pavićević, who was present in the square in Foča.
32. Dedijer, *War Diaries*, i. 29–30.
33. *Ibid.*, i. 88, 92.
34. *Ibid.*, i. 79.
35. Information from Dr Pavićević.
36. Djilas, *Tito*, 92.
37. Information from Olga Humo.
38. Djilas, *Wartime*, 75, 256, 370; information from Dušanka Barović (who served with the Partisans) and Olga Humo.
39. Dedijer, *War Diaries*, i. 91.
40. Roberts, 43.
41. Dedijer, *Tito Speaks*, 175–6; Clissold, *Yugoslavia and the Soviet Union*, 142.
42. Clissold, *Yugoslavia and the Soviet Union*, 145–6; Roberts, 58.
43. Clissold, *Yugoslavia and the Soviet Union*, 143; Dedijer, *Tito Speaks*, 176.
44. Roberts, 58.
45. Tito to the Communist leaders in Bosnia, 8 Apr. 1942 (Clissold, *Whirlwind*, 86–87).
46. Roberts, 54–55; Deakin, *Embattled Mountain*, 173–6; Dedijer, *War Diaries*, i. 131–2; ii. 84–85, 168.
47. Dedijer, *War Diaries*, i. 157.
48. Jones, *Twelve Months with Tito's Partisans*, 78–79.
49. Dedijer, *War Diaries*, i. 307–8; Radošić, 'Culture and Art in the National Liberation War' (*War and Revolution in Yugoslavia*, 208–9, 211).
50. Dedijer, *War Diaries*, ii. 21, 40, 56, 91–93, 133–4, 180, 310, 352–3, 356, 387–8, 397, 410, 430; iii. 39, 69–70; Deakin, *Embattled Mountain*, 36.
51. Dedijer, *War Diaries*, i. 144, 188; Djilas, *Wartime*, 370.

52. Roberts, 61.
53. *Ibid.*, 62–64, 75.
54. *Ibid.*, 113.
55. Information from Slavenka Oughtred (Petnički).
56. Roberts, 114.
57. *Ibid.*, 77; Pijade, *About the Legend that the Yugoslav Uprising owed its Existence to Soviet Assistance*, 20; Clissold, *Yugoslavia and the Soviet Union*, 150.
58. Roberts, 77–78.
59. Information from Milka Kufrin.

Chapter 16: The March Negotiations and the Sutjeska

1. Bennett, *Ultra and Mediterranean Strategy*, 395–6.
2. M. R. D. Foot, 46–47.
3. Information from Ralph Bennett; Roberts, 89.
4. Information from Sir W. Deakin.
5. Gilbert, vi. 1120.
6. Churchill, *Second World War*, iii. 331–3.
7. Gilbert, vi. 1122.
8. Information from John Platts-Mills.
9. My personal recollections; see also *Labour Monthly*, Nov. 1942.
10. Roberts, 66.
11. *Ibid.*, 90–91.
12. Deakin, *Embattled Mountain*, 154.
13. Roberts, 67.
14. Information from Ralph Bennett.
15. Churchill, *Second World War*, iv. 708; Roberts, 88.
16. Information from Sir W. Deakin.
17. Biddle to Cordell Hull (*FRUS*, 1943, ii. 987–8); Roberts, 93.
18. Dedijer, *War Diaries*, ii. 196–7.
19. Deakin, *The Brutal Friendship*, 185.
20. Roberts, 105.
21. *Ibid.*, 106–8.
22. Information from Dr Velebit.
23. Bennett, 334.
24. Roberts, 101.
25. Information from Dr Velebit; Djilas, *Wartime*, 230.
26. Djilas, *Wartime*, 229–31, where there appears to be some contradiction as to the exact date (between 8 and 11 March) of his discussions with Tito.
27. For the negotiations of Djilas, Koča Popović and Velebit with the

Germans, see Leković, *Martovski Pregovori 1943, passim*; Djilas, *Wartime*, 232–44; Hoettl, 163–6; Roberts, 108–11; Broucek, *Die Erinnerungen Glaises von Horstenau*, iii. 34–35, 220–1; Hory and Broszat, 144; information from Dr Velebit and Milovan Djilas; Dedijer, *War Diaries*, ii. 134.

28. Djilas, *Wartime*, 242.
29. Memorandum signed by Djilas, Popović and Velebit, 11 Mar. 1943 (Leković, 256).
30. Dedijer, *War Diaries*, ii. 160.
31. Djilas, *Wartime*, 238–9.
32. Kasche to Ribbentrop, 17 Mar. 1943 (Hory and Broszat, 144).
33. Hoettl, 167 (my translation).
34. Ribbentrop to Kasche, 21 Apr. 1943 (Hory and Broszat, 145).
35. Information from Dr Velebit.
36. Bennett, 335.
37. Maclean, *Disputed Barricade*, 206. Maclean was told this by Tito.
38. Roberts, 102.
39. Minić, *Oslobodilački ili Gratanski Rat*, 79, 119.
40. Roberts, 91.
41. Dedijer, *War Diaries*, ii. 260.
42. *Ibid.*, ii. 264–332.
43. *Ibid.*, ii. 264.
44. Information from Čaldarović.
45. Dedijer, *War Diaries*, ii. 266–7.
46. *Ibid.*, ii. 273; Deakin, *Embattled Mountain*, 3–8.
47. Deakin, *Embattled Mountain*, 7.
48. Dedijer, *War Diaries*, i. 80, 310; ii. 276.
49. *Ibid.*, ii. 294–7, 299, 310–13.
50. *Ibid.*, ii. 295–6; Deakin, *Embattled Mountain*, 18–19.
51. Information from Sir W. Deakin.
52. Deakin, *Embattled Mountain*, 20.
53. *Ibid.*, 25.
54. *Ibid.*, 26–32.
55. Proclamation of 21 July 1943 (in Spomen Park, Kumrovec).
56. Roberts, 122.
57. Tito, *Forty Years of Struggle of CPY*, 44.
58. Seen by me in Aug. 1947.
59. Information from Milka Kufrin.

Chapter 17: Fitzroy Maclean

1. Maclean, *Eastern Approaches*, 83–121; McLynn, *Fitzroy Maclean*, 40, 43–48, 68–72.

2. Maclean, *Eastern Approaches*, 281.
3. *Ibid.*, 308, 316.
4. Information from Sir F. Maclean.
5. Maclean, *Eastern Approaches*, 308–16.
6. Deakin, *Embattled Mountain*, 246.
7. Information from Dr Velebit.
8. Maclean, *Disputed Barricade*, 28.
9. Maclean's report, 6 Nov. 1943 (PRO/FO 371/37615/XC 22801).
10. Woodhouse, 'Summer 1943: the Critical Months' (*British Policy towards Wartime Resistance in Yugoslavia and Greece*, 118–19).
11. Dedijer, *War Diaries*, iii. 431–51.
12. Woodhouse, in *British Policy towards Wartime Resistance*, 129–30, 132.
13. Myers, 'The Andarte Delegation to Cairo' (*ibid.*, 150–5).
14. Myers (*ibid.*, 157–9).
15. Myers (*ibid.*, 159–63).
16. Churchill to Lady Randolph Churchill, 25 Apr. 1898 (Randolph Churchill, *Winston S. Churchill*, i. 383); Churchill, *Savrola*, passim; Churchill, *Thoughts and Adventures*, 223–4; Churchill, *Great Contemporaries*, 125–33.
17. Churchill, *Second World War*, vi. 198.
18. Gilbert, vii. 586; Moran, *Winston Churchill*, 143.
19. *Marshal Tito Speaks*, 5–6, 12–13, 16–17.
20. Tito, 'The Significance of the Decisions of the Anti-Fascist Council of National Liberation of Yugoslavia' (in Tito, *Marshal Tito Speaks*, 18–24).
21. Information from Asil Zulsikarpašić.
22. Maclean, *Eastern Approaches*, 401–3.
23. Information from Sir Anthony Nutting.
24. Djilas, *Converstaions with Stalin*, 102–3.
25. Maclean, *Eastern Approaches*, 433; Deakin, *Embattled Mountain*, 264; Roberts, 205.
26. Churchill's draft of his speech, and Eden to Churchill, 19 Feb. 1944 (PRO/FO 371/44248/R 2947).
27. Hansard, 22 Feb. 1944.
28. Roberts, 74, 126, 137, 157.
29. Draskovich, 89; Dedijer, *War Diaries*, ii. 26–27.
30. Cicely Adams (Rebecca West) to Sir O. Sargent, 20 Feb. 1944; Sir O. Sargent to Rebecca West, 25 Feb. 1944 (PRO/FO 371/44269).
31. Dr N. Grisogono's report, 8 May 1944; Edith Wedderburn to Eden, 20 May 1944; Rose to Elisabeth Barker, 31 May 1944 (PRO/FO 371/44271).
32. Lees, *The Rape of Serbia*, 75.

33. Report of Ba Congress, 6 Feb. 1944; statement of National Agency for Democratic Yugoslavia, 8 Feb. 1944; Stevenson to Foreign Office, 22 Feb. 1944; Colville to Lawford, 10 and 13 Mar. 1944 (PRO/FO 371/44269/R 2757, R 3052, R 3330, R 4095); Roberts, 199.
34. Roberts, 179–80, 226–7; Lees, 256–8, 262.
35. Roberts, 226.
36. Lees, 331. For the supplies sent by air, see Thompson, *New Zealanders with the Royal Air Force*, iii. 226.
37. Information from George Mason; Strutton, *Island of Terrible Friends*, 64–68.
38. Information from Dr Velebit.
39. Djilas, *Memoir of a Revolutionary*, 101, 287; information from Admiral Morgan-Giles.
40. Information from Olga Humo.
41. *The Army Air Forces in World War II*, ii, 558–9, 579–80, 591; Djilas, *Wartime*, 399–400; information from Slavenka Oughtred (Petnički).
42. Information from Slavenka Oughtred (Petnički).
43. Information from Mrs Vasja Brown (Kekez's daughter).
44. Deakin, *Embattled Mountain*, 250–4.
45. Dedijer, *War Diaries*, ii. 160, 172–3, 227–8.
46. Information from Dr Velebit.
47. *Ibid.*
48. *Ibid.*; McLynn, 197–9.

Chapter 18: From Drvar to Belgrade

1. Information from General Jovanić.
2. Broucek, iii. 412–13.
3. Tito's statement of 15 Apr. 1974 (in *Borba*, 1 June 1974; Kumm, *Vorwärts Prinz Eugen*, 220).
4. For the attack on Drvar and Tito's escape, see Stefanović, *Potpis: Tito*, 145–6; *Drvarska Operacija*, 53–56; Colonel V. Stewart, 'Diary of Movements of Marshal Tito from 25 May . . . to 3 June', ff.1–2 (in PRO/WO 106/3284 (XC/A/034320)); Hilary King, 'The British Mission at Drvar', ff. 15, 20–28; Tito's statement of 15 Apr. 1974 (in *Borba*, 1 June 1974); Kumm, 182–3, 209–10, 215–23; information from General Jovanić; information from Hilary King; Kalewert, 'Attack on the Bolshevists' Nest', (in Dedijer, *War Diaries*, iii. 382–3); Maclean, *Eastern Approaches*, 449–52; Broucek, iii. 412–13; *The War and Revolution of the Peoples of Yugoslavia*, 143–5.
5. Information from Hilary King.
6. Information from General Jovanić.

7. Broucek, iii. 413.
8. Djilas, *Wartime*, 394.
9. Information from Olga Humo.
10. Broucek, iii. 413.
11. T.B.L. Churchill, *Commando Crusade*, 238.
12. For Tito's journey to Bari, see Stewart, 'Diary of Movements of Marshal Tito from 25 May to 3 June' (PRO/WO 106/3284 (XC/A/ 034320)); Hilary King, 'The British Mission at Drvar', ff. 17–20; information from Hilary King; Tito's statement of 15 Apr. 1974 (in *Borba*, 1 June 1974; Kumm, 223); Maclean, *Eastern Approaches*, 452–4; Gray, 'Objective Tito' (in *War Monthly*, 36–44 (Mar. 1979)); Vinterhalter, 372; Huljić, *Vis*, 362–3.
13. Information from Hilary King.
14. Huljić, 363–8.
15. Information from Žarko Broz.
16. *Hansard*, 24 May 1944.
17. Churchill to Eden, 1 Apr. 1944 (Churchill, *Second World War*, v. 422).
18. Churchill to Eden, 15 July 1944 (Roberts, 239).
19. Roberts, 231.
20. *Ibid.*, 236–7.
21. *Ibid.*, 134–5; Churchill, *Second World War*, v. 358.
22. Huljić, 373.
23. *Ibid.*, 372–3.
24. Information from Geoffrey Harris.
25. Huljić, 373–6; Vinterhalter, 378–80.
26. Information from a former member of the Communist Youth who does not wish to be named.
27. Huljić, 378.
28. Maclean, *Eastern Approaches*, 462–4.
29. *Ibid.*, 464; Maclean, *Disputed Barricade*, 275.
30. Information from Žarko Broz.
31. For the talks between Churchill and Tito on 12 and 13 Aug. 1944, see Minutes of the meeting with the memoranda and other documents in PRO/FO 371/44277/R 13760; see also Maclean, *Eastern Approaches*, 465–6; Tito in interview on Belgrade TV on 9 May 1975 (in Tito, *Yugoslavia – Revolution and After*, 55).
32. Moran, 165.
33. See supra, p. 47.
34. Tito in TV interview on 9 May 1975 (in Tito, *Yugoslavia – Revolution and After*, 55).
35. PRO/FO 371/44278/R 15715.
36. Huljić, 379, 382.
37. T.B.L. Churchill, 235, 238.

38. Information from Major E. D. Roberts.
39. Information from Admiral Morgan-Giles.
40. Tito's speech at Vis, 12 Sept. 1944 (from manuscript supplied by George Mason).
41. Information from Admiral Morgan-Giles; Broad to Macmillan, 20 Sept. 1944 (PRO/FO 371/44278/R 14964); Maclean, *Eastern Approaches*, 498.
42. Dedijer, *Tito Speaks*, 231; information from Žarko Broz.
43. Information from Olga Humo.
44. Information from Admiral Morgan-Giles.
45. Maclean, *Eastern Approaches*, 498.
46. Broad to Maclean, 27 Oct. 1944 (PRO/FO 371/44280/R 17146/G).
47. Dedijer, *Tito Speaks*, 234; Djilas, *Wartime*, 407.
48. Dedijer, *Tito Speaks*, 234.
49. Kirk to Stettinius, 23 Sept. 1944 (*FRUS*, 1944, iv. 1410–11).
50. Tito in interview on Belgrade TV on 9 May 1975 (in Tito, *Yugoslavia – Revolution and After*, 56).
51. Beloff, *Tito's Flawed Legacy*, 115.
52. Janevski 'Od ustaše do potpukovnika JNA' (in *Ilustrovana Politika*, Nov. 1990).
53. Information from Dr Pero Damjanović.
54. Dedijer, *Tito Speaks*, 218; Lees, 320–1.
55. Tito's speech at Skopje, 2 Apr. 1975 (Tito, *Yugoslavia – Revolution and After*, 19).
56. Maclean, *Eastern Approaches*, 519. Sir Fitzroy Maclean told me in 1990 that Tito's remark was 'perhaps rather cheeky'.
57. Smuts to Churchill, 26 Sept. 1944 (Churchill, *Second World War*, vi. 184).
58. Gilbert, vii. 1082.
59. Macmillan to Foreign Office, 6 Oct. 1944 (PRO/FO 371/44278/R 5978, p. 236).
60. Floydforce Intelligence Survey, 31 Oct., 27 Nov. 1944; Shipley to Eastern Adriatic Rear HQ, 14 Dec. 1944 (PRO/WO 170/4009 A/J.21); 'Report on Operations with Floydforce in Jugoslavia', Oct–Dec. 1944 (G. Harris Archives); information from Geoffrey Harris; information from E. D. Roberts; information from George Mason. See also Col. Ghetman 'Unpublished Facts: How Tito assisted the Nazi Retreat from the Balkans' (in *Free Bulgaria*, v. 314, 1 Nov. 1950).
61. Floydforce Report No. 13, 26 Feb. 1945 (PRO/WO 170/7526/J.3, pp. 15–16).
62. Information from George Mason and Geoffrey Harris; Lt. Col. J. P. E. Lineham's report on operations in support of Partisan attack on Split, 28 Oct. 1944 (PRO/WO 170/4009A).

63. Floydforce Report No. 13, 26 Feb. 1945 (PRO/WO 170/7526/J.3).
64. OOT's report, 2 Dec. 1944 (PRO/WO 170/4009 A/J).
65. Information from Sir F. Maclean; Report to Floydforce, 18, 22 Nov. 1944 (PRO/WO 170/4009 A/M 18, M 22); for the disputes between the British and the Yugoslav Partisans in Bari, and Maclean's intervention, see Broad to Macmillan, 17 Oct. 1944; Foreign Office to Bari, 1 Nov. 1944 (PRO/FO 371/44280/R 17343, p. 48, and R 17343/8/9).
66. Churchill, *Second World War*, vi. 198.
67. Statement of a Greek Communist leader on British TV.
68. Information from Ivor Porter, who was in the British mission in Bucharest; Porter, *Operation Autonomous*, 238.
69. Gilbert, vii. 1194.
70. Information from Sir F. Maclean.
71. Information from Milovan Djilas and Olga Humo.
72. Patterson to Stettinius, 11 Jan. 1945 (*FRUS*, 1945, v. 1175–6); Roberts, 299.
73. Information from George Mason.
74. Maclean, *Eastern Approaches*, 485–9; Ivanović, *LX Memoirs of a Jugoslav*, 265.
75. Karapandžic, *Kočevjo, Tito's Bloodiest Crime*, 29, 38.
76. German radio broadcast, 30 Apr. 1945; Gilbert vii, 1325.
77. Tito's broadcast on Radio Belgrade, 9 May 1945 (in Tito, *Yugoslavia – Revolution and After*, 11).

Chapter 19: Victory and Revenge

1. Tito's broadcast on Radio Belgrade, 9 May 1975 (in Tito, *Yugoslavia – Revolution and After*, 15).
2. Information from General Basta.
3. Sargent to Churchill, 28 Apr. 1945; Stevenson to Macmillan, 28 Apr. 1945 (PRO/PREM 3/495/6, ff. 125–7).
4. Churchill's memorandum, 20 May 1945 (PRO/PREM 3/513/8, p. 12). For the grossly inaccurate dossier on Tito prepared for Churchill, see Millard to Peek, 14 June 1945; Lawford to Rowan, 18 July 1945 (*ibid.*, pp. 7–10, 13–14).
5. Churchill to Sargent, 20 Apr. 1945 (Gilbert, vii. 1304).
6. Tito, *Forty Years of Struggle of CPY*, 21.
7. Dedijer, *Tito Speaks*, 28.
8. Tito to Stevenson, 13 May 1945 (Tito, *Sabrana Djela*, xxviii. 37).
9. For the handing over of the refugees in Austria by the British to the Partisans, see Tolstoy, 'The Klagenfurt Conspiracy', (in *Encounter*, May 1983, 26, 28, 31–37); Tolstoy, *The Minister and the Massacres*,

95–175; Karapandžic, 46–52; Basta, *Rat je Završen 7 Dana Kasnije*, 360–70; The accuracy of many statements in these sources has been disputed. See also Wright to Foreign Office (Nov. 1944) (PRO/FO 371/44280/pp. 215–17).

10. M. Djilas, *Memoir of a Revolutionary*, 371; Dedijer, *War Diaries*, i. 331–2.
11. Karapandžic, 54–76.
12. Tolstoy, *The Minister and the Massacres*, 134.
13. Tito's article in *New Yugoslavia*, 1 Mar. 1944 (in Tito, *Marshal Tito Speaks*, 21); and see Floydforce Intelligence Summary No. 6, 14 Dec. 1944 (PRO/WO 170/4009 A/p.3).
14. Tito to all Army commanding officers, 12 Jan., 11 Feb. 1945 (in Tito, *Sabrana Djela*, xxv. 209; xxvi. 78–79).
15. Information from Dr Znidarčić, who was briefly interned and soon released.
16. Tito, *Sabrana Djela*, xxviii. 43.
17. Information from General Basta and General Babić; Djilas, *Wartime*, 446–7; Urban (in *Encounter*, Dec. 1979, 40–42).
18. M. Djilas, *Memoir of a Revolutionary*, 146.
19. Angelo Seligman's Diary (Seligman, 'Tagebuch', 186 (23 Feb. 1945) Richard Seligman's Archives).
20. For the number of victims killed by the Partisans given by Chetnik supporters and anti-Tito writers, see Sirc, *Between Hitler and Tito*, 79; Lees, 328–9.
21. Aarons and Loftus, *Ratlines*, 24–47, 68–119.
22. Louise Rayner, *Women in a Village*, 209.
23. Djilas, *Tito*, 175–6; Draskovich, 31.
24. *Weekly Review*, 25 Apr. 1946.
25. Information from Živadin Simić.
26. Information from John Platts-Mills.
27. *Review of Policy at Home and Abroad made at Mladenovac . . . by Marshal J. B. Tito*, 1, 5–7.

Chapter 20: The Cold War

1. Clissold, *Yugoslavia and the Soviet Union*, 47–48; *Weekly Review*, 24 Apr. 1947.
2. Byrnes's statement on British TV.
3. McCullough, *Truman*, 375–6.
4. Labour party election slogan in general election of 1945.
5. Information from Ivor Porter; Porter, *Operation Autonomous*, 238.
6. Churchill, *Second World War*, vi. 198.

7. My personal observation in 1947.

8. Information from Marijo and Marina Bauer, of Zagreb, who attended meetings of the Pioneers at school.

9. Dedijer, *Tito Speaks*, 271–2; Djilas, *Conversations with Stalin*, 82.

10. Clissold, *Yugoslavia and the Soviet Union*, 165.

11. *Correspondence between CPY and CPSU*, 4.

12. Tito's speech in Ljubljana on 27 May 1945 (*ibid.*, 3; Clissold, *Yugoslavia and the Soviet Union*, 166).

13. Clissold, *Yugoslavia and the Soviet Union*, 166.

14. Sadchikov to Molotov, 5 June 1945 (*ibid.*, 166–7).

15. Djilas, *Tito*, 122.

16. Information from Živadin Simić; Djilas, *Wartime*, 447–8. The account of Mihailović's capture in Dedijer, *Tito Speaks*, 254–5, is inaccurate.

17. Dedijer, *Tito Speaks*, 255–6.

18. Information from Dr Feine.

19. For the trial, see *The Trial of Dragoljub-Draža Mihailović, passim*.

20. *Ibid.*, 499.

21. 'Proceedings and Report ... of the Committee for a Fair Trial for Draja Mihailovich' (in Martin, *Patriot or Traitor*, 193–493).

22. Roberts, 221.

23. Kirk to Stettinius, 11 Dec. 1944 (*FRUS*, 1944, iv. 1431).

24. See *Daily Review* (Prague), 20 Mar. 1947.

25. Information from Dr Velebit.

26. For the shooting down of the American planes and the diplomatic repercussions, see *The Times*, 19, 20, 21, 22, 23, 24, 26 Aug., 10 Oct. 1946; Dedijer, *Tito Speaks*, 259–61.

27. Djilas, *Conversations with Stalin*, 119.

28. Tito, *Position of the Catholic Church*, 1–2 (where 'as a Catholic myself' has been changed to 'as a Croat myself'. See *infra*, note 29).

29. Djilas, *Rise and Fall*, 39; Beloff, 33.

30. Information from Dr Velebit.

31. Tito, *Position of the Catholic Church*, 3.

32. Information from Sir W. Deakin.

33. Wilson, *Tito's Yugoslavia*, 42; Avakumović, 124.

34. For the trial of Stepinac, see Maclean, *Disputed Barricade*, 328–34; *The Times*, 12 Oct. 1946. For the accusations against him, see Betty Wallace, *The Trial of Dr Aloysius Stepinac*, 5–9; for the criticism of Stepinac by Tito's government, see *Yugoslavia: the Church and the State*, 17–31.

35. Information from Dušanka Barović, Živadin Simić, Colonel Milan Petrović (who worked for many years in Tito's office) and Olga Humo. The widespread belief that Vera Miletić and Zdenka were sisters is incorrect.

REFERENCES

Chapter 21: The Break with Stalin

1. Clissold, *Yugoslavia and the Soviet Union*, 48.
2. Maclean's report to Foreign Office, 23 Sept. 1947 (PRO/FO 371/ 67440/R 13091/1430/92).
3. Dedijer, *Tito Speaks*, 302–5.
4. For the alleged disagreement between Zhdanov, Molotov, Malenkov and Stalin, see Beatrice Heuser, *Western Containment Policies in the Cold War*, 24–28; see also Kardelj, *Reminiscences*, 83; Beloff, 160.
5. For Tito's relations with Albania, see the Tito-Enver Hoxha correspondence, in Arkiv Jugoslavije; and see Dedijer, *Tito Speaks*, 310–13, 318, 320, 328–9.
6. Dedijer, *Tito Speaks*, 322–33; Djilas, *Conversations with Stalin*, 164–5.
7. Djilas, *Conversation with Stalin*, 102.
8. Dedijer, *Tito Speaks*, 333.
9. Tito to Molotov, 20 Mar. 1948 (*Correspondence between CPY and CPSU*, 21–22).
10. Stalin and Molotov to Tito, 27 Mar. 1948 (*ibid.*, 23–28, where Stalin and Molotov are not named as the signatories of the letter); for the passages cited, see pp. 25, 27–28.
11. Information from Dr Velebit.
12. Tito and Kardelj to Stalin and Molotov, 13 Apr. 1948 (*Correspondence between CPY and CPSU*, 29–41, especially 38–39). For the meeting of the Central Committee of the CPY on 12 Apr. 1948, at which it was decided to send this reply, see Dedijer, *Tito Speaks*, 345–53.
13. Stalin and Molotov to Tito, Kardelj and the CC of CPY, 4 May 1948 (*Correspondence between CPY and CPSU*, 45, 59, 63).
14. Tito and Kardelj to Stalin and Molotov, 17 May 1948 (*ibid.*, 65) (my translation).
15. Clissold, *Yugoslavia and the Soviet Union*, 55, 198. For the meeting of the Politburo of the CPY of 9 May 1948 at which it was decided to expel Hebrang and Žujović from the party, see Arkiv Jugoslavije, Minutes of Politburo, ff. 248–50.
16. Dedijer, *Tito Speaks*, 360. For an indignant denial of this story by the Bulgarian Communists see Kolarov and Chervenkov, 'Unbounded Baseness' (in *Free Bulgaria*, iv, 347, 15 Nov. 1949).
17. Stalin and Molotov to Tito and CC of CPY, 22 May 1948 (*Correspondence between CPY and CPSU*, 66–69); Arkiv Jugoslavije, Minutes of Politburo, ff. 251–2 (13 June 1948).
18. Statement of Cominform, 28 June 1948 (Clissold, *Yugoslavia and the Soviet Union*, 202, 207) (my translation).
19. See especially Draskovich, *passim*.

Chapter 22: Defying the Lightning

1. Dedijer, *Tito Speaks*, 374.
2. Information from Sir F. Maclean; Djilas, *Tito*, 31.
3. Tito, *Political Report to CC of CPY*, 5, 21, 35, 44, 77, 96–97, 102–3, 128, 130, 133, 135–6.
4. Maclean, *Disputed Barricade*, 393.
5. For the Danube Conference and Jovanović's attempted flight, see Dedijer, *Tito Speaks*, 396–8.
6. Damjanović, 'Geneza ismisao sukoba Staljin-Tito 1948 godine' (in *Tito i Koncepcije Socijalizma*, 72).
7. Policy Planning Staff Memorandum (*FRUS*, 1948, iv. 1081).
8. Foreign Office to British Embassy in Belgrade, 2 July 1948 (PRO/FO 371/72579/R 407/92).
9. Cecil King to Foreign Office, 30 June 1948 (PRO/FO 371/78715).
10. Cannon to State Department, 30 June 1948 (PRO/FO 371/72579 Desp. 936).
11. Bevin to British Embassy in Belgrade, 30 June 1948 (PRO/FO 371/78715/R 7769/407/92).
12. PRO/FO 371/78716/R 2168, 15 Feb. 1949.
13. British Embassy in Paris to Foreign Office, 30 June 1948 (PRO/FO 371/72579).
14. PRO/FO 371/78715/R 2160/10345/92.
15. Bevin to State Department, 21 Feb. 1949 (PRO/FO 371/78715/R 2057).
16. Auty, 320.
17. Djilas, *Tito*, 81–82.
18. Information from Živadin Simić.
19. This account of conditions in Goli Otok and in Jasenovac is derived from information given to me by an inmate of both camps who does not wish to be identified because 'you never know what may happen in the Balkans'.
20. Djilas, *Tito*, 86–87.
21. Dedijer, *Tito Speaks*, 76.
22. *New Times*, 14 Dec. 1949.
23. Reans to Marshall, 24 June 1949 (*FRUS*, 1949, v. 903).
24. Heuser, 63.
25. Peake to Foreign Office, 28 Jan. 1949 (PRO/FO 371/78716/R 1067); Heuser, 92.
26. Bevin to British Embassy in Belgrade, 26 Apr. 1949 (PRO/FO 371/78768/R 4224/1634/92).
27. Peake to Bevin, 28 Apr. 1949 (PRO/FO 371/78678/R 4457).
28. Maclean to Bevin, 7 May 1949 (PRO/FO 371/78716/R 5235).

29. Maclean's report to Foreign Office, 10 May 1949 (PRO/FO 371/78716/ R 4734/1051/92 G).
30. Peake to Bevin, 28 Apr. 1949 (PRO/FO 371/78768/R 4460).
31. Heuser, 91–92.
32. *The Times*, 6 Apr. 1950.
33. *Pravda*, 26 Mar. 1950; *Zeri i Popullit*, 25 Mar. 1950 (in PRO/FO 371/ 87603/RG 10392/13).
34. Heuser, 93–94, 244 n. 106.
35. *Ibid.*, 109—10.
36. Foreign Office to UK delegates at UN; Parliamentary Under-Secretary to McNeil, 21 Sept. 1949; Gladwyn Jebb's memorandum, 20 Sept. 1949; Peake to Foreign Office, 26 Sept. 1949; Cadogan to Foreign Office, 27 Sept. 1949; Foreign Office to British Embassy in Belgrade, 3 Oct. 1949 (PRO/FO 371/78822/No. 3014, UN 1962, UN 1979, UN 1988); PRO/FO 371/78823, 3 Oct.); Hickerson's memorandum, 27 Sept. 1949 (*FRUS*, 1949, ii. 254); *Hansard*, 23 Nov. 1949; Heuser, 109–12.
37. Peake to Foreign Office, 1 Oct. 1949 (PRO/FO 371/78823/ UN 2021).
38. Minutes of Cabinet Meeting, 20 Oct. 1949 (PRO/CAB 128/16/ Cabinet 60, p. 40).
39. H. Rumbold's memorandum, 28 Sept. 1949 (PRO/FO 371/78822/ UN 1962/212/78).
40. Heuser, 111–12.
41. Bevin to UK delegates to UN, 20 Oct. 1949 (PRO/FO 371/78823/ UN/ R 220/212/78).
42. Acheson to Allen, 7 Feb. 1950 (*FRUS*, 1950, iv. 1365–6).
43. Acheson to Fowler, 11 Feb. 1950 (*FRUS*, 1950, iv. 1370).
44. Allen to Acheson, 19 Feb. 1950 (*FRUS*, 1950, iv. 1370–1).
45. *Khrushchev Remembers*, i. 335.
46. Heuser, 193–4.
47. For the voting in the Security Council and the General Assembly on Korea, see *United Nations Peacekeeping* ii, 160–72; Wilson, 123.
48. Heuser, 173.
49. For Stalin's plans to invade Yugoslavia and the Kremlin meeting in Jan. 1951, see Heuser, 127–9, and the first-hand sources cited by her.
50. Study by the Joint Chiefs of Staff, 15 Jan. 1951 (*FRUS*, 1951, i. 63).
51. Heuser, 160–2.
52. *Ibid.*, 156.
53. *Ibid.*, 174.
54. Information from Živadin Simić.
55. PRO/DEFE 4/46 JP(51)139(Final), Annex, 21 Aug. 1951.
56. Heuser, 167.
57. Joint Strategic Plans Committee, 'The Position of the United States with

respect to Yugoslavia', 7 Apr. 1951 (USNA/JSPC 969/2, Enclosure E. Para. 14, p. 16).

58. Memorandum from Washington to Ministry of Defence in London, 7 Mar. 1951 (PRO/DEFE 7/216, No. 4).

59. Savage's memorandum, 23 May 1951 (*FRUS*, 1951, i. 839–40).

60. Minutes of 136th meeting of (British) Chiefs of Staff Committee, 27 Aug. 1951 (PRO/DEFE 4/46, Confidential Annex, pp. 2, 5, 6, 9, 11).

61. R. H. Scott, 'Account of the visit of the Yugoslav President to attend the funeral of King George VI', 18 Feb. 1952 (PRO/FO 371/102281/ W7 1941/3).

62. *Official Programme* of the funeral; *The Times*, 16 Feb. 1952; *Evening Standard*, 14, 15, Feb. 1952.

63. McLynn, 303; information from Lady Antonia Fraser.

64. Kardelj, *Socialist Democracy*, 29–30.

65. Wilson, 76.

66. Dedijer, *Tito Speaks*, 95–96, 100–1.

67. Wilson, 77.

68. Mallett to Eden, 26 Sept. 1952 (PRO/FO 371/102181/WY 1052/51).

69. Dedijer, *Tito Speaks*, 411–12, 416–17.

70. For the official Titoist line on Hebrang, see Milatović, *Slučaj Andrije Hebrang, passim*.

71. *The Uprooting*, 113.

72. Information from Dr Pavićević; and see Kljakić, *Dosije Hebrang, passim*; Vonte *Hebrang, passim*.

73. Kljakić, 293; Milatović, 129.

74. Information from Dr Velebit.

75. For the Tito–Eden talks on 18 Sept. 1952, see PRO/FO 371/102181/ WY 1053/45. For Tito's speech at the lunch for Eden on 18 Sept. 1952, see PRO/FO 371/102181/ WY 1052/50.

76. Wilson, 87.

Chapter 23: The Triumphant Tito

1. *The Times*, 13, 16, 17, 18, 19, 21 and 23 Mar. 1953. For the KGB plot to assassinate Tito in London, see *ibid.*, 26 Mar. 1994.

2. *Ibid.*, 20 Mar. 1953.

3. Speech of Peter Smithers, MP, in Winchester (*ibid.*, 23 Mar. 1953).

4. Tito, *Marshal Tito on Trieste and Italo-Yugoslav Relations*, 6.

5. Djilas, *Tito*, 65.

6. Khrushchev, 'Stalinist Friendship of Peoples' (in *Pravda*, 21 Dec. 1949) (*Khrushchev Speaks*, 13, 19).

7. Statement by Miša Broz to me on 17 June 1993. For the criticism, see Djilas, *Tito*, 93–95.
8. My observation at 15 Užička Street, Belgrade.
9. Information from Emina Kurtagić.
10. Information from Miša Broz.
11. Information from Ranko Bugarčić (Tito's secretary).
12. Information from Miša Broz.
13. The information about Tito's visits to Kumrovec (on pp. 322–4) is from his cousin Martin Broz.
14. Djilas, *Tito*, 77.
15. Information from Tito's Foreign Ministers Miloš Minić and Josip Vrhovec.
16. Information from Miša Broz, Slavenka Oughtred (Petnički), Ranko Bugarčić and Ljerka Radović. See also Djilas, *Tito*, 127.
17. Beloff, 36 (quoting Enver Hoxha's statements).
18. Information from Ranko Bugarčić.
19. Information from Dušan Makavejev, the film director.
20. Information from Dr Velebit and Mrs Vera Velebit.
21. Djilas, *Land without Justice*, 25.
22. Djilas, *Memoir of a Revolutionary*, 126, 175.
23. Urban, in *Encounter*, Dec. 1979, 23–24.
24. Djilas, *Conversations with Stalin*, 134, 136.
25. Clissold, *Djilas*, 236.
26. *Ibid.*, 244.
27. *Ibid.*, 246; Djilas, *Tito*, 43, 152.
28. For the proceedings against Djilas, see Clissold, *Djilas*, 247–55; Djilas, *Tito*, 163.
29. Clissold, *Djilas*, 247–8.
30. *Ibid.*, 251; information from Miša Broz.
31. Clissold, *Djilas*, 255.
32. Djilas's statement to me on 9 Jan. 1993.
33. Bevan to Tito, 1 Feb. 1954; Tito to Bevan, 22 Feb. 1954 (Michael Foot, *Anuerin Bevan*, ii. 420–3; see p. 422 for the passage cited).
34. Clissold, *Djilas*, 257.

Chapter 24: Khrushchev: The Crisis of 1956

1. Djilas, *Tito*, 164–6; Clissold, *Djilas*, 245.
2. Clissold, *Djilas*, 263–5.
3. *Khrushchev Remembers*, i. 377.
4. Wilson, 97.
5. Djilas, *Tito*, 165.

6. Wilson, 99.
7. For Khrushchev's anti-Stalin speech, see *Khrushchev Remembers*, i. 559–618.
8. For Tito's visit to the Soviet Union, see Mićunović, *Moscow Diary*, 58–75.
9. *Ibid.*, 66.
10. *Ibid.*, 75.
11. *Ibid.*, 330.
12. *Ibid.*, 79.
13. *Khrushchev Remembers*, i. 432–3.
14. Wilson, 104.
15. For Khrushchev and Malenkov's visit to Brioni on 2–3 Nov. 1956, see Mićunović, 131–43; *Khrushchev Remembers*, i. 420–2.
16. Mićunović, 145, 152.
17. *Ibid.*, 147–51, 154–6.
18. For Tito's speech, see Tito, *Reden und Schriften*, iii(ii). 297–313.
19. Clissold, *Djilas*, 269; Djilas, *Parts of a Lifetime*, 362–8; *The Times*, 20, 23 Nov. 1955.
20. Clissold, *Djilas*, 269.
21. Information from Žarko Broz.
22. P. Simić, 112.

Chapter 25: Non-Alignment

1. Mićunović, 169–70.
2. *Ibid.*, 170–83.
3. *Ibid.*, 105–6.
4. *Ibid.*, 287–90.
5. See *supra.* p. 331.
6. Djilas, *The New Class*, 69.
7. Clissold, *Djilas*, 272.
8. For the Moscow meeting, see Mićunović, 313–25.
9. *Ibid.*, 327.
10. *Ibid.*, 371; Wilson, 120.
11. Mićunović, 397.
12. *Ibid.*, 403–4.
13. Tito, *Forty Years of Struggle of CPY*, 10, 12, 14–17, 43–45, 47.
14. Marx and Engels, *Communist Manifesto*, 96.
15. Information from Tito's master of the hunt, Dr Miodrag Zečević, who was present on the second occasion when Ceaușescu cheated, and was then told by Tito about the first occasion.

16. Tito, *Yugoslav Foreign Policy* (speech to UN General Assembly on 22 Sept. 1960), 8, 11–12, 23, 25, 30, 33, 38, 40.
17. Statement of former CIA agent on British TV.
18. Information from a friend of André Philip.
19. Wilson, 131.
20. Djilas, *Parts of a Lifetime*, 296–7 (my translation); Clissold, *Djilas*, 278–81.
21. Clissold, *Djilas*, 281.
22. Tito's speech, 3 Sept. 1961 (Tito, *Reden und Schriften*, iii(ii). 379–96). See also Vratuša, in *Tito – Non-Alignment – Contemporary Times*, 98–100. For a critical Western view, see Wilson, 132–3; Boyd, 'Belgrade Notebook' (in *Encounter*, Nov. 1961, 56–61).
23. This was widely rumoured at the time, and is believed today (to de Gaulle's credit) by the Serbian Chetniks. It is based on the fact that de Gaulle and Tito never met. But they exchanged friendly greetings in Apr. 1969; see Stefanović, *Svet i Tito*, 423–4.
24. Wilson, 133.
25. For the Chetnik and Ustasha propaganda in the United States, see, e.g., Draskovich, 127–37, 180–8, 241–9, 264–83, 316–27; and see Beloff, 170.
26. Wilson, 134.
27. Clissold, *Djilas*, 285–6.
28. Djilas, *Conversations with Stalin*, 169–73.
29. *Ibid.*, 171.
30. For Djilas's trial and sentence, see Clissold, *Djilas*, 286–7.
31. *Ibid.*, 287.
32. Tito's speech, 13 Dec. 1962 (Tito, *Reden und Schriften*, iii (ii). 396–400).

Chapter 26: Liberals and Hardliners

1. *Hronologija*, Mar. 1953–Oct. 1979.
2. Information from Živadin Simić.
3. Information from Slavenka Oughtred (Petnički).
4. *Ibid.*
5. *The Times*, 7, 19, 21, 23, 24 Sept. 1963.
6. *Ibid.*, 30 Sept., 8 Oct. 1963.
7. *Ibid.*, 18, 23 Oct. 1963; *Yugoslav Life*, Nov. 1963; information from Milena Glušac, who was in the Yugoslav consulate in New York at the time.
8. *The Times*, 18 Oct. 1963.
9. Information from Milena Glušac; see also *The Times*, 23 Oct. 1963.

10. *The Times*, 27 Oct. 1963.
11. Wilson, 124.
12. Information from Dr Velebit.
13. Wilson, 46–48.
14. For the economic policies of Tito's govenment, see *ibid.*, 125–30, 142–5, 151–8.
15. Djilas, *Tito*, 45, 73, 75.
16. Wilson, 142.
17. *Intervju*, 11 Aug. 1989.
18. Wilson, 145.
19. *Ibid.*, 138.
20. Minutes of 'Secret Meeting of the Enlarged Executive Committee' of 14 Mar. 1962 (Živadin Simić Archives).
21. Wilson, 138–9.
22. Information from Živadin Simić.
23. For Kardelj's private visit to London, information from Živadin Simić.
24. Information from Živadin Simić.
25. Wilson, 196.
26. Information from Milka Kufrin.
27. *Ibid.*
28. Makavejev, on British TV.
29. Wilson, 147.
30. Wilson, 168–9; *The Times*, 23, 24 Sept., 7, 14 Nov. 1966.
31. Information from Milka Kufrin.
32. This account on pp. 376–7 of the charges against Milka Kufrin, her meetings with Ranković, and her visit to Tito in Brioni, is derived from information from Milka Kufrin.
33. Wilson, 160.
34. *Ibid.*, 159 (my translation).
35. *Ibid.*, 160.
36. Information from Mika Tripalo.
37. Wilson, 161.
38. Information from Mika Tripalo.
39. Information from Milka Kufrin.
40. Information from Živadin Simić.
41. Information from Sir F. Maclean and Sir W. Deakin.
42. Information from Mika Tripalo.
43. Information from Milka Kufrin.
44. Information from Živadin Simić; Wilson, 162–3; Maclean, *Tito*, 105–6.
45. See, e.g., Clissold, *Djilas*, 293–4.

Chapter 27: The Prague Spring and the Crisis of 1968

1. Wilson, 141.
2. For the language dispute, see *ibid.*, 172–3.
3. *Ibid.*, 146.
4. Tito's report to 8th Congress of Yugoslav League of Communists, 7 Dec. 1964 (*Practice and Theory of Socialist Development in Yugoslavia*, 24–29).
5. Wilson, 183; Beloff, 173.
6. Information from General Jovanić.
7. 'Audience with Comrade Tito of the representatives at the Meeting on the October Revolution on 14 Nov. 1967' (Damjanović Archives).
8. Wilson, 184.
9. *Ibid.*, 179–80.
10. *The Times*, 10 June 1968; Maclean, *Tito*, 107; information from Sir F. Maclean; Djurić and Bengsch, *Der Zerfall Jugoslawiens*, 68.
11. The five Communist parties to the Czechoslovak Communit party (the 'Warsaw Letter'), 15 July 1968 (Windsor and Roberts, *Czechoslovakia 1968*, 150–6).
12. Schwartz, *Prague's 200 Days*, 199; Dubček, *Autobiography*, 171.
13. Schwartz, 226–7.
14. Wilson, 185–6.
15. *Ibid.*, 184–5.
16. Beloff, 174; Maclean, *Tito*, 107–8; information from George Mason.
17. Schwartz, 237.
18. Maclean, *Tito*, 107.
19. Beloff, 177.
20. *Tito – Non-Alignment – Contemporary Times*, 64.
21. *Ibid.*, 175.
22. *Ibid.*, 157.
23. Tito's speech (Tito, *Reden und Schriften*, iii(ii). 503–4, 510).

Chapter 28: Curbing the Croats

1. Wilson, 195–6.
2. *Ibid.*, 196.
3. Information from Miša Broz.
4. Information from Dr Miodrag Zečević.
5. Wilson, 216–19.
6. *Ibid.*, 201.
7. *Ibid.*
8. Information from Mika Tripalo.

9. Tito's speech at Brežice, in Wilson, 203.
10. *Ibid.*
11. Information from Mika Tripalo.
12. The account of the incidents during Tito's visit to Zagreb are derived from information from Mika Tripalo. See also Wilson, 204.
13. For Tito's foreign visits, see *Hronologija*, vol. i., and *The Times* (15 Oct. – 9 Nov. 1971).
14. Wilson, 205.
15. *Ibid.*, 206.
16. Information from Mika Tripalo and Ž. Simić.
17. Wilson, 206.
18. The account of the meetings on 1 and 2 Dec. is derived from information from Mika Tripalo.
19. Wilson, 206.
20. Information from Mika Tripalo.
21. *Ibid.*
22. Information from Zvjezdana Znidarčić-Begović, who took part in the demonstrations and was arrested.
23. Information from Mika Tripalo.
24. Information from President Franjo Tudjman.
25. Information from Josip Vrhovec.
26. Wilson, 211–12.
27. Djurić and Bengsch, 38, 65; Beloff, 212–13.
28. Beloff, 216.
29. Information from Makavejev.
30. Col. Ghetman, 'Unpublished Facts: How Tito assisted the Nazi Retreat from the Balkans' (in *Free Bulgaria*, v. 314, Nov. 1950).
31. Published in German as *Die geheime Front* under the pseudonym Wilhelm Hagen. The English translation *The Secret Front* in 1954 was published under the author's real name, Walter Hoettl. In *The Secret Front*, pp. 163–7 deal with the March negotiations.
32. Roberts, 108–11.
33. The account of Velebit's unsuccessful attempt to publish the truth about the March negotiations is derived from information from Dr Velebit.
34. Phyllis Auty's letter in *TLS*, 27 Nov. 1970.
35. Information from Dr Velebit.
36. Mićunović, 98–99, 105–6.
37. Information from a Cominform supporter who does not wish to be identified.
38. Pacepa, *Red Horizons*, 347–8.
39. *Ibid.*, 350–3; *The Times*, 1, 26 Oct., 27 Dec. 1975; 22 June, 6 July 1976; information from Niko Barović.
40. The account of the trial of Dapčević, the bomb explosion in Zagreb,

the trial of the five Croats, and the fatal accident to Barović, is derived from information from Barović's son, Niko Barović.

41. Information from Miša Broz.
42. Information from Tito's foreign ministers Miloš Minić and Josip Vrhovec.
43. V. S. Pritchett, 'Tito' (*PEN Broadsheet*, winter 1975–6).
44. Information from Dr Zečević.
45. Information from Olga Humo.
46. Information from Milka Kufrin.
47. Tempo's statement to journalist Bora Krivokapiĉ, published in *Politikin Svet*, No. 2, July, 1990.

Chapter 29: The Last Days

1. Information from Dr Velebit.
2. See Illustration No. 28.
3. Information from Ranko Bugarčić.
4. Information from Milan Jovanović.
5. Information from Ranko Bugarčić.
6. Information from Ranko Bugarčić and Miša Broz.
7. This is clear from a photograph of them dancing together shown to me by General Jovanić.
8. Information from the friend, who does not wish to be identified.
9. Marković and Vlahovec, *Zivot na dvoru Jovanka Broz*, 121.
10. *Ibid.*, 143–4.
11. *Ibid.*, 150–1.
12. *Ibid.*, 138–9.
13. *Ibid.*, 164; information from Dr Pero Damjanović.
14. Information from Dr Damjanović, who was told by General Stanojević.
15. *The Times*, 19 Oct. 1977.
16. *Hronologija*, vol. i., and *The Times*, 6 and 7 Dec. 1977; McLynn, 361.
17. *The Times*, 11 Mar. 1978.
18. Information from Dr Zečević.
19. Minić, *Medjunarodne Teme*, i. 116, 157, 164; *Daily Telegraph*, 1 Sept. 1979.
20. For the New Year lunch, the bulletins on Tito's health from 3 Jan.–3 May 1980, and the Central Committee's announcement of his death, see *Bilo je časno živjeti s Titom*, 6–35.
21. Information from Miša Broz.

Chapter 30: Yugoslavia after Tito

1. Information from Živadin Simić.
2. Information from Ranko Bugarčić.
3. Information from Dr Milan Jovanović.
4. Djurić and Bengsch, 204.
5. Slogan of Croatian demonstrators in Vienna, seen by me in Sept. 1991.
6. President Tudjman's statement to me on 19 September 1993.
7. Information from Olga Humo.
8. Marx, *The Eighteenth Brumaire of Louis Bonaparte*, 119.
9. Entry by Vuković Željko of Bihac in the visitors' book at the Spomen Park in Kumrovec, dated 15 Sept. 1993, and seen by me on 16 Sept. 1993.

Bibliography

MANUSCRIPT SOURCES

Arkiv Jugoslavije, Belgrade
M. Čaldarović Archives, Zagreb
P. Damjanović Archives, Belgrade
English PEN Archives, London
G. Harris Archives, Tunbridge Wells
Hrvatski Povijesni Muzej Archives, Zagreb
H. W. King Archives, Isle of Luing
G. Mason Archives, Uppingham
Public Record Office Archives, Kew
E. D. Roberts Archives, Steeple Aston
R. Seligman Archives, Melbourne, Australia
Ž. Simić Archives, Belgrade
Spomen Park Archives, Kumrovec
United States National Archives, Washington, DC

PRINTED SOURCES

AARONS, M., and LOFTUS, J., *Ratlines* (London, 1991)
The Army Air Forces in World War II (ed. Craven W. F. and Cate, J. L.)
   (Chicago, 1948–53)
AUTY, PHYLLIS, *Tito* (London, 1970)
AUTY, PHYLLIS and CLOGG, R. (eds.), *British Policy towards Wartime Resistance in Yugoslavia and Greece* (London, 1975)
AVAKUMOVIC, I., *History of the Communist Party of Yugoslavia* (Aberdeen, 1964)
BAILEY, S. W., 'British Policy towards General Draža Mihailović', *see* Auty, Phyllis and Clogg, R. (eds).
BARKER, ELISABETH. 'Some Factors in British Decision-Making over Yugoslavia 1941–4'. *See* Auty, Phyllis and Clogg, R. (eds.)

BASTA, M. *Rat je Završen 7 Dana Kasnije* (Zagreb, no date)

BELOFF, NORA. *Tito's Flawed Legacy* (London, 1985)

BENNETT, R. *Ultra and Mediterranean Strategy* (New York, 1989)

Bila je časno živjeti s Titom (Preface by M. Krleža) (Zagreb, 1980)

BOYD, A., 'Belgrade Notebook' (*Encounter*, Nov. 1961, 56–61)

British Policy towards Wartime Resistance. See Auty, Phyllis, and Clogg, R.

BROUCEK, P. (ed.), *Ein General im Zwielicht: Erinnerungen von Edmund Glaises von Horstenau* (Vienna, 1980–8)

BUBER, MARGARETE, *Under Two Dictators* (London, 1950)

Cahier-Partisan (Belgrade, 1946)

CENČIĆ, V., *Enigma Kopinić* (Belgrade, 1985)

CESARINI, D., *How Britain became a Refuge for Nazi War Criminals* (London, 1992)

CHURCHILL, RANDOLPH S., *Winston S. Churchill*, vols. 1–2 (London, 1966–7). *See also* Gilbert

CHURCHILL, T.B.L., *Commando Crusade* (London, 1987)

CHURCHILL, WINSTON S., *Great Contemporaries* (London, 1937)

— *Savrola* (London, 1900)

— *The Second World War* (London, 1948–54)

— *Thoughts and Adventures* (London, 1932)

CLISSOLD, S., *Djilas: The Progress of a Revolutionary* (Hounslow, Mddx, 1983)

— *Whirlwind: An Account of Marshal Tito's Rise to Power* (London, 1949)

— (ed.), *Yugoslavia and the Soviet Union 1939–1973* (London, 1975)

The Correspondence between the Central Committee of the Communist Party of Jugoslavia and the Central Committee of the All-Union Communist Party (Bolsheviks) (Belgrade, 1948)

Crime without Punishment: Genocide against the Serbs (Belgrade, 1991)

Daily Herald (London, 1933)

Daily Review (Prague, 1947)

Daily Telegraph (London, 1979)

DAMJANOVIĆ, P., 'Geneza ismisao sukoba Staljin-Tito 1948 Godine' (*Tito i Koncepcije Socijalizma*, pp. 56–73, Belgrade, 1990)

DAMJANOVIĆ, P., BOSIĆ, M., LAZAREVIĆ, D. (eds), *Peta Zemaljska Konferencija KPJ* (Belgrade, 1980)

DAVIDSON, B., *Partisan Picture* (Bedford, 1946)

DEAKIN, F.W.D. (Sir W.), *The Brutal Friendship: Hitler, Mussolini and the Fall of Italian Fascism* (London, 1962)

— *The Embattled Mountain* (London, 1971)

DEDIJER, V., *Josip Broz Tito* (Belgrade, 1953)

— *Novi prilozi za Biografiju Josipa Broza Tita* (Belgrade, 1981)

— *Tito Speaks* (London, 1953) (the English version of *Josip Broz Tito*)

— *The War Diaries of Vladimir Dedijer* (Ann Arbor, 1990)

DEGRAS, JANE (ed.), *The Communist International 1919–1943: Documents* (London, 1956–65)

DEUTSCHER, I., *The Prophet Outcast: Trotsky 1929–1940* (London, 1963)

DIMITROV, G., *After Munich*, (London, 1938)

DJILAS, A., *The Contested Country* (Cambridge, Mass., 1991)

DJILAS, M., *Conversations with Stalin* (London, 1962)

— *Land without Justice* (London, 1955)

— 'Le Village Mort' *see Cahier-Partisan*

— *Memoir of a Revolutionary* (New York, 1973)

— *The New Class: An Analysis of the Communist System* (London, 1957)

— *Parts of a Lifetime* (New York, 1975)

— *Rise and Fall* (London, 1985)

— *Tito: The Story from Inside* (New York, 1980)

— *Wartime* (London, 1977)

— 'Yugoslavia in Danger' (*Encounter*, London, July 1979)

DJURIĆ, R., and BENGSCH, B., *Der Zerfall Jugoslawiens* (Berlin, 1992)

DRASKOVICH, S. M., *Tito, Moscow's Trojan Horse* (Chicago, 1957)

Drvarska Operacija. See Sarenac.

DUBČEK, A., *Hope Dies Last: The Autobiography of Alexander Dubček* (London, 1993)

EDWARDS, L. F., *Yugoslavia: People and Places* (London, 1972)

EHRMAN, J., *Grand Strategy* (London, 1956)

Eleventh Congress of the League of Communists of Yugoslavia (Belgrade, 1978)

ENGELS, F., *Herr Eugen Dühring's Revolution in Science* (London no date) (*Anti-Dühring*)

— 'Hungary and Panslavism' *see* Marx and Engels, *The Russian Menace to Europe*

— *See* Marx

Evening Standard (London, 1952)

FALATOV, V., MILOŠEVIĆ, B., POPOVIĆ, M., *Tito i Koncepcije Socijalizma 1948–1958–1988* (Belgrade, 1990)

FEST, J.C., *Hitler* (London, 1974)

FILIPOVIĆ, F., *Sabrana Dela* (ed. P. Damjanović), vol. xiv (Belgrade, 1989)

FOOT, MICHAEL, *Aneurin Bevan* (London, 1962–73)

FOOT, M.R.D., *S.O.E. The Special Operations Executive 1940–46* (London, 1984)

Foreign Relations of the United States: Diplomatic Papers (Washington, DC, 1966–80) (referred to as 'FRUS')

France (London, 1941)

Free Bulgaria (Sofia, 1949–50)

[457]

FRUS. See Foreign Relations of the United States

The General Council of the First International 1864–1866: Minutes (Moscow, 1963)

GHETMAN, A., 'Unpublished Facts: How Tito assisted the Nazi Retreat from the Balkans' (*Free Bulgaria*, v. 314, Sofia, 1 Nov. 1950)

GILBERT, M., *Winston S. Churchill*, vols. iii–viii (London, 1971–88) *See also* Churchill, Randolph S.

GRAY, R., 'Objective Tito' (*War Monthly*, London, Mar. 1979)

GRIFFITHS, R., *Fellow Travellers of the Right* (London, 1980)

Hansard, *Parliamentary Debates, Official Report* (London, 1919–49)

HEUSER, BEATRICE, *Western 'Containment' Policies in the Cold War: The Yugoslav Case, 1948–53* (London, 1989)

HIGGINS, ROSALYN, *United Nations Peacekeeping* (London, 1969–81)

History of the Communist Party of the Soviet Union (Bolsheviks) (London, 1943)

HITLER, A., *Mein Kampf* (Munich, 1935)

HOETTL, W., *The Secret Front* (London, 1954)

HOMONNAY, E., *Atrocities committed by Tito's Communist Parties in Occupied Southern-Hungary* (Cleveland, Ohio, 1957)

HOPTNER, J. B., *Yugoslavia in Crisis 1934–1941* (New York, 1962)

HORY, L. and BROSZAT, M., *Der Kroatische Ustascha-Staat 1941–1945* (Stuttgart, 1964)

Hronologija. See Ilić and Čirković

HUGHES, EMRYS, *Bolshevik Bogey in Britain* (Glasgow, 1943)

HULJIĆ, V., *Vis 1939–45* (Split, 1979)

ILIĆ, B., and ČIRKOVIĆ, V., *Hronologija Revolucionarne Delatnosti Josipa Broza Tita* (Belgrade, 1978–80)

Indictment Presented by the Prosecutor-General of the Bulgarian People's Republic in the Case of Traicho Kostov and his Accomplices (New Times Supplement, Moscow, 7 Dec. 1949)

Intervju (Belgrade, 1989–93)

IVANOVIĆ, V., *LX, Memoirs of a Jugoslav* (London, 1977)

JOLL, J., *The Second International 1889–1914* (London, 1955)

JONES, W., *Twelve Months with Tito's Partisans* (Bedford, 1946)

Josip Broz Tito Memorial Centre (Belgrade, no date)

Jugoslovensko-Britanski Odnosi: Yugoslav-British Relations (Belgrade, 1988)

KARAPANDŽIC, B. M., *Kočevje, Tito's Bloodiest Crime 1945–1965* (Cleveland, Ohio, no date)

KARDELJ, E., *Reminiscences* (London, 1982)

— *Socialist Democracy:* Speech of 1 Apr. 1952 (Belgrade, 1952)

— 'Yugoslav Attitude on Korea' (in *Yugoslav Fortnightly*, Belgrade, 15 Sept. 1950)

KARTUN, D., *Tito's Plot against Europe: The Story of the Rajk Conspiracy* (London, 1949)

KHRUSHCHEV, N., *Khrushchev Remembers* (ed. E. Crankshaw, and S. Talbott) (London, 1971) referred to as *Khrushchev Remembers*, vol. i)

— *Khrushchev Remembers: The Last Testament* (ed. S. Talbott) (London, 1974), (referred to as *Khrushchev Remembers*, vol. ii)

— *Khrushchev Remembers: The Glasnost Tapes* (ed. J. L. Schecter and V. V. Luchkov) (Boston, Mass., 1990) referred to as *Khrushchev Remembers*, vol. iii)

— *Khrushchev Speaks: Selected Speeches . . . 1949–1961* (ed. T. P. Whitney) (Ann Arbor, 1963)

KLJAKIĆ, D., *Dosije Hebrang* (Belgrade, no date)

KLJAKIĆ, S., 'Utakmica se Odlaže' (in *Politika*, 24 Oct. 1993)

KING, H. 'The British Mission at Drvar' (Anglo-Jugoslav Historical Colloquium, 13–15 Dec. 1982)

KOESTLER, A., *Scum of the Earth* (London, 1941)

KOLAROV, V., and CHERVENKOV, V., 'Unbounded Baseness' (*Free Bulgaria*, Sofia, 15 Nov. 1949)

KUMM, O., *Vorwärts Prinz Eugen* (Osnabrück, 1978)

KUSIĆ, M., 'Pod Uticajem Spijunskih Filmova' (in *Intervju*, Belgrade, 1 Oct. 1993)

Labour Monthly (London, 1942)

LEES, M., *The Rape of Serbia* (San Diego, Ca., 1990)

LEKOVIĆ, M., *Martovski Pregovori 1943* (Belgrade, 1985)

LENIN, V. I., *The War and the Second International* (London, 1931)

— *What is to be Done?* (in Lenin, *Collected Works of V. I. Lenin*, vol. iv (New York, 1929)

— *See* Zinoviev

LEONHARD, W., *Child of the Revolution* (London, 1957)

LINDSAY, F., *Beacons in the Night* (Stanford, Ca., 1993)

LOCKHART, R. H. BRUCE, *Memoirs of a British Agent* (London, 1932)

LOW, R., *La Pasionaria* (London, 1992)

MACAN, T., and ŠENTIJA, J., *A Short History of Croatia* (Zagreb, 1992)

MACLEAN, Sir Fitzroy, *Disputed Barricade* (London, 1957)

— *Eastern Approaches* (London, 1949)

— *Tito: A Pictorial Biography* (London, 1980)

MACMILLAN, HAROLD, *Tides of Fortune 1945–1955* (London, 1969)

MARKOVIĆ, NATAŠA, and VLAHOVEC, D., *Život na Dvoru Jovanka Broz* (Belgrade, 1990)

MARTIN, D., *Patriot or Traitor: The Case of General Mihailovich. Proceedings and Report of the Commission of Inquiry for a Fair Trial for Draja Mihailovich* (Stanford, Ca., 1978)

— *The Web of Disinformation* (San Diego, Ca., 1990)

MARX, KARL, *Capital* (Chicago, 1926)
— *The Civil War in France* (London, 1933)
— *The Class Struggles in France (1848–1850)* (no date or place)
— *Communist Manifesto*, see Marx and Engels
— *Das Kapital*, see *Capital*.
— *The Eighteenth Brumaire of Louis Bonaparte* (London, 1926)
— *Marx's Political Writings* (ed. Q. Hoare) (*New Left Review*) (London, 1974)
— *Revolution and Counter-Revolution in Germany in 1848* (London, 1896)
MARX, KARL, and ENGELS, F., *Manifest der Kommunistischen Partei* (*Marx und Engels, Werke und Schriften* vol. vi, Berlin, 1932)
— *Manifesto of the Communist Party* (Moscow, 1969)
— *The Russian Menace to Europe: A Collection of Articles, Speeches* (ed. P. W. Blackstock and B. F. Hoselitz) (London, 1953)
MCCULLOUGH, D., *Truman* (New York, 1992)
MCLYNN, F., *Fitzroy Maclean* (London, 1992)
MEYER, H., 'Karl Marx und die deutsche Revolution von 1848' (*Historische Zeitschrift*, vol. clxxii) (Munich, 1951)
MIĆUNOVIĆ, V., *Moscow Diary* (London, 1980)
MILATOVIĆ, M., *Slučaj Andrije Hebranga* (Belgrade, 1952)
MINIĆ, M., *Medjunarodne Teme* (Novi Sad, 1985)
— *Oslobodilački ili Gratanski Rat u Jugoslaviji 1941–1945* (Novi Sad, 1993)
MINNS, E. H., 'Slavs' (in *Encyclopaedia Britannica*, 10th edition xxv. 230, London, 1910)
MORAČA, P. (ed.). *Proleter 1929–1942* (Belgrade, 1968)
MORAN, LORD *Winston Churchill: The Struggle for Survival 1940–1965* (London, 1966)
Morning Post (London, 5 Jan. 1920)
MYERS, E. C. W., 'The Andarte Delegation to Cairo: August 1943' *see* Auty, Phyllis and Clogg, R. (eds.)
The National Liberation Movement of Yugoslavia: A Survey of the Partisan Movement, April 1941–March 1944 (War Office, London, June 1944)
NETTL, J. P., *Rosa Luxemburg* (London, 1966)
NEUBACHER, H. *Sonderauftrag Südost 1940–1943* (Göttingen, 1956)
Never Again (ed. M. Bulajić, A. Miletić and D. Lukić) (Belgrade, 1991)
New Times (Moscow, 1946–51)
Official Programme of the Funeral of King George VI (London, 1952)
Organizovani Radnik (Zagreb, 1926)
PACEPA, I. M., *Red Horizons* (London, 1988)
PAVLOVIĆ, Z., *Bilans Sovjetskog Termidora* (Belgrade, 1940); reprinted in *Intervju*, 14 July 1989

PAVLOWITCH, S. K., Tito: *Yugoslavia's Great Dictator* (London, 1992) *Yugoslavia* (London, 1971)

Penguin Book of Twentieth-Century Speeches (ed. B. MacArthur) (London, 1992)

Peta Zemaljska Konferencija KPJ. See Damjanović, P., Bosić, M., Lazarević, D.

PETROVITCH, W. M., *Hero Tales and Legends of the Serbians* (London, 1914)

PIJADE, M., *About the Legend that the Yugoslav Uprising owed its Existence to Soviet Assistance* (London, 1950)

Politikin Svet, No. 2 (Belgrade, July 1990)

PORTER, I., *Operation Autonomous* (London, 1989)

Practice and Theory of Socialist Development in Yugoslavia: VIII Congress of the League of communists of Yugoslavia (Belgrade, 1965)

Pravda (Moscow, 1950)

PRITCHETT, V. S., 'Tito' (*PEN Broadsheet*, London, winter 1975–6)

Proleter 1929–1942. See Morača, P.

Questions Actuelles du Socialisme, vols. 7–8 (Belgrade, July–Aug. 1975)

RANELAGH, J., *CIA: A History* (London, 1992)

RAYNER, LOUISE, *Women in a Village* (London, 1957)

Razgovor o Knjizi Vladimira Dedijera 'Novi Prilozi za Biografiju Josipa Broza Tita' (Belgrade, 1982)

ROBERTS, W. R., *Tito, Mihailović and the Allies 1941–1945* (New Brunswick, N. J., 1973)

RUSINOW, D., *The Yugoslav Experiment 1948–74* (New York, 1977)

SARENAC, R., (ed.), *Drvarska Operacija* (Belgrade, 1986)

SCHWARTZ, H., *Prague's 200 Days* (London, 1969)

SERGE, V., *Memoirs of a Revolutionary 1901–1941* (London, 1963)

SHUB, D., *Lenin* (Harmondsworth, 1966)

SILVERLIGHT, J., *The Victors' Dilemma: Allied Intervention in the Russian Civil War* (London, 1970)

SIMIĆ, P., *Tito Agent Kominterne* (Belgrade, 1990)

SIRC, L., *Between Hitler and Tito* (London, 1989)

Socialist Thought and Practice: A Yugoslav Monthly, vols. xv, xx (Belgrade, 1975–80)

STANOJEVIĆ, T., *Tito u Palanci* (Belgrade, 1984)

STANOJEVIĆ, T. and MARKOVIĆ, D., *Tito, His Life and Work* (Zagreb, 1962)

Statement of the Central Committee of the Communist Party of Yugoslavia in regard to the Resolution of the Information Bureau of Communist Parties on the Situation in the Communist Party of Yugoslavia (Belgrade, 1948)

STAUBRIGER, Z., *Najteža Bitka Josipa Broza Tita 1892–1992* (Belgrade, 1992)

STEFANOVIĆ, M., *Potpis: Tito* (Zagreb, 1980)

— *Svet i Tito* (Zagreb, 1988)

STRUTTON, B., *Island of Terrible Friends* (London, 1961)

SWEET-ESCOTT, B., 'SOE in the Balkans', *see* Auty, Phyllis and Clogg, R. (eds.)

TAYLOR, A. H. E., *The Future of the Southern Slavs* (London, 1917)

TEMPERLY, H. W. V., *History of Serbia* (London, 1917)

Tenth Congress of the League of Communists of Yugoslavia (Belgrade, 1975)

THOMAS, HUGH, *The Spanish Civil War* (London, 1961)

THOMPSON, WING COMMANDER H. L., *New Zealanders with the Royal Air Force* (Wellington, N.Z. 1953–9)

The Times (London, 1919–80)

The Times Literary Supplement (London, 1949–72) (referred to as *TLS*)

TITO, J. B., *Ausgewählte Reden* (Berlin, 1976)

— *Forty Years of Struggle of the Communist Party of Yugoslavia* (Belgrade, 1959)

— *The LCY in the Struggle for the Fuller Development of Socialist Self-Management in the Country and the Role of the League of Communists of Yugoslavia* (speech to Tenth Congress) (Belgrade, 1975)

— *Marshal Tito on Trieste and Italo-Yugoslav Relations: Full Text of the Speech made at Okroglica on 6 September 1953* (London, 1953)

— *Marshal Tito Speaks* (London, 1944)

— *Marshal Tito's Speech at the Closing Session of the Communist Party of Croatia* (London, 1948)

— *The People's Front of Yugoslavia: Speech delivered on 27 September 1947* (London, 1947)

— *Political Report of the Central Committee of the Communist Party of Yugoslavia* (Belgrade, 1948)

— *Political Report delivered by Marshal Tito April 9, 1949* (Belgrade, 1949)

— *Position of the Catholic Church: Declaration made to a Delegation of the Catholic Clergy of Croatia on 2 June 1945 by the Prime Minister (Marshal J. B. Tito) Together with the Prime Minister's Reply to a Pastoral Letter* (London, 1945)

— *Practice and Theory of Socialist Development in Yugoslavia* (Belgrade, 1965)

— *Real Reasons Behind the Slanders against Yugoslavia: Speech of 27 December 1948* (Belgrade, 1949)

— *Reden und Schriften Band III: 1945–1979. Teilband 2: Aussenpolitik* (ed. P. Damjanović, K. D. Grothusen, W. Höpken) (Stuttgart, 1984)

— *Review of Policy at Home and Abroad made at Mila Denovac in the Kosmaj District of the Serbian Sumadija on 9 July 1945 by the Prime Minister (Marshal J. B. Tito)* (London, 1945) (Tito's speech was in fact made on 7 July, not 9 July)

— *The Role of the League of Communists of Yugoslavia in the International Workers' Movement in the Struggle for Peace and Socialism in the World* (Belgrade, 1964)

— *Sabrana Djela,* vol. xiv (ed. P. Damjanović) (Belgrade, 1989)

— *The Struggle and Development of the Communist Party of Yugoslavia Between the Two Wars* (Tito's speech at Kumrovec on 26 March 1977) (Belgrade, 1979)

— *Workers Manage Factories in Yugoslavia* (Belgrade, 1950)

— *Yugoslav Foreign Policy* (Speech to Fifteenth Session of the United Nations General Assembly on 22 Sept. 1960) (Belgrade, 1960)

— *The Yugoslav Road* (Speech at Bandung University on 26 Dec. 1958) (Belgrade, 1959)

— *Yugoslavia – Revolution and After* (Belgrade, 1977)

— *See Eleventh Congress: Tenth Congress*

Tito i Koncepcije Socijalizma 1948–1958–1988. See Falatov, V., Milošević, B., Popovic, M.

Tito – Non-Alignment – Contemporary Times. Collection of Papers from the International Scientific Meeting held on December 15–17, 1986, on Brioni Islands (Belgrade, 1989)

TOLSTOY, N., 'The Klagenfurt Conspiracy' (*Encounter*, London, May 1983)

— *The Minister and the Massacres* (London, 1986)

The Trial of Dragoljub-Draža Mihailović. Stenographic Record (Belgrade, 1946)

TROTSKY, L., *My Life* (London, 1930)

ULLMAN, R. H., *Britain and the Russian Civil War* (Princeton, N.J., 1968)

United Nations Peacekeeping. See Higgins, Rosalyn

United Nations Resolutions (ed. D. J. Djonovich) (New York, 1988)

The Uprooting. See Zečević, E.

URBAN, G., 'A Conversation with Milovan Djilas' (*Encounter*, London, Dec. 1979)

VAKSBERG, A., *Hôtel Lux* (Paris, 1993)

VINTERHALTER, V., *In the Path of Tito* (Bombay, 1972)

VLAHOVIĆ, D., and KAČAREVIĆ, S., *Velika Obmana Blago i Raskoš Josipa i Jovanke Broz* (Belgrade, 1990)

VONTE, Z. I., *Hebrang* (Zagreb, 1988)

WALLACE, BETTY, *The Trial of Dr Aloysius Stepinac Archbishop of Zagreb* (London, 1947)

War and Revolution in Yugoslavia 1941–1945 (Belgrade, 1985)

The War and Revolution of the Peoples of Yugoslavia 1941–1945 (Belgrade, 1961)

WAUGH, E., *The Diaries of Evelyn Waugh* (ed. M. Davie) (London, 1976)

— *The Letters of Evelyn Waugh* (London, 1980)

Weekly Review (London, 1946–7)

WERTH, A., *Russia at War 1941–1945* (London, 1964)

WEST, REBECCA *Black Lamb and Grey Falcon* (London, 1942)

WHEELER, M. C., *Britain and the War for Yugoslavia 1940–1943* (New York, 1980)

WILKES, J., *The Illyricans* (Oxford, 1992)

WILSON, SIR D., *Tito's Yugoslavia* (Cambridge, 1979)

WINDSOR, P., and ROBERTS, A., *Czechoslovakia 1968* (London, 1969)

WOODHOUSE, C. M., 'Summer 1943: The Critical Months'. *See* Auty, Phyllis and Clogg, R. (eds.)

Yugoslav Fortnightly (Belgrade, 1945–80)

Yugoslav Life (Belgrade, 1963)

Yugoslavia; the Church and the State (London, 1953)

ZEČEVIĆ, E., (ed.), *The Uprooting* (London, 1992)

ZEMAN, Z. A. B., and SCHARLAU, W. B., *The Merchant of Revolution: The Life of Alexander Israel Helphand (Parvus)* (London, 1965)

Zeri i Popullit (Tirana, 1950)

ZILLIACUS, K., *Tito of Yugoslavia* (London, 1952)

ZINOVIEV, G. and LENIN, V. I., *Socialism and War* (London, no date)

ZULSIKARPAŠIĆ, A., *Put u Foců Bosanski Pogledi* (Vienna, 1957)

INTERVIEWS

Colonel-General Petar Babić, Belgrade, 22 Oct. 1993

Nana Baranac, Belgrade, 18 Oct. 1993

Nikola Barović, Belgrade, 10 Jan. 1993

Lieutenant-Colonel-General Milan Basta, Belgrade, 22 Oct. 1993

Marijo and Marina Bauer, Zagreb, 20 June 1993

Dr Ralph Bennett, London, 12 June 1991

Vasja Brown, Southend, 4 Jan. 1993

Josip Broz, Kumrovec, 22 June 1993

Martin Broz, Zagreb, 12 and 14 Sept. 1993

Miša Broz, Zagreb, 17 June 1993

Žarko Broz, Belgrade, 19 Oct. 1993

Margarete Buber-Neumann, London, 30 April 1953

Ranko Bugarčić, Belgrade, 22 Oct. 1993

Mladen Čaldarović, Zagreb, 18 Sept. 1993
Vladislav Celik, on the journey from Belgrade to Budapest, 12 Jan. 1993
Dr Pero Damjanović, Belgrade, 11 Jan. and 20 Oct. 1993
Sir William Deakin, London, 10 May 1991 and 29 June 1993
Milovan Djilas, Belgrade, 9 Jan. and 19 Oct. 1993
Dr Gert Feine, London, 16 Jan. 1952
Milena Glušac, Belgrade, 18 Oct. 1993
Giovanni and Marion Greco, Tunbridge Wells, 17 Apr. 1993
Geoffrey Harris, Tunbridge Wells, 12 Jan. 1991
Jean Howard, London, 16 May 1991
Colonel-General Djoko Jovanić, Belgrade, 24 Oct. 1993
Duška Jovanović, Belgrade, 19 Oct. 1993
Professor Dr Milan Jovanović, Belgrade, 7 Jan. 1993
Milan Jovanović, the painter, Zemun, 28 Oct. 1993
Hilary King, Isle of Luing, 12 Nov. 1993
Milka Kufrin, Zagreb, 23 June and 18 Sept. 1993
Sir Fitzroy Maclean of Dunconnell, London, 24 Nov. 1990
Dušan Makavejev, London, 17 Nov. 1993
George Mason, Uppingham, 26 June 1992
Dr Miloš Minić, Belgrade, 24 Oct. 1993
Rear-Admiral Sir Morgan Morgan-Giles, London, 10 June 1993
Sir Anthony Nutting, London, 16 Apr. 1992
Slavenka Oughtred (formerly Petnički), Chorley Wood, 20 Apr. and 23 July
    1990
Dr Branko Pavićević, Belgrade, 25 Oct. 1993
John Platts-Mills, QC, London, 26 Aug. 1992
A prisoner in Jasenovac and Goli Otok who does not wish to be identified,
    Zagreb, 21 June 1993
Ljerka Radović, Belgrade, 19 Oct. 1993
E. D. Roberts, Steeple Aston, 23 July 1990
Professor Stojan Sedmak, Belgrade, 10 Jan. 1993
Živadin Simić, Belgrade, 17 and 29 Oct. 1993
Colonel-General Miloš Šumanja, Belgrade, 22 Oct. 1993
Mika Tripalo, Zagreb, 15 Sept. 1993
President Franjo Tudjman, Zagreb, 19 Sept. 1993
Dr Vlatko Velebit, Geneva, 13 Mar. 1993, and Zagreb, 18 June and 16
    Sept. 1993
Dragan Vlahovec, Belgrade, 27 Oct. 1993
Josip Vrhovec, Zagreb, 18 Sept. 1993
Dr Miodrag Zečević, Belgrade, 21 Oct. 1993
Dr Lav Znidarčić, Zagreb, 23 June 1993
Zvjezdana Znidarčić-Begović, Zagreb, 23 June 1993

Index

Abakumov, Viktor, 333
Acheson, Dean, 304–5
Adamic, Louis, 193
Addis Ababa, 365
Adenaur, Chancellor Konrad, 335
Adler, Viktor, 60, 61
Afghanistan, 20, 21, 417
Agadir, 57
Agitprop, Djilas in charge of, 145, 185, 327, and intellectuals, 145, 191, propaganda, 186, 250, 261, asked to help wounded, 208, and Stalin, 291, 328, mentioned, 209, 230, 277, 359
'Aid for Russia' campaign, 200
Albania, and Romans, 26, conquered by Dušan of Serbia, 31, under Turkey, 31, 38, in Second World War, 158, 163, 350, and Greece, 264, 284, 302, and Kosovo, 283, 366, 400, and Yugoslavia, 283, 284, 302, 307, 309, 350, arrest of Xoxe, 299, Anglo-American involvement in, 307
Albanians, 41, 366
Alexander, King of Servia, 41, 51
Alexander I, King of Yugoslavia, as prince, 73–4, 79, 80, *coup d'etat*, 104–5, assassination, 116, mentioned, 24, 95, 99, 103, 106, 149, 187, 218, 221, 238, 239, 246, 255, 298, 319, 327, 328, 343, 349, 381, 391, 392, 397, 414
Alexander I, Tsar of Russia, 265
Alexander II, Tsar of Russia, 51
Alexander, General (afterwards Field-Marshal) Sir Harold, 201, 230, 241, 251
Algeria, 342, 354, 358
Allen , George, 302
Anarchists, 51, 74, 79, 80, 93, 132
Andropov, Yuri V., 346
Angola, 414
Anti-Dühring (Engels), 107, 160
Anti-Fascist Council of National Liberation of Yugoslavia *see* AVNOJ
Anti-Socialist and Anti-Communist Union, 109
Apartheid, 351, 358
Arabs, 184, 281, 332, 342, 384, 388
Archangel, 70, 75
Arms and the Man (Shaw), 40
Assad, President, 21
Athens, 162, 249, 250, 264, 302, 303, 331
Atherton, Major, 190–1
Attlee, Clement, 266, 308, 311

Augustinčić, Anton, 326
Austria, feudal system, 29, war with Turks, 32–3, and Napoleon, 33, and revolution 37, and Congress of Berlin, 38, and political assassinations, 41, and education, 46, and Socialism, 52, 112, and Pan-Slavism, 52, 63, annexes Bosnia and Herzegovina, 52, 57, and First World War, 60, 61, 62, 63, 64, 65, 73, and Versailles treaty, 72, bankruptcy of Kreditanstalt Bank, 109, volunteers in Spanish Civil War, 131, Germany invades, 136, groups escaping to, 251–2, 253, 254, 255, occupation zones, 255, refugees handed over to Partisans, 256, and escape of war criminals, 260, emigration from Yugoslavia to, 374, mentioned, 42, 48, 113, 117, 129, 205, 309, 391, *see also* Vienna; names of Austrian people
Auty, Phyllis, 135, 179, 402–3
AVNOJ (Anti-Fascist Council of National Liberation of Yugoslavia), 195, 220, 221, 230, 231, 233, 238, 239, 240, 241, 244, 246
Azaña, President, 131

Ba, 226
Babić, General Petar, 310
Bailey, Colonel, 202
Bakar, 89
Bakarić, Vladimir, 240, 372, 378, 396, 398, 399, 412
Bakunin, Mikhail, 51, 52, 79, 80
Balance Sheet of the Soviet Thermidor (Pavlović), 173
Baldwin, Stanley, 125, 197
Balkan federation, idea of, 284, 285
Balkan Pact (1954), 331
Balkans, 27, 28, 29, 30, 32, 38, 40, 73, 196, 249, 418
Balkan Wars (1912–13), 57, 159, 175
Banija, 164
Bao Dai, 304, 319
Bari, 227, 228, 230, 236, 237, 238
Barović, Jovan, 404, 405–6
Barre, Raymond, 20
Barthou, Louis, 116
Bartoš, Professor, 86
Basil II, Emperor, 28
Basle, Congress of Second International at, 58, 60

Basta, General, Milan, 253, 258
Bastasi, 233, 234
Batista, general Fulgencio, 350
Baudouin, King of Belgium, 20
Bauer, Lucia (Johanna Koenig), 121, 137, 314, 344
BBC, 189, 192, 193, 197, 199, 200, 226, 228
Beaverbrook, Lord, 199, 200, 232
Bebel, August, 89
Bebler, Aleš, 281, 293, 301, 303
Becić, Vladimir, 326
Belgium, 20, 53, 60, 131, 151, 198
Belgrade, funeral of Tito in, 19, 20, 21–3, Austrian capture of, 32, Communist election success in, 78, Communist demonstrations in, 87, Alexander's *coup d'etat*, 104, Delbos visits, 136, volunteers at Czech embassy in, 141, 142, demonstrations in, 144, 149, 159–60, 161, bombing of, 161, inhabitants flee from, 161–2, Tito and Communist party in, 166–7, 168, 169, 170, sabotage of Zagreb-Belgrade railway, 168, 176, 195, 206, 207, Tito leaves to take command of Partisans, 173, Germans execute Chetnik supporters in, 201, American air raid on, 228, liberation by Partisans and red Army, 246, 247–8, US sends envoy to Tito in, 251, British embassy in, 254, 255, 278, 295, 301, 303, 312, Red army behaviour in, 269–70, proposal to establish Cominform secretariat in, 282, Dimitrov sees Djilas in, 288, International Danube Commission in, 293, 294, US ambassadors in, 295, 302, 304, French ambassador in 296, 308, 358, Soviet embassy in, 312, 388, Eden visits, 315, Tito's residences in, 319, 320, 375, Greek king and queen visit, 331, Khrushchev and Bulganin visit, 333, Gerö invited to, 336, conference of Non-Aligned States in 358, 389, as capital of Yugoslavia, 381, 1968 demonstrations in, 385–6, Nixon visits, 388, Elizabeth II visits, 389, Brezhnev visits, 396, Thatcher visits, 413, attitude to Tito in, 420
Belgrade University, 86, 115, 159, 160, 385–6, 392
Belje, 414
Beloff, Nora, 84
Belousova, Pelagea (Polka) see Broz, Polka
Beneš, President Edvard, 141, 142
Benzler, Felix, 171, 182
Berchtesgaden, 159, 171
Beria, Lavrenti P., 318, 333, 334, 380
Berlin, Communist rising in, 72, fire in Reichstag, 111, surrenders to Russians, 252, Gestapo reports in, 312, Western allies in, 350, 355, crisis (1961), 355, 358–9, 362, Wall, 355, 374, British demonstration about, 358
Berlin, Congress of (1878), 38, 40

Bernstein, Edvard, 329
Bevan, Aneurin, 304, 330, 332
Bevin, Ernest, 266–7, 268, 280, 291, 295, 296, 300, 301, 302, 303–4, 311
Bidault, Georges, 267, 280
Bihać, 191, 192, 194, 195, 204, 220, 420
Black Lamb and Grey Falcon (West), 123, 225
Bled, 276, 284, 319, 331
Bleiburg, 260
Blue Division, 198
Blum, Léon, 124, 129, 154
Bohemia, 54, 55, 72
Böhme, General Franz, 178
Bolivia, 365
Böll, Heinrich, 407
Bolsheviks/Bolshevism, and Russian Revolution, 66, 67, 68, 69, 70, 71, 74, 76, and Hungarians, 71, 72, and Allied leaders, 74–5, refugees from, 80, and tenth anniversary of October Revolution, 92, 93, arguments among, 93–4, as target of purge, 126, Germany intends to destroy, 159, mentioned, 77, 79, 109, 125, 139, 142, 144, 164, 171, 180, 184, 186, 197, 253
Borba, 78, 101, 185, 186, 327, 328, 330, 333, 346, 382
Boris, King of Bulgaria, 158
Boškovic see Filipović, Filip
Bosnia, Christian missionaries to, 27, conversions to Islam, 31, Orthodox use of Julian calendar in, 32, unaffected by French revolution, 33 unaffected by 1848 revolutions, 38, and Congress of Berlin, 38, Austria continues occupation of, 41, Broz family originates from, 43, Social-Democratic party formed in, 52, annexed to Austrian Empire, 52, 57, and creation of Yugoslavia, 72, Communists fail to achieve election success in, 79, Anarchist influence on Socialism in, 79, Muslims in, 24, 95, 222, 282, 292, 400, annexed to Croatia, 163, Ustashas in, 169, 183, Partisans based in, 183, 184, 201, 208, 233, Serbs in, 183, 184, 221, recruitment for Waffen SS in, 184, Agitprop propaganda in , 186, Maclean visits Tito in, 215, and CPY, 292, and free market economy, 368, 374, after death of Tito, 417, 418, 420, mentioned, 26, 28, 170, 218, 276, 309, 319, see also Bosnians, names of places in Bosnia
Bosnians, 27, 44, 59, see also Bosnia
Bradley, General Omar, 310
Brajići, 178, 179
Brankov, Lazar, 291, 300
Brazil, 365
Brezhnev, Leonid, attends Tito's funeral, 20, 21, comes to power, 362, and arrest of Mihajlov, 376, and Nasser, 384, and Czechoslovakia, 385, 386, 388, and possible

invasion of Yugoslavia, 387, and Nixon, 388, 'Brezhnev doctrine', 394–5, and Croatia, 394–5, 396, mentioned, 389, 392, 401

Brežice, 395

Brioni, island of, 319, 325, 338, 339, 340, 343, 369, 376, 377, 379, 389, 403, 406, 409, 410

Britain, and boycott of Olympic Games, 20, representatives at Tito's Funeral, 20, Communist party, 20, 92, 145–6, and Ireland, 36, and Turkish power in Balkans, 38, and assassination of king and queen of Serbia, 41, in First World War, 60, 65, 70, attitude to Serbia, 73, and Bolsheviks, 92, relations with Soviet Union before Second World War, 93, 94, 110, 111, 119, and Alexander's *coup d'etat*, 104–5, and Japan, 109, relations with Germany before Second World War, 111, 125, 136, 141, and Spanish Civil War, 124, 131, 132, Munich Agreement, 141, enters Second World War, 145, helps Finland, 148, lays mines in Norwegian waters, 151, tries to draw neutrals into war, 157, warns Soviet Union about German invasion, 167, discusses Yugoslav guerilla activities, 175–6 sends Hudson to Yugoslavia, 178, drops supplies to Chetniks, 179, 180, Partisans suspicious of, 180, decides to support Mihailović, 180, wishes to stop fighting between Chetniks and Partisans, 188, sees Mihailović as only possible leader, 189, signs friendship treaty with USSR, 190, and identity of Tito, 193, 194, leftist mood in, 197–200, asks Mihailović to blow up bridge, 201, Mihailović denounces, 202, learns about Operation *Weiss*, 204, discovers about Partisans' meeting with Germans, 207, decides to send military mission to Partisans, 208, officers witness Fifth Offensive, 210, decides to support Tito rather than Mihailović, 197, 217–8, 223, policy in Greece, 218, 219, 220, intentions about Yugoslavia, 220, Stalin's reaction to policy of, 223–4, opposition to pro-Tito policy, 225–6, Mihailović attempts to impress, 226, withdraws military mission with Mihailović, 226, sends supplies to Tito, 227, air raids on Yugoslav mainland, 228, invites Tito to send military mission to Cairo, 229–30, Velebit's mission to, 230–2, headquarters in Bari, 236, 237, Tito's position in relation to, 239, 244, Tito discusses proposals of, 239–40, Tito's relationship with officers from, 242–3, tensions between Partisans and, 243, 248, 249–50, troops arrive in Trieste, 252, opposed to Partisans remaining in Trieste and Carinthia, 255, 271, policy over refugees, 255–6, 257, 259, 260, sends observers to Yugoslav elections, 262, at Potsdam

conference, 265, 266, change in policy to Soviet Union, 266–7, policy in Iran, 267–8, sympathy for Mihailović, 273, receives Marshall Aid, 280, Tito unable to rely on support of, 291, and International Danube Commission, 293, and split between Tito and Stalin, 295, and Tito's policy in Greece, 300, 301, 302, 303, as permanent member of UN Security Council, 303, and Yugoslav election to UN Security Council, 303–4, sees Tito as undesirable ally, 308, willing to send arms to Tito, 309, attitude to Yugoslavia, 308, 309, 310–11, reluctant to use atom bomb, 309, 310, Conservatives win election in, 311, economic aid to Yugoslavia, 312, Tito's state visit to, 316–7, and Trieste, 317, 318, and Egypt, 332, 336, 337, 338, 342, troops in Berlin, 355, bans CND demonstration, 358, MPs protest about arrest of Djilas, 359, Thatcher becomes prime minister, 417, mentioned, 184, 186, 206, 214, 221, 246, 251, 278, 281, 351, 374, 401, 418, *see also* London; names of British people

Browder, Earl, 120

Broz, Franjo (father of Tito), 42, 44, 45, 46–7, 48, 49–50

Broz, Hinko (son of Tito), 83

Broz, Josip *see* Tito, Josip Broz

Broz, Jovanka (née Budisavljević; wife it Tito), 22, 314–5, 320, 321, 325, 334, 410–3, 415, 416

Broz, Marija (née Javeršek; mother of Tito), 42, 44, 77

Broz, Martin (brother of Tito), 49

Broz, Martin (cousin of Tito), 322

Broz, Martin (grandfather of Tito), 43–4

Broz, Miša (son of Tito), 59, 167, 319–20, 321, 322, 391–2, 407, 415, 416

Broz, Polka (née Belousova; wife of Tito), 71, 76, 77, 83, 102–3, 121, 137, 314, 343–4

Broz, Žarko (son of Tito), 83, 102, 103, 121, 137–8, 238, 241, 245, 321–2, 344, 415, 416

Broz, Zlatica (daughter of Tito), 83

Broz family, 43 *see also* names of family members

Brussels, 35, 60, 403

Bucharest, 275, 288, 289, 291, 335, 345, 387, 388, 397, 404

Budapest, revolution suppressed in, 37, Tito at fencing championships in, 59, Communist government proclaimed in, 72, Romanian troops enter, 73, 74, Germans make a stand before, 249, falls to Russians, 251, trial of Rajk in, 299–300, anti-Communist demonstrations in, 337, Red Army in, 338, 340, Hungarians in Yugoslav embassy, 340–1, 345, mentioned, 48, 63, 291

Budisavljević, Jovanka *see* Broz, Jovanka

Bugarčić, Ranko, 411

Bukharin, Nikolai, 94, 126, 139, 214, 360, 361
Bulat, General, 408, 409
Bulganin, Marshal Nikolai A., 285, 319, 333, 334
Bulgaria, early history of, 31, 32, and Congress of Berlin, 38, war with Serbia, 40, and Pan-Slavism, 52, proclaims independence from Turkey, 52, and Balkan Wars, 57, and First World War, 73, Communist party of, 120, 282, 288, 292, 386, and Second World War, 158, 159, 163, 218, 246, 248, and Greece, 264, commercial treaties with Soviet Union, 275, and Yugoslavia, 284, 290, 297, 307, trial of Kostov in, 300, Khrushchev visits, 348, and Czechoslovakia, 386, 387, mentioned, 116, 268, *see also* Bulgarians
Bulgarians, 27, 28, 111, 162, 165, 177, 248, 349
Burma, 331, 364
Burton, Richard, 325
Byrnes, James, 265, 267, 280

Čačak, 173, 178, 179, 181
Cairo, 162, 180, 181, 196, 197, 201, 202, 214, 218, 219, 222, 226, 229, 230, 384, 389, 396
Čaldarović, Mladen, 209
Callaghan, James, 20
Cambodia, 390, 414
Campaign for Nuclear Disarmament (CND), 355, 358
Canada, 131, 379, 396
Cannon, Cavendish, 295, 296, 302, 325
Canton, 94
Carinthia, 255, 256, 258, 270, 271
Carl XVI Gustaf, King of Sweden, 20
Carlos I, King of Portugal, 51
Carnot, President Sadi, 51
Carpathians, 63, 64, 319
Carter, President Jimmy, 21, 410, 413
Carter, Lillian, 23
Casablanca, Conference in, 201
Caserta, 241, 246, 248, 274
Castro, Fidel, 350, 353, 355, 356, 414, 415
Cavaignac, General, 37, 110
Ceauşescu, President Nicolai, 21, 352, 353, 387, 388, 397, 403
Central Intelligence Agency *see* CIA
Cerni, Admiral, 227
Cesargrad Castle, 48
Cetinje, 202, 249
Chamberlain, Sir Austen, 93
Chamberlain, Neville, 141, 197
Charlemagne, 28, 29
Chartwell, 125
Cheka, 70, 75
Chetniks, aims of, 175, joint operations with partisans, 176, claim credit for attacks on Germans, 176, meet with Partisans, 177, compared with Partisans, 177, receive arms

from British, 179, 180, agreement with Partisans, 179, attack Užice, 179, 180, Britain decides to support, 180, Germans order crushing of, 181, negotiations with Partisans, 181, Germans march against, 182, kill Muslims, 184, 222, Partisan treatment of, 185, fire on Partisans in Foca, 185, and Agitprop propaganda, 186, Britain wishes to stop fighting between Partisans and, 188, radio broadcasts about, 189, 192, Tito radios Comintern about, 189, 190, and Atherton's murder, 191, British information about, 196, 197, 200, supporters executed by Germans, 201, Bailey unimpressed by, 202, collaborate with Italians, 202–3, Italians cease to supply arms to, 203, ready to attack Partisans across Neretva, 204, fight with Partisans in Montenegro, 207–8, occasional skirmishes, 217, tito willing to accept, 222, Churchill's statement about, 224, 225, draw closer to Germans, 226–7, Red Army encounters, 246, Tito sends divisions against, 251, Tito tries to prevent escape of, 253, Partisans' desire for revenge on, 254, 257, surrender to Partisans, 260–1, and CIA, 296, 327, mentioned, 178, 206, 210, 221, 229, 249, 258, 262, 263, 312, 316, 346, 359, 366, 381, 414, 417, 418
Chiang Kai-shek, 94, 105, 265, 266, 284–5, 303, 305, 350
Chile, 365
China, representatives at Tito's funeral, 21, Chiang Kai-shek against the Communists in, 94, 265, 266, 284–5, 303, 350, and Japan, 109, 265, and United Nations, 303, 305, 306, 358, and Korea, 306, 307, and Third World, 351, and Soviet Union, 356–7, 414, and Tito, 356, 383, 388, 410, 414, and India, 362, Nixon's policy towards, 388, mentioned, 105, 347, *see also* names of leaders
Chou-En-lai, 357
Christianiaty, 27, 28, *see also* Orthodox Church; Roman Catholic Church
Churchill, Lieutenant-Colonel Tom, 242
Churchill, Mrs, 199, 200
Churchill, Winston, Tito alleged to be illegitimate son of, 43, attitude to Bolsheviks, 74–5, anti-Communist views, 92–3, attitude to Mussolini, 93, speech about Japan, 109–10, and Spanish Civil War, 124–5, changing attitude to Soviet Union, 125, British government rejects policy of, 125, 141, speech in Paris, 126–7, and Soviet invasion of Poland, 148, becomes prime minister, 151, warns Soviet Union about German invasion, 167, sets up SOE, 175, hears about guerillas in Yugoslavia, 175, 176, Partisans' view of, 180, Molotov has talks with, 190, and Deakin, 196, 197, supports

Soviet Union, 198–9, encourages enthusiasm for Soviet Union, 199–20, meets Roosevelt at Casablanca, 201, goes to Turkey, 201, goes to Cairo, 201–2, sends Maclean to Tito, 214–5, receives Maclean's report, 217, 222, policy in Greece, 218, 219, 220, 250, 251, attitude to revolutionaries, 219–20, policy in Yugoslavia, 220, 222–3, at meeting in Teheran with Stalin and Roosevelt, 220, and Stalin, 220, 223, makes statement on Yugoslavia, 224–5, receives Ba conference resolutions, 226, and Velebit, 230, 231, 232, seeks reconciliation between Tito and King Peter, 238, suggests landing on Dalmatian coast, 239, meets Tito in Naples, 241–2, Tito cautious in dealings with, 244, and Tito's departure from Vis, 245, changes attitude to Tito, 248, 254, meets Stalin in Moscow, 250, loses patience with King Peter, 251, Sargent writes to, 253–4, agrees to extradite prisoners to Soviet Union, 255, speech about iron curtain, 268, becomes prime minister, 311, and Tito;s state visit to Britain, 316, 317, Tito's respect for, 323, mentioned, 22, 162, 265, 266, 274, 308, 319, 328, 418

CIA (Central Intelligence Agency; formerly OSS), 296, 327, 355, 361, see also OSS

Cierna-nad-Tisou, 386

Ciliga, Anton, 142

Citrine, Walter, Lord, 154

Cizinski, Josip see Gorkić, Milan

Clemenceau, Georges, 74, 75

Clementis, Vladimir, 315

Clissold, Major, 241

CND (Campaign for Nuclear Disarmament), 355, 358

Cold War, 19–20, 24, 264–79, 281, 311, 331, 351, 352, 361, 388, 389, 417

Collins, Michael, 219

Colombo, 389, 412

Colville, John, 198, 199

Cominform ('Informbureau'; Communist Information Bureau), formation of, 282, inaugural meeting of, 282, proposal to establish headquarters in Belgrade, 282, attacks CPY, 288, Yugoslavia expelled from, 288–9, 290, 291, 292, 295, propaganda against Tito, 294, 299, 301, 315, supporters in Yugoslavia, 296–7, 346, 403, and Yugoslav fears of attack, 308, 309, and Hebrang, 313, 314, mentioned, 300, 305, 312, 328, 344, 349, 364, 402

Comintern (Communist International), and Tito's identity, 42, Tito writes curriculum vitae for, 43, foundation of, 72, calls for strike to save Communist Hungary, 73, CPY jois, 78, calls for boycott of Italian goods, 93, and Bukharin, 94, and Social Democrats, 95, 122, opposes united Yugoslavia, 95, sends

Milković to CPY, 95–6, and Polka Broz's escape, 103, and Alexander's coup d'etat, 105, Dimitrov as leading official of, 111, and forged passports, 113, Gorkić as agent of, 114, Tito known as 'Walter' by, 115, opposed to imperialist war, 116, Tito sent to report to, 118, officials stay in Hotel Lux, 120, Tito introduced to members of, 120, Balkan section of, 120–1, Seventh Congress of, 121–2, Dimitrov elected general secretary of, 122, reaches compromise on CPY, 123, makes mistake with Tito's passport, 123, purge of officials in, 127, 128, 129, and Spanish Civil War, 129, 130, 132, and creation of separate Croatian communist party, 134, asks Gorkić to go to Moscow, 134, ratifies Tito's appointment as general secretary of CPY, 135, 144, agrees that Tito should stay in Paris, 135, and translation of History of the Communist party of the Soviet Union, 139, Tito denounced to, 139, 140, and campaign to aid Czechs, 141, 142, attitude to Second World War, 146, 147, 151, 154, tells Tito to return to Yugoslavia, 149, instructs Tito to purge party, 152, 1941 May Day manifesto, 162–3, Tito maintains secret radio contact with, 166, sends orders to Yugoslav Communists, 168–9, 172, Partisans' response to, 176, Tito deals with correspondence to, 187, radio messages between Tito and, 189, 190, launches campaign against Mihailović, 193, and Bihać conference, 194, and Partisans' meeting with Germans, 207, dissolved, 209, mentioned, 59, 80, 98, 100, 104, 136, 137, 138, 150, 153, 160, 161, 185, 188, 192, 220, 226, 245, 254, 268, 282, 286, 346, 354

Committee of 100, 358

Commune, Paris, 39–40

Communism/Communists, in Afghanistan, 20, at Tito's funeral, 20–1, Tito's devotion to, 23, 24, 84, 143, and Marxist ideas, 35–7, reasons for Tito to join, 45, 48, affected by Socialists' support for First World War, 61, and Bolshevik propaganda, 71, attempt to seize power in Berlin, 72, proclaim government in Hungary, 72, overthrown in Hungary, 73–4, early activities in Yugoslavia, 78–9, 80–1, 82, 86–7, 89, 96–7, 98, 99, 114, situation in 1927, 92, condemn Mussolini, 93, struggle with Chiang Kai-shek in China, 94, 265, 266, 284–5, 303, 350, treatment in Yugoslav prisons, 103, 105–6, view of economic problems, 109, and Nazis, 110–11, in retreat in Europe, 112, behaviour as prisoners, 115–16, and Ustashas, 116, in Austria, 117, and Spanish Civil War, 124, 130, 131, 132, and aim of world revolution, 126, purge,

Communism/Communists – cont'd.
125–6, 127, 128–9, 137, 138, against Fascist
aggression in Czechoslovakia, 141, reactions
to injustices in Soviet Union, 142–3, attitudes
to war, 145–6, 147, and economic
inequality, 152–3, German reaction to
sabotage by, 171, and Socialist revolution,
172, and SOE, 196–7, British sympathies for,
197–8, Churchill's changed attitude to, 198,
201, Maclean's attitude to, 214, 215,
political intentions in Yugoslavia, 216, 222,
in Greece, 218, 219, 250, Wintringham's
involvement with, 219, and Poland, 223,
code of sexual conduct, 227, Britain seen as
enemy of, 264, and independence
movements, 265, give voluntary help in
post-war Yugoslavia, 269, denounce
Marshall Aid, 280–1, coup d'etat in
Czechoslovakia, 285, US policy towards,
296, 307, 308, disillusionment, 297, reports
of Korean war, 306, and Hungarian crisis,
337, 338, 339, 342, Djilas attacks, 347, in
Cuba, 350, 355, 356, Chinese style of, 356,
357, in Romania, 352–3, in Vietnam, 383,
388, changes in Czechoslovakia, 385,
denounce invasion of Czechoslovakia, 387,
see also, Bolsheviks; Cominform; Comintern;
Communist party; Communist party of
Soviet Union; Communist party of
Yugoslavia; Partisans; names of Communist
activists and Communist countries
Communist Information Bureau see Cominform
Communist International see Comintern
Communist Manifesto, The, 35–6, 37
Communist party, Albanian, 283, Britain, 20,
92, 145–6, Bulgaria, 120, 282, 288, 292,
386, Croatian, 113, 134, 155, 204, 256, 382,
383, 392, 395, 396, 398, 399, Czechoslovak,
282, 385, 386, Denmark, 348, East Germany,
386, Egypt, 332, Finland, 120, French, 92,
145, 146, 147, 151, 266, 282, 287, 387,
German, 111, Greece, 120, Hungary, 282,
288, 300, 336, 337, 386, India, 92, Israel,
332, Italy, 266, 282, 287, 387, Norway, 348,
Poland, 282, 336, 386, Romania, 120, 282,
Serbian, 382, 400, 408, Soviet Union see
Communist party of Soviet Union, Spain,
120, United States, 92, Yugoslavia see
Communist party of Yugoslavia, attitude of
members serving in army, 64, and History of
the Communist party of the Soviet Union,
138, attitudes to Second World War, 145–6,
147, demand for Second Front, 231,
members' sympathy for Yugoslavia on
expulsion from Cominform, 290,
resignations following suppression of
Hungarian rising, 341
celebrates fortieth anniversary of October
Revolution, 347

members prohibited from entering US, 353,
meeting of twelve parties in Moscow, 357,
leaders meet after Six Day War, 384,
reactions to invasion of Czechoslovakia, 387,
see also Cominform; Comintern;
Communism/Communists; Communist party
of Soviet Union; Communist party of
Yugoslavia; names of individual Communist
party members
Communist party of Soviet Union (CPSU), and
Lenin, 70, Tito's early contact with, 77,
problems in, 94, History of the Communist
party of the Soviet Union, 138–9, 155, and
outbreak of Second World War, 146,
principle of inequality approved by, 153,
member of Cominform, 282, and idea of
Balkan federation, 284, disagreements with
CPY, 287–8, Tito's view of, 289, publication
of correspondence with CPY, 293 Krushchev
becomes general secretary of, 318,
Khrushchev's speech to Twentieth Congres
of, 334, Tito's criticism of, 341, 343, Chinese
condemnation of, 357, meeting at end of Six
Day War, 284, and Czechoslovakia, 386,
mentioned, 120, 286, 398
Communist party of Yugoslavia (CPY), and
Hungarian revolution, 73, in 1920 elections,
78–9, suppression of, 79, and terrorism,
79–80, 100, made illegal, 80, 81, 86, 87, 91,
92, 99, Tito's early association with, 24, 81,
82–3, 84, 85, 88–9, 91, 99, 100, 113, 114,
attitude to Bukharin, 94, special problems of,
95, secret Congress in Zagreb, 95–6, and
Social Democrats, 96, reaction to Radić's
assassination, 97, Pijade imprisoned for being
member of, 103, condemns country's change
of name, 104, directed from Vienna, 113,
114, Gorkić dominates, 114, attitude to war,
116, Politburo moves to Czechoslovakia,
117–8, Tito elected member of Politburo,
118, and Comintern, 120, 123, Filipović as
member of, 127, sends volunteers to Spanish
Civil War, 131, Croat Communist party
becomes distinct from, 134, invites Tito to
Paris, 134, Tito becomes general secretary of,
135, 144, condemns annexation of Austria,
136, and NKVD, 137, works with patriotic
groups, 114, and intellectuals, 144–5,
attitudes to Second World War, 146, 148,
160, 161, 163, organizes demonstration, 149,
purges of dissidents, 152, salaries, 153,
increase in membership, 153, Fifth National
Conference, 153–4, Simić leaks document to,
157–8, and call-up, 158, 162, and
demonstrations, 160, 161, leaves Belgrade,
161–2, and Tito's report to Comintern, 163,
help given to, 166, headquarters moved to
Belgrade, 166–7, and German attack, 168,
dangers faced by, 169, plans uprising, 170,

Stalin's instructions to, 172, Tito's speech in
Foča, 188, ignorance of Tito's identity, 193,
and victory over Hitler, 221, Stalin's attitude
to, 223–4, post-war aims, 239, losses in war,
254, propaganda, 261, achieves successful
Communist revolution, 268, Kardelj
comments on, 271, commercial treaty with
Soviet Union, 275, and Roman Catholic
Church, 276, 277, member of Cominform,
282, as supporters of Zhdanov and Molotov,
283, congratulates Czechoslovakia on coup,
285, receives letter from Stalin and Molotov,
286, disagreement with CPSU, 287–8,
attacked by other Cominform parties, 288,
expelled from Cominform, 288–9, 290, Fifth
Congress, 291–3, publication of
correspondence with CPSU, 293, Cominform
supporters in, 296–7, Sixth Congress, 326,
renamed League of Communists, 326, Djilas
resigns from, 330, fortieth anniversary of
foundation, 349–50, and Pan-Serbian
hegemony, 392, celebrates fortieth
anniversary of Tito's appointment as general
secretary, 410, mentioned, 244, 300, 327,
331, 381, 394, *see also* League of
Communists
Communist Youth, 153, 158, 163, 221, 240
Congo, the, 351, 354, 419
Conservatives, in Britain, 93, 94, 104–5, 111,
119, 124, 125, 197, 216, 219, 220, 266, 311,
317, 337, in Greece, 250, in Yugoslavia, 101,
149, 170, 251
Conspiracy of Silence (Weissberg), 311–2
Constantinople, 27, 28, 31, 32, 52, 73
Conversations with Stalin (Djilas), 359, 401
Copenhagen, 123, 136
Čopić, Vladimir, 120, 138, 139, 349·
Corse, La (ship), 130, 131, 134
Ćosić, Dobrica, 299
Cosiga, President, 20
Cossacks, 65, 255, 308, 319, 414
Cralova, 245
Cranborne, Viscount, 198
Crimea, 110, 283, 294, 334
Cripps, Sir Stafford, 167, 232
Croatia, Tito born in, 23, missionaries in, 27,
and Charlemagne, 28, conquered by
Hungary, 28, feudal system in, 29, 30,
peasant revolt in, 29, under Ferdinand, King
of Hungary and Bohemia, 31, 32, adopts
Gregorian calendar, 32, under Austria, 33,
birth records in, 43, Broz family emigrate to,
43, priests in, 45, anti-Semitism in, 46,
hardships of peasants in, 47, Hungary has
increased control in, 48–9,
Social-Democratic party formed in, 52,
franchise, 52, Pan-Slavism, 52, Catholic
opposition to Socialism in, 54, and creation
of Yugoslavia, 72, Tito returns to, 77, 82,

Communists fail to achieve election success
in, 79, Communists try to organize strikes in,
87, Tito as secretary of Metalworkers Union
in, 89, Croatian Peasant party demands
autonomy for, 95, reaction to assassination
of Radić, 97–8, Alexander determined to
stamp out nationalism in, 104,
unemployment in, 109, Communist party of,
113, 134, 155, 204, 256, 382, 383, 392, 395,
396, 398, 399, degree of autonomy granted
to, 162, Germans promise to create
independent state of, 162, refuses to release
Communist prisoners, 162, becomes
independent state under Ustashas, 163,
Ustasha massacres in, 163–6, 169, 171, 183,
sabotage activity in, 168, 176, 206, Jones
visits Partisans in, 208, Karadjordjević
dynasty unpopular in, 215, Allied air raids
on, 228, new Peasant party founded in, 261,
Tito's problems with Catholic Church in,
276–8, lack of support for Cominform in ,
297, Hebrang as hero in, 313, and free
market economy, 368, 374, liberalism strong
in, 372, and UDBA files, 379, Matica
Hrvatska revived in, 382, language, 382,
income spent outside of, 391, growth of
liberalism and nationalism in, 392, Tito
unsure of how to deal with problems in,
392–3, students unrest in, 394, 397, 399,
Tito and Tripalo discuss situation in, 394,
Brezhnev offers to sort out situation in
394–5, Tito's official visit to, 395–6, Tito is
urged to take firm action about, 396, 397,
Tito meets leaders from, 397–8, discussed at
Party Presidium, 398–9, Tito takes action on,
399–400, Serbian Communists protest
against repression in, 400, Bulat's views on,
408, 409, since Tito's death, 417, 419,
mentioned, 24, 26, 53, 83, 122, 152, 167,
190, 195, 200, 201, 202, 221, 226, 239, 244,
320, 410, 414, *see also* Croats; Ustashas;
names of places
Croatian Anti-Fascist Youth, 137
Croatian Peasant party, 95, 97, 149, 162, 261
Croats, early history of, 27, 28, in army of
Eugène of Savoy, 32, in Austrian army, 33,
help suppress revolution in Vienna and
Budapest, 37, intermarriage, 44, child deaths
among, 45, anti-Semitism, 46, conflict with
Hungarians, 48–9, emigrate to US, 49, desert
to Russians, 63–4, 65, Serbian attitude to,
95, opposed to Marković, 96, massacred by
Serbs, 166, 417, 418, massacred by Chetniks,
184, killed by Partisans, 260, fear of
Yugoslav idea, 381, accused of attempting to
assassinate Tito, 405, mentioned, 24, 41,
177, 186, 195, 202, 238, 259, 278, 292, 365,
406, *see also* Croatia; Ustashas
Cromwell, Oliver, 419

Crvenkovski, Krsto, 378
Cuba, 21, 350, 354, 355–6, 358, 361–2, 415
Curragh Mutiny, 200
Cvetković, Dragiša, 149, 155, 162, 261
Cvijić-Štefek, Stjepan, 349
Cyrillic alphabet, 27–8, 164, 382, 383
Czechoslovakia, and Versailles peace treaty, 72,
  and 'Little Entente', 73, 95, invades Slovakia,
  73, Politburo of CPY moves to, 117, German
  aggression against, 140–1, and Munich
  Agreement, 141, atmosphere in, 268–9, and
  Cominform, 282, Communist *coup d'etat* in,
  285, denounces CPY, 290, nominated for
  seat on UN security Council, 303, 304, and
  Red Army plans for invasion of Yugoslavia,
  307, as atomic target, 310, show trial of
  Slánský, Clementis and others, 315, CPY
  support for, 350, Husák as leader in, 375,
  Prague Spring, 385, 386, letter from
  Communist parties of Soviet Union and
  Eastern Europe, 386, Soviet invasion of, 386,
  mentioned, 92, 114, 122, 297, 313, 361,
  388, 394, 395, *see also* Czechs
Czechs, 37, 54, 55, 63, 65, 70–1, 73, 74, 76,
  116

Dabčević-Kučar, Savka, 394, 395, 396, 397,
  398, 399, 400
Daily Express, 199
Daily Herald, 111
Daily Mail, 111, 301
Daily Worker, 193
Daimler-Benz factory, 55, 56
Daladier, Édouard, 141, 145
Dalmatia, 26, 27, 28, 32, 33, 152, 163, 166,
  184, 212, 227, 228, 239, 243–4, 372
Dalton, Hugh, 175, 176
Damjanović, Pero, 100
Danube, 293, 309, 346
Dapčević, General Peko, 264, 294, 328
Dapčević, Colonel Vlado, 294, 403–4
Davidson, Captain Basil, 196, 197
Deakin, Captain William, 20, 196, 197, 201,
  208, 210, 211, 214, 216, 222, 229, 278, 281,
  418
Declaration of Human Rights (1975), 401
Dedijer, Olga, 211
Dedijer, Vladimir, information about Tito, 45,
  47, 54, 55, 57, 62, 63, 64, 65, 68, 69, 71, 83,
  89, 100, 112, 128, 142, 192, Tito stays in flat
  of, 136, view of British motives and actions
  180, and Muslim atrocities, 184, as Djilas's
  assistant at Agitprop, 185, knows Atherton,
  190, informed about dissolution of
  Comintern, 209, and British mission to
  Partisans, 209–10, death of wife, 211, travels
  to Cairo for treatment, 229, friction with
  British authorities, 230, publishes biography
  of Tito, 312, speaks in defence of Djilas, 330,

Bevan friendly with, 330, Tito wants
  reconciliation with, 332, Kardelj denounces,
  332–3, trial, 333, Tito's remarks on
  economy to, 368, information about March
  negotiations, 402, 403, mentioned, 81, 183,
  188, 191
Degeyter, Pierre, 23
Delbos, Yvon, 136
Delhi, 365
Delo, 375–6
Denikin, 110
Denmark, 151, 198, 348
Deutsch and Grunwald, 45, 46
Deutscher, Isaac, 402
Diaz, José, 120
Dimitrov, Georgi, as defendant in Reichstag
  Fire Trial, 111, 112, meets Tito, 120, elected
  general secretary of Comintern, 122, Tito
  writes to, 136, 137, Tito grateful to, 140,
  brother-in-law hides in flat of, 142, instructs
  Tito to purge party, 152, is warned of
  German invasion of Soviet Union, 168, Tito
  deals with own correspondence to, 187, and
  Balkan federation, 284, 285, talks to Djilas,
  288, 290, denounces CPY, 290, Kostov
  charged with plot to assassinate, 300,
  mentioned, 135, 144, 155, 349
Diocletian, Emperor, 26
Dippold, Lieutenant-General, 205
Divci, 181
Dixon, Pierson, 241
Djerdap Gorge, 309
Djilas, Milovan, information about Tito's life in
  army, 62–3, accuses Tito of exaggerating role
  in Russian revolution, 69, Communist
  activities as student, 86, experiences torture,
  99, 105, believes Tito to have bombs in his
  possession, 100, information about Tito's
  time in prison, 103, views on duties of
  Communist prisoners, 115, draws attention
  to Tito's inaccuracy in translation, 139, and
  Krleža, 145, attitude to outbreak of Second
  World War, 146, 147, helps organize
  demonstration, 149, has problems in deciding
  correct party line on war, 160, decides
  against anti-government demonstration, on
  27 March 1941, 161, insists on sexual
  morality in party life, 169, at Politburo
  meeting (1941), 170, refuses to accept
  Petkovac into Partisan forces, 173, persuades
  Dedijer to join Communist party, 180, as
  head of Agitprop, 145, 185, 327, and
  Zdenka, 187, plays chess with Tito, 192, and
  March negotiations, 205, visits Zagreb, 206,
  402, 403, launches anti-British campaign,
  250, organizes propaganda campaign before
  Yugoslav elections, 261, remarks on
  behaviour of Red Army, 270, 285, 286,
  admits Tito does not bear grudges, 271–2,

Djilas, Milovan – *cont'd.*
unhappy about Tito's remarks about being a Catholic, 277, at inaugural meeting of Cominform, 282, visits Stalin, 284, 285, talks to Dimitrov, 288, 290, believes Tito's ill health due to anxiety, 291, and Goli Otok, 297, 299, visits Attlee, 308, and Trieste Zones, 318, background, 327, as prisoner, 327, disgusted by Stalin's behaviour, 327–8, disgusted by Molotov's behaviour, 328, articles in *Borba*, 328, and wife of Dapčević, 328, protests against, 328–9, case considered at special meeting, 329–30, friendly with Bevan, 330, resigns from party, 330, effect of Tito-Soviet relations on, 331, 346–7, 357, Kardelj faces problems from, 332–3, trial, 333, angered by Tito's speech at Pula, 342, publishes article in US, 343, tried and imprisoned, 343, publishes *The New Class*, 347, further trial and sentence, 347, released from prison, 357, publishes *Conversations with Stalin*, 359–60, arrested, 359, trial, 360–1, and workers' self-management, 368, treatment compared with case of Ranković, 380, released from prison, 380, UDBA take no further action against, 401, publication of *Wartime*, 401, mentioned, 77, 136, 152, 155, 167, 176, 209, 227, 258, 283, 302, 326, 348, 382, 404, 406
Djilas, Stefica, 361
Djodan, Šime, 391
Dodd, Senator, 366
Dolanc, Stane, 406, 407, 408, 410, 411, 413
Dollfuss, Engelbert, 112, 113
Donja Stubica, battle of, 320
Donje Lipovo, 202
Doriot, Jacques, 142
Doronjski, Stevan, 22
Draga, Queen of Serbia, 41, 51
Dresden, 259–60, 292
Drvar, 233, 234, 236, 319, 408
Dubček, Alexander, 385, 386, 387, 392, 397
Dubrava, 153
Dubrovnik, 27, 28, 212, 249 *see also* Ragusa
Duff, Mountstuart Elphinstone Grant, 40
Dušan, Tsar of Serbia, 24–5, 30–1, 164
Düsseldorf, 110
'Duties of Communists in Prison , The' (article by Tito), 115, 116
Duxford, 317
Dzerzhinsky, Felix, 70

EAM (National Democratic Front), 218, 219, 250, *see also* names of countries
Eastern Orthodox Church, *see* Orthodox Church
East Germany, 20, 290, 347, 355, 374, 386
Economist, The, 106

Eden Anthony, visits Hitler and Stalin, 119–20, talks with Molotov, 190, anxious about Churchill's speech, 198, meets Myers, 219, further talks with Molotov, 223, and Churchill's statement on Yugoslavia, 224, 225, and Velebit, 230, 231, and Churchill's comments on Yugoslavia, 238, visits Moscow, 245, returns to office as foreign secretary, 311, Mallett writes about Tito to, 312, official visit to Belgrade, 315, invites Tito on state visit, 316, talks on Trieste, 317, becomes prime minister, 319, and Egypt, 337, 342, mentioned, 241, 267, 328
EDES guerillas, 218
Egypt, 21, 33, 201, 282, 331–2, 336, 337, 338, 342, 364, 383–4, 388
Eisenhower, Dwight D., 231, 319, 337, 350
ELAS, 218, 219, 250, 264, 268, 280, 284, 300, 301, 302
Elizabeth, Empress of Austria, 51
Elizabeth II, Queen of England, 316, 317, 323, 330, 389, 396, 414
Elstob, Peter, 133
Engels, Friedrich, and *The Communist Manifesto*, 35–6, and Pan-Slavism, 37–8, 52, sends money to Marx, 39, expels Bakunin from International, 51, attitude to war, 57, *Anti-Dühring*, 107, 160, mentioned, 126, 138, 139, 153, 216–7, 292, 350, 351, 356
England, 29, 35, 53, 70 *see also* Britain
Erdödy, Countess Barbara, 48
Erdödy, Counts of, 43, 45, 46
Esperey, General Franchet d', 73
Estonia, 255
Ethiopia, 364–5
Eugène of Savoy, Prince, 32, 62

Farouk, King of Egypt, 332
Fascism, Mussolini founds movement, 93, advances in Europe, 112, Comintern's attitude to, 122, and Spanish Civil War, 124, 130, 132, 133, and bombing of civilians, 148, Yugoslav opinion against, 160, 161, 163, collaborators killed by Partisans, 176, international legion of (Waffen SS), 184, mentioned, 117, 136, 141, 142, 155, 168, 172, 180, 186, 239, 244, 257, 261, 264, 389, 390
Feine, Dr Gert, 272–3
Ferdinand, Emperor of Hungary, 43–4
Ferdinand, King of Hungary and Bohemia, 31, 32
Fidlerica, Mrs, 104, 299
Fifth Offensive (Operation *Schwarz*), 208, 209, 210, 211, 214, 229
Filipović, Filip ('Boskovic'), 127, 349
Finland, 67, 148–9, 180
First Dalmatian Brigade, 243

First International *see* International
First Proletarian Brigade, 183, 205
FLN, 358
Florin, Wilhelm, 139–40
Floydforce, 249, 402
Foča, 183, 185, 187, 189, 190, 191, 192
Foggia, 228
Formosa, 303
Fotić, Konstantin, 225
Fourth Offensive, 204, 206, 402, 403
Fowler, William A., 305
France, sends representatives to Tito's funeral,
20, feudal system in, 29, Revolution, 33, 35,
formulation of Socialist ideas in, 35,
Commune, 39–40, growth of Socialism in,
52, and First World War, 60, 61, 65, 70, and
Versailles peace treaty, 72, attitude to Serbs,
73, Communist party in, 92, 145, 146, 147,
151, 266, 282, 287, 387, reaction to
Alexander's *coup d'etat*, 104–5, dominates
League of Nations, 109, Fascist movement in,
112, assassination of King Alexander in, 116,
signs defence pact with Soviet Union, 119,
125, and Spanish Civil War, 124, 129, 131,
132, and Czechoslovakia, 141, and Munich
Agreement, 141, enters Second World War,
145, surrenders to Germany, 151, Allied
invasion of, 231, joins discussions on peace
treaty, 267, and International Danube
Commission, 293, suspicious of Tito, 295–6,
as permanent member of UN Security
Council, 303, angry at Tito's policy in
Indo-China, 304, anti-Tito attitude, 307, Tito
requests arms from, 308–8, and Egypt, 337,
338, 342, and Algeria, 354, 358, troops in
Berlin, 355, withdraws ambassador from
Belgrade, 358, and Vietnam, 383, Tito stays
in, 413, mentioned, 38, 54, 57, 58, 70, 87,
88, 95, 111, 122, 126, 142, 144, 148, 149,
154, 158, 163, 175, 197, 223, 276, 351
Franco, General, 124, 129, 147, 198, 308
Franz Ferdinand, Archduke, 59–60, 288
Franz Joseph, Emperor of Austria, 37, 46, 48,
52, 56, 62, 63
Free Yugoslav Legion, 238, 246, 247

Galeb (yacht), 316, 412
Galliffet, General, 39, 40, 110
Gandhi, Indira, 21
Gandhi, Mohandâs, 103
Garibaldi, Giuseppe, 219
Garibaldi Brigade, 212
Gaulle, Charles de, 266, 358
Geneva Agreement (1954), 318–9
Genscher, Hans Dietrich, 20
George, King of Greece, 218, 219, 250
George VI, King of England, 157, 219, 311
Germany/Germans, leaders pay tribute to Tito,
21, encourages Croats to declare
independence, 24, feudal system in, 29,
Socialist ideas formulated in, 35, 1848
revolution, 37, and Slavs, 38, growth of
Socialism, 52, Tito works in, 55, 57, and
First World War, 60, 61, 63, 65, 73, helps
Lenin, 66, 67, gives money to Bolsheviks, 67,
Lenin thinks Bolsheviks should make peace
with, 70, revolution breaks out in, 72, and
Versailles peace treaty, 72, unemployment,
109, Hitler comes to power, 110, 111,
Communists in, 110–1, Reichstag Fire Trial,
111–2, and Spanish Civil War, 124, 131,
Churchill's attitude to, 125, pavilion at Paris
exhibition, 131, annexes Austria, 136,
aggression to Czechoslovakia, 140–1, and
Munich Agreement, 141, Prince Paul's
attitude to, 144, pact with Soviet Union, 145,
enters Second World War, 145, air raids on
civilian targets, 148, invades Denmark and
Norway, 151, seen as threat by Stalin, 154,
and Tripartite Pact, 159, invades Yugoslavia,
161–2, alters map of Yugoslavia, 163,
prepares to invade Soviet Union, 167, invades
Soviet Union, 168, 170, expects trouble from
Yugoslav Communists, 169, appoints Nedić
as ruler of Serbia, 170, attitude to Ustasha
policy, 171, meets resistance in Serbia, 171,
Chernik intentions towards, 175, Partisan
attacks on, 176, Mihailović claims credit for
attacks on forces of, 176, strength of forces
in Yugoslavia, 177, Partisans and Chetniks
discuss joint action against, 177, 181, kill
Serbs, 178, advances in Soviet Union, 178,
188, and meeting with Mihailović, 181, enter
Užice, 182, march against Chetniks, 182,
further offensive against Partisans, 183,
Chetniks fight with, 186, 189, 190, 224, 225,
Partisans not given credit for action against,
189, 192, Third Offensive against Partisans,
191, identify Tito correctly, 193–4, British
information about Partisan struggle with,
196, 197, 200, 201, Mihailović not active
against, 202, Tito exchanges prisoners with,
203–4, 205–6, 207, Fourth Offensive against
Partisans, 204, Partisan negotiations with,
205–6, reject Partisan's proposals, 207, Fifth
Offensive against Partisans, 208–11, offers
reward for capture of Tito and Mihailović,
212, Sixth Offensive against Partisans, 212,
227, Maclean's report on Partisan action
against, 217, Greek resistance to 218,
Mihailović takes action against, 226, Allied
air raids against German targets in
Yugoslavia, 228, bomb on Partisan military
mission to Cairo, 230, Seventh Offensive
against Partisans, 233–5, retreat from
Belgrade, 248, stand before Budapest, 249,
evacuate Vojvodina, 251, announce fall of
Hitler, 252, Soviet citizens in army of, 255,

Yugoslav liberation from, 268, Mihailović accused of collaboration with, 272, 273, Khrushchev demands peace settlement for, 350, 355, mentioned in Tito's speech at UN, 354, emigration from Yugoslavia to, 374, publication of information about March negotiations with, 401, 402, 403, mentioned, 24, 58, 74, 103, 116, 147, 155, 198, 215, 220, 223, 240, 253, 254, 258, 259, 261, 265, 266, 267, 277, 278, 280, 358, 419, *see also* names of German people and places, East Germany; West Germany

Gerö, Ernö, 336, 337, 341

Gestapo, 166–7, 168, 231, 279, 312, 313, 314, 319, 351

Gheorghiu-Dej, Gheorghe, 335

gipsies, 163, 164, 165, 166

Glan, Beti, 134

Glenconner, Lord, 196

Glinka, Mikhail, 87

Globus, 382

Goebbels, Joseph, 127, 221

Goldwater, Barry, 366

Goli Otok, 297–9, 312, 327, 332, 355, 400, 403, 414

Gomulka, Wladislav, 336, 340, 349, 386

Gorbachev, Mikhail, 417

Gorkić, Milan (Josip Cizinki), 114, 115, 117, 120, 123, 129, 134, 349

Gorky, Maxim, 89

Gornji Vakuf, 205

Gottwald, Klement, 122, 285, 294

Gough, General Sir Hubert, 200

GPU, 102, 119, 212, 226, *see also* Cheka; KGB; NKVD

Grady, Henry F., 303

Graham, Sir Ronald, 93

Greece, Orthodox use of Julian calendar in, 32, and Balkan Wars, 57, Mussolini attacks, 158, German troops on way to, 159, Churchill's policy to, 218, 219, 220, 238, 251, 254, resistance to Germans, 218–9, British forces land in, 249, Communist revolt suppressed in, 239, 250, Tito's support for Communists in, 264, 266, children evacuated from, 264–5, Stalin's views on, 266, 284–5, Soviets denounce British policy in, 268, US involvement in, 280, votes with Arabs at UN, 281–2, Albania supports ELAS in, 264, 284, Tito's policy in, 300–1, 302, 303, possibility of Red Army attack on, 309, 310, signs Balkan Pact, 331, mentioned, 150, 198, 201, 226

Gregorian calendar, 32

Gregory XIII, Pope, 32

Gromyko, Andrei, 20, 359, 361

Gubec, Matija, 29, 48, 320

Haas, Herta, 151, 154. 167, 170, 206, 207, 314

Habsburg family, 29, 31, 32, 33, 58, 62, 320

Haile Selassie, Emperor, 352, 358, 364–5

Haji Amin Husseini, 184

Hankey, Sir Maurice, 125

Hanoi, 304, 387

Havana, 389, 414, 415

Haw Haw, Lord (William Joyce), 259

Hebrang, Andrija, 115, 116, 203–4, 277, 287, 288, 289, 291, 292, 312–3

Heimwehr, 113

Helsinki, 148, 389, 401

Henderson, Arthur, 154n

Herzegovina, 38, 52, 57, 163, 169, 176, 368

Heydrich, Reinhard, 165

Himmler, Heinrich, 247

Hiroshima, 260

History of the Communist Party of the Soviet Union (Bolsheviks), 138–9, 155, 247

Hitler, Adolf, lives in Vienna, 56, hates Jews, 56, 110, comes to power, 110, 111, 112, suppresses Communist party, 111, Simon and Eden visit, 119–20, Comintern attitude to, 122, supports Franco, 124, and cult of personality, 131, marches into Austria, 136, threatens Czechoslovakia, 140–1, and Munich Agreement, 141, invades Poland, 145, secret agreement with Stalin, 147, attacks France, Belgium and Holland, 151, and Prince Paul, 157, 159, decides to attack Soviet Union, 158, sees Yugoslavia as enemy, 160, and Ustasha policy, 171, sends Grand Mufti of Jerusalem to recruit Muslims in Bosnia, 184, opposes Italian help to Chetniks, 203, agains negotiations with Partisans, 207, gives Macedonia to Bulgaria, 218, wishes to capture Tito, 233, 235, German radio announces fall of, 252, mentioned, 22, 143, 144, 154, 197, 198, 199, 208, 209, 246, 255, 256, 259, 266, 268, 283, 308, 316, *see also* Germany/Germans

Ho Chi Minh, 304, 305, 383, 387

Hoettl, Walter, 402

Holland, 151, 198

Holy Roman Empire, 28, 29

Honecker, Erich, 20

Horstenau, General Glaise von, 205, 206, 230, 234, 235, 260, 273

Horthy, Admiral Niklos, 110, 300, 341, 342

Horvatin, Kamilo, 138, 349

Hotel Lux, Moscow, 120, 121, 128, 129, 135, 137, 138, 319, 346, 353

Howie, A. S., 123

Hoxha, Enver, 283, 284, 325

Hudson, Colonel, 178, 180, 181, 202

Humanité, l', 151

Humo, Avdo, 187, 408

Humo, Olga (née Ninčić), 187, 228, 234, 241, 242, 408

Hungarians, 28, 30, 37, 48–9, 71, 72, 162, 169, 258, 259
Hungary, and Charlemagne, 28, conquers Croatia and parts of Dalmatia, 28, feudal system, 29, and Turks, 31, 32, 1848 revolution, 37, and conflicts in Croatia, 48–9, extension of franchise in, 52, Communist government proclaimed in, 72, and Versailles peace treaty, 72, destruction of Communist government in, 73–4, supports Germany, 141, annexes parts of Serbia, 163, fierce fighting in, in 1944, 249, and Cominform, 282, denounces CPY, 290, Brankov defects to, 291, trial of Rajk in, 299–300, 361, and possible invasion of Yugoslavia, 307, crisis in 1956, 336–7, 338–42, 343, Nagy and followers in Yugoslav embassy in 340–1, 345, arrest of Nagy and others in, 345, Nagy executed in, 349, and Czechoslovakia, 386, 387, mentioned, 43, 116, 121, 239, 268, 297, 346, 393
Husák, Gustav, 375
Hussein, King of Jordan, 21
Hvar, island of, 212, 227, 242

Igalo, 321
Illiricum, 26, 27, 28
Illyrians, 26
India, 21, 92, 103, 331, 332, 359, 362, 364, 365, 396, 419
Indo-China, 265, 304
Indonesia, 265
International (International Working Men's Association), First, 23, 39, 40, 51, 52, Second, 52, 57, 58, 60, 61, 78, 329, Third, 72 see also Comintern
International Brigade, 129, 131–2, 133, 147, 219, 300
International Danube Commission, 293, 294
'Internationale, L'', 23, 24
International Leninist School, Moscow, 121
International Red Cross, 65
International Working Men's Association see International
IRA, 219
Iran, 20, 267, 354, 396
Iraq, 21, 311
Ireland, 36, 219
Irkutsk, 76
Israel, 281, 332, 337, 342, 383, 384, 388
Isanbul, 150, 331
Istria, 72, 244, 248, 270
Italy/Italians, representatives at Tito's funeral, 20, dispute with Yugoslavia about Trieste, 20, missionaries from, 27, and Napoleon, 33, and terrorism, 51, and Versailles peace treaty, 72, Mussolini founds Fascist movement, 93, and Ustashas, 116, and Spanish Civil War,

124, 131, pavilion at Paris exhibition, 131, and Munich Agreement, 141, air raids on civilian targets, 148, troops enter Yugoslavia, 162, Pavelić cedes part of Dalmatia to, 163, Jews escape to, 166, 184, Partisans and Chetniks discuss joint action against, 177, Chetniks fight with, 182, 186, 189, 190, 201, 202–3, 224, 225, attack on Partisans, 182–3, ceases to supply Chetniks with arms, 203, signs armistice with Allies, 212, Tito persuaded to escape to, 236, Tito attends talks in, 240–2, Partisans control areas of, 252, Communist party, 266, 282, 287, 387, and Trieste, 317–8, mentioned, 54, 122, 129, 144, 151, 155, 198, 221, 229, 239, 248, 254, 256, 260, 276, 283, 309, see also names of Italian people and places
Ivan Susanin (Glinka), 87

Jadovno district, 164
Jägerhöhe, 247
Jajce, 220, 222, 230, 231, 233, 244, 408
Janeković, Dara, 409
Jan Sobieski, King of Poland, 32
Japan, 70, 92, 109, 188, 265
Jasenovac concentration camp, 163–4, 165, 166, 185, 260, 278, 298, 313, 393–4
Jaurès, Jean, 57, 60
Javeršek, Marija see Broz, Marija
Javeršek, Martin (grandfather of Tito), 44, 46
Jelačić, Count, 37, 392, 396
Jerusalem, 162, 175, 323
Jews, 46, 56, 74, 110, 111, 126, 163, 164, 165, 166, 171, 184, 281, 308, 315
Jince-Čenkov, 54, 55
Johnson, Dr Hewlett, Dean of Canterbury, 199, 200
Johnson, President, 383
Jones, Captain, 208
Jordan, 21
Josip Broz tito (Dedijer), 100
Jovanić, General Djoko, 234, 384, 410, 412
Jovanović, General Arso, 294
Jovanović, Janko, 139
Jovanović, Milan, 411
Julian calendar, 32
'July Days, the', 67
Justinian, Emperor, 27

Kadar, János, 340, 345, 384, 386
Kaganovich, Lazar M., 334, 346
Kamenev, Leu B., 94, 119, 125, 129
Kamnik, 54
Kapoital, Das (Marx), 39, 104, 109, 115
Karadjordj (Black George), 33, 34
Karadjordjevic family/dynasty, 41, 159, 160, 165, 176, 215, 279
Karadjordjevo, 397, 399, 415
Karadžić, Vuk, 382

Karaivanov, Ivan, 140

Kardelj, Edvard, experiences torture, 99, meets Tito, 114–5, attitude to Second World War, 146, at 1941 Politburo meeting, 170, view of British motives and actions, 180, escapes from Drvar, 234, goes to Bari, 236–7, joins in Šubašić discussions, 240, talks to Sadchikov about Tito, 271, accepts Soviet commercial treaty, 275, and shooting down of US planes, 276, at inaugural meeting of Cominform, 282, visits Stalin, 284, 285, and problems with Soviet Union, 287, 288, and Goli Otok, 297, 299, speech in National Assembly, 311, important in Tito's government, 324, 326, 327, accusations against Djilas, 329, faces problems with Djilas, 332–3, at talks on Hungarian crisis, 339, visits Romania, 346, and new forms of Marxism, 347, goes to Moscow, 347, 348, and workers' self-management, 367–8, 369, leads liberal faction, 369, speaks at Executive Committee of League of Communists, 370, goes to London, 371–2, responsible for drafting new constitution, 393, death, 406, mentioned, 170, 187, 188, 334, 374, 380, 382, 411, 419, 420

Kasche, Siegfried, 207, 254, 255

Kaunda, President, 21

Keble, Brigadier, 196, 197, 200, 201–2

Keitel, Field-Marshal, 171, 178, 181

Kekez, Mr, 229

Kennedy, President John F., 354–5, 356, 359, 361–2, 365, 366

Kerensky, Alexander, 66, 67

KGB, 102n, 313, 316, 344, 410 see also Cheka; GPU; NKVD

Kharkov, 137, 178

Khartoum, 371

Khomeini, Ayatollah, 20, 400

Kidrić, Boris, 286, 324, 406

Kiev, 178

Kim il Sung, 21, 305, 306

King, Cecil, 295

King, Captain Hilary, 236

Kirghiz tribe, 71, 75–6

Kirk, Alexander C., 274

Kirov, Sergey Mironovich, 119

Klugmann, James, 196–7, 274, 418

Kočevje, 257, 259

Koenig, Joanna see Bauer, Lucia

Kolben-Daněk steel works, 54

Kolchak, Admiral, 71, 75, 76, 110

Koliševski, Lazar, 23, 416

Komunist, 151

Končar, Rade, 153, 256–7

Kordun, 164

Korea see Korean War; North Korea; South Korea

Korean War, 305–6, 307

Korneyev, General, 224, 230, 236, 237–8, 243, 245, 270

Kosovo, 31, 41, 283, 288, 368, 393, 400, 417

Kostov, Trajko, 300, 402

Kosygin, Alexei Nikolayevich, 386

Kragujevac, 178, 186

Krajačić, Stevo, 297

Kraljevica, 87, 88, 89, 91, 122, 353

Kraljevo, 309

Krleža, Miroslav, 134, 144–5, 326, 382, 383, 399

Krum, 28

Krupanj, 174

Khrushchev, Nikita, becomes general secretary of CPSU, 318, attitude to Stalin, 318, 334, intiates policy of conciliation in international affairs, 318, relaxes Stalinist repression, 318, attends summit meeting, 319, pursues policy of reconciliation with Tito, 333–4, speech to Twentieth Congress of CPSU, 334, and Tito's state visit, 334, 335, behaviour, 335, and Nasser, 335–6, and Poland, 336, and Egypt, 337, and Hungary, 338, 339–40, 341, 342–3, 345, wishes to restore friendship with Tito, 345, requests amnesty for Yugoslav Cominform supporters, 346, 403, attempt to overthrow, 346, meets Tito in Romania, 346, 347, at fortieth anniversary of October Revolution, 348, criticizes Yugoslavia for receiving US aid, 348–9, receives protest about execution of Nagy, 349, visits US, 350–1, walks out of Paris summit, 351, at 1960 UN General Assembly, 353, more liberal policies, 355, 360, 376, and Kennedy, 355, and Berlin crisis, 355, 358–9, China objects to denunciation of Stalin by, 356, 357, and publication of book by Djilas, 360, and Cuba, 361–2, visits Yugoslavia, 362, falls from power, 362, views on art, 375, mentioned, 313

Kufrin, Milka, 195, 212, 372–3, 376–7, 379, 408, 409

Kuibishev, 188, 193

Ku Klux Klan, 351

Kumrovec, Tito born in, 42, Broz family in, 43, 44, 49, situation, 43, Tito spends childhood in, 46, 47, hardships in, 45, 48, right to vote in, 52, Tito returns home to, 53, 54, 77, Polka Broz settles in, 102, Polka Broz leaves, 102–3, Tito ordered to reside in, 108, Tito returns to, 112, Tito leaves, 113, Tito fears danger of visiting, 134, Tito stays in, 321, 322, Tito visits school in, 322–3, Tito goes hunting in, 323–4, mentioned, 23, 58, 84, 115, 135, 193, 319, 325, 353, 364, 411

Kun, Béla, 121

Kungur, 65, 66, 68

Kupreško Polje, 236

Kuusinen, Otto, 120, 122, 346

Labour party, 75, 93, 94, 151, 197, 231–2, 266, 267, 308, 310, 317, 342
Lach, Bishop, 43
Ladislaus II, King of Hungary, 31
Laos, 354
Laski, Harold, 232
Latin America/South America, 250, 351, 354, 365, 394, 419
Latvia, 255
Law for the Protection of the State (1921), 80, 81, 86, 89, 91, 99, 100, 103, 130, 142
Lazar, 'Tsar', Prince of Serbia, 31
League of Communists (formerly Communist party of Yugoslavia), CPY renamed, 326, Seventh Congress of, 348, division between liberals and hardliners in, 369, 370, Third Plenum of Central Committee, 377–8, and commission to investigate UDBA, 378, 379, expulsions from, 380, Fourth Plenum of Central Committee, 383, condemns Soviet invasion of Czechoslovakia, 387, Tito warns about grave situation in, 394, meeting of Party Presidium to discuss Croatia, 397, 398, informs nation of death of Tito, 415, Milošević as leader of, 417, mentioned, 371, 372, 399, 413, see also Communist party of Yugoslavia
League of Nations, 109, 116, 119, 136, 141
Lebedev, V. Z., 193
Lees, Captain Michael, 226
Lenin, Vladimir Ilyich, attitude to war, 58, 61, 146, launches propaganda campaign against war, 66, helped by Germany, 66, 67, and Russian Revolution, 69–70, 71, 92, and Hungarian Communists, 72, condemned by Churchill, 74, Social Revolutionaries against, 75, plot to assassinate, 80, criticized by Mihajlov, 376, mentioned, 81, 89, 138, 139, 153, 265, 292, 319, 320, 329, 350, 356, 401
Leningrad, 119, 145, 148, 149, 178, 334
Leninism, 93, 116, 140, see also Marxism-Leninism
Lepoglava, 100, 102, 103, 104, 106, 149, 162, 299, 353
Leskovac, 251
Le Vernet concentration camp, 147
Liberals, 79, 93, 98, 106, 109, 111, 124, 144, 149, 250, 261, 354, 355
Libya, 266
Lički, Osik, 411
Liebknecht, Karl, 60, 72, 120
Life for the Tsar, A (Glinka), 87
Lika, 164, 314, 394, 408, 410, 411
Lincoln, Abraham, 39
Lisak, Colonel, 278
List, Field-Marshal F. M., 171, 181
Lithuania, 255
'Little Entente, the', 73, 95, 116

Ljotic, Dimitrije, 170, 171, 201, 217, 251, 253, 257
Ljubičić, General, 396, 397, 406, 407, 408, 410, 411
Ljubljana, 19, 21, 54, 113, 114, 116, 117, 146, 270, 319, 348, 391, 415
Ljubljana gap, 307
Lloyd George, David, 54, 74, 75
Lockhart, Robert Bruce, 66
London, Marx in, 39, 40, recruiting office for Finland in, 148, exiled Yugoslav government in, 175, 178, 179, 187, 193, 194, 226, leftist sympathies in, 199, 200, Velebit's mission to, 230–2, meeting to discuss peace treaty with Germany, 267, meeting of UN Security Council, 268, Djilas visits Attlee in, 308, funeral of George VI in, 311, Tito's state visit to, 316–7, 323, Trieste settlement reached in, 318, conference about Suez Canal, 336, CND demonstration in, 358, Kardelj's visit to, 371–2, mentioned, 22, 54, 74, 180, 189, 190, 214, 219, 239, 241, 286, 295, 364, 389, 396, 402, 414
London, Jack, 89
Londonderry, Lord, 125
Louix XIV, King of France, 56
Louis XVI, King of France, 417
Luburic, Max, 164, 260, 298
Lukić, Vojslav, 378, 379, 380
Lumumba, Patrice, 354
Lusaka, 389
Lüters, General, 211
Luxemburg, Rosa, 58, 60, 72, 103, 120

MacArthur, General Douglas, 306, 307
McCarthy, Senator, 143
Macedonia, 31, 78, 96, 104, 163, 218, 249, 264, 368, 372, 374, see also Macedonians
Macedonians, 122, 195, 400 see also Macedonia
Maček, Vlatko, 149, 155, 162, 165, 261
McKinley, President, 51
Maclean, Fitzroy, attends Tito's funeral, 20, believes Tito had bombs in possession, 100, talks to Tito about Soviet purges, 142, mission to Tito, 214–7, recommendations of, 217–8, 222–3, meets Velebit, 232, attends Tito's talks with Churchill, 241, opinion about Yugoslav liberation, 246, meets Tito in Belgrade, 248, visits Tito in Zagreb, 281, talks with Tito about Greece, 301–2, opinion of Ranković, 379, and new Yugoslav constitution, 393, mentioned, 143, 197, 224, 228, 250, 291, 311, 418
McLennan, Gordon, 20
Macmillan, Harold, 248–9, 350, 353
Madrid, 129, 198, 260, 350
Magyars, 38
Maisky, Ivan, 125, 141, 167

Majstorović, Filipović, 165
Makavejev, Dušan, 375, 401
Malaya, 265
Malenkov, Georgi M., 283, 339, 340, 346, 362
Malešević, Branko, 153
Mallett, Sir Ivo, 312
Manchuria, 109
Mannerheim, Field-Marshal Carl Gustav Emil von, 110
Mannheim, 55
Manuilsky, Dmitri Zakhorovich, 120, 121, 122, 137, 146, 147, 154
Mao Tse-Tung, 284, 305, 306, 347, 348, 356, 360, 362, 383, 387, 388
March negotiations (1943), 205–6, 401–2, 403
Margaret, Princess, 323, 389
Maria Theresia, Empress of Austria, 46
Maribor Prison, 106, 107
Marko Kraljević, Prince, 30
Markos, General, 280, 300–1
Marković, Moma, 279
Marković, Sima, 95, 96, 114, 349
Marseilles, 116, 130, 350
Marshall, General, 280
Marshall Aid, 280–1, 295
Martin, Kingsley, 231–2
Marty, André, 122
Marx, Karl, founds International Working Men's Association, 23, 39, and *The Communist Manifesto*, 35–7, joins Radicals in Germany, 37, writes *Das Kapital*, 39, and Communards, 40, and Bakunin, 51, 52, attitude to war, 57, and economic crisis, 109, mentioned, 74, 104, 126, 138, 139, 153, 292, 350, 351, 356, 420
Marxism/Marxists, 35–41, 110, 140, 347, 369, 406, *see also* Marxism-Leninism
Marxism-Leninism, 61, 62, 63, 84, 100, 103, 106, 121, 180, 292, 311, 327, 332 *see also* Marxism/Marxists
Masaryk, Jan, 141
Masaryk, T. G., 70
Matica Hrvatska, 382, 399
Matl, Captain, 181, 202
Maximilian II, Emperor, 29
Mayakovsky, Vladimir Vladimirovich, 145
Medvode, 114
Mein Kampf (Hitler), 56
Memoir of a Revolutionary (Djilas), 105
Mensheviks, 74, 76
Mesić, Marko, 246–7
Metalworkers Union, 54, 87, 88–9
Metaxas, General, 218
Metohija, 368
Mexico, 54, 276, 365
Mićunović, Veljko, 334, 335, 339, 341, 346, 349
Middle East, 20, 196, 332, 358, 364, 400, *see also* names of countries

Milhailović, Colonel Draža, background and beliefs, 159, impresses British, 159, raises force of Chetniks, 175, communicates with exiled Yugoslav government, 175, 179, 193, 194, hates Communists, 176, claims credit for attacks on Germans, 176, meets Tito, 177–8, 178–9, 181, Hudson visits, 178, decides to attack partisans at Užice, 179–80, asks Hudson for British aid, 180, Britain decides to support, 180, meets Germans, 181, retreats from Ravna Gora, 182, announces vengeance on Croats, 184, Britain wishes to influence, 188–9, praised on radio broadcasts, 189, 192, 193, promoted by King Peter, 189, and death of Atherton, 191, denounced on Radio Free Yugoslavia, 192–3, Comintern launches campaign against, 193, Soviet attitude to, 193, scornful of Tito, 194, Britain switches support from, 197, and British public opinion, 200, fails to blow up bridge for British, 201, Bailey visits, 202, and collaboration with Italians, 202–3, prepares to attack partisans at Neretva, 204, reward offered for capture of, 212, Maclean advises no further aid to, 217–8, 222, discussions between Britain and Soviet Union about, 223, mentioned in Churchill's statement on Yugoslavia, 224, 225, support in Britain for, 225, tries to impress British, 226, calls conference at Ba, 226, draws closer to Germans, 226–7, Churchill wishes King Peter to dismiss, 238, Popović leads forces against, 251, escapes, 260, captured, 272, trial of, 272–4, 279, execution, 274, monument erected to, 418, mentioned, 186, 190, 208, 214, 215, 221, 229, 246, 253, 291, 358, 361, *see also* Chetniks
Mihajlov, Mihaljo, 375–6
Mikoyan, Anastas Ivanovich, 334, 346
Milatović, M., 313
Miler, Ozren, 139, 247
Miletić, Mirjana, *see* Milošević, Mirjana
Miletić, Petko, 140, 172–3
Miletić, Vera, 279
Milković, Comrade, 95–6
Milocer, 130
Miloš (Obrenović), Prince of Serbia, 34, 38
Milošević (neé Miletić), Mirjana, 279
Milošević, Slobodan, 279, 417
Minić, Miloš, 413
MKM group, 346
Mladenovac, 262
Mohacs, 31
Mollet, Guy, 337
Molotov, Vyacheslav, M., signs German-Soviet pact, 145, receives warning of German invasion, 167, receives declaration of war, 168, takes part in talks in London, 190, talks with Eden about British support of Tito,

Molotov, Vyachaeslav, M. – cont'd.
223, discloses Tito's visit to Moscow, 245, meets Truman, 266, opposes admission of France to discussions, 267, angry at Tito's speech, 271, and Yugoslav shooting down of US planes, 276, leads group with belligerent policy to US, 283, letter to Tito and CPY, 286, 287, 293, Djilas disgusted by, 328, and policy of reconciliation towards Tito, 333, and attempt to overthrow Khrushchev, 346, mentioned, 280, 334, 362
Mondale, Walter, 21
Mongolia, 346
Mongols, 31
Mont de Moussan, 413
Montenegrins, 27, 44, 115, 177, 195, 327, 400, see also Montenegro
Montenegro, Orthodox use of Julian calendar in, 32, unaffected by French Revolution, 33, unaffected by 1848 revolutions, 38, and creation of Yugoslavia, 72, Communist success in elections in, 78, 79, Communist supporters in, 86, plan to transport volunteers to Spain from, 130, becomes independent kingdom, 163, Chetniks regroup in, 182, Partisan activity in, 185, 190, Chetnik involvement with Italians in, 201, 202, 203, Partisans fight Chetniks in, 207–8, Partisans obtain Italian arms in, 212, strong Slav sympathies in, 291, support for Cominform in, 297, Tito visits, 321, and free market economy, 368, 374, Nikšić steel mill in, 369, mentioned, 26, 31, 152, 170, 178, 210, 218, 249, 372, see also Montenegrins; names of places
Moran, Lord, 241
Moravia, 72
Morgan, Admiral, 243
Morgan-Giles, Lieutenant-Commander, 245
Morocco, 57
Moscow, and Olympic Games, 20, German ambassador assassinated in, 70, sends Sabić to Yugoslavia, 80, performance of Ivan Susanin in, 87, tenth anniversary of October Revolution in, 93, Radić visits, 95, sends Milković to Yugoslavia, 95, Fourth Congress of Comintern in, 96, Polka Broz arrives in, 103, Dimitrov and companions go to, 112, Tito's visits to, 118, 119, 120–2, 124, 127, 133, 135, 136–40, 143, Hotel Lux, 120, 121, 128, 129, 135, 137, 138, Seventh Congress of Comintern in, 121–2, show trial in, 125–6, vulnerability of foreign Communists in, 127–8, 137, NKVD agents recalled to, 132, Gorkić called to, 134, Maclean's period in, 142, 214, 215, German-Soviet pact signed in, 145, meeting of Comintern leaders in, 146–7, receives warnings of German invasion, 167, 168,

Radio Free Yugoslavia broadcasts from, 192, 200, meetings of Stalin and Churchill in, 220, 250, Eden has talks with Stalin and Molotov in, 223, Tito goes to, 245, 248, Tito and Djilas sign friendship treaty in, 270, Stalin summons Tito and Dimitrov to, 284, Jovanović in, 294, Tito's state visit to, 334, 335, meeting of twelve Communist party leaders held in, 347–8, 357, Macmillan visits, 350, Tito addresses Supreme Soviet in, 362, Mihajlov visits, 376, meeting about Six Day War in, 384, discussions about Czechoslovakia in, 385, Dubček and Czechoslovak leaders taken to, 387, mentioned, 22, 24, 59, 72, 83, 101, 123, 150, 152, 153, 188, 189, 199, 207, 232, 238, 247, 275, 280, 282, 283, 286, 287, 312, 319, 327, 340, 346, 349, 359, 375, 392, 410, 413, see also Radio Moscow
Most, Johann, 79
Mostar, 420
Mugabe, Robert, 389
Muk, Adolf, 130
Munich, 55, 110, 394
Munich Agreement (1938), 141–2
Munnich, Ferenc, 340
Murphy, Robert D., 274
Muslims, in Afghanistan, 20, Bosnian, 24, 41, 95, 183, 186, 282, 292, 400, and Turks, 31, killed by Ustashas, 183–4, recruited by Grand Mufti of Jerusalem, 184, kill Serbs, 184, killed by Chetniks, 184, 222, Partisans try to win confidence of, 184, prepared to accept Tito's authority, 276, in Kosovo, 283, fear of Yugoslav Idea, 381, reasons for Tito's policy towards, 400 after Tito's death, 417, 418, mentioned, 177, 202, 414
Mussolini, Benito, founds Fascist movement, 93, appointed prime minister, 93, 125, supports Churchill's attitude to, 93, 125, supports Ustashas, 116, supports Franco, 124, 129, 131, and Munich Agreement, 141–2, attacks Greece, 158, 218, complies with Hitler about supply of arms to Chetniks, 203, 207, arrested, 212, captured and shot, 252, mentioned, 110, 122, 163, 197, 244, 283, 364
Myers, Colonel, 219

Nadj, General Kosta, 193, 318
Nagy, Imre, 336, 337, 338, 339, 340, 341, 345, 349
Naples, 241, 408
Napoleon, 33, 265
Napoleon, III, 39, 57
Nasser, Colonel, 331–2, 335–6, 337, 342, 352, 358, 383–4, 388
National Liberation Army, 251, 252
National Liberation Forces, 169

NATO, 275, 307, 308, 309, 310, 311, 339, 351, 352, 358, 360
Nazis, 110, 111, 113, 117, 125, 127, 136, 144, 147, 168, 198, 205, 247, 266, 300, 308, 351
Nazor, Vladimir, 191–2, 326
Nechayev, Sergei, 51
Nedić, General, 157, 170, 171, 181, 182, 201, 217, 221
Nehru, Jawaharlal, 306, 331, 352, 358
Neretva, River, 204, 206, 207, 402, 403
Neumann, Heinz, 110–1
New Class, The (Djilas), 347, 357
New Leader, 343
News Chronicle, 199
News of the World, 148
New Statesman, 231
New York, 193, 281, 347, 353, 359, 365, 366
New York Stock Exchange, 109
New York Times, 332, 361
New Yugoslavia, 221–2
Nicephorus, Emperor, 28
Nikolić, Baron, 95, 320
Nikolić, Baroness, 320
Nikšić, 369
Ninčić, Olga *see* Humo, Olga
Niš, 159, 228
Nixon, Richard M., 355, 388, 396
Nkrumah, Kwame, 358
NKVD, executes Béla Kun, 121, many executions by, 126, supplies workers for labour camps, 126, kills Filipović, 127, arrests made at Hotel Lux, 128, members sent to Spain, 132, Yugoslav Communists arrested by, 137, Horvatin probably executed by, 138, Karaivanov has influence in, 140, Dimitrov's brother-in-law hides from, 142, chauffeurs as agents of, 153, and Mihailović;s capture, 272, Jovanović as agent of, 294, Krajačić a member of, 297, methods exposed in *Conspiracy of Silence*, 311–2, chiefs executed, 318, and Tito's state visit to Moscow, 335, mentioned, 102n., 135, 152, 414, *see also* Cheka; GPU, KGB
Non-Aligned States, 19, 352, 355, 357, 358, 360, 361, 362, 364, 389, 400, 412, 414
Normandy landing, 237
North Korea, 21, 305, 306, 307, 410
Nova Gorica, 391
Novak, Father Marcel, 112, 113
Novi Sad, 62, 382
Novorossiysk, 334
Novotný, Antonin, 385
Nyerere, President, 352, 358

Obrenović dynasty, 41, 396
October Revolution, 69, 71, 92, 93, 341, 347
Odessa, 70, 150, 178
Ogulin, 89, 90, 97, 107, 108, 112
Okna, 64

Okroglica, 317
Olaf V, King of Norway, 20
Old Partisan Fighters, 397
Olympic Games boycott, 20
Omsk, 68, 69, 71, 75, 76, 77
One Day in the Life of Ivan Denisovich (Solzhenitsyn), 360
Operation Barbarossa, 167
Operation *Schwarz see* Fifth Offensive
Operation *Weiss see* Fourth Offensive
Orthodox Church, 27, 28, 31, 32, 38, 76, 82, 164, 165, 166, 276, 283, 314
Orwell, George, 392
OSS (later renamed CIA), 274, 296, *see also* CIA
Ott, Dr, 203, 206
OZNA (later UDBA), 257, 263, 272, 278, 287, 296 *see also* UDBA

Pacepa, Ion, 403
Pakistan, 21
Palacký, František, 37
Palermo, 37
Palestine, 184, 281, 332, 358
Pan-Slavism, 23, 37–8, 52, 60, 62, 63, 64, 80
Pantovčak, 95, 320, 321
Paris, 1848 revolution, 37, Commune, 39–40, Jaurès assassinated in, 60, Fascists attempt to seize power in, 112, Politburo of CPY in, 123, 129–30, 134, Tito travels to, 123, 133, Churchill lectures in, 126, interntional exhibition in, 131, Tito organizes volunteers for Spain in, 131, Tito summoned to, 134, problems for Tito in, 135, Tito departs from, 136, Germans in, 151, Albanian Communists operate from, 283, Khrushchev walks out of summit conference in, 351, mentioned, 110, 276, 385, 413
Partisans, and Spanish Civil War, 132–3, 147, uniform, 172, policy to dissidents, 172, hostile to Petkovac, 172–3, shoot Pavlović, 173, Tito goes to take command of, 173–4, attack Germans, 176, meet Mihailović and Chetniks, 177–8, compared with Chetniks, 177, Hudson visits, 178, attacked by Chetniks at Užice, 179–80, misunderstand British motives and actions, 180, further negotiations with Chetniks, 181, evacuate Užice, 182, retreat, 182–3, organization, 183, reach Bosnia, 183, try to win confidence of people in Bosnia, 184, treatment of prisoners, 184–5, volunteers for, 185, and Agitprop propaganda, 186, requisition buildings as headquarters, 187, British wish Soviets to exert influence on, 188–9, not given credit for achievements on radio broadcasts, 189, 192, 193, Tiot radios Comintern about, 189, 190, Soviets promise aid to, 189–90, meet Atherton, 190–1, Third

Partisans, and Spanish Civil War – *cont'd.*
Offensive against, 191, 201, retreat from
Foča, 191, hardships faced by, 191, Nazor
joins, 191–2, recreational activities, 192,
reach Bihać, 194, delegates to Bihać
conference, 195, British information about
anti-German activity by, 196, 197, 200,
Chetniks, collaborate with Italians, against,
202–3, exchange prisoners with Germans,
203–4, 205–6, 207, Fourth Offensive
against, 204, and March negotiations with
Germans, 205–6, Germans reject proposals
of, 207, fight against Chetniks, 207–8, Fifth
Offensive against, 208–11, British mission to,
208, 209–10, seize Italian arms, 212, Sixth
Offensive against, 212, Italians desert to,
212, and Maclean's discussions with Tito,
215, 216, 217, Maclean's report about,
217–8, aims in Yugoslavia, 216, 217, 221,
resent Tito's offer of amnesty, 222,
mentioned in Churchill's statement on
Yugoslavia, 224, 225, navy, 227, sexual
conduct among, 227, attitude to Tito, 228,
helped by Allied air raids, 228, and death of
Kekez, 229, and death of Lola Ribar, 230,
Germans attack at Drvar, 233–5, escape
from Drvar, 235–6, arrive at Bari, 236–7, go
to Vis, 237, lavish hospitality of, 240, and
agreement with Šubašić, 240, 244, British
make difficulties for, 240–1, tensions
between Allies and, 243, Tito wants
liberation to be achieved by, 246, 247–8,
enter Belgrade, 248, friction between British
and, 249–50, Chetniks surrender to, 251,
260–1, 272, refugees hope for protection
from, 251–2, 253, desire revenge, 254,
refugees handed over to, 256, treatment of
enemies, 254–5, 256–61, 366, role in
liberation of Yugoslavia, 268, Red Army
behaviour towards, 269–70, forced to
withdraw from Carinthia, 270, shoot Vera
Miletić, 279, work with Albanian
Communists, 283, Tito pays tribute to
achievements of, 350, publication of
information about March negotiations of,
402, 403, mentioned, 226, 239, 245, 263,
287, 292, 294, 298, 312, 314, 326, 327, 328,
329, 352, 357, 372, 387, 404, 405, 408, 412,
414, *see also* names of individuals associated
with Partisans
Pašić, Nikola, 80
Pauker, Ana, 293, 294
Paul, Prince Regent of Yugoslavia, 130, 144,
157, 158, 159, 160, 173, 238, 381, 391
Paunović, Davorjanka *see* Zdenka
Pavelić, Ante, refugee in Rome, 116, as leader
of Ustashas, 116, 162, rules Croatia as
regent, 163, grants religious toleration to
Orthodox Serbs, 166, visits Hitler, 171,

escapes and remains free, 260, dies in 1959,
260, mentioned, 204, 207, 253, 258, 278,
312, 322, 392, 394
Pavlović, Zivojin, 173
Peake, Charles, 301, 302
Peking, 413
PEN, 133, 407
Penezić, Slobodan, 257, 357
Penza, 137
People's Will party, 69
Perm, 65, 66
Perpignan, 133
Peter Karadjordjevic, King of Serbia (later King
of Yugoslavia), 41, 72–3
Peter II, King of Yugoslavia, personal rule
proclaimed, 160, applies pressure to Vatican,
165, approves of Mihailović's policy, 175,
government in exile, 175, 176, 177, 187,
188, 194, promotes Mihailović, 189, meets
Roosevelt, 192, discussed by Tito and
Maclean, 215, British relations with, 217,
mentioned in Tito's address to AVNOJ
conference, 221, 222, Britain wishes Tito to
co-operate with, 224, alarmed by British
support for Tito, 225, and US, 225,
Mihailović pledges loyalty to, 226, Soviet
intelligence wants information about, 231,
Churchill's plan concerning, 238, Stevenson
as British ambassador to, 239, and
Tito-Šubašić agreement, 240, 251, Churchill
suggests meeting between Tito and, 242,
Stalin's remarks to Tito about, 246, Churchill
loses patience with, 251, Šubašić resigns as
prime minister for, 262, mentioned, 193,
223, 243, 268, 274, 279
Peterwardein Castle, 62, 63
Petkovac, 172, 173
Petnički, Slavenka, 46, 159–60, 228–9
Petričević, Colonel Branko, 294
Petrograd, 66, 67, 68, 69 *see also* St Petersburg
Philip, Prince, Duke of Edinburgh, 20, 316, 389
Philip, André, 356
Pieck, Wilhelm, 120–1, 122, 136, 140
Pijade, Mosha, in prison, 103–4, 115, 116,
172–3, receives letter about Atherton, 190,
hears about Tito's plans for March
negotiations, 205, important in Tito's
government, 326, 327, attacks Djilas, 329,
death, 346, 406, mentioned, 149, 187, 225
Pilsen, 55
Pirker, Pero, 394, 398, 399
Pius VI, Pope, 276
Pius XII, Pope, 165, 198, 314
Plastiras, General, 302, 303
Platts-Mills, John, 199–200
Podgorny, Nikolai Viktorovich, 386
Polak, Samuel, 78, 84
Poland, feudal system in, 29, in First World
War, 63, and Versailles peace treaty, 72, gas

chambers in , 85, 165, Soviet ambassador assassinated in, 92, supports Germany, 141, Hitler invades, 145, Red Army invades, 147–8, Stalin's aims in, 223, free democratic elections promised by Yalta agreement, 266, 267, and Cominform, 282, denounces CPY, 290, British trade agreement with, 301, demonstrations at Poznan, 336, 341, Gomulka appointed prime minister in, 336, and Czechoslovakia, 386, 387, mentioned, 110, 268, 297, 346, *see also* Poles

Poles, 37, 92, *see also* Poland

Politika, 136, 190, 402

Pol Pot, 414

Popović, Koca, 205, 206, 234, 251, 260, 309, 334, 345, 384, 401, 403

Port Said, 337, 338

Portugal, 124, 131, 413

Posreda, 44

Potoci, 236

Potsdam Conference (1945), 265

Pottier, Eugène, 23

POUM, 132

Požarevac, 279

Pozega, 173–4

Poznan, 336, 341

Prague, 37, 123, 141, 159, 285, 290, 385, 386, 387

Prague Spring, 385, 386, 387, 393

Pranjani, 181

Pravda, 302, 346, 349

Prica, Srdjan, 371

Priština, 394

Pritchett, V. S., 407

Problems of Leninism (Stalin), 100

Proleter, 173, 349

Prussia, 63, 72

Pula, 302, 339, 340, 341, 342, 343, 345

Pula Film Festival, 401

Putilov engineering works, Petrograd, 66, 67

Pyatakov, Grigory L., 126

Pyongyang, 306, 413

Radek, Karl, 126

Radić, Stjepan, 95, 97, 104

Radio Free Yugoslavia, 189, 192, 193, 200

Radio Moscow, 128, 193, 297

Radio Prague, 297

Radović, Petar, 227–8

Ragusa, 26, 27 *see also* Dubrovnik

Rajk, László, 299–300, 312, 337, 338, 361, 402

Rákosi, Mátyás, 288, 300, 336, 337, 338, 339, 340, 341, 342, 349

Ranković, Aleksander, experiences torture, 99, organizes demonstration, 149, problems in deciding correct party line on war, 160, decides against anti-government demonstration, on 27 March 1941, 161, at

1941 Politburo meeting, 170, meets Mihailović's representatives, 181, quarrels with Zdenka, 187, plays chess with Tito, 192, informed by Tito about March negotiations, 205, takes control when Tito is wounded, 211, advises Velebit to help Soviet intelligence, 231, tells Tito about arrest of Mihailović, 272, and OZNA, 272, 278, 287, 296, visits Stalin, 284, and Hebrang, 291, 312, and Žujović, 291, and Goli Otok, 297, 299, mentioned at trials in Hungary and Bulgaria, 300, concentrates on state security, 327, and UDBA, 327, 367, 372, 373, accuses Djilas, 329, informs Dedijer of Tito's wish for reconciliation, 332, at talks about Hungarian crisis, 339, visits Romania, 346, goes to Moscow, 347, 348, leads hardliners, 369, speaks at Executive Committee of League of Communists, 370, and Kardelj's visit to London, 371, appointed vice-president of Yugoslavia, 372, and Milka Kufrin, 373, 377, Tito decides to get rid of, 377, visits Soviet Union, 378, and bugging of Tito's telephone, 379, expelled from League of Communists, 380, 406, treatment compared with case of Djilas, 380, and Tudjman, 399, and Kosovo, 400, mentioned, 286, 302, 326, 343, 374, 392, 394

Ravna Gora, 175, 177, 178, 181, 182

Rayner, Louise, 260–1

Reagan, President, 417

Red Army, in Russian civil war, 74, Tito attends school of, 121, invades Poland, 147–8, invades Finland, 148, 149, fails to meet German invasion, 170, Žarko Broz joins, 238, in Romania , 245, 246, and Bulgaria, 246, 248, and liberation of Yugoslavia, 246, 247, 248, 268, fights for Budapest, 249, attacks Berlin, 252, White Russians handed over to, 256, Byrnes congratulates Stalin on achievements of, 265, in Iran, 267, behaviour of, 269–70, 285, and possible invasion of Yugoslavia, 294, 307, 308, 309, in Hungary, 337, 338, 339, 340, arrests Nagy and others, 345, supports Khrushchev, 346, plans for war against China, 357, mentioned, 80, 172, 186, 199, 200, 221

Red Cross, 65

Red Guard, 68, 71, 172

Reichstag Fire Trial, 111–2, 120

Ribar, Dr Ivan, 221, 262, 311

Ribar, Lola, 149, 158, 181, 195, 221, 230

Ribbentrop, Joachim von, 145, 207

Ribnikar, Vladislav, 170

Rijeke (Fiume), 244

Rio de Janeiro, Cardinal Archbishop of, 365

Robaje, 174, 177

Roberts, Walter, 402

Roman Catholic Church, missionaries in Croatia and Bosnia, 27, and Charlemagne, 28, adopts Gregorian calendar, 32, and Austria, 32–3, thinks Tito is a Jew, 43, Tito brought up in, 45, attitude to Socialism, 54, Tito attends funeral conducted by, 82, in Spain, 132, and Ustashas, 164, 165, 260, forcible baptism, 165–6, Tito's handling of, 243, 276–8, 314, 316, and Tito's visit to Brazil, 365, mentioned, 184

Romania, President attends Tito's funeral, 21, and Congress of Berlin, 38, and Versailles peace treaty, 72, and 'Little Entente', 73, 95, invades Hungary, 73, Churchill's proposals to Stalin about, 220, Tito flown to, 245, Red Army in, 245, 246, Tito meets Free Yugoslav Legion in, 247, Stalin agrees to Churchill's proposals about, 250, commercial treaties with Soviet Union, 275, and Cominform, 282, denounces CPY, 290, Tito's ambassador defects to, 291, and International Danube Commission, 293, and possible invasion of Yugoslavia, 307, and atomic targets, 310, Tito visits, 335, Nagy held prisoner in, 345, Tito and Khrushchev meet in, 346, 347, Nagy brought back from, 349, Communist regime in, 352–3, fears of Soviet invasion, 387, and Czechoslovakia, 388, Dapčević taken by UDBA in, 403, 404, mentioned, 268, 334

Romans, 26, 27, 28

Rome, 26, 27, 28, 93, 116, 165, 237, 315, 411

Rommel, Erwin, 201

Roosevelt, President Franklin D., 24, 192, 201, 220, 225, 239, 248, 255, 265, 274, 319

Rosenberg, Oskar, 84, 85

Rösselsprung (Seventh Offensive), 233

Roumelia, 38, 40

Rude Pravo, 288

Rudo, 183

Rühr, the, 55

Russell, Bertrand, 358

Russia (up to the end of Civil War), Orthodox use of Julian calendar in, 32, fails to support Karadjordj's revolt, 33, and Pan-Slavism, 37, and Turkey, 38, and political assassinations, 41, Marx and Engels support war against, 57, and First World War, 60, 61, 63, 64, 65, 66, Tito as prisoner of, 64, 65–6, Lenin launches propaganda campaign in, 66, Civil War in, 69–76, refugees from, 80, mentioned, 58, 77, 92, see also Soviet Union; names of Russian people and places

Ruthenia, 72, 114

Sabić, Stevo, 80, 81

Sadat, President, 21

Sadchikov, L. V., 271

Saddam Hussein, President, 21

Saigon, 304, 351

St Petersburg, 61, 66 see also Petrograd

Sakić, Dinko, 260

Salazar, Dr, 124

Samobar, 134

Sarajevo, 59, 114, 184, 205, 288, 420

Sargent, Sir Orme, 225, 253

Sava, River, 309

Savinkov, Boris, 75, 219–20

Schmidt, Helmut, 20, 21

Schusnigg, Kurt von, 117, 123, 129

Second International see International

Secret Front, The (Hoettle), 402

Serbia, economic and social system in early period, 29–30, culture and legends of, 30, conquests made by Dušan of Serbia, 30–1, conquered by Turks, 31, Orthodox use of Julian calendar in, 32, and wars between Austria and Turks, 32–3, unaffected by French Revolution, 33, revolt led by Karadjordj in, 33, rising under Miloš Obrenović, 33–4, unaffected by 1848 revolution, 38, and Congress of Berlin, 38, at war with Bulgaria, 40, Social-Democratic party formed in, 52, Pan-Slavism in, 52, universal suffrage granted in, 52, and Balkan Wars, 57, and First World War, 60, 62, 63, and creation of Yugoslavia, 72, dominates Yugoslavia, 73, 95, 104, Communists achieve election success in, 79, and terrorism among Socialists in, 79, Nedić orders concentration camps in, 157, opposition to Germany in, 159, Communist prisoners released in, 162, Albania annexes parts of, 163, Tito sees chance of starting a rising in, 169, Nedić's coalition government in, 170–1, spread of resistance to Germans in, 171, German operations in, 178, 181, 182, 186, views on Allied air raids in, 228, Red Army enters, 246, Chetniks hold out in, 251, 253, Tito criticized in, 260, support for Tito in, 261, Tito addresses meeting in, 262–3, army hunts for Mihailović in, 272, importance of 28th June in history of, 288, Slav sympathies strong in, 291, possibility of flooding discussed, 309, economic situation, 368, and free market economy, 374, fears of domination by, 381, language, 382, Communist party, 382, 400, 408, Croatian leaders resent attending meeting in, 397, after Tito's death, 417, 418, mentioned, 26, 28, 188, 201, 215, 221, 226, 279, 312, 326, see also Serbs; names of places

Serbian Fascists, 201, 251, 253

Serbs, early history of, 27, 28, culture of, 30, attitudes to Turks and Austrians, 32–3, rebel against Turks, 33, intermarriage, 44, admired by British and French, 73, attitudes to other ethnic groups, 95, as Communist prisoners,

115, as prison warders, 116, volunteer for
Spanish Civil War, 141, killed by Ustashas,
163, 164, 165, 183, 260, 278, retreat to
mountains, 166, 169, join resistance fighters,
171, as Chetniks, 177, killed by Germans,
178, killed by Muslims, 184, killed by Allied
air raids, 228, and plot to assassinate Tito,
280, Kosovo sacred to, 283, in Croatia, 382,
394, 408, urge action against Croatia, 396,
Muslims as balance to power of, 400,
resentment at influence of, 406, and Jovanka,
410, after Tito's death, 417–8, mentioned,
24, 41, 63, 186, 195, 202, 221, 259, 365,
395, see also Serbia
Šešelj, Vojislav, 417
Sevastopol, 168
Seventh Offensive (Rösselsprung), 233
Sèvres, 337
Shanghai, 94
Shaw, George Bernard, 40
Šibenik, 228
Siberia, 61, 65, 68, 69, 71, 76, 109, 122, 142
Simić, Stanoye, 293
Simić, Zivadin, 157–8, 370n, 371–2, 379–80
Simon, Sir John, 119
Simović, General, 160, 162, 175
Sisak, 50, 52, 84, 319
Six Day War (1967), 384
Sixth Offensive, 212, 226, 227
Skopje, 228, 309, 359, 369
Slánský, Rudolf, 315, 361, 385
Slavonia, 163
Slavs, 31, 37, 38, 63, 255, 291 see also
Pan-Slavism
Sljeme mountains, 59
Slovakia, 72, 73
Slovenes, 27, 44, 54, 95, 96, 177, 195, 259,
292, 381, 400, 406, see also Slovenia
Slovenia, and Charlemagne, 28, governed by
German dukes, 28–9, and Habsburg family,
29, 32, 33, as part of Austria, 29, 32, 33,
adopts Gregorian calendar, 32, and
Napoleon, 33, Tito's mother comes from, 44,
Tito stays with grandfather in, 46, and
creation of Yugoslavia, 72, Communists fail
to achieve election success in, 79,
Communists try to organize strikes in, 87,
unemployment in, 109, secret conference of
Communist party in, 114, Germany and Italy
annex, 163, Partisan activity in, 176, Herta
Haas transfers to Partisans in, 207, groups
retreat to Austria from, 251, no vengeance
taken on Ustashas and Chetniks in, 258, and
free market economy, 368, 374, forces of
liberalism in, 372, motorway plans
abandoned, 391, demands independence,
417, mentioned, 26, 43, 48, 134, 152, 170,
200, 201, 226, 239, 293, 329, 364, see also
Slovenes; names of places

Smederevska Palanka, 88
Smodlaka, Josip, 240
Smith, Ian, 389
Smuts, Field-Marshal, 248
Snagov, 346, 347
Snowdon, Earl of, 389
Social Democrats, reject terrorism and
revolution, 51, parties formed in Croatia,
Slovenia, Serbia and Bosnia, 52, call for
strike, 54, attitudes to war, 58, 60, Lenin's
view of, 61, against Bolsheviks, 74, 75, Social
Democratic party of Yugoslavia, 78, 96, 98,
100, Communist attacks on, 94–5, seen as
enemy of proletariat, 111, suppressed in
Germany, 111, and Comintern policy, 122,
and Spanish Civil War, 124, 131, agree to
collaborate with Communists against
Fascism, 136, Tito condemns, 154, 155,
refuse to attend Seventh Congress of League
of Communisms, 348, mentioned, 53, 72, 82,
126, 144, 148, 158, 261, 337
Socialism/Socialists, ideas in The Communist
Manifesto, 35, 36, and universal suffrage, 52,
and Pan-Slavism, 52, Catholic Church
opposed to, 54, attitudes to war, 57–8,
reaction to outbreak of First World War, 60,
61, and terrorism, 79, condemn Mussolini,
93, and smoking, 107, and Nazi atrocities,
111, suppressed in Austria, 112, 113, 117,
Tito sees Soviet Union's importance for, 142,
Stalin's attitude to Socialist revolution, 172,
and Churchill's Greek policy, 250, Tito
surveys history in Yugoslavia, 292, and
Nasser, 332, and Hungarian crisis, 339, 342,
and Djilas, 347, 360, 380, Tito speaks about,
348, and Third World, 351, alarmed by US
policies, 352, 356, and workers'
self-management, 369, new ideas about, 382,
and Czechoslovakia, 386, 387, 388, Kardelj
develops theories about, 406, mentioned,
132, 140, 148, see also
Communism/Communists
Social Revolutionaries, 69, 70, 74, 75
SOE (Special Operations Executive), 175, 196,
197, 201, 254, 274
Sofia, 246, 248, 275, 348
Solzhenitsyn, Alexander, 355, 360
South Africa, 351, 358
South America/Latin America, 260, 351, 354,
365, 394, 419
South Korea, 305, 306, 307, 311
Soviet Union, invades Afghanistan, 20, sends
representatives to Tito's funeral, 20, pays
tribute to Tito, 21, national anthem, 23, and
world opinion, 92, British boycott of goods
from, 93, Trotsky banished from, 94, British
break off relations with trade unions in, 94,
attitude to Radić, 95, Polka Broz returns to,
103, and Japan, 109, and Nazi rise to power,

Soviet Union – *cont'd.*
111, Britain prepared to enter friendly
relations with, 119, Churchill's attitude to,
125, purges in, 125–9, 133, 135, pavilion at
Paris exhibition, 131, and Spanish Civil War,
132, Gorkić killed in, 135, Tito tries to stay
out of, 135, pays financial rewards to
workers, 139, supports Czechoslovakia, 141,
Tito loses illusions about, 142, Tito retains
loyalty to, 142–3, makes pact with Germans,
145, invades Poland, 147–8, invades Finland,
148–9, accepts economic inequality, 152,
sees Germany as threat, 154, Yugoslav
Communists' attitude to, 155, Tito's attitude
to, 155–6, Hitler decides to attack, 158, 159,
receives warnings of German invasion,
167–8, Germany invades, 168, fails to resist
German army, 170, Pavlović denounces
atrocities in, 173, Partisans hope for
liberation by, 178, 186, and Agitprop
propaganda, 186, requested by Britain to use
influence on Partisans, 188–9, and
Mihailović, 189, 193, promises to send help
to Partisans, 189–90, signs treaty with
Britain, 190, British attitudes to, 197, 198,
199–200, Churchill's support for, 198–9,
uninterested in proposal for Anglo-Soviet
mission to Partisans, 208, Maclean's attitude
to, 214, Churchill wishes to collaborate with,
220, reaction to British support for Tito, 223,
224, sends military mission to Tito, 224, asks
Velebit to obtain intelligence information,
230–1, members of mission flown to Bari,
236–7, members of mission arrive at Vis,
237–8, helps Tito leave Vis, 245, policy in
Greece, 250, 268, 280, 'Stalin constitution'
of, 262, Greek children evacuated to, 264,
and Potsdam Conference, 265–6, hardening
of British attitude to, 267, opposed to
inclusion of France in discussions, 267, and
Iran, 267, and beginning of Cold War, 268,
and liberation of Yugoslavia, 268, tensions
between Yugoslavia and, 269–71, signs
commercial treaty with Yugoslavia, 275,
denounces Marshall Aid, 280–1, votes for
Israel at UN, 281, disagreements in policy
towards US, 283, not consulted about Balkan
federation, 284, Kardelj promises to consult
about foreign policy, 285, withdraws experts
and advisers from Yugoslavia, 285–6, and
letter to Tito and CPY leaders, 286–7, and
arrest of Hebrang and Žujović, 287–8,
responsible for Yugoslav expulsion from
Cominform, 289, problem of Yugoslav
loyalty to, 291, Tito fears war with, 291,
mentioned in Tito's speech at Fifth Congress
of CPY, 292, and International Danube
Commission, 293, propaganda against Tito,
294, and disillusioned Yugoslav Communists,

297, imposes economic sanctions against
Yugoslavia, 300, and Tito's policy in Greece,
302, as permanent member of UN Security
Council, 303, and Yugoslav election to UN
Security Council, 303, 304, and Korea, 305,
306, prepares to invade Yugoslavia, 307–8,
Tito plans defence of Yugoslavia against,
309, and nuclear bomb, 307, 309, 310,
criticized in Yugoslavia, 311–2, and death of
Stalin, 315, Khrushchev comes to power in,
318, and 1955 summit meeting, 319, art in,
326, 375, Djilas leads propaganda against,
328, relations with Yugoslavia, 331, 333,
334, 335, 343, 345, 346, 347, 348, 349, Tito
pays state visit to, 334–5, and Egypt, 336,
337, and Hungary, 336, 337, 338, 339, 340,
341, 342, 343, 345, Polka Broz in, 344,
attempt to overthrow Khrushchev in, 346,
and resumption of Cold War, 351, and
Non-aligned states, 352, 358, more liberal
policies in, 355, 360, and Berlin crisis, 355,
and China, 356–7, Djilas criticizes, 360, and
Cuba, 361–2, Tito visits, 362, Brezhnev
comes to power in, 362, summary of Tito's
relationship with, 362, frontier control, 374,
Mihajlov visits, 376, Ranković visits, 378,
and Six Day War, 384, and Czechoslovakia,
385, 386, 387, 388, Tito fears invasion by,
387–8, Nixon's policy towards, 388, and
Helsinki conference, 389, 'Brezhnev
doctrine', 394–5, and Croatia, 395, signs
Declaration of Human Rights, 401, fails to
find out about March negotiations, 402,
Dapčević in, 403, supports Vietnam against
Cambodia, 414, and Gorbachev, 417,
collapse of empire, 419, mentioned, 83, 102,
104, 110, 112, 116, 122, 127, 136, 146, 161,
169, 176, 180, 194, 195, 206, 216, 217, 218,
246, 253, 254, 295, 317, 359, 364, 369, 380,
416, *see also* Communist party of Soviet
Union; Moscow; Red Army; Russia; names
of people and places
Spain, and terrorism, 51, Civil War, 124–5,
129–33, 219, Tito does not go to, 133, 135,
Tito's identity made public in, 194,
mentioned, 54, 139, 147, 148, 172, 198,
225, 226, 260, 276, 300, 350
Spalato, 26, 27, *see also* Split
Special Operations Executive *see* SOE
Split, 27, 28, 129, 130, 160, 212, 228, 229,
323, 370, 371, *see also* Spalato
Sremska Mitrovica, 343, 361
Stalin, Josef, and national anthem, 23, and
Russian Revolution, 71–2, and Trotsky, 94,
and Bukharin, 94, attitude to Social
Democrats, 95, 122, author of *Problems of
Leninism*, 100, Neumann visits, 110–1,
reaction to Hitler's rise to power, 111, and
assassination of Kirov, 119, Eden visits, 120,

attends Seventh Congress of Comintern, 121,
Churchill prepared to ally himself with, 125,
and purges, 126, 128, and Spanish Civil War,
129, 132, cult of personality, 131, and
*History of the Communist Party of the Soviet
Union*, 138, 139, 155, Tito's attitude to, 140,
143, makes pact with Germany, 145, and
attitudes to outbreak of Second World War,
146, 147, asks Finland to cede territory, 148,
perceives Germans as threat, 154, refuses to
believe Germans will invade, 167, 168,
attitude to Socialist revolution, 172,
disapproves of some practices of Partisans,
183, Churchill hopes to reach agreement
with, 220, meets Churchill and Roosevelt in
Teheran, 220, reaction to British support for
Tito, 223–4, demands Second Front, 231,
against Churchill's proposal to land forces in
Dalmatia, 239, Tito seeks intervention from,
244–5, 246, and Mesić, 247, agrees to
Churchill's proposals about Yugoslavia,
Romania and Greece, 250, policy in Greece,
250, 284–5, and Yalta conference, 250, 255,
256, 267, prisoners extradited to, 255–6,
British public's attitude to, 259, intentions at
end of war, 265, at Potsdam Conference,
265, instructions to Communists in other
countries, 266, US attitude to, 266, resents
Truman's criticisms, 267, Tito causes
problems for, 268, offended by Djilas's
remarks about Red army, 270, 285, and
capture of Mihailović, 272, opposes Marshall
Aid, 281, and UN vote on Palestine, 282,
suggests Cominform should have
headquarters in Belgrade, 282, becomes
suspicious of Tito, 282–3, and disagreements
in policy towards US, 283, and relationship
between Tito and Hoxha, 283, and Balkan
federation, 284, Tito sends representatives to,
284–5, applies pressure on Kardelj, 285,
letter to Tito and CPY leaders, 286, 287,
suspects OZNA of spying on Soviets, 287,
breaks with Tito, 289, Cominform countries
support, 290, Yugoslav support for, 291,
signature deleted from published
correspondence to Tito, 293, and campaign
against Tito, 294, 299, and Korea, 305, 306,
307, plans invasion of Yugoslavia, 307–8,
Churchill wants summit conference with,
311, criticized in Yugoslavia, 311, and
Hebrang, 313, death, 315, Khrushchev
praises, 318, Tito shares joke about, 323, as
Marxist theoretician, 326–7, Djilas disgusted
by behaviour of, 327–8, Khrushchev
criticizes policy of, 333, 334, and Hungarian
situation, 337, 338, 339, Stalin era ends in
Soviet Union, 346, 356, 360, China as
supporter of, 357, Djilas denounces, 359,
360, and Tito's Five Year Plan, 367, and art,

375, mentioned, 22, 24, 152, 153, 188, 194,
199, 200, 217, 248, 269, 292, 296, 301, 316,
331, 336, 341, 344, 349, 356, 364, 376, 380,
392
Stalingrad, 265, 285, 334–5, 356
Stambolić, Petar, 376
Stanojević, Tihomir-Tice, 413
Steel, David, 20
Stefanović, Svetislav, 370, 372, 373, 378, 379,
380
Stepinac, Aloysius, Archbishop of Zagreb, 165,
276, 277, 278, 279, 314, 316, 361
Stevenson, Sir George, 239, 240, 254, 255
Stockholm, 394
Stojadinović, Milan, 88
Street, Colonel Vivian, 236
Struganik, 177
Stuart, Captain, 208, 211
Stuttgart, Congress of Second International at,
57
Šubašić, Ivan, 238, 239, 240, 241, 243, 243,
244, 248, 251, 262
Sudan, 364, 371
Sudetenland, 140, 141
Suez Canal, 336, 337, 342
Sukarno, President, 352, 358
Suslov, Mikhail Andreivich, 333
Sutjeska, River, 23, 208, 209, 212, 260, 353,
Battle of, 23, 210, 319
Sutla, River, 43, 134
Sviashsk, 64
Sweden, 20, 411
Switzerland, 92
Syngman Rhee, 311
Syria, 21, 33, 388
Szklarska Poreba, 282

Taiwan, 305, 350
Tamburlane, 31
TASS, 231
Taylor, Elizabeth, 325
Teheran, 220, 396
Tempo, General (Svetozav Vukmanović), 218,
286, 328, 371, 409
Thatcher, Margaret, 20, 21, 22, 24, 413, 417
Third International *see* International
Third Offensive, 191, 201
Third World, 351, 360, 361, 389
Thorez, Maurice, 147, 282
Tibet, 362
Times, The, 21, 105, 332
Timoshenko, Marshal, 199
Tito, Josip Broz, funeral, 19–25, factors
shaping life of, 40, birth, 42, 43, stories
about identity of, 42–3, family background,
43–5, childhood, 45–9, reasons for
becoming Communist, 45, 48, works as
locksmith's apprentice, 50, 52, works as
metalworker, 53, 54, 55–6, relationships

Tito, Josip Broz – *cont'd*.
with women, 55, 57, visits Vienna, 56–7, joins army, 58–9, imprisoned in Peterwardein Castle, 62–3, fights in First World War, 63–4, as prisoner of war, 64–6, goes to Petrograd, 66–7, in prison in Petrograd, 67–8, escapes to Omsk, 68, and Russian Revolution, 69, 71–2, and Kirghiz tribe, 71, 75–6, marries Polka, 76, returns to Yugoslavia, 77, joins Communist party, 77, 78–9, works at Veliko Trojstvo, 78, works for illegal Communist party, 81, gives speech at comrade's funeral, 82, married life with Polka, 83, births and deaths of children, 83, becomes professional revolutionary, 84–5, becomes shop steward of Metalworkers Union, 87, works at Kraljevica shipyards, 87–8, organizes strike, 88, writes article about conditions in wagon-works, 88, appointed as full-time trade union official, 88–9, arrest, 89, imprisonment, 89–91, trial, 91, carries on underground work for Communist party, 91–2, attends secret conference of Zagreb Communist party, 95–6, organizes May Day demonstration, 96–7, eventual arrest of, 98, and torture, 98–9, trial in Zagreb, 99–101, in Lepoglava prison 102, 103–4, 106, transferred to Maribor prison, 106–7, in Ogulin prison, 107–8, ordered to reside in Kumrovec, 108, in Kumrovec, 112, goes to Zagreb, 113, goes to Vienna, 113–4, goes to Ljubljana, 114–5, used pseudonyms, 115, writes article on duties of Communists in prison, 115, 116, further journey to Vienna, 117, goes to Brno with Politburo, 117–8, visits Moscow, 118, 119, 120–2, 124, 127, 133, 135, 136–40, 143, explains new Comintern policy in Yugoslavia, 122, organizes strikes, 122–3, uses forged passports, 123–4, continues to support Soviet Union, 128, organizes volunteers for Spanish Civil War, 129–31, does not go to Spain, 132–3, and founding of separate Croatian Communist party, 134, afraid to visit Kumrovec, 134, summoned to Paris by Politburo, 134, becomes general secretary of CPY, 135, problems in Paris, 135, organizes demonstration to greet Delbos, 136, stays with Dedijer, 136, helps translate *History of the Communist Party of the Soviet Union*, 138–9, denounced to Comintern, 139, 140, loses illusions about Soviet Union, 142, remains loyal to Soviet Union, 142–3, 155–6, confirmed as general secretary of CPY, 144, good relationship with Krleža, 144–5, leaves for Moscow, 145, drafts manifesto about war, 146–7, returns to Yugoslavia, 149–51, lives with Herta Haas, 151, purges party, 152, enjoys good living, 152, privileges as general secretary, 153, report to Fifth National Conference, 154–5, returns to Belgrade, 161, launches campaign to free Communist prisoners, 162, orders Communists to undergo military training, 163, reports to Comintern, 163, moves from Zagreb to Belgrade, 166–7, and German invasion of Soviet Union, 168, faces danger in Belgrade, 169, takes Zdenka as mistress, 169–70, attends meeting of Politburo, 170, leaves to take command of Partisans, 173–4, meets Mihailović, 177–8, 178–9, 181, meets Hudson, 178, leaves Užice, 182, attacked by Italians, 183, forms First Proletarian Brigade, 183, makes headquarters at Foča, 183, treatment of prisoners, 184–5, impresses volunteers, 185, efficiency, 185, appoints Djilas as head of Agitprop, 185, remains aloof, 186–7, meets staff and Politburo members regularly, 187, relationship with Zdenka, 187, speech at Foča, 187–8, radio communications with Comintern, 189, 190, suspicious of Atherton, 190–1, plays chess, 192, speculation over identity of, 193, correctly identified by Germans, 193–4, calls conference at Bihać, 194–5, and British public opinion, 200, negotiations with Germans, 203–4, anxious about Fourth Offensive, 204–5, plans March negotiations with Germans, 205, Herta Haas avoids, 207, informs Comintern about negotiations, 207, orders Partisans to fight Chetniks rather than Germans, 208, anxious about wounded comrades, 208, discusses matters with Dedijer, 209, moves Čaldarović to other duties, 209, and British mission, 210, wounded, 211, escapes Germans, 211, reward offered for capture of, 212, sees Milka Kufrin, 212–3, Maclean's mission to, 214–7, Maclean advises support for, 217–8, 222–3, sends Tempo to Macedonia, 218, gives advice to Greek Communists, 218–9, Churchill's enthusiasm for, 220, Stalin minimizes achievements of, 220, addresses second AVNOJ conference, 220–1, writes article about ideas on post-war Yugoslavia, 221–2, offers amnesty, 222, Britain decides to support, 222, 223, 224, Soviet Union sends military mission to, 224, praised in Churchill's statement on Yugoslavia, 224, 225, opposed by some in Britain, 225–6, receives arms from Britain, 227, Partisans' attitude to, 228, gives permission for Allied air raids, 228, sends military mission to Cairo, 229, sends Velebit to London, 230, Germans try to capture, 233–5, escapes to Bari, 236–7, at Vis, 237–40, 242–5, realises difficulty of his position, 239, signs agreement with Šubašić, 240, invited to talks

in Italy, 240–1, talks with Churchill, 241–2, goes to Moscow, 245, meets Stalin, 245–6, requests that Red Army should enter Yugoslavia, 246, meets Free Yugoslav Legion, 247, Nazis still wish to capture, 247, orders Partisan units to accompany Red Army, 247–8, acts as head of Yugoslav government, 248, British attitude to behaviour of, 248–9, refuses permission for British to move inland from Dubrovnik, 249, maintains good relationship with Maclean, 250, receives US envoy, 251, calls up men for armed forces, 251, takes action against Chetniks, 251, anxious to take Trieste, 252, broadcasts news of German defeat, 252, orders forces to prevent escaping fighters, 253, Churchill turns against, 254, asks for Yugoslav occupation zone in Austria, 255, treatment of refugees handed over to, 257–8, 260, holds elections, 261–2, sets aside agreement with Šubašić, 262, addresses meeting at Mladenovac, 262–3, attitude to Britain, 264, helps ELAS in Greece, 264, supports revolutionary movements world-wide, 265, denounces British policy in Iran, 267–8, causes problems for Stalin, 268, adulation of, 269, signs friendship treaty with Soviet Union, 270, speaks about friendship with Soviet Union, 270, Ljubljana speech seen as critical of Soviet Union, 270–1, Kardelj comments on, 271, tells Stalin about Mihailović's capture, 272, refuses to commute death sentence on Mihailović, 274, signs commercial treaty with Soviet Union, 275, agrees to pay compensation to US, 276, relations with Roman Catholic Church, 276–8, 316, and death of Zdenka, 279, intensifies political repression, 280, unable to accept Marshall Aid, 281, seen as supporter of Zhdanov and Molotov, 283, relationship with Hoxha, 283, and idea of Balkan federation, 284, congratulates Czechoslovak Communists on *coup d'etat*, 285, writes to Molotov, 286, correspondence with Soviet Union, 286–7, accepts Velebit's resignation, 287, and break with Cominform, 289, defies Stalin, 289, Yugoslav support for, 290, anxious after break with Stalin, 290–1, speech to Fifth Congress of CPY, 292–3, publishes correspondence between CPSU and CPY, 293, avoids meeting delegates from Cominform countries, 293, and Jovanović, 294, Stalin wishes to be reconciled with, 294, Western ideas about Stalin's split with, 294–5, CIA encourages revolt against, 296, and Cominform supporters in CPY, 296–7, and Goli Otok, 297, 298, 312, intervenes to protect individuals, 299, campaign against, 294, 299, 315, mentioned in trials in

Cominform countries, 299, 300, 315, Western attitude to, 300, policy in Greece, 300–3, proposes election of Yugoslavia to UN Security Council, 303, supports Ho Chi Minh, 304, 305, asserts independence of Yugoslavia, 305, and Korea, 305–6, does not wish to join NATO, 307, strength of forces, 308, requests arms, 308, plans for defence of Yugoslavia, 309, not consulted about possible use of atomic bomb, 310, biography published, 312, and Hebrang, 312, 313, 314, offers to release Stepinac, 314, marries Jovanka, 314, invites Eden on official visit, 315, state visit to London, 316–7, and Trieste, 317–8, hardships endured during life of, 319, residences, 319–21, relations with sons, 321–2, visits school at Kumrovec, 322–3, hunting, 323–4, uninterested in economics, 324, interested in foreign policy, 324, daily routine, 324, food and drink 324–5, leisure activities, 325, clothes, 325–6, and arts, 326, 375, attractive to women, 326, not a Marxist theoretician, 326–7, and meeting about Djilas, 329, 330, draws closer to Western powers, 331, travels abroad, 331, and Nehru, 331, and Nasser, 331–2, 335–6, 342, conversations with Khrushchev, 333–4, 335–6, state visit to Soviet Union, 334–5, and Hungarian crisis, 336, 338, 339, 340, 341–2, 343, 345, speech at Pula, 341–2, angers Khrushchev, 342–3, and Djilas, 343, 346–7, 357, 359, 360, Polka does not keep in touch with, 344, refuses amnesty to Yugoslav Cominform supporters, 346, meets Khrushchev in Romania, 346, recognizes Communist government in East Germany, 347, absent from meeting in Moscow, 347–8, speech about Khrushchev's criticisms, 348–9, speech for fortieth anniversary of foundation of CPY, 349–50, remains neutral in Cold War, 351, 352, becomes leader of the Non-Aligned States, 352, relationship with Ceauşescu, 352–3, at 1960 UN General Assembly, 353–4, disappointed with Chinese Communists, 356, presides at conferences of Non-Aligned States, 358, angry at threat of US withdrawal of aid, 359, addresses Supreme Soviet in Moscow, 362, relationship with East and West, 362–3, celebrates seventieth birthday, 364, foreign travels, 364–6, and economic policy, 366, 367, 368, 369–70, and Kardelj, 371–2, suggests creation of post of vice-president, 372, and tourism, 373, and Milka Kufrin, 373, 377, and Mihajlov, 376, and Council of Ministers, 376, decides to get rid of Ranković, 377, speaks to Central Committee of League of Communist, 377–8, telephone bugged, 378, 379, and expulsion of Ranković, 380, and

Tito, Josip Broz – *cont'd.*
Yugoslav Idea, 381, speech about freedom of writers, 383, sympathises with Vietcong, 383, and Six Day War, 383–4, and Czechoslovakia, 385, 386–7, 388, broadcasts about demonstrations, 386, fears Soviet invasion, 387–8, Nixon visits, 388, supports Egypt, 388, receives foreign visitors, 389, and conferences of Non-Aligned States, 389, and Africa, 389, addresses Helsinki conference, 389–90, health problems, 391–2, and problems in Croatia, 392–3, 394, 395–6, 397–400, and new constitution, 393, 400–1, orders purge of Serbian Communist party, 400, and Kosovo, 400, creates new nationality of Muslims, 400, and intellectuals, 401, and publication of information about March negotiations, 402, 403, unable to forgive Cominform supporters, 403, alleged assassination attempt against, 404–5, relies on Ljubičić and Dolanc, 406–7, more leisured lifestyle, 407–8, difficulty of contacting him, 408–9, celebrates eighty fifth birthday, 410, relationship with Jovanka, 410–3, foreign visits, 413–4, not happy at development of events, 414, attends sixth conference of Non-Aligned States, 414–5, illness and death, 415, events after death of, 416–20
Tito Speaks (Dedijer), 100
Tito's Pioneers, 269
Togliatti, Palmiro, 120, 122, 132, 282
Tolbukhin, Marshal, 246
Tomašević, Captain (later General), 63, 64, 255
Tomislav II, King of Croatia, 163
Topalović, Živko, 226
Topčider, 273, 291
Transylvania, 72
Trbovlje, 122–3
Trepča mines, 123
Trieste, 20, 54, 72, 242, 248, 252, 253, 255, 256, 266, 271, 317
Tripalo, Mika, 378, 379, 394, 395, 396, 398, 399, 400
Tripartite Pact (1941), 159, 160, 162, 163, 272
Tripolitania, 265–6
Trotsky, Leon, 61, 67, 70, 71, 74, 94, 103, 126, 127, 139, 142, 205, 219, 286, 287, 295, 360
Trotskyists, 132, 138, 139, 142, 155, 172, 197, 214, 292, 334
Truman, President Harry S., 265, 266, 267, 274, 280, 291, 296, 308, 309, 311, 319
Tsaldaris, General, 301, 302
Tshombe, Moise, 354
Tudjman, Franjo, 392, 399, 419
Tukhachevsky, Marshall, 126
Turks/Turkey, 30, 31, 32, 38, 52, 57, 73, 165, 201, 283, 288, 331

UDBA (formerly OZNA), and Goli Otok, 299, and security measures around Tito, 321, 323, 324, Ranković in charge of, 327, officer talks to Djilas, 357, and tourism, 367, 373, 374, Stefanović as head of, 372, 378, Lukić as second-in-command of, 378, commission appointed to investigate, 378–9, expulsion of leaders from League of Communists, 380, action against Croatians, 399, 401, 414, power of, 400, 401, and Cominform supporters, 403, arrest of Dapčević, 403, 404, and Barović's death, 405, 406, *see also* OZNA
Ufa, 71, 189, 192
Ukraine, 26, 74
Ukrainians, 74, 165
Ulbricht, Walter, 386
Umberto I, King of Italy, 51
United Committee of Americans of South Slav Origin, 225
United Nations, sexcretary-general attends Tito's funeral, 21, and Yugoslav elections, 261, 1946 Security Council meeting, 268, relief and Rehabilitation Agency, 274–5, United States threatens Tito with action in, 276, votes on Palestine, 281–2, election for Security Council, 303–4, and Korea, 305–6, Yugoslavia threatens to raise matter of Nagy in, 345, 1960 General Assembly, 353–4, and underdeveloped nations, 358, 1963 General Assembly, 365, peace-keeping force in Egypt, 383
United States, and Afghanistan, 20, and Olympic Games boycott, 20, and Tito's funeral, 21, Lincoln elected as president of, 39, Croats emigrate to, 49, Tito considers emigrating to, 84, Communists in, 92, economic crisis in, 109, sends volunteers to Spanish Civil War, 131, speculation about Tito's identity in, 193, demonstrations about Yugoslavia, 225, air-raids on Yugoslav mainland, 228, sends envoy to Tito, 251, and Yalta conference, 255–6, 266, and fate of refugees, 259, Tito hostile to, 264, 268, 271, and Greece, 264, 280, 285, and Potsdam Conference, 265–6, beginning of friction with Soviet Union, 266, and discussions about peace treaty, 267, and beginning of Cold War, 268, Tito's critics in, 268, 289, and Mihailović, 273, 274, 279, bad relations with Yugoslavia, 274–5, violation of Yugoslav air space, 275, 276, planes shot down by Yugoslavs, 276, criticizes Stepinac's sentence, 278, 279, and Marshall Aid, 280–1, attacked in UN by Vyshinsky, 281, votes for Israel at UN, 281, Soviets disagree on policy towards, 283, and *coup* in Czechoslovakia, 285, Tito unable to rely on support of, 291, attitudes to Tito, 295, 300,

policy towards Communism, 296, 307, 308, instructions to CIA, 296, and Tito's policy in Greece, 300, 302, 303, as member of UN Security Council, 303, supports Yugoslav election to UN Security Council, 303, 304, angry at Tito's support for Ho Chi Minh, 304–5, and aid to Yugoslavia, 305, 312, 348, 352, 359, 365, 367, and Korea, 305, 306, wishes Yugoslavia to be involved in Western defence plans, 307, ready to go to war with Soviet Union, 308, supply of arms to Tito, 309, and possible use of atomic bomb, 309–10, and Trieste, 317, 318, 1955 summit meeting, 319, and Israel, 332, and Mićunoović, 335, and Egypt, 337, 338, Djilas publishes article in, 343, and China, 350, and Cuba, 350, 355–6, 361–2, Khrushchev visits, 350–1, and resumption of Cold War, 351, and Third World, 351, nuclear policy, 351, 352, and Non-Aligned States, 352, 358, Act of Congress (1952) on Communists, 353, UN Asssembly meets in, 353, and Berlin crisis, 355, 358–9, 362, Djilas publishes books in, 359, 360, 401, summary of Tito's relationship with, 362, Tito visits, 365–6, and Vietnam, 383, and Six Day War, 384, Nixon becomes President of, 388, Tito visits again, 410, 413, Reagan becomes President, 417, mentioned, 24, 143, 206, 221, 231, 311, 331, 339, 402, 414, 419, *see also* New York; Washington; names of American people

UNRRA (United Nations Relief and Rehabilitation Agency), 274–5

Ustashas, member assassinates King Alexander, 116, subsidized by Mussolini, 116, and Communists, 116, support Germans, 162, come to power in Croatia, 163, murders by, 163–5, 183–4, 260, and Roman Catholic Church, 164, 165–6, German views on, 171, offensive against Partisans, 183, Partisan treatment of, 185, exchange of prisoners, 203, 204, 205–6, Mesić a member of, 246, Tito tries to prevent escape of, 253, Partisans want revenge on, 254, captured by partisans, 254–5, handed over to Partisans, 257, Tito offers amnesty to, 257, Basta refrains from vengeance on, 258, escape, 260, Tito ready to forgive, 322, and Tito's visit to US, 366, and revival of Croatian nationalism, 392, continue to represent a threat, 393–4, mentioned, 167, 169, 202, 221, 229, 261, 277, 278, 298, 308, 314, 316, 346, 359, 381

Užice, 172, 173, 176, 178, 179, 180, 181, 182, 185, 189, 224, 244, 305, 357

Van der Lubbe, Marinus, 111, 112
Vandervelde, Emile, 60
Varesco, Vladimirovna, 137

Velebit, Vera, 315, 411

Velebit, Vladimir, brings passport to Tito, 150, operates secret radio transmitter, 166, cares for Hera Haas, 167, takes part in March negotiations, 205, 401, visits friends in Zagreb, 206, spends time with Herta Haas, 207, discusses future of Yugoslavia with Deakin, 216, in military mission to Cairo, 229–30, in mission to London, 230–2, and Soviet intelligence, 230–1, welcomes Tito at Bari, 237, and Tito's invitation to meet British leaders, 240, and commercial treaty with Soviet Union, 275, accused of spying, 286–7, resigns as assistant foreign minister, 287, joins Ministry of Foreign trade, 287, asks US for arms, 308–9, Jovanka Broz stays with, 315, and economic affairs, 324, and publication of information about March negotiations, 402, angry at Tito's remarks about March negotiations, 403, mentioned, 326

Velika Trojstvo, 78, 81, 82, 83

Venezia Giulia, 253

Venice, Republic of, 28, 33,

Versailles, Treaty of (1919), 72, 73, 293

Veselinov, Jovan, 371

Viborg, 67

Victor Emmanuel III, King of Italy, 212

Victoria, crown princess of Germany (the Empress Frederick), 40

Victoria, Queen of England, 51

Vienna, Turks march on, 32, revolution in, 37, documents alleged to be in , 42, Tito's brother works in, 49, Tito visits, 56–7, Hitler lives in, 56, public opinion about First World War in, 60, street fighting in, 112, CPY directed from, 113, 114, 115, Tito visits on CPY activities, 113–4, 117, Politburo moves from, 123, Hebrang's contact in, 313, 314, Kennedy and Khrushchev meet in, 355, 362, discussion on Serbo-Croat language in, 382, mentioned, 48, 55, 129, 319

Vienna, Congress of, 33

Vietcong, 383, 388

Vietnam, 21, 304, 318–9, 351, 383, 384, 388, 389–90, 414

Vis, island of, 212, 227, 236, 237, 238, 239, 240, 242, 243, 245, 248, 270, 274, 408

Vis Agreement, 240, 244, 248, 262

Viviani, René, 60

Vjesnik, 409

Vladivostok, 70, 71

Vlahović, Veljko, 137

Vojvodina, 72, 73, 169, 173, 251, 259, 364, 368, 393, 414

Volgograd, 356, *see also* Stalingrad

Voroshilov, Marshal Kliment Y., 334

Vrhovec, Josip, 398, 399

Vujković, S., 105, 173, 176, 255

Vujović, Rade, 349
Vukmanović, Svetozar, *see* Tempo
Vyshinsky, Andrei Y., 188, 193, 268, 281, 293, 304

Waffen SS, 184, 251
Wahnsee Conference (1942), 165
Waldheim, Kurt, 21
Wales, 114
Wall Street, 109, 281
Warsaw, 272, 386
Warsaw Pact, 20, 338, 339, 358
Wartime (Djilas), 401
Washington, 24, 192, 225, 266, 274, 309, 355, 356, 359, 362, 365, 366, 388, 396
Waugh, Evelyn, 242–3
Weissberg, Alex, 311
West, Rebecca, 123, 159, 225, 253
West Germany, 20, 309, 347, 351, 372, 374
White Guards, 71, 74, 75, 80, 251, 253, 257
White Russians, 87, 92, 253, 256
Wiener-Neustadt, 55, 56, 57
Wilson, President, Woodrow, 74
Wilson, Sir Henry Maitland, 230, 240, 241
Wintringham, Tom, 219–20
World News and Views, 151

Xoxe, Koci, 299

Yagoda, Genrikh, 380
Yalta conference/agreement (1945), 250, 255, 256, 266, 267
Yalu River, 306
Yezhov, Nikolay Ivanovich, 125, 380
Yezhov Purge, 125–6
Yugoslavia, historical background, 26–34, creation of, 72–3, and 'Little Entente', 73, dominated by Serbia, 73, 95, occupies Vojvodina, 73, support for strike to save Communist Hungary, 73, 1920 elections, 78–9, Communists suppressed by government in, 79, 80, problems with union of nations of, 95, change of name, 104, unemployment in, 109, Communists spread disaffection in armies of, 116, new drive against Ustashas and Communists in, 116, Communists wish to strengthen defence of, 122, and volunteers for Spanish Civil War, 129–30, 131, 132, alarmed by annexation of Austria, 136, response to call for aid to Czechs, 141, 142, Communists show patriotism for, 144, coalition government, 149, takes action against Communists, 157, Germany requests entry of troops into, 158, signs Tripartite Pact, 159, Peter II proclaimed as ruler, 160, Germany invades, 161–2, Germany changes map of, 163, guerilla activity during Second World War *see* Chetniks; Partisans, Stalin and Comintern

oppose social revolution in, 172, government in exile, 175, 176, 177, 187, 188, 194, 217, German troops in, 177, Bihać conference about future government of, 194–5, not yet a major issue for Allies at Casablanca Conference, 201, discussions about post-war future, 216, 222–3, Churchill's intentions about, 220, Tito calls on AVNOJ to form provisional government of, 220–1, Tito develops ideas about post-war future of, 221–2, Churchill makes statement on, 224–5, Allied air raids on, 228–9, Churchill wishes to find satisfactory political solution for, 238, Tito wishes to establish Communist state in, 239, Tito-Šubašić agreement about, 240, 244, 251, Churchill persuades Tito to make statement about aims in, 242, Tito wishes to interest Stalin in future of, 244–5, Tito and Stalin discuss situation in, 246, Red Army enters, 246, Tito acts as head of government in, 248, Churchill realises situation in, 254, demands occupation zone in Austria, 255, refugees handed over to, 256, elections held in, 261–2, becomes Communist state with Tito as dictator, 262, constitution, 262, Tito's speech about, 263, and ELAS guerillas, 264, 280, own role in liberation, 268, atmosphere in, 268–9, tensions with Soviet Union, 269–72, bad relations with United States, 274–6, relations between Roman Catholic Church and government, 276–8, political repression intensified in, 280, refuses Marshall Aid, 281, abstains at UN vote on Palestine, 281, and Balkan federation, 284, deteriorating relations with Soviet Union, 285–6, unable to depend on support from Western powers, 291, Tito surveys history of Socialism in, 292, represented at International Danube Commission, 293, CIA project in, 296, economic sanctions against, 300, stands for election to UN Security Council, 303–4, recognizes Ho Chi Minh, 304–5, and Korea, 305–6, faces possibility of invasion, 307–11, more freedom in, 311–2, 392, economic controls relaxed in, 312, relationship with Soviet Union, 331, 333–4, 335, 343, 345, 346, 349, Hungarians seek asylum in embassy of, 340–1, 345, and Tito's speech at Pula, 341, 342, protests about arrest of Nagy, 345, West Germany breaks off diplomatic relations with, 347, receives aid from US, 305, 312, 348, 352, 359, 365, 367, policy explained in Tito's speech at UN, 354, US policy towards, 356, Djilas unable to publish book in, 359, divisions between liberals and hardliners in, 364–80, attitude to Tito's foreign travels, 366, economy, 366–70, tourism, 372–4, foreign travel allowed, 374–5, writers and artists in, 375–6, and Yugoslav Idea, 381, fear of Soviet invasion, 387–8, new constitution, 393, 400, Tito warns against civil war, 395, events since death of Tito, 416–20, for policies followed under Tito *see* Tito, Josip Broz, *see also* Chetniks; Communist party of Yugoslavia; Partisans; names of villages, towns, regions, ethnic groups, political groups and people

Zachariades, Nikos, 301
Zadar, 228, 376
Zagreb, Tito works in, 53, 54, Tito in army in, 58, 59, Tito joins Communist party in, 77, Communists achieve election success in, 78, 79, Tito as secretary of Metalworkers Union in, 88, 89, Tito in hiding in, 91, secret Congress of Communist party in, 95–6, Communist demonstrations in, 96–7, 98, Tito tried in, 99, Tito imprisoned in, 102, Tito returns from Kumrovec to, 113, Djilas meets Kardelj in, 146, Tito returns from Moscow to, 151, Fifth National Conference of CPY in, 153–4, Germans enter, 162, Ustasha persecutions in, 164, Tito in danger in, 166, Herta Haas remains in, 167, 170, sabotage of Zagreb-Belgrade railway, 168, 176, 195, 206, 207, Hebrang captured in, 204, 312, March negotiations in, 205–6, Partisans enter, 258, Tito visits after liberation, 270, Maclean visits Tito in, 281, palace in, 319, 320–1, student demonstrations, 392, 394, 397, 399, Tito's official visit to, 395–6, alleged assassination attempt against Tito in, 404–5, Tito and Jovanka in, 412–3, after death of Tito, 419, mentioned, 37, 106, 116, 123, 133, 134, 136, 150, 155, 160, 161, 167, 185, 193, 194, 231, 233, 254, 278, 292, 309, 313, 328, 376, 378, 382, 402, 403, 408, 414
Zagreb, Bishop of, 29
Zajača, 179
Zambia, 21
Zapolya, Jan, 31
Zečević, Miodrag, 407–8, 414
Zdenka (Davorjanka Paunović), 169–70, 173, 187, 192, 207, 228, 234, 235, 237, 239, 245, 279, 314
Zemun, 32
Zeri i Popullit, 302
Zervas, General, 218
Zhdanov, Andrei Alexandrovich, 282, 283, 326, 375
Zhukov, Marshal, 308, 346, 362
Zia, General, 21
Zilliacus, Konni, 99, 100, 262
Zimbabwe, 389
Zinoviev, Grigory E., 94, 119, 125, 126, 129, 361
Žugelj, Milan, 313
Žujovic, Sreten (Crni), 187, 234, 287, 288, 289, 291, 292, 312, 314
Zulsikarpašić, Adil, 222